CHEMISTRY AND PHARMACOLOGY OF NATURAL PRODUCTS

Series Editors: Professor J.D. Phillipson, *Department of Pharmacognosy, The School of Pharmacy, University of London*; Dr D.C. Ayres, *Department of Chemistry, Queen Mary and Westfield College, University of London*; H. Baxter, *formerly at the Laboratory of the Government Chemist, London.*

Also in this series

T0324103

Chemistry and Pharmacology of Natural Products

Saponins

This is the first comprehensive monograph to look in depth at saponins. Saponins are glycosides of triterpenes, steroids or steroid alkaloids which have a very wide distribution in plants and some marine organisms. Their biological activity includes haemolysis and fish poisoning, and the steroid saponins are essential for the manufacture of oral contraceptives and sex hormones. Saponins have also been exploited commercially as soap substitutes and in several other industrial applications. This book gives detailed information on the occurrence and distribution of saponins, their structural types, isolation, analysis and structure determination. Biological and pharmacological activities are discussed, as are aspects of commercial and industrial use. The volume provides a valuable source of data for the different classes of compound and includes an extensive list of references.

The Origins and Development of Financial Markets and Institutions

Collectively, mankind has never had it so good despite periodic economic crises of which the current sub-prime crisis is merely the latest example. Much of this success is attributable to the increasing efficiency of the world's financial institutions as finance has proved to be one of the most important causal factors in economic performance. In a series of original essays, leading financial and economic historians examine how financial innovations from the seventeenth century to the present have continually challenged established institutional arrangements forcing change and adaptation by governments, financial intermediaries, and financial markets. Where these have been successful, wealth creation and growth have followed. When they failed, growth slowed and sometimes economic decline has followed. These essays illustrate the difficulties of coordinating financial innovations in order to sustain their benefits for the wider economy, a theme that will be of interest to policy makers as well as economic historians.

JEREMY ATACK is Professor of Economics and Professor of History at Vanderbilt University. He is also a research associate with the National Bureau of Economic Research (NBER) and has served as co-editor of the *Journal of Economic History*. He is co-author of *A New Economic View of American History* (1994).

LARRY NEAL is Emeritus Professor of Economics at the University of Illinois at Urbana-Champaign, where he was founding director of the European Union Center. He is a visiting professor at the London School of Economics and a research associate with the National Bureau of Economic Research (NBER). He is the author of many books, including *The Rise of Financial Capitalism* (Cambridge, 1990) and *The Economics of Europe and the European Union* (Cambridge, 2007).

The Origins and Development of Financial Markets and Institutions

From the Seventeenth Century to the Present

Jeremy Atack
Larry Neal

CAMBRIDGE
UNIVERSITY PRESS

CAMBRIDGE UNIVERSITY PRESS
Cambridge, New York, Melbourne, Madrid, Cape Town, Singapore,
São Paulo, Delhi, Dubai, Tokyo, Mexico City

Cambridge University Press
The Edinburgh Building, Cambridge CB2 8RU, UK

Published in the United States of America by Cambridge University Press, New York

www.cambridge.org
Information on this title: www.cambridge.org/9780521154765

© Cambridge University Press 2009

This publication is in copyright. Subject to statutory exception
and to the provisions of relevant collective licensing agreements,
no reproduction of any part may take place without the written
permission of Cambridge University Press.

First published 2009
First paperback edition 2010

A catalogue record for this publication is available from the British Library

ISBN 978-0-521-89517-0 Hardback
ISBN 978-0-521-15476-5 Paperback

Cambridge University Press has no responsibility for the persistence or
accuracy of URLs for external or third-party internet websites referred to in
this publication, and does not guarantee that any content on such websites is,
or will remain, accurate or appropriate.

For Becky and Peg
to whom we owe much

Contents

Figures

Tables

Contributors*

JEREMY ATACK is Professor of Economics and Professor of History at Vanderbilt University. He is a research associate with the National Bureau of Economic Research (NBER) and serves as co-editor of the *Journal of Economic History*. For seventeen years he was Larry Neal's colleague at the University of Illinois. Professor Atack has worked primarily on nineteenth century US agricultural, business, industrial, and transportation history but his close contact with Larry Neal has led to his enduring fascination with financial intermediation, markets, and policies. He is co-author of *A New Economic View of American History* (1994).

MICHAEL D. BORDO is Professor of Economics and Director of the Center for Monetary and Financial History at Rutgers University. He was previously Pitt Professor at Cambridge University (2006–2007) and has previously held positions at the University of South Carolina and Carleton University in Canada. He has held visiting positions at the University of California Los Angeles, Carnegie Mellon University, Princeton University, the IMF, the Federal Reserve Banks of St. Louis and Cleveland, the Federal Reserve Board of Governors, the Bank of Canada, the Bank of England, and the Bank for International Settlement. He is also a research associate with the National Bureau of Economic Research (NBER). Recent publications include: *Essays on the Gold Standard and Related Regimes: A Retrospective on the Bretton Woods International Monetary System* (with Barry Eichengreen); *The Defining Moment: The Great Depression and the American Economy* (with Claudia Goldin and Eugene White); and *Globalization in Historical Perspective* (with Alan Taylor and Jeffery Williamson). He is also series editor for *Studies in Macroeconomic History* published by Cambridge University Press.

---

* Larry Neal's professional contributions inspired this volume and all of the contributors are, in one way or another (as detailed below), connected with him and his work.

RICHARD C.K. BURDEKIN is Jonathan B. Lovelace Professor of Economics at Claremont McKenna College. His main research interests include the Chinese economic reforms, inflation and deflation, central bank policymaking, and economic history. Burdekin has published in such journals as the *American Economic Review*, *Economica*, *Economic Inquiry*, the *Journal of Financial Economics*, the *Journal of International Money and Finance*, and the *Journal of Money, Credit, and Banking*. His latest book entitled *China's Monetary Challenges: Past Experiences and Future Prospects* was published by Cambridge University Press in 2008.

ALAN DYE is Associate Professor of Economics at Barnard College, Columbia University. He has also been a visiting professor at Yale University, the University of Michigan, and the Universidad Carlos III de Madrid. He is author of *Cuban Sugar in the Age of Mass Production: Technology and the Economics of the Sugar Central, 1899–1929* (1998) and his dissertation, "Tropical Technology and Mass Production" (supervised by Larry Neal), was awarded the Alexander Gerschenkron Prize from the Economic History Association in 1993. His published work examines the role of institutions and historical processes in the economic history of Latin America.

MARC FLANDREAU is Professor of Economics at the Institut d'Etudes Politiques de Paris, where he has held the Chair of International Finance since 2005. He is also a research fellow at the Centre for Economic Policy Research, London, and a consultant to the research department at the Bank of France, IMF, OECD, and investment bank Lehman Brothers, among others. He has published extensively on international monetary and financial history. Recent books include *The Glitter of Gold: France, Bimetallism and the Emergence of the International Gold Standard, 1848–1873* (2004) and, with Frédéric Zumer, *The Making of Global Finance 1880–1913* (2004). Flandreau discovered Larry Neal's, *The Rise of Financial Capitalism* (Cambridge, 1990) while working on his PhD at the University of California, Berkeley.

CHRISTOPHE GALIMARD is a former PhD student in the Graduate Institute in Geneva and in Sciences Po, Paris. He has conducted research on bankers' networks and commercial bills in the eighteenth century while working as compliance officer for BNP-Paribas in Luxembourg and Geneva. He is now a senior auditor with BNP-Paribas, Paris, dealing with the many issues that have been raised by the sub-prime crisis. He insists that he will eventually return to economic history.

OSCAR GELDERBLOM is a researcher at Utrecht University. He received his PhD in history in 2000. Larry Neal's encouragement and stimulating criticism of his work have helped to shape his current research interest in the organization of long-distance trade and the evolution of financial markets in Europe before the Industrial Revolution.

CLEMENS JOBST spent a year as an exchange student at the University of Illinois at Urbana-Champaign while completing his undergraduate degree at the University of Vienna. While at Illinois, a reading course with Larry Neal led to a lasting reorientation in his historical interests towards financial and monetary topics. After receiving his PhD from Sciences Po, Paris, he is now working in the Economic Analysis Division at the Austrian National Bank. His research interests focus mainly on the nineteenth century and include the working of the international monetary system and the evolution of modern central banking.

JOOST JONKER is Lecturer and Research Fellow Economic History at Utrecht University. Starting out as a historian of twentieth century Dutch banking, he soon found himself sliding back into the eighteenth century and further, which brought him into touch with Larry Neal and his work.

PILAR NOGUÉS-MARCO is a PhD student in monetary and financial history. Her dissertation is supervised by Marc Flandreau at the Chaire Finances Internationales – Institut d'Etudes Politiques de Paris. Her research focuses on international monetary integration in the Early Modern period with a special emphasis on Spain's international monetary and financial relations, and has been very influenced by Larry Neal's pioneering research on financial market integration in the eighteenth century. She has recently published (with Camila Vam Malle) "East India Bonds, 1718–1763: Early Exotic Derivatives and London Market Efficiency" in the *European Review of Economic History*.

LARRY NEAL is Emeritus Professor of Economics at the University of Illinois at Urbana-Champaign, where he was founding director of the European Union Center. He is a visiting professor at the London School of Economics and a research associate with the National Bureau of Economic Research (NBER). He is a past president of the

Economic History Association and the Business History Conference and, from 1981 to 1998, he was editor of *Explorations in Economic History*. He is author of many books including *The Rise of Financial Capitalism* (Cambridge, 1990), *The Economics of Europe and the European Union* (Cambridge, 2007) and *A Concise Economic History of the World* (with Rondo Cameron), as well as numerous articles in American and European economic and financial history. He was a Guggenheim Fellow and a Fulbright Research Scholar in 1996–1997 and an Alexander von Humboldt Fellow in 1982. His current research deals with development of microstructure in securities markets and risk management in the first emerging markets in modern Europe.

STEPHEN QUINN is Associate Professor of Economics at Texas Christian University. Steve, a native of Rockford, Illinois, took his doctorate in Economics at University of Illinois from 1988 to 1994. Larry Neal was his thesis advisor and mentor. During those golden days of Illinois economic history, he was also shepherded by Lee Alston, Jeremy Atack, and Charles Calomiris. He writes on the development of the financial systems in Early Modern England and Holland. More importantly, he strives to balance life's demands with the grace ever demonstrated by Peg and Larry Neal.

WILLIAM ROBERDS is an economist with the Research Department of the Federal Reserve Bank of Atlanta. His research interests focus on the theory of money and payments, including such topics as the design of large-value payment systems, financial privacy and identity theft, and the optimal pricing of card payments. More recently he has co-authored a number of papers with Stephen Quinn on various topics in monetary history. Roberds holds a PhD in economics from Carnegie-Mellon University.

GARY S. SHEA has been a financial consultant in Tokyo, an economist at the Federal Reserve in Washington, DC, and has taught at Pennsylvania State University, the University of Exeter, and the University of St. Andrews, where he is currently Reader in Financial Economics. His current research interests are in the development of early British financial markets, corporations, and corporate law and their contributions to Britain's growth prior to and immediately after the Industrial Revolution. His favorite research topic, however, is the South Sea Bubble – a research interest which he was first tempted to explore by Larry Neal in the early 1990s.

RICHARD SICOTTE is Assistant Professor of Economics at the University of Vermont. He completed his PhD at the University of Illinois at Urbana-Champaign in 1997, under the direction of Larry Neal. His research focuses on the economic history of transportation industries, especially ocean shipping, and on the economic history of Latin America.

RICHARD J. SULLIVAN is Senior Economist at the Federal Reserve Bank of Kansas City. Larry Neal's influence helped to draw Sullivan into the economic history community during his doctoral studies at the University of Illinois and Larry Neal was an active member of his dissertation committee. Larry Neal has also been very supportive during Sullivan's career whose research has focused on three areas: (1) the economics of invention, innovation, and patenting; (2) the performance and development of the banking industry; and (3) development and risk in the payments system. In all of these research endeavors the methods and viewpoints of economic history have been particularly valuable.

RICHARD SYLLA is Henry Kaufman Professor of the History of Financial Institutions and Markets, Professor of Economics at New York University's Stern School of Business, and a research associate of the NBER. He is a past president of the Economic History Association and the Business History Conference, and a former co-editor of the *Journal of Economic History*. He is co-author of *A History of Interest Rates* (2005) and co-editor of *The State, the Financial System, and Economic Modernization* (Cambridge, 1999). He shares with Larry Neal a passion for understanding the influences of financial development on economic growth during the modern era.

FRANÇOIS R. VELDE is a senior economist at the Federal Reserve Bank of Chicago. He previously taught at the Johns Hopkins University and received his PhD from Stanford University. He and Larry Neal share an interest in financial markets in eighteenth century Europe and the ceaseless wonders of John Law's adventures. If that weren't enough in common, Velde's father calls the University of Illinois at Urbana-Champaign his *alma mater*.

KIRSTEN WANDSCHNEIDER is Assistant Professor of Economics at Occidental College in Los Angeles, California. She earned her PhD from the University of Illinois in 2003 under the supervision of Larry Neal. From 2003 until 2006 she was Assistant Professor of Economics at Middlebury College, Vermont. Her research focuses on the development of financial markets and institutions in early twentieth century Europe.

MARC D. WEIDENMIER is the William F. Podlich Associate Professor of Economics and George Roberts Faculty Research Fellow at Claremont McKenna College. He is also a faculty research fellow at the National Bureau of Economic Research and a member of the editorial board of the *Journal of Economic History*. He graduated from the University of Illinois writing his thesis under the supervision of Larry Neal. His research focuses on monetary and financial history. He has published in many journals as the *American Economic Review*, the *Journal of Financial Economics*, the *Economic Journal*, the *Journal of International Economics*, the *Journal of Money, Credit, and Banking*, and the *Journal of Economic History*.

DAVID C. WHEELOCK is an assistant vice president and economist at the Federal Reserve Bank of St. Louis. Dr. Wheelock received his PhD in economics from the University of Illinois where he wrote his dissertation, *The Strategy and Consistency of Federal Reserve Monetary Policy 1919–1933*, under the supervision of Larry Neal. Dr. Wheelock was awarded the Allan Nevins prize from the Economic History Association in 1987. He is a member of the editorial board of the Cambridge University Press series, *Studies in Macroeconomic History*. His research interests include monetary and financial history, monetary policy, and the performance of depository institutions.

EUGENE N. WHITE is Professor of Economics at Rutgers University and a research associate at the NBER. His most recent book is *Conflicts of Interest in the Financial Services Industry: What Should We Do About Them?* (2003), co-authored with Andrew Crockett, Trevor Harris, and Frederic Mishkin. He has published over sixty articles on stock market booms and crashes, deposit insurance, banking regulation, and war economics. A former graduate student of Larry Neal, they have co-authored several papers on the evolution of the microstructure of stock exchanges.

Preface and Acknowledgments

Most of the papers in this volume (Chapters 2–7 and 9–14) were presented at a conference on "The Development of Financial Institutions and Markets," held April 28–29, 2006 at the University of Illinois at Urbana-Champaign. The purpose of the conference was to celebrate the contributions of Larry Neal upon the occasion of his retirement from active teaching at the University of Illinois. Financial historians who had interacted with Professor Neal over his career at Illinois, several of them former students of Larry's, were invited to contribute an original paper in their current area of research. Individually, the papers showcase the variety of approaches and theories that continue to motivate scholars in financial history. Together, they demonstrate various aspects of financial innovation and the evolution of financial institutions over time, which has been the focus of Neal's teaching and research for three decades.

Chapters 1, 8 and 15 were written later and serve to set the scene, recognize the contribution of one of Larry's co-authors, Lance E. Davis, who was not well enough to participate, and emphasize the lessons from these studies of the past for the present and future.

Discussants on each paper provided a perspective and began broader discussion of the issues raised in each among the audience. These included (listed alphabetically): Michael Bordo (Rutgers University), Charles Calomiris (Columbia University), Ann Carlos (University of Colorado and University College, Dublin), Conception Garcia-Iglesias (University of Helsinki), Charles Kahn (University of Illinois), Joseph Mason (Drexel University), and Maria Valderama (National Bank of Austria). Brief biographies of the volume contributors appear below.

The conference and this volume were made possible by the efforts of several individuals and institutions whom we thank for their help and support. Most of the local arrangements were handled efficiently and expeditiously by Lynnea Johnson at the Center for International Business Education and Research (CIBER) at the University of Illinois. Funding for the conference was provided by CIBER, the College of

Law, and the Lincoln Educational Foundation at the University of Illinois, and by *Explorations in Economic History* (editor Robert A. Margo). The editors have been assisted in proof-reading and copy-editing of the final drafts of the conference papers by Jessica Lingo of Nashville, Tennessee.

Very special thanks, however, go to Thomas S. Ulen, Swanlund Professor of Law at the University of Illinois at Urbana-Champaign, for his help and generous support.

1   Financial innovations and crises: The view backwards from Northern Rock

Jeremy Atack

On September 17, 2007, the UK experienced its first bank run in over 140 years.[1] Early that morning, nervous depositors all over the UK began queuing outside their local branches of Northern Rock bank to redeem their deposits (often their life savings) while the bank still had the cash to meet their demands. They had heard the reassuring words over the preceding weekend from Bank of England Governor Mervyn King, including the announcement that the Bank had extended a $4.4 billion line of credit, and they were worried.[2] British deposit insurance rules limited full coverage to just the first £2,000 of a deposit and only 90 percent of the balance up to the insurance cap of £35,000.[3] As a result, many depositors had substantial sums at risk. The run ended only when the Chancellor of the Exchequer, Alistair Darling, overruled the British regulator of banks, the Financial Services Authority, by suspending deposit insurance rules and promising unlimited 100 percent coverage to all existing depositors in the bank as of midnight, Wednesday, September 19, 2007 for the duration of the crisis.[4] Nevertheless, as 2008 began, the crisis was still on-going with no end in sight. As of mid-December 2007, the Bank of England and the British taxpayers had extended at least £25 billion in credit to the bank (about $50 billion) but Northern Rock depositors have continued to withdraw their funds. There were even ministerial discussions about whether or not to nationalize the bank to protect the taxpayers' investment.[5] These discussions became reality when Britain's Parliament passed the Banking (Special Provisions) Act on February 21, 2008, transferring all shares in Northern Rock to the government.[6]

No other recent event better illustrates the themes of this book – the evolutionary nature of financial intermediaries and financial markets, the

[1] Collins, "Overend"; Patterson, "Home Monetary Drains."
[2] *BBC*, "Northern Rock Besieged"; *International Herald Tribune*, "Crisis Deepens."
[3] *New York Law Journal*, "International Banking"; Demirguc-Kunt *et al.*, "Deposit Insurance."
[4] *Financial Times*, "Darling Steps in."   [5] *The Guardian*, "Ministers Prepare Plan."
[6] *Reuters*, "Britain Passes."

critical role played by institutional arrangements in organizing and regulating these activities, and the risks that people bear as these work their way through the system. Getting the rules and organizations "right" brings economic growth and riches. Getting them "wrong" spells economic turmoil and decline.

In the past three decades, the world has witnessed dramatic changes in the organization and operations of financial intermediaries and markets both within and between countries as globalization has spurred global competition. Beginning in the late 1920s and early 1930s and lasting until successive waves of financial deregulation spread around the world beginning around 1980 – a process often referred to in each country as the "big bang" – most financial intermediaries and markets enjoyed a high degree of domestic protection. Now, they are once again subject to common pressures and we are seeing what Justice Brandeis once called "a race to the bottom" as these institutions scramble to remake themselves and compete more effectively.[7]

For example, once upon a time, banks derived their loanable funds from depositors, which they used to make loans to credit-worthy customers. These were then held to maturity thereby building up a "relationship" with customers on both the asset and liabilities side of the balance sheet. Nowadays, however, many banks – including Northern Rock – depend upon impersonal capital markets and other financial institutions for their funds, and they increasingly repackage and resell their loans to third parties. In the process, they pocket one-time loan origination, debt servicing and securitization fees in place of the stream of interest income they once received. They also pass risk along to the investors downstream. This behavior changes their incentives from concern about the long-term outcome to immediate cash income. Indeed, it was Northern Rock's inability to borrow on the capital and credit markets to refinance maturing short-term borrowing that precipitated the crisis.[8] The bank no longer had the funds with which to buy new mortgages, a situation which suddenly and dramatically decreased the liquidity of their asset portfolio as well as threatening their income stream.

To understand why the recent turmoil in the global financial markets resonates so strongly with financial historians, it is useful to review the tensions created by financial innovations. Many of these stem from the different roles which financial intermediaries (mainly banks but also insurance companies, pension funds, and the like) and capital markets (mainly thought of as stock markets dealing in bonds and equity shares, but including secondary markets in short-term debt ranging down to the

---

[7] *Liggett* v. *Lee*.   [8] *Financial Times*, "Confidence."

overnight market in interbank debt) play in finance. Traditionally, financial intermediaries have provided five valuable services to the economy: (1) liquidity; (2) resolving denomination mismatches; (3) reducing credit risk; (4) mediating maturity differences; and (5) bearing interest rate and exchange rate risk.

Some of these same services have also been provided by financial markets, albeit typically in somewhat different forms. The distinctions, however, are rapidly disappearing, putting direct and indirect finance into head-to-head competition with one another. Both financial intermediaries and financial markets, for example, increase liquidity – the ease (speed and price) with which a debt can be converted to cash, and ownership transferred to another party – but they do this in different ways. Financial intermediaries increase liquidity by exchanging the more risky claim against the debtor for a less risky claim against the intermediary, taking advantage of their specialist knowledge and their ability to monitor the debtor. Financial markets, on the other hand, increase liquidity by bringing together buyers and sellers and establishing trading rules which are clear to all parties. In these markets, specialists also emerge to ensure that the market is complete so that a buyer exists for every seller.

Both financial intermediaries and markets also resolve a matching problem between the sums that lenders wish to lend and those that borrowers wish to borrow – often referred to as denomination divisibility. Banks do this by mobilizing and pooling the savings of many small depositors on the liabilities side of the balance sheet to grant fewer and larger loans to debtors on the asset side of their balance sheet. Financial markets accomplish the same task by securitization – dividing the debt into many small, homogeneous and tradable parts either as equity or debt instruments.

Banks seek to defray credit risk – the risk that the borrower might default on the obligation – through the screening and monitoring of their customers. Sometimes this is accomplished through the structure of the loan – for example, an amortized loan. Other times it might be accomplished through a demand for collateral. It is also achieved through long-term banker–customer relationships and repeat trading. Financial markets seek to achieve some of these same benefits through signaling via bond ratings, the issuance of revenue bonds, the use of mortgage bonds, credit-default swaps, or through the reputation of the underwriter. In the case of the sub-prime crisis, there is growing evidence that these controls failed. Rating agencies failed to appreciate the extent and magnitude of the risk of default, and reputable agents all too willingly lent their names in the marketing of these securities.

Figure 1.1 "Passing on the Risks."
Source: The Economist, "Passing on the Risks," (November 2, 1996) Vol. 341, Issue 7990, p. 73. Courtesy of the artist, David Simonds.

Only two areas have really distinguished financial intermediaries from financial markets. First, banks performed the vital service of maturity mediation which arises from the desire of depositors to lend short-term and to have ready access to their funds, and the wishes of borrowers to borrow long-term so as to not jeopardize their investment. Second, by virtue of this maturity mediation, banks also bear the risk that rises in interest rates will depress asset prices, especially for longer term investments. However, even these last two bastions of financial inter-mediation services have become blurred by debt securitization. Banks increasingly initiate loans, supposedly taking advantage of their specialist knowledge, but do not hold the loans for very long. Instead, these are bundled, repackaged and resold as standardized financial instruments in tranches with the bank simply acting as servicing agent (Figure 1.1).[9]

Each of these activities, whether supplied by banks and other financial intermediaries or through financial markets, are now generally regarded as growth-promoting and serve as causal factors in economic growth rather than simply by-products of an expanding economy.[10] Few today – and certainly not the contributors to this volume – believe Joan Robinson's assertion that "where enterprise leads, finance follows."[11] Instead, a preponderance of empirical evidence as well as theoretical

[9] *The Economist*, "Passing."
[10] Levine, "Financial Development" and "Finance and Growth."
[11] Robinson, "Generalisation."

argument support the case that greater financial depth measured, for example, by the ratio of some broad definition of money (say, M3) to GDP, is associated with faster economic growth. Moreover, this relationship holds true even after correcting for prices and population across countries and over time.[12]

As these essays show, some institutional designs have worked better than others. As financial innovations work their way through the existing financial institutions and structures, crises have occurred. Each time, critics have railed against the innovations that appear to have played a role in the crisis, arguing that the unseemly profits for the early innovators could not be justified by the real contribution to the economy. Furthermore, they claim that these returns distracted capable people from continuing to do honest and productive work in their traditional métiers. Examples of such complaints would include Jay Cooke's profits from Union bond sales during the American Civil War and the construction of the Union Pacific,[13] and Michael Milken's earnings from high yield – a.k.a. "junk" – bond sales in the 1980s.[14] Each time, however, provided that the rest of the financial system adjusted to the crisis with the help of both private and public initiative and incentives to "get it right," the benefits of faster economic growth increased the material benefits to society and led it to new heights.

When the financial system did not adjust but rather stifled the financial innovations that seemed to be at the root of the crisis, stagnation and long-term decay (at least in relative terms) typically followed. One such case – the restrictions on French finance following the collapse of John Law's system – is touched upon in two of the essays that follow.[15] This is why it is crucial for governments to respond in a constructive manner to the credit crunch that struck in the summer of 2007 and "get it right" so that the gains being achieved by financial globalization will be sustained.

Why, then, did the initial response to Northern Rock's problems by the British financial authorities not work? After all, central bank transparency and co-insurance of bank deposits, both in evidence as the British authorities reacted to the Northern Rock crisis, had long been touted by academics as desirable changes, precisely to prevent such crises.[16] However, the Bank of England's transparency in the public

---

[12] See Rousseau and Sylla, "Financial Systems."

[13] Oberholtzer, *Jay Cooke*; Josephson, *Robber Barons*.

[14] Bruck, *Predators'*; Stone, *April Fools*; Stewart, *Den*.

[15] de Pinto, *Essay*; Soboul, *La France*.

[16] Geraats, "Central Bank"; Athey *et al.*, "Optimality"; Poole, "Transparent." For an argument contra, see Mishkin, "Central Bank."

announcement of a line of credit to Northern Rock worked no better than earlier public acknowledgments of bank troubles. For example, the Congressional "naming of names" of banks receiving aid from the Reconstruction Finance Corporation simply increased pressure on those banks.[17] During the Savings and Loan crisis of the 1980s in the US, criticism and scorn were heaped upon the American deposit insurance system for its 100 percent insurance coverage.[18] Indeed, while the insurance cap ($100,000) under the FDIC was already generous by world standards, some large institutions such as Continental Illinois enjoyed unlimited protection as they were deemed "too big to fail" and, absent other solutions to their balance sheet problems, the FDIC would sponsor and underwrite the purchase of their assets and assumption of their obligations.[19] Co-insurance was, instead, touted as the solution for deposit insurance's moral hazard because it forced bank depositors to consider the credit practices and financial health of their depository institutions. But, as we have seen in the Northern Rock episode, it was precisely these same incentives which precipitated the bank run.

Northern Rock's problems are a small part of a much larger, global problem – the sub-prime lending crisis. This segment of the market began to gain market share in the late 1990s, making up about 13 percent of all mortgages in 2000–2001, but when delinquency and foreclosure rates rose during the recession and following 9/11, their share declined to under 10 percent until 2003–2004. By 2006, such mortgages accounted for about one-quarter of all mortgages issued in the US. The crisis began in late 2006 as higher interest rates in the US began to filter through to borrowers with adjustable rate home mortgages. Many of these individuals had been given mortgages for which their past credit history or current financial status should have disqualified them. Predictably, as borrowing costs rose and asset price rises stalled or reversed, foreclosure rates began to rise sharply in that segment of the market with less than perfect credit, and especially for those with adjustable rate sub-prime mortgages (Figure 1.2).[20] High rates of delinquency and foreclosure

---

[17] Mason, "Political Economy" and "Reconstruction Finance."

[18] See, for example, Calomiris, "Deposit Insurance." For a follow up on the issue, see Dreyfus et al., "Deposit Insurance."

[19] See, FDIC, History, especially Ch. 7.

[20] According to Federal Reserve Board Chairman Bernanke ("The Subprime Mortgage Market") 14.4 percent of sub-prime mortgages were in default by May 2007 while Schloemer et al., "Losing Ground," estimate that one in five of the sub-prime loans made in 2005–2006 will end in foreclosure. More recent data from the Congressional Budget Office and the Mortgage Bankers Association (CBO, Budget, Figure 2–1) indicate that sub-prime fixed and adjustable rate mortgages had approximately equal delinquency rates of about 10 percent at the start of 2005 but, by the third quarter of

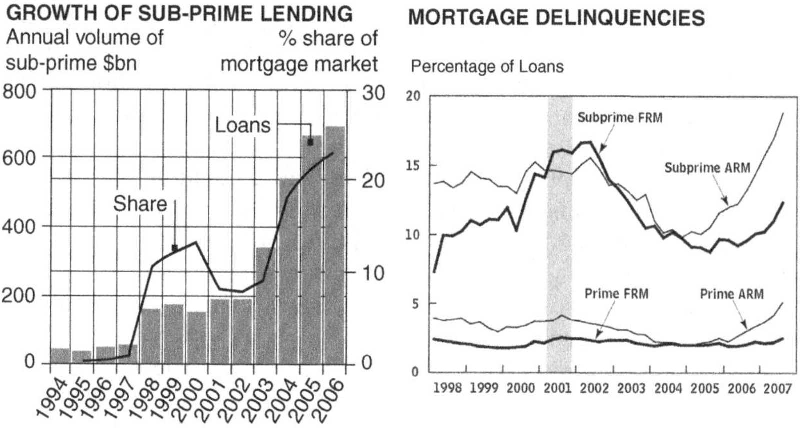

Figure 1.2 Crisis in the US mortgage market: sub-prime loan volume, sub-prime mortgages as share of all mortgages and mortgage delinquency rates by mortgage type.
Source: Center for Responsible Lending/Inside Mortgage Finance; Congressional Budget Office.

have also made it painfully clear that risk might have been under-priced in the global search for interest premiums in excess of the historic low rates prevailing in the economy at that time. These mortgage market problems have been further complicated by mortgage securitization which has sliced, diced and repackaged the underlying mortgages in ways that makes untangling the true risk exposure of each difficult, if not impossible. Consequently, current and future pricing has become highly uncertain and price volatility has increased.[21]

The $150+ billion Savings and Loan crisis of the 1980s transformed the mortgage market in the US. In 1985, there were 3,274 S&Ls nationwide. By 1992, their number had shrunk almost 50 percent to just 1,645 and their numbers have continued to decline.[22] As of 2006, there were just 1,279 federally regulated thrift institutions, down from a peak of 4,842 in 1966.[23] These specialized financial institutions favored by public policy since the Federal Home Loan Bank Act of 1932 had

2007, while fixed rate sub-prime delinquencies had only climbed to about 12 percent those for adjustable sub-prime mortgages had almost doubled.
[21] The absence of a reliable market has led to the abandonment of "marking to market" to "marking to model."
[22] Curry and Shibut, "Cost," Table 4.
[23] Office of Thrift Supervision, 2006, Table 2.1, p. 5.

amassed considerable expertise in the granting and management of home mortgages. As they have disappeared, they have been replaced by mortgage brokers who have little or no interest in holding mortgages. Rather, their earnings came from loan origination, securitization and debt servicing fees instead of from the interest on the amortized mortgage loan. Volume replaced quality and the latter could always be disguised through diversification and subdivision as a part of securitization.

By late summer 2007, sub-prime lending problems in securitized assets were endangering financial institutions on the European continent even before their presence was widely recognized in the US (let alone officially acknowledged). In Germany, in early August, for example, some \$4.8 billion in emergency credit was extended to IKB Deutsche Industriebank and a number of asset-backed security funds were closed in order to halt large withdrawals by investors which were forcing asset sales on a deteriorating market. Similar closures affected funds in France, notably those associated with BNP Paribas, a large French bank.[24] Later that same month, SachsenLB, a Leipzig savings bank, was forced into a merger with Landesbank Baden-Württemberg (LBBW) in an effort to resolve the former's growing liquidity crisis.[25]

These widening problems, among others, doubtless played a role in the European Central Bank's initial decision to offer \$130 billion in low-interest credit to the European financial markets,[26] and then a stunning \$500 billion in mid-December[27] – a far more aggressive action than the Federal Reserve's more belated and conservative actions to lower interest rates and provide liquidity. Rather than intervene directly, the American monetary authorities tried a variety of other responses. Citicorp, the largest commercial and investment bank in the world, for example, tried to create a joint guarantee fund with a consortium of other international commercial and investment banks.[28] In the past, similar efforts had worked quite well. In 1890, for example, the Bank of England had coordinated a bailout of Baring Brothers merchant bank[29] and in 1997, the New York Federal Reserve had coordinated a bailout of Long Term Capital Management.[30] This time, however, no credible coordinating agent of the scale required appeared, and the effort failed.[31] In January, 2008, Citicorp took an \$18+ billion write down in its assets, yet speculation remains of more write-offs to come.[32] Meantime, the US Treasury tried to provide the needed coordination but, because of moral

---

[24] *New York Times*, "Shaky Markets."   [25] *Spiegel On-line International*, "Bail-Out."
[26] *International Herald Tribune*, "ECB."   [27] *BBC News* "EBC."   [28] CNN "Banks."
[29] Ford, "Argentina"; della Paolera and Taylor, *Straining*, Chs. 3 and 4.
[30] *New York Federal Reserve*, "William J. Mcdonough"; *New York Times*, "Fallen Star."
[31] *Washington Post*, "Banks."   [32] *Wall Street Journal*, "Citigroup."

hazard concerns, it has only succeeded in getting the major mortgage lenders to agree to extend their efforts to work out alternatives to foreclosure for their most recent and weakest customers who are not yet delinquent in their payments.[33] The continued uncertainties about how to "get it right," not just in terms of meeting the immediate crisis, but also in terms of the long-run evolution of the global financial system, is simply prolonging the crisis as this book goes to press.

Northern Rock itself had also participated in these sub-prime lending activities and securitization schemes by entering into a partnership with Lehman Brothers. As the company's press release put it, the goal was "to offer near-prime, sub-prime and self certified loans to customers. The credit risk on these loans will not be borne by Northern Rock, but we will earn fee income for the loan introduction."[34]

Nor was this the only way in which Northern Rock serves as a metaphor for changes in the global financial system during the past thirty years or so. The Northern Rock Building Society was formed by the merger of two venerable building societies – both mutual savings companies – in 1965.[35] In the late 1990s, amid an on-going controversy about the dissipation of past and future company worth for the benefit of current depositors, it demutualized and re-formed as a joint-stock bank listed on the London Stock Exchange.[36] British financial institutions were slower in making the switch from mutual organizations to joint stock companies. By the time that Abbey National demutualized in 1989 – the first building society to take advantage of the opportunity under the Building Societies Act of 1986 – almost 900 American mutual savings associations had filed petitions to demutualize, and 769 changes had been approved. By 2006, 1,451 mutual savings associations regulated by the Office of Thrift Supervision in the US had become joint stock entities.[37]

Similarly, the structure of Northern Rock's balance sheet mirrored changes that had long been on-going in American banking circles. According to a mid-year statement in 2006:

Funding through securitization remains an integral part of Northern Rock's funding strategy. During the first half of 2006 two residential mortgage issues were completed raising £9.0 billion through our Granite vehicles. The January deal at £6.0 billion was our largest to date. Diversification of our investor base continued with 75% of the securitized bonds being issued in US dollars or euros.[38]

[33] *New York Times*, "Mortgage Plan."
[34] Northern Rock, "Stock Exchange."   [35] Northern Rock, "Corporate Profile."
[36] Northern Rock Foundation, "History."
[37] Martin and Turner, "Demutualization"; Office of Thrift Supervision, *2006*, Table 2.8, p. 12.
[38] Northern Rock "Highlights."

Such borrowings had long been of increasing importance to American banks. In the mid-1990s, borrowings had accounted for a little more than 16 percent of the liabilities of US commercial banks while deposits (transaction and non-transaction) made up over 60 percent.[39] By 2005, however, borrowings had grown to 23 percent, largely at the expense of deposits.[40] Moreover, by participating in the global market far beyond their home bases, financial institutions have also found themselves facing exchange rate risk in addition to credit risk and interest rate risk.

The essays that follow represent original research, and take up the difficulties in making innovations in banking and financial markets work as complements for the long-run benefit of the economy, especially when their services are increasingly substitutes for one another. The papers begin with the efforts of the Dutch Republic in the seventeenth and eighteenth centuries to innovate first in the field of banking and subsequently in the marketing of government debt. These are followed by discussions of how France and Britain tried to imitate and improve upon the Dutch successes. The growing volume of long-distance trade throughout the eighteenth century forced merchants to develop the means to mediate interest rate and exchange rate risk and facilitate trade through international bills, an instrument that was familiar to the first Secretary of the Treasury of the US: Alexander Hamilton. Hamilton tried to integrate the various intermediation and market innovations from western Europe into a coherent financial system for the new nation and largely accomplished that goal. The system that Hamilton put in place initially flourished until populist politics in the 1830s forced a regress that was to last until the Civil War. The breathing space provided by this hiatus enabled Britain to recover the lead in finance, albeit it only temporarily, as nations jockeyed to capitalize on the most successful new innovations. The case studies presented here highlight the complexity of getting banking and capital markets to work effectively as complements in the long-run.

The twentieth century has witnessed a number of financial experiments, many of them (such as the gold exchange standard and foreign control of domestic finances) failures. A few, such as central bank open market purchases of assets other than government debt, seem to have succeeded but were not institutionalized and have yet to be repeated. Others, such as growing central bank intervention, have met with mixed success. This returns us to the question of what lessons we have learned from these diverse national experiences with financial intermediation

---

[39] Federal Reserve, *Bulletin*, August 1995, Table 1.26.
[40] Federal Reserve, *Bulletin*, December 2007, Table 1.26.

and markets to improve our chances of "getting it right" in the twenty-first century and thereby capturing the benefits of more rapid economic growth.

I.   Dutch origins

Many of the basics of financial markets and intermediation were invented by merchants in the Mediterranean area, especially in the Italian city-states of Genoa and Venice, by the fourteenth and fifteenth centuries, but were innovated and improved in northern Europe beginning in the late sixteenth century.[41] The Dutch Republic, created in 1581 by an alliance of seven provinces against the Hapsburg government of Philip II of Spain, lay on the northern fringes of the Holy Roman Empire which, as Voltaire was to famously note, was neither holy, nor Roman, nor an empire. As a small, strategically-placed but resource-poor country surrounded by many, even smaller countries, the Dutch earned much of their income through trade that was paid for in foreign coin from neighboring principalities and duchies. This foreign coin increasingly came to dominate as the circulating medium within the Dutch Republic. Its rise as a circulating medium, however, was not the benign result of its ready availability, but rather was actually encouraged and rewarded by the policies of foreign mints on the Dutch Republic's borders per Gresham's Law (bad money drives out good money). These mints stood to gain from seigniorage resulting from the incremental debasements of local coin by reductions in the precious metal content whenever their exchange value was set by custom or regulation. Indeed, the legal assignment of exchange values to specific coins through mint ordinances exacerbated the problem by adding the force of law to Gresham's economic law: whenever a debtor was given the choice of payment in two or more coins, payment was always made in the least valuable coin. Moreover, coins with high precious metal contents but low legal value were continually being re-minted into light, debased coins for use in payment whenever the seigniorage on the new coin was less than the saving to the debtor from paying off the creditor in the new coin. Competition among mints and between countries limited the amount of this seigniorage and kept the incremental debasements small, but the inducement was ever-present and on-going.

In an effort to resolve this problem, the Dutch established an exchange bank in 1609 to convert foreign coin into domestic payment – the *Wisselbank*. The bank, also known as the Bank of Amsterdam, stood

---

[41] See, for example, Munro, *Bullion*; Mueller, *Venetian*.

ready to receive deposits of coin that met its strict standards for weight and purity for safekeeping in return for a fee (*agio*) payable every six months. In return, the depositor was issued a bank receipt that was denominated in bank money, *banco shillengen*. This receipt could be used either to redeem the original deposit (a là Cloakroom banking) or, as in earlier deposit banks such as the Casa di San Giorgio in Genoa and the Rialto bank in Venice, could be used to make book entry – giro – payments between customers at the bank. These receipts were also tradable. Unlike a modern deposit bank, however, the Wisselbank made no loans – indeed overdrafts on one's account were penalized – but it did offer foreign exchange services for its customers, much as currency boards do today.

For a while, the bank struggled to win universal acceptance of the banco shillengen as an alternative medium of exchange, but it eventually proved its worth by protecting creditors from payments in debased coins. At the same time, book entry settlement proved a more efficient means of payment. Moreover, the city of Amsterdam guaranteed the deposits, and the deposits were secured from attachments by creditors. Since the bank did not make loans or grant overdraft privileges, use of the banco shillengen verified the credit-worthiness of a customer. Debasement of foreign coin accelerated as the Eighty Years War wound down and deposits with the Wisselbank surged. As a result, the banco shillengen became the preferred medium of exchange, representing the de facto creation of a fiat monetary standard. This process was completed by the late seventeenth century when bank money could no longer be redeemed for the original deposit. As a result, Quinn and Roberds, in Chapter 2, characterize the Wisselbank as the first true central bank in the world – a major accomplishment for a nation that was at war until the Peace of Westphalia in 1648.[42]

Not only did the Dutch improve upon Italian banking practices, they also innovated on the financial instruments that had been issued by governments and other public entities in the Italian city states. For example, in 1171, the Venetian state had funded a naval fleet for war against the Byzantine emperor by forcing taxpayers to accept bonds paying 5 percent interest until repaid.[43] Even before the Dutch Revolt, the city-states of the Hapsburg Netherlands had developed transferable book debts in the form of life-annuities.[44] By the seventeenth, and especially the eighteenth, centuries, Amsterdam increasingly financed

---

[42] Gillat, *La Banque*, finds echoes of the *Wisselbank* in the structure and functions of the European Central Bank.

[43] See Pezzolo, "Italian Monti" quoting Luzzatto, *Il debito*, p. 11.

[44] Tracy, *Financial Revolution*.

the defense of the Dutch state by issuing general obligation bonds that were more readily transferable. In Chapter 3, Jonkers and Gelderbloom document how these new debt instruments, together with equity issued by joint-stock companies, most notably the Dutch East India Company (VOC), gradually supplanted real estate holdings in the portfolio of wealthy institutional investors such as orphanages, hospitals and the poor house. These assets were generally purchased from middlemen, indicative of a growing secondary market, and seem to have been accurately and competitively priced.

Compared with the life annuities and real estate which they displaced, these new financial instruments proved to be more easily resold, less idiosyncratic in their pricing, and of shorter duration to maturity. As a result, they exhibited much less price volatility, and bond-holders were able to reduce their average cash balances and increase their income-earnings assets. For example, in the middle of the seventeenth century, the Amsterdam orphanage often had a cash balance of 60–80,000 guilders whereas during the eighteenth century this balance was reduced to just 4,000 guilders. Experience with these new instruments in the charitable endowments also educated the trustees about their advantages and encouraged greater use of such instruments among the wealthy as part of their portfolio of assets.

II.   Innovations of Dutch finance in France and the UK

The accumulation of staggeringly large government debts by the major participants of the War of the Spanish Succession and the concurrent Great Northern War in the Baltic region led France and the UK to endeavor to imitate the Dutch innovations in banking and securities markets as best they could. In France, the prime mover was economist John Law, the originator of what would become known as the "real bills doctrine" which was adopted as the cornerstone of Federal Reserve credit policy when the institution was created in 1913.

Born in 1671 to a family of bankers–goldsmiths in the Scottish county of Fife, Law had fled to the European continent as a young man after being convicted of murder following a duel in which his opponent was killed. While there, he spent much of his time in Amsterdam, which was still the center of finance and banking, and in Paris, the center of culture.[45] While in Paris, he gained the confidence of the Duke of Orleans, regent for young Louis XV, and, as a result, had the opportunity to put

---

[45] Murphy, *John Law*.

his ideas into practice: taking over French public finance in a creative public-debt-for-private-equity swap.

According to François Velde, in Chapter 4, the subsequent events are regarded quite differently in Britain and France. In the UK, the focus has been on the price of stock. There, the episode is referred to as the Mississippi Bubble and the events are seen as the precursor of other speculative bubbles in Amsterdam and London that ended in 1720. The French (and Dr. Velde), on the other hand, take a more holistic view and refer to the episode as Law's system.

In Chapter 4, Velde lays bare the details of the debt-for-equity swap which underlay Law's audacious scheme and asks the question "Could it have worked?" If the answer is "Yes" then, Velde argues, the system was not a bubble despite its appearance. Law's system began with the establishment of a private bank, the aptly named "Banque Générale Privée" ("General private bank") in May 1716. The bank's principal asset was a specific type of French government debt known as *billets d' état* ("bills of state"). Unlike most sovereign debt today issued by leading countries, these were regarded as relatively risky assets, and Law's bank had acquired much of this debt in exchange for equity in the bank.

The bank, in turn, issued paper money which was accepted in payment of debts to the government, a privilege that Law had won thanks to his friendship with the regent, and was redeemable upon demand in legal tender coin. On the other side of the balance sheet, the bank generated its earnings from the interest payments on the national debt by discounting bills, and by selling foreign exchange. Despite this seemingly thin financial base, the bank was successful and had a note circulation of between forty and fifty million livres per year against which it maintained a fairly conservative reserve ratio of around 50 percent. This assured that the bank's notes were widely accepted and easily redeemed at par at the bank.

A year later, Law branched out by taking over a newly created trading company, the Mississippi Company, and renaming it the Company of the West (*Compagnie d'Occident*), the name of a defunct trading company created to trade with New France. To raise capital for this new venture, Law once again offered the public a chance to buy equity using national debt instead of cash. This time, however, the public got a better deal. In exchange for their risky sovereign debts, they received, instead, an uncertain commercial debt, one whose assets were the same risky sovereign debt plus French Louisiana. Subscriptions were slow at first but, as the value of the company stock took off, holders of debt grew increasingly eager to swap their sovereign debt for equity in the company.

To achieve some of these early price gains and subsequently to maintain the price, the company often entered the market as a buyer on its own account using loans from Law's new bank – the *Banque Royale*, whose notes did not have to be redeemed in coin. The resulting price gains in Mississippi stock from priming the pump were crucial in persuading the public to swap their sovereign debt for equity in the expanded *Compagnie des Indes*.

In early 1720, the Banque Royale merged with the Compagnie des Indes, and the Banque's notes were made interchangeable with the Compagnie's shares at a fixed price of 9,000 livres. However, Law (along with many others, including Richard Cantillon who made a fortune speculating against the Compagnie) soon realized that this price was too high. As a result, he tried to reduce the Banque's issues of notes and to reduce the support price of Compagnie shares, arguing (to no avail) that his sudden deflation of the money supply had maintained the real value of the Compagnie's shares. Instead, investors withdrew their savings as fast as they could and share prices collapsed.

Given the earnings from the various enterprises that comprised the greatly enlarged Compagnie des Indes by the end of 1719 – including the mints, the tax farms, the settlement of Louisiana, the tobacco monopoly, sugar monopoly and trade with Asia – Velde asks whether a share price of 9,000 livres per share in the Mississippi Company was justified in early 1720. His answer is "No." However, Velde argues that Law's innovations were legal under French jurisprudence and prevailing custom. So, the system could have survived had Law not run up the price of stock to speed up the debt for equity swap and then tried to sustain that price.

Dutch financial practices also spread to England as a result of the Glorious Revolution which placed William of Orange on the British throne and brought his advisors to the country. This event has been celebrated by North and Weingast as the triumph of the rule of law in the UK, putting all citizens on a more or less equal footing and ending the arbitrary exercise of power by the monarch.[46] Key to the rule of law was certainty regarding legal outcomes and the sanctity of contracts. In Chapter 5, Gary Shea challenges the rosy picture of an abrupt transformation in law and custom in his examination of the legal fallout from the South Sea Bubble.

One of the largest speculators in South Sea stock, and an important supporter of Tory efforts to create a competing company for the Whig-dominated Bank of England and East India Company, was Henry

---

[46] North and Weingast, "Constitutions."

Bentinck, the first Duke of Portland and one of William's closest advisors. The Duke had purchased a fortune of forward contracts for South Sea stock at optimistic, even surreal, prices from a number of parties including Sir George Caswall (arguably the savviest and most active stockbroker in the London market). However, after prices collapsed in May 1720 and a fortune was at stake, the Duke reneged upon his commitments.

Caswall, himself a member of the House of Commons until he was temporarily expelled in 1721 on ethics charges arising from the bubble, held forward contracts from the Duke to buy South Sea stock valued in excess of £250,000. Many of these remained unconsummated when the bubble burst, and Sir George sought specific performance from the Duke as his legal remedy.

In a story reminiscent of that later told by Charles Dickens in *Bleak House* in the case of *Jarndyce* v. *Jarndyce*, this legal conflict spanned the generations. The first Duke of Portland died in 1726 with the case still unresolved but posing a large potential liability against his estate (then valued at £850,000). Legal proceedings dragged on for another fifteen years beyond the first Duke's death, prosecuted by Sir George's son, until it was eventually rejected by the courts on the grounds that Sir George had failed to pursue his claim in a timely manner and with sufficient vigor. Sir George died shortly thereafter.

In his various pleadings against specific performance on the contracts, the Duke's lawyers faced a dilemma: on the one hand, prevailing legal opinion appears to have held that forward contracts where the future price was vastly in excess of the current market price violated rules on usury. However, to assert a claim that Caswall was guilty of usury would be to admit the legality of the underlying contracts.

Nor was the Duke of Portland's case the only one in which a member of the aristocracy managed to escape their legal obligations in the wake of the bubble. Antoin Murphy in his biography of Richard Cantillon tells of Cantillon's suit against Lady Mary Herbert, the daughter of the Duke of Powis, who similarly failed to honor her Mississippi Company contracts not because she could not do so, but because it would have been too expensive for her.[47] Clearly, during the first half of the eighteenth century it still mattered who the counter-party was in any litigation, regardless of the legal reforms introduced as a result of the Glorious Revolution. However, the key point is that the British courts did not invalidate the contracts per se as the French courts had done after the

---

[47] Murphy, *Richard Cantillon*.

collapse of Law's system. Consequently, active trading on the London stock market was able to resume while in France it stagnated.

III.   Spreading commercial financial networks

In Chapter 6, Marc Flandreau and his co-authors derive new estimates of interest rates in the eighteenth century, based upon the commercial bills market, in three important and closely-linked markets: London, Amsterdam and Paris. Whereas mercantilist governments monitored trade flows quite closely, the commercial bills market lay largely outside of the scope of government regulation and legislation and was global in scope. Unlike other markets, it relied almost exclusively on private personal arrangements based upon the reputation of the principals and so, the authors argue, a London bill drawn, for example, on an Amsterdam bank represented an ideal vehicle in which to hide a loan while the payment of interest could be disguised within the exchange rate. This was an important advantage in markets generally subject to a variety of usury caps on interest rates, and it facilitated the international flow of funds among the important trading nations of western Europe by "flying below the radar screen" of nationalistic governments.

Since the principals involved in this market were well-known players involved in repeated games, the authors claim that interest rates which they derive are essentially risk-free rates – certainly more so than interest rates on sovereign debt at the time. Moreover, the series which they derive are more consistent with one another and across time than those previously available.[48] As a result, these interest rate estimates are likely to find widespread use among those working on eighteenth-century finance.

The key to developing these interest rate estimates is to recognize that the bills of exchange have two components – one an interest rate, r (defined as an annual rate), the other, an "exchange rate." This "exchange rate," a_{ij}, is the price that bankers in one market, i, are willing to pay for currency in market j at some future date. Thus, for example, on a sight bill payable in 90 days, the calculation would be:

$$a_{ij} = \frac{1}{1 + \frac{r}{4}}$$

This allows merchants to quote (unregulated) exchange rates rather than (regulated) interest rates and this formula can easily be modified to allow for differences in risk between markets.

---

[48] For example, Homer and Sylla, *History*.

In deriving these interest rates, Flandreau *et al.* build upon the work of Eric Schubert, a former student of Larry Neal's.[49] War finance had created a raft of public debt. This took a variety of forms; 3 percent Consols in the UK, bearer obligations in Holland. Both were negotiable instruments, easily transferred among merchants thereby increasing the number of ways in which they could settle their accounts with each other, regardless of nationality.

Throughout the eighteenth century, London merchants enjoyed interest rates that were only slightly higher than those in Amsterdam. Paris merchants, on the other hand, had to pay higher rates but these were still below those required of merchants in Italy and Spain. Moreover, Paris credit arrangements, managed largely independently of the monarchy after reforms undertaken in 1726, provided more stability than either London or Amsterdam. While state finances in Europe were being transformed by the on-going financial revolutions of the eighteenth century, the payments system for private trade by European merchants managed to flourish, notwithstanding the occasional shocks to the system from war finance.

Following the adoption of the Federal Constitution, the US embarked upon a series of financial reforms under the leadership of its first Secretary of the Treasury, Alexander Hamilton. In the space of three years, Hamilton transformed the finances of the nation. He persuaded Congress to establish a US Mint, adopt the bimetallic standard, repudiate the Continental dollar, consolidating sovereign interest-bearing debt under the federal government, ensured the regular payment of interest on that obligation, and established a joint-stock independent central bank. The breadth and nature of these accomplishments prompt Richard Sylla to assess the relative merits of US and UK finance. He concludes that between 1789 and 1830 the US grew more rapidly than the UK largely as a result of Hamilton's financial reforms. By 1830 its financial system had at least achieved parity, if not superiority, with the UK's. Unfortunately, these gains were dissipated by Jackson's brand of democracy, a.k.a. populism. Specifically, Jackson's veto of the renewal of the Second Bank of the United States' charter, led to the extinction of central banking in the US in 1836.[50] In the seventy-plus years that followed the demise of the Second Bank, the US grew relatively more slowly than the UK, and throughout that same period the UK's financial institutions were superior to those in the US. The UK's success,

---

[49] Schubert, "The Ties."
[50] See, for example, Temin, *Jacksonian*; Rockoff, "Money."

however, was not due to her superior innovation during the intervening period but rather to US reverses under Jackson.

In assessing the role of finance in economic development in Chapter 7, Sylla identifies six key elements. First, in his report on Public Credit, Hamilton set forth a clear statement of the importance of public credit and laid down a roadmap by which to restore confidence in the government both at home and abroad. Second, the essentially worthless Continental dollar was replaced by new coins based upon a bimetallic standard and all bank money was to be exchangeable upon demand into this legal tender. Third, Hamilton created the first of two nineteenth-century central banks in the US, the First Bank of the United States. This joint-stock bank was 20 percent owned by the federal government and had an authorized capital of $10 million – a huge sum relative to money supply at the time – which gave it the economic power to serve as regulator of the commercial banking system in addition to its role as banker to the federal government. From the beginning, the First Bank was a branch bank with six branches in the nation's major centers of commerce. In contrast, the Bank of England did not establish branches until 1826 and it remained a purely private institution until after 1944. Fourth, the task of chartering individual commercial banks was left to the individual states which were able to fine-tune their size and organizational structure to best suit heterogeneous local conditions. By 1830, these states had chartered more than 500 of them, each with rights of note issue, convertible upon demand into legal tender.[51] These banks financed business and provided intermediation services through a mix of short-term loans to outsiders and longer term loans to insiders, the latter essentially acting as a closed-end mutual fund. Fifth, the US established a securities market. Indeed, there were several securities markets in major population centers in the US such as Boston and Philadelphia as well as New York whereas the UK had only one. These security markets traded both equities and bonds derived from a variety of public and private corporations including canal companies, turnpikes, state and local governments, as well as manufacturing enterprises and banks. The markets were also successful in selling American securities to foreigners. Lastly, the US had a much more liberal attitude regarding corporate charters and the creation of joint-stock corporations in the private sector. Indeed, the legal basis for these institutions was already well established by 1819 when Chief Justice John Marshall declared that a corporation was "an artificial being existing only in contemplation of the law."[52]

---

[51] The best accounting for state banks in America is by Weber, "Early State Banks."
[52] Marshall, J. "Trustees."

Jackson's squabble with the Second Bank of the United States and its president, Nicholas Biddle, however, spoiled it all, eventually plunging the country into a financial crisis from which it did not recover until the early 1840s. Moreover, the federal government was hobbled in its dealings with the public and with the financial markets for much of the rest of the century by the absence of a central bank (despite the creation of the independent Treasury in the 1850s which took over some of its more mundane day-to-day banking activities).

The US was not alone in its failure to successfully imitate the superior financial structures that emerged in the UK after 1825. Surprisingly, other products of Britain's much-touted parliamentary democracy – the gold standard and common law basis for enforcement of contracts and private property that are taken as key elements for its financial success – also fall short of their success in the mother country. In Chapter 8, Larry Neal reviews Lance Davis and Robert Gallman's monumental work on international capital flows and emerging capital markets in the nineteenth century to see what common lessons these scholars draw from their intensive examination of the financial developments in the UK, the US, Canada, Argentina and Australia.[53]

Each of the four frontier economies received huge inflows of British capital to finance their development. Consequently, each had firsthand experience with British financial organization and practice, albeit in somewhat different forms in each. Argentina and Australia imported the institutions themselves with British banks setting up overseas branches in each. This proved to be a mistake when, in the deflationary crises of the 1890s, the British-based banks favored the interests of the home country over their adoptive country. The US, on the other hand, had developed a capital market which financed business and substituted for bank loans while, in Canada, the capital market complemented the nationwide bank branching system. Although these two countries differed in their approach, the institutional innovations in both appear motivated to maintain financial independence from Britain, and the essential lesson is the need to make capital markets complementary to the operation of a country's banking system regardless of how that system might be constituted.

In Chapter 9, Richard Sullivan follows up on Lance Davis's well-known work that showed a dramatic narrowing of large regional variations in US interest rates during the last quarter of the nineteenth century.[54]

---

[53] Davis and Gallman, *Evolving*.
[54] See Davis, "The Investment Market." For a long time following the publication of Davis' work, the story was of segmented local credit markets during the antebellum

Davis attributed this narrowing of interest rate differentials to the development of the national commercial paper market. Subsequently, John James and Richard Sylla attributed it to increased competition within the banking industry, albeit from somewhat different sources. James credited it to easier entry into banking, including state banking.[55] Sylla tipped his hat to the easing of federal regulation of national banking charters, especially the lowering of capital requirements, in the Gold Standard Act of 1900.[56]

Sullivan uses estimates of regional national bank profit rates as a proxy for the incentives to enter or exit the banking industry and posits that systematic differences would be due to differences in financial risk between regions. His results show that the market efficiency steadily improved between 1870–1884 so that essentially all differences were eliminated between 1885 through the end of the century. However, differences re-emerged after 1900, due possibly, as Sylla had argued, to the easing of federal regulations in the Gold Standard Act which allowed the entry of new, inexperienced banks. These increased uncertainty in the cost structure of banks and also led to poorer performance in the loan portfolio. Moreover, national banks faced renewed competition from state banks which staged a dramatic comeback following the widespread adoption of the check as a means of doing business thereby competing away any excess returns. Moreover, other non-bank financial intermediaries, most notably trust companies, increasingly competed for business.[57] Thus, the US eventually "got it right" in making its banks complementary to its capital markets, even though the process was uneven as the forces of competition worked through its developing financial structure.

IV.   Banking and financial market innovations in the twentieth century

The disruptions of the European banking systems and capital markets during World War I led to boom times for the New York Stock Exchange in the 1920s. However, its members soon found that competitive forces from other securities markets across the US and across the street threatened that success by nibbling away at their business. During

period, followed by the integration of these regional markets in the years following the Civil War. Subsequent work by Bodenhorn and Rockoff, "Regional Interest Rates," however, shows a similar convergence of regional interest rates taking place in the pre-Civil War era only to be disrupted by the war with its devastating effect upon southern banking.

[55] James, "Development."   [56] Sylla, "Federal Policy."   [57] Neal, "Trust Companies."

the stock market boom of the 1920s, the volume of daily trades sorely stressed the order mechanism on the exchange. Brokers frequently fell behind in executing orders. Meanwhile, the expansion of stock market activity led more firms to seek market listings and more investors to participate. One solution to this problem was to increase the number of markets but, for matters of prestige and liquidity, most firms sought to be listed on the New York Stock Exchange rather than a regional or the Curb Market (later known as the American Exchange). Because the existing brokers could not physically execute more orders, despite efforts to improve their technology and trading systems, an obvious solution was to increase the number of brokers. However, doing so would divide the commission pool in more ways and so was contrary to individual interests. As a result, such proposals tended to be voted down by the membership. But, as the bull market of the 1920s continued, opposition to this solution weakened and, on February 18, 1929, the exchange declared a one-quarter seat dividend for each member. These quarter seats by themselves were of no use whatsoever, but they could be sold and combined to make a whole seat, subject to the approval of the membership committee of the New York Stock Exchange. For example, J.P. Morgan and his son Junius and John D. Rockefeller each sold their dividend rights after the market had peaked in early September 1929 but before the market crashed. Each sold his quarter seat for $125,000 making the real price of a seat on the New York Stock Exchange the highest it would ever be in the exchange's history. Since these brokers were the ultimate market insiders, Eugene White examines the data on seat sales and prices for insight into market sentiment during this crucial episode in our history in Chapter 10.

White finds that those who bought these dividend seats were, for the most part, not the experienced market pros. Instead, they were either "new money" who wanted the prestige of a seat on the New York Stock Exchange and perhaps the privilege of rubbing shoulders with the likes of Morgan and Rockefeller or they were persons with some market experience but usually in some junior capacity such as a page or a clerk. Seats also sold on regional markets though, there, the market was often much thinner. The NYSE pattern carries over to these other markets; in the run up to the crash, the more experienced brokers were increasingly pessimistic, but their reticence went unnoticed by the less experienced market neophytes.

With the onset of the Great Depression, US authorities attempted a variety of policy responses, most of which seemed at the time and in retrospect to be inadequate to the challenges.[58] Burdekin and Weidenmier

---

[58] Friedman and Schwartz, *Monetary History*; Meltzer, *A History*.

explore the results of one unusual – and largely overlooked – attempt by the US Treasury to pump liquidity into the system: the Silver Purchase Program initiated by the Roosevelt Administration in 1934. At the time, interest rates were already low – a fraction of 1 percent – and could not be forced much lower. There were those in the system who argued that the low interest rates were indicative of abundant and easy credit. Yet unemployment was high, business activity low, and the public overwhelmingly pessimistic. As a result, more economic stimulus was desired but traditional open market operations by the US Federal Reserve would likely be ineffective, given the low interest rates then prevailing. Indeed, recent history, particularly the experiences of the Bank of Japan during the 1990s facing a similar set of circumstances, indicates that even had such operations been attempted they might well have failed or have been prohibitively expensive.

In any event, President Franklin Delano Roosevelt yielded to the silver lobby, which had been vocal and active since the early 1870s, and initiated a policy to buy silver for monetary purposes beginning in June 1934. Just as in 1878, and again in 1890, the US Treasury generally issued silver certificates for the silver received rather than minting coin. These silver certificates circulated as legal tender for all debts public and private and could be redeemed at the US Treasury for silver dollars. In less than a year, the US Treasury accumulated more than 13,000 tons of silver, only a small fraction of which (under 800 tons) was newly mined. In the process, they reversed the long-run decline in the share of silver in the US currency. By 1932, this had dwindled to about 12 percent. Six years later its share had almost doubled, and domestic silver production, most of it from western states, had more than doubled. Although several other authors including Friedman and Schwartz, and Allan Meltzer have noted this silver purchase program, Burdekin and Weidenmier argue, in Chapter 11, that these other authors failed to fully appreciate the expansionary significance of this action, particularly in the western, silver producing states whose political weight was much greater than their economic significance at the national level.[59] Burdekin and Weidenmier's examination of state-level data shows a very favorable impact of the Silver Purchase Act on the silver-producing states and their near neighbors in the western US.

In Chapter 12, Alan Dye and Richard Sicotte look at the role played by US trade policy during the Great Depression on the financial performance of Cuban sugar manufacturers and the impact which this had

---

[59] Each thinly populated state in the west had two Senators and at least one Representative in Congress.

on their New York investment banks. In the wake of the Spanish–American war of 1898, the US had imposed the Platt amendment on the Cuban government. The brainchild of Secretary of War Elihou Root, this amendment defined US–Cuban relations until 1934. Among its various provisions, the US received Guantánamo – a right that the US has still not given up – and Cuba was denied full sovereignty rights. For example, the Cuban government was prohibited from entering into any foreign debt agreement unless interest payments were guaranteed from ordinary revenue, and she was blocked from entering into foreign treaties except with the US. The *quid pro quo* for this agreement was that Cuban sugar producers would receive a 20 percent reduction in the US tariff.[60] Under this arrangement, the Cuban sugar industry prospered. On the eve of World War I, Cuba accounted for almost one-quarter of the world's sugar production and sugar was generating perhaps 80 percent of the country's export earnings.

The prosperity enjoyed by Cuban–American sugar producers, how-ever, depended critically upon the world price for sugar and the US tariff policy. At the height of the post-World War I boom, sugar prices had peaked at 23.6 cents per pound. In the next few months, however, they fell by more than 80 percent. In the face of these low prices, Cuban sugar companies were forced into bankruptcy and faced foreclosure by the US banks that had financed their expansion in the prewar decades. In the wake of these takeovers, the US banks reorganized the Cuban sugar industry into a more oligopolistic structure. What new financing flowed into Cuba was invested in cost-reducing measures rather than in modernizing the industry at a time when Cuba's position in the US marketplace was being eroded.

In 1922, the US raised tariff rates on sugar in the Fordney–McCumber tariff. More importantly, however, Puerto Rico gained ground on Cuba and they were further rewarded under the Smoot–Hawley tariff of 1930. When worldwide sugar prices collapsed at the end of the 1920s to as little as 2–2.5 cents per pound, Cuban sugar produ-cers could no longer stay in business, despite cost reductions, and the banks which had foreclosed on the sugar industry in 1920–1921 now faced huge losses. For example, in 1931 the National City Bank was forced to write down its $25 million investment in Cuban sugar to just $1 million. This had a big effect on the balance sheet of US banks, exacerbating their solvency and liquidity problems. Dye and Sicotte use this largely ignored episode to show the complementary roles of banks and security markets, this time in mutual misery.

[60] Pérez, *Cuba*.

In Chapter 13, Kirsten Wandschneider examines the performance of four central banks operating under the interwar gold exchange standard. Her central question is whether central bank independence was a substitute or a complement to a fixed exchange rate regime. This addresses the important historical and economic issue of how best to solve the "trilemma," the need for an open economy to choose only two of the three desirable policy regimes possible: fixed exchange rates, monetary independence and free capital movements.[61] The gold exchange standard, which tried to replicate the advantages of the classical gold standard after the massive monetary and debt expansions created by World War I, enjoyed only a brief life between 1925 and 1931.[62] Under this system, no gold coins circulated but rather countries held foreign currency which was itself convertible into gold upon demand.

Initially, both Austria and Poland pegged their currency to the Swiss franc, although Austria eventually switched to the US dollar. Hungary, on the other hand, linked its fortunes with London and the pound sterling, while Czechoslovakia managed to stabilize its currency without foreign support. Indeed, it even participated in the international loans to Austria and Hungary. In time, it had substantial credits from France, chiefly for military rearmament.

All four countries were obliged to maintain fixed exchange rates against currencies pegged to gold. In adopting fixed exchange, each country faced the problem of determining the rate of exchange at which to re-establish convertibility. Each opted for convertibility at a small fraction of their prewar exchange rates. Britain, however, refused to recognize reality and tried instead to maintain London's position in the international capital market by keeping its promises. To this end, Winston Churchill returned the country to the gold standard at the prewar rate of exchange in May of 1925 but with a chronically overvalued currency. Eventually, in September 1931 the UK was finally forced off the gold standard. This clearly had a negative impact upon Hungary which had linked itself to the British pound.

The four case studies in Wandschneider's analysis represent quite different combinations of circumstances. Three of the countries were successor states to the Austro-Hungarian Empire while the fourth, Poland, lay sandwiched between Germany and Russia. The central banks in Austria and Hungary had been created under the League of Nations with an implicit mandate to serve the interests of international creditors first, rather than support domestic policies. That is to say, these

[61] See, for example, Obstfeld *et al.*, "Monetary Sovereignty."
[62] Eichengreen, *Golden Fetters*.

banks had a high degree of central bank independence from domestic pressure. Nevertheless, she finds that none of the banks fully committed to the "rules of the game" of the gold exchange standard despite the attempts by the League of Nations Financial Commission and the private investment banks committed to sustaining the market value of their foreign debts. The two democracies – Austria and Czechoslovakia – were most responsive to domestic political pressures, despite the nominal independence of the central bank in Austria and the explicit government control of the central bank in Czechoslovakia. This finding is consistent with the observation by Eichengreen and others that post-World War I democracies made it impossible for central banks to adhere strictly to the gold standard ideals of fixed exchange rates.[63] Similarly, more recently emerging market economies and new democracies have found it difficult to maintain fixed exchange rates with their major trading partners. On the other hand, the central banks of Hungary and Poland, with their authoritarian regimes, responded mainly to signals from Berlin until exchange controls removed all responsiveness to external finance.

In Chapter 14, Michael Bordo and David Wheelock examine the relationship and the timing between asset price appreciation and the business cycle for a number of OECD countries for the twentieth century. Their goal is to determine what role macro-economic policy played in creating asset price appreciation and in bringing about depreciation of asset prices. Although their theory probably applies to all assets, they focus solely on equity prices rather than other assets, such as housing, in part because there have been too few cycles in the housing market. Moreover, they confine their attention to expansions and ignore declines. Their data cover six western European countries: the UK, Germany, France, Italy, the Netherlands and Sweden; and three outposts of European settlement in the New World: Australia, Canada and the US; and one Asian country, Japan. For each, they have monthly stock prices adjusted for inflation from the second or third decade of the twentieth century through the end of the century. They define a stock market boom as any period of three or more years from trough to peak in which there was and average annual rate of stock price growth of 10 percent per year or more.

Consistent with economic theory, they find that monetary policy plays a positive role in asset price appreciation working through falling interest rates. This asset price appreciation, however, comes to an end when interest rates finally begin to rise as a result of more restrictive monetary policy, excess demand for loanable funds, or a rise in the inflation rates.

---

[63] Eichengreen, *Golden Fetters.*

The importance of their finding lies in its general application across the varied financial structures of the countries in their sample, as well as across the variation in financial regimes that each country maintained through the successive traumas of the twentieth century – recovery from World War I, the worldwide depression of the 1930s, the devastation of World War II and the economic miracles that followed until the oil shocks of the 1970s. The importance of complementarity between banks' relationship financing and the pricing of traded securities is underscored for today's policy makers.

In the final chapter, Larry Neal, in whose honor these individual studies were presented, poses the ultimate question: can governments and regulatory institutions today learn valuable lessons from the past as global financial markets bounce from one crisis to another like the steel ball in a pinball machine? His guarded answer, readers will be happy to know, is basically optimistic. Even though governments have tended to kill the financial goose, whether the eggs it laid were silver, gold, or sound fiat money, in the long-run a growing number of countries have managed to "get it right," thanks to the strength of private incentives and the creativity of the human mind in working around regulations and problems and finding creative new solutions.

References

Athey, S., A. Atkeson and P.J. Kehoe. 2001. "On the Optimality of Transparent Monetary Policy," Federal Reserve Bank of Minneapolis Working Paper 613.

BBC News, international version. "Northern Rock Besieged by Savers," September 17, 2007: http://news.bbc.co.uk/2/hi/business/6997765.stm.

"EBC Lends $500bn to Lower Rates," December 18, 2007.

Bernanke, Ben. "The Subprime Mortgage Market." Speech to the Federal Reserve Bank of Chicago's 43rd Annual Conference on Bank Structure and Competition, Chicago, Illinois. May 17, 2007: www.federalreserve.gov/newsevents/speech/bernanke20070517a.htm.

Bodenhorn, Howard and Hugh Rockoff. 1992. "Regional Interest Rates in Antebellum America," in C. Goldin and H. Rockoff (eds.). *Strategic Factors in American Economic History: A Volume to Honor Robert W. Fogel*. Chicago: University of Chicago Press for NBER: 159–87.

Bruck, Connie. 1988. *The Predators' Ball: the Inside Story of Drexel Burnham and the Rise of the Junk Bond Raiders*. New York: Simon and Schuster.

Calomiris, Charles. May 1989. "Deposit Insurance: Lessons from the Record," *Economic Perspectives*: 10–30.

CNN Money.com. October 15, 2007. "Banks Seen Readying $100B Bailout. Reports: Citigroup, Others Working with Treasury Department to Protect against Further Securities Collapses."

Collins, M. 1992. "Overend Gurney Crisis, 1866," in P. Newman (ed.). *The New Palgrave Dictionary of Money and Finance*. London: Palgrave Macmillan.

Congressional Budget Office. *Budget and Economic Outlook*, January 2008.

Curry, Timothy and Lynn Shibut. December 2000. "The Cost of the Savings and Loan Crisis: Truth and Consequences," *FDIC Banking Review*, 13(2): 26–35.

Davis, Lance E. September 1965. "The Investment Market, 1870–1914: The Evolution of a National Market," *Journal of Economic History*, 25(3): 355–99.

Davis, Lance and Robert Gallman. 2001. *Evolving Capital Markets and International Capital Flows: Britain, the Americas, and Australia, 1865–1914*. New York: Cambridge University Press.

della Paolera, Gerardo and Alan M. Taylor. 2001. *Straining at the Anchor: the Argentine Currency Board and the Search for Macroeconomic Stability, 1880–1935*. Chicago: University of Chicago Press.

de Pinto, Isaac. 1774. *An Essay on Circulation and Credit*. London: J. Ridley.

Demirguc-Kunt, A., B. Karacaovali and L. Laeven. April 2005. "Deposit Insurance around the World: a Comprehensive Database," World Bank, unpublished working paper.

Dreyfus, Jean-Francois, Anthony Saunders and Linda Allen. 1994. "Deposit Insurance and Regulatory Forbearance: Are Caps on Insured Deposits Optimal?" *Journal of Money, Credit & Banking*, 26.

The Economist. November 2, 1996. "Passing on the Risks," 341, 7990: 73–4.

Eichengreen, Barry. 1992. *Golden Fetters: the Gold Standard and the Great Depression, 1919–1939*. New York: Oxford University Press.

FDIC. *History of the 80s: Volume I: An Examination of the Banking Crises of the 1980s and Early 1990s*. Available online from FDIC at: www.fdic.gov/bank/ historical/history/vol1.html.

Federal Reserve. *Bulletin*, various issues.

Financial Times. "Confidence in Northern Rock Collapses," September 14, 2007 "Darling Steps in to Halt Bank Run," September 18, 2007.

Ford, A. G. 1956. "Argentina and the Baring Crisis of 1890," *Oxford Economic Papers*, New Series, 8(2): 127–50.

Friedman, Milton and Anna Jacobson Schwartz. 1963. *A Monetary History of the United States, 1867–1960*. Princeton: Princeton University Press.

Geraats, Petra. March 2002. "Central Bank Transparency," University of Cambridge Working Paper.

Gillat, Lucien. 2004. *La Banque d'Amsterdam et le florin européen au temps de la Republique néerlandaise, (1610–1820)*. Paris: EHESS.

Guardian. "Ministers Prepare Plan to Nationalize Northern Rock," December 14, 2007.

Homer, Sidney and Richard Sylla. 2005. *A History of Interest Rates*. Hoboken: Wiley, 4th edition.

International Herald Tribune. "ECB Gives Banks Another Cash Injection," August 13, 2007.

"Crisis Deepens for Northern Rock," September 17, 2007: www.iht.com/ articles/2007/09/17/asia/17northern.php.

James, John A. December 1976. "The Development of the National Money Market, 1893–1911," *Journal of Economic History*, 36(4): 878–97.

Josephson, Matthew. 1934. *The Robber Barons: the Great American Capitalists, 1861–1901*. New York: Harcourt, Brace.

Levine, Ross. June 1997. "Financial Development and Economic Growth: Views and Agenda," *Journal of Economic Literature*, 35: 688–726.

2005. "Finance and Growth: Theory and Evidence," in Philippe Aghion and Steven Durlauf (eds.). *Handbook of Economic Growth*. The Netherlands: Elsevier Science.

Liggett v. Lee, 288 US 517 (1933).

Luzzatto, G. 1963. *Il debito pubblico della Repubblica di Venezia*. Milano-Varese.

Marshall, John. 1819. *Trustees of Dartmouth College v. Woodward*, 17 US (4 Wheat.) 518.

Martin, Ron and David Turner. 2000. "Demutualization and the Remapping of Financial Landscapes," *Transactions of the Institute of British Geographers*, 25(2): 221–41.

Mason, Joseph. 2001. "Reconstruction Finance Corporation Assistance to Financial Institutions and Commercial & Industrial Enterprise in the US Great Depression, 1932 – 1937," in Stijn Claessens, Simeon Djankov and Ashoka Mody (eds.). *Resolution of Financial Distress*. Washington, D.C.: World Bank Press: 167–204.

April 2003. "The Political Economy of RFC Assistance during the Great Depression," *Explorations in Economic History*, 40(2): 101–21.

Meltzer, Allan H. 2003. *A History of the Federal Reserve*: Chicago: University of Chicago Press.

Mishkin, Frederic S. October 2004. "Can Central Bank Transparency go too far," NBER Working Paper 10829.

Munro, John. 1992. *Bullion Flows and Monetary Policies in England and the Low Countries, 1350–1500*. Hampshire: Variorum.

Mueller, Reinhold C. 1997. *The Venetian Money Market: Banks, Panics, and the Public Debt, 1200–1500*. Baltimore: Johns Hopkins Press.

Murphy, Antoin E. 1986. *Richard Cantillon, Entrepreneur and Economist*. New York: Oxford University Press.

1997. *John Law: Economic Theorist and Policy-maker*. Oxford: Clarendon Press.

Neal, Larry. Spring 1971. "Trust Companies and Financial Innovation, 1897–1914," *Business History Review*, 55: 35–51.

New York Federal Reserve Bank. "William J. Mcdonough, President Federal Reserve Bank of New York Before the Committee on Banking and Financial Services," US House of Representatives, October 1, 1998.

New York Law Journal. "International Banking," September 7, 2005.

New York Times. "Fallen Star: the Regulators; Fed Chief Defends U.S. Role in Saving Giant Hedge Fund," October 2, 1998.

"Shaky Markets Prompt Rumors of Who's in Trouble," August 10, 2007.

"In Mortgage Plan, Lenders Set Terms," December 7, 2007.

North, Douglass and Barry R. Weingast. December 1989. "Constitutions and Commitment: the Evolution of Institutions Governing Public Choice in Seventeenth-Century," *Journal of Economic History*, 49(4): 803–32.

Northern Rock. "Corporate Profile": http://companyinfo.northernrock.co.uk/investorRelations/corporateProfile/.

"Highlights": http://companyinfo.northernrock.co.uk/investorRelations/results/stockEx062607.asp.

"Stock Exchange Announcement Northern Rock PLC: Trading Statement for the 9 months to 30 September 2006," issued October 2, 2006: http://companyinfo.northernrock.co.uk/investorRelations/results/stockEx061002.asp.

Northern Rock Foundation. "History": www.nr-foundation.org.uk/about_history.html.

Oberholtzer, Ellis P. 1907. *Jay Cooke, Financier of the Civil War*. Philadelphia: G.W. Jacobs & Co.

Obstfeld, Maurice, J.C. Shambaugh, and A.M. Taylor. Special Issue 2004. "Monetary Sovereignty, Exchange Rates, and Capital Controls: The Trilemma in the Interwar Period," *IMF Staff Papers* 51: 75–108.

Office of Thrift Supervision. *2006 Fact Book*, June 2007.

Patterson, R.H. 1870. "On our Home Monetary Drains, and the Crisis of 1866," *Journal of the Statistical Society of London*, 33(2): 216–42.

Pérez, Jr., Louis A. 1986. *Cuba under the Platt Amendment, 1902–1934*. Pittsburgh: University of Pittsburgh Press.

Pezzolo, Luciano. "Italian Monti: the Origins of Bonds and Government Debt," Yale University Working Paper.

Poole, William. November 30, 2001. "How Transparent Should a Central Bank Be?" The Philadelphia Fed Policy Forum, Federal Reserve Bank of Philadelphia.

Reuters, "Britain Passes Northern Rock Nationalization Law," February 21, 2008: http://www.reuters.com/article/businessNews/idUSL2138183920080221?feedType=RSS&feedName=businessNews.

Robinson, Joan. 1952. "The Generalisation of the General Theory," in Joan Robinson, *The Rate of Interest and Other Essays*. London: Macmillan.

Rockoff, Hugh. 1971. "Money, Prices and Banks in the Jacksonian Era," in Robert W. Fogel and Stanley L. Engerman (eds.). *The Reinterpretation of American Economic History*. New York: Harper & Row: 448–58.

Rousseau, Peter and Richard Sylla. 2003. "Financial Systems, Economic Growth and Globalization," in M. Bordo, A.M. Taylor and J.G. Williamson (eds.). *Globalization in Historical Perspective*. Chicago: University of Chicago Press: 373–416.

Schloemer, Ellen, Wei Li, Keith Ernst and Kathleen Keest. December 2006. "Losing Ground: Foreclosures in the Subprime Market and Their Cost to Homeowners," Center for Responsible Lending.

Schubert, Eric Stephen. 1986. "The Ties that Bound: Market Behavior in Foreign Exchange in Western Europe during the Eighteenth Century," unpublished Ph.D. thesis, University of Illinois at Urbana-Champaign.

Soboul, Albert. 1966. *La France à la veille de la Révolution*. Paris: Société d'Édition d'enseignement Supérieur.

Spiegel On-line International. "Bail-Out for Subprime Casualty: Baden-Württemberg Bank to Buy SachsenLB," August 27, 2007: www.spiegel.de/international/business/0,1518,502203,00.html.

Stewart, James B. 1991. *Den of Thieves*, New York: Simon & Schuster.

Stone, Dan G. 1990. *April Fools: an Insider's Account of the Rise and Collapse of Drexel Burnham*. New York: D.I. Fine.

Sylla, Richard. December 1969. "Federal Policy, Banking Market Structure, and Capital Mobilization in the United States, 1863–1913," *Journal of Economic History*, 29(4): 657–86.

Temin, Peter. 1969. *The Jacksonian Economy*, New York: W. W. Norton.

Tracy, James D. 1985. *A Financial Revolution in the Habsburg Netherlands: Renten and Renteniers in the County of Holland, 1515–1565*. Berkeley: University of California Press.

Wall Street Journal. "Citigroup Swings to a Loss, Plans to Raise More Capital," January 16, 2008.

Washington Post. "Banks Drop Plan Aimed at Easing Credit Crunch," December 22, 2007.

Weber, Warren E. June 2006. "Early State Banks in the United States: How Many Were There and When Did They Exist?" *Journal of Economic History*, 66(2): 433–55.

2 An economic explanation of the early Bank of Amsterdam, debasement, bills of exchange and the emergence of the first central bank[*]

Stephen Quinn and William Roberds

The early Dutch Republic experienced a monetary problem called incremental debasement, for mints repeatedly reduced the precious metal content of coins by small amounts. Adam Smith termed this the "small-state" problem because small, open economies often made substantial use of foreign coins, so debased foreign mints flowed into ports like Amsterdam. Around 1600, The Dutch Republic was awash in foreign coins and these were widely used as media of exchange.[1] The fragmented nature of minting authority within the Dutch Republic meant that debasement had a domestic component as well. Whether foreign or domestic, a debasement led to uncertainty in the value of payments, creating transaction costs that hampered commerce.

The Dutch authorities attempted to deal with this debasement problem through laws and regulations, but these were often slow and ineffective. It took decades, for example, for the Republic to establish full control over its numerous independent mints. By contrast, laws assigning coin values were enacted early and often, but these did not solve the problem of debasement. While these were intended to simplify the use of coins by giving them a known value (tale) in terms of a unit of account, we argue that these laws, called *mint ordinances*, had the unintended consequence of making the situation worse. The disconnect between legal and intrinsic value encouraged people to bring old coins with high intrinsic, but low legal value to the mint in order to repay their debts with newly debased coins. The mints benefited as well from the consequent increase in business and their government owners benefited

[*] The authors would like to thank Jeremy Atack, Joost Jonker, Charles Kahn, Larry Neal, Francois Velde, and David Weiman for comments on an earlier draft, Oscar Gelderblom for tips on numerous references, and especially M. S. Polak for sharing Volume II of his book *Historiografie En Economie Van De "Muntchaos."*

[1] Eight hundred foreign coins were officially recognized by the end of the sixteenth century (Dehing and 't Hart, "Linking the Fortunes", p. 40).

from the increase in seigniorage. Then as now, there was no free lunch, as the garnering of seigniorage through debasement imposed an onerous burden on the Dutch economy.

Another regulatory approach was the creation of an exchange bank or *Wisselbank*. Exchange banks were intended to address the debasement problem by limiting deposits to coins above a certain quality. When debt was settled through the exchange bank, lenders were protected from repayment in debased coin. To generate participation, municipalities, starting with Amsterdam in 1609, required that commercial debts embodied in bills of exchange had to be settled through the city's exchange bank. Because such bills were the dominant vehicle for international trade credit, merchants were compelled to open an account with the exchange bank.[2]

This chapter argues that the creation of the exchange bank, known as the Bank of Amsterdam or *Amsterdamsche Wisselbank*, was effective at reducing debasement.[3] The settlement of bills in bank money blunted debasement incentives by, ultimately, decoupling the connection between common coins and their ordinance value in the Dutch unit of account called the florin.[4] By shielding creditors – the beneficiaries (also called payees) of bills of exchange – from payment in debased coins, the exchange bank diminished the mints' ability to extract profits from these beneficiaries.

The initial success of the Wisselbank, however, was less than complete because much of the Republic's payment system remained outside the Republic's control. The final stabilization of Dutch coinage required the emergence of effective control by the central government over the domestic mints. Also, the regulations controlling the exchange bank were initially adjusted in unhelpful ways, so the development of the payment system took unexpected turns. This chapter tracks the institutional evolution of the Wisselbank within this nexus of regulations,

---

[2] Bills of exchange came to dominate short-run international finance in Northern Europe during the second half of the sixteenth century (de Vries and van der Woude, *First Modern Economy*, p.130). While bills of exchange dominated contracts for less than three months, bills obligatory (IOUs) were very important for three to twelve month borrowing (Gelderblom, "The Governance", p. 627).

[3] We present an abbreviated version of this argument in Quinn and Roberds, "Leap to Central."

[4] Synonymous with the guilder or *gulden*. The silver florin of Charles V was a coin set to be worth twenty stuiver coins, but the debasement of stuivers drove florins out of circulation in the sixteenth century (see Dehing and 't Hart "Linking the Fortunes," p. 38); van Dillen ("The Bank of Amsterdam," p. 82). By the founding of the Wisselbank in 1609, the unit of account in most of the Dutch Republic remained the florin despite there no longer being florin coins.

coins and bills of exchange in order to explain why the bank was founded, what effect it had, and how it evolved.[5]

One noteworthy, though unintended, consequence of the Wisselbank's success and peculiar regulatory changes was the creation of a new, parallel unit of account for major commercial transactions. A receipt for ten florins held *in banco* (the term for exchange bank money) came to represent more money than ten florins *current* (the term for local money). Though unwieldy to modern eyes, this system of parallel units of account seemed to have worked extremely well in practice.[6]

Another unintended consequence of the Wisselbank took even longer to evolve, but was ultimately even more revolutionary in nature: the emergence of bank money as a fiat monetary standard. By the late seventeenth century, exchange bank money lost the right of redemption into coins altogether, and the Wisselbank came to have no obligation to redeem its deposits on demand. Anticipating today's fiat money regimes, the predominant unit of account, the bank florin, was then no longer bound to any particular coin. Instead, the value of balances held at the Wisselbank derived from their ability to discharge debts. This development represented a historic shift in the nature of money, one that leads us to characterize the Wisselbank as the first true "central bank." In its mature form, the Bank of Amsterdam allowed the inhabitants of the Dutch Republic to,

[R]eap the advantages of a fixed exchange rate for their international trade and finance, encouraging their own merchants as well as foreign merchants to use their financing facilities for long-distance trade and long-term finance. At the same time, they were able to maintain the shock absorber benefits of a flexible exchange rate for their domestic economic activity.[7]

In a previous paper (Quinn and Roberds, "The Big Problem") we set out a formal model of the problematic monetary situation in the early years of the Republic and the impact which the Bank of Amsterdam had on this situation. Though stylized, the model allows for an examination of some, perhaps under-appreciated, general-equilibrium aspects of the Dutch "debasement problem." This chapter reviews the narrative history of the early years of the Bank of Amsterdam and demonstrates the

---

[5] Our view of the Amsterdam Wisselbank agrees with Gillard (*La banque d'Amsterdam*), but our focus is on the Republic's domestic monetary system rather than the florin's international standing.

[6] A modern analog might be the custom, common in some countries, of pricing large transactions in US dollars and smaller ones in the local currency.

[7] Neal, "How it all Began," p. 122.

explanatory power of our stylized model despite the complexities of the Dutch economy of the seventeenth century.[8]

I.   Debasement, the underlying problem

Around 1600, the fundamental monetary problem facing the Dutch Republic was that debtors (or their agents, called cashiers) had an incentive to pass debased coins to their creditors. This opportunity to profit from light coins existed because bills of exchange were debts denominated in the unit of account (florins), but the florin did not correspond to any particular coin. Rather, the value of various coins in terms of florins was specified through mint ordinances. When a debtor had two coins with the same ordinance value (tale), he and/or his cashier had incentives to pass the lighter one on to his creditor in a "Gresham's Law"[9] type decision.[10]

A key constraint in this story is that the debtor willingly gave his heavy coins to be debased into lighter coins. The debtor eventually profits only if the amount of silver (seigniorage) he pays to the mint for the new, lighter coin is less than the amount of silver he avoids paying his creditor. In other words, a debasement is successful only if the mint and the debtor can share the silver that they are denying the creditor, in which case both mint and debtor have an incentive to "collude" against a creditor.[11]

Establishing the debtor's incentive to participate in the debasement is important. Lacking this incentive, mints could offer debased coins, but

---

[8] Many of the original documents relevant to the history of the Wisselbank are available in a collection compiled by van Dillen, *Bronnen*. Given our limited facility with seventeenth-century Dutch, we rely heavily on van Dillen's ("Oprichting" and "Bloeitijd") account, which is largely based on these documents. An English-language summary of this account can be found in van Dillen, "The Bank of Amsterdam." Coinage data are from Polak, *Historiografie en Economie, Deel I and Deel II*.

[9] We use the term "Gresham's law" with considerable caution, as our approach is inconsistent with some common interpretations of this "law."

[10] For expositional convenience, our discussion will proceed "as if" a debt would always be repaid in coin. As discussed in more detail below, debts were more commonly repaid by either (a) transfer of balances held with an intermediary known as a *cashier*, or (b) assignment of a bill of exchange. Below we will argue that this institutional detail is inessential for our argument, since these forms of payment typically represented claims redeemable only in debased coin, or non-debased coin at a substantial premium above its legal value.

[11] Again this story should not necessarily be taken as literal description. Debasement might also occur at the hands of cashiers or moneychangers, who were in fact widely condemned for this practice (see below). Debtors holding undervalued coins could also "synthetically" subject these to debasement by using them to import goods which could then be sold for lighter coin.

no one would supply them the silver from which to mint them.[12] For example, an attempt to debase coins could cause the market price of heavy coins to rise, so people lose their incentive to bring heavy coins to the mint, and the debasement would fail. In fact, the market price of coins commonly exceeded their legal value, and this helped keep heavy coins from vanishing from circulation.

When retiring a debt, however, a creditor could insist on payment in coin valued at its ordinance value rather than its market value. A debtor can respond by finding some of the new, lighter coin that could discharge the debt at the legally set value. The point is not that heavy coins will not be used to settle debts; rather, that the threat of passing light coins establishes the debtor's best alternative to no agreement. If the creditor insists on heavier coin, then the creditor has to pay the debtor extra for it. The increase in the market price of heavy coins does not help the creditor if the debtor has light but legal coins with which to settle the debt.

The need to retain a legal value acted as the brake on the incentive to debase. Too great a debasement could cause creditors to challenge a coin's legal standing. For example, the Republic appears to have promulgated regulations stating that creditors had a right to insist that debt settlement use the coinage standards in force when a debt was contracted.[13] However, the costs of legal action were substantial, and early modern merchants appear to have rarely resorted to formal legal procedures. Instead, problems that resisted the threat of legal action were dealt with using "amicable settlement" or the acceptance of a loss, "rather than engaging in endless litigation."[14] The incentive to enforce such a right would increase with the rate of debasement and the size of the debt, so small debasements had a clear advantage.

Each debasement tended to be relatively small – a drop in the silver content of a few percent at most.[15] As lighter coins became the standard, however, the system recalibrated, and the incentive to debase again returned, leading to a pattern of mild but persistent debasement. Moreover, incentives to debase could be equally great at neighboring

---

[12] Rolnick et al., "The Debasement Puzzle."

[13] Oscar Gelderblom has kindly informed us that such a regulation is mentioned in a legal advice to the High Court of Holland that published in the mid-seventeenth century "Waerdije van eenige Munte veranderd zijde, moet men insien de Waardij, dieze hadde ten tijde van het contract ende niet ten tijde van de betalinge" Consultatien, Advysen en Advertissementen, gegeven ende gechreven bij bverscheyden Treffelijcke Rechts-Geleerden in Hollandt, zes delen" (Rotterdam, J. Naeranus, 1645–1666; volume IV: 69).

[14] Gelderblom, "The Governance," p. 634.

[15] On the other hand, a debasement also had to be large enough to generate incentives to bring metal into the mint.

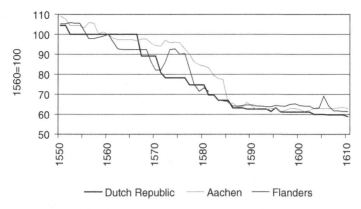

Figure 2.1 Indices of silver per coin.
Source: Metz 1990.

mints whose coins infiltrated the Dutch monetary stock.[16] Figure 2.1 shows the general pattern of official coin valuations for the Dutch Republic and two of its neighbors over the second half of the sixteenth century. Over this period, the fine-metal content of silver coins within the Republic fell by about 1 percent per year, on average. Most of the decline coincides with the pressures financing the Dutch Revolt (also called the Eighty Years War) that began in 1568, paused in 1609, resumed in 1621 and finally ended in 1648.[17]

Authorities could attempt to adjust minting-ordinance values quickly, but a move to raise ordinance values to match the market prices of heavy coins just locks-in the losses to creditors. Again, debtors may be willing to give heavy coins, but the higher price per coin means that creditors still see less silver than they expected. In practice, ordinance adjustments lagged actual price changes.

Creditors could try to insulate themselves by adding a risk premium when agreeing to accept a bill of exchange. The result would weaken the Dutch exchange rate and reduce bill-financed trade.[18] This approach, however, does not discourage a debtor from participating in a debasement. Indeed, a debtor would need to participate in a debasement in order to cover the risk premium already contracted into the bill of exchange.

---

[16] Dehing and 't Hart, "Linking the Fortunes," pp. 37–8.
[17] Fritschy, "A 'Financial Revolution.'"
[18] In the words of Adam Smith "if foreign bills of exchange are paid in this currency [such as the florin], the uncertain value of any sum, of what is in its own nature so uncertain, must render the exchange always very much against [a country such as the Republic], its currency being, in all foreign states, necessarily valued even below what it is worth (*Wealth of Nations* IV.3.12)."

An important question is whether these problems could have been circumvented through purely private means.[19] In his discussion of the events preceding the founding of the Wisselbank, van Dillen[20] casts doubt upon the efficacy of private remedies. Settling debts in a specific coin or amount of metal would have been prohibitively expensive. In practice, debts were routinely settled through assignment of bills, or transfer of accounts on the books of cashiers (primitive banks); as there was simply not enough coin to accommodate the payment needs of a commercial center such as Amsterdam. Attempts were made to outlaw the settlement of debts through assignment (1602) and to prohibit cashiers outright (1604 and again in 1608) but these were quickly abandoned. The "netting" function provided by these types of payment was deemed essential, particularly at times of year such as June and November, when bills of exchange traditionally came due.[21]

The activities of the cashiers and their fellow intermediaries, the moneychangers, were in turn quite difficult for the authorities to monitor.[22] Moneychangers were bound by oath to uphold the minting ordinances, but the availability of "illegitimate" moneychangers weakened adherence to these oaths. In discussions of this situation with the Dutch monetary authorities, the Amsterdam business community voiced a preference for settlement on the books of a municipal bank of "superior authority" to the private cashiers. The Amsterdam city council (*vroedschap*) favored a plan under which the Republic would establish an exchange bank in each commercial city,[23] but this plan was ignored by the governing body of the Republic, the States General. In response, the city council took unilateral action, creating the Wisselbank in January 1609.[24]

II.   Complications

A.   Cashiers

In our basic story, mints and debtors use debasement to take advantage of the rigid ordinance values of coins. Actual settlement appears to have more often involved the use of intermediaries known as cashiers or

---

[19] Rolnick *et al.*, "The Debasement Puzzle."   [20] van Dillen, "Oprichting," pp. 340–5.

[21] This discussion obviously begs the even deeper question, which we cannot address here, of why debts were denominated in florin and not units of precious metal.

[22] Cashiers and moneychangers were legally distinct types of intermediaries, but this distinction was not always observed in practice.

[23] This proposal for a geographically dispersed system of central bank-like institutions anticipated (by about three centuries) similar proposals in late nineteenth-century US.

[24] van Dillen, "Oprichting," p. 333.

kassiers. Like modern banks, cashiers held deposits and provided certain other financial services, most notably local payment by "giro" or book-entry.[25] As financial intermediaries, cashiers were in a stronger position than the typical merchant to have the numismatic sophistication to cull out heavy coins and knowingly accept and pass light coins. While the small percentages of silver involved with debasement may have seemed a minor issue for a merchant, the same silver would have been a substantial part of a cashier's income as that income was derived from processing other people's money.

Of course, cashiers could take a similar approach to withdrawals of deposits and other financial transactions. In this sense, cashiers played the role of the "debtor" benefiting from debasement, while anyone using a financial intermediary was a suffering creditor. At the time of the Wisselbank's founding, cashiers were under frequent condemnation for these practices. An attempt by Amsterdam in 1604 to ban cashiers noted that cashiers "allow for fraudulent activity, especially the removal of heavy gold and silver coins, and their transport to prohibited and other mints, in order to be converted into new (light) coins, which are then circulated within the community."[26]

B.   Multiple mints

Another institutional wrinkle that promoted debasement was the diffuse political structure of the Dutch Republic. Fourteen government mints and forty private mints meant plenty of opportunities for mints to serve local revenue needs.[27] Because all were legally recognized and created a common pool of coin, debasement was a form of "tragedy of the commons" whereby the rewards went to the first to debase.

Another significant source of debased coins was the Southern Netherlands. Here, the twist is that Dutch heavy coins did not have to be melted down to produce light coins because the export of goods could finance debasement instead. A great deal of light coin was minted in the southern Netherlands and shipped to the Dutch Republic to finance the south's trade deficit with the Republic. Causation could clearly run both ways: the profitable export of light coins by the Southern Netherlands "pulled" extra export goods from the Republic, just as trade imbalances

---

[25] A crucial exception being international remittances, which were largely accomplished through bills of exchange.
[26] Our translation of van Dillen, "Oprichting," p. 344.
[27] Dehing and 't Hart, "Linking the Fortunes," p. 39; Korthals Altes, "De Geschiedenis," p. 41.

helped to "push" silver into the Republic, silver that happened to be light coins.[28]

A piece of evidence in favor of the "pull" interpretation is that the southern coins were not treated as bullion (a commodity) to be minted into Republic coin. Instead, the debased coins were adopted into circulation because merchants and cashiers wanted them in that form. Debased coins were in demand since these could be used to short change creditors. The incentive to use southern coins was substantially increased when the Mint Ordinance of 1622 gave them a favorable fixed value in the Republic.[29] The Spanish Netherlands minted massive quantities of light coin for export to the Dutch Republic because of a massive demand for the light coins in the Dutch Republic.[30] The inflow of light coins could have been financed by an outflow of Republic coins, but export goods were preferable. The Southern Netherlands already had access to plentiful Spanish silver, while the Republic had higher valued uses for silver in the Baltic and Asia.

C.   Distance between debasement and creditors

Another feature of our story is that the instigating shock is not arbitrage. Instead, a well-timed debasement serves as a type of tax or taking, whereby legal recognition of light coins denies creditors expected silver. The debtors who accept the light coin need not be literally the parties who supply mints with silver. Indeed, the extraction of seigniorage from minting a light coin, and the taking of silver from creditors, could be spread out along a chain of transactions.

For example, a Flemish merchant could have silver gained through trade with Spain. The Flemish merchant has the silver minted into light coin that is the coinage standard of Flanders. The Flemish merchant then makes a local purchase using his local coin. The new holder of the light coin then passes it onto a Dutch merchant to pay for the importation Dutch manufactured goods. The Dutch merchant accepts the light coin at some discount to cover transportation expenses, but the Dutch merchant also expects his cashier in Amsterdam to accept the coin at tale.

---

[28] See for example, Polak, *Historiografie en Economie*, p. 205.

[29] This occurred less than a decade after a failed 1613 attempt to ban the importation of "counterfeit Burgundian silver dollars" (Korthals Altes, "De Geschiedenis," p. 51).

[30] We take the adjective *massive* from de Vries and van der Woude, *The First Modern Economy*, p. 83, "The enormous trade deficit that the Southern Netherlands ran with the North throughout the first half of the seventeenth century resulted in a massive flow of these coins into the Republic."

The cashier in Amsterdam accepts the light coin at tale because it can be used to satisfy creditors' demands with less silver than other coins.

The chain could be much longer if light coin migrates north via numerous local transactions. The point is that the process only requires someone willing to supply a mint with silver at the start of the chain and someone having to pay creditors at the other.

III.   Minting and melting

Once the shock of debasement occurs, then arbitrage causes the monetary system to adjust, and it is this process of arbitrage that produces the dynamic process seen in the Netherlands. To analyze the interaction of multiple coins with legally fixed exchange rates, this section uses a framework developed by Redish (1990), Sargent and Smith (1997), Sargent and Velde (2002) and Sussman and Zeira (2003). The conclusion is that persistent debasement gives rise to inflation, a weakening exchange rate, calls for adjustment of mint ordinance prices, and, if adjustment is too slow or insufficient, demonetization of heavy coins.[31]

The dynamics of adjustment in a monetary system under a metallic standard hinges on the fact that coins always have two values, the value of the metal in them (intrinsic value) and the value of their coined form (tale) as set out by regulations like mint ordinances. When the tale value is greater than the intrinsic value by enough to cover minting and seigniorage costs, people will bring precious metal to the mint to be converted into coins. In contrast, when the intrinsic value is greater than the tale value, people will melt coins into bullion or, equivalently, treat coins like bullion rather than as a circulating means of payment.

Taking into account ordinance prices, metallic content, minting costs and seigniorage, each coin has a minting point (which Redish calls the *mint price*) and a melting point (called the *mint equivalent*). The mint price is the value to someone of bringing precious metal to a mint so the metal can be converted into coin. The mint equivalent is the value to someone of melting a coin back into bullion. The difference between the two prices is the cost of the minting process, so the mint equivalent is higher than the mint price because the cost of minting has already been paid for a finished coin. Figure 2.2 gives the minting and melting points for a particular coin, the rixdollar or *Rijksdaalder*, at the time of the Wisselbank's founding in 1609. If the value of a mark[32] of pure silver

---

[31] While bimetallic issues are also important, we focus on only silver, for silver appears to have been the focus of both debasement and specie flows.

[32] Eight troy ounces.

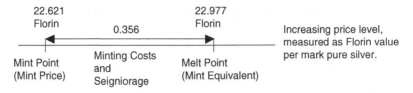

Figure 2.2 Mint points for the rixdollar in 1609.
Source: Polak 1998a: 70.

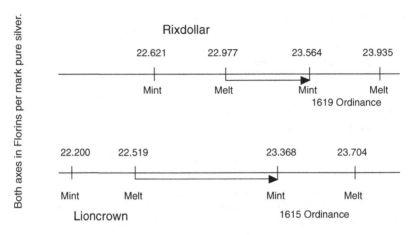

Figure 2.3 Mint points for the rixdollar and lioncrown, 1609 and 1615.
Source: Polak 1998a: 70–1.

was less than 22.621 florin, then one had an incentive to bring the silver to the mint. In contrast, it the value of a mark of pure silver was greater than 22.977 florin, then one had the incentive to treat a rixdollar coin as bullion and so demonetize it.[33]

When a system has two coins, then the mint–melt points of both coins can be placed on the same price continuum, but the mint and melt points are unlikely to match exactly. Smaller coins have relatively higher production costs, so their mint points tend to be lower than larger coins. Also, mint ordinances may not correctly relate prices to intrinsic values. For example, the lioncrown, or *Leeuwendaalder*, was a Dutch silver trade coin that was 95 percent of the weight of the rixdollar. Figure 2.3 gives

---

[33] The difference between mint price and mint equivalent of the rixdollar is approximately 1.5 percent, which is typical for silver coins of this period. Thus, even a relatively small debasement of one coin could demonetize or cause appreciation in the market values of competing coins.

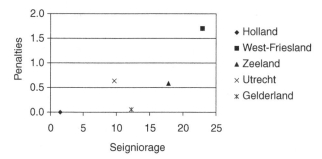

Figure 2.4 Seigniorage and penalties for rixdollars in 1607, in florins per day.
Source: Polak 1998b: 103–68.

the mint and melt points for both coins in 1609. At this time, the lioncrown's melt point is to the left of the rixdollar's mint point, so the incentive is to melt lioncrowns, and, if prices are low enough, mint rixdollars.

To maintain circulation, the market price of lioncrowns rose above the mint ordinance value, with the effect that the mint–melt points shifted to the right when market prices were used. In 1615, the rising price was recognized by a new ordinance, and the new mint–melt points are plotted in gray in Figure 2.3.[34] Now rixdollars were undervalued relative to lioncrowns, and the market price of rixdollars rose. In 1619, yet another ordinance raised the legal value of rixdollars, and now lioncrowns were discouraged.[35] The desire of authorities to have ordinance prices match market prices created a destabilizing process, and, however well-intentioned, the ordinances provided creditors no assurance against future revaluations. Indeed, a sufficiently aggressive increase in a coin's legal value could itself amount to a backhanded sort of debasement.

Debasement also shifted mint–melt points for the same type of coin produced by different mints. The lighter coin will lie to the right of the heavier coin, so the mint producing the lighter coin gets work and earns seigniorage. For example, Figure 2.4 shows the production of the rixdollar in 1607 for five provincial mints.[36] These mints are for the large provinces of Holland, Zeeland, Utrecht, West-Friesland and Gelderland.

---

[34] van Dillen, "Oprichting," p. 355.

[35] The province of Holland unilaterally raised the legal valuation to 2.6 florins (van Dillen, "Oprichting," p. 355).

[36] 1607 is used because it is just before the founding of the Wisselbank, and it is the year in this period for which the most mints are reported (Polak, *Historiografie en Economie, Deel I*, pp. 103–49).

Mint output, measured as legitimate seigniorage income, was highly correlated with the amount of debasement per mint. Debasement income is an estimate by Republic officials of the income derived by each mint for coins falling below official tolerances of weight and fineness (Polak 1998a: 112–13). These numbers are available because Republic officials audited mint output using weighing and trial by fire.[37] In 1607, Holland had the most accurate rixdollar production (no assessments for light coins), but Holland also had the least demand for its minting services. In contrast, West Friesland had the most minting activity (seigniorage) and the most debasement.

IV.   Systemic adjustment

To connect mint behavior with the general economy, Sargent and Velde (2002) convert the unit of measurement from the price of bullion to the price of a composite consumption good, i.e., the domestic price level. Consider the situation when an economy has only one type of coin. If domestic prices are too low (below the mint point), then people can increase their domestic purchasing power by exporting consumer goods to where their prices are higher, then importing the resulting silver from the sale, and finally have the silver minted into coin. High prices (above the melt point) reverse the incentives.

The advantage of viewing the process from the perspective of the price of goods instead of the price of silver is that a process of systemic adjustment emerges.[38] When people follow these incentives, the money supply and price level change until the incentive is eliminated, so minting and melting points create a self-adjusting process that is a type of specie-flow mechanism.[39] Minting coins increases the domestic money supply and can cause inflation. Enough inflation raises the price level above the melting point, and the process reaches an equilibrium. Melting works in reverse.

At first glance, debasement does not appear to trigger an international flow of metal because the existing metal stock is simply being re-minted into a new form with a higher nominal value, more coins, each worth the same number of florins as before. Consider this in terms of the equation

---

[37] Details of how these data were collected are discussed in Polak (1998a: 107–39).

[38] In practice, one can measure changes in domestic price level using price indices such as a consumer or commodity price index. For example, see Sargent and Velde, *The Big Problem*, pp. 35, 159, 193–4. Alternatively, one can measure the international exchange rate to gauge the value of the local unit of account. For example, see Quinn, "Gold, Silver and the Glorious Revolution."

[39] Sargent and Velde, *The Big Problem*, pp. 15–36.

of exchange $MV=Py$ where M is the nominal monetary stock, P is the price level, y is real GDP and V is the velocity of money. In a frictionless world, the increase in P would be matched by an equal increase in nominal M. In other words, the real monetary stock remains unchanged, so no change in real income or velocity was necessary.

This does not hold, however, if mints siphon metal out of the money stock of the economy. Such a drain would have easily resulted from military expenditures by provinces and cities during the wars against Spain.[40] Another drain would have resulted from Dutch metal crossing the border to foreign mints specializing in rival coins or counterfeits. In these situations, it can be shown algebraically that the increase in M stemming from a debasement is less than the minimum feasible increase in P.[41] Unless velocity (V) can be increased, real GDP (y) falls for the transitory period and the export of goods is required to "rebuild" the real money stock (M/P) and return the economy to its previous level of activity.[42] We are not in a position to estimate the scale of the resulting welfare loss, but the persistence of debasement and inflation in the Netherlands in this era suggests a substantial effect.[43]

It can also be shown that this systemic adjustment can be mitigated, if the market price of the heavy coin rises in response to a debasement, shifting its mintmelt points to the right. The coin develops a market price greater than its mint-ordinance price. While this keeps the heavy coin from being melted, it does not help creditors who face repayment in either lighter-than-expected coins or fewer-than-expected heavy coins. When a new mint ordinance eventually recognizes the higher price of old, heavy coins, it still does not compensate a creditor caught in the debasement. Only instantaneous adjustment of the minting ordinance

---

[40] An important component of military expenditure was the feeding of armies in the field, which in turn involved the importation of grain.

[41] Detailed calculations are given in Quinn and Roberds, "The Big Problem."

[42] I.e., debasement served as a form of taxation, levied by coin holders on themselves. Given that coinage freely flowed across borders, debasement offered cash-strapped governments the possibility of taxing not only their own economy but simultaneously the economies of their neighbors.

[43] Of course, there is always the temptation of informed conjecture. Before the founding of the Wisselbank, the metallic content of the Republic's coinage was dropping at a rate of about one percent per florin per year. The resultant welfare loss depends on the velocity of circulation, about which little is known. Available estimates suggest that in the eighteenth-century Republic velocity was extremely low, on the order of 1.5, based on money and income estimates reported in de Vries and van der Woude, *The First Modern Economy*, pp. 86, 702. Taking a figure of 1.5 as a lower bound for velocity and 10 for an upper bound (the number for the late nineteenth-century US), a velocity of 2–3 seems a reasonable "guesstimate" for the early Republic. This would then imply an annual loss of one-third to one-half percent of national income due to debasement, a considerable hindrance to the dynamic performance of the economy.

that lowered the price of debased coins would have offered protection; obviously this was not practical.

V.   The Wisselbank

If debasement, as described in the previous sections, was the monetary problem plaguing the Dutch Republic, then a solution was to end the incentives to debase. The most direct mechanism was to value debased coins correctly when those coins were used to discharge a debt. The Amsterdam city council partially achieved this goal when it created the exchange bank in 1609. Exchange banks (government-owned deposit banks) had developed in the Mediterranean as a substitute for private, fractional reserve banks.[44] In response to banking instability, cities like Venice created municipal exchange banks that did not lend reserves, so the system of payments based on bills of exchange had a stable monetary base.[45] A public bank arose in Genoa as an adjunct to an institution that managed the public debt.[46] The Bank of Amsterdam was modeled on the Venetian institution, but the primary focus was on stabilizing the coinage rather than the banking system.[47]

For Amsterdam, the key aspect of the exchange bank was that any deposit of illegal coins would be valued by the bank based solely on their metal content (intrinsic value). Withdrawals, in contrast, would be paid in certain types of coin, called trade coin or *negotiepenningen*), of a consistent weight and value. In this way, debts payable through the exchange bank would be protected from debasement because any deposit of debased coin would have its value at the Wisselbank proportionally reduced. The incentive to debase would be removed, so the thinking went, because debtors would no longer have the option of (however indirectly) settling debts in "overvalued" debased coin.

To put this in practice, the Wisselbank had to become the intermediary that paid creditors on behalf of debtors. Cashiers had been doing just this, but, unlike cashiers, the Wisselbank would not pass on

---

[44] Usher, *The Early History*.   [45] See Mueller, *The Venetian Money Market*.

[46] See Fratianni and Spinelli, "Did Genoa and Venice Kick."

[47] De Vries and van der Woude characterize the motivation as, "The great concern of the city fathers was to protect and enlarge the supply of good, full-valued coin. This they regarded as far more important to the prosperity of a commercial economy than the proliferation of circulating bills" (*The First Modern Economy*, p. 131). We differ in asserting that the Wisselbank was designed to promote bills of exchange through the supply of heavy coin. We would add that the city prohibited bill assignment because bill circulation was seen as a means by which cashiers could hold back heavy coin (van Dillen, "Oprichting," p. 345). Moving bill settlement to the Wisselbank solved this problem.

light coin. To provide incentives to use the Wisselbank, the Amsterdam city council included two regulations on private finance: (1) bills of exchange over 600 florin had to be settled through the Wisselbank (reduced to 300 florin in 1643) and (2) cashiers were outlawed.[48] The limit was reduced to 300 guilders in 1643.[49] The enforcement of these restrictions, however, was evidently less than perfect. As by 1615, the city council felt the need to pass a resolution explicitly forbidding the settlement of bills outside of the Wisselbank.[50]

Despite these difficulties, settlement of bills through the Wisselbank became the norm. Merchants could open an account at the Wisselbank or purchase "bank funds" through an intermediary. The Wisselbank did not charge a fee for bill settlement, and the process was quick because settlement occurred through the transfer of funds from debtor to creditor account. The city guaranteed deposits and the deposits were secured against attachment by creditors.[51] The reduction in settlement costs for merchants was substantial, for "In the years leading up to the establishment of the Wisselbank in Amsterdam about 20 percent of the more than four hundred accounts in [an examined merchant's] ledgers related solely to the settlement of bills of exchange."[52]

The Wisselbank did not offer overdraft facilities, and having insufficient funds could lead to penalties.[53] In this way, the Wisselbank monitored debtors and disseminated news of default.[54] The coordination of information needed to promote a reputation mechanism was particularly valuable for a city that was the intersection of different trading routes, for reducing the need for sector specific information assisted the blending of bills into a unified secondary market. Such market depth increased the liquidity of bills payable through the Wisselbank.

VI.   Regulatory dilemma

The initial structure of the Amsterdam Exchange Bank provided some protection to creditors who held bills payable through the Wisselbank; however, its municipal nature limited its reach. Other cities (Middelburg 1614, and Delft 1621 subsequently moved to Rotterdam in 1635) eventually opened exchange banks also, but the rest of the Dutch

---

[48] The prohibition on cashiers was reversed in 1621; however, strict regulations forbade cashiers from holding customer money for more than three days (van Dillen, "Oprichting," p. 353). Still, cashiers played an active role as intermediaries who arranged for payments in Wisselbank funds or receipt of the same.
[49] Korthals Altes, "De Geschiedenis," p. 49.   [50] van Dillen, "Oprichting," p. 349.
[51] van Dillen, "Oprichting," pp. 349–53.   [52] Gelderbloom, "The Governance," p. 635.
[53] van Dillen, "Oprichting," p. 50.   [54] Neal, *The Rise of Financial Capitalism*, p. 7.

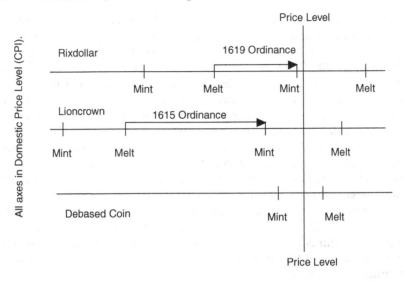

Figure 2.5 Mint points for heavy and debased coins, 1610 to 1620.
Source: see text.

economy remained outside the system, and debasement of Republic coins continued. Simultaneously, the flow of light coins from the southern Netherlands increased during the Twelve Years' Truce with Spain (1609–1621). As a result, the silver *patagon* and *ducatoon*, both coins from the Southern Netherlands, became common in Amsterdam by 1612.[55]

Continued debasement meant that the market price of heavy coins had to rise in order to keep them in circulation. Figure 2.5 presents this phenomenon by comparing the relative mint–melt points for a debased coin to the mint–melt points for full-weight rixdollars and lioncrowns in the 1610s. We lack measures of actual metal content of debased coins, so the picture provides an abstract rather than concrete schematic. Also, the metric is the domestic price level which highlights the process of systemic adjustment. With debased coins creating incentives to melt full-weight coins, the market price of rixdollars and lioncrowns increased, and that slid their de facto mint–melt points to the right. Again, the mint ordinances of 1615 and 1619 were simply official validation of the market prices of these coins.

[55] van Dillen, "Oprichting," p. 355. These coins were expressly designed to compete with the Republic's coins, in retaliation against the ongoing debasement of coins within the Republic (Korthals Altes, "De Geschiedenis," pp. 50–1). The *patagon* was also known as the "cross rixdollar."

The ordinances of 1615 and 1619 satisfied one regulatory goal, keeping ordinance prices in line with circulating prices. However, the ordinances also undercut the Wisselbank's mission to protect creditors. The Wisselbank was obliged by statute to follow ordinance prices, so the official increase in lioncrown and rixdollar values reduced the value of a deposit at the bank because the same number of florins now purchased fewer coins upon withdrawal. The effects of debasement were visited on creditors despite all the efforts to insulate them because regulators forced Wisselbank valuations to match those from the debased side of the economy. The situation followed from having one policy tool, mint ordinances, trying to achieve two policy goals, insulating creditors from debasement while adjusting official prices to the reality of debasement.

VII.   Regulatory odyssey

During its first fifty years, the Wisselbank was repeatedly caught between these two regulatory goals. The mint ordinances regulating the structure of the Dutch monetary system were repeatedly tweaked to either reflect the debasement that had occurred or to undo the effects of debasement. Each change produced unintended consequences for both the Wisselbank and the monetary system. Eventually but erratically, regulators began to accept the solution to the dilemma, i.e., that the value of coins at the Wisselbank should differ from the value of the same coins in general circulation.

A.   The mint ordinance of 1619

The mint ordinance of 1619, which raised the official price of rixdollars, touched off a surge of minting. To show why this happened, we need to separate the coins depicted in Figure 2.5 above into domestic coins and the light coins moving up from the Spanish Netherlands. We focus on the Republic's primary trade coin, the rixdollar, and its mimicker from south, the patagon. By debasing rixdollars, Dutch mints could achieve mint points above the melt points on patagons. This situation produces seigniorage for the debasing mints.

There is some indirect evidence that this is what actually happened. Figure 2.7 shows the amount of silver the minted as lioncrowns and rixdollars.[56] For later reference, the graph superimposes the dates of

---

[56] The data are derived from Polak, *Historiografie en Economie, Deel II*, pp. 103–45. Mint periods of less than 60 days (of which there were six) are excluded because they have insufficient denominators for reliable relative measures. If two observations included the same year, then the one with more days in that year was used.

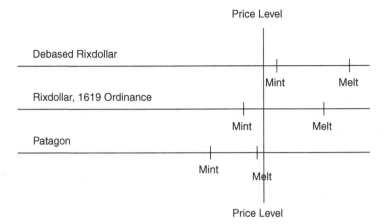

Figure 2.6 Mint points for the rixdollar, the debased rixdollar and the *patagon*, 1619–1621.
Source: see text.

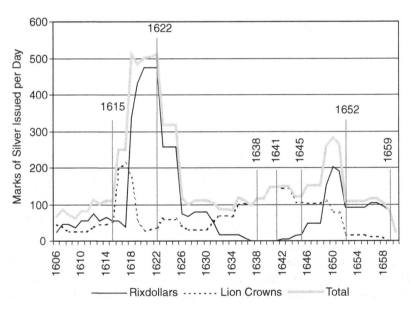

Figure 2.7 Production of heavy silver coins at five provincial mints.
Notes: dates within the graph indicate major mint ordinances.
Source: calculated from Polak 1998b: 103–68.

major mint ordinances. The measure of mint output is incomplete in that it only covers five provincial mints and has periods of missing observations.[57] The mints are Dordrecht in Holland; Hoorn, Enkhuizen and Medemblik in West-Friesland; Middelburg in Zeeland; Utrecht; and Harderwijk in Gelderland. The series are also lumpy, in that a mint's production total could encompass many years, so, although all production levels have been converted into a per-day basis, the same value can run over many years. Lioncrown production spikes in 1617 as the 1615 ordinance value encouraged lioncrown production relative to rixdollars (see section III, above). The process was focused in Utrecht, the mint on the southern frontier with the Spanish Netherlands. The rise and fall of lioncrown minting in 1616–1618 was evidently driven by a surge in Utrecht production of lioncrowns in 1616. Utrecht then switched from lioncrowns to high levels of production of rixdollars as the next ordinance favored the minting of rixdollars.

Was the surge in minting driven by debasement? Figures 2.8 and 2.9 plot the amount of seigniorage that would have been earned by the five mints if they had produced full weight lioncrowns (Figure 2.8) and rixdollars (Figure 2.9). The figures also chart the penalties the mints were assessed for producing debased coin. These penalties were assessed by Republic mint officials in an effort to maintain the quality of the coinage. Interestingly, the penalties themselves were due from a mint's master to the owner of the mint, i.e., the province. In other words, monitoring and assessment of penalties by the national government created an incentive for provinces to condone debasement. We cannot speak to what other economic relationships existed between mint masters and their provinces, but the potential for mutual gain through debasement is obvious.

For both coins, the relationship between demand for a coin (legitimate seigniorage) and penalties for debasement is striking. Again, the seigniorage values are for (hypothetical) full-weight coins, so the amount of additional seigniorage from coins being below tolerance is not known. Of course, the five mints varied in both the amount of minting they engaged in and the amount of debasement they were penalized for. Figure 2.10 plots the seigniorage and penalties for debasement by mint for the year 1620, the peak of rixdollar production. Again, demand for a mint's business is positively related to its readiness to debase.

---

[57] This is also a somewhat biased sample, as unfortunately there are no data during this period for the municipal mints, which were on the whole less inclined to hold to the minting ordinances.

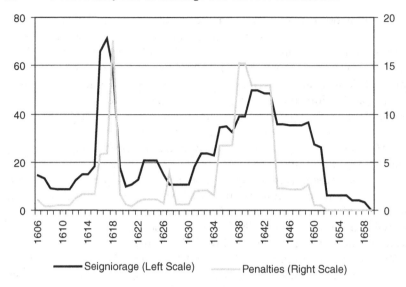

Figure 2.8 Lioncrown seigniorage and penalties, in florins per day.
Source: calculated from Polak 1998b: 103–68.

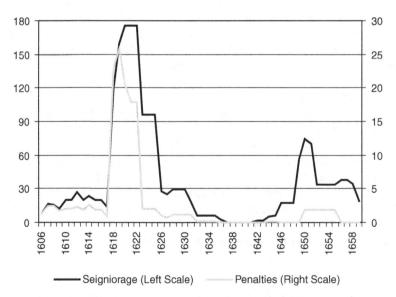

Figure 2.9 Rixdollar seigniorage and penalties, in florins per day.
Source: calculated from Polak 1998b: 103–68.

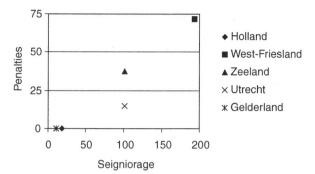

Figure 2.10 Seigniorage and penalties for rixdollars in 1620, in florins per day.
Source: Polak 1998b: 103–68.

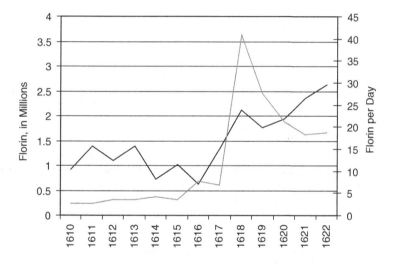

—— Deposits at the Amsterdam Wisselbank (Left Scale)

—— Debasement Penalties on Rixdollars and Lioncrowns (Right Axis)

Figure 2.11 Wisselbank deposits and debasement.
Source: Wisselbank deposits from van Dillen 1934: 117; penalties derived from Polak 1998b: 103–49.

What did the surge in debasement mean for Amsterdam's Wisselbank? It appears to have promoted deposits despite the revaluation of coins in 1615 and 1619. Figure 2.11 shows that deposits at the Wisselbank grew rapidly in 1617 and 1618 when debasement of the

Wisselbank's primary silver coins, rixdollars and lioncrowns, peaked. Available evidence also suggests that the number of accounts held at the Wisselbank also grew over this time period; Van Dillen[58] puts the number of accounts at 708 in 1611 and 1202 in 1620. As debasement continued in the following years, so did the growth in Wisselbank deposits. Unlike the other mints, Holland abstained from debasement, so coin minted for the Wisselbank maintained content.

Finally, we should stress that Figure 2.11 does not include debasement from other sources, for example, small silver coins from municipal mints, patagons from the southern Netherlands, etc., so ours is very incomplete measure of overall debasement. For example, the start of the Thirty Years' War in Central Europe in 1618 led to five years of severe debasement and inflation throughout the German states (Sargent and Velde 2002: 257–60).[59] Rixdollars and lioncrowns, however, were the basic coins of the Wisselbank, so their debasement elsewhere was a direct threat to the creditors that used the Wisselbank.

B.   The mint ordinance of 1622

In 1622, the Dutch Republic changed its regulatory approach. Instead of increasing the official price of rixdollar and lioncrown coins, it instead created a legal value for the patagons "invading" from the Southern Netherlands. The mint ordinance created a fixed legal exchange rate between the insurgent patagons and the Republic's system of coins. The 1622 ordinance set a legal value for the patagon at 2.35 florins, and it rolled the rixdollar back to 2.5 florins, so the rixdollar-to-patagon ratio became 1.064.[60] The market values of the coins, however, were close to 2.6 florins for rixdollars and 2.5 florins for patagons, so the market's ratio was 1.04.[61] This corresponds with the finding that southern coins had, "silver contents 4 percent lower than those of comparable Dutch coins."[62] In short, official prices overvalued rixdollars relative to patagons, and Figure 2.12 draws the situation.

One result was that people lacked an incentive to bring patagons to the Wisselbank or to the mints, so the minting of Dutch rixdollars declined precipitously.[63] Our characterization of the 1622 ordinance is

---

[58] See "Bloeitijd," p. 406.   [59] Sargent and Velde, *The Big Problem*, pp. 257–60.

[60] van Dillen "Oprichting," p. 356. Holland had increased rixdollars to 2.6 florins the previous year.

[61] van Dillen "Oprichting," pp. 355–6.

[62] de Vries and van der Woude, *The First Modern Economy*, p. 83.

[63] With the renewal of war with Spain in 1621, the loss of seigniorage from the decline in minting was particularly counterproductive for the Republic. 1621 begins an era of rapidly increasing long-term borrowing (Fritschy "A 'Financial Revolution,'" p. 66).

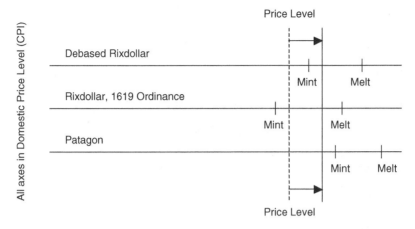

Figure 2.12 Mint points for the rixdollar, lioncrown and *patagon*, 1622–1638.
Source: see text.

that it shifted the patagon rightwards, so that the incentive to mint rixdollars ended as domestic prices rose. Returning to Figure 2.9, the amount of rixdollars produced by the five mints returned to pre-1616 levels under the new ordinance.

At the same time, the ordinance increased incentives to import patagons into the Dutch Republic. The first half of the seventeenth century witnessed a surge in mint production in the Southern Netherlands, and, from 1613 through 1656, the value of average annual mint output for the Southern Netherlands was 4.2 million florins.[64] In contrast, the combined rixdollar and lioncrown production for these five mints only produces a rough estimate of 1.6 million florins.[65] While much of the southern coinage was then exported by the Dutch Republic to the Baltic, Levant and Asia, what remained, "became the dominant circulating currency" in the Republic.[66]

At an aggregate level, the inflow of light coin promoted inflation. Figure 2.13 plots both the level of combined rixdollar–lioncrown minting and a consumer price index (CPI). The price level situation is not a simple money supply story, for the Dutch Republic and Spain resumed war in 1621; however, the mint ordinance of 1622 also marked

---

[64] de Vries and van der Woude, *The First Modern Economy*, p. 86.
[65] Using a per-day output of 191 marks at 23.5 florins per mark.
[66] de Vries and van der Woude, *The First Modern Economy*, p. 83.

Figure 2.13 Dutch CPI and production of heavy silver coin.
Source: mint numbers from Polak (1998b); prices from van Zanden (2004).

the beginning of a period of renewed fiscal, and hence, inflationary pressures.[67]

Was the Wisselbank able to protect creditors in this era? We answer "yes but only partially," for the Wisselbank was able to limit declines in the external value of its deposits during an era of substantial domestic inflation. Table 2.1 contrasts changes in the exchange value of the florin, relative to the English pound, with changes in the Dutch domestic price level. Because the exchange rates are in averages for five-year periods, the other values have also been calculated as changes between five-year averages. The inflation from the early 1620s to the early 1630s corresponds with a much smaller decreases in the florin. At the same time Wisselbank deposits continued to grow rapidly. We take this as evidence that the Wisselbank succeeded in protecting bills of exchange in Amsterdam, yet the exchange bank could not fully control the aggregate price level.

C.   *The toleration of 1638 and the crisis of 1641*

By the late 1630s, patagons were circulating above their ordinance value. The production of rixdollars had dwindled to only Holland and Zeeland,

---

[67] In 1621, military expenditures "immediately doubled, exceeding 20 million per year in the mid-1630s" (de Vries and van der Woude, *The First Modern Economy*, p. 100).

Table 2.1. *Changes in external and internal value of the florin*

	Change in florin's exchange rate	Change in CPI	Change in Wisselbank deposits
1606–1610 to 1611–1615	−1%	2%	
1611–1615 to 1616–1620	1%	0%	40%
1616–1620 to 1621–1625	−2%	16%	52%
1621–1625 to 1626–1630	−1%	14%	51%
1626–1630 to 1631–1635	−2%	0%	10%
1631–1635 to 1636–1640	1%	−2%	50%
1636–1640 to 1641–1645	−6%	1%	31%
1641–1645 to 1646–1650	11%	10%	13%
1646–1650 to 1651–1655	−4%	5%	−8%

Source: exchange rates from McCusker, "Money and Exchange," p. 55; price changes derived from van Zanden, "The Prices"; and Wisselbank changes from van Dillen, "The Bank of Amsterdam," pp. 117–18.

for both provinces had exchange banks. Lioncrowns were being minted primarily in West Friesland and Gelderland, but those two mints were also being assessed for debasement. In 1638, a new effort was made to reconcile ordinance prices with circulating reality, so the value of patagons was raised by a temporary "toleration" of over 6 percent from 2.35 to 2.5 florins each – the same as the official value for rixdollars. Not only did the official premium on rixdollars disappear, but patagons were lighter than rixdollars, so rixdollars suddenly became officially undervalued.[68] In terms of mint–melt points (Figure 2.14), the toleration of 1638 pushed patagons far to the right.

This created a strong incentive to withdraw heavy rixdollars from the Wisselbank. People complained that rixdollars were flowing out of the bank, not to finance trade, but to send to the mints in the Southern Netherlands for conversion into light southern coins.[69] Production of

[68] van Dillen, "Oprichting," p. 360.   [69] van Dillen, "Oprichting," p. 360.

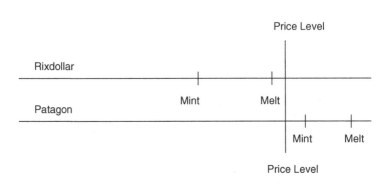

Figure 2.14 Effects of the 1638 toleration.
Source: see text.

rixdollars ceased (see Figure 2.9), and merchants complained that it was impossible to get good, heavy silver coins. In the process, "rixdollars and lioncrowns completely disappeared from circulation to be exclusively used as commercial coins for export."[70]

The Wisselbank apparently ran out of rixdollars sometime in 1640–1641, so the Wisselbank violated its own governing ordinances and began to give out *patagons* and *ducatoons*, another "light" Southern Netherlands coin, for withdrawals.[71] This change was subsequently recognized by municipal ordinance in October 1641.[72] The change removed the incentive behind the withdrawal process, but it also marked a failure of the Wisselbank to defend creditors and the value of bills of exchange. Once Amsterdam had declared the southern coins to be bank money, the exchange banks in Middelburg and Rotterdam quickly followed.[73] In turn, the florin exchange rate dropped 6 percent from its average value in the late 1630s to the early 1640s (see Table 2.1). Deposits at the Wisselbank first surged by 44 percent from January 1638 to January 1640, then held steady for the year 1640, but then collapsed to below their 1638 levels.[74]

---

[70] van Dillen, "The Bank of Amsterdam," p. 88. Of course, coins exported to finance trade might easily re-enter the Republic as *patagons*.

[71] In contrast, Rotterdam dealt with the shortage of heavy coin in 1639 by allowing English Merchant Adventurers (the primary debtors having bills payable there) to circumvent the Rotterdam exchange bank (van Dillen 1964a: 362).

[72] van Dillen, "Oprichting," p. 361.   [73] van Dillen, "Oprichting," p. 361.

[74] The five-year averages used in Table 2.1 miss this drop in 1641 because of a one-year surge in deposits in 1644.

D. *The agio and the mint ordinances of 1645*

After the crisis of 1641, the Dutch Republic struggled with how to deal with the patagons, for they were by then the standard circulating coin and the de facto standard for the Wisselbank. The process was chaotic, for regulators could not reconcile themselves to the same coin, the patagon, having a different value in the Wisselbank relative to outside.

The regulatory mayhem began in March 1645, when the Republic passed a new mint ordinance that was a return to the old 1622 system. The change was wrenching, for it meant that patagons were no longer legal money for withdrawal despite patagons having become the basis of the monetary system. Not surprisingly, Amsterdam merchants complained to the city for the regulation threatened the liquidity of the Wisselbank.

Two months later, in May 1645, the city relented and empowered the Wisselbank to defy the mint ordinance and again issue patagons for withdrawals, but the withdrawal rate was set at 2.4 florins.[75] While this change did allow withdrawals, it would also created a 2 percent "haircut" for depositors, for patagons were valued at 2.35 florins when deposited. Perhaps the price differential was a concession the Wisselbank had to make to gain regulatory relief, but it would have been another failure to protect depositors had not the Wisselbank sought a remedy.

The very next month, June 1645, the Wisselbank requested, and the city of Amsterdam agreed, to raise the lawful value of patagons for deposit purposes, so deposit value equaled withdrawal value.[76] While the June rate adjustment protected new depositors, it did not help existing depositors. In August 1645, when the Wisselbank was again running out of heavy coins and expected to cover withdrawals in patagons, the exchange bank gained permission from the city to adjust the rate to reflect the lightness of the coin.[77] The adjustment was called the agio, and it meant that more patagons were given out than their ordinance value would dictate, so the intrinsic value of deposits was maintained.

Because the Wisselbank charged a small withdrawal fee, a market developed for buying and selling deposits on the Wisselbank. People had been contracting to avoid these fees from the opening of the Wisselbank, but now, for the first time since the decline of the rixdollar in 1622, the same coin was commonly on both sides of the exchange, so by the late 1640s the market deepened as a standard type of trade emerged. Buyers and sellers of Wisselbank funds against "current money" (that which

---

[75] van Dillen, "Oprichting," p. 362.   [76] van Dillen, "Oprichting," p. 362.
[77] van Dillen, "Oprichting," p. 362

circulated outside the bank) would meet every morning at the square in front of the Amsterdam Town Hall. Often these were cashiers, who had by now established themselves as intermediaries in Wisselbank funds.[78] The emergence of Wisselbank funds as a tradable commodity was a critical step in the evolution of the Wisselbank away from the medieval model of an exchange bank and towards something more closely resembling a central bank.[79]

The term "bank money" was already in use at this time, but initially this meant nothing more than "coin such as is kept at the Wisselbank." The only difference between a patagon in the bank (banco) and a patagon outside the bank (current) was the fee and the difference in official prices. The exchange rate that developed was also called the agio, but it was a market swap rate (current coins for deposit balances) rather than the actual rate used by the Wisselbank to calculate the amount of coins delivered upon withdrawal of a deposit. Indeed, arbitrage meant that the actual withdrawal rate created an upper limit on the market agio. The agio was measured as the ratio of current florin over bank florin. For example, if patagons circulated at 2.5 florin, then the agio would be $[(2.5/2.4)-1]*100 = 4.166$ percent, less a small amount for a share of the withdrawal fee.

The agio allows a direct measure of the current price of patagons, relative to the Wisselbank price, and Table 2.2 presents agio values from 1645 through 1657. Although unstable, the development of the agio was a crucial step in the protection of creditors, for the agio allowed systemic adjustment while keeping the metal value of Wisselbank deposits constant. Debasement of circulating coins could be met with a virtually simultaneous increase in the agio, so debtors gained no advantage. Similarly, authorities could adjust the legal price of circulating coins, via tolerations, without upsetting the Wisselbank. Part of the process was that Wisselbank customers were becoming comfortable with the distinction between bank prices and current prices, comfortable with an exchange rate between the two units of account, and comfortable with brokers and dealers managing the market between the two kinds of money.

E.   Period of transition, 1646–1658

The agio of 1645 brought a new dynamic to the Dutch monetary system. For example, 1646 brought two new trends that lasted until 1651–1652:

[78] van Dillen, "Oprichting," pp. 366–7.
[79] We believe this market to be the world's first "open market" in central bank funds.

Table 2.2. *The* agio *(premium) on* Wisselbank *deposits*

Year (* mint ordinance)	Agio
1645*	4 1/6 to 4.75%
1646	0.75–2%
1647	1.125–1.25%
1648	1.75–2%
1649	2.53%
1650	2.32%
1651	3.06%
1652*	3.38%
1653*	1.94%
1654*	2.10%
1655	2.42%
1656	2.20%
1657	3.00%
1658	No observation

Source: 1645–1648 observations from van Dillen, "Oprichting," p. 363; 1649–1657 observations from McCusker, "Money and Exchange," p. 46.

(1) the production of rixdollars suddenly recovered, and (2) the CPI began to increase. Back in 1619–1621, rixdollar production had surged while prices were steady. After 1622, prices surged while rixdollar production collapsed. Now, both were increasing, and the difference was that rixdollars were no longer part of the circulating monetary stock. Rixdollars were now only produced and used for export. The production reflects a boom in international trade between the end of Eighty Years' War in 1648 and the First Anglo-Dutch war in 1652. Put another way, the mint–melt points for rixdollars used to describe earlier eras were no longer relevant.

What *was* relevant was the quality and quantity of coins circulating in, but not minted in, the Dutch Republic. We have no direct measure of either, but we do have the agio. The initial agio of 1645 disappears by 1646 (see Table 2.2). That dramatic change suggests that the Wisselbank stopped offering to supplement withdrawals and that patagons were circulating at around 2.45 florins. The rise in the agio from 1646 through 1652 suggests that patagons were rising in current price towards 2.5 florins, so it took ever so slightly more of them to purchase a deposit at the Wisselbank. The increase in domestic prices over the same period, however, was far more dramatic. If the agio tells us that the florin value

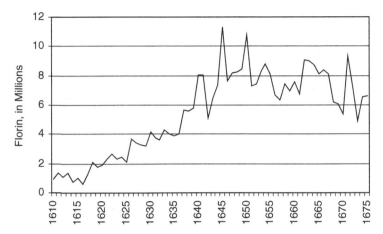

Figure 2.15 Deposits at the Amsterdam *Wisselbank*.
Source: van Dillen 1934: 117–19.

of patagons was not surging, then the quantity of them in circulation was. Debasement may have contributed to the influx of patagons, but it would not have been the primary story. Instead, during this period "real-side" effects likely took precedence over monetary adjustments. The Dutch economy expanded strongly following the 1648 Treaty of Westphalia, which ended the war with Spain. Prices rose with the recovery and patagons streamed in to finance the resumption of trade with the South, and the growth of the economy more generally.

During this same era, deposit levels at the Wisselbank stopped growing. Figure 2.15 plots annual deposit levels, and, despite one-year peaks in 1645 and 1650, a slowing of the Wisselbank's growth is evident. Instead of viewing this as a sign of the Wisselbank failing, however, we view this as a sign that the campaign against debasement was succeeding, for less debasement reduced demand for Wisselbank balances. While we have no measure for the amount of debasement occurring across all the relevant mints, Figure 2.7 does show a decline in the debasement of lioncrown coins by the provincial mints in this era. Moreover, the surge in rixdollar production around 1650 was apparently accompanied by little debasement.[80]

A number of factors were coming together to discourage Dutch debasement at mid-century. The development of the agio meant the successful protection of creditors and reduced incentives to debase. The 1645 mint ordinance reduced the number of coins holding official

[80] Polak, *Historiografie en Economie, Deel II*, pp. 103–49.

valuations, so fewer types of coins could be used to short-change creditors. The end of the Eighty Years' War in 1648 reduced government demand for seigniorage. Finally, rixdollars were now viewed as an export coin, so the surge in production suggests a recovery in international trade.[81]

Authorities eventually responded to this situation by adjusting their lawful price in 1652 and 1653.[82] The tolerations did not apply to the Wisselbank, so the same coin, the patagon, was lawfully valued at 2.4 florins at the exchange bank but at a higher price in circulation.

Still, government authorities were not happy with the *patagons* and the agio, and van Dillen suggests that a spurt of ordinance tinkering occurred in the 1650s. The 1645 mint ordinance was renewed in 1652 and 1653, but tolerances for circulating coins were added. A mint ordinance of 1654 complains that the agio was high and uncertain. It was high because, as a moneychanger, the Wisselbank was only to charge a modest withdrawal fee, typically less than 0.5 percent. After 1645, the agio was greater than this, and it increased from 1646 to 1652. The agio was uncertain because it was a market price. In response, the mint ordinance of November 1654 increased the Wisselbank price of a patagon to 2.45 florins while the lawful circulating price was 2.5.[83] This created another "haircut" for depositors, for there is no mention of a special withdrawal agio to compensate depositors. Less than two years later, the 1654 ordinance was revoked. The Amsterdam city council felt that the coins of the Wisselbank had fallen into "decadence." To improve the situation, the value of patagons was reduced back to 2.4 florins and the withdrawal fee was set at 1/8 percent. All this is based on obscure references found by van Dillen, but the overall picture suggests that authorities just did not know what to do with the agio.

F.   The mint ordinance of 1659

The strangeness of the Dutch monetary situation derived from a monetary base built on foreign coin. The Republic did not receive seigniorage from these coins, nor control their quality. Similarly, the Wisselbank

---

[81] Here we would be remiss not to mention the role of the "financial revolution" in the Dutch Republic. Effectively, this meant that war expenditures were financed through funded, long-term debt that bore relatively low interest rates (see 't Hart 1997). Debt levels (temporarily) stabilized following the cessation of hostilities in 1648. The Wisselbank was not directly impacted by these developments, since it was not concerned with the management of public debt, but it did ultimately benefit through the lessening of the provinces' incentives to debase.

[82] van Dillen, "Oprichting," p. 364.   [83] van Dillen, "Oprichting," p. 364.

defended the quality of coins available to depositors but could not mint high-quality versions of the coins used for withdrawal. To undo the situation, the Republic introduced new coins in 1659 that mimicked the coins from the Southern Netherlands. The silver *dukaat* and the silver *rijder* were made slightly lighter than their respective southern substitutes, the patagon and the dukaton. The new coins quickly replaced the old coins, and the change ushered in an era of stable coinage.[84]

To facilitate acceptance of the new coins, the existing pricing system was maintained, so a silver dukaat was officially made worth 2.4 florins at the Wisselbank and 2.5 florins as current money outside of the exchange bank. The distinction between the banco unit of account and current unit of account was codified at the national level, to the double pricing that had begun fifteen years earlier was recognized and made a permanent part of the system. Another aspect of how the 1659 ordinance minimized disruption of the monetary system was that the new silver dukaat came to be called the rixdollar in everyday use. The old rixdollar came to be called the bank rixdollar. Similarly, the new rijder was called the ducaton in usage.

G.   Summary

To summarize this long section, from the 1610s to the 1650s, the Amsterdam Wisselbank was buffeted by a series of mint ordinances, for the exchange bank was caught in offsetting policy goals. Policy makers desired to stabilize both coin content and coin values. Unfortunately, each new fixed-price regime created unstable dynamics, and some directly undermined the Wisselbank's ability to protect creditors.

Ironically, the road to stability was to embrace flexible coin prices. This was managed by allowing a floating exchange rate, the agio, to exist between deposits at the Wisselbank and money circulating outside the exchange bank. Official recognition of the agio, however, occurred only at the end of a bewildering chain of regulatory missteps. By 1659, just getting the Dutch Republic to again use its own coins was a greater concern than the cognitive dissonance of a coin having two prices. Once the new set of Dutch coins was well established, the dual pricing

---

[84] Complete victory remained elusive. A rise in the price of silver during the second Anglo-Dutch war (1665–1667) and during subsequent hostilities severely cut into the business of the mints. This resulted in a wave of marginal debasement by mints outside of Holland and a slight depreciation in the value of current money (Korthals Altes, "De Geschiedenis," pp. 54–9). The value of Wisselbank money was unaffected, however. A fully stable national coinage was finally achieved after passage of the mint ordinances of 1691 and 1694 (de Vries and van der Woude, *The First Modern Economy*, p. 83).

structure of the agio was an accepted and, we assert, a beneficial part of the monetary system. Superficially the agio on bank money resembled the historically common "overvaluation" (*stygeringhe*) of heavy coin. But the key difference was that the unit of account for commercial transactions was unambiguously tied to the essentially non-circulating heavy coin in the vault of the Wisselbank.

VIII.   Genesis of a central bank

From its inception, the Amsterdam Wisselbank carried out one of the key functions of modern central banks, the operation of a "real-time gross settlement system," i.e., a giro or book-entry payment system that allowed for efficient settlement of the high volume of commercial transactions flowing through Amsterdam.[85] Total balances at the Wisselbank were relatively modest, always less than twenty million florins in the late seventeenth century, and less than thirty million in the eighteenth.[86] By way of comparison, de Vries and van der Woude (1997: 90) estimate the total money (coin) stock of the Republic at 120 million florins in 1690 and 200 million a century later.

The low levels of Wisselbank deposits no doubt understate their importance to the Dutch economy, however, as the velocity of transactions in Wisselbank balances was probably quite high. Writing in 1766, Jacques Accarias de Sérionne[87] put the daily value of Wisselbank transactions at ten to twelve million florins per day. Given a mid-eighteenth century national income of around 250 million florins,[88] this would in turn imply that the Wisselbank "turned over" transactions equal to the annual value of the Republic's GDP within a space of less than six weeks. This pace is not quite as frenetic as that of modern large-value payment systems, which routinely turn over their host countries' annual GDP within a week or less (Committee on Payment and Settlement Systems 2006). It is nonetheless an astonishingly high figure for an economy that has often been described as "pre-industrial."

The mint ordinance of 1659 set the stage for the Wisselbank to assume additional central-bank-like responsibilities. As guardian of a separate, privileged medium of exchange with its own unit of account, the Wisselbank was implicitly entrusted with a mission of maintaining price stability. This mission proved problematic as long as the value of

---

[85] Neal, "How it all Began," pp. 121–2.
[86] van Dillen, "The Bank of Amsterdam," pp. 117–23.
[87] Cited in Braudel, *The Perspective*, p. 240.
[88] de Vries and van der Woude, *The First Modern Economy*, p. 702.

Wisselbank deposits was rigidly bound to the value of the coins within its vault. The agio could and did fluctuate erratically with market conditions, and a sufficient drop in the agio could cause account holders to withdraw coin from the bank. The French invasion of 1672 saw an apparent negative agio (no precise figures are available) and a run on the Wisselbank ensued.[89] While the bank was able to withstand the run, ongoing fluctuations in the agio no doubt contributed to an appetite for institutional reform.

In 1683 a facility was created whereby Wisselbank account holders could "park" gold and heavy silver coins at the bank for a period of six months.[90] Anyone making use of this facility received a credit on the books of the bank as well as a receipt. When the six-month period expired, the receipt holder could, in return for payment of a minuscule amount of interest, either renew the agreement or repurchase his coins. Coins not so reclaimed then fell to the bank (van Dillen 1964b: 394–5).[91]

The introduction of the "receipt" system transformed both Amsterdam financial markets and the Wisselbank itself. The receipts are recognizable to modern eyes as European call options on the deposited coin, or equivalently, put options on Wisselbank funds. The availability of these options, which were freely assignable, greatly improved the liquidity of the Amsterdam market in precious metals.[92] Receipts were readily traded against Wisselbank funds, as described by Adam Smith, "The person who has a receipt . . . finds always plenty of bank credits, or bank money to buy at the ordinary price; and the person who has bank money . . . finds receipts always in equal abundance (*Wealth of Nations IV.3.20*)."

Since it was generally cheaper to purchase an option than to withdraw funds (and so incur withdrawal fees), redemptions became uncommon. As a result, at some point, probably in the late seventeenth century, the Wisselbank quit redeeming deposits. Wisselbank money itself had become a "virtual currency." Unfortunately for this change in policy, surely one of the most momentous in monetary history, "no ordinance nor any precise date can be assigned."[93]

[89] van Dillen, "Oprichting," pp. 369–71; Korthals Altes, "De Geschiedenis," p. 55.
[90] Later on receipts were issued against uncoined precious metal and even current money (with a "haircut" reflecting the prevalent agio). Vault inventories reported in van Dillen (1925) suggest that the presence of this haircut discouraged the deposit of current money.
[91] van Dillen (1964b: 395) suggests that these transactions were not in fact loans but repurchase agreements.
[92] van Dillen, "Bloeitijd," p. 395. Receipts against deposits were already required in 1654, suggesting some earlier experimentation with the post-1683 system.
[93] van Dillen, "Oprichting," p. 101.

To us, such a story requires a remarkable indifference to the right of withdrawal. The end of withdrawal was, practically speaking, a termination of debt that affected thousands of wealthy people. Any collective or noisome response would have had a very strong position, so likely a low threshold of perceived harm would trigger a response. The lack of a discernable response suggests that withdrawals were rare and that the expectation of ever wanting to make a withdrawal was rare. Such low expectations of withdrawal mean that developments in and out of the Wisselbank combined in a powerful way.[94]

Absent withdrawal, a way had to be found to maintain the value of Wisselbank balances. The hit-upon method, which would again seem quite natural to modern observers, was open market operations, meaning the sale and purchase of receipts against bank funds. By this means, the Wisselbank was able to keep the agio on bank money over current money in a very narrow range over most of the eighteenth century, between 4 1/4 and 4 7/8 percent.[95] Moreover, the Wisselbank could use the agio as a "sluice gate" to manage specie flows.[96] Again this does not quite correspond to our modern day notion of "open market operations" as the sale and purchase of government securities, but it is obviously quite close to the modern practice, common in many countries, of pegging the value of a currency through intervention in markets for foreign exchange.

The Wisselbank's use of open market operations marked a significant development in the evolution of central banks (Gillard 2004).[97] Earlier public banks (in Barcelona, Genoa and Venice) had operated giro payment systems. Separate, commercial units of account had existed both in cities with a public bank[98] and in cities without.[99] Through its open market operations, the Wisselbank put the pieces together in a new way: by trading receipts, it could shore up the market's confidence in its inconvertible money as settlement medium, while simultaneously enhancing the liquidity of the precious metal whose value underpinned the Republic's monetary system.

In summary, by the end of the seventeenth century, Amsterdam's Wisselbank performed three functions that are routinely carried out by central banks today: operating a large-value payment system, creating a form of money not directly redeemable for coin, and managing the value of this money through open market operations. Ironically, the Bank of

---

[94] Gillard, *La banque d'Amsterdam*, stresses the role of cashiers.
[95] van Dillen, "Oprichting," p. 404.   [96] Neal, "How it all Began," p. 122.
[97] Gillard, *La banque d'Amsterdam*.
[98] For example, Genoa; see Fratianni and Spinelli, "Did Genoa and Venice Kick."
[99] For example Florence; see Sargent and Velde, *The Big Problem*.

Amsterdam may be best remembered for what it did *not* do, i.e., take on what are now viewed as the definitive central-bank functions of circulating note issue, operation of a discount window, and the purchase of government securities.[100] Even so, the activities of the Wisselbank set a strong precedent. As the seventeenth century came to a close, the idea of a central bank was a proven concept, and ready for its now-famous voyage across the North Sea.

References

Braudel, F. 1894. *The Perspective of the World, Civilization and Capitalism 15th-18th Century.* New York: Harper & Row.

Committee on Payment and Settlement Systems. 2006. *Statistics on Payment and Settlement Systems in Selected Countries – Figures for 2004.* Basel: Bank for International Settlements.

Dehing, P. and M. 't Hart. 1997. "Linking the Fortunes, Currency and Banking, 1550–1800," in M. 't Hart, J. Jonker and J. L. van Zanden, eds., *A Financial History of the Netherlands.* Cambridge, Cambridge University Press: 37–63.

De Vries, J. and A. van der Woude. 1997. *The First Modern Economy, Success, Failure and Perseverance of the Dutch Economy, 1500–1815.* Cambridge: Cambridge University Press.

Fratianni M. and F. Spinelli. 2005. "Did Genoa and Venice Kick a Financial Revolution in the Quattrocento?" Oesterreichische Nationalbank Working Paper 112.

Fritschy, W. 2003. "A 'Financial Revolution' Reconsidered: Public Finance in Holland during the Dutch Revolt, 1568–1648," *Economic History Review* 56: 57–89.

Gelderblom, O. 2003. "The Governance of Early Modern Trade: The Case of Hans Thijs, 1556–1611," *Enterprise and Society* 4: 606–39.

Gillard, Lucien. 2004. *La banque d'Amsterdam et le florin européen au temps de la République neerlandaise, 1610–1820.* Paris: EHESS.

Hart, M. 't. 1997. "The Merits of a Financial Revolution: Public Finance, 1550–1700," in M. 't Hart, J. Jonker and J. L. van Zanden, eds., *A Financial History of the Netherlands.* Cambridge: Cambridge University Press: 11–36.

Korthals Altes, W. L. 2001. *"De Geschiedenis van de Gulden, Van Pond Hollands tot Euro" [History of the Guilder, from the Holland Pound to the Euro].* Amsterdam: Boom.

McCusker, J. 1978. *Money and Exchange in Europe and America, 1600–1775.* Chapel Hill: University of North Carolina Press.

Metz, R. 1990. "Geld, Währung und Preisentwicklung, der Niederrheinraum im europäischen Vergleich, 1350–1800 (Frankfurt am Main)", in Rudolph M.

---

[100] We are abstracting from the relative minor amounts lent on occasion to the Amsterdam city treasury and the Municipal Loan Chamber. Also, the receipts were arguably banknote-like in some respects, as they circulated freely and had value in exchange.

Bell and Martha Howell, eds., *The Medieval and Early Modern Data Bank*, 1998. Accessed online at: www.scc.rutgers.edu/memdb.

Mueller, R. 1997. *The Venetian Money Market, Banks, Panics and the Public Debt, 1200–1500*. Baltimore: Johns Hopkins University Press.

Neal, Larry. 1990. *The Rise of Financial Capitalism, International Capital Markets in the Age of Reason*. Cambridge: Cambridge University Press.

2000. "How it all Began, the Monetary and Financial Architecture of Europe during the First Global Capital Markets, 1648–1815," *Financial History Review* 7: 117–40.

Polak, M. S. 1998a. *Historiografie en Economie van de "Muntchaos", De Muntproductie van de Republiek 1606–1795*, Deel I [*Historiography and Economics of the Coinage Chaos, Coin Production in the Dutch Republic 1606–1795, Part I*]. Amsterdam: NEHA.

1998b. *Historiografie en Economie van de "Muntchaos", De Muntproductie van de Republiek 1606–1795*, Deel II [*Historiography and Economics of the Coinage Chaos, Coin Production in the Dutch Republic 1606–1795, Part II*]. Amsterdam: NEHA.

Quinn, S. 1996. "Gold, Silver and the Glorious Revolution, Arbitrage between Bills of Exchange and Bullion," *Economic History Review* 49: 473–90.

Quinn, S. and W. Roberds. 2005. "The Big Problem of Large Bills, The Bank of Amsterdam and the Origins of Central Banking." *Federal Reserve Bank of Atlanta Working Paper* 2005: 16.

2007. "The Bank of Amsterdam and the Leap to Central Bank Money," *American Economic Review* 97: 262–5.

Redish, A. 1990. "Evolution of the Gold Standard in England," *Journal of Economic History* 30: 789–805.

Rolnick, A. J., F. R. Velde and W. E. Weber. 1996. "The Debasement Puzzle, an Essay on Medieval Monetary History," *Journal of Economic History* 56: 789–808.

Sargent, T. J. and B. D. Smith. 1997. "Coinage, Debasement, and Gresham's Laws," *Economic Theory* 10: 197–226.

Sargent, T. J. and F. R. Velde. 2002. *The Big Problem of Small Change*. Princeton: Princeton University Press.

Sussman, N. and J. Zeira. 2003. "Commodity Money Inflation: Theory and Evidence from France 1350–1436," *Journal of Monetary Economics* 50: 1769–93.

Usher, A. P. 1943 [1967]. *The Early History of Deposit Banking in Mediterranean Europe*. New York: Russell and Russell.

Van Dillen, J. G. 1925. *Bronnen tot de Geschiedenis der Wisselbanken [Sources for the History of the Exchange Banks]*. The Hague: Rijksgeschiedkundige Publicatieen.

1934. "The Bank of Amsterdam," in, J. G. van Dillen, ed., *History of the Principal Public Banks*. The Hague: Martinus Nijhoff: 79–124.

1964a. "Oprichting en Functie der Amsterdamse Wisselbank in de zeventiende Eeuw 1609–1686," [Establishment and Functioning of the Amsterdam Exchange Bank in the 17th Century] in J. G. van Dillen, ed., *Mensen en Achtergronden, Studies uitgegeven ter gelegenheid van de tachtigste jaardag van de schrijver*. Groningen: J. B. Wolters.

1964b. "Bloeitijd der Amsterdamse Wisselbank 1687–1781" [High Tide of the Amsterdam Exchange Bank 1687–1781] in J. G. van Dillen, ed., *Mensen en Achtergronden, Studies uitgegeven ter gelegenheid van de tachtigste jaardag van de schrijver*. Groningen: J. B. Wolters.

Van Zanden, J. L. 2004. "The Prices of the Most Important Consumer Goods, and Indices of Wages and the Cost of Living in the Western Part of the Netherlands, 1450–1800." Accessed online at: www.iisg.nl/hpw/data.html #netherlands.

3 With a view to hold: The emergence of institutional investors on the Amsterdam securities market during the seventeenth and eighteenth centuries[*]

Oscar Gelderblom and Joost Jonker

Institutional investors such as insurance companies and mutual funds are a prominent feature of today's financial systems. To some extent they serve as a hallmark of modernity and as such Richard Sylla has included them in his list of six features of successful financial revolutions inaugurating economic leadership.[1] Sylla did not specify his reasons for doing so, but we may summarize the importance of institutional investors as, on the one hand, providing access to the securities market for savers otherwise unable to enter it, and on the other hand as providing a ready demand for secure investments suited to fund long-term liabilities.

Institutional investors in themselves are an old phenomenon in Europe. Already by the late Middle Ages ecclesiastical institutions derived income from the land and houses which they owned. In several parts of early modern Europe revenue from real estate contributed to the funding of hospitals and orphanages.[2] Investment in financial assets remained limited, however.[3] Only in sophisticated financial markets, i.e., Venice,[4]

[*] We are indebted to Irene Mangnus, Kirsten Hulsker, and Heleen Kole for excellent research assistance. Our analysis of the asset management of Amsterdams *Burgerweeshuis* builds on the MA Thesis of Irene Mangnus on this very subject. Jan Lucassen and Piet Lourens shared their data on the property of Dutch guilds in 1799 with us. We have greatly benefitted from comments on an earlier draft by Jeremy Atack, Jean-Laurent Rosenthal, Erika Kuijpers, and Maarten Prak.

[1] Sylla, "Financial Systems."

[2] For example the endowments of hospitals in Paris and Bologna: Ramsey, "Poor Relief"; Terpstra, "Apprenticeship."

[3] Three recent surveys on poor relief and healthcare in a large number of countries in pre-industrial Europe suggest that only in Italy and the Low Countries charities were funded with income from financial assets: Grell and Cunningham, *Health Care*; Grell, Cunningham, and Jütte, *Health Care*; Grell, Cunningham, and Roeck, *Health Care*.

[4] Venetian hospitals and confraternities owned real estate as early as the thirteenth century, and government bonds (issued from bequests but also occasionally bought on the

Genoa,[5] and Amsterdam, did charities have portfolios with a considerable volume of public and private securities.[6] Until the eighteenth century, when the first joint-stock insurance companies were created in London, there were no large insurance firms or pension funds either.[7] Non-permanent syndicates of underwriters remained the norm throughout pre-modern Europe.

The link between institutional investors and financial development would appear to be twofold. First, the rise of financial markets during the early modern era enabled some institutional investors to diversify their portfolio and shift from real estate to financial assets such as bonds thereby contributing, in their turn, to the further evolution of those markets. Second, new forms of institutional investors appeared, such as tontines, life insurance companies and mutual funds. These new types of institutional investors had a different purpose from the older ones in that the long-term generation of income gave clients new ways of managing life-cycle and other income risks. These two elements would seem to be interrelated. At present we know next to nothing about the early history of institutional investors, but it would seem that a financial market offering paper assets of sufficient liquidity and long-term security would enable both the asset shift of older institutions and the rise of the new type.

In this chapter we focus on institutional investors in Amsterdam between 1500 and 1800. Even before its rise to economic and financial primacy the city turns out to have harboured a variety of institutional investors, including orphanages, poor houses, hospitals, and craft guilds. The rapid growth of Amsterdam's population, from 30,000 to 200,000 people between 1580 and 1670, created an equally rapid expansion of

---

market) from at least the late fourteenth century onwards: see Mueller, *Venetian*, pp. 463–4, 490, 494, 545.

[5] Besides monasteries, religious fraternities, and chapels, Jacques Heers refers to charities owning government bonds (luoghi di San Giorgio) in the fifteenth century, albeit without further specification: Heers, *Gênes*, pp. 184–90.

[6] McCants, *Civic Charity*. To be sure, there are examples of charities outside Amsterdam with financial assets in their portfolio. See for example Prak, "Goede buren," pp. 153–8.

The allegedly limited spread of investment in financial assets across Europe may simply reflect the current state of the historiography on social welfare. For example in the eighteenth century the *Misericórdias* responsible for social welfare in Portugal derived their income from taxes, bequests and from loans made to local aristocratic elites. Individual cases explored in greater depth do reveal other holdings of financial assets: Lopes, "Poor Relief," pp. 142–63. 146, 149. In a brief history of Danzig's hospitals after 1500, Maria Bogucka ("Health Care") mentions "nine urban hospitals, each richly endowed with land and annuities."

[7] For England: Harris, *Industrializing*, pp. 100–7. The two fire insurance companies that existed in the Dutch Republic in the eighteenth century are described in: Langenhuyzen, "Zekerheid," pp. 203–22. 211–15. The absence of other insurance companies and pension funds in the Dutch Republic can be deduced from Leeuwen, *De rijke*.

the social safety net provided by these institutions, and consequently in their funds. All of them relied to a greater or lesser degree on investments to fund their expenditure. We analyze the financial administration of several of these institutions, and several other sources, to explore their asset shift from real estate into securities. When did it occur, why, and can we say anything about the consequences of that shift for the securities market? In addition we trace the rise of new types of institutional investors from the 1670s.

The paper proceeds as follows. Section II analyzes the investment portfolio of Amsterdam's municipal orphanage, the *Burgerweeshuis*. Section III looks at other charities, including Amsterdam's commissioners of the poor, its hospitals, and homes for the elderly. Sections IV and V extend the analysis to the investment income generated by the city's churches and craft guilds. Private institutional investors such as tontines and mutual funds are discussed in section VI. A final section summarizes our findings and discusses implications for our understanding of the evolution of financial markets.

I.   The endowment of Amsterdam's public orphanage

Around 1520 the Amsterdam city council founded the Burgerweeshuis to care for the city's growing number of orphans. The institution derived its funding from four main sources: subsidies from the city; donations and regular public collections; the right of usufruct on the estates of orphans in its care; and investment income. This last source probably existed from the orphanage's inception because rich inhabitants donated real estate to the Burgerweeshuis.[8] In 1578 the orphanage's endowment increased substantially when Amsterdam switched to the Protestant side and joined the Dutch Revolt against Spain. The city council expropriated Catholic Church possessions and turned over some of the assets to the Burgerweeshuis. The institution itself moved into a dissolved monastery on the Kalverstraat, now part of the museum of Amsterdam's history, while the orphanage also received real estate in and around the city to serve as a source of income, thus radically reducing its dependence on subsidies and charity.

Indeed, for most of the seventeenth and eighteenth centuries the Burgerweeshuis ran a budgetary surplus which the board of trustees channelled into expanding its portfolio of investments.[9] As a consequence the orphanage became largely self-supporing. Income rose from around

---

[8] McCants, *Civic Charity*; Eeghen, "Excursie," pp. 52, 121–5. 121; Engels, *Kinderen*, p. 14.
[9] McCants, *Civic Charity*, pp. 157–65.

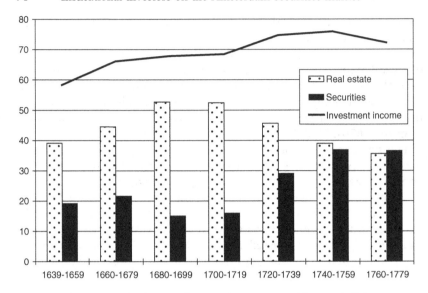

Figure 3.1 The income from real estate, securities, and all investment as a percentage of total income at the *Burgerweeshuis*, 1639–1779. *Source:* McCants, *Civic Charity*, 174.

80,000 guilders in the 1630s to between 120,000 and 130,000 guilders during the second half of the eighteenth century. Prior to the 1720s most of the investment income derived from real estate. The orphanage's board of trustees managed a varied portfolio ranging from farm lands and residential housing to inns and the city's main theatre, which happened to be its most profitable source of income overall. At times the Burgerweeshuis also acted as property developer by building residential housing on vacant plots of land in the city.[10] In addition to real estate, the orphanage invested its wealth in private and public securities, most notably bonds of the States of Holland. The combined income from property and securities increased steadily from 57.6 percent in 1639 to stabilize at around 70 percent from 1668, edging up slightly during the first half of the eighteenth century only to sink back again (Figure 3.1).[11]

The contours of the board's financial policy came out in the first spell of adversity in the 1670s.[12] Cost overruns on a property development, a growing numbers of orphans in care, and sharply rising costs of living caused by the war years 1672–1678 pushed up expenditure and created

---

[10] Ridder, "De Beerebijt," pp. 52, 56–65; McCants, *Civic Charity*, pp. 154–8.
[11] McCants, *Civic Charity*, pp. 156, 164, 174.   [12] Ibid. 165–70.

a budget deficit. Keeping the endowment intact as much as possible was the first priority. Confident that the crisis situation would not last, the trustees covered the deficit by borrowing rather than selling assets. Between 1671 and 1680 they took out loans with a total value of 180,000 guilders. When the selling of property proved inevitable, the trustees sold securities rather than real estate, so holding on to the latter clearly formed a second priority.

Renewed financial difficulties encountered during the 1690s led the board to scrutinize the orphanage's portfolio and rearrange its holdings once again. In 1700 fifteen rural properties were sold off as structural underperformers. With the proceeds the Burgerweeshuis cleared its debts and returned to budget surpluses.[13] This sale marked the beginning of a very gradual portfolio shift from real estate into securities. The budget surpluses were now reinvested in securities and the board also exchanged some more underperforming rural properties for securities. As a consequence, the orphanage's real estate holdings declined relative to the amount invested in securities (Figure 3.1).

The Burgerweeshuis was already an active investor in securities since 1578. Its portfolio originated in the same policy decision made by the city council regarding expropriated church assets; along with the real estate, the orphanage also received financial assets. As early as 1590 the Burgerweeshuis had a total of 26,364 guilders invested in this way, which yielded almost 14 percent of its total income. At the time loans to individual persons generated two-thirds of the income from financial assets. Term annuities issued by the estates of Holland and by the city of Amsterdam made up the rest.[14] Over time the reinvestment of budget surpluses boosted the securities portfolio to a peak of more than 400,000 guilders in 1670. As for the spread of investments, the amount put into private loans had declined in favor of formal securities. Securities issued by the States of Holland and the city of Amsterdam now formed the mainstay of the portfolio, in which bonds from the Amsterdam admiralty and from the Dutch East India Company (VOC) also figured.[15] Still, the trustees' preference for real estate meant that the income from securities and loans as a percentage of the total remained stable at around 20 percent for another half century (Figure 3.1).

---

[13] Ibid. 174–6, noting that other Amsterdam investors moved out of rural property at the same time.

[14] Ibid. 160–3; GAA 367 reg., pp. 226–50; no. 194; no. 196, fol. 1–13, 122–31; no. 197–200; no. 202; no. 204; no. 226 fol. 64–94, fol. 159–88.

[15] Ibid. 154–6 for the portfolio around 1670; her figures were appended by Mangnus, "Tot behoef," 23–5.

A marked shift towards government bonds occurred only in the first half of the eighteenth century. Between 1700 and 1715 the trustees doubled the amount of States of Holland obligations to 400,000 guilders. Most of these bonds were directly purchased from the receivers' offices, but during the next quarter century the trustees turned to the secondary market, because the States of Holland had stopped issuing debt. Through local brokers the Burgerweeshuis bought bonds, separately or in batches, and raised its total bond holdings to almost one million guilders in 1740. Finally, between 1755 and 1770 the orphanage bought, again through Amsterdam brokers, batches of obligations issued in Amsterdam and in other Holland towns for a total of 250,000 guilders. By 1770 the orphanage's portfolio was equally divided between real estate and financial assets.[16]

At first sight the growing preference for public debt seems curious. Holders of Holland's bonds paid a 1.5 percent property tax on their holdings which effectively reduced the nominal interest rate to 2.5 percent.[17] With a return of 4.3 to 4.5 percent real estate should have been the better investment. Why then did the orphanage's trustees reconfigure the portfolio? Ann McCants has argued that realizing the investment premium of city property over securities required considerable care and attention from the trustees and therefore really represented a donation in kind which securities did not require them to make. In addition, she states that the price of city property appears had risen to the point where the Burgerweeshuis no longer wanted to buy, presumably because the board considered the ratio of price to earnings insufficiently attractive.[18] After 1670 the real estate market probably diverged as Amsterdam's population stagnated and the city's rapid expansion halted. The walls built to accommodate further growth proved too wide and large tracts of land enclosed within the perimeter for the planned increase in residential housing remained empty until late into the nineteenth century. As a result residential developments like the Noordsche Bosch lost their attraction, but at the same time property in busy districts such as the Kalverstraat, where the Burgerweeshuis owned many houses, rose in price, preventing further purchases. Consequently, securities were really the only option to invest budget surpluses.

Two other factors would seem to explain the rearrangement of the portfolio. First, for most of the eighteenth century the Burgerweeshuis

---

[16] The composition of the Burgerweeshuis' bond holdings can be gleaned from: Amsterdam City Archives, Inventory 349, nr. 153; McCants, *Civic Charity*, pp. 176–7, lists all assets in 1772, albeit omitting the municipal theatre, which burned down in May of that year. If one includes that particular property and securities were about equal.

[17] Fritschy and Liesker, *Gewestelijke financiën*.   [18] McCants, *Civic Charity*, pp. 176–7.

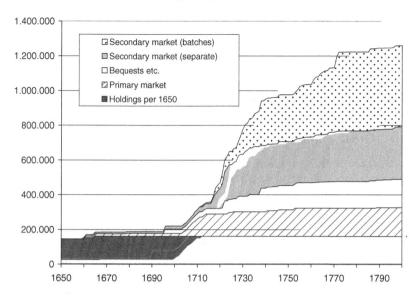

Figure 3.2 Government bonds purchases by the *Burgerweeshuis*, 1650–1800.
Source: GAA Archief 367.A, Inv. Nr 152 (Nieuw Rentenboek).

was probably exempt from the 1.5 percent property tax, so the bonds did in fact give 4 percent interest.[19] Second, in all likelihood the bonds yielded more, for the orphanage's purchases on the secondary market were probably made at prices below par. Two price currents published in October and November 1747 by a local bookseller in Amsterdam show Holland's obligations trading at prices between 65 and 90 percent.[20] In Leyden the prices of Holland's bonds stood at 92 percent in 1720, at 97 percent in 1742.[21] A bond bought at 90 percent on the secondary market would yield a 4.4 percent return on investment – slightly above that of real estate. Third, the board of the Burgerweeshuis probably also preferred bonds because they offered further advantages over real estate. The trustees gradually learned that first-class securities with a liquid

[19] McCants' reconstruction of the orphanage's portfolio in 1772 does reckon with the payment of a 1.5 percent tax on government bond holdings. However, the financial accounts of the Burgerweeshuis reveal that in the early 1780s bonds still yielded 4 percent. Only in 1786 the records show a reduction of the interest paid to 2.75 and 2.5 percent (Amsterdam City Archives, Inv. 349, nr. 153).
[20] V. Dillen, "Effectenkoersen," pp. 2–4. The price current of 6 November 1747 is printed on pages 13–14.
[21] Leiden "Notarial," courtesy of Maarten Prak.

market were as good as cash, if only because such paper could always be lombarded at little cost.[22] Consequently, the board reduced its cash holdings to a minimum. Until 1660 the amount of cash at year-end was usually in the region of 60–80,000 guilders; during the eighteenth century it was typically 4,000 guilders, and the board took care to invest any surplus money as quickly as possible.[23]

II.   Other public welfare institutions

The Burgerweeshuis was not the only public institution that relied on investment income. There were several other civic welfare institutions in Amsterdam: two poor relief funds, an orphanage, a hospital, and a madhouse. The surviving accounts of some of these institutions enable us to analyze their sources of income. Not all had the means to invest. The Aalmoezeniersweeshuis, for instance, which cared for the children left by inhabitants who were not Amsterdam citizens, does not appear to have accumulated sufficient surpluses with which to buy either real estate or securities. Instead, the orphanage was run by city officials and derived its main income from the public garbage collection and the right to half a percent of the revenues from all public sales of merchandise.[24]

Amsterdam's poor houses did have some capital. From the early fifteenth century (and possibly earlier) the city council annually appointed officials known as *huiszittenmeesters* to oversee the urban poor. In 1419 their responsibilities were divided along the lines of the city's two parishes, thus creating the Oudezijds and Nieuwezijds Huiszittenmeesters. Initially the officers provided accomomdation and occasionally also food and fuel. After 1600 the *Nieuwezijds* and *Oudezijds Huiszittenhuizen* principally provided the poor with peat, bread, butter, and cheese from Christmas to Easter.[25] In summertime the *Aalmoezeniers*, first appointed by the town magistrate in 1613, took care of the poor. This division of responsibilities changed in 1682 when the two poor houses took on the distribution of food and fuel throughout the year.

The financial administration of the two poor houses shows them to have been substantial institutional investors.[26] In 1698 the bookkeeper of the Oudezijds Huiszittenhuis, in the eastern part of the city, put the value of the poor house's portfolio of annuities and bonds issued by

---

[22] Riley, *International Government* 31.
[23] McCants, *Civic Charity*, pp. 160–2 (data), 178 (cash policy).
[24] Amsterdam, "Inleiding."
[25] Mothers of newly-born children received an additional twenty stivers per week.
[26] Melker, "Inleiding." See McCants, *Civic Charity*, pp. 155–6; the Burgerweeshuis had a bigger portfolio, but only 156,800 guilders of it in Holland debt.

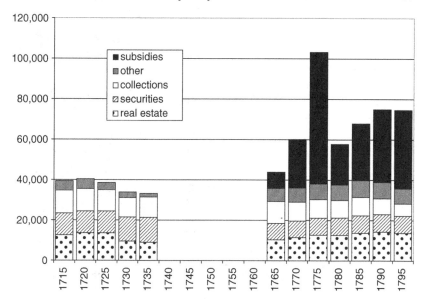

Figure 3.3 The composition of the annual income of Amsterdam's
Oudezijds Huiszittenhuis in the eighteenth century.
Source: Amsterdam City Archives, Inv. 349, Nrs. 244, 245.

Holland at nearly 270,000 guilders, more than what the Burgerweeshuis
owned in 1670.[27] We can reconstruct the main revenue flows for the first
and last third of the eighteenth century (Figure 3.3). Until 1735 public
collections, real estate, and securities each yielded about 30 percent of
gross income. After 1765 total income increased considerably but not
as a result of a larger investment portfolio. In fact, a provincial tax of
1 percent on public debt holdings cut the net income from securities by
3,000 guilders a year. The income grew because the city of Amsterdam
granted large subsidies to allow the Oudezijds Huiszittenhuis to continue her poor relief.

The revenues of the sister poor house, the Nieuwezijds Huiszittenhuis, located in the western part of the city, seems to have been quite
similar in volume and composition.[28] The institution's accounts show
that, from the late sixteenth century until the late seventeenth century,

---

[27] Amsterdam City Archives Inv. 349, Nr. 301.
[28] Van Leeuwen estimated the average annual income of the Oudezijds and Nieuwezijds
Huiszittenhuizen combined at 136,000 guilders between 1687 and 1799. Leeuwen,
"Amsterdam." Our reconstruction of the annual income of the Oudezijdshuiszittenhuis
between 1713–1736 and 1762–1800 reveals a total of 62,500 guilders.

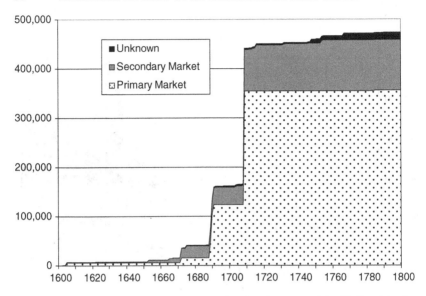

Figure 3.4 The nominal value of obligations issued by Holland in the portfolio of Amsterdam's *Nieuwezijds Huiszittenhuis*, 1600–1800.
Source: Amsterdam City Archives, Inv 349, Nrs. 402, 421.

houses and land generated most of its income, with public collections and interest on securities contributing smaller sums. Initially the securities portfolio consisted mainly of Amsterdam city annuities and 15,700 guilders of Holland annuities and bonds but on two occasions, during 1689–1691 and again in 1709, the Nieuwezijds Huiszittenhuis bought very large amounts of Holland debt, for a total of some 350,000 guilders (Figure 3.4). Most of these bonds were bought directly from Holland's receiver in Amsterdam, but after 1709 purchases were made on the secondary market.

The Amsterdam hospitals also built up considerable possessions. In the second half of the eighteenth century the madhouse held 120,000 guilders worth of Holland bonds, probably in addition to other investments.[29] The main hospital *Binnengasthuis*, which was formed when two medieval hospitals merged in 1582, appears to have followed an investment strategy similar to that of the Burgerweeshuis, and from an identical point of departure.[30] Initially the hospital, having obtained two convents from the expropriated church assets, concentrated on real estate

[29] Amsterdam City Archives, Inv. 342, Nrs. 1006, 1007.
[30] Eeghen, "Gasthuis", pp. 59–63.

Table 3.1. *The investment portfolio of St. Peter's Hospital in Amsterdam, 1650 and 1750*

	1650		1750	
	Principal sum	Percentage of total	Principal sum	Percentage of total
Securities				
Holland	85,800	16	86,875	28
Amsterdam	56,000	10	114,000	37
Six major towns	10,928	2	11,228	4
Hoorn			16,000	5
Friesland	14,000			5
Obligations – polders	4,600	1		
Obligations – VOC	4,000	1		
Subtotal	161,328	30	242,103	78
Private loans				
Obligations	107,420	20		
Mortgages	76,812	14	5,310	2
Term annuities	15,282	3	4,250	1
Subtotal	199,514	37	9,560	3
Real estate[a]	178,798	33	58,152	19
Total	539,640	100	309,815	100

Source: Amsterdam City Archives, 342 (Gasthuizen) Nrs. 1601, 1604, 1605; (a) The principal sum of real estate in 1650 is estimated on the basis of the total income from housing rents, and the value and rents paid (4.6 percent on average) for some of the individual houses; The value of real estate in 1750 is estimated on the basis of the total rental income and the average return for all other investments in that year (3 percent).

by building residential accomodation on its lands. The trustees subsequently enlarged and diversified the investment portfolio which, by 1650, had reached a value of 540,000 guilders (Table 3.1). Nearly 40 percent consisted of loans to private individuals in various forms, 33 percent was in real estate, and 28 percent in public securities, notably those of Holland (18 percent), and the city of Amsterdam (10 percent).

During the eighteenth century the hospital's financial position deteriorated as a consequence of rising expenses.[31] The board of trustees had to liquidate part of the portfolio, which by 1750 had shrunk from 540,000 to 310,000 guilders. At the same time the trustees changed their investment policy. As with the Burgerweeshuis, the reconfiguration particularly hit the private loans, of which only a very small amount

[31] Ibid. 61–3.

remained. By contrast, the hospital board clearly came to prefer securities over real estate, because the former category went up and the latter went sharply down, so that the balanced portfolio of 1650 made way for one heavily weighted with securities. Even so the yield on the investment portfolio declined from 4.5 percent in 1650 to 3 percent in 1750, causing the hospital to become increasingly dependent on subsidies from the city.

This preliminary investigation shows Amsterdam's civic welfare institutions possessing substantial investment portfolios, with an estimated total of 4.3 million guilders at the end of the eighteenth century. The Burgerweeshuis, with 2.5 million, was the single biggest institutional investor, followed by the two public poor houses with 1.5 million together, and the hospital and madhouse closed the ranks with a total of about 430,000 guilders. We need further research to assess the position of these institutions in greater detail and to clarify the various policy shifts, but two main trends appear to be clear. First, over time these institutions phased out private loans in favor of other, especially securitized, investments, so private borrowers must have turned to other creditors instead. Second, although some of the institutions retained a preference for real estate, the relative importance of securities, notably Holland bonds, rose markedly. This was a clear consequence of market circumstances. Profitable real estate opportunities became more scarce; in addition, Holland's debt almost tripled between 1670 and 1720, creating a flood of bonds which left investors with few options but to buy. At the same time the secondary market for public bonds apparently widened to offer both more choice and greater liquidity. We will return to this important finding in the conclusion.

III.   The churches

The rapid growth of Amsterdam's population in the seventeenth century raised the demand for social welfare of all kinds. To alleviate the financial burden of the public welfare institutions, the town magistrate devolved the responsibility for poor relief and orphan care to the various religious communities. The charity board of the Lutheran Church, formally established in 1595, distributed food and fuel among a growing number of mostly German immigrants.[32] In the first half of the seventeenth century both the Walloon Church and the Portuguese Jewish community created their own separate orphanages in addition to a poor relief program. The welfare work commenced by several prominent

---

[32] Kuijpers, "Een zeventiende-eeuwse."

Catholic families in the 1630s was gradually extended to include regular poor relief, two orphanages, a home for the elderly, and three of Amsterdam's twenty-odd *hofjes* (almshouses) that provided small-scale housing for persons in need. Probably the most extensive program was offered by the city's official church, the *Nederduits hervormde gemeente*. To support the poor, the charity commissioners of this congregation ran their own bakery and brewery, and they founded an orphanage (1657), an almshouse for the elderly poor (1683), and the Corvershof residence (1723).

The financing of these arrangements differed from congregation to congregation. The Lutheran charity commissioners appear to have depended almost entirely on revenue from collections and bequests.[33] The Portuguese Jewish congregation received gifts and bequests, and also generated income through its meat hall, the sale of graves, and the levy of taxes within the community –on commercial turnover at first, and later also on its members' wealth.[34] Amsterdam's Catholics boosted the income from collections and bequests with revenues from investment in real estate and financial assets.[35] By the end of the eighteenth century the total assets of both their *Armenkantoor* and the *Maagdenhuis*, its orphanage for girls, amounted to more than one million guilders.

The rebuilding of Catholic endowments, however, took considerable time. After Amsterdam switched sides in 1578 the Catholic welfare program simply disappeared for some thirty years.[36] Shortly after 1600 a few Catholic families again started helping the poor of their community. This led to the creation of a regular fund, the *Beurs voor Catolijke Armen*, around 1632. The *beurs* had an initial endowment of half a house, 13,000 guilders in cash, and loans to private individuals worth 30,000 guilders. The board of four trustees gradually extended its activities, establishing separate orphanages for boys and girls during the 1660s. The *Oude-Armenkantoor*, as it became known, subsequently concentrated on poor relief. By 1690 its assets, including 25 houses in Amsterdam, amounted to 100,000 guilders; in 1760 the investment portfolio stood at 400,000 guilders. At the turn of the nineteenth century real estate and

---

[33] Ibid.; Leeuwen, "Amsterdam," pp. 138, 140. In the first half of the nineteenth century the financial assets of the Lutheran diaconate yielded an average annual income of less than 4,000 guilders – indicative of a portfolio worth less than 100,000 guilders. Leeuwen, *Bijstand.* 324.

[34] On the various income sources in 1683: Pieterse, *Daniel Levi.* pp. 73–4. On taxes levied on commercial turnover: Vlessing, "Portuguese-Jewish." Cf. also Kaplan, "De joden."

[35] Wolf, *Geschiedenis*.

[36] One exception was the Begijnhof, or Beguinage, a fourteenth-century urban enclosure with houses and a church used by unmarried lay women.

Table 3.2. *The annual income from real estate, securities, and other revenue sources of the Roman Catholic* Maagdenhuis, *1600–1800*

Income source	1610	1643	1692	1732	1738	1750
Houses	300	–	2,500	6,373	7,244	–
Securities	200	800	–	5,904	7,000	7,800
Knitting wages	200	1,000	2,500	3,759	5,000	–
Collections	–	–	–	4,825	–	–
Bequests	–	–	–	7,995	–	–
Total	–	–	–	**28,856**	–	–

Source: Meischke, R. (1980). *Amsterdam. Het R.C. Maagdenhuis, het huizenbezit van deze instelling en het St. Elisabeth-gesticht.* 's-Gravenhage: Staatsuitgeverij.

securities worth one million guilders generated almost 30 percent of annual revenue.[37]

The trustees of the Catholic girls' orphanage also created a large endowment but again it took considerable time.[38] In 1610 the Maagdenhuis had owned just a few houses and annuities of no more than 6,000 guilders. Collections, gifts, and bequests covered expenses, with the older girls contributing the wages of their knitwork to the institution's purse. Over the years that followed, rich Catholics donated so much property to the Maagdenhuis that in 1655 the provincial authorities issued a formal ban on any further gifts and bequests to Catholic institutions. As a result donors adopted usufruct constructions, transferring the revenues of property set aside for welfare work. In 1715 the Maagdenhuis succeeded in getting an exemption from the ban but it did not obtain the waiver of the 1.5 percent tax on financial assets which most public welfare institutions enjoyed.

Even so the orphanage accumulated a substantial investment portfolio. In 1732, the one year for which we can detail the income of the Maagdenhuis, real estate worth 163,000 guilders and public securities worth 240,000 guilders brought in 40 percent of all revenue (Table 3.2). The institution's endowment continued to grow over the next half

[37] The rapid growth of the Armenkantoor's wealth in the second half of the eighteenth century is documented in: Wolf, *Geschiedenis*, pp. 61–5. The portfolio was probably divided equally between real estate and securities. In the first half of the nineteenth century the securities of the Armenkantoor yielded 20,000 guilders per year. Assuming an average yield of 4.5 on these assets, at that time the financial assets were worth 450,000 guilders. Leeuwen, *Bijstand in Amsterdam*, p. 324.

[38] The following is based on: Meischke, *Amsterdam*.

Table 3.3. *The revenues of the* Hervormde Diaconie, *1770*

Source	Income	Share
Collections	224,992	40%
Bequests and donations	179,415	32%
Bank and cash	54,060	10%
Sales obligations	44,101	8%
Interest	28,894	5%
Rents	17,878	3%
Other	19,530	3%
Total	568,869	100%

Source: Hoeven, *Geheime notulen*, 177.

century, totaling over 1.25 million guilders by 1797. By that time the trustees had changed their investment policy, for public securities formed no less than 80 percent of assets.

The investment portfolio of the Dutch Reformed Church's *diakonie* or welfare fund during the second half of the eighteenth century has been documented in some detail. The most striking feature of its budget is the very high annual income of almost 600,000 guilders in 1770 (Table 3.3).[39] Collections during services and donations into the many boxes installed in public buildings generated 40 percent of revenues and bequests and gifts 30 percent. At 6.5 percent the contribution of investments in real estate and securities seems paltry by comparison, though this figure was probably a little higher if we take into account that the interest payments on loans were entered into the ledgers amongst the general receipts.

Even so the church possessed an impressive portfolio. A reconstruction of the asset holdings of the Hervormde diaconie by H.W. van der Hoeven indicates an estimated value of 2.5 million guilders in 1771. With a total value of 1.4 million guilders public securities, largely consisting of Holland obligations, were the single most important property, but the diaconie also owned private obligations and shares in Dutch and English joint-stock companies. If we assume that the yield of these financial assets equalled that on the 39 houses and warehouses owned by the church (2.6 percent in 1771), the value of this real estate portfolio can be estimated at almost 700,000 guilders.

The diaconie had accumulated this portfolio largely through bequests and donations, so we cannot use the 1771 reconstruction to speculate

[39] Hoeven, *Geheim notulen*. See also: Leeuwen, "Amsterdam", pp. 139–43.

Table 3.4. *The investment portfolio of the* Hervormde Diaconie *in 1771*

	Capital sum	Annual income	Implied yield
Real estate	(687,600)	17,877	
Public securities			
Obligations Holland	1,160,174	28,933	2.5%
Lottery loans Holland	115,950	2,742	2.4%
Obligations Friesland	84,600	1,692	2.0%
Obligations States General	68,300	2,049	3.0%
Private securities			
VOC shares and obligations	121,625	5,987	4.9%
Annuities	78,009	1,908	2.4%
Kustingen and *schepenbrieven*	37,325	1,162	3.1%
Obligations	36,413	952	2.6%
Foreign securities			
Shares South Sea Company,			
Bank of England	89,217	2,125	2.4%
Obligations	22,686	507	2.2%
Unspecified	3,100	433	14.0%
Total	2,505,000	66,368	2.6%

Source: Hoeven, *Geheime notulen*, 178–80.

about its financial policy. What we do know, however, is that the commissioners did not hesitate to use the endowment for bridging shortfalls in revenue (Table 3.4), either by selling securities or by using them as collateral for loans in about equal proportions.[40]

IV.   The guilds

The city and the church were not the only providers of financial support for poor, sick, and elderly Amsterdam inhabitants. Besides the support of family members and friends – a largely invisible but presumably very important safety net for the majority of urban dwellers – most of the city's guilds ran mutual funds (*bussen*) to provide for sick members and the widows of deceased masters. Initially such funds derived the bulk of their income from members' contributions. However, as Sandra Bos has pointed out, several guilds in Amsterdam were able to save money and create an endowment to fund their welfare expenditure. The accounts of

[40] Hoeven, *Geheim notulen*, pp. 184–5, 35, 69.

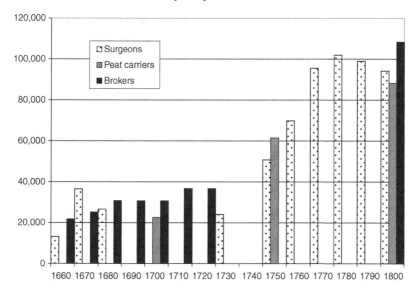

Figure 3.5 The value of financial assets in the portfolios of several Amsterdam guilds, 1650–1800.

Source: The data for surgeons and peat diggers is from: Bos, S. (1998). *"Uyt liefde tot malcander" Onderlinge hulpverlening binnen de Noord-Nederlandse gilden in international perspectief (1570–1820).* Amsterdam: Stichting Beheer IISG. 77, 126; The data for brokers is from: Amsterdam City Archives, Inv. 366, Nrs. 1257/1258.

three of these guilds suggest that by 1650 they had already built up investment portfolios (Figure 3.5).

The available data do not allow a detailed reconstruction of the financial policies of these guilds, but several features stand out. One is the slow growth of the securities portfolios in the second half of the seventeenth century. In the 1660s the brokers'guild waited several years before putting surplus cash into more bonds.[41] The importance of financial assets greatly increased during the first half of the eighteenth century, i.e. more or less parallel to other institutional investors such as the Burgerweeshuis. In 1737 the peat carriers' guild sold off its last piece of real estate.[42] Between 1733 and 1770 the financial portfolio of the surgeons' guild increased fourfold, enabling it to fund welfare for elderly members and widows entirely from the return on securities.[43] At the same time the guilds show varying investment preferences. After 1675

[41] Amsterdam City Archives, Inv. 366, Nr. 1257.
[42] Bos, *Uyt liefde*, p. 125.   [43] Ibid. 76–9.

Table 3.5. *The value of property owned by Amsterdam guilds in 1799, according to their own statements*

Property	Number of guilds	Value	Share
Holland's debt	42	1,271,196	68.9%
Other loans	32	121,166	6.6%
Real estate	23	385,880	20.9%
Cash	34	33,215	1.8%
Plate, furniture, etc.[a]	19	6,600	0.4%
Unknown	2	26,183	1.4%
Total value	48	1,844,239	100.0%

Source: ARA Wet Col 507; Missive 11–01–1799 N. 71 (Courtesy Jan Lucassen and Piet Lourens); (a) money value estimated on the basis of property of three guilds.

the brokers held only Holland bonds, but the surgeons preferred VOC shares and obligations of the city of Amsterdam.[44]

Each of these guilds possessed financial assets worth between 90,000 and 110,000 guilders at the end of the eighteenth century. If other guilds owned just as much, the total holdings of Amsterdam's guilds may have been of a similar magnitude to that of the civic charities and churches. Data from a 1799 enquiry into property held by the soon to be abolished guilds suggests that this was indeed the case. Data from forty-eight Amsterdam guilds surveyed show that no fewer than 42 of them owned financial assets. Public bonds, and primarily Holland bonds, amounted to almost 70 percent of the total guild assets; the share of real estate was only one-fifth (Table 3.5).[45]

Table 3.6, drawn from the same database, shows another interesting aspect, the exceptional nature of the Amsterdam guilds' investments. Of all major cities in Holland only the Rotterdam guilds owned substantial financial assets. These amounted to about one-sixth of those of the Amsterdam guilds, which corresponds neatly to Rotterdam's size in relation to Amsterdam.[46] Elsewhere in the province, the guilds possessed a few thousand guilders worth of securities at most.

---

[44] Ibid. 76–7.

[45] We thank Jan Lucassen and Piet Lourens for sharing their dataset containing the complete contents of the letters sent by all guilds in the Dutch Republic. It should be noted that the missives are not complete. For example, one conspicuous absence is that of the surgeons' guild of Amsterdam.

[46] For a comparison with towns in other parts of the Dutch Republic, notably Bois-le-Duc and Utrecht, see Bos, *Uyt liefde.*

Table 3.6. *The property of guilds in several towns in Holland in 1799*

Town	Number guilds	Total capital	Debt Holland	Other securities	Real estate	Other	Property not valued
Amsterdam	48	1,844,239	69%	7%	21%	4%	
Rotterdam	37	278,079	39%	41%	5%	-	6 houses
Haarlem	30	98,250	46%	21%	3%	-	5 houses, 14 graves, 1 almshouse
Hoorn	12	43,035	11%	89%	-	-	5 houses
Dordrecht	17	41,489	17%	41%	-	-	3 houses, 17 graves, 1 chapel
Den haag	14	21,907	69%	28%	1%	1%	3 houses
Schiedam	13	21,067	84%	10%	6%	-	
Enkhuizen	17	11,049	14%	81%	5%	-	7 houses
Alkmaar	18	9,834	70%	24%	6%	-	14 houses, 1 warehouse
Delft	15	9,144	59%	41%	-	-	2 houses, 1 guild chamber
Vlaardingen	9	6,713	77%	17%	1%	6%	
Gorinchem	8	1,630	74%	26%	-	-	
Naarden	3	531	19%	65%	16%	-	
Purmerend	3	206	97%	-	3%	-	1 house (partially)
Edam	1	4	-	-	100%	-	
Delfshaven	7	40	-	-	100%	-	
Alphen	1	-	-	-	-	-	
Gouda	2	-	-	-	-	-	

Source: Courtesy Jan Lucassen and Piet Lourens

As with the Burgerweeshuis and the diaconie, securities enabled the Amsterdam guilds to pursue a more active financial policy. In 1799 ten guilds declared to have used these assets as collateral for borrowing money.[47] Guilds in other Dutch towns might have been familiar with this financial technique but its use only shows in two other towns, perhaps not surprisingly Rotterdam and Haarlem – the numbers two and three on the list of wealthy guilds in 1799.

V.   New types of institutional investors

The institutional investors treated so far do not figure in the literature on financial markets in the industrial era which focuses on insurance companies, pension funds, and private investment funds. At first sight the new kind of institutions would seem to be absent from Amsterdam. The city's large maritime insurance sector, for example, was largely in the hands of private syndicates and partnerships.[48] In the eighteenth century only two joint-stock companies for fire insurance existed in the entire Republic. Apart from the Burgerweeshuis and the hospitals which took on the Noordsche Bos development, there appear to have been no corporate real estate investors or property developers in Amsterdam. Pension funds proper did not, as yet, exist. There were many mutual funds for life-cycle risks, notably to give financial assistance to widows. As often as not the members' contributions barely covered the benefits paid out, so the funds never built up sufficient savings to invest.[49]

From 1670 a different form of mutual old-age pension took off in the form of private tontine societies. The tontine, essentially a pooled life annuity where the benefits to the survivors rise as death reduced the number of participants, originated in Italy where the Montes de Pietate issued them.[50] During the 1650s the instrument gained wider currency when Lorenzo Tonti proposed plans for loans based on this principle to the French statesman Cardinal Mazarin. Consequently tontines have become best known as interest tontines, a public debt instrument.[51] In the Dutch Republic such interest tontines were mostly issued by cities and semi-public bodies such as church congregations and militia

---

[47] ARA Wet Col 507; Missive 11–01–1799 N. 71. Interestingly, the guilds were required to pledge 3,000 guilders worth of bonds for a loan worth 1,000 guilders, witness to the then very low price of Dutch government bonds.

[48] Spooner, *Risks at Sea*.   [49] Bos, *Uyt liefde*.

[50] Maassen, "De montes"; Haaften, "Een tontine," 189–90.

[51] Jennings and Trout, *The Tontine*; Velde and Weir, "The Financial Market"; Weir, "Tontines"; Poterba, "Annuities"; Rouwenhorst, "Origins."

corporations.[52] In October 1670, the city of Kampen issued the first such loan. The estates of Holland considered issuing tontines twice, in 1670 and in 1735, only to choose a different type of loan for reasons unknown. Some 45 interest tontines are known to have been issued between 1670 and 1799, for a total of over 6.5 million guilders. The largest of them raised three million guilders for the provincial estates of Zeeland, but 50,000–100,000 guilders was a more typical loan size.[53]

Tontines achieved more prominence as vehicles for private old-age pension and in this form, usually known as capital tontines, they were much closer to institutional investors such as modern life insurance companies and investment trusts. A typical contract would bind together a group of investors subscribing to shares in a block of securities, the interest payments or dividends being shared out amongst the individuals named in the contract until their death. A specified number of last survivors eventually obtained the securities. The first such partnership was probably set up in Amsterdam in 1670, and whereas interest tontines were issued all over the Republic, capital tontines remained by and large an Amsterdam phenomenon. They enjoyed an immediate popularity. Nearly 200 mutual tontine contracts were concluded between 1670 and 1700 and by 1687 printed standard forms had appeared. After 1703 interest waned somewhat after a scandal about fraud committed by the manager of a large number of tontines, but a further 100 contracts are known to have been concluded during the eighteenth century.[54]

Initially most tontines had between ten and thirty participants, but during the eighteenth century a number of fifty became more or less standard and contracts with 100 or even more participants were not uncommon. The shares in known contracts totalled some 8,500 which, assuming 500 guilders as the average sum per share, would amount to a total of 4.3 million guilders invested in this way.[55] Many of the early tontines were based on VOC shares, which since the 1630s had sharply risen in price as a consequence of regular and generous dividends.[56]

[52] For example the tontines issued by the Dutch Reformed deaconate in Amsterdam in the 1790s: Hoeven, *Geheime notulen*, p. 39.
[53] Wagenvoort, *Tontines*, pp. 118–20.   [54] Ibid. 126–52.
[55] Ibid. 102 and 145, for a contract from from 1671 with 450 guilder per share and one from 1748 with fifty shares and 28,500 invested; Rouwenhorst, " Origins," p. 251, for a contract from 1687 with 10,000 guilders on 20 lives; Liefrinck-Teupken, "Een merkwaardig," p. 153, for a 1745 tontine with 500-guilder shares; Haaften, "Gegevens omtrent," p. 234, for a 1736 tontine with 500-guilder shares; Haaften, "Een tontine," p. 63, for a 1772 tontine with 500-guilder shares; Haaften, "Een Remonstrantse," pp. 161–2, for a tontine with 100-guilder shares; Haaften, "Een oud Tontineproject," pp. 91–2, for a project with 250-guilder shares.
[56] Gelderblom and Jonker, "Amsterdam," p. 198.

Since these shares were commonly traded with a standard nominal value of 3,000 guilders, the 500-guilder tontine shares presumably derived their popularity from the fact that they considerably widened access to the VOC dividends.[57] The company even allowed one of its senior book-keepers to manage a group of these tontines, perhaps because the directors considered them a convenient way to cement shareholder loyalty and dampen share price fluctuations. The man at the heart of the 1703 accounting scandal had been the VOC bookkeeper.[58] Gradually the scope of tontines widened to include other securities such as provincial and central government bonds and bonds issued by the Elector of Brandenburg, the King of Prussia, and the Austrian Emperor. Some tontines even adopted diversified portfolios and thus acquired a close resemblance to mutual investment funds, the main difference being the tontine's lack of transferable shares and a different objective.[59]

Mutual investment funds originated in the practice of loan securitization developed by the firm of Jean Deutz & Soon. Deutz held an exclusive agency to sell mercury for the Austrian emperor, during the course of which the firm gave regular advances to the emperor. In 1695 Deutz transformed a 1.5 million guilder loan into a *negotiatie*, i.e., a fund managed by the firm in which investors could buy a share. This negotiatie was, in effect, a unit trust, that is to say a mutual investment fund focusing on one particular security. Subsequently Deutz and other firms used this innovative construction to repackage further loans to Austria, but in 1753 it was again the Deutz firm that took the technique one step further by bundling and repackaging mortgages on Caribbean plantations into negotiaties. The success of this type of fund triggered a boom in plantation loans which is estimated to have raised some eighty million guilders until it collapsed with the 1772–1773 crisis.[60]

This crash helped to bring about another innovation, the mutual fund proper. In 1774 an Amsterdam securities broker, expecting investors to want to spread risks after the shocks sustained, launched a mutual fund with 500,000 guilders invested in a portfolio of ten different securities, including three plantation loans. Within a few years, two more funds followed for a combined total invested of 2.5 million guilders. By issuing

---

[57] Wagenvoort, *Tontines*, pp. 102–5; the supposition that the tontines used new shares issued by the VOC is incorrect, because the company did not raise its capital after its flotation in 1602.

[58] Ibid. 108–10.

[59] Ibid. 126–53. We know of one case in which the capital was invested in an Amsterdam inn, Haaften, "Een tontine op een Amsterdamsche," p. 34; Haaften, "Tontines uit 1671," p. 323; Rouwenhorst, "Origins," p. 253.

[60] Jonker and Sluyterman, *At home*, pp. 91, 122; Jonker "De vroege geschiedenis," p. 114; Rouwenhorst, "Origins," pp. 253–4.

shares of 500 guilders, the funds targeted the same investment public as the tontines but they did not succeed in generating sufficient interest to place all the shares, and in the medium to longer term, their results remained disappointing.[61]

The idea of mutual funds with diversified portfolios was probably ahead of its time, for unit trusts continued to enjoy popularity. Several such funds were organized during the 1780s on various French public loans, but the total amount raised is difficult to make out.[62] Between 1786 and 1804 unit trusts investing in US public bonds raised more than thirty-three million guilders. By repackaging the American securities into negotiaties of the Deutz type, these investment funds made them liquid, because the funds' shares were transferable in Amsterdam whereas a transfer of the original bonds required a power of attorney in the US. Moreover, the funds enabled investors to hold the paper without having to bother about the chore of half-yearly interest collection on the other side of the Atlantic. Finally, the first-rank merchant houses organizing the negotiaties appeared to give them an aura of solidity which no doubt helped to sell the shares, even though at 1,000 guilders apiece they appear to have been targeted at a different market segment from the mutual funds and tontines.[63]

VI.   Conclusion

The evolution of institutional investors on the Amsterdam market falls into three fairly distinct phases. Funding welfare institutions with revenue from endowments was essentially a medieval practice, but with the transfer of expropriated church property to two social welfare institutions in 1578 the Amsterdam city council raised this technique to a new level. Subsequently other institutions for poor relief, health- and orphan care also strove to finance their expenditure with the revenue from endowments. During the eighteenth century the endowments of most institutions grew, as revenues from bequests, donations, and investments outpaced the fairly stable expenses. Between 1730 and 1780 Amsterdam's guilds also accumulated substantial surpluses which were directed into investment. By 1790 the public welfare institutions had collective endowments of at least 4.5 million guilders, the various organized churches at least 5.5 million, and the guilds some two million guilders.

---

[61] Berghuis, *Ontstaan*, pp. 62–73; Rouwenhorst, "Origins," pp. 254–62; Slot, *Iedereen*, pp. 84–5.
[62] Riley, *International Government Finance*, pp. 181, 182–5.
[63] Winter, *Het aandeel van den Amsterdamschen*, Vol 2, pp. 124–5, 141, 145, 466–75; Rouwenhorst, "Origins," pp. 262–5.

Real estate dominated most portfolios until about 1720, and remained a prominent investment in subsequent years. Most institutional investors also owned financial assets from an early date. Initially they favored loans to private borrowers, but the importance of public securities gradually increased during the seventeenth century and, between 1670 and 1700, they almost entirely replaced the private loans in portfolios. From 1720 the purchases of these securities rose exponentially and by 1780 they were the single most important asset held by the institutions. At this stage we possess insufficient comparative yield data to give a proper assessment of institutional investment policy, but the main trends are clear enough. Real estate was favored, but difficult to get and to manage; securities were easy to get and manage, liquid and, given the widely available borrowing facilities, really a form of interest bearing cash. With bond prices generally below par after 1715 the institutions could get an attractive yield, which the waiver of the property tax allowed them to keep. The data on the property held by guilds elsewhere in Holland suggest that the substantial and varied portfolios of institutional investors in Amsterdam were very much the exception.[64] By all appearances the city's dynamic market did not extend very deep into its hinterland.

These institutional investors all had the form of foundations; it was only during the second phase of evolution, which began during the 1670s, that mutual funds appeared in the form of interest tontines designed as vehicles for private pension funding. During the third phase, from about 1750, mutual funds really took wing. As institutional investors, these funds were entirely different from the foundations: far more dynamic, offering innovative commercial products, and targeting a middling sort of investors with their 500-guilder shares. They also attracted far greater sums of money for a large variety of purposes, rarely for buying real estate or public bonds. Amsterdam may have been the first financial centre to have spawned this type of institutional investor on such a scale; we know of nothing similar in the Italian cities or in eighteenth-century London.

---

[64] The available literature on orphanages in other towns in Holland suggests a similar pattern. Rotterdam's orphanage was a wealthy institution with a portfolio of securities worth 770,000 in 1795. Schoor, *In plaats*. The same may be said of Delft's reformed orphanage which in 1772 owned financial assets worth 270,000, and real estate worth between 130,000 and 200,000 guilders. Hallema, *Geschiedenis*. On the other hand, the annual income from real estate and securities of Alkmaars orphanage between 1769 and 1772 suggests total assets worth some 180,000 guilders. Bruinvis, *De geldmiddelen*. In the same period Woerden's orphanage owned securities worth only 26,000 guilders. Vis, *Het weeshuis*. The annual income of the civic orphanage of Schoonhoven from financial assets amounted to between 1,000 and 2,300 guilders before 1800. Molen, *Ordentelyck*.

Finally, the behavior of Amsterdam's institutional investors reveals a new and very important feature of the financial market there, i.e. the existence of a secondary market for public debt. Larry Neal and others have argued that the Dutch Republic had no such market because there were too many issuers, too many types of debt, and no uniformity of conditions. Besides, bonds were rarely secured on specific revenue flows as in France or England, adding to the uncertainty.[65] However, during the seventeenth century institutional investors already had sufficient confidence in the bonds' liquidity to invest large amounts, which suggests a ready market for them did exist. During the eighteenth century the institutions no longer bought their bonds directly from the receivers, but rather from a secondary market served by specialized brokers.

The discovery of this secondary market sheds new light on the history of Dutch public credit. From the early 1700s, public borrowers must have shaped their financial policy in response to market signals. Moreover, the emergence of this market attracted a widening circle of customers as investors discovered that liquid bonds were better than cash. Merchants had discovered the advantages of holding securities for such purposes early in the seventeenth century with the shares of the VOC, but at 6.4 million guilders the company's stock remained a rather limited means of credit. The secondary market for public bonds opened a vastly greater reservoir, a boon for lenders and borrowers alike. The next urgent research priority therefore becomes detailing how and when that market developed.

References

Amsterdam City Archives, "Inleiding" in: *Inventaris archief van de Aalmoezeniers, sinds 1682 regenten van het Aalmoezeniersweeshuis.* Online, available at: http://gemeentearchief.amsterdam.nl/archieven/oi/overzicht/343.nl.html, consulted July 8, 2007.

Berghuis, W.H. (1967). *Ontstaan en ontwikkeling van de Nederlandse beleggingsfondsen tot 1914.* Assen: Van Gorcum.

Bogucka, M. (1997). "Health Care and Poor Relief in Danzig (Gdansk). The Sixteenth- and First Half of the Seventeenth Century." In *Health Care and Poor Relief in Protestant Europe 1500–1700* (eds., Grell, O.P. and Cunningham, A.). London/New York: Routledge, 204–19.

Bos, S. (1998). *"Uyt liefde tot malcander" Onderlinge hulpverlening binnen de Noord-Nederlandse gilden in internationaal perspectief (1570–1820).* Amsterdam: Stichting Beheer IISG.

Bruinvis, C. W. (1909). *De geldmiddelen van het burgerweeshuis te Alkmaar sedert de oprichting (1558).* Haarlem: J.W. de Waard.

---

[65] Neal, "How it all Began"; Homer and Sylla, *History* p. 175.

Dillen, J.G. van (1931). Effectenkoersen aan de Amsterdamsche beurs, 1723–1794. *Economisch-Historisch Jaarboek* 17, 1–46.

Eeghen, I.H. van (1965). Excursie naar het voormalige Burgerweeshuis. *Maandblad Amstelodamum* 52, 121–125.

(1981). Van gasthuis tot academisch ziekenhuis. In: *Vier eeuwen Amsterdams binnengasthuis* (idem, D. du Moulin and R. Meischke, eds.). Amsterdam, 47–104.

Engels, J.T. (1989). *Kinderen van Amsterdam, Burgerweeshuis, Aalmoezeniersweeshuis, Diaconieweeshuis, Sociaalagogisch Centrum.* Amsterdam.

Fritschy, W. and Liesker, R. (2004). *Gewestelijke financiën ten tijde van de Republiek der Verenigde Nederlanden. Deel IV Holland (1572–1795).* The Hague: Instituut voor Nederlandse Geschiedenis.

Gelderblom, O. and Jonker, J. (2005). "Amsterdam as the Cradle of Modern Futures Trading and Options Trading, 1550–1650." In: *The Origins of Value. The Financial Innovations that Created Modern Capital Markets* (eds., Goetzmann, W.G. and Rouwenhorst, K.G.). Oxford: Oxford University Press, 189–205.

Grell, O.P. and Cunningham, A. (1997). *Health Care and Poor Relief in Protestant Europe 1500–1700.* London/New York: Routledge.

Grell, O.P., Cunningham, A., and Jütte, R. (2002). *Health Care and Poor Relief in 18th and 19th Century Northern Europe.* Aldershot: Ashgate.

Grell, O.P., Cunningham, A., and Roeck, B. (2005). *Health Care and Poor Relief in 18th and 19th Century Southern Europe.* Aldershot: Ashgate.

Haaften, M. van (1919). "Een oud Tontineproject." *De Verzekeringsbode* 38.

(1943a). "Gegevens omtrent tontines in Nederland tot 1750." *De Verzekeringsbode*, 234–5.

(1943b). "Tontines uit 1671 op aandeelen van de Oost-Indische Compagnie." *Verzekeringsarchief* 24, 314–26.

(1944). "Een tontine op een Amsterdamsche logement uit 1772." *De Verzekeringsbode* 63.

(1948). "Een tontine voor uitgestelde lijfrente uit 1739." *De Verzekeringsbode* 67.

(1953). "Een Remonstrantse tontine te Boskoop in 1799." *De Verzekeringsbode* 72.

Hallema, A. (1964). *Geschiedenis van het Weeshuis der Gereformeerden binnen Delft.*

Harris, R. (2000). *Industrializing English Law. Entrepreneurship and Business Organization, 1720–1844.* Cambridge/New York: Cambridge University Press.

Heers, J. (1961). *Gênes au XVe siècle. Activité économique et problèmes sociaux.* Paris: S.E.V.P.E.N.

Hoeven, H.W. van der (1985). *Uit de geheime notulen van de eerwaarde groote vergadering – het beleid van de Diakonie van de Hervormde kerk te Amsterdam van 1785 tot 1815.* 's-Gravenhage: Boekencentrum.

Homer, S. and Sylla, R.E. (1991). *A History of Interest Rates.* New Brunswick and London: Rutgers University Press.

Jennings, R.M. and Trout, A.P. (1982). *The Tontine from the Louis XIV to the French Revolutionary Era.* Philadelphia: University of Philadelphia.

Jonker, J. (2002). "De vroege geschiedenis van de firma Insinger & Co." *Jaarboek Amstelodamum* 94, 110–31.

Jonker, J.P.B. and Sluyterman, K.E. (2000). *At Home on the World Markets: Dutch International Trading Companies from the 16th Century until the Present.* The Hague: Sdu Uitgevers.

Kaplan, Y. (1995). "De joden in de Republiek tot omstreeks1750 – religieus, cultureel en sociaal leven." In: *Geschiedenis van de joden in Nederland* (eds., Blom, J.C.H., Fuks-Mansfeld, R.G., and Schöffer, I.). Amsterdam: Balans, 129–76.

Kuijpers, E. (2004). "Een zeventiende-eeuwse migrantenkerk. De lutheranen in Amsterdam." In: *Amsterdammer worden. Migranten, hun organisaties en inburgering, 1600–2000* (ed., Lucassen, L.). Amsterdam: Vossiuspers, 39–59.

Langenhuyzen, T. (1998). "Zekerheid en brand vóór 1800." In: *Studies over zekerheidsarrangementen. Risico's, risiocbestrijding en verzekeringen in Nederland vanaf de Middeleeuwen* (eds., Leeuwen, M.H.D.v. and Gerwen, J.v.). Amsterdam/Den Haag: NEHA/Verbond van verzekeraars, 203–22.

Leeuwen, M.H.D.v. (1992). *Bijstand in Amsterdam, ca. 1800–1850: armenzorg als beheersings- en overlevingsstrategie.* Zwolle: Waanders.

(1996). "Amsterdam en de Armenzorg tijdens de Republiek." *NEHA Jaarboek* 59, 132–161.

(2000). *De rijke Republiek. Giden, assuradeurs en armenzorg, 1500–1800.* Den Haag/Amsterdam: Verbond van verzekeraars/NEHA.

Liefrinck-Teupken, W.F.H. (1920). "Een merkwaardiug lijfrentecontract uit de eerste helft van de 18e eeuw." *Verzekeringsarchief* 1, 153–163.

Lopes, M.A. (2005). "Poor Relief, Social Control and Health Care in 18th and 19th Century Portugal." In: *Health Care and Poor Relief in 18th and 19th Century Southern Europe* (eds., Grell, O.P., Cunningham, A., and Roeck, B.). Aldershot: Ashgate, 142–63.

Maassen, W.W.J (1947) "De montes en de tontine." *de Verzekeringsbode* 66, 41–42.

Mangnus, I. (2004). "Tot behoef der arme wezen." Het effectenbezit van het Amsterdamse Burgerweeshuis in de 17e en 18e eeuw. Utrecht University: Unpublished MA thesis.

McCants, A.E.C. (1997). *Civic Charity in a Golden Age. Orphan Care in Early Modern Amsterdam.* Urbana and Chicago: University of Illinois Press.

Meischke, R. (1980). *Amsterdam. Het R.C. Maagdenhuis, het huizenbezit van deze instelling en het St. Elisabeth-gesticht.* 's-Gravenhage: Staatsuitgeverij.

Melker, B.R. de "Inleiding." In: *Inventaris Archieven van het Nieuwezijds en het Oudezijds Huiszittenhuis en van de Regenten over de Huiszittende Stadsarmen.* Online, available at: http://gemeentearchief.amsterdam.nl/archieven/oi/printversie/349.nl.pdf, consulted March 17, 2007.

Molen, H. van der (2000). *Ordentelyck, stil ende manierlyck: het Schoonhovense weeshuis, 1581–1940.* Rotterdam.

Mueller, R.C. (1997). *The Venetian Money Market. Banks, Panics, and the Public Debt, 1200–1500.* Baltimore and London: The Johns Hopkins University Press.

Neal, L. (2000). "How it all Began: the Monetary and Financial Architecture of Europe during the First Global Capital Markets, 1648–1815." *Financial History Review* 7, 117–140.

Pieterse, W.C. (1968). *Daniel Levi de Barrios als geschiedschrijver van de Portugees-Israelietische Gemeente te Amsterdam in zijn 'Triumpho del Govierno Popular'.* Amsterdam: Scheltema & Holkema NV.

Poterba, J.M. (2005). "Annuities in Early Modern Europe." In: *The Origins of Value. The Financial Innovations that Created Modern Capital Markets* (eds., Goetzmann, W.G. and Rouwenhorst, K.G.). Oxford: Oxford University Press, 207–24.

Prak, M. (1994). "Goede buren en verre vrienden. De ontwikkeling van onderstand bij armoede in Den Bosch sedert de Middeleeuwen." In: *Op lange termijn. Verklaringen van trends in de geschiedenis van samenlevingen* (eds., Flap, H. and Leeuwen, M.H.D.v.). Hilversum: Verloren, 147–70.

Ramsey, M. (2002). "Poor Relief and Medical Assistance in 18th and 19th Century Paris." In: *Health Care and Poor Relief in 18th and 19th Century Northern Europe* (eds., Grell, O.P., Cunningham, A., and Jütte, R.). Aldershot: Ashgate.

Ridder, B. de (1965). De Beerebijt en de Keizerskroon. *Maandblad Amstelodamum* 52, 56–65.

Riley, J.C. (1980). *International Government Finance and the Amsterdam Capital Market 1740–1815.* Cambridge: Cambridge University Press.

Rouwenhorst, G.K. (2005). "The Origins of Mutual Funds.rdquo; In: *The Origins of Value. The Financial Innovations that Created Modern Capital Markets* (eds., Goetzmann, W.G. and Rouwenhorst, K.G.). Oxford: Oxford University Press, 249–70.

Schoor, A. van der (1995). *In plaats van uw aardse ouders: geschiedenis van het Gereformeerd burgerweeshuis te Rotterdam.* Rotterdam.

Slot, B. (2004). *Iedereen kapitalist, de ontwikkeling van het beleggingsfonds in Nederland gedurende de 20ste eeuw.* Amsterdam: Aksant.

Spooner, F. (1983). *Risks at Sea: Amsterdam Insurance and Maritime Europe, 1766–1780.* Cambridge: Cambridge University Press.

Sylla, R. (2002). "Financial Systems and Economic Modernization." *The Journal of Economic History* 62, 277–92.

Terpstra, N. (1994). "Apprenticeship in Social Welfare: From Confraternal Charity to Municipal Poor Relief in Early Modern Italy." *Sixteenth Century Journal* 25, 1–120.

Velde, F. and Weir, D.R. (1992). "The Financial Market and Government Debt Policy in France, 1746–1793." *The Journal of Economic History* 52, 1–39.

Vis, G.N.M. (1996). *Het weeshuis van Woerden: 400 jaar Stadsweeshuis en Gereformeerd Wees- en Oude Liedenhuis te Woerden, 1595–1995.* Hilversum: Verloren.

Vlessing, O. (1995). "The Portuguese-Jewish Mercantile Community in Seventeenth-Century Amsterdam." In: *Entrepreneurs and Entrepreneurship in the Orbit of the Dutch Staple Market* (eds., Lesger, C. and Noordegraaf, L.). The Hague: Stichting Hollandse Historische Reeks, 223–43.

Wagenvoort, H. (1961). *Tontines, een onderzoek naar de geschiedenis van de lijfrenten bij wijze van tontine en contracten van overleving in de Republiek der Nederlanden.* Utrecht.

Weir, D.R. (1989). "Tontines, Public Finance, and Revolution in France and England, 1688–1789." *The Journal of Economic History* 49, 95–124.

Winter, P.J. van (1933). *Het aandeel van den Amsterdamschen handel aan de opbouw van het Amerikaansche Gemeenebest.* The Hague: Nijhoff.

Wolf, H.C. de (1966). *Geschiedenis van het R.C. Oude-Armenkantoor te Amsterdam.* Hilversum/Antwerpen: Uitgeverij Paul Brand.

4   Was John Law's System a bubble?
The Mississippi Bubble revisited

François R. Velde

From 1715 to 1720, a Scotsman named John Law undertook a radical restructuring of French public finances. Because the entire operation appeared to be based on rational principles, it has been called in the French historiography Law's *Système*. In the English-language historiography, it is perhaps better known as the Mississippi Bubble, because an essential element of the scheme was the issue of shares in a trading company, whose prices rose prodigiously in a short period of time and then collapsed.

It is one of Larry Neal's achievements to have placed this bubble in the European context of 1720, tracing the links it had with near-simultaneous bubbles in London and Amsterdam. I wish to revisit the question posed by the title, in the light of more recent work on John Law[1] and my ongoing research. In doing so, I will adopt a narrower approach, focusing essentially on the purely French aspect of the question.[2]

The bubble, or more precisely the rise in the price of the shares of Law's company, were but a cog in the vast operation that Law planned, or at any rate carried out (how much it was planned remains debatable), radically to transform French public finances. I will argue that the market whose prices we observe was managed, if not manipulated. Law ultimately had a target for his share price, partly motivated by misconceptions on the effect of monetary expansion on the interest rate, and therefore on the discount rate; partly motivated by the need to maintain the forward momentum of his operation. I will also "crunch the numbers" and determine whether this target could be justified.

I.   The rise and fall of John Law (1716–1720)

What was the nature of Law's operation? It involved the floating of shares in a private company, the issue of paper money, and the conversion of

---

[1] See Murphy, *John Law*, and Hoffman *et al.*, *Priceless Markets*.

[2] Neal, *Rise*, relied on the existing state of research, notably Harsin, *Doctrines*, Harsin, *Crédit public*, Faure, *Banqueroute*.

government debt into a sort of government equity. The System ultimately unraveled with a coincident, and dramatic, fall in the market value of both the money and the equity.

The System unfolded from the founding of Law's first company in May 1716 to Law's departure from France in December 1720, in three (not necessarily consecutive) stages. The first stage was the creation of a private joint-stock bank that issued notes. Its notes were denominated in coins, were not legal tender, and were redeemable on demand in coin. The bank operated successfully in this form from May 1716 to December 1718, when its shareholders were bought out by the crown, and it became an instrument of the government. Law used it to replace the existing commodity money with fiat money, at first on a voluntary basis, later relying on legal restrictions, in what was the first full-scale attempt at replacing the metallic medium of exchange with paper in Europe.

The second stage was the creation of another joint-stock company, one that was initially involved in developing the crown colony of Louisiana and exploiting associated trade monopolies. This company, to be known as the (French) Indies Company, formed slowly in 1717 and 1718, but from the summer of 1718 it became extremely active, mainly in buying up other trade monopolies and various tax farms. It financed its acquisitions by selling equity on an increasingly buoyant market.

In the third stage, the Indies Company morphed into a very different entity. Tax collection became its principal activity, and in August 1719 it started a scheme that was essentially a non-compulsory conversion of the French national debt into equity of the Company.

At its peak, in January 1720, the System was headed by Law as CEO of the Company (and director of the bank), but also as minister of finance enjoying the full confidence of the Regent. The bank's notes were purposefully taking the place of specie. The unofficial street market for shares had reached extraordinary heights, with prices going from 500 in May 1719 to 9,000 in January 1720.

The downfall soon followed. John Law, for a variety of reasons (in particular to induce the bondholders to literally buy into his conversion scheme) pegged the price of shares above their market level, leading to a massive issue of notes in exchange for shares. To control the inflation that was bound to follow, he tried to change the relation between notes and unit of account, just as his predecessors routinely did during and after monetary reformations. This broke the trust in his System, both in the public and in government (May 1720). Law spent six months trying to rescue his company by unwinding the debt conversion scheme and repurchasing bank notes, until the company's impending bankruptcy forced him to throw in the towel and leave France.

A.   The bank

The first component of the system was a bank, as one could have expected of him. The texts he wrote between 1700 and 1715, all more or less in support of his banking projects, placed a note-issuing or money-creating bank at the center. Whether in Scotland, in Turin or in Paris, the plan's basic structure was the same: the bank, by creating money, would stimulate the economy and enrich its owners as well as the sovereign enlightened enough to charter it. But the plans varied in their details, both reflecting the peculiarities of the country for which they were proposed, as well as the evolution of Law's own thinking away from land-based credit.

The bank Law initially proposed to create in France fit in with the existing financial network of tax collectors and royal cashiers. The liabilities of Law's bank would be, in his scheme, the privileged medium for the financial flows from the provinces to Paris and from taxpayers to the state, as well as the reverse flows out of Paris and to state debtors, employees, and contractors. Law's proposal was thus intended to resolve a rather technical payments problem. The proposal was rejected by the Regent's cabinet in October 1715 because the French government was facing at the time a major crisis. It had neither cash nor credit left. This meant that the niceties of the payments system were far from the most urgent matters, and making a government-sponsored paper compulsory for anything would only make the crisis of confidence worse.

It took more time for Law to implement his initial plan. In May 1716, after a series of operations (partial debt default, emergency loans from financiers, a major recoinage) had gained some breathing space, the cabinet approved a revised plan. The only thing Law asked for now was a charter for a privately-owned note-issuing bank. The bank was given an effective monopoly on note issue because, at the same time as it was chartered, a royal edict prohibited privately issued bearer bills.[3] Other than that, it initially received no special treatment.

To raise the bank's capital, Law made a public offering of 1,200 shares at 5,000L each. Subscribers could purchase shares with a mix of cash and a certain type of government bond (*billets d'État*). The bank was private, but from the start Law bought a quarter of the shares and the king almost as much. The bank was structured similarly to a modern limited liability company. A general assembly was to be held twice a year, at which shareholders voted in proportion to their shareholdings, management reported profits and dividend payments were announced. The bank's main activities were to discount bills, sell foreign exchange, take

---

[3] Antonetti, "Observations."

deposits and manage current accounts, and issue notes payable in specific silver coins (*écus*) on demand to the bearer. It was not allowed to engage in trade or to borrow.

Several features of Law's System are already apparent from the start. Although the bank was ostensibly a private company, the government was involved from the start through the king's shareholdings. The offering was also a hybrid of private and public: capital was raised from the public, but the bank's initial asset was government debt. The bank's shareholders were government creditors who were given a chance to convert their (risky) bonds into a chartered commercial venture.

Getting the notes to circulate and not return constantly to the bank for redemption was critical to the bank's profitability. Three factors played in their favor. The first is that the Regent and several influential and wealthy backers deposited large sums at the very early stages; so the first note issues were made against deposits, not discounting, and the depositors were willing to hold the notes they received and not redeem them. The second is that the notes were given partial protection from the seigniorage tax levied on the whole money stock when a general recoinage was ordered in 1718. Finally, the elements of Law's original bank proposal were introduced one by one. In October 1716 tax collectors were obligated to redeem the bank notes into cash on demand. In April 1717 the notes became legal tender in the payment of taxes. In September 1717 the government's tax accountants and cashiers were ordered to keep accounts and make receipts and payments in notes.

The bank was rapidly successful, in spite of initial doubts and rumors. It issued a fairly large amount of notes, 40 to 50 million L per year on average, while maintaining a reasonable specie reserve (about 50 percent). The notes circulated at par. Law claimed to have lowered the commercial paper rate in Paris, because his bank discounted at rates from 4 to 6 percent. It provided valuable foreign exchange services to the government and to private clients as well. The bank's total dividend payments (three half-yearly payments from 1716 to 1718) amounted to a respectable 15 percent rate of return on the cash price of the initial shares, though perhaps not as high as one would expect given the note circulation. The returns to shareholders included a sizeable capital gain. The only indication for the price of its shares is that they were 3 percent above par in cash in January 1718: this represents almost 90 percent appreciation over the purchase price a year and a half before (assuming a share fully paid with 1/4 cash and 3/4 billets d'État at a 60 percent discount).

Having succeeded in creating a solid note-issuing institution, Law made a puzzling move: he had it nationalized in December 1718. He had made the suggestion even earlier, in May 1718, after barely two years' activity. The Crown bought out all the existing shareholders in cash at the face value of the shares (5,000L). The bank would henceforth be managed by Law on behalf of the king, and all profits turned over to the Royal Treasury. This nationalization had two consequences: it shows the gains to be made by investing early in a company launched by Law, and it gave the king a functioning printing press for the first time.[4] How did the bank's credit survive nationalization? Three years earlier, such a takeover would have been the kiss of death for its reputation. The difference was that the Regent's government in December 1718 was in a different position. Led by the duc de Noailles until January 1718, the government had succeeded in bringing some order to public finances with an array of traditional means (defaults, punitive taxation on war profiteers, seigniorage, tax increases) as well as introducing better accounting practices. Furthermore, the Regent's power had become more secure; he had won a showdown with the Paris Parlement over the recoinage of May 1718, and dispensed with a cumbersome system of committees filled with the dominant figures of the court and the army. The Regent, and Law, were poised for bolder action.

B.   The company

The next component of the System was further removed from anything one finds in Law's earlier writings, and would later overtake the bank in importance. In early 1717, a group of merchants and outfitters were making plans for a small company to develop the vast colony of Louisiana, which consisted in the whole watershed of the Mississippi river. The territory had been French for over forty years but no one had yet made a profit from it. Law took over the project with government approval and made it far more ambitious, creating the Company of the West (*Compagnie d'Occident*) in August 1717.[5]

The creation of the company followed two well-tried models. One was the model for developing land in the New World: governments typically handed over the territory to a company (while retaining nominal sovereignty) and expected to profit from its private development through tax collection. Here, the company was given a twenty-five-year monopoly on trading with the colony as well as on the beaver fur trade in Canada.

---

[4] The earlier instruments issued in France with the name of "billets," such as the *billets de monnaie* and *billets d'État*, were interest-bearing bonds with no convertibility and no redemption date, rather than non-interest bearing bearer demand notes.
[5] See Giraud, *Histoire*, vol. 3, pp. 3–27.

The other classic model was to convert government debt into equity of a government-instituted monopoly, potentially riskier but also more rewarding. The model had just been used for the bank, but the scale was now much larger: the bank had raised six million L while the company would raise 100 million L, all of it payable in billets d'État. In fact, the offering began on September 14, 1717, but was not closed until July 16, 1718, after measures were taken up to speed up payment, notably by introducing a down-payment system (a subscriber paid 20 percent of the price to secure an option on a share, with the rest payable within five months, else he forfeited the down-payment).

For a holder of a billet d'État, subscribing to the IPO meant converting a 4 percent bond into a share in a company whose main assets were the same bond and Louisiana. The government's debt was unchanged: indeed, the company had an arrangement with the government to consolidate the billets d'État received during the subscription for perpetual annuities accruing from January 1717. There seemed to be only upside potential for the subscriber, and no benefit for the government. The idea of substituting the returns on Louisiana for the interest on the bonds (the key idea behind Law's System) was explicitly negated in the terms of the company's charter, and thus not part of the original plan.

The subscription dragged on for so long partly because the company's claim on the government, the interest on the 4 percent bonds, was assigned on a tax farm that was already encumbered with other liens. Other state revenues were later assigned as surety for the interest, including the tobacco farm revenues. In July 1718, the company proposed to take over the tobacco farm directly. The current annual lease price was four million L, exactly the sum that the government would owe the company as interest on the subscribers' bonds. The lease price would cancel out the interest payment, and the company would, as any tax farmer, take on the risky part of the tobacco monopoly's yield. Law believed that he could run the monopoly better, expecting to generate six to eight million L per year (a reasonable expectation, as it turned out). And, by running the farm himself, he was sure of being paid his interest. This operation would provide the template for the whole System.

Law's company was not a shell. Even as the subscriptions dribbled in, Law took over the assets of Louisiana's previous owner, including one ship. He hired competent and knowledgeable people as directors and they proceeded to purchase, lease and build new ships, so that by December 1718 the company had a dozen ships at its disposal and had already made several voyages to Louisiana.[6]

---

[6] See Giraud, *Histoire*.

At the same time, the company grew by a series of mergers and acquisitions. After the tobacco monopoly, the company bought out other companies holding trading monopolies: the Company of the Senegal in December 1718, Company of the Indies, the Company of China and the Company of Africa in June 1719, the Company of Santo Domingo and the monopoly over the Guinea slave trade in September 1720. This gave the company an effective monopoly on almost all French overseas trade. The company also extended its tax farming activities, first with the lease on the royal mints in July 1719, then with the lease on the *Fermes Générales* (General Farms), which collected most of the excise taxes in France and about 30 percent of government revenues, and finally with the buy-out of the collectors of all direct taxes (*recettes générales*, about 55 percent of revenues).

While the first acquisition, that of the tobacco farm, was financed with the company's initial asset (the 4 percent bonds), most of the other acquisitions were financed with new share issues, each new share having equal standing with the older shares although the offer price rose over time. The initial issue (200,000 shares) was offered at 500L each, payable in government bonds (billets d'État) at face value. The June 1719 issue (50,000 shares) was offered at 550L each in cash, the July 1719 issue (50,000 shares) at 1,000L each in cash, and the final issue in September and October 1719 (300,000 shares) at 5,000L each in cash.

The second and third issues took the form of a rights offering: a subscriber to the June issue had to own four original shares (which came to be known as the "mothers," as opposed to the July shares known as "daughters"), and a subscriber to the July issue had to own four mothers and one daughter to purchase one "granddaughter." This requirement helped turn the secondary market in the older shares into a frenzy. Law also demonstrated the profits to be made in a bull market by introducing Parisians to options, buying call options on shares of the company in March–April 1719, and cashing in after the merger with the Indies Company had helped boost the price of his company.

After making a down-payment, a subscriber received a certificate that entitled him to a share upon full payment of all the installments. By missing an installment he forfeited his share, and (in some cases) all previous payments made. This feature, noted by John Cochrane,[7] made the certificates into options on shares rather than shares, with a strike price paid over time (when the payments were refundable, the option was a standard European one). This feature also characterized the fourth issue, generally called *soumissions*.

---

[7] Cochrane, "Book Review."

C.   The System

The turning point of Law's enterprise was in late August 1719. Within the four months that followed, the enterprise changed from an ambitious trading and banking concern into a radical experiment in public finance.

The experiment had two components, corresponding to the two liabilities of Law's enterprise: the company's shares and the bank's notes. The first component was an all-share buy-out of the national debt by the company, creating what I call "government equity." The second was an all-note buy-out of the money stock. At the end of the operation the company was owned by the former creditors of the state. It collected all taxes, owned most colonies, monopolized all overseas trade, and freely issued fiat money which was sole legal tender. Its director, John Law, became minister of finance on January 5, 1720.

How did this happen? The buy-out of the national debt started on August 27, 1719, when the company made two offers to the government, which were accepted. One was to take over the lease on the General Farms for 52 million L, which was 3.5 million L more than the current lease. The other was to lend 1,200 million L (soon raised to 1,600 million L) to the government at 3 percent. The forty-eight million L interest almost canceled the fifty-two million L lease payment, as had happened with the (much smaller) tobacco monopoly operation of the previous summer. The government would use the 1,600 million L to buy out the funded debt (perpetual annuities) and miscellaneous other debts. This buy-out was compulsory but perfectly legal, because perpetual annuities and offices, by their legal nature, included a call option: the creditor could never demand repayment of the capital, but the debtor could reimburse at any time, in legal tender. This much-vaunted feature of the British consols was in fact present much earlier in the French rentes, and Law's operation took full advantage of it. Interestingly, the king's debt to the company was irredeemable for twenty-five years. Bondholders were to receive drafts from the Royal Treasury on the company, payable by the company's treasurer in specie or bank notes at the bondholder's option.

How could the company finance a loan twice the size of France's metallic money stock? The initial plan was to borrow the same amount (1,200 million L) from the public by selling 3 percent bonds.[8] But early on the company changed its financing strategy and turned to equity. On August 26, before the repayment of the debt was announced, the company's share stood at 3,600L. By September 11, it had reached an

---

[8] Although Murphy, *John Law*, p. 200, disagrees, the terms of the decree of August 27, 1719 are quite clear.

all-time high of 5,400L. That day, the company asked the government permission to raise 500 million L by selling shares at 5,000L in cash. The success of the share issue led to two other share issues of the same size and at the same price on September 26 and on October 2, thus bringing the total sum raised through equity issue to 1,500 million L and covering the company's loan to the king. Moreover, shares ceased to be sold for cash; instead, only the vouchers issued by the Treasury to reimbursed bondholders and other government bearer debt were accepted. In the end, the company never issued the 3 percent bonds.

In other words, since government bonds were accepted in payment of the shares, the operation was simply a gigantic swap of government bonds, bearing on average 4.5 percent, for company equity.[9] The company's profits came from the 3 percent interest it was owed by the government, plus any profits on its commercial and tax-farming activities.

The end result of the process was that the company collected about 90 percent of taxes in France, passed on a fixed nominal amount to the government, and distributed the rest as dividends to its shareholders. Figure 4.1 illustrates the System. Prior to the System, taxes were collected by various tax collectors and a fixed sum was passed on to the state. The state was in turn creditor for an annual payment of roughly 90 million L, which I label as "constant" between quotation marks because of the government's unreliability; what is left is spent on government purchases. In the System, the company has consolidated all tax collection, and has also inserted itself between the state and its creditors. The company now owes a variable amount no less than forty-eight million L to its shareholders, and the state has more to spend.

The second component of the System, the buy-out of the money stock, took place gradually. Recall that the bank had been bought out by the king in December 1718. The following month, the bank ceased to issue notes denominated in specific silver coins and issued instead notes denominated in units of account. They remained payable on demand into coin, but at a rate that could vary, because the relation between coin and unit of account was not fixed.[10] At the same time, the notes progressively acquired legal tender status while gold and silver lost theirs. In February 1720, the bank was merged with the company, payments in gold and silver were limited to 100L, and private holdings of gold and silver in excess of 500L were to be exchanged for notes. The notes

---

[9] The debt-for-equity swap has been noted by Hoffman *et al.*, *Priceless Markets*, pp. 83–4, although they date its inception to March 1720, when the swap actually ended.

[10] Velde, "Chronicle."

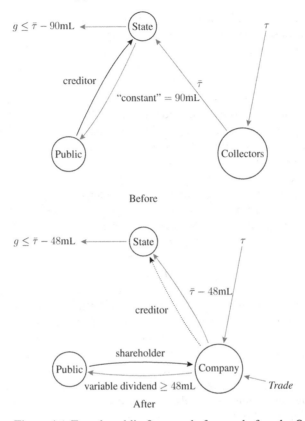

Figure 4.1 French public finances before and after the System.

remained payable on demand in coin, but coin was relegated to subsidiary status: in effect, France was on a fiat money standard.

II.   The Mississippi "Bubble" revisited

Figure 4.2 plots (on a logarithmic scale) the price of shares in John Law's company, from August 1718, when the initial offering closed, to March 1721 when the company went into receivership. In July 1718, after the initial offering closed, the price of a share in the Company of the West was around 250L. After the company's restructuring in 1723, the share price (adjusting for share splits and changes in the units of account) was equivalent to 320L. In-between, the price of shares peaked at 9,525L on December 2, 1719 (and possibly close to 10,000L just before Christmas), and bottomed around 50L in March 1721.

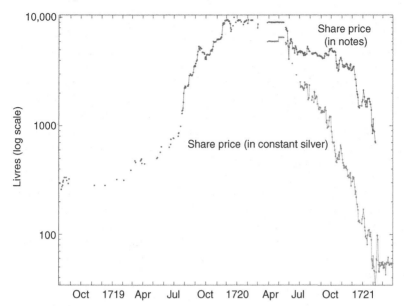

Figure 4.2 Prices of shares in the *Compagnie des Indes*. From June 1720 to February 1721.

Can the price of an asset rise by a factor of thirty in less than two years, and fall by as much in a little more than two years, purely because of reasonable beliefs about prospective returns on this asset? The intuitive answer is "no," and, as far as the existing literature goes, suffices. It seems enough to notice the price rise, without paying much attention to what, exactly, the rising price was pricing.

The foregoing narrative suggests two points that I develop in this section. One is that the bubble did not arise spontaneously. The English name of the episode, the Mississippi Bubble, is less telling than its French name, *le système de Law*. It was Law's scheme, after all. Whether or not he knew from the start where he was going remains debatable; what is beyond doubt is that a man was behind the company, and the market. It is worth noting here that, while the South Sea Bubble in London witnessed a proliferation of schemes and companies and a broad-based rise in the market for shares, the French bubble concerned only one company.[11] Not only is the market only for Law's company,

---

[11] Part of Law's scheme was to buy out other trading companies, taking them out of the market. Of other companies there is little trace. Contemporary Dutch newspapers mention plans for a trading company of the North Seas in the fall of 1719, but nothing

but Law actively managed the market, and the prices that we see rising in late 1719 are not "pure" market prices. Law had been influencing, if not manipulating, the price of his company's shares for a long time.[12]

The second point is that Law's company was in the business of identifying and acquiring a large collection of profitable opportunities. The rise in the price of shares reflects the fact that these opportunities were turned into publicly traded assets. Thus, a rise in the price, in of itself, is not informative. The real question is: how profitable were the opportunities? Did the price collapse merely reveal their true value, or was it caused by other events?

Any economic definition of a bubble will rely on a divergence between a fundamental value based on future earnings and the market value. Was Law's company overvalued? Amazingly, no one has so far tried to answer this question, at least not since Nicolas Dutot.[13] Here, I carry out a crude price/earnings calculation. To do this, I need P (the price, shown in Figure 4.2), E (the expected earnings) and some discount rate to which we can compare the ratio.

A.   A "managed" market

The market whose prices are plotted in Figure 4.2 was Law's market, in more ways then one. The prehistory of the French *bourse* is not well known. In the Middle Ages, currency traders in Paris gathered at the "exchange bridge" (*pont au change*) near the mint. In the late sixteenth century official positions of exchange traders were created, but there was no official location where they met. When Law's company set up its offices in the rue Quincampoix, it provided a focal point for the kind of trading in government securities that undoubtedly existed before. The market had become visible, and it could be tolerated or repressed but not ignored. Finally, the government decided to acknowledge and regulate the market and gave it a permanent location in September 1724.

Law did not only create the market in a physical sense. He also introduced the French to the kinds of financial instruments familiar to Dutch and English traders. In May 1718, the subscription of the Company of the West was still languishing. Law publicly announced his willingness to buy American call options on the shares, "for the convenience of those who have shares in the Company of the West." The announcement, published in the *Gazette d'Amsterdam* (May 23, 1718,

---

else is known. One company led by the previous owner of Louisiana, the banker Crozat, issued shares in 1718 to build a canal in Provence.
[12] Lüthy, *Banque*, vol. 1, pp. 310, 319.   [13] Dutot, *Réflexions*, vol. 1, p. 92.

p. 43), reproduced the text of the proposed option's contract. In exchange for a 2 percent premium, the writer of the option would commit to delivering one share (along with any unmatured dividend coupon) at any time of Law's choosing within the following year, at the price of 70 percent of face value. As the announcement pointed out, this guaranteed the owner of 100L in billets d'Etat a minimum 76L payoff: the 4 percent minimum dividend on the share in the course of the year, the 70 percent strike price and the 2 percent premium of the option. This compared favorably with the current market price of 65 percent on billets d'Etat.

A similar offer appeared a year later in the *Amsterdamse Courant*.[14] This time, Law was buying European options on the new company (presumably the renamed Indies Company) at a price of 200L in January 1720.[15] In this instance, rather than providing insurance to hesitant subscribers, Law was signaling that he believed the stock was heading up.

But it is in the fall 1719, after the debt conversion got under way, that the company became an active participant in the market, especially at times when the share price sagged.

One such episode took place in late September 1719. The debt conversion had been announced on August 28, pushing the price of shares within the day from 3,100L to 3,500L. One share issue worth 500 million L had been announced on the evening of September 14, when share prices were exactly 5,000L. Shares gained another 300L within three days, but then began to fall below 5,000L in the second half of September. By the time a second issue of the same size was announced on September 30, the shares fell to between 4,100L and 4,200L. Rising to 4,335L on October 2, they fell back to 4,200L on October 3 when the third issue of 500 million L was announced. Giraudeau's manuscript shows the shares back at 4,500L on October 4, 5, and 6 but the contemporary newspapers tell a different story. According to the *Amsterdamse Courant*, the shares fell to 3,800L, at which point Law called a meeting of the directors of the company to deplore that the price of such a good security should be so low, and to discuss the possible remedies. The next day, shares opened at 4,000L and closed at 4,250L; that day, October 5, the bank announced that it was willing to buy shares at 4,500L; the next day the shares rose to that price and on October 7 to 4,750L. On October 13 the bank was still buying shares at that price,

---

[14] *Amsterdamse Courant* 1719, n. 78.

[15] The announcement states a price of 200L. The price of the share stood at the time around 150 percent of par, or 750L. It is quite possible that the proposed strike price was 200 percent of par; the confusion between N par and N livres is frequent in contemporary documents.

and the market was barely above 4,500.[16] Finally, a royal decree dated October 12, explicitly alluding to rumors of further share issues, formally promised that no other shares would be sold in any manner or form, thus putting to rest the risk of share dilution. The following week, shares rose to 4,900L.

Another episode of falling prices countered by Law's intervention took place in December 1719. The problem here was not share dilution, but a liquidity crunch due to the upcoming deadline for making payments on the subscriptions. Recall that the subscriptions were options on shares, and to keep the option alive the owner had to make periodic payments. In late October the first monthly payment on the September issue was coming due, but obligingly a decree of September 20 consolidated the monthly payments into quarterly payments and postponed the first one to December. This allowed the share price to pass the 6,000L mark, although the *Amsterdamse Courant* wryly noted that the market being led by successive decrees like an orchestra, it might well end up jumping a whole octave.[17] In late December, then, the first payment was due on the September issue, and since it combined three monthly payments, it amounted to 1,500L. Speculators started selling some of their subscriptions in order to finance the payment on the rest, and this pushed prices down. From a peak of 9,525L on December 2, the price of the shares had drifted down to 9,250L on December 9 and then plummeted to 7,430L on December 14. Likewise, the subscriptions fell from 5,700L on December 2 to 3,000L on the morning of December 14. That day, the bank once again intervened by posting a purchase price of 4,000L, and by the evening the subscriptions were back at 4,500L. Nevertheless, the company maintained the existing schedule for the down payment on the subscription, dashing the hopes of those who had counted on a postponement to mid-January, and keeping the price of subscriptions lingering around 4,000L. Then talk of the upcoming general assembly of shareholders on December 30 gathered momentum. The original shares reached their recorded all-time high on December 23, at 10,000L.

Throughout this period, the bank also lent 2,500L at 2 percent per annum against the security of a share, effectively putting a floor on the share price as well as fueling speculation with easy money. The total lent under this program amounted to 276 million L.[18] On December 30, 1719, at the General Assembly, the company decided to open a window where shares and subscriptions could be bought and sold for prices

---

[16] *Gazette d'Amsterdam* 1719, n. 84.   [17] *Amsterdamse Courant* 1719, n. 131.
[18] Dutot, *Histoire*, pp.183,197, states that the Bank began lending in March 1719, which is not plausible given that the share price at that date was less than 500L.

posted each day.[19] The office operated intermittently: it closed temporarily between January 10 and 15, then again from January 29 to February 10; each closure brought a fall in the share price. Finally, the price of shares was officially pegged at 9,000L on March 5. By May 1720, the company had bought 800 million L worth of shares, or about 16 percent of its capitalization, with a corresponding addition to the money supply.

From January 1720 at the latest, probably from November or December 1719, one cannot consider the "market" price to represent anything but Law's policies.

The market was thoroughly managed, if not manipulated, and for good reason. It was a crucial aspect of Law's scheme that the share price remain high. As long as the PE ratio was higher than the comparable effective ratio on government bonds as of August 1719 (about 22), the conversion of bonds into shares was worthwhile for the company and the government. However, the call-option feature of the subscriptions meant that bondholders (who were obligated to accept repayment of the bonds but not necessarily in the form of shares) could back out if the price of shares fell too low for their liking and lead to the scheme's unraveling, and there is evidence that the former bondholders were not all in a hurry to convert their bonds into shares.

This manipulation had disastrous consequences for Law, as he probably realized if we can judge by the inconsistencies and sudden reversals that mark his policies between late February and early March 1720. On February 22, 1720, the bank was merged with the company with the intention of preventing it from lending to the king. Also, the company stopped its price support. The effect on prices was immediate: from the support price of 9,425L the market price of shares fell to 8,000L by March 1, while the subscriptions fell from 6,600L to 5,450L. Law quickly reversed course on the price of shares and, on March 5, opened another office for the buying and selling of shares at a fixed price of 9,000L. At the same time, the outstanding subscriptions lost their option and were all converted into shares at a 2:3 ratio, while reimbursements of the public debt continued to be made, but in bank notes. This removed the problem of enticing bondholders to convert their bonds, since they were now reimbursed in what had become full legal tender; but, of course, at the cost of transforming a debt-equity swap into a pure monetization of the debt, with predictable consequences for exchange rates and inflation. From March to late May 1720, the company spent another 1,319.5 million L in notes to buy 28 percent of its stock, resulting in a colossal increase in outstanding notes.

---

[19] Faure, *Banqueroute*, pp. 307–8, 319, 340.

The seeds of destruction were sown, and Law was soon forced to control the nominal money supply, by either reducing the number of outstanding notes or reducing the face value of each note. He tried the latter on May 21, 1720, resulting in a collapse of confidence. He tried the former from June to August 1720, buying back notes with coins, bonds, new shares, and bank account balances, to little or no avail. On August 15, a gradual demonetization of the notes was announced and carried out. By November 1720, the monetary experiment was over, and Law's company was insolvent. Law went into exile on December 18, and it was left to others to pick up the pieces.

B.   *Was Law's company overvalued?*

I have argued that, if the company was overvalued, it was not so much the market's doing as Law's. But was it overvalued?

A P/E ratio compares the ratio of price to earnings with some rate of return. Our price will be 9,000L, roughly the peak of Figure 4.1 and Law's fixed price of March 1720. I now look at earnings and at the appropriate rate of return. Law's companies paid dividends twice a year, and dividends were announced in advance. The dividend announced on December 29, 1719, at the peak of the System, is of particular significance. Was the dividend of 200L per share announced by Law plausible, and could it justify a price of 9,000L?

The earnings I try to estimate can be thought of as "steady state" or long-term projections.

Writing in 1723, Law counted that he needed revenues of eighty million L to pay the 200L dividend to 400,000 shares, omitting 100,000 shares held by the company as collateral for loans, and a like amount owned by the King (which were ultimately given for free to the company in June 1720).[20] He presented some estimates of likely earnings to the general assembly, and Dutot presented slightly lower estimates (see Table 4.1). I now evaluate those estimates.

The minting profit was obviously a one-time gain, which Law could not expect to make on a continuous basis, especially given his plan to replace gold and silver with paper money.

Trade was overestimated, as the history of the Indies company after 1720 indicates. The average dividend paid per share, inclusive of repurchases of shares in 1730–1733, is 117L (at sixty L per marc) or 6.5 million L in aggregate, in 1719 livres.

---

[20] Law, *Œuvres*, vol. 3, pp. 312–13.

Table 4.1. *Expected revenues from the Company's activities as of December 1719*

Source	Law (1)	Law (2)	Dutot	Revised
King's debt	48	48	48	48
General Farms	12	8	15	10
Recettes Générales	1	1	1.5	1
Mints	12	10	4	0
Tobacco	6	5	2	10
Trade	12	8	10	6.5
Total	91	80	80.5	75.5

Note: Law (1) was presented in December 1719 to the shareholders; Law (2) was made in May 1723.
Source: Harsin, *Doctrines*, p. 174, and see text.

The most difficult piece to estimate is the profit on the general farms. The price of Law's lease was fifty-two million L, which was an increase over the previous lease of 1718 (forty-eight million L). Dutot states that the revenues during the lease year 1720 were 90.4 million L, but he does not take into account the fact that the livre was on average at eighty per marc during that period: at sixty L per marc, this would amount to 67.6 million L, or a 15.6 million L profit; which is about the profit claimed by the company after the fact, in April 1721 and used as a basis to compensate the company for the loss of the lease.[21] There is evidence that profits would have increased over the next few years. The farms were managed directly by the government for the next few years, and the receipts rose from sixty-one million L in 1721 to 91.5 million L in 1725 in that period.[22] That would have yielded an average profit of 22.8 million L, but these would not have lasted. During the Carlier lease which followed (1726–1732), the average profit was 4.9 million L (5.9 million L in 1719 livres), but over a lease price of eighty million L. That is, the government ratcheted up the lease price when the lease came up for renewal. The experience of the eighteenth century suggests that the government might leave in the five to fifteen million L range as profit to the farms, or roughly 10 percent of gross receipts.[23] Of course, had Law's System continued in place, the government's power and incentives in its bargaining with the company would have been quite different,

---

[21] Dutot, *Réflexions*, vol. 2, p. 214; Giraud, *Histoire*, vol. 3, p. 80; Archives Nationales M1026, Premier recueil, pp. 113–23.
[22] White, *France*.   [23] Marion, *Histoire*, vol. 1, pp. 145–6.

Table 4.2. *Total revenues of the tobacco monopoly, broken down into lease price and farmers' profits, in current livres per year*

Year	Lease	Profit	Year	Lease	Profit
1698–1714	1.5	?	1730		7.0
1715–1716	2.0	?	1731–1732	7.5	4.5
1717	2.2	?	1733–1738	7.8	6.5
1718–1721	4.0	2.4	1739–1744	8.0	10.5
1722	1.2	?	1745–1750	8.0	13.3
1723	1.8	?	1751–1756	13.0	12.1
1724	7.9	7.9	1757–1762	15.0	8.7
1725	7.4	7.4	1763–1768	22.2	?
1726		6.9	1769–1774	23.1	0.9
1727		6.9	1775–1780	24.1	2.3
1728		7.1	1781–1786	26	?
1729		6.8	1786–1789	27–31	?

Notes: the lease years run from October 1 to September 30. The Company owned the monopoly from 1724 to 1747, and did not farm it from 1724 to 1730, hence there is no lease price for those years.
Sources: Dutot, *Réflexions*, vol. 2, pp. 222–6; Morellet, *Mémoire*, Marion, *Dictionnaire*, p. 525, Clamageran, *Histoire*, vol. 3, pp. 254, 402, 444; Matthews, *Royal General Farms*, pp. 29–30.

knowing in particular that part of the profit it was leaving to the company would have been paid to former bondholders.

There is better information on the tobacco monopoly: Table 4.2 reports information on lease prices paid by successive farmers and, when known, the farmers' profits. The average revenue from 1724 to 1789 was about twenty-five million L (at sixty L per marc), from which a lease price must be deducted to obtain the company's expected profits. In 1719, the company paid three million L per year, but, as with the General Farms, the difficulty is in estimating what lease prices would be negotiated in the future. Table 4.1 assumes a fairly generous ten million L average profit.

As shows, it is not too difficult to come up with an estimate within 10 percent of Law's projection,[24] and one can perhaps justify a 200L dividend in steady state, with the important caveat that, in steady state, Law could not expect to pay no dividends to the king's shares, or to those shares held as collateral for loans. Paying dividend on those additional

[24] Harsin's estimate of ninety-nine million L (cited in Faure, *Banqueroute*, p. 304) is perhaps overly generous.

Table 4.3. *Prices of* Fermes Générales *shares (FG) and government*
rentes sur l'hôtel de Ville *(rentes), 1718–1719*

Prices are expressed as percentage of face value.					
Date	FG	rentes	Date	FG	rentes
9 Nov 1718	56.5	62	29 Jun 1719	91, 92	
10 Dec 1718		67	30 Jun 1719		100
14 Jan 1719		65	26 Jul 1719	105	
4 Feb 1719		75	27 Jul 1719	92	66
9 Mar 1719	64		31 Jul 1719	108	
11 Mar 1719	67	70	2 Aug 1719	105 to 108	
14 May 1719	76		10 Aug 1719	99	
24 May 1719	78		17 Aug 1719	106	
25 May 1719	80		21 Aug 1719	101, 102	
17 Jun 1719	80.5		24 Aug 1719	100	80 to 82

Source: Gazette d'Amsterdam.

shares, based on the earnings estimate of Table 4.1, would bring the
dividend down to 125L.

Even granting the 200L dividend, can one accept a valuation of 9,000L
per share, a P/E ratio of 45? Law clearly thought so, as he explicitly set a
target interest rate of 2 percent for his System.

As described above, there are several distinct components to the
company's revenue stream. Each component can be priced with a different factor.

The trade component (6.5 million L) can be evaluated by looking at
the Indies Company as it survived after 1725. Its price was quoted on
the market, and we see that the price-dividend ratio fluctuated widely
between four and twenty-four, and averaged about fifteen.

The fiscal component (tobacco, general farms, collection of direct
taxes, amounting to twenty-one million L) was probably subject to similar
risks as the Indies trade, since the main source of risk were foreign wars.
The shares in the General Farms issued by the Paris brothers in 1718
confirm this. From the *Gazette d'Amsterdam* we have a few market prices
for these shares, along with some observations on the price of government bonds. The shares were expected to earn on average 7 percent. In
late August 1719, the share price rose above par on rumors of an 8
percent dividend.

Not much growth could be expected to boost the ratio, except perhaps
in the tobacco monopoly, which shows 1.5 percent annual real revenues
growth. Overall fiscal revenues grew by about 0.6 percent annually in

Table 4.4. *Valuation of Law's Company*

	Revenue	Factor	Value
King's debt	12.5	48	600
General Farms	10	12.5	125
Recettes Générales	1	20	20
Tobacco	10	15	150
Trade	6.5	15	97.5
Total	75.5		992.5

Source: as described in the text.

real terms from 1726 to 1789, slightly above the estimated 0.5 percent GDP growth.[25]

The largest component of revenues (almost two-thirds) was the King's debt. What was its market price at the time? Before the System, in 1718, the cash price of 4 percent debt in 1718 was 50 percent of face value.[26] After the Visa, the average market price of liquidation certificates, which were convertible into 2 percent debt, was 22 percent of face value.[27] These figures suggest a PE ratio of 11 to 12.5. Of course, these valuations of French government debt come from a time when default risk was probably seen as fairly high. A market interest rate of 8 percent or 9 percent on French debt is about 5–6 percent higher than the rate on Dutch debt at the same time, or English debt around 1730. By the early 1730s, French 2.5 percent debt had risen to 40 percent of face value, a 6.25 percent interest rate.

Table 4.4 yields a valuation of 992.5 million L for 600,000 shares, or a share price of 1,650L. This summarizes the values and multiples and puts the peak share price of 9,500L as overvalued by a factor of 5.8. Even if we use Law's estimates of income (and capitalize the mint revenue at twenty) we get a share price of 2,130L.

The big difficulty with justifying Law's valuation is not the income, but the discount factor. The calculation isn't quite fair to Law, who used a discount rate of 2 percent, and who would have argued that his System was bound to reduce interest rates on government debt, both by making the debt more secure and by lowering interest rates in an economy lacking in financial intermediation. He also argued that his System

[25] Maddison, *World Economy*.

[26] Law, *Œuvres*, vol. 3, p. 199; Forbonnais, *Recherches*, vol. 6, p. 67.

[27] From prices reported in the *Gazette d'Amsterdam* from February 1722 to February 1724; see also Dutot, *Réflexions*, vol. 1, p. 343.

would boost economic growth, and these claims taken at face value all tend to raise the PE ratio. However, to justify the market valuation on the basis of seventy-five million L in earnings would require, say, Dutch interest rates of 3 percent and a growth rate of 1.5 percent, which no European country enjoyed before the start of the Industrial Revolution. Assuming alone that Law's System would have brought interest rates to Dutch levels would leave overvalued by a factor of 2; this seems to me as far as one can go on behalf of Law. It seems difficult to avoid the conclusion that the company was overvalued several times over.

III.   Conclusion

Although Law's experiment has been called a "bubble" in the English language since at least the mid-eighteenth century, it is not a classic example of a bubble in the modern sense of the word.[28] Law's ambition was a wholesale transformation of French public finances, achieved through two radical innovations: the replacement of metallic with fiat money, and the replacement of government debt with equity.

Both conversions were to be voluntary, as they had to be if the goal was to endow France with the kind of credit that would give it the necessary edge over its Dutch and British rivals for European dominance. But this required Law to manage the market's expectations more and more forcefully and reach a price peg for his company's shares that was too high. I find that the peg was two or three times too high. In that sense, the company was overvalued, not by a frenzied and irrational market, but by Law himself.

References

Amsterdamse Courant. Amsterdam: imprint varies. Various issues.

Antonetti, Guy. 1978. "Observations sur certains aspects du système de Law." *Revue historique de droit français et étranger* 2e série 56, no. 4: 681–2.

Clamageran, Jean-Jules. 1867–1876. *Histoire de l'impôt en France.* Paris: Guillaumin et Cie.

Cochrane, John H. "Book Review of 'Famous First Bubbles' by Peter M. Garber." *Journal of Political Economy* 109, no. 5 (2001): 1150–4.

Dutot, Nicolas. 1935. *Réflexions politiques sur les finances et le commerce.* Paris: E. Droz.

---

[28] Whatever Swift meant by the title of his poem on the South Sea, "bubble" as verb or noun meant "swindle." Law's decision to invest his fortune into French real estate does not suggest a bubble in the eighteenth-century sense either.

Histoire du Système de John Law (1716–1720). Paris: Institut national d' études démographiques, 2000.

Faure, Edgar. 1977. *La Banqueroute de Law*. Paris: Gallimard.

Forbonnais, François Véron Duverger de. *Recherches et considérations sur les finances de France, depuis l'année 1595 jusqu' à l'année 1721*. Liége, 1758.

Gazette d'Amsterdam. Amsterdam : imprint varies. Various issues.

Giraud, Marcel. 1966. *Histoire de la Louisiane française*. Paris: Presses universitaires de France.

Harsin, Paul. 1928. *Les doctrines monétaires et financières en France du XVIe au XVIIIe siècle*. Paris: F. Alcan.

1933. *Crédit public et banque d'état en France du XVIe au XVIIIe siècle*. Paris: E. Droz.

Hoffman, Philip T., Gilles Postel-Vinay, and Jean-Laurent Rosenthal. 2000. *Priceless Markets: the Political Economy of Credit in Paris, 1660–1870*. Chicago: University of Chicago Press.

Law, John. 1934. *Œuvres Complètes*. Paris: Librairie du recueil Sirey.

Lüthy, Herbert. 1959–1961. *La Banque protestante en France de la révocation de l' Édit de Nantes à la Révolution*. Paris: S.E.V.P.E.N..

Maddison, Angus. 2001. *The World Economy: A Millenial Perspective*. Paris: Development Center of the OECD.

Marion, Marcel. 1914. *Histoire financière de la France* (vol. 1). Paris: Arthur Rousseau.

1923. *Dictionnaire des institutions de la France aux XVIIe et XVIIIe siècles*. Paris: A. Picard.

Matthews, George Tennyson. 1958. *The Royal General Farms in Eighteenth-Century France*. New York: Columbia University Press.

Morellet, André. 1769. *Mémoire sur la situation actuelle de la Compagnie des Indes*. Paris: Desaint.

Murphy, Antoin E. 1997. *John Law: Economic Theorist and Policy-Maker*. Oxford: Clarendon Press.

Neal, Larry. 1990. *The Rise of Financial Capitalism: International Capital Markets in the Age of Reason*. Cambridge: Cambridge University Press.

Velde, François R. 2007. "Chronicle of a Deflation Unforetold." Working paper, Federal Reserve Bank of Chicago.

White, Eugene N. 2001. "France and the Failure to Modernize Macroeconomic Institutions." In *Transferring Wealth and Power from the Old to the New World: Monetary and Fiscal Institutions in the Seventeenth through the Nineteenth Centuries*, edited by Michael D. Bordo and Roberto Cortes-Conde: 59–99. New York: Cambridge University Press.

5   Sir George Caswall vs. the Duke of Portland: Financial contracts and litigation in the wake of the South Sea Bubble

Gary S. Shea[*]

In one of the more influential papers in economic history of the past twenty years, North and Weingast (1989) described the connections between a singular event, the English Glorious Revolution of 1688, and the subsequent evolution of political institutions and capital markets in the UK. Although it is usually difficult to argue that a particular series of events represents a true watershed in history, the arguments presented in their paper are quite persuasive in regards to public finance. In terms of both scale and unit cost of public finance, there is little similarity between the reigns of the Stuart and of the early Hanoverian monarchs. From about 1688, events were put in motion that would transform the relation between government and finance. North and Weingast persuasively argued that these events were: (1) royal political revolution, followed by (2) the complete seizure of taxation powers by parliament and by (3) an extension of parliamentary oversight of expenditure – all of which were made necessary by the financial exigencies of prolonged large-scale European warfare. These processes were coupled with the rise of a market for tradable government debt, which was in turn accompanied by the development of a smaller market for joint-stock company equity securities. All of these developments are part of the collection of events that is now called the Financial Revolution in England.

This watershed in history can be demarked by a number of events. The Treaty of Utrecht (1712–1713) marks the end of large-scale European warfare and the beginning of an extended period of comparative peace until there was world war again later in the eighteenth century. Although the Northern War was to trundle on to 1720, the core impetus for the European conflagration of the previous fifty years, French expansionism was ended with the Utrecht treaty. The Hanoverian

[*] The author wishes to thank Jeremy Atack, Larry Neal and Ann Carlos for reading and commenting upon previous versions of this paper.

Succession (1715) too is useful as a marker because it was part of a new political settlement between the Crown, parliament and the English people. The political settlement had several important aspects: the permanent establishment of frequent parliaments; the stabilization of ministerial control of parliamentary business; the establishment of a stable role for religion in public life and a clear demarcation of the Crown's role in foreign affairs. But it is the South Sea Bubble of 1720 that particularly interests us as the demarcation of the historical divide described by North and Weingast. In Section VI of their paper, they argued that growth and security of *private* capital markets paralleled similar growths in the markets for public finance. During the South Sea Bubble and afterwards, however, it was by no means clear that such a parallel development would take place. It did not appear in 1720 that English law was in any way prepared, or was being prepared, to accommodate many of the innovations of the Financial Revolution.

The Bubble Act (June 1720) imposed upon incorporated business enterprise certain limitations which were intended to discourage joint-stock capital structures for companies. New company organization was thereafter to be encouraged along the lines of partnerships or trusts. The relation between the law and business was left to be worked out in practice and in case-law, but rarely spelled out in the clear terms of legislated law. This argument is one qualification to the North and Weingast thesis that is already well-documented.[1] In this chapter we shall attempt to establish another qualification by examining how prepared and how friendly the legal system was towards the development of *secondary* markets for securities – the very markets in which private property rights to financial assets were exchanged.

There has been no extensive description of the legal environment or aftermath of the South Sea Bubble. Dickson describes how the litigation between the public and the South Sea Company was largely prevented,[2] but a history of private litigation between individuals has not been told except in Banner's description of some of the arguments and judgments that appeared in printed law reports.[3] What can such a history usefully reveal? It can reveal what was the custom in financial contracting and yield insights into the costs and efficiency of financial dealing and markets. The efficiency of financial markets and their completeness will probably be at the heart of any future theory of the South Sea Bubble. Scholars are far from a formal theory of this great stock market crash, but whenever such a theory is achieved, it will probably depend upon

---

[1] See Harris, *Industrializing English Law.*   [2] See fn. 5, section II.
[3] See fn. 8, section II.

much better information than we currently have about the costs and efficiency of financial contracting in 1720. A second reason for doing such a history is that the cases studied will be revelatory of peoples' hopes and expectations during the South Sea Bubble. This not only fleshes out the social history of the Bubble, but may reveal clues as to what people thought the fundamental value of the South Sea Scheme was. A final reason for commencing a legal study of the Bubble's aftermath is so that it can become a part of the legal history of contract and liability. London was arguably the birthplace of modern financial markets and financial contracts and it would be surprising if the special demands of financial contracting as practiced in London did not leave some special mark on the development of contract law. The plan for this chapter is to use the story of the first Duke of Portland as a means of entry into the study of the legal history of the South Sea Bubble and private financial contracts.

The next section is an outline of some important features of the South Sea Scheme and the resulting Bubble. Section II describes the scope of possible legal conflict concerning financial contracts stemming from the events of 1720. Much of this section is a review of what little literature we have on such legal conflicts. In section III I describe the circumstances of trade in South Sea Company liabilities in 1720 and how they defined the special features of the legal conflicts that were to follow. Section IV is a short introduction to the Duke of Portland himself and sources that are useful for the study of his role in the South Sea Bubble. In section V I look at Portland's actions in the markets for securities and show how he came to his financial and legal difficulties. Section VI describes the Duke's legal struggle to escape financial ruin. Section VII contains my conclusions and suggestions for further research.

I.   The South Sea Scheme and the South Sea Bubble

What was the South Sea Bubble? More properly, in posing such a question we should employ the term used by people in 1720 and first ask, "what was the South Sea Scheme?" A commonly-held modern misconception of the South Sea Scheme is that it was primarily a stock flotation, as would occur with the projection of a new railway company in the nineteenth century or the public offering of stock in an internet company in the late twentieth century. There was certainly flotation of new stock in 1720, but it occurred in a stock market very unlike anything we know of today. The most important thing to know about the stock markets of 1720 is that the overwhelming numbers and values of stocks traded and issued in them were stocks in the three so-called "great moneyed companies." Since the foundation of the Bank of England in

1694, the re-organization of the East India Company in 1710 and the foundation of the South Sea Company in 1712, these three institutions tried to expand their respective businesses and competed with each other for more complete control of the supply of the most important component of the asset-side of their balance sheets – the interest-paying debt obligations of the government itself. Although the trading interests of each of these three institutions were quite different, the very existence of each institution depended upon the simultaneous privilege and obligation of lending to the national government.

It was thus for their own survival and to strengthen their legal foundations that the three companies occasionally competed with each other for the political favors of the government. The South Sea Scheme was one such competition in which the South Sea Company sought for itself the complete management of the government's debt. This was by far the grandest of all such competitions. Indeed, it was thought to be so grand and dangerous that, by the end of 1720, the political nation decided that there would never be another such competition. In the post-Bubble legislative settlements of 1721 the relations between the three great moneyed companies were given stability and the shape they would retain well into the nineteenth century.[4] It was the connection in peoples' minds between the large-scale revolution in public finances implied by the South Sea Scheme and the future of private property rights that resonates so well with the themes discussed by North and Weingast. To many people in 1720, however, the South Sea Scheme appeared more as a threat to private property rights rather than as a harbinger of better property rights in capital markets.

Before the legislative settlements of 1721 were put in place, however, there was the famous Bubble speculation about the shape and ultimate success of the South Sea Scheme. The real core of the speculation was about the future structure of national public finances. The times then were so different and the Scheme, even in its own context, was so grandiose that it is impossible to offer analogies that would make the concerns of people in 1720 understandable to modern readers. The arguments in the great majority of the polemical literature and the emphasis in debates in parliament and in private correspondence concerning the South Sea Scheme were not so much about possible earnings, profits and payouts; the arguments were mostly about private property rights, legal rights, control of public finance, control of parliament and the very control of government itself.

---

[4] This summary of the more long-term effects of the South Sea Bubble are those discussed in more detail by Dickson, *Financial Revolution*, Chapter 8.

II.   The legal conflict to come

The extent and direction of liability in financial contracts was at the heart of many of the debates stemming from the South Sea Scheme in 1720. There has been little literature on this debate, especially in terms of how it actually played out in the courts. A good way to organize our discussion is to first consider two basic strands in the controversy: (1) there was one debate on the liability that came from the South Sea Company's relations with the public and (2) there was another debate on liabilities between private persons that were generated in the course of the South Sea Bubble.

The debate on the liabilities generated between the public and Company can itself be broken into two parts: (1) there was the more important issue surrounding the Company's proper relationship with the holders of government annuities and (2) the less important questions about the Company's proper relationships with the public subscribers for shares in cash. The former is given prominence in the histories of the Bubble and concerns the terms by which those government annuitants were to obtain South Sea securities in return for the annuities they held in 1720. When the resulting terms were shown to be unfavorable to the annuitants, public interest was turned towards the proper restitution (if any) that should be undertaken. The resulting political struggle threatened the very foundations of public finance in Britain that had been successfully laid more than two decades previously. That threat was finally brought to an end by the legislative maneuverings of Robert Walpole.[5]

Less extensively discussed is the debate about the Company's relationships with its cash subscribers. This was arguably not as important a debate as the one concerning the annuitants. Only a small portion of the South Sea Company's equity liabilities was affected by the cash subscriptions for shares in 1720; in the South Sea Scheme the liability side of the Company's balance sheet was being restructured primarily by the issue of large amounts of new debt (to be held by the Treasury, for the most part) and large amounts of new equity that were going to be issued directly to owners of government annuities. Nevertheless, until the Company's new relations with the government and the annuitants were put on a final footing, the cash subscriptions for shares in 1720 were the primary means by which the Company raised cash for its operations.[6] Many persons saw the cash subscriptions as the means by

---

[5] Dickson, *Financial Revolution*, Chapters 7 and 8.
[6] The Company also managed to raise short-term cash (£1 million) by borrowing Exchequer Bills from the Treasury.

which the Company financed its most nefarious behavior in 1720. The legal and political standing of the cash subscriptions is analyzed in another paper.[7]

The only study relevant to private financial contracting during and after the South Sea Bubble is Banner's survey of treatises, judgments and reports on cases.[8] Of direct concern to this study are his conclusions with regard to absolute liability in contract. In section III of Chapter 2 he starts with a brief analysis of Sir David Dalrymple's treatise[9] on time bargains and then reviews the implications for the judgments handed down in Thomson vs. Harcourt.[10]

There were several South Sea pamphlets of the 1720s that were evidently written by lawyers. The most extensive and interesting document of this type was Dalrymple's *Time Bargains*. It is an important document because it is argued closely and is careful in its definition of terms. Dalrymple also did not fear to reveal his authorship (which was unusual) and, as a prominent legal officer serving in the government until shortly before the South Sea Bubble,[11] his opinion might be accorded some special authority. Dalrymple was indeed impressed with his own authority, wrote contemptuously of what he called coffee-house talk, and his writing was dedicated ironically to "my Brethren Animals, the Impudent and Ignorant." His overriding concern was to address the large question of "what will become of Time Bargains? Will they be good or not?"[12] He declined to discuss the Common Law's view on the matter because, as he admitted, it was too great a subject for his small volume. He took his arguments from Equity and the Civil Law, on which he could write with more authority as a one-time Scottish law officer. One of his first points was that on the question of time bargains alone, parliament must come in with an act or acts to regulate or put an end to disputes: "I think this one Question affords such a fund for Law Pleas, that is Consequence enough to deserve the Parliament's Notice (. . .) The Parliament ought to give their Determination in all Cases, which they take Notice of, according to the Laws of Nature and Nations, and the universal Rules of Equity."[13]

---

[7] Shea, "Financial Market Analysis," in particular, Appendix II.

[8] Banner, *Anglo-American*, Chapter 2, section III and Chapter 3, section III.

[9] Dalrymple, *Time Bargains*.

[10] Thomson vs. Harcourt, 1 Brown 193, 1 *English Reports*. See also *Cases of the appellant and respondent in the House of Lords* (HL/PO/JU/4/3/4, HLRO).

[11] Sorenson, "Dalrymple."   [12] Dalrymple, *Time Bargains*, p. 4.

[13] Ibid. Parliamentary intervention in such matters was delayed by a resolution of December 19 in the Commons. (Boyer, *The Political State*, vol. 20, pp. 584–5). Dalrymple discussed these matters at further length in *Time Bargains*, pp. 41–2. The need for a general "annulling Act" was a theme in many other tracts written in the period

He wrote that in Equity and Civil Law a contract must be *quid pro quo*. Since no one expects to be a loser going into a contract, if they are a loser coming out by being wronged, "then the Law ought to assist him."[14] The Civil Law is hostile to bargains that result in sales at less or more than a good is worth, but the Common Law is more *laissez-faire* in this regard, with everyone to be left to make the best bargains they can.[15] As far as time bargains were concerned, Dalrymple distinguished between three types: (a) Bargains on Stock; (b) Bargains on first and second subscriptions and (c) Bargains on third and fourth subscriptions.

Bargains on Stock were of three types: (1) transfers of stock; (2) the assignment of subscription receipts or (3) the taking of security (bills, bonds or other) for the price "between the Buyer and Seller, the Stock &c. still remaining in the Name and Possession of the Seller." The form of the bargains was of two sorts: (a) "the Stock, &c. was sold a great deal above the Market Price at the Time, and a Bill or Bond taken for the Money payable at some time after" or (b) "Others were sold at the Market Price, and a Bond or Bill taken for the Price with Common Interest from the Date. This last sort hardly deserves the Name of Time Bargains. However, we shall now consider them as such, and discuss them first, because whatever Argument is good in Law against them, will be good against every one of the rest."[16]

If the Directors were in no way culpable and if the Stock was bought of a man in no way concerned in the mismanagement of the Company, then if a man was mistaken in the

real Value of the Thing bought (. . .) (h)is promise therefore being founded *in Presumptione facti quod non ita se habet*, is in itself void, and by the Civil Law, the buyer is certainly Free, because the *Læsio* or Loss he sustains by the Bargain, is *ultra dimidium valoris rei venditæ*: And likewise because there was a latent Defect in the Thing Sold, which if the Buyer had known, he would never had promised so much for it.

and he has grounds for an action against the seller even if the seller was ignorant of the defect.[17]

Dalrymple was also sympathetic to the application of the statutes against usury against certain styles of time bargains (such as in Thomson's and Harcourt's contract). For example, he would have certainly argued

and, of course, soon such acts became a reality with 7 Geo. 1, c. 5 and 7 Geo. 1, stat. 2. More details are found in the analysis of Appendix II in Shea, "Financial Market Analysis."
[14] Dalrymple, *Time Bargains*, pp. 5–6.   [15] Ibid. pp. 6–8.   [16] Ibid. pp. 10–11.
[17] Ibid. pp. 12–13. This is a basic theme, which is echoed in much other pamphlet literature such as (Anon.), *Queries*.

that when forward buyers and sellers were mutually agreed that future values would be high, then if they contract to deliver stock forward at a high price relative to the present price, the forward seller is certainly practicing usury upon the buyer.[18] As we shall see, Portland's advisors were quite interested in the argument that the Duke was a hapless victim of usury.

Banner cites the final judgments in Thomson vs. Harcourt and concludes that the rule of absolute liability that prevailed in courts of law was easily adapted to cases involving financial contracting during the South Sea Bubble and afterwards. This conclusion is reinforced in section III of Chapter 3 in which he recites the case reports that show, "From the beginning, the courts were willing to enforce contracts to buy or sell securities to the same extent as contracts to buy and sell any other item".[19] In the reports which he reviews he concludes that all involved cases in which sellers were trying to hold buyers to their agreements to buy securities at agreed higher pre-crash prices. None of these cases failed on grounds that the agreements were themselves *executory agreements* – requiring performance in exchange of monies and securities in the future. In his opening summary of the section he even goes so far to write, "Judges tended to give as much latitude as possible to the securities market, by enforcing even the more speculative transactions and narrowly construing would-be statutory limits on trading."[20]

However well rules of absolute liability were affirmed in cases like Thomson vs. Harcourt, there is still much we need to learn from the processes in which they were applied. In particular we need to know how long and costly legal processes were. On June 18, 1720, Thomson agreed to deliver to Harcourt South Sea stock at a future unknown date (dependent upon when the South Sea Company was willing to transform government annuities into company stock) at the rate of £920 per share. This date was just a few days prior to the closing the Company's ledgers for transferring stock in order to make up the midsummer dividend on the stock. The closing period was anticipated to be about two-months long. There are many instances in the historical record of persons agreeing to forward purchases and sales of stock for an array of dates after the transfer books were to be reopened at the end of August 1720 and the Thomson/Harcourt agreement was but a typical example. What was also typical of their agreement is the forward delivery premium that was built into it. On June 18 the value of South Sea share for immediate delivery was about £750 per share. The forward premium in

---

[18] Dalrymple, *Time Bargains*, pp. 31–2.   [19] Banner, *Anglo-American*, p. 111.
[20] Ibid.

their contract was thus large; £920 is 22.67 percent higher than £750 and, considering that the forward contract could have been expected to be completed in about three month's time, this would imply a forward premium of about 100 percent p.a. This is a large number, but it is not an atypically large number for the early summer of 1720.[21] There could be several reasons for such a premium. Perhaps everyone at that time, including Thomson and Harcourt, were mutually optimistic and in agreement on probable future values for South Sea shares. Or on the other hand, perhaps there were a significant number of forward sellers who worried about the substantial risk that future South Sea share values might turn out to be low. In writing an array of forward contracts such persons might expect that the typical forward buyer would attempt to renege on his contracts. A premium to compensate forward sellers for this risk might have been typical in forward delivery contracts. It is hard to imagine forward premia of this size being common in a legal environment in which the rule of absolute liability in executory agreements was readily, cheaply and certainly applied. After all, small forward premia are achieved in modern-day forward markets, not through enforcement in courts, but through marking-to-market settlement systems that are a feature of modern-day futures exchanges. Thomson's route to justice and restitution was a long and (probably) an expensive one, and his suit was only partially successful.

Banner's work here depends primarily on printed law reports. Law reports were written and collected to be used in arguments and were at times accepted in court as precedents. They would thus tend to highlight aspects of cases that would be most useful for those purposes. The case that was most likely to go unreported was one in which all the legal principles involved were already well established. Although Banner's survey establishes that the eighteenth-century financial contract for future performance was considered to be just another form of executory agreement, it does not show whether it was as easy or cheap to enforce as any other executory agreement. In particular, it does not tell us if the balance of litigation that followed in the wake of the South Sea Bubble favored reneging buyers or fairly protected the sellers. To answer these questions would require an extensive survey of the bills presented, cases heard and their resolutions. No matter how well financial contracting fitted into the existing principles of contract law, there may have been something about financial contracts during and after the South Sea Bubble that made them easy to void. If so, and more importantly, if it was widely understood to be so, surely this would have implications for

---

[21] This was an example of one type of bargain on stock described by Dalrymple. cf. fn. 16.

how people drew up contracts and valued them.[22] To perform this research is a large task, but we argue that one very good place to start would be to look at a sample of cases outside of those that found their way into the law reports. It would be especially useful if these cases have a history that is also supported by private legal documents. Unlike a law report on a case in judgment, if we could look at how lawyers prepared strategically, how they looked at the law and formed strategies to use in the defense of their clients' interests, we might discover something more like the true dimensions to the problem of obtaining efficiency in financial markets. I will argue that the Portland cases are one such sample of cases.

III.   Private financial contracts in 1720

It was typical in this period that ledgers become occasionally disabled from normal day-to-day work so that they could be used to bring up to date the company's larger scale bookkeeping. The primary instance of this would be when stock ledgers would be closed so that a company's clerks could use them to calculate and allocate dividends. Or whenever there was going to be any general change in the definition of the Company's nominal capital, such as in a rights issue or in an exchange of shares for government annuities, the lumbering pace of eighteenth-century bookkeeping would require the stoppage of recorded trades in a company's liabilities. In the South Sea Company's case there were two periods in 1720 in which the stock ledgers were closed: (a) they were closed for an announced two-month period from June 22 through August 22, 1720 and (b) they were closed on August 31, to remain shut until September 22, but were suddenly reopened on September 12.[23] This latter closing of the transfer books was a product of the South Sea directors' usual chaotic style of financial management. As soon as a fourth cash subscription for shares was announced, there was discussion in committees about how it would subsequently be managed and whether it might not be converted into a rights issue for original shareholders or whether yet another (fifth) issue of shares should be a rights issue. While these matters were discussed, the Directors determined it would be best

---

[22] Further evidence is found section III and supplementary Appendix III (re the South Sea Company's third-subscription shares) in Shea, "Financial Market Analysis can go Mad."

[23] A forward financial contract whose performance was tied to the re-opening date that ended this period was the object of dispute in Maber vs. Thornton. We find the Company decision to close the ledgers in BL, Add. MS 25, 499, *Court minutes*, August 26, 1720. In the same source the ledgers are ordered (September 11) to be reopened the next day.

if the transfer ledgers were shut. Whether on a regularly announced basis or not, private persons had to be prepared to occasionally make their own markets for trade in company liabilities as best they could. Private financial contracting was instrumental in this process.

Private financial contracting was also used to make the markets in company liabilities more complete. There clearly was a demand for contingent claims (options) in company liabilities. A large part of this demand may have been met in the ready-made markets for subscription shares,[24] but there may have been much other demand that could only be met through private contracting. Call options on shares were the most common from the evidence that we have. Options would use very much the same contractual forms as were used in forward delivery agreements. That is, the contracts would be written as bilateral contracts, using very similar legal language to bind one party and the other to perform in the contract.[25]

IV.   The Duke of Portland: background and sources

Henry Bentinck (1682–1726) was the son of William Bentinck, who was a great favorite of William III and who rose in the King's service as a diplomat and soldier. He was given the revived title of Earl of Portland, a title that the son (Henry) assumed upon the father's death in 1709. In 1716 Henry was created the first Duke of Portland. The fortune that had been accumulated by his father in England was greater than the estates in Holland to which Henry's half brother, Willem, succeeded.[26] The Duke supplemented this inherited fortune by marriage to Elizabeth Noel (d.1736), first daughter of the second Earl of Gainsborough. As will be shown later, it was by borrowing from his own estate trust that Bentinck was able to leverage much of his speculative activity during the South Sea Bubble. It was also in his role as trustee that he later tried to protect some portion of this fortune from his creditors.

The Portland (London) manuscripts at the University of Nottingham (class Pl) are a collection of legal, financial and estate records that came to Nottingham in 1947 after sustaining considerable war damage in the London law offices of Bailey, Shaw and Smith, solicitors to the Dukes of

---

[24] My thesis in "Understanding Financial Derivatives during the South Sea Bubble" is that the Company's subscription shares were a form of compound call option on the firm's own shares.

[25] Examples of option contracts from this period are not numerous, but what few exist are quite alike in their legal language. See BL, Add. Ms. 22,639, fff. 193,195 and 203, as examples.

[26] Dunthorne and Onnekink, "Bentinck, Hans Willem, First Earl of Portland (1649–1709)."

Portland since the late 1830s. This collection is the main repository of legal and financial records of the Portland estate that go back to the early eighteenth century. There is also that portion of the Portland Manuscripts taken from Welbeck Abbey, not residing with the rest of the Portland Manuscripts at the British Library, which reside at the University of Nottingham (class Pw). These too contain many papers that are complementary to the Pl-class financial and legal papers.

Although Bubble historians have long known that Portland suffered some great reverses in 1720, without the Pl and Pw classes of papers, no real history of his troubles could be written. Many of the papers are highly disordered and so a timeline can be difficult to discern in Portland's legal affairs. Many of the papers are also unavailable whilst they await conservation. The manuscript curators at the University of Nottingham, however, have gone to great lengths to bring forward the conservation schedule for some of the most important documents so that they can be consulted and in other ways provided information from other papers that simply cannot be handled by anyone but a professional conservator. It is only thanks to the efforts, co-operation and permissions of the Manuscripts and Special Collection staff at The University of Nottingham that this chapter is possible.

V.   The Duke of Portland: his actions during the Bubble

The Portland manuscript collection contains several distinct sources of information about the Duke's speculative contracts:

a) Contracts and draft contracts – there are twenty-four such contracts and drafts in the Pl class, but there are a number of others in the Pw class, amongst which are the contracts most ruinous to the Duke. Table 5.1 describes some of the rough details of Pl-class contracts. The reader should not at this point work too hard in making sense of the contractual terms. Some of the contracts' special characteristics, such as side-agreements and guarantees, will be explained later;

b) small ledgers and notebooks recording contracts – complementing the contract documents are several notebooks and ledgers in which payments associated with some of the contracts were recorded. Importantly, these notebooks also contain references to contract-related payments for which no manuscript contracts exist. We have placed a transcript of one of the more useful of these (Pw B 164) in Appendix A[27] and

---

[27] Three other such sources are also useful, Pw B 165 and Pl F2/6/179 and Pl F2/6/310.

c) memoranda discussing the contracts and resulting transactions – the details of many other contracts and related transactions can also be had from references in letters and legal documents. The memoranda often contain quite detailed legal analyses.

From these sources we can trace the rough outlines of the Duke's speculative activities. The Duke was known to a wide circle of individuals who helped him in his financial stratagems. For reasons never stated, it appears that the Duke decided on a highly aggressive attempt to control as much South Sea stock as he could through leverage. We do not know what his holdings were near the beginning of 1720, but by the time that the South Sea Scheme was fully underway with the South Sea Company's Act (6 Geo 1, c.4) coming into force by later April, the Duke was starting to move aggressively.[28]

The first such action that we can identify was his borrowing of £83,575 from the Portland estate trust. Created in 1689, the trust was augmented by extensive grants to the Duke's father and by the Duke's marriage to Elizabeth Noel in 1704. The trustees were the Duke's two lawyers Sir John Eyles and M. Joseph Eyles and the banker Comrade de Gols. The Duke used the money, supplemented with his own cash to buy 160 South Sea shares.[29] According to a later (and perhaps deliberately misleading legal strategy document) the 160 shares were to be under control of the estate trustees with instructions to collect payouts and to sell the shares if their value fell to £700 or below. How the trustees were to have control of the shares, however, is difficult to see for the shares were re-transferred to six other individuals, exclusive of the trustees.[30] We see these individuals named again as contracting to sell back to the Duke these shares (with the 10 p.c. midsummer stock dividend) at about £705 a share for the opening of the transfer ledgers.[31] Portland's own promise to re-purchase the shares for about £705 each was the only protection accorded to the trust's outlay of £83,575. In a hypothetical case document from May 1722, counsel's opinion was

---

[28] Portland was certainly at as a high, probably higher, social level than either Lord Londonderry or Chandos in 1720. Yet the dealings of these two were more varied and sophisticated than are Portland's dealings. It does not appear that his dealings had a logical direction except one based upon presumed advances, forever and upward, in South Sea shares values. For Londonderry's and Chandos' South Sea histories, see Neal, "'For God's Sake, Remitt Me.'"

[29] I follow the usual convention in defining £100 nominal South Sea stock as one South Sea share.

[30] Pl F2/6/179, p. 12.

[31] Pw B 165, pp. 23–4. The Earl of Warwick contract contained in Table 5.1 is one of these contracts and is dated May 31, 1720.

asked whether trustees, who failed to collect dividends and who failed to sell the stock they held in trust at values higher than the monies lent out on that stock, were liable to make good the monies lost.[32] The hypothetical discussion contained in this document was clearly a trial argument to see if the blame for the estate trust losses could be pinned on the trustees and not on the Duke.

The Duke's next move was to borrow £8,000 and then £70,000 from the South Sea Company on the security of another 160 shares (twenty shares transferred to South Sea Director Robert Surman and 140 shares transferred to a Mr. Shaw).[33] This is remarkable and shows that the Duke was especially favored by the Company in the allocation of loans on stock in which the Company's stated by-laws on the loan program stipulated that no more than £4,000 would be lent to any individual nor would monies be lent at a higher rate than £400 per pledged share.[34] A parallel record of these loans can be found in the South Sea Company's ledger of the loans on stock. This was a document of some importance in the deliberations of the Parliamentary Committee of Secrecy at the end of 1720.[35] Under a heading for June 13, the Duke is shown to have borrowed from the Company £84,000 (not £78,000) on the pledged security of 151 original shares and twenty shares in the first cash subscription.

In the meantime the Duke was creating a number of forward purchase agreements with a wide range of people. From what contracts or drafts of contracts that exist (see Table 5.1), the Duke typically agreed to repay money lent to him by individuals and in return received back from them some South Sea stock. The contracts also typically stated that the Duke would undertake the receipt of the stock (making him liable to an action on the case, if he were to default), and also stated that the other party held the stock in trust only as a trustee (also making that party liable to an action), and the money to be repaid was a loan to the Duke (additionally making the Duke liable to an action of debt). In some of the contracts an exchange of securities was specified. For example, a certain amount of South Sea securities in the counterparty's hands could be sold if stock prices fell to a sufficiently low level. Sometimes these securities

---

[32] Pl F2/6/180.

[33] This is probably Joseph Shaw, a broker with heavy dealings with the South Sea directors. Abstracts of his ledgers showing his dealings with the directors are found in Box 158, parchment collection, HLRO.

[34] There were several different packages of loans that were made to shareholders. The first was in late April and the so-called Third Loan was in June 1720. See discussion of these loans in BL, Add. Ms. 25, 499, *Court Minutes*.

[35] *An abstract of the ledgers of the loan on stock*, Box 157, parchment collection, HLRO.

Table 5.1. Contracts in the Portland (London) manuscripts

Acc. No.	Date	Stock	Payment	Settlement terms	Seller
Pl F2/6/111	23 April 1720	£2,000	£6,400	12 Aug 1720 or next opening	Charles Ottway
Pl F2/6/112	16 May 1720	£2,000	£8,200	On or before Xmas 1720	Thomas Seabright
Pl F2/6/113	1 June 1720	£1,000	£6,400	On or before next closing	Earl of Uxbridge
Pl F2/6/114	31 May 1720	£1,000	£7,050	On or before next shutting or within 3 days of the opening	Earl of Warwick
Pl F2/6/115	1 June 1720	£3,000 1st Sub	£12,000	For the opening	Henry Temple
Pl F2/6/116	1 June 1720	£2,000	£12,800	On or before next shutting	Richard Bayliss
Pl F2/3/117	1 June 1720	£2,000	£11,600	On or before next shutting	Thomas Martin
Pl F2/6/118	1 June 1720	£1,000	£5,900	On or before next shutting	John Shurkbrugh
Pl F2/6/119	1 June 1720	£1,000	£9,350	For the opening	Sir William Gage
Pl F2/6/120	10 June 1720	£5,000	£50,000	On or before 25March 1721	Edward Eure
Pl F2/6/121	28 June 1720	£1,000	£10,000	Within 14 days of opening	Alexander Gordon
Pl F2/6/122	18 June 1720	£2,000 1st Sub	£10,000	On demand (the Duke executes almost immediately)	Robert Surman
Pl F2/6/123	23 June 1720	£1,000	£8,900	For the opening	John Marke, goldsmith
Pl F2/6/124	23 June 1720	£1,500	£13,875	For the opening	Daniel Carroll
Pl F2/6/125	23 June 1720	£1,000	£6,650	For the opening	Isaac Hern. Nunes
Pl F2/6/126	23 June 1720	£1,000	£6,550	For the opening	Phosaunt Crisp
Pl F2/6/127	23 June 1720	£1,000	£8,900	For the opening	John Marke
Pl F2/6/128	23 June 1720	£5,000	£33,000	For the opening	Sir George Caswall
Pl F2/6/129	2 July 1720	£3,000 1st Sub	£11,000	Within 8 days of the opening	Thomas Martin
Pl F2/6/130	22 Aug 1720	£1,100	£7,300	On 23 Nov 1720	Isaac Hern. Nunes
Pl F2/6/131	23 Aug 1720	£3,500	£22,000	On or before 24 Nov 1720	William Bowles
Pl F2/6/132	23 Aug 1720	£3,000	£17,600	On or before 23 Nov 1720	John Edwin
Pl F2/6/133	23 Aug 1720	£5,500	£36,300	On or before 24 Nov 1720	Sir George Caswall
Pl F2/6/134	23 Aug 1720	£1,100	£7,200	On or before 24 Nov 1720	Phosaunt Crisp

Source: Portland Manuscripts. See Column 1 for accession numbers.

were to be held in trust by yet another party (e.g. the Sword Blade Bank) and there could even be a provision that additional stock would be given to such trustees if stock prices fell. A final guarantee usually built into these contracts was the traditional double penal sum long found in written contracts of debt. Given the stupendous size of some of the Duke's contracts, it is striking to see this penal sum provision retained in an unreduced form.[36]

The Duke was active in forming forward purchase agreements in the spring of 1720, usually for settlement before the closing of the transfer ledgers at the end of June 1720. We have some evidence that the Duke was successful in fulfilling these contracts.[37] At the same time he was settling these earlier contracts, he was promising to undertake delivery of more stock at even higher prices for the opening of the Company's ledgers at the end of August. He also formed some more long-term forward purchase agreements for settlement in the autumn and end of year 1720, with two more large contracts for settlement in March 1721. It was these latter contracts that were the largest and therefore potentially the most ruinous to the Duke's fortunes.

In Table 5.1 we see three of the contracts that were to give Portland difficulties. There was first the relatively long-term forward purchase agreement with Edward Eure. The manuscripts show that Eure planned to make a good tender of shares to Portland, for there is a letter from Eure to Portland commanding his presence on March 21, 1721 to take receipt of the fifty shares for the contract price of £1,000 a share.[38] But elsewhere we find a signed statement by three clerks of the South Sea Company that March 21 was not a regular transfer day, therefore to make a good tender Eure would have had to attend at the South Sea House all day, which he did not do.[39]

In a number of the Portland cases it is alleged, at least as a trial argument, that good tender of stock was not made at the stipulated time. This argument appears in a number of unrelated cases found in the *English Reports* as well. If these allegations are to be believed, incredible as it may seem, some people, when given opportunity to sell shares from £900 to £1,000 p.s. when they were worth only about £150 p.s.,

---

[36] We shall see later that a penal sum of £200,000 originating from the Duke's two £50,000 forward purchase agreements with George Caswall was the final claim still in dispute between Caswall and the second Duke in 1741.

[37] Pw B 165 is filled with descriptions of the terms under which these contracts were settled.

[38] Pw B 143.

[39] Pl F2/6/145. The tender of shares had to be made at South Sea House where the transfer ledgers were lodged.

apparently passed up the opportunity to do so.[40] In other papers we see the Duke's advisors checking that the Eure contract was properly registered and that Eure was actually in possession of sufficient stock to make the tender when the contract was signed. These were all requirements under the 1721 Act 7 Geo. 1, stat. 2 and were systematically checked for in many other contracts to which Portland was a party.[41] The Eure contract, if fairly settled, would have cost Portland about £43,000 net and he could have been liable for £100,000 in a penal sum in the worst case scenario.

The second contract that gave the Duke trouble was the contract for £17,600 with John Edwin. Edwin and his brother (Charles) adopted a particularly aggressive and uncompromising stance towards the Duke. The first discoverable communications from these brothers to Portland were in the most threatening tones.[42] We know also that they were the most active in trying to build legal coalitions against Portland amongst his other contract partners.[43] They even tried latterly to have Portland's goods and chattels distrained.[44] There are two contracts with Sir George Caswall in Table 5.1, the second being just a compounding of the first contract. To that contract we must add two others, both for fifty shares at £1,000 p.s., each with £200,000 penal sums contained therein.[45] These were the main contracts that the Duke, his widow and his successor, the second Duke fought so strenuously to renege upon throughout the 1720s and, in the case of the Caswall contracts, as late as 1741.

---

[40] We later see that Sir John Meres actually did this because, as he wrote, he thought it was accommodating to Portland to be allowed more time to settle with Meres. Perhaps other contracting parties felt the same way. Certainly Caswall's correspondence with the Duke regarding Portland's account with the Sword Blade bank also expresses this sentiment. See fn. 59.

[41] Such references are found in a number of places, but mostly in Pl F2/6/145.

[42] Pw B 36–7.

[43] In March 1722 Sir John Meres (Pw B 57 and Pw B 64/1) was asked by the Edwins to join them in suits against the Duke. Similarly, in Pw B 74–8, Thomas Wynne plaintively wrote to the Duke just before his departure for Jamaica that he was being pressurised by the "unmerciful Edwins" to join them against the Duke. For his contract with the Duke, see Pw B 164 (Appendix A). In their letters to the Duke, Charles and John Edwin state that they have successfully brought others into their hounding of the Duke. On October 14 they remind him their affairs with him involve others quite prominent, "one is a gentleman of Norfolk a relation of Mr Walpoles & Neighbor of Lord Townsends who has very little to do in the South Sea affairs except in this unfortunate transaction with your Grace, another is a Daughter of your neighbour Sir Roger Hill who has once had the honour to be acquainted with her Grace the Duchess, a third is a Lady of her acquaintance." Pw B 36.

[44] Pl F2/7/7, a letter reference to a writ of *distringas*, purchased by the Edwins, which was in the hands of the Sheriff of Buckinghamshire in December 1725.

[45] See fn. 66.

On the contracts to Eure, Edwin and Caswall alone Portland's net liability would have been about £180,000 if fairly settled. Added to that there would have been about another £100,000 in net liability stemming from all his other unfavorable forward purchase agreements that we have discovered. His potential liabilities from these contracts would have been a very large portion of his potential net worth at that time and may have well sunk the entire Portland fortune if they had been fully honored.[46]

VI.   Portland's defense

What defensive stratagems did Portland adopt? One thing that is clear from the manuscripts is a substantial uniformity in his contracts. If he could not discover a legal stratagem that would defeat them all, they would have to be defeated piecemeal, with perhaps the weakest opponents being singled out for the most ruthless dismissal. There is strong evidence that Portland's advisors chose their adversaries in this way. They of course opposed those persons who posed the greatest threats to the Bentinck fortune. They ignored the claims of those who, out of post-Crash poverty, were too weak to pursue Portland legally.[47] The first thing was to discover every potential opponent's weaknesses. Portland's lawyers, directed by John Lucas, were first ordered to check each contract thoroughly to see if had been properly registered at the South Sea House as stipulated in 7 Geo 1, stat. 2. Second, every possible bit of evidence, no matter how far fetched, that would show that a forward seller was not diligent in the proper presentation of his claims to the Duke was gathered. Finally, the best legal opinion of the day was polled on the validity of the contracts themselves.

It is in the statements of strategic legal opinion that we find the most interesting papers amongst the Portland manuscripts. Whilst pleas can be found in archives and whilst judgments can be found in the legal reports, it is rare to find a collection of communications between lawyers and clients in which a range of legal strategies is discussed. Such communications show the known extent to which legal opponents could use the law to achieve their purposes. Such documents appear in the Portland collection from about September 1721. At that time the prominent

---

[46] Dunthorne and Onnekink report that the value of his father's estate was about £850,000 when it was passed to the Duke in 1709. The estate was heavily encumbered with debts even prior to the South Sea Bubble. See Pl F2/6/106–110.

[47] Such were the fates of Alexander Gordon and the Duke's agent and financial correspondent, Pheasunt Crisp. See Pw B 38–41 and Pw B 21.

King's Sergeant, Sir John Chesshyre,[48] was asked to look over the Edwin contract and to give his opinions.[49]

The legal questions and opinions are patently directed at defending against actions that might arise from the contract dated August 23 with John Edwin.[50] There is little joy in Sergeant Chesshyre's opinions for the Duke. Amongst the "facts" put to the lawyer was that the £17,600 the Duke was supposed to pay on November 23, 1720 for thirty South Sea shares was split into a loan of £16,000 and £1,600 interest for three months. The claim is made that this amounts to a loan at an interest rate of 40 p.c. p.a. and is clearly usurious.[51] When asked whether the Duke could claim the statutes of usury, Chesshyre is quite clear that the agreement will not be looked upon as usurious merely on the Duke's or any other person's say-so.[52] The legal opinion was that he will have to prove the "Loan to be or having an usurious sum for forebearance" and it must be "in such a case the proofs be clear and manifest."[53] Chesshyre also warns in so many words that the Duke cannot simultaneously deploy all the legal weapons that he has at his disposal. If he is going to seek relief on the grounds of usury, he cannot simultaneously take Edwin to task for not performing on the contract. If the Duke were to claim that Edwin took unfair advantage of him under the terms of the contract, he would also affirm the contract's legality.

To set these arguments in their financial context, consider that when the contract was signed on August 23, South Sea shares were worth about £750 p.s. One or both parties to the contract were clearly pessimistic about the future value of such shares on November 23 when the contract was to expire. £17,600 promised in payment for thirty shares would imply a delivery price of a little more than £580 p.s. The facsimile contract, which Chesshyre was inspecting, specified that Edwin could sell the thirty shares he was holding if their value fell below £600 p.s. and the Duke would still guarantee that on November 23 he would pay Edwin the residual up to the fully specified £17,600. Certainly by the second re-opening of the firm's share ledgers (September 12), South Sea share values had not fallen below £600 p.s. What the Duke's legal advisers wanted to claim, however, was that Edwin had got rid of the thirty shares well before September 12. This would have put Edwin into a double bind. In the first instance, the original contract stated that the

---

[48] Lemmings, "Chesshyre, Sir John (1662–1738)." Chesshyre was to become the King's First Serjeant in 1727.

[49] Pl F2/6/200, reproduced here in full as Appendix B. My thanks to Kathryn Summerwill who helped in the decipherment of Serjeunt Chesshyre's difficult hand.

[50] Pl F2/6/132.   [51] App. 2, lines 1–16.

[52] App. 2, line 36, "Paroll proofs . . . will not be allowed"   [53] App. 2, lines 40 and 53.

shares were the Duke's and Edwin was holding them in trust. Therefore the use of the shares for Edwin's benefit would be against the terms of the contract. Secondly, by the time Chesshyre was doing his work, 7 Geo 1, stat. 2 required that for contracts that had yet been unperformed, sellers of stock had to be in possession of adequate stock within six days of the contract's date. If Edwin had disposed of the thirty shares too quickly, the Duke would be liable to purchase only the shares Edwin was actually in possession of within the six-day window around the contract date. These were the issues addressed to Chesshyre and to which he responded.[54]

In his last advice, Chesshyre warned the Duke that if he claimed there were wrongful advantages to Edwin resulting from his dealing in the Duke's stock, he had better make sure that the advantages to Edwin actually exceeded the Duke's liability to Edwin under the contract. For by making this argument, the Duke would again affirm the validity of the contract.[55] Such a balance was not very likely to be in the Duke's favor. In a small book, which we might call an inventory and collection of memoranda about the Duke's contracts, we find that Portland's advisors had discovered, while looking at the South Sea stock ledgers, that Edwin was in possession of only six shares on August 31, 1720. The value of South Sea shares at the signing of the contract was about £750 p.s. and was certainly still above £600 p.s. until about September 14. So, according to the contract Edwin would have prematurely disposed of twenty-four shares he was holding for the Duke. But the maximum net advantage to Edwin of having done this (prior to further price declines below £600 p.s.) would be only $24 \times (£750-£600) = £3,600$. Balanced against this the Duke, by affirming the contract, would have obliged himself to (at the very least) a liability to purchase the six shares for about £586 p.s., when they were worth then only about £150 p.s. The danger of admitting to this liability is that Edwin might even still later prove that he had control of all the required thirty shares by trust arrangements with others. At least this was the claim made by Edwin that was noted in another source.[56]

In the end, Edwin may or may not have fulfilled his side of his contract, but the Duke was in the position of having to affirm the validity of the contract in order to discover in court whether this was true or not. What did he do? We have not yet discovered the full proceedings of Edwin against the Duke; all we know so far is that they were strenuous and threatening and from this we might guess that Edwin was pursuing

---

[54] App. 2, lines 18–22, 29–30 and 61–70.   [55] App. 2, lines 77–80.
[56] Pl F2/6/137.

the Duke for full performance of the contract, plus costs, at least. This would have been an obligation to repurchase all thirty shares for £17,600 when they were worth only £4,500. Furthermore, Edwin might have pursued the Duke for the penal sums resulting from default on the contract, £35,200. In an undated memorandum we see noted only some instructions to delay the Edwins' actions by presenting a bill to relieve the Duke of his contract with Edwin on the grounds of usury and improper use and benefit of the thirty shares – precisely the two grounds that Chesshyre warned should not be used simultaneously.[57]

We have outlines of how the Duke was planning to proceed against his other antagonists. We have seen that against Edwin and Crisp the Duke was going to proceed on the grounds that, under 7 Geo 1, stat. 2, these persons were deficient in the stock they needed to have when the contracts were signed. There were also a few instances in which his advisors believed they had discovered that contracts had not been properly registered, as required under that Act. The most important instance of this concerned the Duke's first contract with Sir George Caswall. Our sources suggest that his legal advisors thought that usury was still useful grounds for relief against the contracts with Edwin, Caswall (3rd contract), Crisp and Bowles. By far the most common defense that was deployed against the creditors, however, is that they failed to make good tender of stock to the Duke. This was to be used against Bowles, Meres, Nunes, Crisp, Eure, Seabright and Caswall.[58] We cannot yet be sure how far in advance or after Chesshyre's advice that the Duke's legal defenses were fully operating, but we do know that from late 1720 and through much of 1722 the Duke was actively reneging and delaying his creditors.

Not all creditors were successfully turned away, although many of the letters in the Portland archives are plaintive appeals to the Duke. The best preserved collection of letters is from Sir John Meres. Alternatively begging, cringingly obsequious and threatening, the Meres letters to Portland provide some of the best amusement to be found in any South Sea archive. That they were ultimately successful with the Duke may be due to their writer's persistence, but it is more probable that, as one of the six clerks in Chancery, Meres was ideally placed to

---

[57] Pl F2/6/145. Because the memorandum is undated, it may very well have predated Chesshyre's advice. The same document shows that the Duke intended to give Pheasunt Crisp the same treatment he was going to mete out to the Edwins. The similar contract with Crisp (Pl F2/6/134, Table 5.1) was to be opposed on the same grounds – usury and not having enough stock within six days of the contract date.

[58] Pl F2/6/137 and Pl F2/6/145, memoranda and observations concerning contracts.

advance his claims against Portland along a legal fast-track – or so he would occasionally darkly threaten.

Feb 15 1721 – My Lord Duke, I may now reasonably Compute that besides the loss of £11170 by the 1st and 2nd Subscriptions which I bought & fairly advanced & paid for to your Grace, I have lost about the value of £5000 by your Grace's Neglect or delay of Accepting the South Sea Stock which you Bought of Me.

I will not trouble Yo'r Grace again with Circumstances or a long Letter, tho' it might be usefull to Your Self & other Sufferes by the South Sea Directors, because I hear the length of my last was Complain'd of: And if I may not be admitted the honour of Discoursing with You, or hearing from Yo'r self on this Occasion, I shall not trouble Yr'r Grace any further than by such or better Agents than You have used towards Mee, if You can think I have deserved no better from You, who (to my great Loss & Inconvience in whatever I have transacted with Yo'r Grace) have shew'd myself to be with all respect & kind intention towards YOU!

I have already intimated to Your Grace how this matter may be made easy, & it will be entirely owing to Your Unkindness if I am any way troublesome or pressing; tho' I meet with no favour on the like Occasions.

Your Grace has brought me under a necessity of doing the same things Thrice already that I might be Supplied with Money for Performing my Contracts with others: And I must once more raise Money at any loss before the Books of the South Sea Company will be again Open'd; however I give Your Grace this Timely Notice that I will so soon as the South Sea Books shall be Open'd for that Purpose Transfer a 2d time or tender to be transferred to your Grace, or Your Order the £3500 South Sea Stock at the price of £22000, which I pray you to accept, or Cause to be Accepted accordingly; It is extremely uneasy to me that I am Compelled to Act thus, who am MY Lord Duke Your Grace's etc.[59]

This was a typical and, by Meres' standards, not a long-winded effort to get satisfaction from the Duke. In March and April of 1722 Meres sent one begging or threatening letter after another to the Duke. He wrote that he had a series of unsatisfactory meetings with the Duke's representatives and that the ever redoubtable Edwin brothers had been at him to join in a coalition against the Duke.[60]

Some further light is shed upon Meres' frustration and irritation with the Duke by the pleading he filed in Chancery at this time.[61] In this document he complained to the Lord Chancellor that Portland was using Meres' loss of a promissory note to claim that the note never existed in the first place. This was not just any promissory note, but was the very note by which the Duke had promised to pay the £22,000 referred to in his letter above. The existence and validity of this note is evidenced in

[59] Pw B 48.   [60] Pw B 55–61.   [61] NA, C11/852/14, March 21, 1722.

numerous places in the Portland papers. In the pleading, Meres asked the Court to compel the Duke to produce the witnesses and evidence for the note, which he knew existed. Meres' persistence soon obtained results to his satisfaction for he wrote on June 5, 1722, "My Lord Duke, Permit Me once more to Kiss Yo'r Grace's hand"[62] in thanks for all the ways in which his demands had been met. His descriptions of these devices were incomplete, but we do know that earlier (March 21, 1721) the Duke had somehow arranged for Meres to purchase (for £5,000) a £8,000 judgment against the Duke that had been enrolled in 1718.[63] Meres had before acknowledged that £5,000 was a bargain price for the judgement because, from the time he had obtained it, other enemies of the Duke (again, the Edwin brothers) had offered more than £6,000 for it.[64] Meres related in his June 1722 letter the final arrangements by which the judgement was released to him. He also mentioned a series of other notes and securities from the Duke that had been finally accepted by Meres' creditors.[65]

The Duke's settlement with Meres was probably quite an expensive one. In a series of agreements brokered by Pheasant Crisp, the Duke had agreed to buy £3,500 South Sea Stock (35 shares) and £1,000 each of receipts in the first and second South Sea subscriptions. By late November 1720 when all these agreements should have been settled, the stocks the Duke had agreed to buy would have been worth no more than £9,000, but he had agreed to pay nearly £32,000 for them. A realistic net liability to Sir John Meres thus would have been on the order of £20,000. Meres was clearly such a dangerous adversary with a large, but not too large, claim upon the Duke's assets that he had to be satisfied. Although Meres might have shared some losses with the Duke and others in the South Sea Bubble, he was in the end not financially disabled. Later in the 1720s he was to remain active in finance and business as an officer in the Royal African Company (sub-governor) and York Buildings Company (Governor).

There was one dangerous antagonist whose claims the Duke clearly could not afford to satisfy, Sir George Caswall. It was not until the 1730s

---

[62] Pw B 63.   [63] Pl F2/7/30.

[64] Pw B 64/1. An enrolled judgment would be a debt senior to other debts, such as the rest of the Duke's debts to Meres. A judgment would not only be paid first, but would also be useful as a legal weapon with which to harry the Duke. It is thus quite telling of the Duke's financial problems in 1721 that his highest grade debt had a market discount of at least 25 p.c.

[65] We do not know what the complete accounting of these arrangements were, but we do know that amongst them was the assignment to Meres of the fee farm rents of Wingham in Kent that Meres would later sell on for £3,400. We also know that a number of East India bonds were sold for Meres' benefit. See Pl E8/6/34,43.

that Sir George Caswall, co-partner with Jacob Sawbridge and Elias Turner in the Sword Blade Bank, began to use legal means to press his claims. Amongst the Portland legal papers of the 1730s we find a "rough draft of the defendant's case and proofs" in which there is a copy of a letter dated to mid-1722 in which Caswall lays before the Duke the totality of the Sword Blade's claims,

A Copy of the letter & Account vizt.
  Rt Honourable
My Lord the very great calamity that hath befallen all persons concerned in Stocks hath in a more particular manner been exceeding grievious to my self & Copartners for over & above the loss of money we have suffered the disgrace of doing that which in the course of 22 years trade we never did before I mean to refuse paying what we owed at demand whereby we have lost 20,000L p.annm.

I have delayed sending your account untill this time because I was persuaded your Grace would cause all your accounts to be stated that you might know what condition your Grace's affairs were in to satisfy the demands upon you The generality I shewed your Grace in the agreements we made with you I doubt not will plead our cause and as we had no views of dissrving your Grace for you might have made large advantages by what you did with us so I can say we shall be as willing as any of your creditors to do the kind part by you I have been a great many times to wait on your Grace at your own house tho in vain I have therefore sent you this letter with your account with us & beg your Grace's answer in writing and commands when & where I shall wait on you being
Your Grace's very sincere and Humble Servant
George Caswall

To his Grace Henry Duke of Portland present
  His Grace Henry Duke of Portland Debit
To Cash on. . . ...5500 S Sea due 24 November. 36300
To ditto. . .. .5500 ditto due 29 Septem. . . .. .50000
To ditto. . .. .5500 ditto due 23 Decem. 50000
To ditto.... . .. . ..600 ditto Ballance of his Account Stock

      17100   136300

To ditto   10000 ditto Deposit on your Grace's & sundry other account deduct for Ballance of his Acct cash 943L14s11d
Interest of 1600L E.I. bonds receiv'd   21L11s9d   965L6s8d

135334L13s4d[66]

A net claim upon Portland's estate in excess of £135,000 was certainly the greatest single liability against which he had to defend himself. From

[66] Pl F2/6/313.

numerous sources it is plain that Caswall took no legal action during the Duke's lifetime, although the same sources allude to frequent attempts to negotiate settlements to the dispute. As a member of the House of Lords and as a serving Royal Officer on mission in Jamaica, the Duke's person was inviolable in actions of debt at Common Law, but there is no apparent reason why Caswall could not have followed a strategy similar to that followed by Meres – harassing the Duke for reply and evidence in equity and establishing a record of complaint and evidence before useful witnesses and records disappeared. The Duke died in 1726 and thereafter the Duke's creditors' best remedies would be found in equity against his executors and heirs. The second Duke, William, would not reach his majority until 1730 and in the meantime Henry's widow, Elizabeth, was the executrix of his estate, which she would remain until her death in 1736 and William became sole heir.[67]

We have not found one coherent source that describes Caswall's attacks and Portland's defenses through the courts. A painstaking comparison of the papers found in the Portland manuscripts with public court records appears now to be the only way to find out conclusively what happened.[68] From the Portland manuscripts perspective only, however, we have the best evidence of the strategy behind the Duke's defenses. The bulk of the papers from the late 1720s and well into the 1730s show that the Duke's representatives defended against Caswall and other creditors by tying up vulnerable assets in trust. Prior to his departure to the Governorship of Jamaica, Portland created a new strict settlement of the remainder of the estate trust for his children. This had to be done with care in 1721 because if an executor or an heir later failed to successfully plead the exclusion from creditors of assets from the deceased Duke's estate, the establishment of the estate trust could be construed as an attempt to circumvent the statute against fraudulent

---

[67] A portion of the estate was created for younger sons in the first Duke's 1704 marriage settlement. After the first Duke's death, Elizabeth petitioned (see Bentinck, 1726) for a Private Bill to remove and manage that portion of the settlement for the benefit of her second son (George, b. 1715) until he should reach his majority. That portion of the estate was thus protected from the actions by the first Duke's creditors. See Private Bill 1Geo. 2, c.5, *An Act to Enable the Guardians of the Lord George Bentinck*.

[68] The National Archives are making great strides in converting finding aids for courts of law and equity into electronic forms. So far, however, most progress has been made in making equity court pleadings name-searchable by defendant and plaintiff. The finding aids for Common Pleas and King's Bench, however, are still quite cumbersome to use. See fn. 85. It would seem strange that a trail of public records for such a series of important cases such as the Duke's would be hard to find, but without some foreknowledge of what courts and in what sessions hearings took place and without the names under which the cases were filed, it is a difficult task indeed.

devises. Such a failure could potentially further expose the estate to charges from creditors of the deceased ancestor.[69]

It appears that Caswall bided his time before he launched his legal attack on the Portland interests. His path would have certainly been eased by the Duke's death in 1726 in Jamaica, for it would have widened his options for action in equity, but we see no evidence that he immediately began an attack on either the Portland estate's executrix, Elizabeth, or the estate trustees. Not until 1735 and 1736 was he purchasing writs of *distringas* in Buckinghamshire (as the Edwin brothers did in 1725) to accompany his pleadings in Exchequer. One object of his actions was to force Elizabeth to produce an inventory of the Portland estate as it would pass to the ultimate heir, the second Duke. When this inventory was eventually produced, it was quite small (less than £7,000) because it clearly excluded all lands and land-derived incomes – as if such assets were not going to pass to the second Duke by descent.[70] This was a clear premonition of one defensive device the second Duke was to subsequently use; he would plead that the bulk of the estate did not come to him by descent (the plea, *riens per descent*) and thus was not assets available to his father's creditors. We have already described the dangers of making a false plea of *riens per descent* and this is the setback that William eventually suffered in Exchequer. To see why this might have happened, we have to go back to 1720 and the first Duke's relationship with the Portland settled estate.

We have already visited the issue of Portland's relations with his estate's trustees.[71] There are papers dating from 1722 in which the idea is tested of shifting the blame of estate losses towards the trustees and away from Portland.[72] This argument was still alive and was raised, as if it were of some possible use, even in 1739. Portland's paid legal advisors were disdainful of its merits and later we find evidence that the estate's trustees were indemnified by the second Duke for any losses to the estate that their actions may have led to. The apparent reason for doing this was so the trustees could be better used as witnesses in the Duke's defense. The second Duke greatly needed such witnesses because he faced several problems in defending the 1721 settlement of the estate; his legal advisors were quite divided as to whether it was a good

---

[69] See 3 Will. & Mary, c. 14, 1691, *An Act for Relief of Creditors against Fraudulent Devises*. For discussion of pleas in defence of creditors' bills against estate heirs in equity, see also Langdell's "A brief survey of the equity jurisdiction."

[70] Details of writs, pleadings and the inventory referred to are found in Pl F2/6/225,226. Elizabeth died March 1736.

[71] See fn. 31, section V and related discussion on page 16.   [72] See fn. 32.

settlement or not. The crux of the issue was whether the first Duke in 1720 had (a) acted in concert with the trustees in applying the trust's cash for allowed uses or (b) whether the Duke had merely borrowed money from the trust. In the latter case, the money would be treated as personal estate and would be available to creditors. In the former case, the money would be simply the Duke's debt to the estate. Several advisors were looking at the same hypothetical case document reproduced in Appendix C. In the opinion of John Browne (KC and MP for Dorchester) if the Duke was not actually a borrower from the original estate, the resettlement of the estate upon his son would be fraudulent and void as it would appear that it was done merely to avoid the claims of creditors, "the principall Difficulty & defect in the Case seems to be the Slight Evidence of John Strongs having really borrowed the 10000L."[73] In another opinion "it seems to be an agreement between the X and the Trustees to layout the 10000 in the Purchase of Stock. . .& if this should come out to be the case it may be of very ill consequence to the family."[74] Finally, in the opinion of no less than Sir Dudley Ryder, the Attorney General,

I think on the whole of this transaction the placing out the trust money in the purchase of SS Stock at 500 p cent cannot be considered as a Loan on governmt. securitys according to the trust & therefore was a breach of trust & as Jo Strong was not only a party to it but procured it to ease himself he would be bound in Equity to make it good the consequence of which is that the settlement made by him of his own estate to repair the Loss was on valueable consideration not void as to creditors & therefore that Robert the Son did not take that estate by Descent from his father. but How far he may safely plead riens per descent will I think depend on the Evidence he is capable of giving of the nature of the transaction. As to the Remainder in Fee it being after an Estate Tail which he barred it has no assets

As to the estate purchas't with the 10000L if that appears to be the fact I am of opinion it was well settled & therefore no assetts of Jo Strong.

As to the trustees being Evidence I rather think they cannot because it is to discharge themselves of the trust money by the purchase of the Stock, to gett themselves indemnify'd so far as the value of the Estate against their breach of trust but this is not quite clear.

D Ryder
18 Sept 1739[75]

---

[73] Pl F2/6/220.   [74] Pl F2/6/219.

[75] Pl F2/6/218. There is a note on the verso of this document that the Mr. Attorney General was due 2 guineas for this opinion. For Ryder's career see, Lemmings, "Ryder, Sir Dudley (1691–1756)."

After the controversial settlement, the first Duke departed for his well-remunerated Governorship of Jamaica. It was not a very successful sojourn, nor in the end did the Duke live long enough to much benefit from the salary.[76] The portion of the estate strictly settled on his son may have remained safe, but the portion that the Duke managed to expose to the deterioration in the South Sea appeared, in his lawyers' eyes, to have remained "assets" available to creditors.

Caswall's direct attacks upon William, as sole heir to the estate, started in late 1737. From this point forward, we have more than just the Portland manuscripts to guide us. We have also the record of rules and orders coming out of Exchequer.[77] In November 1737 the Buckinghamshire sheriff summoned the second Duke to answer one of Caswall's bills in Exchequer.[78] We have not yet discovered Caswall's pleadings in Exchequer, but we have the Portland manuscripts copies of them and they claim the penal sums for non-performance on the three contracts described in his original letter (reproduced above) of 1722 to the first Duke.[79] In June 1739 we know that the court was moved that Portland be allowed to plead that "the deed was not the Duke's and the plaintif did not tender stock." There follow several notices of trial and motions for delay until it appears that May 14, 1741 was to be the day of reckoning. For that day there are notices to the South Sea Company to prepare to deliver transfer ledgers for 1720, cash books and the register of contracts to be at the court's disposal. Paperwork was also ordered to trace the accounts of not only Caswall, but also those of the Portland trustees (Eyles, Eyles and de Gols).[80]

---

[76] He was appointed in September 1721, but did not arrive in Jamaica until December 1722. At the Crown's request, the Jamaican Assembly reluctantly granted him an expenses/salary budget of £5,000 p.a., twice the usual £2,500 p.a., received by Governors of Jamaica. He unsuccessfully negotiated with the Assembly on revenue bills. He had poor relations with the Royal Navy establishment in Jamaica and had even tried to alleviate the problems of piracy with direct offers of grants and pardons to pirates. In short, he had all the usual problems of Jamaican governors in this period. He also experienced the usual death of Jamaican governors; fatal disease was rarely a lingering disease and he was quickly carried off by a fever on July 4, 1726. Neither was his sojourn in Jamaica financially successful. Although the Jamaican Assembly, upon his wife's petition, made good the remnants of the Duke's salary, her requests for relief from the Duke's accumulated debts met with rebuff. See Cundall, *The Governors of Jamaica. . .*, Chapter 7. An official sojourn in the Caribbean to escape creditors and to make money was common. It was a ploy nearly undertaken by Thomas Pitt the elder in 1717 and undertaken by Lord Londonderry in 1727. See Larry Neal's "The Money Pitt."

[77] This is series NA, E12.

[78] Pl F2/6/225 in the Portland manuscripts. Corroborating evidence comes from the 1738 entries in the Exchequer series NA, E12/40.

[79] Pl F2/6/230, dated 1738.

[80] These are all in the series Pl F2/6/261–272. All these orders and actions are corroborated in NA, E12/41.

What happened? By this time Sir George's son was contesting the action alone. Perhaps Sir George was too ill to attend to his legal affairs, although he was not to die until the autumn of 1742. In a memorandum of July 16, 1741 of a meeting between the Duke's counsel and the younger Caswall, Caswall apparently tried to come to some salvaging arrangement with the Duke.

That if it had been in his power he would deliver up that contract {referring here to Pl F2/6/133} as well as the other two which he did deliver to the Duke and that he was ever ready if the Duke desir'd to make an assignment of said two contracts. . . . That Sir George does not know of his giving up the Contracts to his Grace . . . That the mony he has expended in the suit has been more than he ever had from his father in his Life since 16 years old.

These passages are the only existing evidence of an attempted settlement between the antagonists. Perhaps the younger Caswall was proposing to accept payment for the contracts, or perhaps such a payment had already changed hands.

Why should Caswall have attempted a settlement? Not everything had gone against the Caswall suit. In a fortuitous reminiscence more than thirty years after the events, Lord Chief Justice Mansfield recalled that, when he was but a junior member of the Duke's defense team, the Duke had suffered a ruling that his plea of *riens per descent* was a false plea and this opened the way for Caswall to enter a claim for the £200,000 penal sums attached to the two contracts referred to in the passage above.[81] By making an analogy between the Caswall case and the case on which he was ruling in 1773, Mansfield revealed something about the course of the suit in 1741. First, he stated that the basis of the false plea ruling was trifling matter; there had been some small error in the accounting of the assets the second Duke had received by descent, but it was not the intent of the statute against fraudulent devises that such small errors should open the heir's estate to the whole debt. With these remarks Mansfield also revealed that Caswall had some success in establishing that debt and that it was not a small debt. The proceedings in May 1741 were either postponed or incomplete because there were fresh rulings for the formation of a new jury in June.[82] This was probably the jury, which Caswall complained, was not allowed to judge his suit. He "had heard the Judg had sent for the Record the night before the tryall to his

---

[81] Lofft, *Reports of cases adjudged in the Court of King's Bench*, page 263.

[82] NA, E12/41. Perhaps there were problems in jury selection. In an early June ruling Caswall was ordered to show cause as to why he should object to presence of nonjurors in his jury.

chamber ... {and} ... That if it had been left to the Jury he was sure he should have had a verdict."[83] Apparently some settlement between the antagonists along the lines suggested in the July memorandum was arranged, although we cannot find the details of it in the Portland manuscripts, since the last mention of the case is a November 1741 order to enter the judgement that the plaintiff was nonsuit.[84]

VII.   Conclusions and directions for further research

The primary goal of this chapter was to begin an examination of the mechanics by which private financial contracts were settled in the wake of the South Sea Bubble. There is a natural and unavoidable bias, however, in the historical sources that we must use since disputed financial contracts tend to leave behind a richer historical record than amicably settled contracts would tend to do. In Banner's seminal work on early security regulation we find a description of the legal principles that were in existence and developed afterwards, but what we really wish to know is how well these principles worked in practice in the settlement of disputes. The South Sea Bubble period should be a particularly fruitful in producing examples of legal proceedings arising from financial disagreements, but we admittedly start here with an examination of cases that were probably not typical of the cases produced in this period. The Duke of Portland's disputes were numerous and involved huge sums of money. In monetary terms the cases may have well been amongst the largest generated by the South Sea Bubble. The historical record of his disputes is unusual in that it pertains to a number of disputed contracts with a variety of people. It also contains expert opinion upon the proper legal strategies for Portland to follow. A broader survey of financial disputes arising from the South Sea Bubble will have to depend, however, upon sources very different from the Portland sources.

We believe that most South Sea cases would probably have been actions on debt in Common Law courts, not Equity. The debts in dispute would probably have been of considerable size and thus it would be more likely they were actioned in the Court of King's Bench, rather than Common Pleas. A survey of disputes that came into the Court of King's Bench, just before and after the South Sea Bubble, will probably reveal more about the common run of disputes than will a study of large disputes such as Portland's, but the challenges presented to such a study will be formidable. The records of the Common Law courts for the 1720s are much less accessible than are the records for the courts in

---

[83] Pl F2/6/312.   [84] NA, E12/41.

Equity in the same period.[85] The search also may not uncover a huge number of cases because the 1720s sit very close to a period of a great decline in civil litigation near the middle of the eighteenth century.[86] In contrast to the period right after the collapse of the Railway Mania, the South Sea Bubble may not have caused a "hurricane of litigation."[87] Nevertheless, hidden in the relatively smaller amount of private litigation there might actually be a high proportion of cases that stem from the South Sea Bubble. Until the results of a broader survey can temper our conclusions, we here attempt what conclusions we can as regards the state of law in its attitudes towards financial litigants.

It is hard to imagine that the first Duke of Portland, if he were alive today, could have possibly remained solvent after having undertaken such a series of large and uniformly ill-advised financial contracts as he undertook in 1720.[88] The Bentinck/Portland house has only recently expired with the 9th Duke of Portland (d. 1981), but we have to conclude that the Bentinck direct line was able to continue its march towards ultimate extinction only on the backs of the eighteenth-century claimants to the Bentinck estate. There was an extensive uniformity in the basic structure of all the Portland contracts in Table 5.1 and elsewhere in the Portland Manuscripts. The Duke and his successor were nevertheless able to discriminate between claimants' demands and strategically decide whose demands could be ignored, whose demands must be satisfied and whose demands must be legally resisted. So far I have found no one who obtained large satisfaction from the Duke except Sir John Meres. Caswall's claims appear to have been harmed by his reluctance to move quickly and aggressively against the Duke. Instead of appreciating Caswall's hesitance, the Duke's defense used Caswall's delay to his own advantage. It is difficult therefore not to have wished the Edwin brothers well in their pursuit of the Duke – their brutal

[85] Court of King's Bench judgments and their finding aids from this period, such as the Entry Books for judgments (NA, KB 168) or the Rule Books (NA, KB 125) are all written in a legal Latin and typically recorded (with numerous specialized abbreviations) in a very small legal hand, a descendant of the court hand of medieval scriptography.
[86] If there was a general rise in numbers of cases started and reaching advanced stages as a result of the Bubble, it would have to have been quite short-lived since it escaped notice in the survey performed by Brooks, The 1720s and 1730s were characterized by very low levels of litigation. See Brooks, "Interpersonal conflict," pp. 360–4.
[87] Kostal, *Law and English Railway Capitalism*, Chapter 2 (The Hurricane of Litigation), describes the litigation aftermath of the Railway Mania of 1844–5 and shows that the Railway Mania was directly responsible in a very large increase in civil litigation.
[88] It is also highly unlikely that the heirs of the late Lord Lovat could have suffered a worse financial fate in 1720 than they suffered in 1995 when (mere) debt and the weight of modern death duties forced the sale of one of the oldest (thirteenth century) estates in the British Isles.

and uncompromising approach was seemingly more fitting to the true dignity[89] of Henry Bentinck than the equally threatening, but more honeyed approach taken by Meres.

In the hands of as resourceful an antagonist as the Duke of Portland, the provisions of 7 Geo. 1, stat. 2 were weapons that could be effectively deployed to deny justice to claimants. The intent of the statute clearly was to draw a line under the South Sea Bubble by hastening an end to vexatious suits, but in the hands of the Portland legal team it could be used, and was used, to make financial lawsuits vexatious. To modern minds it is somewhat incredible that two cornerstones of Portland's defense were the arguments that his creditors (a) could not manage properly to ask the Duke to perform on his contracts and simultaneously (b) could not manage to properly register their contracts as required under 7 Geo. 1, stat. 2. Yet these were the two arguments that were raised and refined repeatedly in the Portland papers in which legal strategies were rehearsed. But perhaps nothing more could have been expected of a duke in the early eighteenth century. Caswall's struggles against Portland are reminiscent of the struggles Richard Cantillon had at the same time with the Lady Mary Herbert, another member of the aristocracy who would not honor her contracts apparently only because it would have been too expensive for her to do so.[90]

For private property rights in capital markets, 1720–1721 was "the best of times, it was the worst of times." In three acts, parliament had radically intermeddled with public finance, company law and the security of contract. The public's ultimate negative reaction to the first of these acts[91] finally forced Walpole's administration to put public finance on a footing that was stable and secure for more than a century afterwards. The second act[92] forced the development of company law onto paths in which change could take place only very slowly. This may ultimately have had its benefits and certainly in many contemporary minds the joint-stock form of incorporation was itself seen as a nuisance which needed to be restricted. On the other hand, joint-stock incorporation had previously been a popular way of organizing business and so it is likely that the Bubble Act did reduce the ability and rights of certain persons to organize businesses into the forms they preferred. In the third act,[93] parliament sought to reduce the proliferation of lawsuits

---

[89] We must remember that Henry Bentinck, or at least some of his advisors, were willing to try the argument that long-term family servants (Eyles) and not the Duke were responsible for the misapplication of estate trust funds – an argument that not one of the Duke's paid legal counsel was willing to countenance.

[90] Murphy, *Richard Cantillon*, Chapter 11.   [91] 6 Geo 1, c. 4.

[92] 6 Geo 1, c. 18, the Bubble Act.   [93] 7 Geo. 1, stat. 2.

resulting from the South Sea Bubble, but this was clearly achieved at the cost of a reduction in the rights of creditors.

Forward markets today usually work on principles that make parties to contracts as faceless as is possible, with no contract being more or less subject to settlement risk than any other. Such was not the case in 1720, however, when parties to forward contracts had to be very careful of whom they contracted with. The shocks delivered by the South Sea Bubble revealed a number of fault lines in law into which the rights of financial contractors could founder. If unilateral acts of parliament did not upset some of those rights, then others could be frustrated by financial defendants, especially if they were members of the aristocracy, who could find refuge in the complexities of the land law. The legal process itself was so slow or could be slowed to the point where the lives of litigants and witnesses alike could not outlast the length of the suits. A long time was to pass after 1720 before property rights in capital markets could be more fully achieved for people who wished to write speculative financial contracts.

Appendix A   Pw B 164
1st Duke of Portland Misc. 9 South Sea Transactions

[pages 1–2]		
His Grace the D of Portland	debit	per Contro Credit
To Sr Jn Eyles, M Jos Eyles &		By 16000 South Sea Stock
Mr Comrade de Gols as Trustees	83575L7s6.5d	Transferr'd to them as a for Mony advanc'd

Security for the 83575L7s6.5d

[pages 3–4]		
His Grace the D of Portland	debit	per Contra Credit
To the South Sea Compy a Loan at 4 p.c.	8000	By 2000 South Sea Stock transferr'd to R Surman
To Interest thereof at 4 p.c.		By the Mid Srm Divid: on the 2000 Stock
		By 14000 South Sea Stock
To the Loan of.	70000	Transferr to Shaw by
To the Int thereof at 5 p.c		Mr Knights order as Deposit

[pages 5–6]		
His Grace the D of Portland to Mr Jn Edwin	debit	per Contra Credit
22 Sep 1720 To Mony Lent	16000	By 3000 South Sea Stock
To Int agd: to be paid to	1600	Transferr'd to him as a
him Dec 22 1720		Security

[pages 7–8]

His Grace the D of Portland to Mr Wm Bowles	debit	per Contra Credit
1720 To Mony Lent	20000	By 3500 South Sea Stock Transferr'd to him as
To Int: agreed to be paid him the {blank} 1720	2000	Security

[pages 9–10]

His Grace the D of Portland to Sr Jn Meers	debit	per Contra Credit
To Mony Lent	20000	By 3500 South Sea Stock
To Int: agd to be paid him the {blank} 1720	2000	Transferr to Mr Tho: Martin by Sr Jn Meers order as a Security

[pages 11–12]

His Grace the D of Portland to Isaac Nunez	debit	per Contra Credit
To Mony Lent	6000	By 1000 South Sea Stock
In Int: till the openg: after Midsmr 1720	650	Transferr'd to him as security
To ditto to the {blank} of Nov	650	By 100 Stock for the Divd: at Midr: on the sd 1000 Stock

[pages 13–14]

His Grace the D of Portland to Phest: Crisp	debit	per Contra Credit
To Mony Lent	5900	By 1000 South Sea Stock
To In: thereof to the openg: after Midsr: 1720	650	Transferr'd to him as a security
To Int: thereof to the {blank}	650	By 100 Stock for the Div:d at Midsmr on sd 1000 Stock

[pages 15–16]

His Grace the D of Portland to Sr George Caswall	debit	per Contra Credit
To Mony lent	30000	By 5000 South Sea Stock
To Int to the openg: after Midsmr	3000	Transferr'd to him as security for the sd 30000
To Int: to the 24 Nov: 1720 for the sd 33000	3000	By 500 Stock for the Mid smr Divd on the sd 5000 stock
		By 500 S Sea Stock deposd as additional Security

[pages 17–18]

His Grace the D of Portland to Sr George Caswall	debit	per Contra Credit
To Mony agreed to be pd on the 29th of Sepr 1720 for the purchase of 5000 South Sea Stock with the	50000	By 5500 Stock to be delivr'd the {blank}

Divd: thereon at Midsmr 1720
being 500 Stock at the rate of 1000
p. ct.

To Mony agreed to be paid on the   50000   By 5500 South Sea Stock to
24th of Decr: for the like Stock and   be delivr'd the {blank}
at the like Price

[pages 19–20]

His Grace the D of Portland to Sr   debit   per Contra Credit
  Tho: Sebright

To Mony agreed to be pd for 2000 SS 8200   By 2000 SS Stock to be
Stock to be Delivr'd his Grace   delivr'd
on or before the Openg: after Xmas   By 200 Stock for the 410 p
1720 at   Cent. Divd: at Midsmr
              1720 also to be delivr'd

[pages 21–2]

His Grace the D of Portland   debit   per Contra Credit
to Mr Ed Eure

To Mony agreed to be paid for 5000 50000   By 5000 SS Stock to be
South Sea Stock to be delivr'd on or   Delivr'd
before the 25th of March 1721 at   By 500 Stock for the
the rate of 1000 p cent   Midsmr:
              Divd: also to be delivr'd
              By The Divid: at Xmas on
              the 5500 Stock

[pages 23–4]

Sword Blade Comp   debit   per Contra Credit
To His Grace the Dk: of Portland

                      Stock

To South Sea Stock deposd: by   By {blank}
  his Grace the Ld Morpeth   4000
By his Grace the Coll Darcey   2000
By his Grace the Coll Cope   1000
By His Grace the Cl Campbell   1000
By His Grace the Gen Wade   2000
By His Grace to Sr George Caswall   500
To Stock undeposited   100

[pages 25–6]

His Grace the D of Portland to Mr   debit   per Contra Credit
  Robt: Surman

To Mony Lent   10000   By 2000 of the 1st Sub
To Int: thereof   receipt deposited with
              him

[pages 27–8]

His Grace the D of Portland   debit   per Contra Credit
To Tho: Wynn Esq   6100
To Alexd: Gordon   4000
To Mr Owen   {blank}

Appendix B   Pl F2/6/200

The fictitious case of Ellis vs. Davis: similar to Edwin vs. Portland with Sergeant Chesshyre's opinions

Facts:

22 Aug 1720 Davis having purchased several large quantitys of SS stock applys (by his broker) to Ellis for 16000L on 3000L stock.

Ellis agrees to lend the money on having 1,600L for the Loan for three Months which is after the rate of 40L p.c. And which 1,600L was agreed to be added to the Sums lent.

Accordingly Ellis pays the 16,000L to the persons of whom Davis had purchased/the residue of the purchase money being paid by Davis/and Ellis has the stock transferred to himself.

In order the evade the Statute of usury the form of the agreement is varied and Indentures of Agreement are reciprocally Executed a Copy whereof is Annexed.

Which agreement please to observe is for Stock as bought by Davis of Ellis for a future day and the 1600L for the Loan is added to the 16000L lent and Davis thereby Covenants to accept the Stock on the 23rd Nov 1720 and pay for the same 17,600L.

Stock continuing to rise Considerably Ellis makes use of Davis's Stock and sells the same as we supposed at a considerable advance for it appears by the SS Books that 9 days after viz.t 31st Aug Ellis had in his name no more than 600L but some few days before the expiration of the Contract he bought in Stock/it being then very considerably fallen/so that on the 23rd Nov 1720 he had 3500L South Sea Stock.

23 Nov 1720 – The contract expired & no notice was taken by either of the partys or the other Ellis did not tender transfer or sell out the stock or did he require Davis's acceptance or payment for it Or on the other side did Davis require the Transfer or offer the money.

(And we doubt not but Ellis has gained very considerably by trading with Davis's stock.)

Q Can Ellis maintain an action against Davis for the 16000L lent notwithstanding this Deed of Agreement if so can Davis plead the Statute of Usury and thereby avoid the payment.

Paroll proofs of the Loan of the money will not be allowed to maintain an action for money lent against this contract of the party reduced into writing under hand and seal But I do not see But the borrower may plead the Statute of usury against any action which the lender can bring to recover the money. In case he can prove the contract or Loan to be or having an usurious sums for forbearance not withstanding the contrivance of the security to blind or avoid the statute.

Q Or must Ellis ground his action for breach of the Covenant by Davis for not accepting the stock and paying the money If so can Davis avoid the payment by the Statute of usury & is it not essentially necessary that Ellis proves the tender of the stock on the day or will a subsequent tender be sufficient.

I think Ellis his remedy must be on the covenant and it will be incumbent in order to assigne a good breach that a tender be avirrd either on the day or before with notice and a tender after will not be sufficient But if he could assigne a good breach I cannot apprehend but Davis may avoid the charge by pleading the usurious contract (this money lent) and (??) writing made in execution of it. In case he carefully prove it but it will be expected that in such a case the proofs be clear and manifest.

Q Can Ellis be relieved on this Agreement in Equity should Davis insist on the statute of usury there.

I conceive that a Court of Equity will not give relief against a statute made to suppress usury in case the party can avoid the contract at law as usurious.

Q In case Ellis shall not Register this Contract pursuant to the Late Act 7 Geo for restoring publick Creditt shall Davis be discharged from this demand of Ellis.

I conceive he will be discharged from soe much as remaynes unperformed.

Q Shall Ellis be accountable for such advantages as he may have made by trading with this stock.

I do not see but he ought and may be made accountable for them In case he did by sale make any & he must by answer admit them or they can be proved upon him.

Q Is it advisable for Davis to Exhibit a Bill in the Court of Equity in order to preserve the testimony of his Witnesses who are now Living and could prove the usurious agreement or for any purpose in order for his relief.

I do not think that a bill can be proper to preserve the testimony of individuals in such a case. But in case Ellis did really make such advantage by the sale of the stock, a bill will be proper to discover it(or that) but then Davis should be sure on the account of those advantages there will come out a balance on his side against Ellis on demand on the contract which Davis will by such bill affirm as legal.

23 Sept 1721 Chesshyre

Appendix C   Pl F2/6/220

The fictitious case of John Strong and Mary Best

1689 . . . . John Strong and Mary Best upon Intermarriage vested in Trustees 20,000L to be laid out in Purchases of Land to be Settled in Strict Settlement with Power to Trustees to lend the Money on Government Securities till purchases could be had 1691 . . . . A Purchase was made of Lands & the Consideration being 10,000L was laid out of Said Trust Money but the Conveyances taken to John Strong & his Heirs

1720 . . . . The said Trustees lent the remaining 10,000L to said John Strong upon 2000L South Sea Stock but no Contract or Defeazance is found between the said Trustees & John Strong nor was the Stock transferred to them from John Strong but by his Direction from other Persons of whom he had bought it at much greater Prices

The said 2000 South Sea Stock being from various Causes reduced in Value to 3000L Money whereby a loss was Sustained of 7000L of said Trust Money & the Purchases directed to be made by the Marriage Articles of Lands to be settled for the Benefit of the Issue of said Marriage could not be made and John Strong being greatly indebted by Bonds & other Specialtys did

1721 . . . . By Deed reciting said Articles & also reciting the Loss of 7000L part of said Trust Money & that thereby the Issue of that Marriage would be so far deprived of the Benefit intended them by the said Marriage Articles the said John Strong at the Pressing Instances of said Trustees for & towards making Satisfaction for said Loss & in Discharge of so much of said Trust Money as the Value of Lands therein mentioned would extend settled the Lands purchased with the 10,000L Trust Money in 1691 & also several other Lands of which he was seized in Fee in such manner as the Lands to be purchased by the Articles were to be settled & soon after dyed leaving several Sons & Daughters

N.B. The Lands of Inheritance so settled were not of Value sufficient to make good the loss of the 7000L Trust Money

Queare Will the Deed of Settlement made by John Strong in 1721 (for the Considerations aforesaid) both of the Lands purchased with the Trust Money & also of his own lands of Inheritance be either in Law or Equity looked upon as made for a valuable Consideration or will all or any of said Lands be Assetts by Descent in the Hands of Robert Strong the Eldest Son with Respect to the Creditors of his Father?

References

(Anon.) 1721. *Queries, whether the South Sea Contracts for Time, and now Pending Unperformed, Ought to be Annulled or not.* London: Warne.

Banner, S. 1998. *Anglo-American Securities Regulation.* Cambridge: Cambridge University Press.

Bentinck, Elizabeth. *The Petition of Eliz, Duchess of Portland, as Guardian to and on behalf of Geo. Bentinck, an infant, her Son, by Henry late D of P, Deceased.* London, 1726.

Boyer, A. 1720–1721. *The Political State of Great Britain*, vols. 19–22. London: Warne.

Brooks, C.W. 1989. "Interpersonal Conflict and Social Tension: Civil Litigation in England, 1640–1830," in Beier, A.L., Cannadine, D. and Rosenheim, J.M., *The First Modern Society: Essays in English History in Honour of Lawrence Stone.* Cambridge: Cambridge University Press: 357–99.

Cundall, F. 1937. *The Governors of Jamaica in the First Half of the Eighteenth Century.* London: The West India Committee.

Dalrymple, D. 1720. *Time Bargains Tryed by the Rules of Equity and Principles of the Civil Law.* London: Goldsmiths'-Kress Library.

Dickson, P.G.M. 1967. *The Financial Revolution in England: a Study in the Development of Public Credit, 1688–1756.* London: Macmillan.

Dunthorne, H. and D. Onnekink. 2004. "Bentinck, Hans Willem, first earl of Portland (1649–1709)," *Oxford Dictionary of National Biography.* Oxford: Oxford University Press.

Harris, R. 2000. *Industrializing English Law: Entrepreneurship and Business Organization, 1720–1844.* Cambridge: Cambridge University Press.

Kostal, R.W. 1994. *Law and English Railway Capitalism, 1825–1875.* Oxford: Oxford University Press.

Langdell, C.C. 1890. "A Brief Survey of the Equity Jurisdiction: VI., Creditors' Bills," *Harvard Law Review*, 4(3): 99–127.

Lemmings, D. 2004. "Chesshyre, Sir John (1662–1738)," *Oxford Dictionary of National Biography.* Oxford: Oxford University Press.

2004. "Ryder, Sir Dudley (1691–1756)," *Oxford Dictionary of National Biography.* Oxford: Oxford University Press.

Lofft, C. 1776. *Reports of Cases Adjudged in the Court of King's Bench from Easter Term 12 Geo. 3. to Michaelmas 14 Geo. 3. . . . . With some Select Cases in the Court of Chancery, and of the Common Pleas.* London: W. Strahan and M. Woodfall.

Maber, E. and Thornton, R. *The Cases of the Defendant and Plaintiff in Error to be Argued at the Bar of the House of Lords 18 January* 1722.

Murphy, A.E. 1986. *Richard Cantillon: Entrepreneur and Economist.* Oxford: Oxford University Press.

Neal, L. 1994. "'For God's Sake, Remit me': The Adventures of George Middleton, John Law's London Goldsmith-Banker, 1712–1729," *Business and Economic History*, 23(2): 27–60.

2000. "The 'Money' Pitt: Lord Londonderry and the South Sea Bubble, or, How to Manage Risk in an Emerging Market," *Enterprise and Society*, 1(4): 659–74.

Shea, G.S. 2007. "Financial Market Analysis can go Mad (in the Search for Irrational Behaviour during the South Sea Bubble," *Economic History Review*, 60 (4): 742–65.

2007. "Understanding Financial Derivatives during the South Sea Bubble: the Case of the Subscription Shares," *Oxford Economic Papers*, 59 (Suppl. 1): i73–i104.

Sorensen, J. 2004. "Dalrymple, Sir David, First Baronet (c. 1665–1721)," *Oxford Dictionary of National Biography*. Oxford: Oxford University Press.

Additional Manuscripts (Add. MS), British Library (BL).

House of Lords Record Office, Parchment Collection (HLRO).

Portland (Welbeck) [Pw] Collection and Portland (London) [Pl] Collection. Manuscripts and Special Collections, The University of Nottingham.

Records of Courts of Chancery (class C), Exchequer (class E) and King's Bench (class KB), National Archives (NA).

Acts of Parliament

3 Will. & Mary, c. 14

6 Geo. 1, c. 4

7 Geo. 1, c. 5

7 Geo. 1, stat. 2

Private Bill, 1 Geo. 2. c. 5

6 The bell jar: Commercial interest rates between two revolutions, 1688–1789[1]

Marc Flandreau, Christophe Galimard, Clemens Jobst and Pilar Nogués-Marco

> Le problème clef, c'est de savoir pour quelles raisons un secteur de la société d'hier que je n'hésite pas à qualifier de capitaliste, a vécu en système clos, voire enkysté; pourquoi il n'a pas pu essaimer facilement, conquérir la société entière.[2]
>
> (Fernand Braudel, *Civilisation matérielle, économie et capitalisme*, Volume 2: *Les Jeux de l'échange*), p. 289

In our opening quotation, Fernand Braudel likens the development of early modern capitalism to a process occurring inside a "bell jar:" insulated from the rest of the economy and unable to expand to the whole society.[3] The key question for him was to understand why, although the main elements of modern capitalism were already present in the Commercial Revolution, it took so long, until the Industrial Revolution, for capitalism to "conquer" society, and become the dominant organizational mode in the West.

Braudel's puzzle has much relevance for modern development economists. Recently, Hernando de Soto suggested that the bell jar metaphor

---

[1] The authors are grateful to the British Library and the archivists from the Nederlandsch Economisch-Historisch Archief for facilitating access to sources. Availability of the Goldsmith-Kress online library, "The Making of the Modern Economy" (MOME) through a free trial access proved critical. We thank Thomas M. Luckett for sending his unpublished dissertation and François Velde for sharing data on French government bonds with us. The comments of Jeremy Atack, Charlie Calomiris, Guillaume Daudin, Larry Neal, Camila Vam Malle, and conference participants are gratefully acknowledged.

[2] "The key problem is to find out why that sector of society of the past, which I would not hesitate to call capitalist, should have lived as if in a bell jar, cut off from the rest: why was it not able to expand and conquer the whole society?"

[3] By using the expression "bell jar" we follow the wording chosen by Braudel's translator and recently popularized by de Soto, whose website displays a logo with a Wall-Street looking city enclosed in a bell jar and surrounded by deserts. As readers of French can notice, Braudel really referred to "*système clos,*" which could be translated as "secluded" or "self-centered." He also writes "*enkysté,*" evoking the image of a (benign or malign) tumor that has limited interaction with the organism in which it is located.

fairly characterizes today's global financial system.[4] During the past twenty-five years, he argues, many countries have formally opened up to global capital flows, but we still need to see the extreme efficiency displayed by New York's sophisticated financial markets benefit the poor rural areas of Peru, Niger, or India, where credit markets are shallow and interest rates remain high. The implication is that capitalism may thrive in certain areas without inducing rapid progress in other areas.[5] This "Braudelian" puzzle is called by de Soto the "mystery of capital."

This chapter revisits some critical aspects of this mystery of capital within the context of the eighteenth century. Our central theme is to provide a new interpretation of the logic of the historical development of financial markets. We argue that the benchmark money market of the early modern period was the commercial bills market, which had grown outside the reach of legislators and regulators. This market had a global scope because it was collateralized by commodities with an international circulation. The global trading network, in other words, turned out to provide the infrastructure of financial development for merchants fortunate to participate in it, regardless of their nationality. Since merchants could transfer funds as a counterpart to their shipping of commodities, capital was bound to be available at a cost that did not diverge much, on average, across markets that traded with one another. This in turn facilitated the extension of the trading system especially in places and for commodities that caused minimum disruption in the rest of the economy, since this limited the regulatory backlash by temporal and religious authorities. Therefore, the contours of the bell jar coincided with the boundaries of world shipping, and the development of capitalism was confined to the realm of global commerce, "unable to conquer the whole society."

Another contribution of this chapter is to construct new series of commercial interest rates in Amsterdam, London, and Paris. Systematic evidence on these is not available from contemporary sources. This absence is in large part attributable to regulations that set caps on interest rates and deterred contemporaries from giving too much publicity to the business of lending. We measure the opportunity cost of lending by recovering the interest-rate component of foreign exchange quotations.

Finally, the new statistical material presented here shows that, although interest-rate levels were quite similar across markets, suggesting sheer integration, cyclical properties varied considerably, with more volatility

---

[4] de Soto, *The Mystery*.
[5] See World Bank, *World Development Report*, pp. 89–91, for a discussion of the policy implications of this situation.

in certain markets than in others (for instance, movements in Paris appear to have been dominated by seasonal variations). This means that the precise operation of the different credit markets located inside the global system is significant in its own right and calls for more research on markets microstructures.

The remainder of the chapter is organized as follows. The first section discusses contemporary views on how much interest rates differed across countries and why. The second section focuses on prime commercial lending and explains why clean series for interest rates are rare in primary sources. The third section develops a simple model of the bell jar and builds on it an arbitrage formula to retrieve "shadow" interest rates from exchange rate quotations. The fourth section discusses our findings in relation to national and international monetary architecture. The fifth section compares our results with other domestic interest-rate series, yield on government debt, and private returns on land. The last section offers conclusions and directions for future research.

I.   Why do interest rates differ?

A.   *Josiah Child, interest rates, and prosperity*

While it is hard to find consistent interest rate series, P.G.M. Dickson (1967) reckons that economists, policy makers and merchants of the seventeenth and eighteenth centuries were actually *obsessed* with international interest-rate comparison. Edward Hatton writes that "the rate of interest is the sum given for the use of 100 *l.* for one year, and it is in some places more, in others less,"[6] and the reasons *why* they were in some places more and in others less intrigued observers. This is because they perceived that deviations in the price of money bore some relation to respective national economic performances. Prosperity (or, in the language of the time, "riches") was found where interest rates were lowest. Amsterdam was the archetype of cheap money and sheer wealth occurring jointly. He who mastered the mystery of capital would also achieve economic prowess.

Thus causality was found to run from cheap money to prosperity: in the language of the first proponent of this view, Josiah Child, low interest rates were the *"causa causans* [the causing cause] of all other riches of [the Dutch]."[7] "The abatement of the interest", Child claimed, "is the cause of the prosperity and riches of any nation," and to drive home his

---

[6] Hatton, *The Merchant's Magazine*, p. 137.   [7] Child, *Brief Observations*.

point Child's statement was typed in upper case letters. The capital market, he concluded, was the philosopher's stone of development.

Gathering empirical evidence, he further argued that his law of an inverse relation between the level of interest rates and riches did never "fail in any particular instance:" in France, where the rates were at 7 percent, the "Gentry lives in good conditions" but "Peazants are little better than slaves." In Italy, where rates stood at 3 percent, "people are rich, full of trade [and] well attired." The result held in Christendom but also "under the Turk Dominions, East-India, and America."[8]

Child's approach anticipated Douglass North and Barry Weingast's celebrated paper on the relation between Britain's development and its "Financial Revolution" in the late seventeenth century.[9] Child's way of looking at economic progress became a genre in the period that followed. The anonymous author of a pamphlet against high interest rates, writing probably in 1695, argued that, "as it is evident in those Countries viz. in Holland and Italy where Money is at 3 percent, trade flourishes, but in Spain, and other places where the interest of Money is at 10 and 12 percent, the people are poor, and have but little trade."[10] One French economist of the mid-eighteenth century mentions that it is "a widespread opinion nowadays that the interest on money has an influence on agriculture and commerce."[11]

Using the numerous books that compared "national" interest rates, we constructed Figure 6.1 (Table 6A.1 in the Appendix gives background data and sources). The chart captures the well-known downward trend in interest rates already emphasized by Carlo Maria Cipolla (1952). Gregory Clark (2005) argues that "the magnitude of this decline [of interest rates] is little appreciated, its cause is a mystery, and its connection to the shift to an economic system with persistent advance is unknown."[12]

Contemporaries for their part were mostly intrigued by the cross-sectional properties of the data. They found that Holland and – perhaps more surprisingly, in view of recent literature on the topic – Italy, were

---

[8] Child, *Brief Observations*.

[9] North and Weingast, "Constitutions," argue that the Glorious Revolution of 1688 caused a profound reorganization of the institutional design of Britain's government, evidence of which is available in the sharp improvement of borrowing terms after 1688.

[10] *An Answer to a Paper Entitled Reasons Against Reducing Interest to Four Percent*, in Miscellaneous papers on banking, London (1695–1750). British Library (8223e7).

[11] Buchet, *Causes de la diversité*, p. 3 "C'est une opinion aujourd'hui généralement reçue, que l'intérêt de l'Argent a une influence sur l'Agriculture et sur le Commerce. Cette opinion admise, il serait superflu d'examiner s'il est important de connaître les causes qui en déterminent le Taux; l'utilité de cette recherche est évidente."

[12] Clark, "Interest Rate," p. 1.

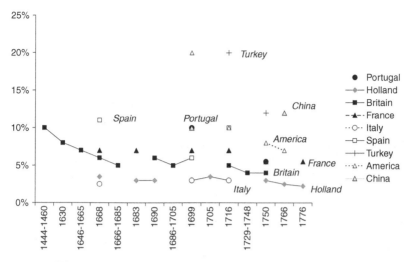

Figure 6.1 Summary of interest rates, 1450–1889.
Source: see Table 6A.1 in the Appendix.

rich countries with low interest rates.[13] Other European nations, such as Britain and France, were found within an interval of about 200 basis points above the two leaders. Britain's spread relative to Holland and Italy declines gradually. On the other hand, non-European countries had much higher rates: China, Turkey, and even such areas of European settlement as the West Indies and the British colonies of North America.

B.   Constitutions, commitments and credit

We have suggested that there is a similarity between contemporary views on the relations between capital markets and development and the ideas articulated more recently by North and Weingast (1989). The parallel is not a superficial one: when they turned to the causes determining the level of interest rates, eighteenth century economists also emphasized institutional and political factors. For instance, one popular explanation of interest-rate differentials was variations in constitutions and commitments. Buchet is a characteristic example, and his rhetoric strikingly "modern:"

This difference [between "national" interest rates] takes its origin in *political and civil constitutions*. If a government can, at will, destroy its obligations whatever its resources and revenues, it will always be riskier to transact with that government, than with another one. *From where it follows that a Monarchy borrows at a higher*

---

[13] On Italy's financial lead, see Fratianni and Spinelli, "Did Genoa?"

rate than a Republic. In the latter, we have individuals transacting with themselves, as members of a society they govern. They do not think of these loans as bearing any further risks than the other loans that are in their hands, and the influence that the various bodies of the state have in most of these governments give to contracts with their general, a degree of trust that the people of a Monarchy never enjoys. If any material proof of this proposition was needed, we would easily find such a state which, while more indebted and with less wealth than others, nonetheless borrows at lower rates.[14]

Buchet was obviously speaking of Britain and his view was not isolated. Dickson identifies this conventional line of thought as the "confidence argument" (a close approximation of what economists call now credibility).[15] It had many other proponents, such as Joseph Massie, who argued: "It is Government, and not nature, which makes Men thus differ from each other."[16] W. Temple emphasized the importance of "safety" for economic development, which could not "grow or thrive" without a "trust in the government, from an Opinion in its strength, wisdom, and justice." Finally, this trust must be grounded "upon the constitutions and order of a state."[17] John Law, who motivated his 1715 project for a French government bank by the need to secure lower interest rates, felt compelled to address, if in the instance to reject, the "*conventional* objection that a government bank would not work [in France], because of the country's political regime and the lack of control on the power of its sovereign."[18] And at the end of the century, Mirabeau summarized: "A constitution: behold the basis of all economics, of all resources, of all confidence, of all power."[19]

---

[14] "Cette différence [entre les taux d'intérêts «nationaux»] prend sa source dans les constitutions politiques et civiles. Si le Gouvernement peut anéantir, quand il le voudra, ses engagements quelles que soient ses forces et ses revenus, les risques seront toujours plus grands dans ses conventions que dans celles d'un autre Etat. De-là vient qu'un Gouvernement Monarchique emprunte à un taux plus haut qu'un gouvernement Républicain. Dans ces Etats ce sont des hommes qui contractent avec eux-mêmes comme membres d'une Société qu'ils forment et qu'ils gouvernent ; ils ne voyent aucuns risques dans ces prêts qui ne soient communs aux biens qui restent dans leurs mains, et l'influence qu'ont dans dans la plûpart de ces Gouvernements tous les ordres de l'Etat donne dans ces conventions au général du peuple une confiance que n'ont Presque jamais au même degré les peuples dans les Monarchies; s'il falloit un exemple pour appuyer cette opinion, on trouveroit aisément un de ces Etats qui quoique plus obéré, et avec moins de richesses que quelques autres, emprunte encore à un Taux plus bas" (Buchet, *Causes de la diversité*, p. 20; emphasis in original).

[15] Dickson, *Financial Revolution*, p. 475.

[16] Massie, *An Essay on the Governing Causes*, p. 57.

[17] Temple, *Observations*, p. 190.

[18] Emphasis added; quoted in Faure, *Banqueroute*, p. 56. Law's *Mémoire* is published in Harsin, ed., *Œuvres complètes*.

[19] Mirabeau, *Suite*, p. 70, quoted in Luckett, *Crédit*, p. 173: "Une constitution: voilà donc la base de toute économie, de toute ressource, de toute confiance, de toute puissance."

Of course, the argument came in various packages. One emphasized the rule of law. Because governments had a responsibility to promote a sound judicial system, the quality of government institutions reverberated on the condition of private credit.[20] Lacking commercial and bankruptcy laws, as well as judges and a police to enforce them, contracts would be plagued with moral hazard and the credit market would disappear.[21] The case was also made by Adam Smith, among many others:

A defect in the law may sometimes raise the rate of interest considerably above what the condition of the country, as to wealth and poverty, would require. *When the law does not enforce the performance of contracts, it puts all borrowers nearly upon the same footing with bankrupts or persons of doubtful credit in better regulated economies. The uncertainty of recovering his money makes the lender exact the same usurious interest which is usually required from bankrupts.* Among the barbarous nations who over-run the western provinces of the Roman Empire, the performance of contracts was left for many ages to the faith of the contracting parties. The courts of justice of their kings seldom intermeddled in it. The high rate of interest which took place in those ancient times may perhaps be partly accounted for from this cause.[22]

A variant emphasized what today's credit agencies refer to as "transfer risks." Poor government credit spills over on private credit because bad governments are likely to expropriate private agents in order to pay off their debts.[23] This view, John Law emphasized, had its origin in medieval conceptions of private ownership, whereby individual agents could not really own assets but only use them as long as the king was gracious enough to let them do so.[24] As a result, governments with poor reputation dragged with them the entire scale of credit toward bankruptcy. As Clavière, a Swiss refugee and financier in Paris, argued: "Lack of public faith would spread general distrust among individuals, because the government can just as well rip off an individual to whom it owes nothing, as it can renege its pledge to those he is indebted to."[25] For how could the law punish private bankruptcies, this same law that has not punished but authorized the general bankruptcy of the government?[26]

---

[20] An anticipation of La Porta *et al.* "Legal determinants" and "Laws and finance."
[21] An anticipation of Akerlof, "Lemons".
[22] Smith, *An Inquiry*, Book I, Chapter ix, p. 133, emphasis added.
[23] Compare Moody's Investor Service, *Revised Country Ceiling Policy*.
[24] See Faure, *Banqueroute* , p. 55.
[25] Quoted in Bouchary, *Manieurs*. "Le manque de foi de la part des gouvernements répandrait une défiance générale entre les individus, car l'Etat peut aussi bien dépouiller l'individu à qui il ne doit rien qu'il peut manquer à sa promesse envers ceux dont il s'est rendu débiteur."
[26] Brissot, *Banqueroute*, as quoted by Luckett, *Crédit*, p. 196.

II.   Challenges of direct evidence

The parallel between contemporary views on credit and modern theories, which the previous section established, is as striking as it is intriguing: seventeenth and eighteenth century economists perceived and analyzed their world in pretty much the same way as today's influential economic historians. On the one hand, this may tell us about the sophistication of contemporary understanding; on the other hand, it may suggest the incompleteness of our current beliefs. Should we trust eighteenth century observers? As Braudel would probably have argued, contemporaries perceive only imperfectly the world in which they live, and we cannot rule out that we too are erring on the wrong side.

A.   Searching for the risk-free rate

The evidence on which contemporaries based their assessment is not airtight. The interest rates reported by Child and included in Figure 6.1 used information from his "acquaintance[s] that had knowledge of foreign countries." We have no idea how Child proceeded or how reliable his acquaintances were. Moreover, there are obviously many interest rates, especially in an underdeveloped economy with huge transaction costs and numerous informational asymmetries.

The issue is illustrated by a fascinating passage of Abbé de Condillac's *Le commerce et le gouvernement* in which he discusses the situation of *"revendeuses des Halles"*, who lived on walking a stock of fresh fish across Paris. They purchased their bundle from the bulk market, the *Halles*, with money borrowed in a way similar to today's "payday loans" (i.e., the loan was repaid as money rolled in from selling out the stock). The interest was *"cinq sols d'intérêt par semaine pour un écu de trois livres,"* enabling Condillac to compute an "exorbitant" interest of 430 percent per year.[27] Condillac argued that such an interest rate must have reflected the market power of the lender and thus is certainly not informative of the "genuine" cost of capital, which he suggested be found in wholesale credit centers. The same would hold of the interest rate at which, say, today's sellers of Biri leaves (a kind of tobacco) in Kolkata's streets secure their capital. There again, the "interest rate" would fail to convey any information on "Indian" interest rates.[28]

---

[27] Condillac, *Commerce*, pp. 147–8

[28] We prefer using this notion rather than the modern concept of "risk free rate," although it was known to contemporaries, as revealed by Massie's sophisticated discussion of "Praemia of Risque." Massie distinguished between sovereign rates, private commercial rates, and the interest rate at which the East India Company secured funds: "Part of the

The matter is further complicated by the existence of usury regulations. The numbers by Hatton (1699, 1716) and included in Table A.6.1 seem to have referred to legal ceilings, not to actual interest rates.[29] A debate exists as to whether legal rates were effective or not. Peter Temin and Joachim Voth (2004) argue they were. They show that the records of Hoare's bank reveal a perfect compliance to ruling usury rates circa 1714, when the legal rate was reduced. This may be too perfect to be true. Historians long emphasized that a current practice was to record a price for the amount of capital to be repaid at a level that would incorporate an adjustment of the official interest rate[30] so that records would look fine. I lend 100£ at 7 percent, but rather than recording this as such, I can record a 102£ loan at 5 percent. Borrowers would certainly not complain, since the alternative was to be turned down. Moreover, once they had agreed to the deal, documents only recorded a lawful interest rate and a capital they had agreed they owed.[31] David Ricardo's own conclusion was that "little dependence for information, then, can be placed on that which is the fixed and legal rate of interest, when we find it may differ so considerably from the market rate."[32]

Praemium which lenders receive under the name of interest, is, in all cases where there is Danger of losing, a Praemium of Risque, and not of Use; and there being a very great Risque of losing, where borrowers have, by their extravagance, spent one half of what was lent to them, a considerable part of the praemium paid for money by such borrowers is certainly a premium of indemnity and not of Use; and to call it interest, is as improper as it would be to call that praemium interest which a Merchant gives an Insurer to have his ship or Merchandize insured against the dangers of the Sea or Enemies: so that what is disguised under the Name of high interest, is in fact no such Thing, but a Praemium of Use and Risque joined together, which may just as well be called high Insurance as high Interest, for it is as much the one as the other," *Essay*, pp. 20–2. Similarly, Temple, *Observations*, dwelled on the differences between "country risk" and "sovereign risk," referred to as "private" and "publick safety."

[29] Indeed, Hatton, *The Merchant's Magazine*, gave 6 percent as the interest rate in Britain. This was the usury rate prevailing at the time. This number is revised to 5 percent in the next edition (1716), following the 1714 abatement of the usury ceiling to 5 percent.

[30] See e.g. Luckett, *Crédit*.

[31] Luckett, *Crédit*: "There probably never was a time in European history when usury laws actually prevented lenders from charging interest, but it should be clear from the foregoing that the formal compliance with these laws shaped the form and function of credit instruments by forcing business people to disguise interest payments as something else . . . Short term credit at interest was disguised as credit without interest by the simple trick of including the interest payment with the principal. Peter purchases from Paul, on credit, a quantity of merchandise priced at 100£, for which he writes out a promise to pay Paul in six months the amount of 102£ 10s. Who is to say that the latter figure was not actually the cash price? Certainly the note itself contains no indication that interest has been charged."

[32] As Ricardo went on: "Adam Smith informs us, that from the 37th of Henry VIII to 21st of James I, 10 per cent continued to be the legal rate of interest. Soon after the Restoration, it was reduced to 6 per cent, and by the 12th of Anne, to 5 per cent. He thinks

Benchmarks   We think the best way to measure the opportunity cost of capital (the "benchmark" interest rate) during the period under study is to look at short-term commercial rates: the rates at which credit was extended to a merchant banker of high standing by his correspondents in other cities.

This benchmark is analytically distinct from, though not necessarily inconsistent with, the approach by Clark (1996), who calculates private interest rates in England using the return on land and on rent charges. It is, however, in contrast with the emphasis on sovereign bond prices in North and Weingast (1989) and more recently in Nathan Sussman and Yishay Yafeh (2006).[33] Our benchmark is recommended by a number of contemporary observers of the capital market. According to the British economist Massie (1750), the "risk free rate" was provided by the rate at which "a reputable Merchant or Tradesman [can borrow money] upon his bond or note." He took such an interest rate as the "standards for determining the rates of interest upon real and personal Securities" and recommended using this interest rate to compute the risk premium paid by other borrowers.[34] As already argued, Condillac concurred that a reliable measure of the cost of capital would be interest rates in leading commercial centers, "because money, in trading centers, has one price, just like corn has a price in markets . . . and money is sold there just like any other commodity."[35]

One further reason for using merchant bankers' interest rates is their long noted ability to escape usury regulations altogether. According to Raymond de Roover (1953), bills of exchange (i.e., promises to pay a certain amount in a given place at a later date) were the instruments of choice whereby promoters of the commercial revolution managed to escape usury ceilings. Unlike other financial instruments, such as France's *billets à ordre*, which had a local circulation and were thus subject to regulation, bills of exchange incorporated a convenient spatial dimension.[36]

---

the legal rate followed, and did not precede the market rate of interest. Before the American war, Government borrowed at 3 per cent, and the people of credit in the capital, and in many other parts of the kingdom at 3 1/2, 4 and 4 1/2 per cent," *Principles*, Chap. XXI.

[33] We return to this point in the last section of the paper.

[34] His conclusion was that "we need only subtract from the Rates paid by other People the Rates paid by the Gentleman, Merchant, or Tradesman, and the remainder will be Praemia of Risque," p. 21.

[35] "Parce que l'argent dans les places de commerce a un prix courant, comme le bled en a un dans les marchés. On traite publiquement, ou du moins on ne se cache point; et on vend son argent comme on vendroit toute autre marchandise" (Condillac, *Commerce*, p. 148).

[36] On *"billets à ordre"*, see e.g. Fuleman, *Traité*, pp. 8–9.

The price they charged on bills of exchange, the bankers emphasized, was motivated by the risks and efforts associated with overcoming the obstacles of foreign settlement.[37] Consequently, foreign exchange bills were an ideal place to hide a loan, and the exchange rate an ideal place to hide an interest rate.

The problem may be stated as follows. Suppose that legislation prevents interest rates from rising above a certain ceiling, which would constitute "usury." This obviously puts a severe constraint on the growth of formal credit markets: instead of charging higher interest rates when market conditions deteriorate, agents face a choice of either cheating or rationing.[38] However, suppose that bankers are entitled to buy and sell bills of exchange payable in foreign centers, and assume again that there is a sudden need to push interest rate above the usury ceiling. In this case, whereas domestic bankers cannot legally lend at the new interest rate, foreign bankers can buy bills on that center at a low price, in effect incorporating the unlawful interest rate. If one has a correspondent in each market, one can then arrange swaps that formally are exchange operations but really are credit operations. For legislators, it is hard to argue that bill prices in foreign centers are low because local interest rates are high, since lending does not exist in the first place or, if it does exist formally, it exists at a price that meets regulations. Moreover, as emphasized by Eric Kerridge, even church regulators had always been kinder with inter-merchant credit, in which they saw agreements between consenting adults.[39] But the fact remains that a low price for bills is the same as a high interest rate.[40]

A statement of this mechanism is provided in an early discussion by Gerard de Malynes (1601, p. 120). In effect, Malynes (a Huguenot) saw global finance as a social "canker," or cancer, given its ability to circumvent legislations. As he explained, there are regulations on interest rates but not on exchange rates, so that a foreign investment (the purchase of a

---

[37] Formal legislation incorporated this principle, which was kept in force all over Europe until the early nineteenth century. De Roover, *L'évolution*, p. 45, gives Napoléon's *Code de Commerce* as a late example.

[38] The point was first made by Montesquieu's *Lettres Persanes*. His critique was formally directed against Muslim's sharia but really targeted Christianity. Adam Smith discusses this point in the passage referred to earlier, and where he likens interest prohibition to a failure of the rule of law: "When the law prohibits interest altogether, it does not prevent it. Many people must borrow, and nobody will lend without such a consideration for the use of their money as is suitable, not only to what can be made by the use of it, to the difficulty and danger of evading the law. The high rate of interest among all Mahometan nations is accounted for by Mr. Montesquieu; not from their poverty, but partly from this, and partly from the difficulty of recovering the money," Smith, *Inquiry*, Book I, Chapter IX, p. 133.

[39] Kerridge, *Usury, passim*.   [40] See Munro, "Origins," for a recent statement.

foreign bill) can produce a bigger interest rate than domestic credit, which British regulations of the time limited to 10 percent:

> The difference betwixt those that deliver their money at interest or by exchange, in regard of usurie, consisteth onely in the name, for they have both an intention of gaine upon money, and do beare an adventure for the losse of their monies, where as the one is certaine to have no more but ten upon the hundredth at the most, and the other doth expect at least 15. or 20. upon the hundredth, in regard whereof he is contended to stand in adventure to lose sometimes (and that seldome) by exchanges, but still the intention remaineth, which should be the surest guide of conscience to take away false or counterfeit pretences.

By the end of the eighteenth century, financial innovation had reached such a level of perfection that bankers could rely on a vast array of credit instruments based on derivatives of bills of exchange. These are described in the various editions of the *Negociator's Magazine*, a leading financial textbook of the time.[41] After a concise presentation of plain vanilla bills of exchange (called "real exchange"), the book gets into a long list of hot ways to use "dry exchange" meant to circumvent regulations and thus perform "usury" – that is, lend locally rather than internationally to yield a return that did not consider usury constraints.

These operations were typically over-the-counter transactions between agents who were "feigning an exchange."[42] For instance, a banker in city A agreed to buy a first foreign bill payable in city B and use the proceeds to purchase at the maturity of that bill a second "return" bill payable in city A, thereby creating what was essentially a local loan. Hayes indicates that such an operation could be either covered or uncovered depending on whether bankers had agreed in advance on the price of the return bill.[43] If the operation was covered then it was bound by arbitrage to yield the same return as a local loan, had such a contract existed. If finance theory is a guide, the price of bills of exchange must have incorporated an implicit interest rate equal to the interest rate that would have been charged every time this could be done in the open, as was the case when interest rates were low or toward the late eighteenth century, as tolerance for credit increased.[44]

In summary, exchange bills were "off shore" financial products that could be combined in many creative ways to replicate missing instruments. This was well recognized by the economists of the time such as

---

[41] Hayes. *Negociator Magazine*.   [42] de Roover. "What is Dry Exchange?"
[43] He states: "In dry exchange, sometimes the Sum to be repaid for the Sum received is fixed, determined, or certain, and sometimes uncertain or accidental," *Negociator Magazine*, p. 3.
[44] Carrière *et al.*, *Banque et capitalisme*, p. 32.

Condillac, who argued that "legislators condemn lending on interest, and they allow it. . . . For, they do not object to exchange bills and they do object to lending on interest. . . . Are lending and borrowing anything else than an exchange transaction?"[45] Condillac's assessment resounds as the late eighteenth century's pragmatic answer to Malynes's earlier moral concerns. Through the agency of bills of exchange, credit had become a fact of life.

The case of the missing commercial rate   We therefore set out to collect data on the interest rate at which merchant bankers involved in long-distance trade would borrow or lend money. This is more easily said than done. Direct evidence on commercial interest rates is exceedingly difficult to come by. Whichever financial center we are looking at, there are no recorded series of "money market" rates for the period before the French Revolution. Rather, such series generally start around the second half of the nineteenth century. This seems to conflict with the earlier indication that contemporaries knew what they were talking about when they mentioned "national interest rates" but it is consistent with the fact that we are dealing with an over-the-counter market. In order for "one" price to be recorded and quoted, a formal centralized market must be organized. This requirement was not met by the credit markets of the time, since interest rates resulted from bilateral drawing arrangements that were in turn put to work as a lever for operating on the foreign exchange market. Formalization and centralization prevailed in the foreign exchange market, not in the money market. As a result, a precise notion of the "general interest rate," meaning probably the typical conditions that the best houses in a center would extend to their correspondent in another center, must have existed as a kind of "mental average" in the mind of contemporary practitioners but was nowhere to be quoted. Yet the "local" interest rate that a banker would extend to his correspondent could not really be made public, since when it was too high it was not supposed to exist at all. Thus, although observers had a precise notion of what interest rates were and meant in time and space, those rates are quite elusive when one tries to catch them.[46]

---

[45] "Les législateurs condamnent le prêt à intérêt et ils le tolèrent . . . . En effet, ils ne blâment pas le change et ils blâment le prêt à intérêt. . . . Le prêt et l'emprunt sont-ils autre chose qu'un change?" *Commerce*, p. 141.

[46] Reflecting on this paradox, Lüthy, *Banque protestante*, p. 435 wondered how contemporary authors could be so sure when they mentioned, say, that discount rates "stood in France at 6%" when "the actual business of local discounting had not come to age" ("D'après les auteurs économistes du temps – mais où prennent-ils cette assurance puisque l'escompte des lettres de change n'est pas encore entré dans les usages? – le taux d'escompte courant en France est de 6%").

These considerations shed light on the significance of the alternative sources that are nonetheless available. One is the interest rates at which banks of issue would discount bills when they did. Since these banks had commercial activities, such rates must have been related to the price at which other institutions engaged in lending activity. On the other hand, banks of issue were typically not merchant banks and hence were subject to public scrutiny. As a result, the indications they provide are a bit off the mark and probably not much better than legal rates. Another possible source is occasional reports in contemporary commercial letters, reflecting what observers felt was "the" relevant rate at a given time in a given commercial community (i.e., financial center). Provided such reports come from relevant persons (i.e., genuine operators) they must be trustworthy. This encourages using archives in order to be as close as possible to where the business of merchant banking was taking place, as opposed to relying on a patchwork of comments in the secondary literature. Ideally, one would want to find systematic information on bilateral drawing conventions between correspondents, since they would state the interest rate at which business would be conducted even as the private nature of these documents helped them eschew legislation. However, archives are not a magic bullet. Sheer luck is involved, and the cost of collecting information can become prohibitive. Beyond the problem of the significance of the material they contain, we want to make sure that we focus on really top signatures, i.e., "risk free", not an "average" merchant, or industrialist of good standing.[47] The intersection of these constraints with what little material is available may be zero.

Thus, interest-rate collectors have tended to be eclectic in their choice of sources, as illustrated by Sidney Homer and Richard Sylla's pioneering work.[48] These authors provide some numbers for the markets on which this paper focuses. For Amsterdam, they follow a British parliamentary report suggesting an interval of between 2 percent to 3 percent for the period 1735–1738.[49] This is below the range (of 3 percent to 3.5 percent) that Pierre de la Court, writer of several financial handbooks, indicated for "commercial interest" in 1671.[50] Elisabeth de Jong-Keesing

[47] For instance, Etienne, *Veuve Cliquot*, p. 183 discusses the case of credit lines that the bank Lowenberg & Leclerc extended to the champagne maker Ponsardin et fils (predecessor of today's Veuve Clicquot) at 6–7 percent in the early nineteenth century. This is substantially higher than the prime banker interest-rate quotes we find for the same date. Ponsardin might have been a first-class house, but the credit in question is more like an industrial credit with default risk included.

[48] See Homer and Sylla's most recent edition of *Interest Rates*.

[49] Clapham, *Bank of England*, vol. I, p. 93; quoted in Homer and Sylla, *Interest Rates*, p. 176.

[50] Saugrain, *Baisse*, p. 108 who reportedly follows books by Aulnis de Bourrouil and d'Avenel.

(1939) studied the crisis of 1763 from bankers' archives and found (unsurprisingly) somewhat higher rates (between 4 percent and 6 percent). As far as we know, there are no continuous series for the Bank of Amsterdam, although it reportedly started to discount bills in the eighteenth century.[51] R.V. Eagly and V.K. Smith (1976) mistakenly refer to a series in N.W. Posthumus (1946) as an "interest rate" series while it is really the agio of the Bank of Amsterdam.[52] More frequent references to market rates in Amsterdam are available toward the later part of the century, and it is likely that a series could be put together with some additional effort. The article by C.H. Wilson (1939) refers to the work by J.G. Van Dillen (ca. 1930, p. 3633), which contains additional evidence.[53]

To our knowledge, no source documents short-term commercial interest rates in London. Homer and Sylla rely on Clapham (1944), who gave some rates for the Bank of England that correspond to bills drawn within Britain and from abroad. They argue that this rate was "usually at or near the legal maximum" (Homer and Sylla 2005, p. 163). This would suggest that the rate fails to reflect the genuine cost of borrowed capital.[54] We are not aware of studies documenting interbank discount rates during the period under study.

Evidence for France is even more patchy. Homer and Sylla rely extensively on a late nineteenth century dissertation by G. Saugrain (1896). Saugrain indicated rates for France in the early eighteenth century ranging between 4 percent and 10 percent, but he stated that rates did not exceed 6 percent after 1776.[55] Direct evidence from bankers' correspondence supports slightly lower rates. René Squarzoni quotes reports in the late 1720s giving 6 percent as the "norm" in Lyons, though "scarcity" may have caused interest rates to rise as high as 9 percent.[56] Sources quoted by Herbert Lüthy (1959) also suggested

---

[51] Vilar, *Or et monnaie.*

[52] The "agio" was the market swap rate between current coins and deposit balances at the Bank of Amsterdam. For a recent discussion see Quinn and Roberds, "Economic Explanation."

[53] "The permanent stimulus to foreign investment was the low rate of interest in Holland. In the seventeenth century it had fallen from 6 1/2 to 3 1/2 and in the eighteenth century it was 3 to 2 1/2 per cent." Wilson, "Economic Decliner," p. 122. We referred to Van Dillen, *Bronnen*, which does not contain more information but does use to original sources: rates for "commercial loans" that the Bank of Amsterdam made to some private merchants.

[54] Note, however, that "usury" (i.e., the maximum legal interest rate) was at 5 percent after 1714 and that the Bank of England rate was at 4 percent during most of the century.

[55] "En réalité, c'est entre 4 et 5% qu'il faut évaluer le taux de l'intérêt au XVIIIème siècle . . . L'escompte ne dépassait pas 6%," Saugrain, *Baisse*, p. 107.

[56] Squarzoni, *Mécanismes*, p. 283. "La puissante maison Sellon confirme ce point de vue en indiquant à nouveau le taux de 6% l'an comme *norme* à Lyon pour les négociants et banquiers de premier rang. . . . Lyon, Sellon père et fils, 6 Novembre 1729 . . . 1 1/2 %

that, from mid century onward, interest rates in France might have been lower: close to 4 percent on average.[57] Sources for the late eighteenth century mentioned Paris interest rates of about 4–4.5 percent in 1790[58] as well as foreign drawing arrangements on Paris at 5 percent in 1789.[59]

A rare discovery is that of Thomas Luckett (1992) who found that, for about fifteen years (1746–1759), *Les Affiches*, a French commercial newspaper that appeared twice weekly, reported indications on interest rates on bills of exchange (*lettre de change*) and for financial bills (*billet de finance*) – that is, secured and unsecured bankers drafts.[60] According to this source, the interest rate for bills of exchange remained at 6 percent from 1746 (when the *Affiches* started being published) to April 1749, was then reported at 5 percent until September 1758, and then returned to 6 percent. Luckett expresses reservations about these quotations, which fail to display the "kind of volatility one would expect from a financial market," and concludes that the rates reported may have represented a "kind of norm."[61] In any case, the series lapses in 1759, and we can only speculate on the reasons for this.

III.   Shadow interest rates

A.   The bell jar: a model

Consider the following thought experiment. The world is made of *n* trading centers. As in Condillac (1776), there are strict controls on domestic credit but no controls on capital movements. Merchant bankers can buy and sell foreign exchange bills, which are promises to pay a certain amount of money in a certain foreign trading center at a certain

qui est le cours d'un seul paiement pour les gens solides comme vous et nous. (6% l'an)." On high rates: "Lyon, Melchior Philibert, 8 avril 1729, notre dit paiement s'est terminé sans aucun dérangement quoique l'argent *soit ici fort rare*, lequel a valu *jusqu' à* 2 1/2 % [i.e., 9% per year]." Squarzoni, *Mécanismes*, p. 284.

[57] Lüthy, *Banque protestante*, p. 434. Lüthy cites Isaac Mallet, a "retired banker" in Geneva who lent at 4 percent. But Geneva is not France. He also mention a French institution, the *Caisse d'Escompte* (created March 23, 1776) that "peut escompter tout papier commercial sans aucune clause de précaution relative à la qualité de ce papier ou de ses signatures; mais son taux d'escompte ne pourra jamais dépasser 4% par an." Note that the *Caisse* was somewhat specific and thus may not be representative.

[58] Letter to Froust and Guinebaud in Nantes, Antonetti, *Une maison*, p. 146.

[59] Arrangement between banker Greffuhle Montz et Cie in Paris and Courtiau Echenique Sanchez in Amsterdam, Antonetti, *Une maison*, p. 146.

[60] By "secured" we refer to bills of exchange that were the counterpart of a commercial transaction; "unsecured" bills were not. The *Affiches* also gave interest rates for promissory notes (*billets à ordre*), but in view of our discussion the bills of exchange are to be preferred.

[61] Luckett, *Credit*, p. 31

time, say two months in the future. To simplify, regulations prevent the emergence of a market for domestic credit so that there is no such thing as a "local" interest rate (an interest rate at which local bankers would lend money to one another). Suppose as well that there are no transaction costs and that all markets use the same currency, so that there is no exchange risk. This convenient assumption will be amended at a later stage.

Now, we let merchant bankers trade their bills of exchange all over the world. In equilibrium, this determines a uniform "world" interest rate, say r. This is because if the rate at which bankers agree to swap their positions differs from unity, then arbitrage is feasible. This also determines the price at which foreign exchange bills trade in each market. Let's call this price the "exchange rate," or a_{ij}. It is the price bankers in market i are prepared to pay in order to purchase one unit of "universal" currency to be paid in market j within, say, two months. If the world interest rate r is expressed in percentage per annum and the maturity of the bill is two-months (one-sixth of a year)

$$a_{ij} = \frac{1}{1+r/6} \tag{1}$$

This shows that merchants need not quote the interest rate r but only the exchange rate. The crucial point to understand is that, despite the lack of a domestic money market, there does exist a global capital market and a global interest rate, thanks to the availability of a global foreign exchange market with time contracts. This global interest rate, however, is a "shadow" interest rate in that it is not recorded in any periodical or price current. It exists only implicitly in the price at which bankers are prepared to trade domestic balances against foreign time deposits. This world displays a peculiar form of financial development; an efficient global market for credit will thrive, despite the lack of domestic markets.

Obviously, if there were local markets for credit, these markets would have to clear at the same price as implied by equilibrium in the global money market (as will be discussed later), so that local interest rates should be identical to global ones. But the point is that such local markets need not exist. Consequently, the existence of local markets is not a precondition for the development of a global money market. This is the essence of the bell jar.[62] Globalization may precede national development.

---

[62] In fact, our model captures the notion that financial development is a process that proceeded "top-down" – that is, from the making of a global market to the emergence of local ones. The Commercial Revolution, by creating a network of correspondent

Two slight complications are now introduced to make our framework more realistic. First, exchange rates can vary. Merchant bankers buying bills denominated in specific currencies must adjust the world interest rate according to their expectations of future exchange rate changes. The result is k potentially different local interest rates whose prices incorporate compensation for expected appreciation or depreciation with respect to the virtual global currency standard. Depreciating currencies will have higher interest rates, appreciating currencies lower ones. Second, there are transaction costs. These entail a lower price (higher interest rates) for bills of exchange that are payable in trading centers characterized by greater frictions. In practice, since transaction costs are likely to be determined by bilateral characteristics (such as the greater or smaller number of correspondents that trading center i has in market j), there are $k-1$ different local shadow interest rates for each individual centre. Obviously, arbitrage ensures that the $k-1$ shadow interest rates for market j differ little from one another, since with zero transaction costs they should be all identical. But the point is that the modern notion of a national interest rate just doesn't exist as such. In this economy, we have only "bilateral" interest rates, i.e., interest rates in city j as seen from i.

Our empirical approach builds on this insight. Specifically, we consider the following arbitrage, which is a generalization of (1). There are two bills of exchange of different maturities traded in a given market (i) and payable in a certain foreign center (j). Denoting by a_{ij} the number of units of currency i that bankers give to get one unit of currency j in country j in n months and x_{ij} the number of units of currency i that bankers give to obtain one unit of currency j in country j on the spot, we have r_j^i as the shadow interest rate in center j "according" to center i:

$$r_j^i = \frac{12}{n} \cdot \left(\frac{x_{ij}}{a_{ij}} - 1 \right) \tag{2}$$

To be precise, r_j^i is the marginal interest rate in center j as given by center i. "Marginal" means the following: suppose that in market i, where bills on j are being traded, there is a number of bankers who have

bankers working along trade relations, fostered the development of a global credit market that could prosper quite apart from the rest of the economy and that must therefore have preceded local development, explaining why local interest rates are hard to come by: the only thing that existed was the concept of the opportunity cost of lending real resources.

various drawing arrangements with their correspondents in market *j*. Banker A can lend and borrow from his correspondent at 4 percent, Banker B at 5 percent, Banker C at 5.5 percent, and so forth. Suppose now that the exchange rate on two-month bills payable in *j* falls to a price such that the shadow interest rate in *j* is 4.5 percent. Only banker A will find it profitable to buy such bills. Consequently, *the shadow interest rate reveals the opportunity cost of a draft on j by the most competitive merchant banker in center i.*

In practice, of course, things must have been dramatically more complex. When one drew a bill on a foreign center, one could never be entirely sure of the conditions there. The correspondent might have changed terms or even gone bust. There was thus an inevitable element of chance. Therefore, the series we are about to uncover reflects a given market's perceptions of the conditions in another foreign market at a given time. This is certainly not the same thing as knowing the actual interest rate in that center, if such an interest rate existed at all. But we must emphasize that in the eighteenth century, that's all there was.

B.   Methodology

In the literature, arbitrage relations between exchange rates and interest rates have been used in two main ways. Some studies have sought to derive the missing term of the equation: to compute implicit interest rates from knowledge of the price of spot and time exchange bills as just explained or, more often, to compute a spot exchange-rate series from knowledge of the price of time bills and interest rates. Foreign exchange quotations recorded the price of "notional" contracts, typically a one, two, or three-month bill payable in a given foreign place.[63] However, comparisons require putting all exchange rates on the same time

---

[63] Reference to future payments has misled a number of authors, who have referred to these quotations as "forward exchange rates." For instance, Juhl *et al.*, "Covered Interest Arbitrage," argue that they introduce a "new weekly database for spot and *forward* US–UK exchange rates." However, these authors really refer to time bills of exchange. This is inadequate because a forward exchange contract implies no current down payment whereas quotations for time bills of exchange recorded outright purchases, implying full payment. Obstfeld and Taylor, "Globalization," refer to the exercises they perform with time bills as "*Covered Interest Parity [CIP] tests*" (a language that is also used by Juhl *et al.*, "Covered Interest Arbitrage." Since CIP is a condition on the pricing of forward markets, these authors must think of time bills as genuine forward instruments.

footing – that is, transforming the various time quotations to a common maturity and contemporaries used such algebra.[64]

Similar computations first appeared in the work of economic historians with Lance Davis and Jonathan Hughes' 1960 construction of what they call a "true" dollar–sterling spot exchange rate series for 1803–1895. Davis and Hughes discount the price of sterling time bills they found in Trotter bank's archive using the interest in New York, arguing: "Had Trotter not purchased time-bills of exchange, he could have invested in American earning assets."[65] However, according to Edwin Perkins (1975, 1978) this approach is inadequate. Time bills on London traded in New York should be discounted using the London rate because, by arbitrage, a London time bill in New York is equivalent to a transfer of funds to London (at the current exchange rate) and a subsequent deposit at the London interest rate. Perkin's approach is now conventional and, in effect, consistent with both economic logic and contemporaries' recommendations. Lawrence Officer provides the general formula for converting the price of time bills into a spot foreign exchange quotation when both the local interest rate r_j and the n-month exchange rate a_{ij} are known:[66]

$$x_{ij}^* = a_{ij} \cdot \left(1 + r_j \cdot \frac{n}{12}\right) \tag{3}$$

---

[64] An illustration of this is found in William Tate's discussion of "arbitrations of exchanges," where he explains how, given an interest rate, "sight" rates can be computed from knowledge of the price of time bill. Tate, *Modern Cambist*, pp. 89–90; "The two places of operation should be taken at a long date as three months, and then discounted . . . according to the rate charged by the two houses of business. . . . To show how to apply this discount properly, we will take the rates at the following example . . .

London on Paris at 3 months is quoted Fr. 25 55 Cents

Paris on London at 3 months – Fr. 25 10 Cents

The discount for 3 months is there stated to be taken at 1 per Cent or 25 Cents (the interest is here reckoned at 4 per Cent per Annum), which is taken from the London rate, and added to the Paris rate to make them Short or Cash rates; rendering the one Frs. 25 30 Cents and the others Frs. 25 35 Cents. The interest is taken from the London rate, because if I send the Bill to Paris, and get it discounted there, the Interest will be deducted; but it is added to the Paris rate, because, if at Paris I want a bill upon London at sight, I shall have more French money to pay for it, than I should have to Pay for a Bill at three months." See also Tate, *Foreign Exchanges*.

[65] They continue in a footnote: "Trotter was, in fact, granting credit to Americans, and thus the bill prices reflect an interest payment. Moreover, *since credit was being granted in the American market, the discount on the bills was the American rate. This is true regardless of what Trotter's British correspondents did with the remitted bills -whether they were held until the British importer paid them at maturity, or had them discounted in Britain,*" Davis, "Dollar Sterling Exchange," p. 53, emphasis added.

[66] Officer, *Gold points*, pp. 61, 295.

Another group of studies has been concerned with matters of market integration.[67] Efficiency requires that local interest rates and shadow interest rates, *when they both exist*, be identical to one another. Formally, these studies have considered the spread between actual and implicit interest rates. Under efficiency, this spread should be zero:

$$r_j^i - r_j = 0 \tag{4}$$

Marc Flandreau and Chantal Rivière explore the theoretical foundations for this relation. They show that the actual interest rate is a *lower bound* for the shadow interest rate. Specifically, shadow rates are kept within a fluctuation band. The upper bound is the actual interest rate augmented by a factor related to arbitrage costs. The key intuition is that agents incur a transaction cost when they move capital from one market to the other: Although bills can readily be cashed in their domestic market, buying them in a foreign exchange market and then repatriating them for purposes of arbitrage entails expenses c. As a result, the shadow interest rate is always above the actual interest rate:[68]

$$r_j \leq r_j^i \leq r_j + \frac{12}{n} \cdot c \tag{5}$$

Focusing on the Paris shadow interest rates and the Paris actual open market interest rates derived from London sources during 1900–1914, Flandreau and Rivière show that (5) performs very well empirically, suggesting no hindrances to credit and foreign exchange operations during that period.[69]

---

[67] Calomiris and Hubbard, "International Adjustment"; Obstfeld and Taylor, "Great Depression"; "Globalization"; Flandreau and Rivière, "Grande Retransformation"; Juhl *et al.*, "Covered Interest Arbitrage."

[68] See Flandreau and Rivière, "Grande Retransformation" for details.

[69] Flandreau and Rivière's claim that the shadow interest rate is, in the context of nineteenth century arbitrage, an upper bound for the actual interest rate is also illustrated in graphs provided by Calomiris and Hubbard, "International Adjustment" (Figures 7.1 and 7.2) for the US dollar. In addition, our Appendix shows that the existence of transaction costs implies that local market conditions do have an effect on the shadow interest rate. This can be understood as follows. Suppose that the domestic interest rate rises. Investors thus sell some foreign assets and switch to domestic ones. The result is a decline in the price of foreign time bills and hence an increase in the computed shadow interest rate. But because there are transaction costs, this may not affect actual interest rates abroad. One should thus expect that, though shadow interest rates are primarily driven by foreign ones, an effect of domestic credit conditions is nonetheless perceivable on the margin.

Table 6.1. *Exchange market money market arbitrage operations: survey*

	Authors	Country pair/period	Output
Arbitrated exchange rate or interest rate			
Shadow exchange rate	Davis and Hughes (1960)	New York/London (1803–1895)	Shadow spot exchange rate dollar/sterling
	Perkins (1978)	New York/London (1835–1900)	Shadow spot exchange rate dollar/sterling
	Schubert (1989)	London/Amsterdam/ Paris/Hamburg/ Lisbon (1731–1795)	Shadow cross rates Amsterdam on Hamburg, Paris, Lisbon through London; London on Hamburg, Paris, Lisbon through Amsterdam
Shadow interest rate	Perkins (1978)	New York/London (1835–1900)	Shadow interest rate in London from New York
	Eagly and Smith (1976)	London/Amsterdam (1731–1789)	In effect: shadow interest rate in Amsterdam from London[*]
	Schubert (1989)	London/Paris/ Amsterdam (1731–1795)	Shadow interest rates in Amsterdam and in Paris from London
	Luckett (1992)	London/Paris (1740–1789)	Shadow interest rate in Paris
	Boyer-Xambeu *et al.* (1995)	London/Paris and Paris/London (1795–1873)	Shadow interest rate in London and Paris
	Boyer-Xambeu *et al.* (2001)	London/Paris (1833–1873)	Shadow interest in Paris from London and in London from Paris
Onshore/offshore spreads			
Compute interest spread	Calomiris and Hubbard (1996)	New York on London: shadow London minus London (1889–1909)	
	Obstfeld and Taylor (1998)	New York on London: shadow London minus London (1870–1914)	
	Flandreau and Rivière (1999)	London on Paris: shadow Paris, and interest arbitrage band for shadow Paris (1900–1914)	

Table 6.1. (*cont.*)

Authors	Country pair/period Output
Boyer-Xambeu *et al.* (2001)	London on Paris: shadow Paris minus Paris; and Paris on London: shadow London minus London rates (1833–1873)
Obstfeld and Taylor (2003)	New York on London: shadow London minus London rate (1870–1880); London on Berlin: shadow Berlin minus Berlin (1877–1914)
Juhl *et al.* (2004)	New York on London: shadow London minus London (1880–1913)

Source: see text.* Eagly and Smith argue that they are computing a London rate, but they actually calculate the Amsterdam interest rate because they use the price of bills on Amsterdam traded in London.

In the rest of the paper, we apply the methodology detailed previously and compute implicit (or, in the language of the time, "arbitrated") interest rates from the exchange rates of the *schelling vlaamsch* Banco of Amsterdam, the British pound sterling, and the French *écu* (of three livres tournois) during the eighteenth century. This follows Eric Schubert who computes point wise eighteenth century shadow interest rates for Amsterdam and Paris, and Luckett (1992), who constructs a series of monthly average French shadow interest rates from exchange rates in London during 1740–1789.[70]

Our goal is to provide more systematic evidence by considering a greater number of countries and longer time periods. We also want to give a more explicit interpretation of the output of such exercises. A convenient, if anachronistic, metaphor would be to liken our new shadow interest rate to the interest rate on money balances denominated in a given currency in an offshore market, such as the Eurodollar market that developed in London in the 1950s following the tightening of credit conditions in New York and the existence of a binding regulation on dollar interest rates – the infamous regulation Q.[71] In other words, what we are really computing is, in a world of credit controls, the interest rate

[70] Specifically, Schubert, "Arbitrage," computes average shadow interest rates from bills in London on Amsterdam and Paris for periods between four and fifteen years and then applies a uniform 4.3 percent to various series to derive spot exchange rates. The 4.3 percent is "in the range of interest rates observed in typical long bills in London on Amsterdam" (p. 3).
[71] Schenk, "The Origins."

on "Euro-*écus*" and "Euro-*schellings*" in London as well as the interest rate on "Euro-pounds" in Amsterdam. The euro-currency metaphor squares nicely with the notion of our "shadow" interest rates being the price that would clear the supply and demand of credit in a cosmopolitan "Republic of Merchants."

IV.   New results, new insights

Previous research by Larry Neal and others has demonstrated the value of "courses of exchange" as reliable sources of information for quantitative financial historians. Consequently, we content ourselves with briefly surveying the sources and move swiftly to the estimation techniques and results.

A.   Minutiae

We have relied on Castaing's *Course of Exchange* (London) and on the *Koers de Koopmanschappen* (Amsterdam). The *Course of the Exchange* is from the collections of the University of London Library and British Museum and the *Lloyd's List*.[72] Our database is more complete than similar ones used in literature.[73] The *Course* provides the implicit interest rate in Amsterdam and Paris only since these are the cities for which both two-month and sight maturities are recorded.[74] We have collected the first quotation of each month; because exchange was quoted twice a week (Tuesday and Friday), the first quotation of the month means the 1st, 2nd, 3rd or 4th of each month.[75] For each date, a

---

[72] *The Course of the Exchange* (1698–1810) University of London Library Collection and British Museum Collection; British Library (St. Pancras). *Lloyd's List* (1741–1826), reprinted in 1969 by Gregg International Publishers Ltd; of Farnborough, England.

[73] McCusker, *Money*, and the most quoted secondary source, Schneider *et al.*, *Statistik*. Our London database is missing only one entry: that corresponding to February 2, 1778, when there was no quotation for Amsterdam. Double quotation for Amsterdam started in November 1720 and for Paris in February 1740. Data stopped between 1793 and 1802 for Paris and between 1795 and 1802 for Amsterdam. Our calculations run only through 1789 in order to avoid the high distortion in data caused by the French Revolution.

[74] Neal, *Rise*, pp. 20–43, compiles a full explanation of stock price lists in London and Amsterdam during eighteenth century. McCusker, *Money*, and McCusker and Gravesteijn, *Beginnings*, provide a description of exchange-rate source locations.

[75] London adopted the Gregorian calendar on September 14, 1752 (September 3 in Julian calendar). The Course of Exchange was first published on Tuesday, September 1, 1752 (Julian calendar) and Friday, September 15, 1752 (Gregorian calendar; September 4, 1752 in Julian calendar). We have converted Julian to Gregorian calendar from 1720 to 1752 to maintain the homogeneity in data collection.

range of exchange rates is provided (lowest/highest). Given our claim that the shadow interest rate reflects the conditions of the most competitive banker, it is natural to focus on the best exchange rate (highest number of domestic unit per foreign unit).

The data collected for Amsterdam is similar to that collected by others.[76] As far as we know, the only European location where it can be read is the EHB in Amsterdam, which holds a series of photocopies from original materials held in Jakarta and Copenhagen, apparently made upon the initiative of N.W. Posthumus after World War II. The original copies of *Prijscouranten-Koers van de Koopmanschappen* are located in *Cophenague Rijksarchief* for 1708–1734 and in *Wordt Arsip Nasional Jacarta* for 1734–1789.[77] The *Koers* provides two different maturities on London and Paris, starting fairly early on.[78] Yet because most of the data for the first quarter of the eighteenth century is missing, we have started our calculations in 1734 for London. Data limitations for Paris encouraged us to leave it aside at this stage, although we return to it later on.

Previous research about the topic considers sight as spot and derives the implicit interest rate by straight application of formula (2).[79] However, it should be noted that sight is *not* spot because there is a time delay between the purchase of a "sight" bill and when it is cashed, since there is the physical delay involved with such things as the time needed for reaching Dover and crossing the Channel, as one late eighteenth century banker does in the opening pages of Charles Dickens' *Tale of Two Cities*. Similarly, for long bills, one must reckon

---

[76] See Schneider *et al.*, *Statistik*.

[77] Except for years 1757, 1759, and 1783, when no *Prijscouranten* has been kept; Posthumus, *Inquiry*.

[78] According to the *Prijscouranten*, not only Paris and London but also Rouen and Hamburg started to be quoted with either one or two "usances" from 1634 on. According to Lespagnol, *Messieurs*, although the Third Anglo-Dutch War (1672–1674) did not create major commercial disruptions, the following period of conflict between England and France (1688–1697) had major consequences on international trade about which see Clark, *Dutch Alliance*. This may explain the discontinuation of double quotation in Amsterdam on several other centers (except for quotations on London, which suffered a break around 1690). Another interesting feature of the primary source is that it is also about that time that we observe a shift, for short maturities, from "usance" to "sight."

[79] See Eagly and Smith, "Domestic and International Integration," p. 201, and Schubert, "Arbitrage," p. 4, for eighteenth century data, though these papers do not show the interest-rate graphs and/or data. See also Boyer-Xambeu *et al.*, "L'intégration," p. 2 for the nineteenth century calculations.

Table 6.2. *Time horizon for "long" and "short" bills*

	"Long"		"Short"
	Maturity	Days of grace	Maturity
In London on Amsterdam[a]	2 months and/or 2.5 months	6	3[d]
In London on Paris[b]	2 months	10	4 + 1 day's date bills
In Amsterdam on London[c]	2 months	3	3[d]

Source: (a) Hayes (1724, pp. 261–5; 1777, pp. 11, 260–5; (b) Hayes (1724, p. 261); Markham *General Introduction*, p. 236); Hewitt (1740, p. 25); (c) Hayes (1724, p. 261); Markham ibid., p. 236); Hewitt (1740, p.25); Hayes (1777, p. 266); (d) Anonymous, *Le Guide d'Amsterdam* (1701, p. 45) which indicates "Les lettres partent deux fois par semaine, savoir les mardis et vendredis à neuf heures du soir, et doivent arriver les lundis et vendredis lorsque le vent est bon".

with the grace period between the day the bill is presented and the day it is paid. Thus, the long exchange rate $a_{ij}[n_l]$ and the short exchange rate $a_{ij}[n_s]$, can be rewritten in terms of an imaginary spot exchange rate x_{ij} as

$$a_{ij}[n_l] = x_{ij} / \left(1 + r_j^i \cdot \frac{n_l}{365}\right) \tag{6}$$

$$a_{ij}[n_s] = x_{ij} / \left(1 + r_j^i \cdot \frac{n_s}{365}\right) \tag{7}$$

Substituting for x_{ij} gives the arbitrage condition that we have used to derive shadow interest rates (details for sources are shown in Table 6.2):[80]

$$r_j^i = \frac{(a_{ij}[n_s] - a_{ij}[n_l]) \cdot 365}{(a_{ij}[n_l] \cdot n_l - a_{ij}[n_s] \cdot n_s)} \tag{8}$$

---

[80] The most used book about exchange rate in eighteenth century London is Hayes, *Negociator Magazine*. See also Marius, *Advice;* Bringhurst, *Stile*; Hewitt, *Treatise*; de Sequeira, *New Merchant's Guide*; Dickinson, *Foreign Exchange* and Tate, *Modern Cambist*.

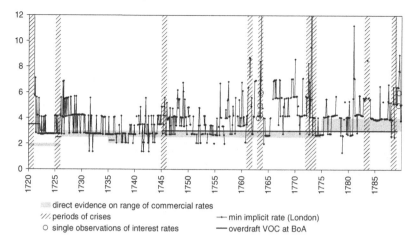

direct evidence on range of commercial rates
periods of crises
single observations of interest rates
→ min implicit rate (London)
— overdraft VOC at BoA

Figure 6.2 Amsterdam shadow interest rate, from London *Course of Exchange* (%).

Sources: shadow interest rates: see text. Range of commercial rates: 1720–1789, Homer and Sylla, *History*; 1720–1725, Ehrenberg, *Capital*; 1726–1734, Wilson, "Economic Decline," and McCulloch, *Essay*; 1735–1738, Clapham, *Bank*; 1738–1774, Wilson, ibid., and McCulloch, ibid.; 1775–1789, Ehrenberg, ibid. Direct observations: 1763, Jong-Keesing, *Economisches Crisis*; 1789, Antonetti, *Une maison*. Overdraft rates: Van Dillen, *Bronnen*.

B.   Individual interest-rate series

Figures 6.2–6.4 depict the results from implementing equation (8) on the data described previously. Figure 6.2 presents the shadow interest rate for London as per Amsterdam; Figure 6.3, the shadow interest rate for Amsterdam as per London; and Figure 6.4, the shadow interest rate for Paris as per London. We have also reported on the charts (whenever this was feasible and meaningful) evidence on the short-term "commercial" interest rates discussed in Section II. Moreover, we also provide overlapping bars representing the financial crises summarized in Table 6.3. To work out this table we relied on Charles P. Kindleberger (1989), Neal (1990), Luckett (1992, 1996), and the sources these authors refer to.[81] Combining direct evidence on interest rates and crises with evidence

---

[81] We have relied on the sources indicated by Luckett, *Credit*, and "Crises" rather than on Luckett's own chronology of financial crises. The reason is that Luckett provides a chronology of financial crises that is suggested by the evidence of spikes in the arbitrated interest rate series he computes. Consequently, it would have been tautological to invoke his chronology as evidence in favor of our interest-rate data.

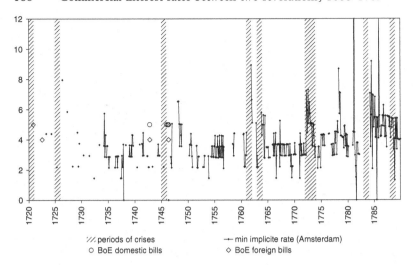

Figure 6.3 London shadow interest rate, from Amsterdam *Course of Exchange* (%).

Sources: shadow interest rates: see text. Bank of England rates: Clapham, *Bank.*

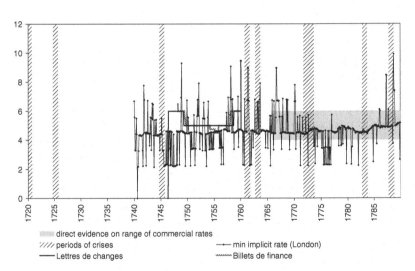

Figure 6.4 Paris shadow interest rate, from London *Course of Exchange* (%).

Sources: shadow interest rates: see text. Range of commercial rates: Homer and Sylla, *History,* from Saugrain, *Baisse.* Interest rate on *lettres de change* and *billets de finance* from data in Luckett, *Credit,* following *Petites affiches.*

Table 6.3. *List of financial crises, 1700–1789*

Crises	Source	Centers affected	Motive
1708–1710	Neal (1990, pp. 46, 134)	London (1708–1710)	Need for government finance in the War of the Spanish Succession (1702–13)
	Lüthy (1959, vol. 1, p. 226)	Paris (1709 only)	Plague, famine, and fall of leading banking houses having lent to the king
1715	Lüthy (1959, vol. 1, pp. 256–5)	Paris	Standstill on French government debt
1720	Kindleberger (1989) Neal (1990)	London, Paris	South Sea, Mississippi
1725	Marion (1914, pp. 124–9)	Paris	Final liquidation of the Law system and devaluation of the *livre tournois*
1745	Neal (1990, p. 169), from Ashton (1959)	London	Jacobite rebellion in Scotland; war of the Austrian succession (1740–8) with heavy influence on Amsterdam
1761	Neal (1990, p. 170), from Ashton (1959)	Panic confined to London	Unknown
1763	Kindleberger 1989; Luckett, (1992, p. 134)	Amsterdam, Hamburg, then London and Paris	End of the Seven Years war, Failure of De Neuvilles
1772–1773	Neal (1990, p. 170); Kindleberger (1989)	Scotland, then London and Amsterdam	Unknown
1783	Bigo (1927, pp. 76–94), Bouchary (1937, p. 43) Luckett (1992)	Paris	Run on Caisse *d'escompte*, end of American War
1788	Luckett (1992)	Paris	Partial default on French debt

reconstructed from foreign exchange data demonstrates the consistency between these alternative sources.

First, our estimates of the shadow interest rate in the three financial centers are quite obviously in line with direct evidence. This suggests that a more intensive search for interest rates in primary sources could lead further insights, especially for those centers that did not benefit from double quotation abroad so that a shadow interest rate cannot be

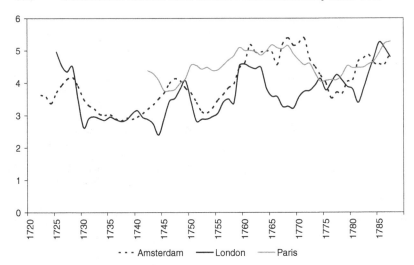

Figure 6.5 Commercial rates, five-year moving averages (%).
Source: see text.

retrieved. An implication of this is that commercial credit was sufficiently developed and efficient since there was little difference between the average interest rate (as indicated by contemporaries) and marginal ones (as measured by the shadow interest rate). This is supporting evidence of a central claim in this chapter.[82]

A second finding is the consistency between the behavior of implicit interest rates and independent evidence on crises, suggesting here again that our computations are very informative. As already emphasized by Luckett (1992), monetary crises were accompanied by high interest rates and this is exactly what we find. Moreover, although many crises were idiosyncratic, we note that some had an impact on several interest rates at once, a finding that accords with our hypothesis of a European-wide but closely knit, fabric of merchant bankers shifting capital from one centre to another. This is especially clear for Amsterdam and London, which exhibit co-movements in periods of stress.

We now take a look at the long-run behavior of the three commercial interest-rate series thus computed. This is done in Figure 6.5, which depicts five-year moving averages. Differentials between series remain

---

[82] Incidentally, note the strong similarity between the implicit interest rate we compute for Paris during the mid-eighteenth century and the one reported in the *Petites affiches*. Luckett discards the evidence in *Petites affiches* on the grounds that the rates do not move much where financial series should fluctuate a lot. The rate reported in *Petites affiches* might not have moved much, but neither does our Paris shadow interest rate.

small throughout, especially for the Amsterdam–London pair. Paris interest rates were slightly higher – say, between 4 percent and 5 percent when London and Amsterdam were between 3 percent and 4.5 percent – but the salient fact is that differences across countries are not large and actually disappear toward the end of the century. Note also that the ranking emphasized by contemporary authors and summarized in Figure 6.1 (whereby Amsterdam rates were lowest, followed by British and French rates in that order) is modified. London catches up very early on and leads the pack thereafter.

In any case discrepancies are dwarfed by common secular trends: specifically, a general tendency for the price of money to rise over time. This finding is interesting in view of many previous historical accounts, which have focused on individual countries and have therefore portrayed these evolutions as essentially idiosyncratic. An illustration of this is the work of Luckett (1992) and Phil Hoffman *et al.* (2000), who have emphasized "French" factors to account for rising interest rates in Paris before the French Revolution. Although making sense of these common trends is still a long shot (an obvious candidate explanation is the mounting international political tensions that followed the US independence), the evidence reported here suggests that we should be dealing with late eighteenth century monetary tensions as European-wide phenomena.[83] An implication would be that the financial distress that preceded the Revolution might have more to do with European trends than with French ones.

C.   Cycles and seasonality

The data also exhibit cyclical patterns. A glimpse at Figures 6.2–6.4 shows that Paris is relatively stable while London is less so and Amsterdam displays much variation. Some authors have argued that these flat interest rates bear no connection with the state of the economy.[84] But computing monthly average spreads against annual averages suggests a more nuanced characterization. As illustrated in Figures 6.6 and 6.7, Paris rates – although stable in the long run – displayed a highly seasonal pattern of fluctuations until 1770. This is also true of London and Amsterdam rates. Of all three economies, the French one was probably the most reliant on agriculture. We thus cannot rule out that money

---

[83] A rare exception emphasizing the international character of tensions in international credit markets of the 1780s is Bouchary, *Le Marché*.

[84] See, for example, Hoffman *et al. Priceless Markets*.

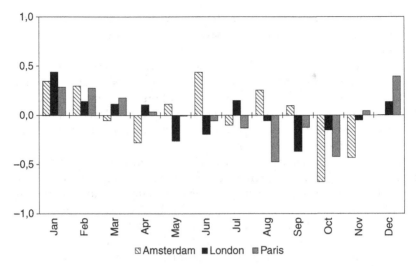

Figure 6.6 Seasonality in interest rates, 1740–1770.
Source: author computations (see text). Data is beginning of month for Paris and Amsterdam, mid-month for London, so "Aug" denotes early August for Paris and Amsterdam but mid-August for London.

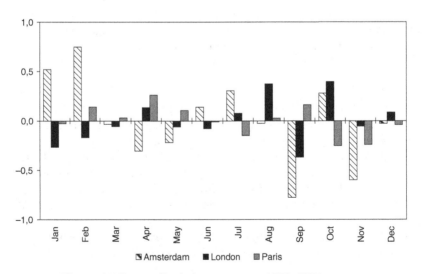

Figure 6.7 Seasonality in interest rates, 1770–1789.
Source: author computations (see text). Data is beginning of month for Paris and Amsterdam, mid-month for London, so "Aug" denotes early August for Paris and Amsterdam but mid-August for London.

markets were influenced by crops and thus bore at least some connection with the state of the economy. Other economic factors may have contributed to cyclical behavior. Carrière *et al.*[85] report substantial effects of the arrival of Spanish galleons in Cadiz in late winter, on European exchange rates. To the extent that the arrival of fleets exhibited seasonality, they might have contributed to the cyclical behavior of interest rates. Changes in the patterns of arrival of bullion might also have triggered changes in the patterns of seasonality.

An intriguing feature of the data, however, is that this pattern disappears toward the latter part of the century. After 1770 we find essentially no seasonality for both Paris and London, with Amsterdam becoming by contrast more cyclical. This takes place precisely when the integration of money markets – as measured by average shadow interest rates – was highest. One explanation could be that certain markets managed to use other markets as lenders of last resort, thus transmitting to them their business cycle.

D.   *Bilateral connections and the structure of the global money market*

To conclude this section we take a look at the association between shadow interest rates in one financial center as measured from two other financial centers. Given our sources, this can only be done for Paris, since this is the only market for which both the London and Amsterdam courses of exchange report two maturities. Paris as from London has already been discussed (see Figure 6.4): now we want to compare it with Paris as from Amsterdam.

This exercise requires some qualification. First, data from London is beginning of month while data from Amsterdam is mid-month, so that there is no time coincidence between the two series. Second, and more importantly, the data on Paris in the Amsterdam course of exchange lacks regularity and consistency. There are many missing observations and many instances where one maturity only is quoted. It is not entirely clear whether this is a problem with the source or whether this pattern reflects some fundamental aspect of the underlying transactions. To support the latter interpretation we have anecdotal evidence that, whereas Amsterdam seems to have been an important source of capital for Parisian bankers, the converse was not true.[86] Paris bills in Amsterdam

---

[85] Carrière *et al.*, *Banque et capitalisme*, p. 87.
[86] See Condillac, *Commerce*. Condillac, obviously briefed by a banker of the time, goes into minute details while explaining how the resources of modern finance enabled bankers in France to take advantage of lower interest rates in Amsterdam when there

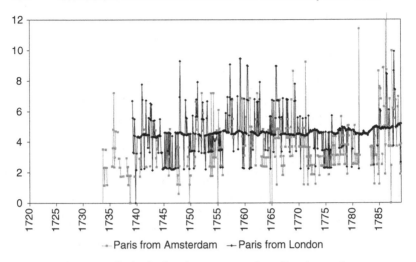

Figure 6.8 Paris shadow interest rate, from London and Amsterdam (%).

may have lacked liquidity, and their price must have behaved in a somewhat erratic way.

In any event, the result from our exercise is depicted on Figure 6.8, which reveals little connection between the two series. Since the Paris shadow interest rate, as priced in London, is consistent with direct evidence on reported average Paris conditions and is also obviously derived from quotation of a liquid instrument, it must be that the "abnormal" series is that constructed from the Amsterdam course of exchange. Subject to the foregoing qualification, this suggests that, within a general tendency toward market integration, a distinct hierarchy was nonetheless observed, with the more popular financial routes being those that were the most liquid, efficient, and thus informative.

This leads us to recognize the existence of a complex web of issues pertaining to the microstructures of the global market for commercial credit. To get things close to the ground, consider the following anecdote, taken from Guy Antonetti (1963, p.146). In the late 1780s, the banking house Greffuhle, Montz & Cie of Paris made a convention with the Courtiau, Echenique, Sanchez & Cie bank of Amsterdam, arranging for drawing on each other. Paris would charge 5 percent and Amsterdam 4 percent; this was said to be in connection with the "usually lower" rate

was a profit to do so. That Paris rates were, on average, higher than Amsterdam ones suggests that the opposite must have been less frequent.

in Amsterdam. In July 1789, when the cost of money rose suddenly in Amsterdam to an "extraordinary level" of about 5–6 percent, Courtiau Echenique, Sanchez & Cie reneged on its promise to Greffuhle and started charging 5 percent. Greffuhle immediately complained, arguing that conditions had changed in Paris, too (this was eight days before the storming of the Bastille): if they were to go by the current rate in Paris then they should be entitled to charge "9 percent, 10 percent, or even 12 percent."

The episode raises many interesting questions. First, the form of the drawing convention between the two firms should be explained. Why did firms engage in fixed-interest rate drawing arrangements as opposed to state-contingent contracts? Second, the unilateral reneging on the contract makes the matter even more puzzling. It is very probable that a firm that did this would seriously compromise its relations with its correspondents. Hence, under what circumstances could reneging be optimal?

V. The bell jar: inside and outside

This chapter would not be complete if we didn't compare our results with other domestic interest-rate series. In what follows, we combine the London and Paris shadow interest rates with yields on government debt and private returns on land. The yield on British government debt is derived from the price of British Consols, which we collected from *The Course of Exchange*; the series for France is the background series for François Velde and David Weir (1992).[87] Returns on land are taken from Clark (2005), who computed a rent charges series for Britain and reports some values for France.

The result (Figures 6.9 and 6.10 for Britain and France, respectively) is revealing. Consider government bonds first. As seen, yields on British consols overlap nicely with London commercial rates measured in Amsterdam. This means that the reorganization of Britain's government following the Glorious Revolution in 1688 essentially established its credit on the same footing as the best commercial signatures in Amsterdam when they borrowed sterling from their London counterparts. And since we have assumed that the best conditions in London as measured in Amsterdam are informative of the opportunity cost of capital in London, we must conclude that the British government was not faring

---

[87] See Velde and Weir, "Financial Market," for details.

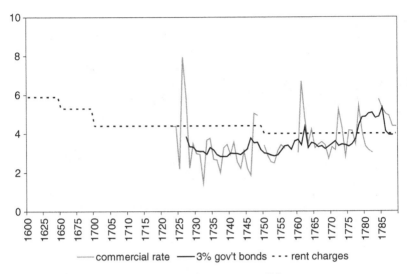

Figure 6.9 Britain: various interest rates (%).
Sources: author calculations; Clark, "Interest Rate."

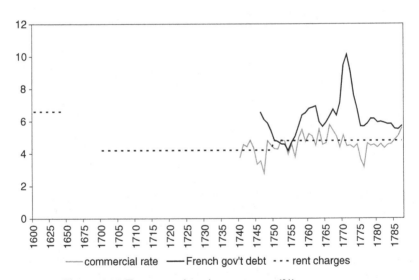

Figure 6.10 France: various interest rates (%).
Sources: author calculations for Paris commercial interest rates; Clark, "Interest Rate" (2005) for rent charges; Velde and Weir, "Financial Market" for yield on government debt. Hoffman *et al.*, "Priceless Market" indicate essentially stable interest rates on notarial credit, citing an interval of 4%–5% for 1720, but do not provide a time series.

better than London merchants. The standard way of looking at things is to argue that the improvement in the reputation of Britain triggered a decline of all interest rates and paved the way for the subsequent development of that country. Yet if Figure 6.9 tells anything, it is that commercial and sovereign credit behaved alike; thus it is not clear what drove what.

Figure 6.10, for its part, shows that the notion of a sovereign ceiling does not apply to the eighteenth century capital market. During most of the period, French government yields are significantly above commercial rates, implying that commercial credit can thrive even in an economy with a delinquent government. Of course there is an issue with the slope of the yield curve since we are comparing short and long term debt, but this cannot be the entire story. At the very least, this casts doubts on the costs-of-transfer risks and institutional moral hazard in the Ancien Régime economy. We conclude that in France, the benchmark interest rate was provided by corporate credit (just as Condillac argued). By the same token, improvement in the government's credibility cannot in itself radically change the prospects for development. To capture this notion, we might describe the financial system of the eighteenth century as displaying a "corporate ceiling" rather than the "sovereign ceiling" that exists today.

Another interesting comparison is with the returns on land. Given that we are now comparing two forms of private credit (commercial credit and land credit), one should expect consistency within both countries. Merchant bankers did invest part of their gains in land and real estate, so that returns on property should converge to returns from commercial investments. Such is indeed what we observe, and in a particularly striking manner for France. This is again consistent with our notion of a corporate ceiling.

In conclusion, we suggest that the views developed in this paper have the potential to explain the long-run decline of interest rates in the late medieval and early modern periods, although verifying this should be the topic of future research. To the extent that merchant bankers connected with one another across Europe and achieved significant financial progress throughout the period, managing to reduce transaction and information costs by a variety of technological improvements, one should expect a decline in the return they required from extending commercial credit. By the same token, one should observe a reflection of this decline in the equilibrium return of all other assets in which these bankers invested. It may therefore be that the financial progress brought about by the Commercial Revolution goes a long way toward explaining the puzzle of declining land return identified by Clark (1996). Those sectors that were fortunate to attract the attention of merchants thus became an inclusive part of the bell jar. The rest were locked out.

VI.   Conclusions

Owing to the fragmentary nature of the data, the evidence in this chapter must remain incomplete. But a number of truly important findings emerge. The first is a fairly radical hypothesis: we have pleaded here for a thorough reassessment of the mechanics of financial development, which would have little to do with revolutions in constitutions or commitments. This is contrary to the hypothesis put forward by neo-institutional economic historians. Their view, we think, is rooted in the modern notion of sovereign ceiling: government bonds are essentially risk-free assets, enjoying the highest grade and trading at the highest price compared to corporate securities. If one believes in the sovereign ceiling argument, then one is naturally led to treat transformations fostering the credibility of the sovereign as critical. They are bound to have trickledown effects on economic development, with the improvement in the quality of the sovereign percolating the economy at large through a reduction of all interest rates. The political transformations that took place in 1688 and after would then be epoch making, since they had the potential to lead to a considerable increase in the credibility of the British government. This familiar narrative places much emphasis on national differences, government quality, and interstate competition.

The alternative that emerges from our discussion is the following. Long before the British government reformed itself to take advantage of the possibilities of the capital market, a deep transformation of this capital market had already taken place. Commercial interest rates were very low quite early, but better still, they were so for merchants all over Europe. In effect, the low interest rates at which the British government managed to secure capital during the eighteenth century, after its reorganization of 1688, were identical to the cost at which Amsterdam or Paris merchant bankers lent money to their London counterparts.

If one were to exaggerate a little bit (but only a little bit), one would argue that there is nothing exciting about the British government catching up on the credit of bankers. That the Glorious Revolution forced the introduction of a heavy dose of business-like manners in government is consistent with our insight that, in the late seventeenth century, "benchmark" rates were provided by commercial credit so that there was no sovereign ceiling. Corporate governance was the basis of credit, and government had to adjust to it. The history of finance in the eighteenth century and afterwards would be that of the delayed catch-up by governments on commercial best practice. Or, to put it in still another way, it is a story of how governments reformed themselves to become included in a "bell jar" that pre-dated their subjecting to parliamentary control.

This way of looking at things advises against writing about early modern financial development from a narrowly national perspective, since the transformation that occurred in finance long before 1688 was international or more rigorously, European. In any case, it was closely related to the making and reinforcement of a global community of merchants. In this context, the key questions would be to understand why and how – despite inept governments that went bankrupt, relished predation, or imposed all kinds of counterproductive regulations – finance found ways to develop, prosper, and integrate internationally long before the late eighteenth century.

We also emphasize, however, that our claim that financial development was in essence an international phenomenon does not mean that financial geography was a *tabula rasa* – a blank slate. This was our second main theme. While we found that interest rates did not differ much between the markets under study (Amsterdam, London, and Paris), we also noted that there were persistent differences in average rates, suggesting different degrees of liquidity. Similarly, we reported that, quite early in the century, London – the capital of what was by then the world's leading commercial power – tended to register the lowest commercial interest rates available anywhere. We also found evidence that some financial routes may have been one-way streets: the peculiar behavior of Paris shadow interest rates inferred from the Amsterdam course of exchange suggests a limited use of Paris credit by Amsterdam bankers, but by contrast there is anecdotal evidence of Paris bankers relying on Amsterdam. The conclusion, therefore, is that within global finance there were capitals, hubs, highways, secondary routes, and a direction of circulation.

Finally, at the intersection of these two issues – the high degree of international financial sophistication within the community of merchant bankers prevailing already in the early eighteenth century, and the chasm that existed between this community and a large variety of economic agents (both public and private) who lived outside the bell jar in abject underdevelopment – lies the key problem facing eighteenth century thinkers of policy making. For them, much as for Hernando de Soto today, the question was not how to develop finance, since finance had already developed, but rather how to develop the rest of the economy to match the levels achieved within the global financial system. Contemporaries thus struggled with the question of how to break open the jar of European financial capitalism so that it would pour its riches over the rest of the economy. Perhaps unsurprisingly, they were naturally led to look for lessons in the way merchant bankers had dealt with development, and in so doing, put the final stone on a construction that had been started much earlier and whose completion may have indeed opened the way for the subsequent material revolution. As Condillac concluded a key chapter of *Le commerce et le gouvernement*: *"Si l'art de mettre en valeur les terres avoit fait les mêmes progrès que l'art de mettre l'argent en valeur, nos laboureurs ne seroient pas aussi misérables qu'ils le sont."*[88]

Appendix A   Evidence on interest rates from secondary sources

Table 6A.1. *Interest rates in the early modern period*

Date	Source	Holland	Britain	France	Italy	Spain	Portugal	Turkey (a)	North America	China
1444– 1460	Massie 1750		10%							
1630	Child 1668		8%							
1646– 1665	Massie 1750		7%							
1668	Child 1668	3%; war 4%	6%	7%		<3%	10%– 12%			
1666– 1685	Massie 1750		5%							
1683	Petty 1690	3%– 3.5%		7%						

---

[88] Condillac, *Commerce*, Chap. 17: "If the art of exploiting land had progressed as much as the art of exploiting money, our peasants would not be as miserable as they are."

Table 6A.1. (cont.)

Date	Source	Holland	Britain	France	Italy	Spain	Portugal	Turkey (a)	North America	China
1690	Barbon 1690	3%	6%							
1699[?]	Hatton 1699	3%	6%	7%	3%	10%		20%	10%	
1686–1705	Massie 1750		5%							
1705	Law 1705	3%–4%								
1716	Hatton 1716	3%	5%	7%	3%	10%		20%	10%	
1729–1748	Massie 1750		4%							
1750	Massie 1750	3%	4%	5%–6%	5%–6%	12%	7%–9%			
1766	Smith 1776	3%						"high"	6%–8%	12%
1776	Condillac 1776	2%–2.5%		5%–6%						

Notes: (a) "Turkey" refers to either "Ottoman Empire" or so-called "Mahometan nations."
Sources: Barbon, "Discourse," p. 80; Child, Brief Observations; Condillac, Commerce, p. 135; Hatton, Merchant's Magazine and Comes commercii; Law, Money, Chap. 2; Massie, Essay, pp. 44, 51; Petty, Political Arithmetick, Chap. I; Smith, Inquiry, book 1, pp. 127–9 and 133. Note that subsequent editions of Hatton (1727, 1734, 1754, 1766, 1794) do not update the data – except for Britain's data (which was probably adjusted for change in regulations; see text).

Appendix B   Incidence on local rates on shadow foreign interest rates: nineteenth century evidence

Table 6A.2 reports the results from simple regressions of the shadow Paris interest rate (computed from the London course of exchange) on the actual Paris interest rate (franc) and the London interest rate (sterling). As the table shows, there is a modest influence of local money market conditions on shadow interest rates, but the predominant driver is the actual interest rate. In the late nineteenth century world of small transaction costs, the limited extent of the local money effect is understandable. We can surmise that this factor was more substantial for earlier periods.

Table 6A.2. Regression output (1900:01–1914:06, least squares)

Dependent variable	Explanatory variable				DW	Adj. R^2	N-obs.
	r_P	r_L	Constant				
r_P^L	0.879956** (34.67501)	0.05569** (3.257247)	0.488423** (9.574705)		1.840358	0.940589	174
	Δr_P	Δr_L	Constant	Error correction			
Δr_P^L	0.830261** (19.52174)	0.043893 (1.489809)	-0.000578 (-0.035164)	–	2.990289	0.711300	173
Δr_P^L	0.904045** (27.17838)	0.022615 (0.998388)	0.306791** (10.00012)	-0.836597** (-10.98731)	2.051867	0.830599	173

Note: Error correction factor is the one-period lagged difference between franc rate in London and the Paris open market rate, or $r_P^L(-1) - r_P(-1)$.

References

Akerlof, G.A. 1970. "The Market for 'Lemons': Quality Uncertainty and the Market Mechanism." *Quarterly Journal of Economics* 84, no. 3: 488–500.

Anonymous. 1701. *Le guide d'Amsterdam, enseignant aux voyageurs et aux negocians sa splendeur, son commerce, et la description de ses édifices.* Amsterdam: Editions Daniel de la Feuille.

Antonetti, G. 1963. *Une maison de Banque à Paris au XVIIIe siècle, Greffulhe Montz et Cie (1789–1793).* Paris: Editions Cujas.

Ashton, T.S. 1959. *Economic Fluctuation in England, 1700–1800.* Oxford: Clarendon Press.

Barbon, N. "A Discourse of Trade" [1690]. In *In Commerce, Culture, and Liberty: Readings on Capitalism Before Adam Smith*, edited by Henry C. Clark. 2003. Indianapolis: Liberty Fund.

Bigo, R. 1927. *La Caisse d'escompte et les origines de la Banque de France, 1776–1793.* Paris: Presses Universitaires de France.

Bouchary, J. 1937. *Le marché des changes de Paris à la fin du XVIIIème siècle 1778–1800*, vol. 1. Paris: Marcel Rivière et Cie.

―――. 1939. *Les manieurs d'Argent à Paris à la fin du XVIIIème siècle*, vol 2. Paris: Marcel Rivière et Cie.

Boyer-Xambeu, M.-T., G. Deleplace, and L. Gillard. 1995. *Bimétallisme, taux de change, et prix de l'or et de l'argent 1717–1873.* Economies et Sociétés: Histoire quantitative de l'économie française, Cahiers de l'ISMEA. Grenoble: Presse Universitaire de Grenoble.

―――. 2001. "L'intégration des marchés monétaires au XIXe siècle. Les places financières de Paris et de Londres (1833–1873)." *Histoire et Mesure* 16, no. 1/2 (Varia).

Braudel, F. 1979. *Civilisation matérielle, économie et capitalisme, XVe–XVIIIe siècle.* Paris: Armand Colin.

Bringhurst, J. 1682. *The stile of exchanges containing both their law & custom as practised now in the most considerable places of exchange in Europe. Unfolding divers mysteries and directing every person, howsoever concerned in a Bill of exchange, to what he ought to do and observe, in any case, in order to his own security.* Translated out of low and high-Dutch, French, and Italian-Latine authors. London: John Bringhurst.

Brissot, J.-P. 1787. *Point de banqueroute ou lettre à un créancier de l'Etat sur l'impossibilité de la banqueroute nationale et les moyens de ramener le crédit et la paix.* London [no name of publisher available].

Buchet du Pavillon. 1757. *Essai sur les causes de la diversité des taux de l'intérêt.* London and Paris: Duchêne.

Calomiris, C. and G. Hubbard. "International Adjustment under the Classical Gold Standard: Evidence for the United States and Britian, 1879–1914." In *Modern Perspectives on the Gold Standard.* 1996. Edited by T. Bayoumi, B. Eichengreen, and M.P. Taylor, 189–217. Cambridge: Cambridge University Press.

Carrière, C., M. Coudurie, M. Gutsatz, and R. Squarzoni. 1976. *Banque et capitalisme commercial, la lettre de change au XVIIIème siècle.* Marseille: Institut Historique de Provence.

Castaing, John. *The Course of the Exchange*. London, various issues.

Child, J. 1668. *Brief Observations Concerning Trade and Interest of Money*. London: Printed for Elizabeth Calvert at the Black-spread Eagle in Barbican, and Henry Mortlock at the Sign of the White-Heart in Westminster Hall.

Cipolla, C.M. May 2, 1952. "Note sul saggio d'interesse, corso dividendi e sconto dei dividendi del Banco di S. Girorgio nel Sec. XVI." *Economia Internazionale*: 255–74.

Clapham, J.H. 1944. *The Bank of England, A History*. Cambridge: Cambridge University Press.

Clark, G.N. 1923. *The Dutch Alliance and the War against the French Trade, 1688–1709*. Manchester: Manchester University Press.

Clark, G. 1996. "The Political Foundations of Modern Economic Growth: England, 1540–1800." *Journal of Interdisciplinary History* 26, no. 4: 563–88.

2005. "The Interest Rate in the Very Long Run: Institutions, Preferences and Modern Growth." Working paper, University of California – Davis.

Condillac, [E. Bonnot] Abbé de. 1776. *Le commerce et le gouvernement considérés relativement l'un à l'autre*. Paris: chez Jombert & Cellot.

Davis, L. and J. Hughes. 1960. "A Dollar Sterling Exchange 1803–1895." *Economic History Review* 13: 52–78.

de Jong-Keesing, E. 1939. *De economische crisis van 1763 te Amsterdam*, Amsterdam: N. v. Intern. uitgevers en h. mij.

de Malynes, G. 1601. *A Treatise on the Canker of England's Commonwealth*. London: Printed by Richard Field for William Iohnes printer.

de Roover, R. 1944. "What is Dry Exchange?: A Contribution to the Study of English Mercantilism." *Journal of Political Economy* 52, no. 3: 250–66.

1953. *L'évolution de la lettre de change. XIVème XVIIIème siècles*. Paris: Armand Colin.

de Sequeira, J.H. 1798. *A new merchant's guide; containing a concise system of information for the port and city of London: together with some observations particularly useful to commercial men and their clerks*. Compiled and digested by I. Sequeira. London: Printed for the author.

de Soto, H. 2003. *The Mystery of Capital: Why Capitalism Triumphs in the West and Fails Everywhere Else*. New York: Basic Books.

Dickinson, W. *Foreign exchanges; being a complete set of tables, calculated from the lowest exchange to the highest usual rates . . . shewing, at one view, any sum of foreign money reduced into British sterling, and British money into foreign*. Revised by Mr. Tate. London: Boosey & Sons, 1819.

Dickson, P.G.M. 1967. *The Financial Revolution in England: A Study in the Development of Public Credit, 1688–1756*. London: Macmillan.

Eagly, R.V. and V.K. Smith. 1976. "Domestic and International Integration of the London Money Market, 1731–1789." *Journal of Economic History* 36, no. 1: 198–212.

Erhenberg, R. 1928. *Capital and Finance in the Age of the Renaissance: A Study of the Fuggers and Their Connections*. Translated from German by H.M. Lucas. London: Jonathan Cape.

Etienne, M. 1994. *Veuve Cliquot Ponsardin*. Paris: Economica.

Faure, E. 1977. *La Banqueroute de Law.* Paris: Gallimard.

Flandreau, M. and C. Rivière. 1999. "La Grande Retransformation? Contrôles de capitaux et integration financière internationale 1880–1996." *Economie Internationale* 78: 11–58.

Fratianni, F. and F. Spinelli. 2006. "Did Genoa and Venice Kick a Financial Revolution in the Quattrocento?" Working Paper No. 112, Oesterreichische Nationalbank (Austrian Central Bank).

Fuleman, M.J.-G. 1739. *Traité sur les lettres de change, contenant l'analyse & démonstration instructive de la valeur des termes qui la composent, de leurs effets & conséquences, &c.* Paris: Hourdel.

Harsin, P., ed. 1934. *Œuvres complètes: John Law, 1671–1729.* Paris: Sirey.

Hatton, E. 1699. *The Merchant's Magazine: Or, Trades-man's Treasury,* 3rd edn. London: Printed for, and sold by Chr. Coningsby.

    1716. *Comes commercii, Or, The Trader's Companion,* 3rd edn. London: D. Midwinter.

Hayes, Richard. *The Negociator Magazine of Monies and Exchanges.* Editions: printed for Richard Hayes (1st, 1719); printed for J. Noon (2nd, 1724); printed for W. Meadows (3rd, 1730); printed for J. Noon (4th, 1739); printed for J. Noon (6th, 1740); printed for J. Noon (8th, 1754); printed for G. Keith (9th, 1764); printed for G. Keith (11th, 1777). London.

Hewitt, J. *A treatise upon money, coins, and exchange, in regard both to theory and practice. As also tables relating to the conformity of different weights and measures.* London: H. Woodfall, 1740; London: G. Keith, 1755.

Hoffman, P.T., G. Postel-Vinay, and J.-L. Rosenthal. 2000. *Priceless Markets, The Political Economy of Credit in Paris, 1660–1870.* Chicago: University of Chicago Press.

Homer, S. and R. Sylla. 2005. *A History of Interest Rates,* 4th edn. New Brunswick: Rutgers University Press.

Juhl, T., W. Miles, and M. Weidenmier. May 2004. "Covered Interest Arbitrage: Then vs. Now." *Economica* 73: 341–52.

Kerridge, E. 2002. *Usury, Interest and the Reformation.* Hants: Ashgate.

Kindleberger, C.P. 1989. *Manias, Panics and Crashes, A History of Financial Crises,* London: Basic Books.

Kours van Koopmanschappen tot Amsterdam. Amsterdam: Bijzondere collecties 674 Economisch Historische Bibliotheek, various issues.

La Porta, R., F. Lopez-de-Silanes, A. Shleifer, and R. Vishny. 1997. "Legal Determinants of External Finance." *Journal of Finance* 52: 1131–50.

    1998. "Law and Finance." *Journal of Political Economy* 106: 1113–55.

Law, J. 1705. *Money and Trade Considered. With a Proposal for Supplying the Nation with Money.* Edinburgh: The Heirs and Successors of Andrew Anderson.

Lespagnol, A. 1997. *Messieurs de Saint-Malo, une élite négociante au temps de Louis XIV,* 2 vols. Presses Universitaires Rennes.

Lloyd's List. London: Edward Lloyd, various issues.

Luckett, T. 1992. *Credit and Commercial Society in France, 1740–1789.* Ph.D. diss., Princeton University.

    1996. "Crises financières dans la France du XVIIIe siècle." *Revue d'Histoire Moderne et Contemporaine* 43, no. 2: 266–92.

Lüthy, H. 1999. *La banque protestante en France: de la Révocation de l'Edit de Nantes à la Révolution*, 2 vols. Paris, 1959; new edition, Paris: EHESS.

Marion, M. 1914. *Histoire financière de la France depuis 1715*. Paris: Arthur Rousseau Editeur.

Marius, J. 1655. *Advice concerning. Bils of exchange. Wherein is set forth the nature of exchange of monies, severall formes of bils of exchange in different languages, manner of proceeding in protest, countermand, security, letters of credit, assignments, and generally the whole practicall part and body of exchanges anatomized. With two exact tables of new stile and old stile*, 2nd edn. London: W.H.

Markham, W. 1739. *A general introduction to trade and business. Or, the young merchant,s and tradesman,s magazine*, 2nd edn. London: Bettesworth.

Massie, Joseph. 1750. *An Essay on the Governing Causes of the Natural rate of Interest: Wherein the Sentiments of Sir William Pettyand Mr. Locke, on that Head, are considered*. London: printed for W. Owen, at Homer's Head, near Temple Bar.

McCulloch, J.R. 1851. *Essay on Interest*. Philadelphia: A. Hart.

McCusker, J.J. 1978. *Money and Exchange in Europe and America, 1600–1775*. Chapel Hill: University of North Carolina.

McCusker, J.J. and C. Gravesteijn. 1979. *The Beginnings of Commercial and Financial Journalism: The Commodity Price Currents, Exchange Rate Currents, and Money Currents of Early Modern Europe*. Amsterdam: Nederlandsch Economisch-Historisch Archief (NEHA).

Mirabeau, Comte de. 1788. *Suite de la Dénonciation de l'agiotage*. N.p..

Montesquieu, C.S., Baron de. 1721. *Lettres Persanes*. Amsterdam: Chez P. Brunier.

Moody's Investors Service. June 2001. *Revised Country Ceiling Policy*. New York: Moody's Investor Service.

Munro, J. 2001. "The Origins of the Modern Financial Revolution: Responses to Impediments from Church and State in Western Europe, 1200–1600." Working Paper, University of Toronto.

Neal, L. 1990. *The Rise of Financial Capitalism: International Capital Markets in the Age of Reason*. Cambridge: Cambridge University Press.

North, D.C. and B. Weingast. 1989. "Constitutions and Commitment: The Evolution of Institutions Governing Public Choice in Seventeenth-Century Britain." *Journal of Economic History* 49, no. 4: 803–32.

Obstfeld, M. and A. Taylor. 1998. "The Great Depression as a Watershed: International Capital Mobility over the Long Run." In *The Defining Moment. The Great Depression and the American Economy in the 20th Century*, edited by M.D. Bordo *et al.*, 353–402. Chicago: University of Chicago Press and NBER.

2003. "Globalization and Capital Markets." In *Globalization in Historical Perspective*, edited by M. D. Bordo *et al.*, 121–90. Chicago: University of Chicago Press.

Officer, L. 1996. *Between the Dollar-Sterling Gold Points: Exchange Rates, Parity and Market Behaviour*. Cambridge: Cambridge University Press.

Perkins, E.J. 1975. *Financing Anglo-American Trade: The House of Brown 1800–1895*. Cambridge: Harvard University Press.

1978. "Foreign Interest Rates in American Financial Markets: A Revised Series of Dollar-Sterling Exchange Rates." *Journal of Economic History* 38: 392–417.

Petty, W. *Political Arithmetick.* 1690. London: Printed for Robert Clavel at the Peacock, and Hen. Mortlock at the Phoenix in St. Paul's Church-yard.

Posthumus, N.W. 1946. *Inquiry into the History of Prices in Holland,* vol. I. Leiden: E.J. Brill.

Quinn, S. and W. Roberds. 2009. "An Economic Explanation of the Early Bank of Amsterdam." *The Origins and Development of Financial Markets and Institutions.* (Cambridge: Cambridge University Press), pp. 32–70.

Ricardo, David. 1821. *Principles of Political Economy and Taxation,* 3rd edn. London.

Saugrain, G. 1896. *La Baisse du taux de l'intérêt, causes et conséquences,* Paris: L. Larose.

Schenk, C.R. 1998. "The Origins of the Eurodollar Market in London: 1955–1963." *Explorations in Economic History* 35: 331–8.

Schneider, J., O. Schwarzer, and P. Schnelzer. 1993. *Statistik der Geld-und Wechselkurse in Deutschland und im Ostseeraum (18 und 19 Jahrhundert).* St. Katharinen: Scripta Mercaturae Verlag.

Schubert, E.S. 1989. "Arbitrage in the Foreign Exchange Markets of London and Amsterdam during the 18th Century." *Explorations in Economic History* 26, no. 1: 1–20

Smith, A. *An Inquiry into the Nature and Causes of the Wealth of Nations.* 1776; [2003] New York: Bantam Dell.

Squarzoni, R. 1976. *Mécanismes monétaires et bancaires du capitalisme commercial au XVIIIeme siècle.* Ph.D. diss., University of Aix-en Provence.

Sussman, N. and Y. Yafeh. 2006. "Institutional Reforms, Fianncial Development and Sovereign Debt: Britain 1690–1790." *Journal of Economic History* 66, no. 4: 906–35.

Tate W. 1819. *Foreign exchanges: being a complete set of tables calculated from the lowest exchange to the highest usual rates . . .,* 1st edn. London: Boosey & Sons.

1834 and 1836. *The modern cambist, forming a manual of foreign exchanges in the direct, indirect, and cross operations of bills of exchange and bullion: including an extensive investigation of the arbitrations of exchange according to the practice of the first British and foreign houses: with numerous formulae and tables of the weights and measures of other countries, compared with the imperial standards,* 2nd edn. and 3rd edn. (with extensive alterations and additions). London: E. Wilson.

Temin, P. and H.J. Voth. 2004. "Financial Repression in a Natural Experiment: Loan Allocation and the Change in the Usury Laws in 1714." Discussion Paper No. 4452, CEPR.

Temple, W. *Observations upon the United Provinces of the Netherland,* London, printed by A. Maxwell for Sa. Gellibrand, 1673. Reprinted in *The Works of Sir William Temple,* vol. 1, 118–19. London, 1814.

Van Dillen, J.G. 1925. *Bronnen tot de Geschiedenis der Wisselbank (Amsterdam, Middleburg, Delft, Rotterdam).* Gravenhage: M. Nijhoff.

1929–1931. *Het economisch leven in de republiek der zeven provincien* [ca. 1920]. In *Nieuwe geïllustreerde wereldgeschiedenis*, edited by J. Romein door J. Suys, S. van Praag, and H.J. Smeding, 3623–42. Amsterdam: Seyffardt.

Velde, F. and D. Weir. 1992. "The Financial Market and Government Debt Policy in France." *Journal of Economic History* 52: 1–40.

Vilar, Pierre. 1978. *Or et monnaie dans l'histoire 1459–1920*, Paris: Flammarion.

Wilson, C.H. 1939. "The Economic Decline of the Netherlands." *Economic History Review* 9, no. 2: 111–27.

World Bank. 2006. *World Development Report: Equity and Development*. Washington, DC: World Bank.

7 Comparing the UK and US financial systems, 1790–1830[*]

Richard Sylla

Liam Brunt, the author of a recent and otherwise admirable article on English country banks as venture-capital firms during the first industrial revolution, states, "We have known for a long time that the English financial market was sophisticated and far in advance of that of any other country."[1] This is a pretty strong claim to make without giving more than cursory examination to what was happening in other countries.

We have been told for such a long time what Brunt says we know that we might think we know it without actually knowing it. Perhaps repetition is not always the mother of learning. For some time, a number of scholars (referred to below) have been studying the early US financial system. They find that it developed very rapidly in the early decades of US national history, and suggest that this financial development might help us to understand more fully the rapid economic growth of the US that, in almost all accounts comparing the two countries, exceeded that of the UK almost all of the time. One way to find out whether what we think is right is to make an explicit and detailed comparison of the UK and US financial systems. That is what I attempt here for the period 1790 to 1830, when the modern US financial system was created and grew, and when many think they know the contemporaneous UK financial system was far in advance of that of any other country. The analysis reveals that in most respects the US had the more developed, more modern financial system by 1830. That is likely an important reason why the US, by 1830, already had achieved rough parity with the UK in levels of real output per person and was already on a higher growth trajectory that would make it the world's largest and richest economy roughly half a century later.

[*] I wish to thank Jeremy Atack, Michael Bordo, Charles Calomiris, Forrest Capie, Ron Harris, Larry Neal, Edwin Perkins, Hugh Rockoff, Eugene White, and Robert Wright for useful comments on earlier drafts of this chapter.
[1] Brunt, "Rediscovering Risk," p. 99.

Economic progress is not always linear, however, especially in finance. Populist politics, an ever-present phenomenon in US history, intervened not long after 1830 to damage what at the time was likely the most effective financial system of any country. Sustaining effective financial systems once they are in place is not always easy. Discovering and maintaining appropriate regulatory responses to innovations in financial institutions, markets, and instruments is a difficult task for statesmen and financial leaders. The Jacksonian financial reversal of the 1830s did not derail the engine of US economic growth, but arguably slowed it down from a speed it might otherwise have attained. As the US was having a financial reversal, the UK, less subject to the whims of populist politics, was making adjustments that improved its financial system so that by the second half of the nineteenth century the UK overall likely did have the superior financial system, while the US engaged in a protracted struggle to restore what once had been the superior system.

I.   Comparing the British and American economies

Several recent developments in economics and economic history make a comparative examination of the financial systems of the UK and the US during the four decades between 1790 and 1830 timely. One is the accumulation of evidence, both historical and contemporary, that financial development leads to economic growth. As Patrick Honohan put it, "The causal link between finance and growth is one of the most striking empirical macroeconomic relationships uncovered in the last decade."[2] Economic historians, of course, have known about this link for some time.

Another finding of interest is that the US perhaps had a higher real income per capita than the UK (and even Great Britain) as early as 1831. According to Marianne Ward and John Devereaux, in 1831 UK GDP per capita was 76 percent (and Great Britain's 92 percent) of US GDP per capita.[3] The US lead in output per worker was even larger; the UK in 1831 on that measure was 58 percent, and Britain 70 percent, of the US level. Four decades ago Robert Gallman had suggested such a possibility for 1840, placing the range of Britain's product per capita from 78 to 120 percent of the US level.[4] Ward and Devereaux are more precise about the comparison and place the US lead a decade earlier than Gallman suggested it might have appeared.

---

[2] As cited by Mishkin, "Is Financial Globalization Beneficial?," p. 4.
[3] Ward and Devereaux, "Relative British and American Income Levels," pp. 252–3.
[4] Gallman, "Gross National Product in the United States," p. 5.

The Ward/Devereaux findings are not uncontested. Stephen Broadberry and Douglas Irwin contend that output per worker in the US from 1840 to 1870 was only 90 to 95 percent of UK levels, and GDP per capita, because of lower labor force participation in the US, supposedly was only 70 to 75 percent of UK levels.[5] Interestingly, although Ward/Devereaux disagree with Broadberry/Irwin on the relative positions of the two countries, they do agree that the UK *gained* relative to the US over the period 1830 (or 1840) to 1860 (or 1870). For reasons hinted at in the introduction and to be further developed, I find the UK relative gain plausible. It might be noted, however, that another investigator, Leandro Prados, finds that the UK and the US had essentially the same GDP per head from 1820 to 1870; the US had caught up with (actually, slightly surpassed) the UK by 1820, marked time with it over the next five decades, and then pulled decisively ahead of the UK after 1870.[6]

A major source of the differences in the findings of Ward/Devereaux and Broadberry/Irwin (in addition to quite different methodologies) seems to be a disagreement over whether US price levels were lower than those of the UK (Ward/Devereaux) or higher (Broadberry/Irwin). There are some reasons to believe that Ward/Devereaux are right on this. In any case, the facts of the matter are something that economic historians should clear up if they want to be taken seriously.

Still a third recent finding of interest is that of Joseph H. Davis, whose index of US industrial production shows high and sustained rates of growth of about 5 percent per year from 1790 all the way into the twentieth century.[7] There was no "kink in the curve" or "industrial revolution" in US history; industrial output grew at high rates from the beginning. A broader measure of US growth, real GDP per capita as estimated by Louis Johnston and Samuel Williamson, behaves much the same way. US real GDP per capita grew peak-to-peak at modern rates of 1.4 percent per year from 1790 to 1833, as well as from 1833 to 1859.[8]

The constancy of real growth from 1790 to 1859 is something of a surprise, as we might have expected from the experiences of other countries that the growth rate of US real GDP per capita would exhibit a gradual acceleration. Assuming that the traditional sector (agriculture) grew more slowly than the modern sector (roughly approximated by

[5] Broadberry and Irwin, "Labor Productivity in the United States and the United Kingdom."
[6] Prados, "International Comparisons of Real Product."
[7] Davis, "A Quantity-based Annual Index of U.S. Industrial Production."
[8] Johnston and Williamson, "The Annual Real and Nominal GDP for the United States." Johnston and Williamson make use of Davis's work, so their GDP series is not entirely an independent estimate.

everything but agriculture) gradual acceleration in the growth of GDP per capita would occur as the initially small modern sector grew rapidly at, say, 5 percent per year (as did industrial production, according to Davis) to become an increasingly larger share of aggregate output. The implications of an apparent absence of gradual acceleration in US real growth per capita deserve more study. Could it be that US agriculture was not so traditional or slow growing in comparison with the modern sector? What might have caused the US to grow at modern rates from 1790 on, almost from the beginning of its history?

Taken together, the recent findings indicate that US economic growth, measured either by industrial production or real GDP per capita, was rather boringly modern roughly from the time George Washington assumed the presidency in 1789. They even suggest a plausible reason why that might have been the case, namely the financial revolution executed by the Federalists, led by Alexander Hamilton, Washington's Treasury Secretary and "prime minister," in the early 1790s. The US financial revolution, the quickest and neatest of any in history, gave the US a thoroughly modern financial system almost from its inception as a nation.[9] The US financial system was the newest new thing of the early 1790s, and there do not appear other viable candidates for a persistent quickening of US economic growth at that time.[10] Given the emerging consensus that financial modernization promotes economic growth, the work of the Federalists in creating a modern financial system during Washington's administration should have had growth effects. That appears to be confirmed, or at least not denied, by the research of Davis on industrial production and Ward/Devereaux on income levels.

II.   Financial revolutions create modern financial systems

A modern financial system has six key institutional components. We can identify them in the successful financial revolutions of the Dutch Republic and the UK long before the US came into existence, as well as

---

[9] Perkins, *American Public Finance and Financial Services*; Wright, *The Wealth of Nations Rediscovered*.

[10] Some (e.g., North 1961) have argued that European warfare commencing in 1793 conferred economic advantages on a neutral US, at least until Jefferson's embargo in 1808, by stimulating demand for US shipping services and other new-world products. It is now evident that both the US financial revolution and a higher, modern rate of growth were in place for several years before 1793. Moreover, it is possible that the trade diversions, domestic political divisions, diplomatic uncertainties, increased borrowing costs associated with interruptions to capital inflows from Europe, and the increased US military and naval expenditures associated with the European wars, actually detracted from economic growth.

in the unsuccessful financial revolution in France attempted by John Law from 1715 to 1720. I list them here with a brief account of what happened in each area during the US financial revolution of 1789–1795 when Hamilton was Treasury Secretary.

- **Public finance and debt management.** In 1789 the US Treasury was virtually empty; in 1795 federal revenues were sufficient to fund government expenses and pay interest in hard-money equivalents on a national debt of $80 million. In 1789, no interest was paid on the national government's domestic debt, five-sixths of the total national debt as it emerged shortly afterwards, and the financial instruments that represented the domestic debt sold at 15 to 25 percent of par value. By 1791–1792, the main issue of new Treasury bonds for which investors had voluntarily swapped the old debt instruments sold at 100 to 120 percent of par in secondary security markets of major US cities.
- **Money.** In 1789, the US money stock consisted of a variety of gold and silver coins of other nations, and fiat paper money issued by state and national governments that fluctuated in value in relation to coin. By 1792, the US had a new dollar unit of account defined as certain weights of gold and silver, and had established a mint to make coins. Increasingly, however, money consisted of bank notes and deposits that were convertible into the specie dollar monetary base.
- **Central bank.** Absent in 1789; by 1792, the Bank of the United States (BUS) chartered by the federal government in 1791 with an authorized capital of $10 million was headquartered in Philadelphia and had branches in Boston, New York, Baltimore, and Charleston.
- **Banking system.** In 1790, three banks operated as local institutions in three cities. Two of them – the Bank of North America in Philadelphia and the Massachusetts Bank in Boston – were limited-liability corporations chartered by state governments, and the third – the Bank of New York – was what the British would term a joint-stock bank without limited liability. By 1795, the states had chartered twenty banking corporations that, along with the five offices of the Bank of the United States, comprised an integrated banking system headed by a large central bank.
- **Securities markets.** These existed in 1789, but trading in them was limited and sporadic. By 1792, securities markets were actively trading government bonds and corporate equities every weekday in Boston, New York, and Philadelphia, and Philadelphia and New York had established stock exchanges. Foreigners were active buyers of securities, transferring capital from Europe to the new American republic. By 1803–1804, European investors had purchased about half of all US

securities, public and private, most of which had been issued after 1789.[11]

- **Corporations, financial and non-financial.** Seven business corporations had been chartered in the American colonial era. In the 1780s, twenty-eight more business corporations were chartered by states. In 1791–1792, as the federal government chartered the BUS and it opened for business, states chartered forty corporations, more in two years than had been created from 1607 to 1790. States chartered 114 corporations during 1790–1795, and another 181 from 1796 to 1800. Thus, US states chartered 295 corporations in the decade 1791–1800.[12]

The effects of the financial revolution on US economic growth appear to have been immediate. Industrial production grew from 1790 to the business-cycle peak of 1796 at 7.4 percent per year, while real GDP per capita grew at 4 percent per year.[13] These are among the highest rates for any peak-to-peak expansion in US history. The US economy was off and running. Financial modernization no doubt was not the only reason, but it was a major reason for the jumpstart to US growth.

How could the US financial revolution, as dramatic in its range as it was compact in time it took to happen, have such a powerful effect. Mishkin suggests an answer:

Why is finance so important to economic growth? The answer is that the financial system is like the brain of the economy: it is a coordinating mechanism that allocates capital to building factories, houses and roads. If capital goes to the wrong uses or does not flow at all, the economy will operate inefficiently and economic growth will be very low. No work ethic can compensate for a mis-allocation of capital. Working hard will not make a country rich because hard-working workers will not be productive unless they work with the right amount of capital. Brain is more important than brawn, and similarly an efficient financial system is more important than hard work to an economy's success.[14]

The US economy in 1790 started fast out of the gate and achieved parity with the Mother Country, home of the industrial revolution, within four decades because it was equipped from the start with a highly developed brain.

That, of course, is only part of the comparative story. We also need to ask why the Mother Country's brain was not quite as developed as the

[11] Sylla *et al.*, "Integration of Trans-Atlantic Capital Markets."
[12] Davis, *Essays in the Earlier History of American Corporations*, vol. 2, Appendix B.
[13] Davis, "Index of U.S. Industrial Production"; Johnston and Williamson, "Real and Nominal GDP."
[14] Mishkin, "Is Financial Globalization Beneficial," p. 3.

US brain during those four decades two centuries ago, so that Britain was unable to maintain an economic lead from being the home of the industrial revolution. Ron Harris in his recent book, *Industrializing English Law*, suggests an answer:

If one accepts my claim that the business institutions that did develop during the period under discussion in this book [1720–1844] were not necessarily the most efficient possible, one should go a step further and agree that they did to a degree shape the development of the British economy. My methodology and research approach enable me only to hypothesize that *in a counterfactual world with early free incorporation, more joint-stock corporations would have been formed in the financial and in some industrial sectors; joint-stock banks would have played a more significant role in industrial finance; the aggregate rate of growth during the period 1760 to 1860, and beyond, would have been somewhat greater; managerial capitalism would have replaced the family firm in a more massive way by mid-nineteenth century; and Britain would have entered the economic decline of the nineteenth century in somewhat different shape.*[15]

I proceed to argue here that Harris's "counterfactual world" that would have made Britain grow faster than it did is, in fact, a pretty good description of the US in the decades after 1789, when the US grew faster than Britain did.

III. Comparing the British and US financial sectors

The six key institutional components of modern financial systems out-lined above provide a convenient framework for analyzing similarities and differences between the UK and US systems in the 1790–1830 period. Here I discuss them one by one, although it should to be remem-bered that "system" implies that the components typically mesh together in a mutually reinforcing manner, and that every now and then problems in one or more of the components reverberate throughout the system, sometimes leading to financial crises and economic fallout.

A. *Public finance and debt management*

The UK and US fiscal systems, at least on the surface, had a lot of simi-larities. Indeed, one of the charges leveled at Hamilton by his critics in the 1790s was that he seemed to be giving the US a "British" fiscal system along with all the corruption that went with the British system in the eyes of many Americans and some British observers. In both countries, govern-ment spending was financed heavily (at the national level) by customs

---

[15] Harris, *Industrializing English Law*, p. 292 (italics added).

duties and excise taxes, supplemented by postal revenues, land and property taxes, and local "rates." There were a few differences. The UK had a wartime income tax from 1798 to 1817; and in some years this yielded as much revenue as customs duties. In the US any direct tax ran into constitutional difficulties at the federal level. Many US state and local governments levied poll taxes, a practice that Britain had abandoned in the seventeenth century. The US government also raised money by selling land, although revenue from land sales seldom accounted for as much as 10 percent of federal revenues in the years from 1790 to 1830.

There was, however, a major fiscal difference between the two countries. In 1830, at the end of the period that concerns us here, the UK national debt stood at nearly £800 million, or more than 200 percent of GDP, and this absolute level of debt was maintained into the 1860s before it began to decline.[16] By contrast, the US national debt was just under $50 million in 1830, about 5 percent of GDP, and was headed toward extinction within a few years thereafter. Unlike the UK, the US was a federal state, and so we might also consider debts of state and local governments. In 1830, US states had about $25 million of debt, to which we might add a small amount of local debt. If we do, it remains that all government debt, about $80 million, was likely no more that 8 percent of GDP, far less than the 200 percent of the UK. In per capita terms, in 1830, the UK (population = 23.8 million) national debt was £33.5 or $161 per head (£ = $4.80), while the US level (population = 12.9 million) was about $6.20.

Even at relative and absolute peaks, there were large differences. For Britain, both peaks likely occurred in 1819, when £844 million of debt represented more that 250 percent of GDP. In the US the relative peak came at the start in 1790, when the debt of about $80 million after Hamilton's restructuring was about 40 percent of GDP. The absolute US peak came in 1816, with a national debt of $127 million, but by then it was only 16 percent of GDP.

There are a number of implications of the huge difference between UK and US debt burdens. The UK government collected in revenue £55.3 million, about 15 percent of UK GDP around 1830, and a little over half of this revenue went to pay interest on the national debt. In the US, on the other hand, federal revenues were only 2.5 percent of GDP, and if state and local revenues are added, the total would come to no more than 4 percent of GDP. The fact that the UK had to collect so much more revenue, which largely derived from customs duties and excise taxes, is the main reason I think Ward and Devereaux are correct

[16] Mitchell and Deane, *British Historical Statistics*, Chaps. 13–14.

in saying that prices in the UK were higher than those in the US. There was little tax in US prices, and a lot of tax in UK prices.[17]

Another implication of the debt differences has to do with the nature of securities markets in the two countries. The par value of equity on the London Stock Exchange (essentially the only UK stock exchange before 1830) is estimated by Peter Rousseau and me to have been £38 million in 1825.[18] Since the UK national debt was more than £800 million at the time, it is clear that the UK securities market was pretty much a government debt market. In the US on the other hand, Rousseau and I show that the equity market in 1825 was about the same size as that of the UK, but since government debt in the US was so much smaller, US securities markets were dominated by corporate equities to a much greater extent than was the case in the UK.

Finally, the relatively large debt burden of the UK relative to the US in the early nineteenth century must have had an impact on the relative growth of the two economies. The UK debt may have tended to crowd out private investment, but that tendency may have been mitigated, as Larry Neal has argued, by the efficiency of international capital markets in transferring foreign capital to Britain in the Napoleonic era.[19] British growth (product per person) did accelerate in the early nineteenth century, although it was acceleration to a relatively low level, 0.52 percent per year in 1801–1831, up from 0.35 percent per year in 1781–1801, according to Nicholas Crafts.[20]

Similar evidence indicates that the comparable growth rate in the period was 1.4 percent per year for the US, where a far more modest public debt was being paid down during the 1820s and 1830s. How much of the difference in real growth was caused by differences in debt burdens is unknown, but it must have been something. In any case, the difference in real growth rates makes it unsurprising, as Ward/Devereaux found, that the US may have caught up with the UK in GDP per capita by 1831, or by 1820, according to Prados. If the US was growing at a rate of 0.8 to 0.9 percent per year faster than the UK (or Britain) from 1790 to 1830, it would have made up a lot of ground over four decades even if it had started behind the UK, as was likely in the aftermath of the War of Independence, which likely disrupted the American economy far more than that of the UK.

---

[17] Taxes, of course, are only one factor that might affect price-level comparisons. Transport costs and the relative importance of different categories of goods and services in consumer budgets are others.

[18] Rousseau and Sylla, "Emerging Financial Markets."

[19] Neal, *Rise of Financial Capitalism*, Chap. 10.

[20] Crafts, "British Economic Growth, 1700–1850"; Neal, *Rise of Financial Capitalism*.

B.   *Money*

Data on the money stocks of the UK (especially) and the US for the early nineteenth century are pretty much in the nature of guesstimates. For the UK, Forrest Capie estimates a range for 1790 of from £63 to 76 million, or say £70 million for a point estimate.[21] The next tolerably complete estimate that I know of is that of Michael Collins, which is £255 million in 1850.[22] If so, the UK money stock from 1790 to 1850 grew at 2.15 percent per year, which on other grounds seems within the realm of plausibility. Growth at that rate would have given the UK a money stock of around £134 million in 1830. From Capie's earlier work, we know that these estimates pertain to a broad M3 version of the UK money stock that includes "non-bank holdings of notes and coins plus all deposits of all residents (both the public and private sectors) within the UK banking sector (including sight and time deposits in sterling and foreign currencies, and time deposits with accepting houses, overseas banks and other banks)."[23] Broad-money M3 is the only version of the UK money stock available before the twentieth century, with the annual time series starting at £540 million in 1870.

Assuming that the estimate of £134 million for 1830 is credible, it implies a per capita money stock of £5.61 or $27 for that year.

For the US, we have the estimates of Peter Temin for a narrower M2 version of the money stock that includes the public's holdings of specie plus notes and deposits of banks.[24] Missing are the monetary liabilities of private bankers and brokers, and, on the asset side, deposits of the US government, with their equivalents seemingly included in the UK data. The estimates are annual, but they move up and down from year to year in ways that suggest data problems rather than economic problems, so I average the estimates of 1825 to 1834 to obtain an estimate for 1830. The result is a US money stock of $129.3 million, or $10 per capita, as compared with $27 per capita for the UK at that time.

Even with allowance for different money stock concepts, M3 vs. M2, it seems evident (and perhaps not surprising) that the UK was the more monetized economy around 1830. Given that the two countries' GDPs per capita were about the same, this might seem something of a surprise. It is less of a surprise when one reflects on other differences between the UK and US economies, an issue to which I return later in the chapter.

[21] Capie, "Money and Economic Development," p. 222.
[22] Collins, *Money and Banking in the UK*, p. 40.
[23] Capie and Webber, *Monetary History of the United Kingdom*, pp. 15ff.
[24] Temin, *Jacksonian Economy*, p. 71.

C. Central banking

On the surface, the Bank of England (BoE) and the Banks of the United States were similar central banks. They were chartered by the central governments of their countries, the Bank of England in 1694 and the BUSs in 1791 and 1816. Hamilton, who promoted the BUS as Secretary of the Treasury and drafted its initial charter, modeled it in some ways on the BoE's charter. Each institution was its government's bank, holding public deposits, transferring public monies, helping the government to manage it debts, and managing international financial transactions. In each country, the central bank furnished a good proportion of total banknote circulation, and held substantial specie reserves. Each acted as a lender of last resort before the theory behind that concept had been fully worked out for orthodox central banking.

But there were important differences. The BoE was owned entirely by private investors, while the US government took a 20 percent stake in the capital of both BUSs. And the BUS was a branch bank from the start. The first BUS (1791–1811) had nine branches counting its Philadelphia headquarters. The second BUS (1816–1836) had twenty-six offices. The BoE was not authorized to open branches until 1826, and was only beginning to do so at the end of the 1820s.

In the period surveyed here, the Bank of the United States was much more of a modern banking corporation than was the Bank of England. In 1830, the BoE's assets consisted of £20.5 million of UK government debt, £3.9 million of other earning assets (discounts mainly), and £10.2 million of bullion (29 percent of its monetary liabilities). Against those assets, the BoE had issued £20.8 million of circulating notes, held £11.2 million of deposits (about half of which were government deposits), and had surplus capital (the so-called "Rest") of £2.6 million.[25] The BoE's total assets and liabilities thus came to £34.6 million, or $166.1 million. The original capital subscribed (and subsequent enlargements by subscription) was not carried on the balance sheet, and indeed had never been so identified. This capital was permanently invested in UK government debt, and so not available for banking purposes. The BoE before mid-nineteenth century was rather like a closed-end government bond fund, passing interest on UK debt, its main asset, to fund shareholders, and holding a large bullion reserve against its note and deposit liabilities. It made additional loans to private-sector borrowers, but those came to less than an eighth of its assets. Indeed, *Course of the Exchange* listed BoE stock as a government security, not a private corporate equity.

---

[25] Mitchell and Deane, *British Historical Statistics*, Chap. 15.

The two BUSs, in contrast, were thoroughly modern banks involved to a greater degree than the BoE in the banking business of the country. The second BUS in 1830 had $35 million of capital, issued $12.9 million in notes, held $16 million in deposits, and had other liabilities of $4.5 million, for a total of $68.4 million. On the asset side, it showed $40.7 million of loans and discounts (almost all to private borrowers, not the US government), "stocks" (mostly US government bonds) of $11.6 million, real estate (including banking houses) of $4.3 million, deposits with and notes of other banks ($4.2 million), and specie reserves of $7.6 million (26 percent of monetary liabilities), again for a total of $68.4 million.[26]

Until 1825, the Bank of England had an effective monopoly of corporate banking in England and Wales, since no other bank had received a corporate charter, and a law dating back to 1707–1708 had decreed that no other bank in that part of the UK could issue notes unless it was a partnership with a maximum of six partners. In 1826, unlimited-liability joint-stock banks with note-issuing privileges were authorized to bank beyond a sixty-five-mile radius of London, and in 1833 such banks were allowed in London provided they did not issue notes. These were measures to improve English banking by allowing joint-stock banks while at the same time allowing the BoE to maintain monopoly privileges. In return for losing some of its monopoly protections, the BoE was granted the right to open branches. But the joint-stock banks that new law allowed had little impact in English banking before the 1830s.

In contrast, both BUSs competed with other corporate banks in the US throughout their charter periods. The advantages of the BUSs included ones enjoyed by the BoE, namely the privilege of being the government's banker and substantially larger capitalizations than other US banks attained. An additional advantage of the BUS was the ability from the start to open branches nationwide, which gave the US effective interstate banking from 1792 to 1836.[27]

Which central bank did a better job of being a central bank? In the fourth edition of *Manias, Panics, and Crashes*, the late Charles Kindleberger lists financial crises around the world from 1618 to 1998.[28] The US from 1790 to 1830 had two crises, one in 1792 and the other in 1819. In each of these the BUS (first and second) was a new institution, and its early actions may well have contributed to the subsequent panic.

---

[26] US Bureau of the Census, *Historical Statistics of the United States*, series X566–79, p. 1018.

[27] Except for the years 1812–1816, after the charter of the first BUS had lapsed and until the second BUS was chartered.

[28] Kindleberger, *Manias*, Appendix B.

The UK ("England," to Kindleberger) on the other hand had six crises, in 1793, 1797, 1810, 1815–1816, 1819, and 1825, and during all of them the BoE was an old, established institution. By that comparison the BUSs appear to have done the better job of central banking by stabilizing its economy. There are other reasons to think that Hamilton, Gallatin, and Biddle, US leaders closely involved with the BUSs, understood central-bank crisis prevention and central banking functions in general better than did any leaders of the BoE during the 1790–1830 period, although others in England such as Sir Francis Baring and Henry Thornton may have had similar understandings.[29] This is another reason to think the BUSs were better at central banking than the BoE during the years when both existed.

D. Banking

Banking developed rapidly in both the UK and the US from 1790 to 1830. But it developed differently. Apart from the Bank of England, UK banks were partnerships. In England and Wales, there were two other types of banks, the London private banks and the country banks. London private banks experienced little growth. Rondo Cameron says there were fifty of them in 1825, the same number as in 1775, although they likely increased their capitals over that period.[30] Country banks numbered some 100 in the 1780s, 200–300 in the 1790s, 783 at the peak in 1810 (official statistics), then down to 521 in 1821, and 439 in 1830.[31] London private banks exhibited stability, whereas country banks – about 300 of them from 1795 to 1825 – failed in droves during UK financial crises. Scotland had fewer banks (thirty-two to thirty-eight between 1825 and 1836) with extensive branch systems (140 to 230 branches, 1825–1836) and Scottish banks were more stable than those of England and Wales.[32] Scotland, however, was but a sixth the size of England and Wales in population. Scotland's banks were not limited to six partners, as in England and Wales, and it was partly to copy Scotland after the financial crisis of 1825 with its numerous country bank failures that England introduced legal changes allowing larger joint-stock banks. Ireland also had a few banks, including the one bank (besides the BoE)

---

[29] See Hammond, *Banks and Politics*; Cowen, *Origins and Economic Impact of the First Bank*; and Wood, *History of Central Banking*, for discussions of the lender of last resort in the 1790–1830 period.
[30] Cameron *et al.*, *Banking in the Early Stages of Industrialization*, p. 33.
[31] Pressnell, *Country Banking*, p. 11.
[32] Cameron *et al.*, *Banking in the Early Stages of Industrialization*, p. 66.

in all of the UK to be listed on the London Stock Exchange in the mid-1820s.

In a banking system of partnerships with unlimited liability, the concept of banking capital is ambiguous. Theoretically, the combined net worth of all the partners could be considered the capital of a banking partnership. Despite the ambiguity, Cameron estimates the capital invested in banking in England and Wales in 1825, including that of the BoE, to have been £11.4 million pounds, or $55 million.[33] Comparable data on capital do not seem to be available for Scotland and Ireland, but if they were available they might show a total UK capital of some $70–80 million.

US banking developed from next to nothing (three state banks) in 1790 to a system of 330 state banks in 1825, plus the BUS with twenty-five branches.[34] Almost all of these banks were corporations with, as a rule, strict limited liability. In addition, there were numerous private bankers whose numbers and assets we do not know. The 330 state banks of 1825 had authorized capitals of $157 million, of which about 70 percent ($110 million) was paid in; in 1830 the data indicate 381 banks with $170 million of capital authorized and about $119 million paid in. To the state bank figures we would have to add the BUS with $35 million of capital, all paid in, giving the US banking corporate banking system a paid-in capitalization of $145–154 million during 1825–1830. This is approximately twice the capitalization of the UK banking system even though the US had only a little over half the population of the UK.

Several consequences follow from the facts that US banks were predominantly corporations with limited liability while UK banks were predominantly partnerships with unlimited liability. One we have just seen: US banks attracted much more capital investment. Because they were more highly capitalized, US banks could create much more credit than their UK counterparts per unit of monetary liabilities; they could lend their capital in addition to lending their notes and deposits. For example, the banking data for New England state-chartered banks, which are more or less complete, indicate that on average in the decade 1825–1834 the banks had notes and deposits of $22.7 million per year, but their loans and discounts averaged $53.9 per year.[35] The data for the

---

[33] Ibid., p. 33.

[34] Sylla, "US Securities Markets and the Banking System," Table 1, p. 86. A more recent annual series on the number of banks and branches in the United States (Weber 2006) differs slightly from the numbers given in Table 1, with most of the differences appearing to result from when a bank was chartered and when, as in Weber's series, it actually commenced operations.

[35] Fenstermaker et al., "Monetary Statistics of New England," pp. 452–3.

Table 7.1. *US state-chartered banks: numbers and authorized capital, by region and total, 1790–1835* (*Capital in millions of dollars*)

Region Year	New England		Mid-Atlantic		South		West		US	
	Number	Capital	Number	Capital	Number	Capital	Number	Capital	Number	Capital
1790	1	0.8	2	2.3					3	3.1
1795	11	4.1	9	9.4					20	13.5
1800	17	5.5	11	11.9					28	17.4
1805	45	13.2	19	21.7	6	3.5	1	0.5	71	38.9
1810	52	15.5	32	29.4	13	9.1	5	2.2	102	56.2
1815	71	24.5	107	67.1	22	17.2	12	6.4	212	115.2
1820	97	28.3	125	74.4	25	28.6	80	28.4	327	159.6
1825	159	42.2	122	71.2	32	33.3	17	9.4	330	156.6
1830	186	48.8	140	73.8	35	37.3	20	10.5	381	170.4
1835	285	71.5	189	90.2	63	111.6	47	35.0	584	308.4

Source: see note 34.

UK are not so systematic, but from casual observation of several English country-bank balance sheets published by Pressnell for the same era, it appears that the credit (loans and discounts) created by banks was less than or about the same as their note and deposit liabilities, in part because – as we might expect – a lack of limited liability meant that UK banks were more thinly capitalized than US banks.[36]

Another consequence of the greater capitalization of US banking corporations is that US banks were much less likely to fail (annual average failure rate of five per thousand, 1782–1837) than English banks, the annual average failure rate of which was eighteen per thousand, 1809–1830. Scottish banks did better than either England or (marginally) the US, failing at an annual rate of four per thousand during 1809–1830.[37]

So US banks by the late 1820s had attracted twice the investment capital of UK banks even though the US had only half the population of the Mother Country, they were able to create far more credit per dollar of monetary liabilities because of that greater capitalization, and they failed considerably less frequently than UK banks. Although proponents of each type of banking system debated the question of which system was better at the time, to us now the answer should seem obvious.[38] The US had much the better system. Anyone who disagrees has to shoulder the burden of explaining why the UK eventually liberalized its banking laws to allow its banks to become limited-liability corporations, which nearly all of them did by the end of the nineteenth century.

E.   Securities markets

Apart from the huge UK–US difference in national debts, and London's trading of foreign debt securities (which was not a feature of US markets), by 1830 the securities markets of the two countries were quite similar in size, at least in terms of the numbers of corporate securities traded (see Table 7.2). In 1830, London was essentially the only UK securities market; provincial markets appeared later. The US had seven markets, but those outside the northeastern states were small. State and local debt securities are included in the US data because they financed some of the same activities companies financed in the UK, for example, canals and utilities.

What about capitalizations of these securities? The paid-up capitalization of the 156 UK joint-stock companies established prior to 1824 is given by E. Victor Morgan and W.A. Thomas as £33.1 million, or

---

[36] Pressnell, *Country Banking.*   [37] Sylla, "Early American Banking," p. 118.
[38] See ibid.

Table 7.2. *Number of company and state/local securities listed in UK and US markets in 1830*

Sector	Lon.	Bos.	NY	Phil.	Balt.	Rich.	Chas'ton	N.O.	US total
Canals, navig.	72		1	8	5			1	15
Insurance	28	17	34	13	7		2	4	77
Utilities	49		1		4				5
Roads	7			4	5				9
Mines	22		2	2	1				5
Railways	4		2		2				4
State/local debt			12	7	4		4		27
Banks		18	20	14	11	3	5	4	75 (71*)
Mfg.		6			2				8
Misc.	24			1					1
Total	206	41	72	48	42	3	9	9	226 (222*)

* The BUS was traded, and counted, in five cities; the asterisked figure eliminates the multiple counting.
Source: London: Harris (2000), p. 219; US cities: Sylla, Wilson, Wright securities database (ICPSR), taken from contemporary newspapers; Boston manufacturing companies from Martin (1898), p. 128.

$159 million.[39] Harris notes 258 companies listed in *Course of the Exchange* in 1825, when there was a boom in UK company formations, but only 206 in 1830, as in Table 7.2, after the boom collapsed.[40] Harris gives no capitalization data for either 1825 or 1830, but Rousseau and I, as mentioned above, estimated it using *Course* at £38 million, or $183 million.[41] Given the disappearance of joint-stock companies from *Course* between 1825 and 1830, the latter figure is probably close to the actual 1830 level.

There is not a corresponding figure available for the US, but Table 7.1 showed that the authorized capital of US state banks in 1830 was $170.4 million. About 70 percent of that capital, or $119 million, was paid up, to which we can add the $35 million capital (all paid up) of the BUS and the $30 million of state and local debts in 1830 used for purposes financed by companies in the UK. The total of these items, which does not include the capital of other sectors (notably a large US corporate insurance sector) is $179 million. Only seventy of the 381 US state banks

---

[39] Morgan and Thomas, *Stock Exchange*, Table III, p. 278.
[40] Harris, *Industrializing English Law*.
[41] Rousseau and Sylla, "Emerging Financial Markets," pp. 8–9.

in 1830 were traded in the markets listed in Table 7.2, but these were the largest banks representing a good portion of the estimated state banking capital of $119 million, and there were local markets for the shares of the other state banking corporations not listed and traded in the major city markets.

Table 7.2 also brings out a glaring difference between the UK and US securities markets. The financial sector hardly appears at all in the UK listings. The Bank of England (not included in Table 7.2 – it was treated as a national-debt security by *Course* and UK investors) and the Provincial Bank of Ireland (included in Miscellaneous) were the only two banks, and the US had almost three times as many insurance companies as the UK, where much insurance underwriting remained private rather than corporate.[42] If financial development matters for economic growth, as seems increasingly evident to those who study the connection, it appears that between 1790 and 1830, securities markets did relatively little in the UK as compared to the US to encourage financial development.

The bottom line is that the data given here indicate that, apart from national and foreign debts, the UK and US securities markets were about equal in size, whether measured in listings or capitalizations, in 1830. And because a majority of the US listings do not enter into these calculations, there is a pretty good chance that a full accounting would show the US equity market to have been substantially larger than the UK's by 1830. Since the US population was only 54 percent of the UK's, the US securities market most likely made a substantially larger contribution to US economic growth than did the Mother Country's securities market.

F.   Corporations

Probably the greatest difference between the UK and US financial and economic systems (as well as between the US and any other nation) was the proliferation of business corporations after 1790. In this area the US developed a large lead from the start over other countries. Those countries did not begin to emulate the US in easing the path of business to incorporation until mid-nineteenth century or after. By that time the US had thousands of business corporations.

The UK lagged behind the US in corporate development largely because the Bubble Act of 1720, which remained in effect until 1825, made it difficult for British entrepreneurs to avail themselves of the

---

[42] Kingston, "Marine Insurance in Britain and America," and "Marine Insurance in Philadelphia."

Table 7.3. *Corporations chartered in the US, 1607–1800*

Colonial era	7		
1781	1	1791	9
1782	0	1792	31
1783	1	1793	15
1784	3	1794	17
1785	3	1795	42
1786	2	1796	32
1787	6	1797	41
1788	5	1798	36
1789	3	1799	33
1790	4	1800	39
1781–1790	28	1791–1800	295

Source: derived from Davis (1917), vol. 2, appendix B, pp. 332ff.

corporate form. Indeed, Harris's study of entrepreneurship and business organization in the UK is something of a lament about this British failure, which only timidly began to be redressed after the 1825 crisis led to repeal of the Bubble Act. And full redress did not come for another two to three decades. Table 7.3, showing corporations chartered in the US between the Jamestown settlement and 1800, demonstrates the British legacy and the effects of the US financial revolution of the early 1790s. Under British rule, 1607–1776, apparently only seven corporations were chartered. Four times as many corporations, though still not a lot by later standards, were chartered in the 1780s as in the entire colonial era. Then more than ten times the number for the 1780s were granted charters in the 1790s. In 1791–1792 alone, in the midst of the financial revolution, more corporations were chartered than in all previous years of US history. The controversial federal charter of the BUS, a very large corporation for its time, seems to have served as a precipitating factor; state governments did not want to be co-opted by the new federal government with its Hamiltonian plans for economic modernization, so they turned favorable ears to charter requests from would-be bankers and other entrepreneurs.

The corporate boom of the 1790s was just the beginning. Between 1800 and 1830, the six New England states chartered 1,722 corporations.[43] New York chartered nearly a thousand companies in these three decades.[44] Maryland, New Jersey, and Pennsylvania chartered

---

[43] Kessler, "Incorporation in New England," p. 46.
[44] Hilt, "Corporate Ownership and Governance."

194, 188, and 428 corporations. The total for these ten northeastern US states is more than 3,500 corporate charters in the first three decades of the nineteenth century. Even Ohio, a new state in 1803, chartered 117 corporations from that year to 1830.[45] Currently, we know little about corporate charters granted in the states to the south and west of these eleven northeastern US states, but we suspect there were fewer of them.

Not all of the corporations states chartered, of course, lasted, and some charters granted may not have resulted in enterprise formations. Of the 827 corporations New York charted before 1826, only 266 (32 percent) appear to have been operating, or at least responded in 1827 when the state asked them to report information. Some may never have commenced business. Others may have stayed in business only a few years before winding up voluntarily or involuntarily. Of these New York corporations, 82 percent of their total paid-up capital of $46 million in 1827 was that of the state's 44 banks and 48 insurance companies.[46] The corporate form seems to have been especially attractive to financial firms in the early US.

If we apply New York's 32 percent persistence rate to the total charters of all eleven states for which we have information, the number of corporations operating in these states around 1830 could be estimated at no less than 1,100 to 1,200. The hard estimate we have for joint-stock companies in the UK nearest to that date is 156 companies established before 1824.[47] The UK had a spate of company formations during 1824–1825, with 624 new ones. By 1827, about 500 of these had disappeared. So it is a fairly safe to say that the UK had perhaps 250 to 300 joint-stock companies around 1830, roughly one-quarter of the corporations operating in eleven states, all but one northeastern, in the US.

Joint-stock companies, moreover, were inferior to corporations as a business form. Liability was unlimited, and British legal cases before 1844 frowned on such companies issuing tradable shares, a legacy of the Bubble Act both before and after it was repealed in 1826.[48] Not all US corporations possessed limited liability, but in general it was the default option unless charters specified other than limited liability. Hence, it appears that in company law and encouragement of forms of enterprise that pooled capital to achieve economies of scale, the US was far ahead of the UK by 1830.

---

[45] Evans, *Business Incorporations in the United States.*
[46] Hilt, "Corporate Ownership and Governance."
[47] Morgan and Thomas, *Stock Exchange*, p. 280.
[48] Harris, *Industrializing English Law*, Chaps. 8–10.

IV.   Assessing financial leadership

It is time to summarize and expand on the above comparative findings. There were some regional and global similarities as well as differences between the two nations, and these have comparative implications. For example, one can view both countries as empires. The UK might be regarded as the center of a vast British world empire, or – as the Scots and the Irish might view it – England and Wales could be regarded as the empire's center, with Scotland, Ireland, and the overseas entities comprising the empire's peripheries. The US empire was more internal, and as of 1830 it was still incomplete, as the northwest border had yet to be determined and the southwest, Alaska, and Hawaii had yet to be brought into the country's borders. The center of the US empire was the Northeast, comprising the New England and Middle Atlantic states including Delaware, Maryland, and the federal capital in the District of Columbia. The US northeast, where much of US financial development had taken place by 1830, can be viewed as in roughly the same position as the UK in one version of the British empire, or as England and Wales in the Scots-Irish version.

A map of the continental US with the UK on the same scale would indicate that the UK would fit comfortably into the US northeast, which in fact is nearly 50 percent larger in area than the UK.[49] In many ways, the US northeast offers a fairer basis for making comparisons with the UK (or England and Wales) than does the entire US. The US northeast by the early 1800s had been settled for approximately two centuries by people quite similar to those of the UK, and had developed a commercial, industrial, and agricultural economy quite like that of the UK.

Other regions of the US were very different. The US south with its semitropical agriculture and low-wage (slave) labor can be regarded as akin to India. The US west, a newly settled area, can be regarded as the US empire's Canada, Australia, and New Zealand. Only a prisoner of nation-state thinking would fail to see grasp such economic similarities between the regions of the US internal empire and those of the British external empire.

In terms of population, the UK was much the larger country in 1830. It had some 23.8 million souls, as compared with 12.9 million in the US. And England and Wales, the Scots-Irish version of the headquarters

---

[49] Such a map appears in Thomas McCraw, ed., *Creating Modern Capitalism* (Cambridge: Harvard University Press, 1997), p. 544. The UK, Germany, and Japan together fit comfortably into the territory of the forty-eight contiguous US states, with about 80 percent of the area remaining for Americans.

of the British Empire, had 13.8 million souls; the US Northeast had 6.1 million. I use these population data and the conceptual framework outlined above to make the following comparative observations, some of which appeared earlier in the chapter, about the two financial systems around 1830.

A.   Public finance and debt

The UK had a national debt of $161 per person. The US had a national, state, and local debt of $6–$7 per person. There is no reasonable basis for attributing these total public debts to particular sub-regions of the UK and US. In terms of willingness to incur public debt, the UK clearly "wins." Although a thriving public debt market trading low-risk government securities is probably a good thing for any financial system and economy, there are reasons for doubting whether this "victory" was all that good for UK economic growth. To service its huge debt, the UK had to tax its industrious classes in order to transfer substantial income to the rentier class.

B.   Money

The UK had a broad M3 money stock of $27 per capita. The US had a narrower M2 money stock of $10 per capita. Again, there is no good way to estimate the money stock of sub-regions in either country; that can be accomplished more readily for bank assets (see below). But even taking into account the different concepts of money, the UK again appears to be the "winner." It had a higher ratio of money to GDP, that is, it had more monetary "depth" or, what is the same thing, a lower velocity of money.

On the other hand, both countries had similar monetary systems, with bank money being convertible (apart from periods in which convertibility was temporarily suspended) into a precious-metal monetary base or central-bank notes. Furthermore, by the 1820s there appear to have been few concerns about the monetary situation in either country. Britons did not generally complain about having too much money (or inflation), and Americans did not generally complain about having too little (or deflation). The two countries were part of an international monetary system (or systems) anchored in precious-metal convertibility that tended automatically to correct any temporary surpluses or shortages of money. Hence, as far as money is concerned, there is no winner or loser.[50] The

---

[50] I thank Charles Calomiris for making this point forcefully in his discussion of this paper at its first public presentation in April 2006.

quantitative monetary differences observed resulted from differences in economic structures rather than from a lead of Britain and a lag of the US in financial and monetary development.

C.   Central banking

In the UK, Bank of England assets per capita came to $6.97 in 1830. In the US, BUS assets per capita came to $5.30. The UK is moderately ahead of the US on this financial measure. Since the main business of the BoE at the time was to hold UK public debt and issue bank notes against it and its specie reserves, there is no reason to allocate its activities among the three regions of the UK. In the case of the US, three-quarters of banking activity took place in the US northeast. If we attribute the same proportion of BUS activity to the northeast where its headquarters and twelve of the twenty-five branches were located, BUS assets per capita in the US northeast were $8.41, greater than BoE assets per UK capita of $6.97. Since the BUS was more of a modern bank actively involved with its banking system than the BoE, and since the US had fewer financial crises, the nod in central banking goes to the US.

D.   Banking system

Data limitations for both countries, particularly the UK, make it difficult to compare the two in terms of banking assets. For the UK, I attempt an estimate by starting with the money stock estimate of £134 million in 1830. To get the bank-money part of this, I subtract an estimate of the coin part. Capie estimates coin in the UK money stock at £44 in 1790, and Collins gives it as £61 million in 1850.[51] A figure in the range of £50–55 million seems reasonable for 1830; I use £50, so as not to short-change the UK banks. Subtracting coin from the money stock yields an estimate of £84 million of bank money (notes and deposits) in 1830. To get a measure of total bank assets via this route of estimating total bank liabilities, there should be added to this the banking capital of the UK. Cameron *et al.* estimate the banking capital of the UK as £11.4 million in 1825, including the capital of the BoE. So perhaps it was £12 million by 1830. Adding capital to bank monetary liabilities thus give an estimate of total UK bank liabilities (and thus assets) of £96 million, or $461 million in 1830. On a per capita basis, this is $19 per head. In 1850, a year when estimates for the UK are fairly complete, the monetary

---

[51] Capie, "Money and Economic Development," p. 224; Collins, *Money and Banking in the UK*, p. 40.

liabilities of banks in England and Wales were 73 percent of those of the UK.[52] Applying this ratio to 1830, I estimate the bank assets of England and Wales at $337 million, or $24 per person in England and Wales, somewhat above the $19 per capita estimated for the whole UK.

For the US, Wright, by applying the ratio of bank assets to authorized capital of banks for which this known (72 percent of them) to the authorized capital of all banks (including the BUS), estimates US bank assets at $403.5 million in 1830.[53] The procedure is rough because only 70 percent of the authorized capital of state banks was paid up (although presumably callable), whereas all of the capital of the BUS was paid up. To refine the estimate of state bank assets, I subtract from Wright's estimate of total bank assets the assets of the BUS ($68.4 million) and the estimated unpaid part of the authorized capital of state banks ($51.1million). This yields an estimate of state bank assets of $284 million, or $22 per capita for the US. To this should be added the $5.30 of assets per capita of the BUS, giving bank assets per capita for the US in 1830 of $27. This is greater than the bank assets per capita of either the UK as a whole or of England and Wales.

Going further, 82 percent of US state banks and 72 percent of authorized state bank capital were in the US northeast in 1830. On the basis of these ratios, I assume 75 percent of US state banking activity, and most likely a similar proportion of the business of the BUS, took place in the northeast. Total US bank assets of $352.4 ($284 state and $68.4 BUS) times 0.75 yields an estimate of bank assets for the US northeast of $264.3 million, or $43 per capita.

Several comparative conclusions about banking in the UK and the US follow from this analysis. In 1830, bank assets per capita for the US ($27) exceeded those of the UK ($19) and even England and Wales ($24). Bank assets per capita in the US northeast ($43) considerably exceeded those of either the UK or England and Wales. In terms of banking, the US northeast most likely possessed the most highly developed system in the world in 1830. And the reason for that is also clear. Although the UK had more money per capita at the time than the US, banking in the US – especially in the US northeast – was far more developed than UK banking because US banks were usually limited-liability corporations that attracted much more capital investment than the thinly capitalized UK banks, held back as they were by unlimited liability and, in England

[52] Cameron et al., *Banking in the Early Stages of Industrialization*; Collins, *Money and Banking in the UK*, p. 40.
[53] Wright, "Early US Financial Development," and Wright, "National Financial Data Estimations."

and Wales, the six-partner rule in effect from 1707 to 1825 to preserve the Bank of England's monopoly of corporate banking. Hence, while the UK may have had more money per capita than the US, the US was able to furnish considerably more bank credit per capita than could UK banks. For economic growth, bank credit matters more than the monetary stock. This is likely a reason the US economy grew faster than did the UK economy in the early nineteenth century. In banking, the US wins. In time, the UK would emulate it.

E.   Securities markets

Comparative conclusions about securities markets follow from the data of Table 7.2. Listed company securities in the UK per million people come to 8.7; for the US the figure is 17.1 (including a number of state debt securities that financed such items as canals that were financed by companies in the UK). Since the London securities market was essentially the only one in the UK in 1830, the same number of company securities that went into the UK calculation yields 14.9 listed securities per million people in England and Wales. For the US northeast, we combine the listings of the markets of Boston, New York, Philadelphia, and Baltimore (leaving out Richmond, Charleston, and New Orleans) to yield 33.3 security listings per million people, more than twice the level for the UK. Again, the early extension of limited-liability corporate privileges seems to have led securities-market development to outpace and surpass that of the UK during the four decades 1790–1830.

Comparing the company securities markets in this manner leaves out, of course, the vast difference between the two countries in the extents of their national-debt markets. It does emphasize, on the other hand, the sector of the capital markets that is most likely to promote economic growth. Unless one is prepared to argue that the huge UK national debt, as well as the high levels of taxation that sustained it, were actually positives for UK growth, the US wins this competition.

F.   Corporations

In this financial-system key component, which figures largely in the US advantage over the UK in banking and securities-market development, the competition between the two countries can hardly be called real competition. Ignoring many states (but perhaps not so many corporations), eleven US states for which we have good data had chartered about 1,200 corporations that were in operation around 1830, or ninety-three corporations per million people. The 300 hundred joint-stock companies estimated for the UK at that time come to about thirteen per million people. If we consider all of those joint-stock companies to be in England and Wales – perhaps largely but not entirely the case – there were twenty-two of them per million people. The US northeast had about 1,100 operating corporations at the time, or 180 per million people. Still to be determined are the relative sizes of companies, joint-stock and incorporated, in the two countries. Still, even without considering the disadvantages of the UK joint-stock company as compared with the US corporation as a form of enterprise organization, the US appears to win hands down.

In ways that mattered for economic growth, the US financial system, quantitatively and qualitatively, surpassed that of the UK by 1830. And the US northeast, the center of the US empire, probably possessed the most developed financial system in the world at that time, one that in most important growth-enhancing respects was certainly more advanced than that of the Mother Country. It was a key reason why the US caught up with the UK as quickly as it did, and why it was on a higher growth trajectory that would lead the US in a few more decades to surpass the UK in growth and development. This was the longer-term legacy of the US financial revolution four decades before, in the early 1790s.

V.   Financial system reversals and leadership changes

Given the evident superiority of the US financial system over that of the UK around 1830, what can account for the widespread impression that the UK always had a superior system? Why does almost everyone think that the UK was the leader of world finance throughout the nineteenth century?

I can think of three reasons. First, the UK system got better after 1830. Second, the US system got worse. Together these changes probably did give the UK the better system during the second half of the nineteenth century, the period that shaped the impressions of economic historians. Third, the UK, an island nation with an overseas empire, had a strong international orientation in finance whereas the focus of US finance during the nineteenth century, in contrast, was almost entirely on the domestic economic development of a nation of continental dimensions. Hence, US financial development in comparison with the UK's was less noticed and experienced by the rest of the world.

The UK system began to improve after 1825 with the repeal of the Bubble Act of 1720 and the ending of Bank of England's monopoly, dating from 1707, of joint-stock banking in England and Wales. As Neal put it in describing reforms to the UK financial system that began in the wake of the UK financial crisis of 1825, "The policy changes that affected the monetary regime ... while minor in each particular and slow to take effect, were cumulatively effective in laying the basis for Britain's dominance in the world financial system until the outbreak of World War I."[54]

From 1826 onward, joint-stock banks with note-issuing powers could be organized sixty-five miles away from London, and in 1833, they could organize in London provided they did not issue notes. In return, the Bank of England obtained the right to open branches, and began to move toward being more of a central bank like the Banks of the United States. Britain had fewer financial crises after 1825.

In 1844, Gladstone's Joint-Stock Companies Registration Act made it possible for a UK company, merely by registering, to enjoy "all the features of incorporation – separate personality, free transferability of shares, and hierarchical management structure – with but one exception: limitation of liability."[55] Even the exception was eliminated in the late 1850s, when the UK at last allowed corporations, including banks, with limited liability.

The UK national debt was stable from the 1820s to the 1860s, and then declined steadily to the turn of the century. The UK banking system eventually consolidated and developed extensive branch networks. It was the resulting late-nineteenth, early-twentieth century UK financial system that became so admired by historians.

Across the Atlantic, Andrew Jackson vetoed Congress's renewal of the charter of the Bank of the United States in 1832, and Congress could not muster the supermajority of votes to override the veto. Thus, the BUS ceased being a central bank in 1836. Not until 1914, when Congress established the Federal Reserve System, would the US again have a central bank.

The 1832 veto unleashed a decade of financial instability, crises, and depression. The US had more frequent financial crises after 1832 than before, while the UK had fewer of them. Moreover, US currency entered an era of messiness and widespread counterfeiting until national legislation of the Civil War era re-introduced federally chartered banking – the national banks – and re-established a more uniform currency – greenbacks and national bank notes, both of which were effectively currencies backed by the credit of the US government.[56] The loss of the BUS with its nationwide branch network also led to further

[54] Neal, "Financial Crisis of 1825," p. 53.
[55] Harris, *Industrializing English Law*, p. 283.
[56] Mihm, *A Nation of Counterfeiters*.

entrenchment of unit banking and proliferation of thousands of small banks rather than, as in the UK, consolidation into larger banks with extensive branch networks. In money, banking, and central banking, the US therefore took steps backward after 1830.

The Civil War raised the US national debt to near-British levels. Only the corporate system and the securities markets remained relatively unscathed by the Jacksonian "great reversal" of US financial development. These key financial components tended to improve rather than become worse after the 1830s, as states introduced general incorporation laws and New York City became the undisputed center of US finance.

Given the favorable UK and unfavorable US financial developments after 1830, it is not difficult to understand why some investigators have found that the UK gained relative to the US in terms of real income per person from the 1830s to the 1870s. The Jacksonian "great reversal" appears as well in yield spreads between the UK and the US. UK consol yields averaged 3.69 percent from 1820 to 1832 (after which US yields are problematic, as the national debt was disappearing), and US Treasuries 4.52 percent, for a spread of 83 basis points (bp). When US debt reappeared in 1842, the spreads were 217 bp in the 1840s, 107 bp in the 1850s, and 207 bp in the 1860s.[57]

A more continuous series of US yields over the same decades is that of New England municipal (state and local) bonds. In the 1820s the spread of this series over consols was 105 bp; in the 1830s it widened to 155 bp, and further to 176 bp and 190 bp in the 1840s and 1850s.[58] Country risk appeared to increase for the US. That might have happened for lots of reasons besides Jacksonian policies, including rising tensions over slavery. On the other hand, the data just mentioned have another, more telling, feature. New England municipals had market yields higher than those of US government bonds from 1820 to 1832. When US government debt reappeared in the markets in 1842, New England municipals sold at lower yields than federal debt did. And well they might. An administration that killed a central bank designed to lend it money when needed should have expected no less of a reaction from domestic and foreign investors when it weakened its financial position.

Further, Rose Razaghian's structural-break analysis of US bond yields indicates a break raising yields when the first BUS failed to be re-chartered in 1811, a break to lower yield levels when the second BUS

---

[57] Homer and Sylla, *History of Interest Rates*, derived from Tables 19 and 38, pp. 192–4 and 282–4.
[58] Ibid.

appeared in 1817, and a break to higher yields when Jackson vetoed the second BUS re-charter in 1832.[59] The evidence is quite strong that Andrew Jackson perhaps unintentionally was something of a bomb-thrower into the state-of-the-art financial system he inherited on assuming the presidency in 1829. He was, of course, neither the first nor the last US leader to abuse the financial system.

The two BUSs from the 1790s to the 1830s were integral parts of Hamilton's well-designed US financial system. When they were terminated for political reasons that from an economic viewpoint have to be viewed as misguided, the credibility of that system – the confidence in it demonstrated by investors – was damaged. After 1830, the US paid a price for damaging its financial system, just as the UK gained from improving its system.

Nonetheless, the negative developments on the US financial scene in 1811 and 1832 should not lead us to forget the splendid financial and economic accomplishments of the US from 1790s to the 1830s when its financial system came to equal, and even to surpass, the older, less liberal system of the UK, which was the best in Europe. The US system was the brain, at that time a more developed brain than the UK had in its financial system, driving US economic development by financing territorial acquisitions, land settlement, transportation improvements, and industrialization.

We give the last word to Tocqueville, the young French aristocrat who visited the US in 1832, who admired both the BUS (just as Jackson was starting to dismantle it) and what he saw happening in the American economy:

The United States of America emerged from the colonial dependence in which England held them only a half century ago; the number of great fortunes there is very small and capital is still rare. There is nevertheless no people on earth that has made as rapid progress as the Americans in commerce and industry. Today they form the second maritime nation in the world; and although their manufactures have to struggle against almost insurmountable obstacles, they continue to make new developments daily.

In the United States the greatest industrial enterprises are executed without difficulty, because the population as a whole is involved in industry and because the poorest as well as the most opulent citizen willingly unite their efforts in this. One is therefore astonished daily to see immense works executed without trouble by a nation that includes so to speak no rich men. Americans arrived only yesterday on the soil they inhabit, and they have already overturned the whole order of nature to their profit. They have united the Hudson to the Mississippi and linked the Atlantic Ocean with the Gulf of Mexico across more than five

---

[59] Razaghian, "Political Institutions and Sovereign Debt."

hundred leagues of continent that separate the two seas. The longest railroads that have been made up to our day are in America.[60]

That was the early 1830s, not the 1920s, 1950s, or 2000s. Perhaps – and just perhaps, pending more investigation of the other countries' financial systems – the uniquely rapid growth of the early US in commerce and industry by the 1830s was a consequence of having a financial system that was the equal of any other country.

References

Broadberry, Stephen N., and Douglas A. Irwin. April 2006. "Labor Productivity in the United States and the United Kingdom during the Nineteenth Century." *Explorations in Economic History* 43: 257–79.

Brunt, Liam. March 2006. "Rediscovering Risk: Country Banks as Venture Capital Firms in the First Industrial Revolution", *Journal of Economic History* 66: 74–102.

Cameron, Rondo, *et al.* 1967. *Banking in the Early Stages of Industrialization*. New York: Oxford University Press.

Capie, Forrest. 2004. "Money and Economic Development in Eighteenth-century England," in Leandro Prados de la Escosura, ed., *Exceptionalism and Industrialization: Britain and its European Rivals, 1688–1815*. Cambridge: Cambridge University Press.

Capie, Forrest., and Alan Webber. 1985. *A Monetary History of the United Kingdom, 1870–1982*. London: George Allen & Unwin.

Collins, Michael. 1988. *Money and Banking in the UK: a History*. London: Croom Helm.

Cowen, David J. 2000. *The Origins and Economic Impact of the First Bank of the United States, 1791–1797*. New York & London: Garland Publishing.

Crafts, N.F.R. July 1987. "British Economic Growth, 1700–1850: Some Difficulties of Interpretation." *Explorations in Economic History* 24: 245–68.

Davis, Joseph H. November, 2004. "A quantity-based annual index of U.S. industrial production, 1790–1915." *Quarterly Journal of Economics* 119: 1177–1215.

Davis, Joseph S. 1917. *Essays in the Earlier History of American Corporations*. Cambridge: Harvard University Press.

Evans, G. Heberton. 1948. *Business Incorporations in the United States 1800–1943*. New York: National Bureau of Economic Research.

Fenstermaker, J. Van, John E. Filer, and Robert Stanley Herren. June 1984. "Monetary Statistics of New England, 1785–1837." *Journal of Economic History* 44: 441–53.

Gallman, Robert E. 1966. "Gross National Product in the United States, 1834–1909." In *Output, Employment, and Productivity in the United States after*

---

[60] Tocqueville, *Democracy in America*, 528–9.

1800. NBER Studies in Income and Wealth 30. Chicago: University of Chicago Press: 3–76.

Hammond, Bray. 1957. *Banks and Politics in America, from the Revolution to the Civil War.* Princeton: Princeton University Press.

Harris, Ron. 2000. *Industrializing English Law: Entrepreneurship and Business Organization, 1720–1844.* Cambridge: Cambridge University Press.

Hilt, Eric. 2006. "Corporate Ownership and Governance in the Early Nineteenth Century." Working Paper, Wellesley College.

Homer, Sidney, and Richard Sylla. 2005. *A History of Interest Rates.* Fourth edition. New York: Wiley.

Johnston, Louis D., and Samuel H. Williamson. "The Annual Real and Nominal GDP for the United States, 1790-Present." Economic History Services, 2006, URL: http://www.eh.net/hmit/gdp/.

Kessler, William C. May 1948. "Incorporation in New England: a Statistical Study, 1800–1875." *Journal of Economic History* 8: 43–62.

Kindleberger, Charles P. 2000. *Manias, Panics, and Crashes: a History of Financial Crises.* Fourth edition. New York: Wiley.

Kingston, Christopher. June 2006. "Marine Insurance in Britain and America, 1720–1844: A Comparative Institutional Analysis," *Journal of Economic History* 66, no. 2: 379–409.

——— 2007. "Marine Insurance in Philadelphia during the Quasi-War with France, 1795–1801." Working Paper, Amherst College.

Martin, Joseph G. 1898. *A Century of Finance: Martin's History of the Boston Stock and Money Markets, 1798–1898.* Boston: The Author.

Mihm, Stephen. 2007. *A Nation of Counterfeiters: Capitalists, Con Men, and the Making of the United States.* Cambridge: Harvard University Press.

Mishkin, Frederic S. 2005. "Is Financial Globalization Beneficial?" NBER Working Paper No. 11891, Cambridge, Massachusetts.

Mitchell, B.R., and Phyllis Deane. 1971. *Abstract of British Historical Statistics.* Cambridge: Cambridge University Press.

Morgan, E. Victor, and W.A. Thomas. 1962. *The Stock Exchange: its History and Function.* London: Elek Books.

Neal, Larry. 1990. *The Rise of Financial Capitalism: International Capital Markets in the Age of Reason.* Cambridge: Cambridge University Press.

——— May/June 1998. "The Financial Crisis of 1825 and the Restructuring of the British Financial System." *Federal Reserve Bank of St. Louis Review* 80: 53–76.

North, Douglass C. 1961. *The Economic Growth of the United States, 1790–1860.* Englewood Cliffs: Prentice Hall.

Perkins, Edwin J. 1994. *American Public Finance and Financial Services, 1700–1815.* Columbus: Ohio State University Press.

Prados de la Escosura, Leandro. January 2000. "International Comparisons of Real Product, 1820–1990: an Alternative Data Set." *Explorations in Economic History* 37: 1–41.

Pressnell, L.S. 1956. *Country Banking in the Industrial Revolution.* Oxford: Clarendon Press.

Razaghian, Rose. 2004. "Political Institutions and Sovereign Debt: Establishing Financial Credibility in the United States, 1789–1860." Working paper, Yale University.

Rousseau, Peter L., and Richard Sylla. January 2005. "Emerging Financial Markets and Early US Growth." *Explorations in Economic History* 42: 1–26.

Sylla, Richard. "Early American Banking: the Significance of the Corporate Form." *Business and Economic History*, Second Series, 14, 1985: 105–23. Accessible at Business History Conference website in BEHonline.

  May/June 1998. "U.S. Securities Markets and the Banking System, 1790–1840." *Federal Reserve Bank of St. Louis Review* 80: 83–98.

Sylla, Richard., Jack W. Wilson, and Robert E. Wright. 2006. "Integration of Trans-Atlantic Capital Markets, 1790–1840," *Review of Finance* 10: 613–44.

Temin, Peter. 1969. *The Jacksonian Economy*. New York: Norton.

Tocqueville, Alexis de. 2000. *Democracy in America*. Translated by Harvey C. Mansfield and Delba Winthrop. Chicago: University of Chicago Press.

US Bureau of the Census. 1975. *Historical Statistics of the United States, Colonial Times to 1970. Bicentennial Edition*. Washington, DC: US Government Printing Office.

Ward, Marianne, and John Devereaux. 2005. "Relative British and American Income Levels during the First Industrial Revolution." *Research in Economic History*, vol. 23. Elsevier.

Weber, Warren E. June 2006. "Early State Banks in the United States: How Many Were There and When Did They Exist?" *Journal of Economic History* 66: 433–55.

Wood, John. 2005. *A History of Central Banking in Great Britain and the United States*. Cambridge: Cambridge University Press.

Wright, Robert E. 2002. *The Wealth of Nations Rediscovered: Integration and Expansion in US Financial Markets, 1780–1850*. Cambridge: Cambridge University Press.

  2003. "Early U.S. Financial Development in Comparative Perspective: New Data, Old Comparisons." Working paper, New York University.

  2003. "National Financial Data Estimations: Canada, New York, the United States, and Great Britain, 1790–1850." Working paper, New York University.

8   Natural experiments in financial reform in the nineteenth century: The Davis and Gallman analysis

Larry Neal

The failure of the United States to build upon the proven success of the early national financial system put in place by Alexander Hamilton is surely one of the most notable examples of the difficulties that confront efforts at financial reform. Even so, the US was not alone as throughout the nineteenth century well-intentioned governments attempted to imitate the successful example of the UK or devise their own system of effective financial intermediation. Meanwhile, the British system kept improving to keep London the financial center of the global capital market that emerged during the classical gold standard of 1880–1913. Continental Europe created new financial institutions based on the *Crédit Mobilier* and *Crédit Foncier* in France and cooperative rural savings banks in Germany to mobilize their resources quickly enough to catch up with the industrial lead of Britain.[1] The most detailed analysis of the problems confronting the construction of an efficient and durable financial system for modern economies remains the monumental study by Lance Davis and Robert Gallman, *Evolving Capital Markets and International Capital Flows: Britain, the Americas, and Australia, 1865–1914* (2001).

Davis and Gallman documented the "natural experiments" that took place in four quite different frontier economies in the late nineteenth century – the US, Canada, Australia, and Argentina – to generate the

---

[1] Alexander Gerschenkron hypothesized that the longer a European country delayed its industrialization, the more resources it would require to catch up with the technological lead of Britain, so financing would require larger firms and eventually the state itself. (Gerschenkron, *Economic Backwardness*). Rondo Cameron focused on the *Crédit Mobilier* in France with its imitators in Germany and the rest of the Continent in later work. (Cameron, *France; Banking*) Hoffman *et al.* (2000) focus on the *Crédit Foncier's* role in creating a much more efficient mortgage market after the land reforms of the French Revolution were legitimized. Timothy Guinnane, "Delegated Monitors," puts the rural cooperative savings banks of Germany into the larger structure of the German financial sector in the latter nineteenth century.

Table 8.1. *Comparison of the breadth and depth of financial markets of the UK and the four frontier economies in the nineteenth century*

	Formal exchange	Regional exchanges	Financial assets/GNP 1850	Financial assets/GNP 1913	Financial institution assets/GNP 1914
UK	1812, London	Yes	4.95	5.70	n.a.
US	1817, New York	Yes	1.33	3.47	1.09
Canada	1852, Toronto	Yes	n.a.	n.a.	0.92
Australia	1865, Melbourne	No	1.18 (1870)	2.90	1.09
Argentina	1854, Buenos Aires	No	n.a.	2.35	0.69

Source: Davis & Gallman, country chapters, p. 770, Table 7:2–1, and p. 773, Table 7:2–2.

necessary institutional innovations to generate the capital flows they required to exploit their natural resources. Each one of these young, empty countries benefited greatly from the long-term capital flows emanating from the UK. So too did the British investors. Davis and Gallman calculate that Britain's contribution to capital formation rose sharply from around 10 percent to 20 percent for the US. It rose to even higher proportions for Canada, Australia, and then Argentina over the course of the late nineteenth century and the first decade of the twentieth. Initially, most of Britain's capital exports focused on the construction of the infrastructure necessary to gain access to the interior of each country. This ultimately meant railroads and their complements – docks, mines, livestock ranches, and land companies, and the like at the terminal points. All this investment led to the remarkable rise in the size of the British merchant marine, whose shipping earnings generated an increasing share of Britain's exports on current account. While the final tangible British investment in the four frontier economies (largely peopled by British migrants) was similar in each case, the form and function of the financial intermediation varied widely from country to country. Consequently, the resistance toward adopting specific British institutions to funnel British savings into each rapidly growing economy (described in detail by Davis and Gallman in the chapters devoted to each country) was obviously driven by non-economic factors.

Table 8.1, based on the pioneering work of Raymond Goldsmith (1985), demonstrates the clear lead of the British financial system on every measure. The ratio of financial assets to gross national product, Goldsmith's preferred measure of the degree of financial development of a given country, was far greater for the UK at nearly five times its GNP than the ratio of 1.33 for the US. The remaining young, empty countries were further behind even the US, reflecting the underdevelopment of both Australia and Canada in 1850 and the legacy of Spanish financial institutions in Argentina. By 1913, all four frontier countries had matured financially, cutting into the British lead even as that country deepened its financial structure. The Canadian figures are especially difficult to reconstruct given the large holdings of Canadian securities by British investors and by American banks. Nevertheless, the last column, giving the ratio of the assets of financial intermediaries (mainly banks, but also insurance and trust companies) to a country's GNP, shows that by 1914 on this measure that Canada was nearly on a par with the US and Australia. The difference between the ratios in the last two columns comes from financial assets held by the household or non-financial firm sectors. The gap is largest for the US, showing the relative importance of capital markets there throughout its history. Argentina remained the least developed of the four in terms of its domestic financial sector, the result of relying on the UK for both bank finance and issues of securities.

The importance of these ratios for Davis and Gallman lies in the role played by financial innovations within each country. These could, in theory at least, shift each country's supply schedule of savings to the right. This rise of savings, in turn, could drive an increase in the investment rate for each country, which in turn would lift its rate of growth and/or its capital/output ratio. Taking the UK as the world's leading innovating country in financial technology at least down to 1870, Davis and Gallman then attribute the massive outflow of British savings to these financial innovations.[2] Consequently, to understand their analysis of the natural experiments in financial innovation that took place in the leading recipients of British savings, we have to examine the financial innovations in Britain that created the increases in British savings.

---

[2] The appendix to Chapter 1, "The Role of Financial Intermediaries in Decisions to Save and Invest," discusses various counter-arguments that have been advanced to explain either the US or British high rates of investment by an outward shift in investment demand rather than an outward shift in the supply of savings. As these arguments usually assume relatively high rates of interest elasticity of savings, Davis and Gallman assert that more reasonable elasticities, in the range of 0 to 0.1, would imply a major role for financial innovations. Note, however, that Davis and Gallman's argument applies to nineteenth century societies that were already high income and market oriented. Financial innovations in today's underdeveloped economies, by contrast, appear to reduce the aggregate savings rate. One theoretical explanation is that increased financial intermediation in the twenty-first century reduces the precautionary demand for savings, which dominates in traditional, non-market, societies.

I.   The essential elements of Britain's financial success

Davis and Gallman describe the basic structure of the British financial sector in 1870 in the following terms:

Commercial banks accounted for about 65 percent of total assets at the beginning of the period and about 60 percent at the end. Loans and advances by those institutions represented about one-third of all assets in 1880, and about one-quarter thirty-four years later. The decline in the relative importance of the commercial banks was almost exactly offset by the increasing relative size of the insurance industry (from just less than 20 percent to about 25 percent of the total).[3]

They argue that Britain's financial structure changed only slightly thereafter up to World War I. They do note in passing, however, that the rise of deposits in Postal Savings Banks at the expense of building associations represented a substitution of government bonds for private mortgages by non-bank intermediaries. This, in their opinion, "did not bode well for private domestic or international capital mobilization."[4] By 1914 and the outbreak of World War I, Davis and Gallman see signs that the British financial sector was stagnating, and perhaps even regressing a bit from the plateau it had reached in 1870. To determine how the British financial sector achieved its apogee by 1870 and then sustained its level of performance for the next thirty-five years, Davis and Gallman then describe the rise of the various financial intermediaries and capital markets that came to form Britain's increasingly complex financial sector in the nineteenth century. First, they take up the rise of joint-stock banks, which quickly replaced private banks throughout the United Kingdom after enabling legislation was passed for England in 1826, and then consolidated into a highly concentrated sector by 1900.

W.T.C. King, in his classic study of the London discount market, identified the crisis of 1825 as bringing about "changes in the banking structure which were responsible for every major influence upon market evolution in the succeeding twenty years."[5] His analysis of the crisis, "when the country came within 24 hours of barter" according to one contemporary, was that the re-financing of government debt after the Napoleonic Wars, which reduced the market yield on Consols below 5 percent, created a speculative surge in demand for Latin American bonds issued by the newly independent Spanish colonies. When most of

---

[3] Davis and Gallman, *Evolving Financial*, pp. 92–3.
[4] Davis and Gallman, *Evolving Financial*, p. 93.
[5] King, *London Discount Market*, p. 35.

the new governments proved unable to maintain their promised interest payments, the prices of their bonds collapsed at the end of 1825. King added as an additional factor that a series of good harvests had made the country banks located in Britain's agricultural districts especially flush with funds, which they foolishly committed to the new Latin American securities.

In terms of conditions in the money market, however, the effects of the stock market crash in December 1825 were limited in duration. By June of 1826, the money market rate had again fallen well below 5 percent and the Bank of England was no longer besieged with requests to re-discount bills. Of more interest to King were the implications for the development of the bill market in London from four changes in the financial structure that occurred in response to the crisis. These were: (1) the beginnings of joint-stock banking, (2) the establishment of Bank of England branches, (3) the cessation of re-discounting by the London private banks, and (4) the assumption of some central banking functions by the Bank of England.[6] The combination of these four factors allowed the rise of the most distinctive feature of the British financial system in the later nineteenth century, the inland bill of exchange market, which was the focus of King's classic account.

The new joint-stock banks had to function outside London (thanks to resistance by the Bank of England) and they had to compete with existing country banks by attracting deposits rather than issuing notes. King does not explain why this was so, noting only that those joint-stock banks that began business by issuing notes gave them up after a few years. The rise of deposits in lieu of note issue by joint-stock banks arose in large part because the Bank of England branches refused to do business with joint-stock banks that issued notes.[7] Given that their business was necessarily local and that they had no notes to redeem, the new joint-stock banks kept minimum reserves, relying instead upon re-discounting bills of exchange to obtain cash whenever they needed to meet withdrawals of deposits. They also had a strong preference for short-term loans in the form of self-liquidating bills of exchange, rather than government securities, as had been the case earlier.[8] These yielded higher returns and could be staggered to mature at the same times as seasonal withdrawals of funds tended to occur. As the country banks wound up their small note business, they also turned increasingly toward deposits and to the behavior of joint-stock banks as described by King.

[6] Ibid., p. 38.   [7] Great Britain, *Monetary Policy*, pp. 427–8.
[8] Pressnell later confirmed this tendency even for country banks, *Country Banking*, pp. 415–34.

King concludes that it was the period from roughly 1830 until the 1860s or 1870s that the inland bill market became the most important way in which domestic credit was redistributed within the UK.[9]

Because joint-stock banks could also operate branches, unlike the private banks, they began to take over previous country banks as branches throughout England and at an accelerating rate after mid-century. "By 1914, when 40 English and Welsh joint-stock banks operated almost 5,300 branches, there remained fewer than 30 private banks controlling a total of less than 100 branches."[10] Reviewing the work of British historians on the effect of the rise and consolidation of joint-stock banking in Britain, Davis and Gallman conclude that British banks continued to supply the investment demands of the British economy after 1870 as before. If the concentration of the industry led to cartel behavior, it was more evident on the deposit-taking side where interest rates could be kept lower than in a more competitive market than on the loan-making side, where there is evidence that customers could successfully threaten to take their business elsewhere and obtain better terms.[11] Overall, British commercial banks serviced their business clients well with short-term loans, often rolling them over repeatedly if the enterprise were successful. Their conservative lending practices, reinforced by increasingly effective interventions in the London money market by the Bank of England, maintained an enviable stability in the banking sector, especially after the Overend, Gurney crisis in 1872.[12]

By 1865, however, the importance of the inland bill market for Britain's commercial banks had begun to decline, from roughly one-third of banks' assets in the period 1840–1880 to less than 13 percent by the end of the 1880s and less than 10 percent by 1914.[13] The nationwide branching system of the major joint-stock banks allowed them to shift funds within their network from surplus regions to deficit regions as the occasion demanded without recourse to bills. As the inland bill market began to decline the foreign bill of exchange became an increasingly important form of negotiable credit. The discount houses in London

---

[9] King, *London Discount Market*, p. 41.

[10] Davis and Gallman, *Evolving Financial*, p. 109.

[11] They take as conclusive the findings reported in Capie and Mills, "British Bank Conservatism."

[12] The failure of Overend, Gurney in 1872, the largest discount house in the world at the time, brought the Bank of England to implement for the first time the practice of lending freely at a penalty rate to offset the internal drain on banking reserves. Since labeled "Bagehot's rule," after Walter Bagehot, the editor of the *Economist* extolled it in his book on Lombard Street, it has become the guiding principle for any lender of last resort.

[13] Davis and Gallman, *Evolving Financial*, pp. 128–9.

expanded their operations to include foreign bills.[14] From 1885 to 1914, the sterling bill market in London was comprised of three large limited companies (National Discount House, Union Discount Company, and Alexander's) and a score of private firms. In the words of Leslie Pressnell, the term "international gold standard" does not truly describe this period; it was, rather, the "international bill-on-London standard."[15]

Non-bank intermediaries such as the London discount houses accounted, moreover, for between 35 and 40 percent of the assets held by all financial institutions in Britain. Of that amount, the share of insurance companies gradually rose from 20 to 25 percent and the share of post office savings banks nearly doubled, from 4.5 to 9 percent.[16] The fall in the interest earned by these non-bank intermediaries on their main investments in the early part of the nineteenth century, namely government debt and mortgages, led them to seek more remunerative investments overseas by the later nineteenth century. British government securities at all levels fell from 17 to 7 percent of insurance companies' portfolios while overseas investments rose from 7 to over 40 percent between 1870 and 1913.[17]

The search for more remunerative outlets for the accumulated deposits of the various non-bank intermediaries was successful, largely because of the continued expansion of the formal securities markets of the UK, centered upon the London Stock Exchange. From a total nominal value of shares quoted on the London Stock Exchange of £1.604 billion in 1863, by the end of 1913 it had reached £11.262 billion, implying a growth rate of about 3.8 percent annually. Over this half century of spectacular growth, the share of government securities had dropped from two-thirds of the total to less than one-half, while railroads had risen to more than one-third, and that of "others" to almost one-fifth.[18] Moreover, the capitalized market share of total foreign securities quoted on the London Stock Exchange had risen from under one-quarter in 1863 to over half in 1913.[19] Further, this stock of securities, comprised mostly of foreign government debt and overseas railroads girdling the globe totaled £6.8 billion, and amounted to 60 percent of the value of all securities quoted anywhere in the world.[20] The increasing importance of foreign securities after mid-century was due in part to one of the felicitous outcomes of the collapse of the first

---

[14] Nishimura, *The Decline.*   [15] Pressnell, *Country Banking*, p. 131.
[16] Davis and Gallman, *Evolving Financial*, p. 131.
[17] Davis and Gallman, *Evolving Financial*, p. 146.
[18] Davis and Gallman, *Evolving Financial*, p. 155.
[19] Davis and Gallman, *Evolving Financial*, Table 2:3–11, p. 157.
[20] Davis and Gallman, *Evolving Financial*, p. 159.

generation of Latin American bonds in 1825. In response, the London Stock Exchange established ever more rigorous rules to establish the legitimacy of any foreign bond or stock before listing it.[21]

Such was the dominance of the British financial system, built on a set of complementary financial intermediaries and securities markets that had arisen in response to government demands for loanable funds and the public demand for convenient means of payment and liquid, interest-earning financial assets. The exogenous shock of the crisis of 1825 was met not with government restrictions on country banks or restraints on stockjobbing, but rather the government's response in 1826 was, in quick succession, to repeal the Bubble Act of 1720, remove restrictions against joint-stock companies engaging in banking, ameliorate the laws governing bankruptcy, and nudge the Bank of England into establishing a nationwide network of branches. The felicitous outcome of these liberalizations was to free up the forces of financial innovation as described by King. In the theoretical framework of Davis and Gallman, the ensuing financial innovations kept shifting the supply curve of British savings to the right. The outpouring and mobilization of British savings then financed not only the British industrial revolution but also the spread of steam transport around the world and creating the first age of globalization. The primary beneficiaries of the excess savings created by continued financial innovation in the UK were, in addition to the British public, the young, empty countries overseas that welcomed British labor, capital, technology, and, to a large degree British legal and political institutions, especially the guarantee of private property rights.

II.   Imitation may be harder than innovation

Despite the obvious success of the British financial innovations even the four countries receiving the largest flows of British savings could not, or would not, simply imitate the British financial innovations. The benefit that various follower countries could have derived from similar financial innovations to increase their domestic supplies of saving to finance their own industrialization was largely forgone. Indeed, even the US after enjoying the fruits of Hamilton's financial revolution, which were clearly modeled on the best features of the English, Dutch, and Scottish financial sectors at the time, actually regressed twice in the following half-century; first, with the termination of the First Bank of the United States in 1810 and then the lapse of the charter of the Second Bank in 1836.

---

[21] Davis and Neal, "Rules and Regulations" and "Structure and Performance."

Davis and Gallman concentrate their analysis on the implications of the four separate trajectories that were followed by each country as they induced British capital inflow to finance their respective transportation infrastructures and related capital stock. The authors point out the distinctive financial innovations each country created to make investment opportunities especially attractive to British investors. As it turns out, each frontier country adopted just the one aspect of the British financial system that seemed most useful for financing construction of that country's railroad network. The US picked British-style merchant banks such as Prime, Ward, and King in New York, which had a long-standing association with the House of Baring, and John E. Thayer and Brother in Boston, which dealt with the British house McCalmont & Co.; Alexander Brown and Sons of Baltimore had a Liverpool correspondent, Brown, Shipley & Co.; August Belmont & Company was established as the result of the Rothschild interest in US opportunities.[22] In commercial banking, however, the US largely ignored Scottish-style banking, with its emphasis on joint-stock ownership and branching. Instead, most states stuck with English-style country banking with its closely held capital stock and no branching, a restriction maintained throughout most of the country until the late twentieth century. By 1915, the 27,390 banks in the US operated only 785 branches, and only twenty-six were branches of National Banks.[23] Canada and Australia, starting later, wisely picked Scottish banking – joint-stock banks with extensive branching – and with a physical presence in London. Reliance on British-based banks, however, proved disastrous for Australia when it was hit by the agricultural depression of the 1890s. The London managements decided to redirect their capital rather than recapitalize their Australian branches. Canada, meanwhile, had managed to create a nationwide banking system based on domestic banking houses by the last quarter of the nineteenth century. The resulting bank networks helped to finance the wheat boom in the first decade of the twentieth century. Both countries, however, relied mainly on the London capital market for marketing the securities issued by their railroads and distribution companies, although mining stocks enjoyed local markets in both countries, as they did in the US, but these were small, speculative, and widely scattered stock markets with few externalities.

Argentina got off to a bad start with Barings early in the nineteenth century, when it defaulted on its original issue of government bonds through the merchant bank. Consequently, it had to accept British

---

[22] Davis and Gallman, *Evolving Financial*, p. 301.
[23] Davis and Gallman, *Evolving Financial*, p. 271.

incorporation of its railroads and banks to get its share of British savings flowing into the construction of its infrastructure. British-based management for Argentine enterprises proved essential if British-based investors were to provide finance.

For the purposes of this volume, the analysis provided by Davis and Gallman of the obstacles in each country that stood in the way of financial innovations and the idiosyncratic ways in which each country overcame its specific institutional barriers are most interesting. Ultimately, each country should have created a complementary set of local banking institutions and secondary capital markets. In this way, they could combine the advantages of confidential relationships between banks and firms for short- and medium-term investment opportunities with the advantages of transparent pricing of publicly traded securities issued by firms for longer-term capital. To see why three of the countries did not and the fourth, the US, delayed for most of the nineteenth century, we take up the Davis and Gallman analysis of the respective developments of the banking sector in each country and then their analysis of how each country established a secondary market for its securities.

III.   Banking developments compared

As Table 8.2 demonstrates (even for the basic institution of a gold standard as the basis for the money supply), the main recipients of British capital took their time in following the British leads. For example, Australia and Argentina delayed formal adoption until the start of the twentieth century. In practice, of course, all four countries had to insert gold clauses in their dealings with British investors. The US had a de facto gold standard after Andrew Jackson's Specie Circular of 1836 and changes in the mint ratio between silver and gold in 1834 and 1837 meant a de facto gold standard even before the outpouring of California gold in the 1850s. The upsurge of world gold supplies then forced all bimetallic countries, regardless of their mint ratios, onto a de facto gold standard.

With respect to banking practices, by contrast, the rest of the UK did not take up the Scottish example of branch banking by joint-stock corporations created in the eighteenth century until enabling legislation was passed in 1826 following the financial crisis of 1825. Even then, branch banking awaited the consolidation of joint-stock banks much later in the century.[24] For the frontier economies, joint-stock banking was necessary from the beginning, but only Australia and Canada combined

---

[24] Capie and Webber, *A Monetary History;* Collins, *Money and Banking.*

Table 8.2. *Comparison of banking systems of the UK and the four frontier economies in the nineteenth century*

	Gold standard	Central bank	Branch banking	Joint-stock banking
UK	1819–	(1694) 1844	18thC (Scotland) 1826 (E&W)	18thC (Scotland) 1826 (E&W)
US	1876–	1790–1810 1816–1836 1914–	Mostly unit	Yes
Canada	1854	1934	Yes	Yes
Australia	1910	1910	Yes	Yes
Argentina	1867–1873 1883–1890 1899–1914	1891	Yes	Yes

Source: Davis and Gallman, ch. 7; della Paolera and Taylor; Powell.

this with branch banking, reflecting perhaps the dominance of Scottish emigrants in their populations. The US remained committed largely to unit banks in the industrial heartland and New England, although these were mostly joint-stock companies closely held by local investors. While both the First and Second Banks of the United States had branches predating branching by the Bank of England, the demise of the Second Bank with Andrew Jackson's veto of the bill to renew its charter in 1836 ended most branch banking in the US. Even in New York, branching was limited to New York City while California's banks were limited to branches in that state, as were banks in the handful of other states that permitted branching. British chartered banks were allowed to operate in Argentina and Canada with branching allowed in Canada, but not in Argentina. The British banks, mostly headquartered in London, dominated the banking system of Australia and spread their branches throughout the six colonies. British commercial banks were largely excluded from the US, although the major investment banks, such as the House of Rothschild, Barings, and J.S. Morgan established US subsidiaries. The advantage of the US investment banks was their membership in the major stock exchanges, a privilege denied to British merchant banks by the London Stock Exchange.[25]

[25] Calomiris, "Corporate-Finance Benefits" and "The Costs of Rejecting," however, argues that US investment banks took advantage of their membership in the stock exchanges with restricted numbers to raise their fees for underwriting services, whereas competition within exchanges in London and Berlin made initial public offerings (IPOs) more affordable.

The resistance of these separate societies to adopting the full range of successful British financial innovations arose from their distinctive political structures and legal systems, not from differences in their respective needs for external finance, much less from differences in their latent profit potential. The rejection of British-style finance by the US stemmed in part from political fears of British retaliation after winning independence, fears exacerbated by the trauma of the War of 1812. Andrew Jackson's victory in the Battle of New Orleans at the end of that conflict, however, secured the Louisiana Purchase for the new republic and laid the basis for its westward expansion over the rest of the century. Each of the new states that entered the republic as it expanded then established its own system of banking, given the absence of controlling legislation from the central government.

The remarkable aspect of the US's record of economic growth, documented in earlier work by Davis and Gallman (1978), was the sustained high rate of domestic savings it managed throughout the nineteenth century. This financed high rates of gross domestic capital formation. High rates of investment, they argued, were the key to establishing the US as the world's largest economy by the beginning of the twentieth century. And, one of the keys to the continued high rates of savings was the continued innovation of financial intermediation both through the easy spread of unit banking and, especially, through the rise of organized secondary markets for government, railroad, and industrial securities throughout the country.

Canada and Australia eventually became self-governing colonies within the British Empire as it expanded and re-organized, but had quite different financial links to the mother country. Canada, throughout most of its history, has struggled to find its optimal political and economic relationship between the UK and the US. The defining moment for modern Canada, however, came with John MacDonald's re-election as Prime Minister in the election of 1878 and implementation of his National Policy. This consisted basically of protective tariffs against the US and construction of the Canadian Pacific Railway to link British Columbia in the west to the industrial and commercial centers in Ontario and Quebec. It had been his initial vision that led to the creation of modern Canada in 1867 as a dominion within the British Empire.

The key to the success of MacDonald's National Policy was the completion of the Canadian Pacific Railway in 1885 and financed by British investors relying on Canadian government guarantees of the bonds. Domestic savings in Canada were devoted to self-financing of business enterprises or deposited in banks that were restricted by their charter to short-term mercantile credit. Consequently, "financing for industrial and infrastructure projects was largely dependent on external capital."[26] At least half of foreign capital came from Britain, much of it through portfolio investment in railroad or telegraph company securities issued in London.

British chartered banks operated throughout Canada, competing with well-capitalized Canadian banks. After the failure of the Bank of Upper Canada in 1866 due to widespread defaults on land mortgages it had made during a speculative land rush in 1857 and 1858, Canada chartered its banks with much higher capital requirements than in the US. These new charters restricted Canadian banks after 1870 from any lending on land or any similar long-lived asset. Despite the absence of restrictions against branching, branching was slow to develop nation-wide, reflecting the vast stretch of undeveloped prairie that lay between Winnipeg and Vancouver. Not until the wheat boom at the beginning of the twentieth century did branching reach its potential, helping Canada achieve unprecedented rates of economic growth in the years 1900–1910. Further, the wheat boom was financed to a much greater extent than in the past by Canada's domestic savings, helped no doubt by the surge of immigrants. From 1897 to 1905, Canadian savings accounted for three-quarters of its gross domestic capital formation. From 1906 to 1913, however, foreign savings recovered to finance 44 percent of Canada's gross capital formation in that period.[27]

Australia, by contrast with either Canada or the US, maintained six separate and largely independent colonies until the creation of a federal government in 1901 that became a Commonwealth within the British Empire. Until that time, Australia lacked the equivalent of Canada's National Policy. Consequently, its infrastructure was fragmented among the individual states as each pursued its own economic policy to exploit the natural resources specific to that territory. Most activity was concentrated in the eastern seaboard colonies of Victoria and New South Wales, especially after the Victorian gold rush that began in 1851. No attempt was made to connect the separate state railroad systems into a national grid. Despite the incoherence of the Australian transportation network in terms of a nationwide system as in Canada, however, the financial system was remarkably uniform throughout the island continent as a result of overwhelming dominance of London-based and British chartered banks and a universal reliance on British savings for funding local government capital expenditures. To build the necessary

---

[26] Davis and Gallman, *Evolving Financial*, pp. 361–72 and quoting Sheila Dow, p. 60 on p. 362.

[27] Davis and Gallman, *Evolving Financial*, p. 358.

infrastructure in each colony, the local government had issued bonds in London, which offered remunerative returns to British savers who also expected the British government to do whatever might be necessary to insure repayment by the colonies. Reliance on British financing extended to encouraging British-chartered banks headquartered in London to establish branches throughout Australia. The result has been labeled "colonial socialism" by Noel Butlin (1959) because each state government became the lender of first resort for each major construction project. In the short run, each colony responded quickly to possibilities of exploiting mineral discoveries or markets for sheep or sugar as they arose. But in the long run, according to Davis and Gallman (and the Australian economic historians they cite), the absence of domestic private sources of financial intermediation left Australia vulnerable to exogenous shocks such as occurred in the 1890s.

The agricultural crisis of the early 1890s, coming as commodity prices continued their decades-long fall, caused the major Australian banks to fail *en masse*. Their London owners withdrew from further investment and no domestic sources of finance were forthcoming. Eventually, each state government stepped in to create land banks to provide the missing finance for the agricultural sector, but the boom days for Australia were over. The rise in commodity prices caused by World War I was followed by a collapse afterwards, leading to increased reliance upon government support and even with recovery in the 1930s, Australia's economic recovery was dependent on preferred access to the British market.

As bad as this outcome was for Australia, the case of Argentina proved even more telling. While Argentina lacked the advantages of British common law and political constraints on arbitrary power by the executive branch, features which gave the other three destination countries a more favorable impression for British investors, it enjoyed an abundance of natural resources and access to the London capital market, especially during the classical gold standard period. It also became a favorite destination for emigrants from the British Isles at that time. Table 8.1, however, highlights the recurring difficulties for Argentina in coming to terms with the requirement of the gold standard, a necessary guarantee of private property rights even to foreigners wishing to repatriate their profits or to liquidate their holdings. The financial innovation employed by British investors, given a disastrous outcome for their initial portfolio investments in 1825 (Neal 1998), was to set up British chartered companies to exploit Argentina's resources, drawing upon British savings funneled to them through British chartered banks, whether in Britain or in Argentina. British investment then took the form of direct investment in British-controlled enterprises in Argentina, rather than portfolio investment in Argentina's railroad or government securities. This stood in stark contrast to the emphasis on portfolio investment for Canada and especially Australia as far as infrastructure capital was concerned. It was similar, however, to the standing companies employed by the British when investing in industrial and commercial enterprises in the US later in the nineteenth century. But while British investment became less and less important for the US over the nineteenth century, it became increasingly important for Argentina's capital formation.

Davis and Gallman summarize the difficulties faced by each: Australia in confronting the agricultural crisis of the 1890s, Argentina's problems in overcoming the aftershocks of the Baring Crisis of 1890 and then the withdrawal of British finance during World War I, and Canada's early lagging development, as "overbanking." By this, they mean that in each country capital formation relied too heavily on its banking sector. The resulting mismatch in maturities between the banking sector's assets (very long-term and with high variance in returns) and its liabilities (short-term and often held by foreigners) created an increasingly precarious financial structure. The specific form of this malady varied for each country, but the effect was to make each country more vulnerable to external economic shocks. The US, by contrast, clearly confronted much more serious shocks to its economy throughout the nineteenth century, including the most expensive and bloodiest war, but somehow it managed to overcome each crisis in fairly short order, thanks, Davis and Gallman argue, to its well-developed and extensive set of securities markets.

IV.   The Davis and Gallman comparison of securities markets

What about the development of securities markets needed to encourage the long-term, large-scale investments necessary for each of these young, empty countries to exploit its natural resources? Table 8.3 summarizes the scattered data available relating to the role of securities markets in each of the frontier economies, compared to the dominant role of the London Stock Exchange. The data are often inconsistent from source to source. For example, the breakdown of activity for the New York Stock Exchange in 1910 is by volume of turnover instead of market capitalization as in the case of London. Nevertheless, the relative absence of government bonds from any level of government in the US clearly distinguishes it in terms of the relative importance of finance through large corporations rather than by government as in the case of Australia. Even Canada and Argentina's relatively low levels reflect not the absence of

Table 8.3. *Comparison of stock markets of the UK and the four frontier economies on the eve of World War I*

	Market capitalization	Government bonds (%)	Railroad securities (%)	All other securities (%)
London Stock Exchange	$52.0 billion	34.8	43.4	21.8
New York Stock Exchange	$26.3 billion	0.25	3.5 (bonds)	96.25 (all stocks)
Canada Stock Exchanges	$2.26 billion	7.0	34.0	59.0
Melbourne Stock Exchange	$0.3 billion	15.0	6.0	79.0
Buenos Aires	$2.0 billion	7.8	30.5	61.7

Source: Davis and Gallman, ch. 7; Michie, "Canadian Securities"; US, Historical Statistics, Series X 531–5; Argentina, calculated from Tornquist, excludes external government debt and *cedulas*.

government but rather the importance of the external debt of both countries, which were favorite investments by British savers. The high proportion of government bonds on the London Stock Exchange reflected the importance of foreign, especially imperial and Commonwealth, government issues there. In other words, the London Stock Exchange provided the complementary capital markets that enabled the banking systems of Argentina, Australia, and Canada to thrive as long as they did.

Each country then adapted the British-style financial institution it had acquired by innovating according to its own unique political and economic dynamic. In the US, the first-generation investment affiliates, mere branches of the British merchant banks, evolved into independent investment banks in the second generation that were responsible for generating the finance for US trunk railroads. The financing of the Union's war effort during the American Civil War was greatly facilitated by Jay Cooke's mass marketing of the Union's war bonds to domestic investors. Davis and Gallman note that his original firm, Clark & Dodge "generally depended on domestic sources of funds."[28] Cooke's firm, along with the Boston firm of Lee, Higginson, and Co., in turn were overtaken by second-generation investment banks, headed by J.P. Morgan & Co. followed by Kuhn, Loeb, Speyer and Co., J.&R. Seligman, and August Belmont & Co., the Boston firms of Kidder, Peabody, and Lee, Higginson and the Philadelphia firm of Drexel & Co. In the first decade of the twentieth century a third generation of investment banks began to market securities on a broad scale for industrial and commercial

[28] Davis and Gallman, *Evolving Financial*, p. 301.

firms, focusing more on equity stocks than bonds that had been the focus of previous investment banking. Goldman, Sachs & Co. and Lehman Brothers, for example, managed 114 offerings for 56 firms over the eighteen years following their initial offering of Sear, Roebuck & Co. stock in 1906.[29]

Canada's financing of its infrastructure depended on government guarantees of bonds issued by railroads, canals, or utilities before these bonds could be placed in the London market. When tapping into Canadian domestic savings, bond houses arose that could place new issues with a narrow circle of Canadian financial institutions and wealthy individuals. Australia's London-based banks developed securitized mortgage bonds so they could indirectly (and ultimately disastrously) invest in overpriced mortgages. Argentina developed a security more directly based on land mortgages, the *cedula*, which became a favorite asset for Argentina's banks, which were mostly foreign and mostly British.

V.   Government regulations

What lessons do Davis and Gallman draw from their detailed examination of each country's financial sector and its innovations in response to the challenges of tapping into the vast pool of savings available in London? Ultimately, the less successful the frontier economy was in financing its development with foreign funds, the better it performed in the long run. Why? Their explanation is that the innovative efforts of the frontier economy's financial sector turned to ways it could attract domestic savings, and these continued to finance domestic capital formation whenever the supply of British funds slackened or stopped entirely. Implicitly, the Davis and Gallman study suggests as well the importance of developing transparent and competitive capital markets. The more a frontier economy's financial innovations were directed toward developing and sustaining its capital markets, as opposed to its banking institutions, the better able it was to recover from shocks inflicted by regime changes, whatever the source or severity of the shocks. This held especially so in coping with the shock of the complete withdrawal of European finance during World War I, as the authors demonstrate in Chapter 8, "Skipping Ahead: The Evolution of the World's Finance Markets, 1914–1990."

In the nineteenth century in the young, empty countries analyzed by Davis and Gallman, the pay-off expected from opening the frontiers to European settlement and production techniques was long-term in agriculture and highly uncertain in mining. Crop failures or competition

---

[29] Davis and Gallman, *Evolving Financial*, p. 311.

from new sources of supply created havoc for Argentina and Australia in the 1890s. Increased diversity of financial institutions as in the US and Canada, starting with investment banks and moving on to insurance companies, helped to lessen the extent of mismatched maturities of financial claims. Further, if a country is equipped with deep, liquid capital markets, these can provide essential safety valves for each set of financial institutions whenever shocks do occur. As Rajan and Zingales (2006) note in their subsequent work (none of which is cited in the Davis and Gallman monograph), it is precisely those liquid capital markets that are most vulnerable to regulation and ultimate reversal by government interventions. Because the markets for publicly traded securities are highly visible and well-publicized in order to generate trading volume, any reversals in prices will elicit public outcries for the government to protect the perceived interests of their most influential constituencies.[30] Such government reactions clearly occurred in the cases of Australia, Canada, and Argentina. In the US, however, despite the rise of progressive reforms in the twentieth century, only the Federal Reserve System emerged for the financial sector, and its initial effects were limited.[31]

In the previous chapter, Richard Sylla documents that Alexander Hamilton, as the first Secretary of the Treasury in the newly-formed US, established a financial system for the US that proved even more effective than the British model upon which it was based. Later political developments driven by westward expansion and the Jeffersonian ideal of agrarian democracy and hostility toward a powerful central government led to the removal of one of the pillars of his system – the first Bank of the United States with its single currency and regional branches. The usefulness of such a bank proved itself even to Jefferson's party during the War of 1812, leading to a renewed charter for the Second Bank of the United States. President Andrew Jackson refused to renew the charter of the Second Bank of the United States in 1836, again showing the political difficulties that regularly confront innovative institutions in the financial sector.

A period of free banking experimentation among the various states ensued, complicated by the regular addition of new states, each of which decided on its unique form of banking regulation. The ensuing period of free banking that lasted until the taxation of state bank notes in 1865 at the end of the American Civil War has been examined in detail by

---

[30] Michie (*Global Securities*) argues that governments' well-meaning interventions through the ages have limited the possible benefits that a global securities market can provide for the private sector, especially in banking.
[31] White, *Regulation and Reform*.

numerous scholars.[32] The general conclusion is that it worked well if the note-issuing bank could establish credible backing for its notes with the help of the state or local government. But the opportunities for opportunistic behavior based on fraud were rampant and, unsurprisingly, exploited if regulation by government or market competition was lax. The National Banking system that essentially took free banking to a national level after the Civil War created a uniform currency throughout the US, essentially by levying a 10 percent tax on state bank notes. But, without a central bank to act either as a regulator or lender of last resort, the integration of the nation's bank credit failed to emerge until the beginning of the twentieth century. Further, even with formal adoption of the gold standard in 1879 and reassertion of this commitment to gold with the Gold Standard Act of 1900, the US financial system was not well integrated with the British financial sector.[33] The puzzle that this creates for economic theory has occupied the attention of a number of financial historians including, Lance Davis, Richard Sylla, John James, Maureen O'Hara, Richard Keehn, and Gene Smiley, and is taken up again in the next chapter by Richard Sullivan.

References

Bagehot, Walter. 1962. *Lombard Street, A Description of the Money Market*. Homewood: Richard D. Irwin.

Bodenhorn, Howard and Michael J. Haupert. August 1995. "Was There a Note Issue Conundrum during the Free Bank Era?" *Journal of Money, Credit, and Banking*, 27:3: 702–12.

Butlin, Noel G. 1959. "Colonial Socialism in Australia, 1860–1900," in Hugh G. Aitken (ed.), *The State and Economic Growth*. New York: Social Science Research Council.

Calomiris, Charles W. July 1993. "Corporate-Finance Benefits from Universal Banking: Germany and the United States, 1870–1914," NBER Working Paper No. 4408.

1995. "The Costs of Rejecting Universal Banking: American Finance in the German Mirror," in Naomi Lamoreaux and Dan Raff (eds.), *The Coordination of Economic Activity Within and Between Firms: Historical Perspective on the Organization of Enterprise*. Chicago: University of Chicago Press.

Cameron, Rondo. 1961. *France and the Economic Development of Europe, (1800–1914)*. Princeton: Princeton University Press.

1967. *Banking in the Early Stages of Industrialization, A Study in Comparative Economic History*. New York: Oxford University Press.

---

[32] Rolnick and Weber, "New Evidence" and "Explaining the Demand"; Rockoff, *Free Banking*; Bodenhorn and Haupert, "Note Issue"; Dwyer, "Wildcat Banking."

[33] Friedman and Schwartz, *A Monetary History*; Neal and Weidenmier, "Crises"; Odell and Weidenmier "Real Shock."

Capie, Forrest H. and Terence C. Mills. July 1995. "British Bank Conservatism in the Late 19th Century," *Explorations in Economic History*, 32:3: 409–20.

Capie, Forrest H. and Alan Webber. 1985. *A Monetary History of the United Kingdom, 1870–1992*. London: Allen & Unwin.

Collins, Michael. 1988. *Money and Banking in the UK: A History*. London: Croom Helm.

Davis, Lance E. and Robert E. Gallman. 1978. "Capital Formation in the United States during the Nineteenth Century," in Peter Mathias and M.M. Postan (eds.), *The Cambridge Economic History of Europe*, vol. VII, *The Industrial Economies Capital, Labour, and Enterprise*, Part 2, *The United States, Japan, and Russia*. Cambridge: Cambridge University Press: 1–69.

2001. *Evolving Financial Markets and International Capital Flows: Britain, the Americas, and Australia, 1865–1914*. Cambridge and New York: Cambridge University Press.

Davis, Lance E. and Larry Neal. 2005. "The Evolution of the Rules and Regulations of the First Emerging Markets: The London, New York and Paris Stock Exchanges, 1792–1914," *The Quarterly Review of Economics and Finance*, 45: 296–311.

2006. "The Evolution of the Structure and Performance of the London Stock Exchange in the First Global Financial Market, 1812–1914," *European Review of Economic History*, 10:3: 279–300.

della Paolera, Gerardo and Alan M. Taylor. 2001. *Straining at the Anchor: The Argentine Currency Board and the Search for Macroeconomic Stability, 1880–1935*. Chicago and London: University of Chicago Press.

Dwyer, Gerald P. December 1996. "Wildcat Banking, Banking Panics, and Free Banking in the United States," Federal Reserve Bank of Atlanta Review, 81:6: 1–20.

Friedman, Milton and Anna Schwartz. 1963. *A Monetary History of the United States*. Princeton: Princeton University Press for the National Bureau of Economics.

Gerschenkron, Alexander. 1962. *Economic Backwardness in Historical Perspective*. Cambridge: Harvard University Press.

Goldsmith, Raymond W. 1985. *Comparative National Balance Sheets*. Chicago and London: University of Chicago Press.

Great Britain, British Parliamentary Papers. *Monetary Policy, General, Vol. 4*, "Session 1821–32," "Report from the Committee of Secrecy on the Bank of England Charter," Shannon Ireland: Irish University Press, 1968.

Guinnane, Timothy. March 2002. "Delegated Monitors, Large and Small: Germany's Banking System, 1800–1914," *Journal of Economic Literature*, 40:1: 73–124.

Hoffman, Philip T., Gilles Postel-Vinay, and Jean-Laurent Rosenthal. 2000. *Priceless Markets: The Political Economy of Credit in Paris, 1660–1870*. Chicago: University of Chicago Press.

King, Wilfred T.C. 1936. *History of the London Discount Market*. London: Routledge.

Michie, Ranald C. Spring 1988. "The Canadian Securities Market, 1850–1914," *Business History Review*, 62: 35–73.

1999. *The London Stock Market: A History.* Oxford: Oxford University Press.
2006. *The Global Securities Market: A History.* Oxford: Oxford University Press.
Neal, Larry. May/June 1998. "The Financial Crisis of 1825 and the Restructuring of the British Financial System," *Federal Reserve Bank of St. Louis Review:* 53–76.
Neal, Larry and Mark D. Weidenmier. 2003. "Crises in the Global Economy from Tulips to Today: Contagion and Consequences." *Globalization in Historical Perspective, National Bureau of Economic Research Conference Report.* (Edited by Michael Bordo, Alan M. Taylor, and Jeffrey G. Williamson). Chicago: University of Chicago Press, pp. 473–513.
Nishimura, Shizuya. 1971. *The Decline of Inland Bills of Exchange in the London Money Market, 1855–1913.* London: Cambridge University Press.
Odell, Kerry and Mark D. Weidenmier. 2004. "Real Shock, Monetary Aftershock: The 1906 San Francisco Earthquake and the Panic of 1907," *Journal of Economic History,* 64: 1002–27.
Powell, James. 2005. *A History of the Canadian Dollar.* Ottawa: Bank of Canada.
Pressnell, Leslie S. 1956. *Country Banking in the Industrial Revolution.* Oxford: Clarendon Press.
Rajan, Raghuram G. and Luigi Zingales. 2004. *Saving Capitalism from the Capitalists,* London: Random House.
Rockoff, Hugh. 1975. *The Free Banking Era: A Reexamination.* New York: Arno Press.
Rolnick, Arthur J. and Warren E. Weber. December 1983. "New Evidence on the Free Banking Era," *American Economic Review,* 73: 1080–91.
January 1988. "Explaining the Demand for Free Bank Notes," *Journal of Monetary Economics,* 21: 47–71.
White, Eugene N. 1983. *The Regulation and Reform of the American Banking System, 1900–1929.* Princeton: Princeton University Press.

9 Regulatory changes and the development of the US banking market, 1870–1914: A study of profit rates and risk in national banks

Richard J. Sullivan[*]

Capital accumulation is central to economic development and economists have had a long fascination with its history. An increase in the savings rate was the fundamental aspect of Walt Whitman Rostow's vision of the stages of economic development, and Robert Solow's path-breaking work showed how standards of living are tied to the level of capital per worker in an economy.[1] In these formulations, the amount of savings directly affects the amount of capital accumulation and ultimately economic development. Lance Davis's seminal work added an important perspective on the process of capital accumulation: improvements in the allocation of scarce savings can raise standards of living (independent of the savings rate) because capital will then be allocated more productively.[2]

Davis focused on the late nineteenth-century US, where he found that regional differences in interest rates charged by national banks were large after the Civil War, but diminished over the subsequent fifty years. He argued that firms selling commercial paper entered the financial market, made them more competitive, and the subsequent operation of the law of one price caused regional interest rates to converge. Later research by Richard Sylla and John James has confirmed Davis's findings but these authors argued that the banking industry itself became more competitive.[3] Whatever the nature of added capital market competition,

[*] I thank Zhu Wang for useful discussion on this topic and Hugh Rockoff, Howard Bodenhorn, Mike Bradley, Larry Neal, Jeremy Atack, Joe Mason, and Concepcion Garcia-Iglesias for valuable comments on an earlier version of this paper. The views expressed in this article are those of the author, and do not necessarily reflect those of the Federal Reserve Bank of Kansas City or the Federal Reserve System.

[1] Rostow, *The Stages of Economic Growth*; Solow, "Contribution."
[2] Davis, "The Investment Market."
[3] Sylla "Federal Policy"; James, "Development."

regional integration helped to improve the allocation of capital and thus aided US development.

In this chapter I explore the Davis–Sylla–James (DSJ) hypothesis in a manner somewhat different from previous work. As Larry Neal points out, measuring capital market integration using interest rates on loans is complicated by factors such as local regulations, risk and duration of loans, and monopoly rents.[4] Consequently, rather than look at regional interest rates, I study differences in the regional profit rates of national banks.[5] Profit rates are germane to the mechanism of capital allocation because they are critical incentives for entry to and exit from the financial market. To anticipate the conclusion, I find substantial support for the DSJ hypothesis: regional profit differentials converged substantially after 1884.

To delve deeper into the extent and causes of profit rate convergence, I apply capital market theory to relate the fluctuations of banks profits to their levels across the different regions of the US. I find that a considerable amount of the observed difference in national bank profit rates can be explained by financial risk.[6] Results also show that risk-adjusted profit differentials across regions were present in the 1870–1884 period, but not in the 1885–1899 period, which is consistent with the DSJ hypothesis. However, there is also a puzzling result: risk-adjusted profit differentials reemerge in the 1900–1914 period, a period where there was an integrated and competitive national banking market. I argue that the easing of entry barriers after the Gold Standard Act of 1900 introduced new inherent risk into the market. New bank entry was characterized by smaller, less capitalized banks and often in newly developed, less economically stable regions. Investors may have required additional returns to compensate.

The pattern of development of banking in the US from 1863 to 1914 is one of a relatively mature industry responding to economic expansion but punctuated by exogenous regulatory changes that influenced interest rates, profits, and financial risk. High capital requirements established in the National Bank Acts during the Civil War created significant barriers to entry, especially on the frontiers and other less populated areas. By

---

[4] Neal, "Integration of Financial Markets."

[5] Sylla ("Federal Policy," pp. 677–9) examines intraregional, but not interregional, profit rates.

[6] For other applications of capital market theory to historical analysis see Atack *et al.* ("Risk"), who examine financial risk, profit rates, and capital investment in US industry for the 1850 to 1870 period, and Neal (*Rise of Financial Capitalism*, Chaps. 3 and 6), who studies the performance of the Amsterdam and London capital markets in the seventeeth and eighteenth centuries.

the mid-1880s, however, financial innovation in the form of commercial paper and the paper check enabled other financial institutions to offer services that competed with national banks. Further change was caused by regulatory competition that gave significant momentum to expansion in the banking industry.[7] State legislators, seeking to increase banking facilities in smaller communities, encouraged state and trust company entry by undercutting national bank capital requirements.[8] The federal government reacted by passing the Gold Standard Act of 1900, provisions of which reduced capital requirements for national banks, but states followed with another round of reductions in their capital requirements.

This chapter reviews previous work on the US banking industry relevant to the DSJ hypothesis in light of industrial dynamics. I then present two statistical tests. The first is a regression analysis of regional profit rate differentials and the second is a regression analysis of profit premia as a function of financial risk (measured by the standard deviation of profit rates). The concluding section summarizes results and discusses their implications.

I.   Interest rate differentials and the industrial dynamics of banking

Because Davis was ultimately concerned with the allocation of savings, he studied the interest rates that banks charged loan customers, properly focusing attention on the outcome of regional allocation of capital on the uses of savings. In his research Davis calculated regional interest rates and inspected a time plot of the results. He found that, after the Civil War, banks in other developing regions of the US charged interest rates on loans that were high relative to Middle Atlantic rates but the spread of regional interest rates narrowed over the period from 1870 to 1914. Davis considered several mechanisms that might channel funds across regions and cause a narrowing of interest rate differentials. In the end he concluded that the most important factor was that bank lending operations faced new competition from the commercial paper market.

Later writers subjected Davis's data to more rigorous statistical tests and have challenged Davis's original hypothesis. Gene Smiley noted that if Davis was correct then measures of the dispersion of regional interest rates would have declined, but his calculations show neither a decline in the coefficient of variation, nor a statistically significant fall in the

---

[7] White, "Political Economy."
[8] Neal ("Trust Companies") argues that the trust company was an important source of financial innovation in the US prior to World War I.

standard deviation of the cross-sectional values of regional interest rates.[9] John Binder and David Brown used dummy variables in a regression analysis to see if there were significant changes in the difference between interest rates in developing regions and those of the Middle Atlantic region for the periods after 1885 and after 1900.[10] They found that coefficients on dummy variables were often statistically insignificant, and that measured declines in interest rate differentials were numerically small. More recently, Scott Redenius analyzed data at the local (town) level for 1890, including the number of banks, bank balance sheet composition, and population.[11] After considering variables such as banks per market, banks per population, lending patterns, and regional loan rates, he concluded that proxies for local market structure used in previous research are weak and that market power does little to explain regional differences in loan rates.[12]

While studying the interest rates charged on loans is relevant, there is another perspective that can be used to study post-Civil War banking. The theory of industrial dynamics focuses on profitability of an industry: if profit rates are high or low relative to some "normal" level, then entry or exit will occur until profit rates are at the normal level. In the context of the DSJ hypothesis, entry restrictions generated monopoly power and allowed persistent super-normal profits in banking for some developing regions in the years immediately following the Civil War. But during the 1880s increased competition gave loan customers an alternative and began to erode the monopoly power of banks. According to Davis, the source of this competition was entry into the loan market by commercial paper brokers. Subsequently, Sylla and James argued that the extra competition may have come from the entry of banks into the market, with Sylla emphasizing entry in rural areas and James stressing entry of state-chartered banks.[13] This dynamic process would have implications on the price charged to customers, since we typically expect monopolistic industries to gain their high profits by charging high prices. We

---

[9] Smiley, "Interest Rate Movement."
[10] Binder and Brown, "Bank Rates of Return."
[11] Redenius, "Bank Market Power."
[12] On its surface it appears that barriers to entry were weak in this period of US history: the number of state and nationally chartered banks rose from 1,937 in 1870 to over 23,000 in 1914. Atack and Passel (*New Economic View*, pp. 510–14) provide an excellent review the interest rate convergence literature and conclude that "the evidence in favor of monopoly banking is weak." However, there is a case to be made for significant local monopoly power for some markets: Redenius ("Bank Market Power," Table 6) shows that of 5,529 towns in his sample, 57 percent had only one state or national bank.
[13] Sylla, "Federal Policy"; James, "Development."

might expect interest rate convergence as banking in the developing regions of the US faced with stronger competition.

But interest rate convergence is not necessarily an indicator of a change from a monopolistic to a competitive banking market because changes other than the competitive structure also influence interest rates. For example, a dispersion of interest rates could occur in a competitive industry due to differences in the cost of banking. Regional differences in costs may have been substantial, due to factors such as different wage rates for labor, different amounts of labor needed to conduct business, transportation costs, and economies of scale with respect to physical capital, which in turn could cause differing interest rates charged to loan customers. Under such circumstances, a regional structure of interest rates would emerge, even with significant loan competition and inter-regional capital flows.[14] Interest rate convergence could also have been due to factors other than competition: labor mobility could have reduced regional wage differentials, and as the regions developed, higher loan volume could have reduced regional differences in the amount of labor or capital per unit output of banks.[15]

Binder and Brown make the same point but argue that regional flow of funds will be related to net returns on assets, and they therefore study income earned by banks net of costs divided by earning assets of banks.[16] However, the net returns on assets will diverge from profit rates (net income divided by equity capital) due to differences in the capital-asset ratio. Mathematically this relationship is shown in the equation

$$\text{profit rate} = \text{net return on assets} / \text{bank capitalization}^{17}$$

where

$$\text{profit rate} = \text{profit} / \text{equity capital}$$
$$\text{net return on assets} = \text{profit} / \text{assets}$$
$$\text{bank captilization} = \text{equity capital} / \text{assets}$$

---

[14] Restrictions on bank branching in this period would have kept banks from low cost regions from easily offering lending services in high cost regions.

[15] Sushka and Barrett ("Banking Structure," pp. 469–71) show that a monopolistically competitive banking structure may also lead to a dispersion of interest rates because banks in regions with a relatively low interest sensitivity of loan demand would charge relatively high interest rates.

[16] Binder and Brown, "Bank Rates of Return."

[17] Formally, let A = assets, C = equity capital, $k = C/A$, ROE = profit rate (return on equity), ROA = net return on assets, and k = bank capitalization. Then ROE = profit/C = (profit/A)(A/C) = $ROA(1/(C/A))$ = ROA/k. Equity capital is measured by paid in capital plus surplus, where surplus is retained earnings of the bank.

Thus regional differences in the net return on assets could be consistent with equal profit rates on capital if bank capitalization was relatively large in the region with higher net returns on assets.

Sylla has documented regional differences in the capitalization ratio of national banks for the year 1900.[18] This ratio was relatively low in the Middle Atlantic region. There are at least two reasons why regional capitalization ratios would represent systematic differences across regions. First, Hugh Rockoff has shown that there were large differences in the rates of bank failure across the various regions of the US.[19] Since capital serves as a buffer against failure, banks in regions with high rates of failure may have held higher ratios of capital to assets, and Rockoff presents correlations that show that regions with high rates of failure were also those with high returns to bank capital. Second, newly established national banks were subject to minimum capital requirements, a constraint that was likely to be more binding in the developing regions of the US, and on average may have led to higher capitalization ratios.

In sum, profit rates incorporate differences in capitalization, and they also account for differences in costs. Profit rates are most relevant to the industrial dynamics of financial markets: commercial paper brokers and potential investors in new banks were not drawn into competition with existing banks because of high interest rates, but rather because of a potential for high returns on their capital investment.

II.   Regional profit rates

The data on regional profit rates for national banks are plotted in Figure 9.1 and summary statistics shown in Table 9.1.[20] The co-movement in the profits rates is evident in Figure 9.1 and so it is clear that regional profits of national banks were subject to similar business cycle influences, especially in contiguous regions, suggesting at least some integration among various banking markets. At the same time, there was a structure to profit rates that suggests that some regional influences were determining profit rates. Table 9.1 shows that national banks in the New England region had the lowest profit rates, averaging 6.57 percent per year for the period from 1870 to 1914. The national banks in the Middle Atlantic region had a higher average profit rate, at 8.28 percent. National banks in the West and Pacific had the highest average profit

---

[18] Sylla, "Federal Policy," p. 660.   [19] Rockoff, "Regional Interest Rates."
[20] Data are from Powlison (*Profits of the National Banks*, pp. 105–7) and represent averages of the profit rates of national banks weighted by the bank's equity capital to total equity capital of all the banks in the region.

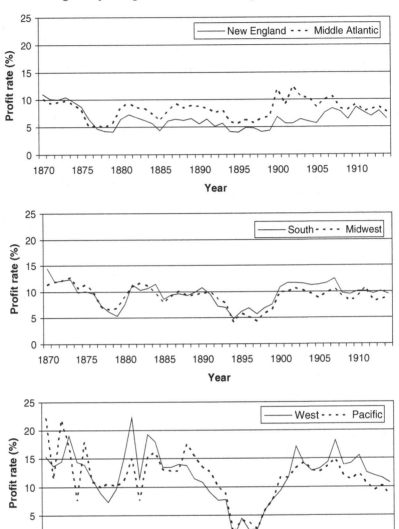

Figure 9.1 Profit rates of national banks by region.

Table 9.1. *Summary statistics for profit rates of regional national banks: 1870–1914*

Region[b]	Average				Standard deviation			
	1870–1884	1885–1899	1900–1914	1870–1914	1870–1884	1885–1899	1900–1914	1870–1914
Middle Atlantic	7.98	7.42	9.44	8.28	1.82	1.27	1.45	1.72
Midwest	10.20	7.59	9.48	9.09	1.98	2.11	0.88	2.04
South	10.06	7.95	10.75	9.59	2.50	1.75	0.97	2.17
West	14.27	8.35	13.43	12.02	4.17	4.44	2.36	4.53
Pacific	13.70	9.49	11.93	11.70	4.71	4.99	1.83	4.37
New England	7.47	5.28	6.98	6.57	2.36	0.94	1.01	1.81

Notes: Profit rates are bank net income divided by equity capital, where equity capital is measured by paid in capital plus surplus, and surplus is retained earnings of the bank. The regions are: *New England* – Maine, New Hampshire, Vermont, Massachusetts, Rhode Island, Connecticut; *Middle Atlantic* – New York, New Jersey, Pennsylvania, Delaware, Maryland, Washington DC; *South* – Virginia, West Virginia, North Carolina, South Carolina, Georgia, Florida, Alabama, Mississippi, Louisiana, Texas, Arkansas, Kentucky, Tennessee; *Midwest* – Ohio, Indiana, Illinois, Michigan, Wisconsin, Minnesota, Iowa, Missouri; *West* – North Dakota, South Dakota, Nebraska, Kansas, Montana, Wyoming, Colorado, New Mexico, Oklahoma; *Pacific* – Washington, Oregon, California, Idaho, Utah, Nevada, Arizona, Alaska.
Source: Powlison, *Profits of the National Banks*, pp. 105–7.

rate over the entire period, and profit rates for the South and Midwest were between those for the West and Pacific and that for the Middle Atlantic. This basic structure (New England with the lowest profit rates, with Middle Atlantic next highest, South and Midwest next highest, and West and Pacific highest) was essentially stable for the three sub-periods 1870–1884, 1885–1899, and 1900–1914.

Also evident from Figure 9.1 are significant differences in the fluctuations of regional profit rates. Table 9.1 shows the standard deviations calculated from the data; the standard deviation of the Middle Atlantic national banks for the period 1870–1914 was smallest, at 1.72 percent, while the standard deviation of the West region was some 2.6 times higher, at 4.53 percent.[21] This suggests that financial risk of investing in banks was not the same across regions which may in turn explain part of the structure of regional profit rates.

---

[21] The coefficient of variation for the Middle Atlantic region was 0.21, while for the West it was 0.38, which is 1.8 times higher than that for the Middle Atlantic region.

The DSJ hypothesis suggests that increased competitive forces led to changes in regional profit rates outside of the Middle Atlantic regions, shifting them closer to the Middle Atlantic profit rates. Unfortunately, simple inspection of Figure 9.1 is not conclusive as to whether such a trend existed. Formal time-series tests for trends in regional profit rates are equally inconclusive (shown in an appendix). With a confidence level of 10 percent, these tests indicate that each of the profit rate series was fluctuating around a constant mean. In so far as this indicates that regional profit rates could not have converged between 1870 and 1914, it contradicts the DSJ hypothesis. But at a confidence level smaller than 10 percent, the tests indicate that the Middle Atlantic profit rate did not have a trend while there was a trend in the profit rates in at least some other regions. It is this that motivates the next section, for it suggests that profit differentials may have changed over time.

III.   A regression analysis of profit rate differentials

If some of the regional profit rates were not stationary series, then what type of trend might they have had? Statistical tests do not suggest either a deterministic or a stochastic trend.[22] Both tests, however, assume that the trend persisted through the entire period, whereas the DSJ hypothesis does not necessarily suggest a smooth convergence in profit rates over the entire period. Consequently, the data may be best characterized as having variable trends. In what follows, this variable trend is modeled as a shift of the mean of the regional profit rates for subperiods of time.

In their analysis of the DSJ hypothesis, Binder and Brown broke the 1870-to-1914 period into three subperiods of equal length, with breaks at 1885 and 1900.[23] The 1885 break is based on Davis's argument that, during the 1880s, the entry of brokerage firms specializing in commercial paper began to erode the monopoly position of bankers.[24] The 1900 break is based on the work of Sylla, who argued that high minimum capital requirements set by the National Banking Acts had been binding outside of the Middle Atlantic and New England regions, imposing entry restrictions and monopoly power in the southern and western parts of the US.[25] The Gold Standard Act of 1900, however, lowered

[22] When time was added to appendix equation (A1) as an explanatory variable, its coefficient was not statistically different from zero. In addition, a stochastic trend was not indicated, because the constant term for a stochastic-trend model (using first-differences of the data) was not statistically significant.
[23] Binder and Brown, "Bank Rates of Return."
[24] Davis, "The Investment Market," pp. 372–3.   [25] Sylla, "Federal Policy."

minimum capital requirements for national banks in small towns, and so eroded the monopoly power of existing banks in these towns.

Consequently, we will look for a shift in the mean regional profit rate relative to a reference region. However, the choice of a reference region is not clear. Because capital requirements were generally not binding there, both the Middle Atlantic and the New England regions would be good candidates. Moreover, the economies of both regions were relatively advanced and both were within the boundaries of the development frontier by 1870.

While New England's banking market was highly competitive, well developed, and soundly run prior to and after the Civil War, it also has some special characteristics that argues against using it as the reference region. Compared to banks in other regions, New England's banks tended to be small with a management dominated by insiders and were organized around kinship groups.[26] This tended to limit their size and led to relatively high levels of insider lending. The conservative nature of New England banks manifested itself in an aversion to deposits as a source of funding so that capitalization rates were high relative to other regions.[27]

This legacy influenced New England banking practices through the entire nineteenth century and distinguished it from other regions. In Table 9.2, for example, we see that New England is the only region in the US where the number of national banks declined after 1900. Moreover, in contrast to other regions, New England did not experience an increase in state chartered banks after 1885, although it did participate in the expansion of trust companies that occurred in all regions of the US.[28] Yet more interesting, the total capital investing in New England national banks declined from $165 million in 1885 to $99 million in 1915.[29] It stands out as the only region in the US where there was disinvestment of capital in national banks between 1885 and 1914.

As a result, the Middle Atlantic banking market provides a better reference region. Its banking practices were likely to be mimicked elsewhere in the country because some of the most influential writers on banking practices in the late nineteenth century came from the area.[30] Moreover, like the developing regions of the US, the banking market was expanding in the Middle Atlantic region up to 1915.

---

[26] Bodenhorn, *A History of Banking*, p. 32; Lamoreaux, *Insider Lending*.

[27] Lamoreaux, *Insider Lending*, pp. 65–70.   [28] Neal, "Trust Companies."

[29] Lamoreaux (*Insider Lending*, pp. 137–44) writes that bankers in the late nineteenth century were aware of the overcapitalization of New England banks and that they used consolidation as a method of reducing bank capital.

[30] Lamoreaux, *Insider Lending*, pp. 114–17.

Table 9.2. *Regional banking characteristics: US, 1870 to 1914*

	Middle Atlantic	Midwest	South	West	Pacific	New England	US Total
Number of national banks							
1870	587	431	93	13	3	494	1,620
1885	739	826	294	243	52	560	2,714
1900	1,023	1,156	596	412	122	561	3,870
1915	1,652	2,101	1,563	1,352	542	434	7,644
Number of state banks							
1885	196	459	232	139	81	17	1,124
1900	333	1,658	1,068	1,045	280	21	4,405
1909	*387*	*3,717*	*3,312*	*3,026*	*831*	*19*	*11,292*
Number of trust companies							
1885	27	2	0	0	0	21	50
1900	211	47	97	18	39	90	502
1909	*475*	*228*	*131*	*34*	*56*	*155*	*1,079*
Total capital of national banks (millions)							
1870	$189	$70	$16	$1.3	$0.4	$154	$430
1885	$172	$120	$44	$19	$7	$165	$528
1900	$208	$165	$68	$32	$19	$137	$630
1915	$331	$291	$183	$74	$91	$99	$1,069

Sources: National bank data are from Comptroller of the Currency, *Annual Report*,1921, pp. 307–45. State bank and trust company data are from Barnett, *State Banks and Trust Companies*, fold out tables at page 248, and are available only up to 1909.

At the same time, developments in the Middle Atlantic region can be viewed as exogenous relative to other regions. Several reasons justify this assumption. First, the Middle Atlantic region was the largest of all regions both in terms of population and of personal income over the entire period from 1870 to 1914; if we view the six regions as several open economies, the Middle Atlantic could be viewed as a large open economy, where changes in any of the other smaller regions would have a negligible impact on the national bank profit rates of the Middle Atlantic region. Second, the Middle Atlantic region was relatively well developed and densely populated, which meant that minimum capital requirements would be less (and possibly not) binding. Third, as noted by Davis, commercial banking in the region was highly competitive, and the commercial paper market was well established, by the time of the Civil War.[31] Thus, the spread of the commercial paper market affected only other regions. Fourth, the main centers of international finance were

[31] Davis, "The Investment Market," p. 372.

located in the Middle Atlantic region so that given international capital flows, it is likely that rates of return to Middle Atlantic national banks were closely tied to "world" rates of return.[32]

To investigate changes in the regional profit differentials, I assume that the Middle Atlantic profit rates of national banks fluctuated around a constant mean. Let

y_t = profit rates of national banks in the Middle Atlantic region for year t, and

μ_o = mean value of national bank profit rates for the Middle Atlantic region.

We have seen that y_t fluctuate around μ_o in a stationary fashion, which suggests that

$$y_t = \mu_o + u_t \tag{1}$$

where u_t represents the difference between actual and mean interest rates. Similarly, let z_t = profit rates for national banks in non-Middle Atlantic regions; $f(t)$ = trend function, where t denotes time.

(For simplicity, subscripts to denote the various regions are assumed.) Suppose that

$$z_t = f(t) + v_t \tag{2}$$

where v_t is also the difference between actual and mean interest rates. The function $f(t)$ represent the mean value of z_t, which is allowed to change through time.

Because we assume that the mean of each regional profit rate has its own deterministic trend, the interregional relation between profit rates will be embodied in the terms v_t and u_t. This relation may be written as

$$v_t = \pi u_t + \varepsilon_t \tag{3}$$

where ε_t is a zero mean error term, which suggests that fluctuations in profit rates are related through the parameter π.[33] If $\pi = 1$, then a 1 percent change in Middle Atlantic profit rates would be associated with a 1 percent change in the regional profit rate. If $\pi \neq 1$, then regional profit rates may rise or fall by more than 1 percent for a 1 percent change in

---

[32] If the profit rates of the Middle Atlantic region were endogenous, then the estimation results would be subject to simultaneity bias. Unfortunately there are no annual data available on a regional basis that would permit an instrumental variables estimation procedure, and so there is no way to test the assumption of exogeneity.

[33] There is no intercept term in equation (3) because any systematic differences between profit rates are accounted for by differences in μ_o and $f(t)$.

Middle Atlantic profit rates. The value of π is determined by the regional supply and demand forces associated with saving and borrowing, as well as the potential flows of funds into the region.[34] In a world of perfect capital mobility, it is reasonable to suppose that $\pi = 1$, but a value of $\pi \neq 1$ does not necessarily suggest independent financial markets, given the costs of transactions as well as differences in risk.[35]

Based on the periodization discussed above, denote for the mean profit rate of regional national banks *other than* Middle Atlantic banks:

$\mu_i =$ region i mean profit rate for the 1870–1884 period;
$\mu_i' =$ region i mean profit rate for the 1885–1899 period;
$\mu_i'' =$ region i mean profit rate for the 1900–1914 period.

Also let

D1885 = 1 for periods after 1884, and zero otherwise;
D1900 = 1 for periods after 1899, and zero otherwise.

Then for each region the trend in the mean profit rate can be modeled as

$$f(t) = \mu_i + (\mu_i' - \mu_i) \, D1885 + (\mu_i'' - \mu_i') \, D1900 \qquad (4)$$

Combining equation (4) with equations (1)–(3) we obtain the basic estimating equation

$$z_t = (\mu_i - \pi\mu_o) + (\mu_i' - \mu_i) \, D1885 + (\mu_i'' - \mu_i') \, D1900 + \pi y_t + \varepsilon_t \qquad (5)$$

Integration of the regions imposes some restrictions on the error term, ε_t, which represents the difference between actual profits in a region and the structural profit given by the other terms on the right-hand side of equation (5).[36] In a world of capital mobility, a non-zero value for ε_t would provide a signal for both regional capital flows as well as entry into or exit from banking. But even with monopolistic restrictions on capital flows and entry, ε_t should signal some adjustments for existing banks. For example, if monopolistic banks used a strategy of limiting profits to

[34] Odell, "Integration."
[35] Given regional differences in risk and transactions cost, it seems imprudent to impose a restriction that $\pi = 1$. Binder and Brown ("Bank Rates of Return," p. 52), in effect, impose such a restriction when they use interregional differences in interest rates as a dependent variable in their regressions.
[36] This discussion is akin to what time-series analysts have called cointegration (Granger, "Developments"). However, in this instance we do not have cointegration because two time-series of data can be cointegrated only if both are non-stationary and as we have seen, the Middle Atlantic profit rates were stationary.

levels that would not encourage entry, a positive value of ε_t might signal a response that would reduce profits, while negative values of ε_t might signal a response that would increase profits.[37] In either case, this adjustment would take time, and so any excess profit may persist for a period of time. Thus the ε_t may be autocorrelated, but the autocorrelation should be such that, over time, any excess profit should diminish towards zero. Stationarity imposes such a restriction. If the ε_t are stationary, then in the absence of further innovations the error terms would decline towards zero. Non-stationarity of the ε_t, on the other hand, would suggest that the interregional profit rates could diverge substantially, implying capital immobility and restricted entry, that is, non-integrated banking markets.

Table 9.3 presents ordinary least-squares estimates of equation (5); since the error terms are autocorrelated, I used a method for finding the standard errors of the coefficients that is consistent with respect to autocorrelation.[38] As can be seen, only for the Southern region was the coefficient on *D1900* statistically different from zero. Accordingly, a second version of the model is also shown in Table 9.3, where the *D1900* variable is removed from the estimation equation. On the other hand, regardless of the specification, we see that for every region the coefficient on the *D1885* variable is statistically significant and less than zero. Because the coefficient represents the difference between the regional profit rates for 1870–1884 and for the period after 1884, these estimates suggests that the mean of regional profit rates for national banks fell after 1884.

Estimates suggest that the fall in profit differentials was completed in the 1885–1899 period because, with the exception of the South, the estimated coefficients on the *D1900* variable are not statistically significant. In the South, however, the coefficient on *D1900* is significant and positive at a 5 percent level, suggesting a rise in average profit rates for Southern national banks after 1900. This finding is consistent with

---

[37] In a formal model of a profit-maximizing bank with monopoly power, Sushka and Barrett ("Banking Structure," pp. 470–1) show that information from other markets would influence the pricing policy and profitability of the bank.

[38] Hansen, "Large Sample Properties." This technique also requires an estimate of the "long-run" variance of the error term ε_t, which requires calculation of a number of the lagged autocovariances of the estimated values of ε_t. Three lagged autocovariances were used, again based on the selection criteria given by Schwert ("Effects of Model Specification," p. 88). The standard errors are also consistent with respect to heteroscedasticity; see White, "Heteroscedasticity-Consistent Covariance Matrix Estimator." In her investigation of regional differences in interest rates, Odell ("Integration," p. 304) had difficulties with heteroscedasticity and as a result used a log transformation. Figure 9.1 and Table 9.1 suggest that the fluctuations in profit rates may have changed for some subperiods, and so a correction for heteroscedasticity seems warranted.

Table 9.3. *Regression analysis of the profit rate differentials for regional national banks, 1870–1914*[a]

		Dependent variable: profit rates of regional national banks								
		Independent variables[b]						Residual analysis		
Region	Regr. Number	Constant	D1885 (D=1 after 1884, D=0 otherwise)	D1900 (D=1 after 1899, D=0 otherwise)	Profit Rate for Middle Atlantic Banks	S_e	R^2	Durbin–Watson Statistic	$\hat{\rho}$	τ[a]
Midwest	1	3.0628** (1.196)	-2.1049*** (0.560)	0.0845 (0.531)	0.8944*** (0.133)	1.099	.729	1.379	0.3012	-4.809**
	2	2.9834*** (1.130)	-2.0671*** (0.407)		0.9043*** (0.127)	1.086	.728	1.387	0.2966	-4.832***
South	3	2.7668** (1.407)	-1.5902*** (0.577)	0.9597** (0.412)	0.9133*** (0.156)	1.231	.701	1.300	0.3034	-5.057**
	4	1.8651 (1.252)	-1.1607** (0.504)		1.0263*** (0.137)	1.266	.676	1.312	0.3075	-4.936***
West	5	2.2740 (2.729)	-5.0691*** (1.334)	2.0396 (1.466)	1.5028*** (0.333)	3.028	.585	1.196	0.3956	-4.348*
	6	0.3578 (3.038)	-4.1561*** (1.135)		1.7429*** (0.372)	3.085	.558	1.110	0.4357	-4.153**
Pacific	7	0.8901 (2.863)	-3.3082** (1.542)	-0.7943 (1.479)	1.6048*** (0.368)	3.327	.460	1.646	0.1485	-5.807***

8	1.6363 (2.838)	−3.6637*** (1.156)		1.5113*** (0.360)	3.300	.456	1.623	0.1569	−5.762***
New	9	2.5087 (1.568)	−1.8382*** (0.667)	0.4430 (0.637)	0.6214*** (0.202)	1.280	.536	0.464	0.7318	−2.800
England	10	2.0925 (1.412)	−1.6399** (0.743)		0.6735*** (0.178)	1.275	.528	0.461	0.7389	−2.716

Notes: ***, **, and * indicate statistically different from zero (or $\rho < 1$ for the last column) at the 1%, 5%, or 10% levels in a one-tailed test. Coefficient estimates are found using ordinary least-squares with 45 annual observations; standard errors of the estimated coefficients are found using a heteroscedasticity- and autocorrelation-consistent method; see White, "Heteroscedasticity-Consistent Covariance Matrix Estimator" and Hansen, "Large Sample Properties." Entries show coefficient estimates; standard errors are in parentheses.

[a] Dickey–Fuller test statistic to test a null hypothesis that $\rho < 1$. Critical values to reject the null in a one-tailed test at the 1%, 5%, and 10% levels are −5.065, −4.3553, and −4.0027 in regressions with four explanatory variables, and −4.6355, −3.9396, and −3.5951 in regressions with three explanatory variables. Critical values are from MacKinnon, "Critical Values."

Davis's discussion of the South as being different from other regions, due to relatively poor banking facilities, binding minimum capital requirements, and inadequate bank-note quotas.[39] These differences may have allowed Southern national banks to earn extraordinary profits even into the twentieth century.

The last column of Table 9.3 shows the Dickey–Fuller tau statistic to test for stationarity of the residuals. The null hypothesis of non-stationary residuals can be rejected for all regions except for the regression for New England national banks, consistent with the argument that the banking market in New England operated independent of other regions.

Two parameters in the model, π and ρ, reflect regional financial integration. The significant positive values for π suggest that the structural profit levels of banks in other regions were tied to those of Middle Atlantic banks. In regions where estimates of ρ indicate stationary error terms, profit rate signals were operating to reduce differences between actual and structural profit rates.[40] Such a result is not surprising, given research that suggests regional integration of financial markets even before the Civil War, which strongly implies integration after the Civil War.[41] Indeed, the autocorrelation coefficients suggest that any "excess" profits measured by the error term were eliminated quickly. Ignoring the New England region, the estimated autocorrelation coefficients range from 0.1485 to 0.4357. This implies that the mean lag for innovations to structural profit rate differences was only 2.5 to ten months.[42] Some underlying mechanism for relative rapid interregional adjustments was operating, perhaps tied the flow of funds through the interbank deposit market.[43] This market was well established by 1880 and grew rapidly at least up to 1910.[44]

The change in profit rates that occurred after 1885 was large, as indicated by changes in profit rate premia. The Middle Atlantic region provides a useful reference point on the grounds that, as a large open economy, its profit rate represents the competitive rate. Its 8.28 percent average returns for the period from 1870 to 1914, and the estimated parameters shown in Table 9.3, are used to calculate a predicted average rate for each of the other regions.[45] The results are shown in Table 9.4.

---

[39] Davis, "The Investment Market," pp. 388–92.
[40] In all cases a first-order autocorrelation model for the error terms was adequate.
[41] Bodenhorn and Rockoff, "Regional Interest Rates."
[42] The mean lag is calculated using $\hat{\rho}/(1 - \hat{\rho})$; see Johnston, *Econometic Methods*, p. 344.
[43] Sylla, "Federal Policy," pp. 335–70.   [44] Redenius, "Bank Market Power."
[45] I calculate profit premia for each region and for each subperiod, where the premia is the predicted regional profit rate minus the profit rate for the Middle Atlantic region.

Table 9.4. *Estimates of premia for profit rates of regional national banks, 1870–1914*

Region	Regression Number	1870–1884	1885–1899	1900–1914
Midwest	2	2.19	0.12	0.12
South-A	3	2.05	0.46	1.42
South-B	4	2.08	0.92	0.92
West	6	6.51	2.35	2.35
Pacific	8	5.89	2.22	2.22
New England	10	−0.61	−2.25	−2.25

Notes: Premia are the predicted profit rate for regional national banks minus the profit rate for Middle Atlantic national banks. Predicted profits are calculated based on the parameter estimates from Table 4.9, and using the average profit rate of Middle Atlantic national banks for the entire period 1870–1914 (see Table 1.9).

In the Midwest, the profit premium was 2.19 percentage points for the period from 1870 to 1884, or roughly a quarter of the profit rates earned by Middle Atlantic banks. This differential virtually disappeared after 1885. In the South, the premium was about 2 percent in the 1870–1884 period, and it fell to 0.46 after 1885, but rose to 1.42 percent after 1900 (Regression 3). The West and Pacific regions had the highest profit premia, at 6.51 percent and 5.89 percent for the 1870–1884 period, which are large values relative to the Middle Atlantic's 7.98 percent average profit for this same period. In each case the premium fell by more than half after 1885.[46]

IV.   Profit rates and financial risk

Financial risk is often measured using the standard deviation of returns to capital. As we have seen (Table 9.1), this changed markedly over time

Equations without the *D1900* variable are used, except for the South, where I present two calculations since either estimation equation is arguably relevant for the South.

[46] The results for the Pacific region need to be interpreted with some caution. As noted by Bodenhorn and Rockoff ("Regional Interest Rates," pp. 183–4), after the Civil War most of the country retained the greenback dollar as a unit of account until specie payment was resumed in 1879, but during the same period the Pacific coast used the gold dollar as a unit of account. According to Bodenhorn and Rockoff's figures ("Regional Interest Rates," p. 185), the greenback appreciated on average by 3.02 percent per year between 1869 and 1879. I have not adjusted for this, because both total profits and total capital would be affected by exchange rate fluctuations in equal percentages, so that their ratio would be unaffected.

and across regions. One reason for the regional profit differentials may be regional risk differentials, so that higher profits may simply have reflected a greater level of risk. In this section, I examine the relation between financial risk and profit rates and, as a starting point, I apply capital market theory.[47] According to this theory, in a well-functioning capital market with unrestricted capital flows, rates of return for efficient portfolios should differ only due to systematic risk, measured by the fluctuation in portfolio returns that are tied to fluctuations in the market rate of return.

It seems plausible to assume that the annual average of profit rates for Middle Atlantic banks represents the return on an efficient portfolio, for two reasons. First, banking in the Middle Atlantic region was competitive, so that capital flows should affect interest rates in a manner that would drive rates of return close to an equilibrium return. Second, the large number of banks underlying our estimate of the annual average profit rate should eliminate risk that was specific to any individual bank. The standard deviation of average profit rates across time should then measure systematic risk. Let $\sigma_o =$ standard deviation of annual profit rates for Middle Atlantic banks.

All efficient portfolios should lie along the capital market line which relates average return to standard deviation. The average and standard deviation for Middle Atlantic national banks should lie on that line; thus

$$\mu_o = p_o + r\sigma_o \tag{6}$$

where p_o is the "pure" (riskless) rate of return and r measures the change in average return for a one-standard-deviation change in financial risk (the "price" of risk).

For national banks in regions *other than* the Mid-Atlantic, let $\sigma_i =$ region i standard deviation of annual profit rates.

Assume that the relation between risk and return is given by

$$\mu_i = p + r\sigma_i \tag{7}$$

Subtracting equation (7) from (8) we get

$$\mu_i - \mu_o = (p - p_o) + r(\sigma_i - \sigma_o) \tag{8}$$

If, as the DSJ hypothesis suggests, monopoly power allows relatively high rates of return, then rates of return for national banks in other

---

[47] Sharpe, *Portfolio Theory*, Chap. 5.

regions should be high at a given level of risk, which implies that $p > p_o$.[48] On the other hand, full regional integration and competitive banking markets would imply that $p = p_o$ and that any observed difference in average profit ($\mu_i - \mu_o \neq 0$) would be caused by a difference in financial risk ($\sigma_i - \sigma_o \neq 0$).

Equation (8) may or may not be the same for each of the subperiods.[49] The initial estimation will allow equation (8) to be different for each subperiod. Let

D1885–99 = 1 for the period 1885–1899, and zero otherwise;
D1900–14 = 1 for the period 1900–1914, and zero otherwise;
($p - p_o$), r = intercept and slope coefficients for the period 1870–1885;
($p - p_o$)′, r' = intercept and slope coefficients for the period 1885–1899;
($p - p_o$)″, r'' = intercept and slope coefficients for the period 1900–1914.

The full estimation equation is

$$\mu_i - \mu_o = (p - p_o) + r(\sigma_i - \sigma_o)$$
$$+ \left\{ (p - p_o)' - (p - p_o) \right\}^* D1885-99$$
$$+ \{ r' - r \} \left[D1885-99^*(\sigma_i - \sigma_o) \right]$$
$$+ \left\{ (p - p_o)'' - (p - p_o) \right\}^* D1900-14$$
$$+ \{ r'' - r \} \left[D1900-14^*(\sigma_i - \sigma_o) \right] + \varepsilon_i \qquad (9)$$

The terms within braces {} will be estimated, and measures the profit-premia, risk-differential relation for a subperiod relative to the 1870–1884 subperiod.

Ideally the values of μ_i should represent equilibrium profit rates. However, if we used actual average profit rates, some of the profit rate would represent the disequilibrium represented by the error term ε_t from equation (5). To measure the equilibrium profit premia more closely, values taken from Table 9.3 (which adjust for the effects of ε_t) are used

---

[48] James ("Portfolio Selection") develops a formal model of portfolio selection under imperfect competition and shows that the return to an asset issued by a bank with monopoly power would consist of a standard financial-risk premium plus a positive return to monopoly power (as measured by the interest sensitivity of loan demand). The difference between p and p_o can be interpreted as a measure of the return to monopoly power.

[49] Sharpe, *Portfolio Theory*, p. 85.

to measure ($\mu_i - \mu_o$). The standard deviations σ_i are measured using the subperiod values for each region and σ_o is measured using the full period value for the Middle Atlantic region from Table 9.1. The special characteristics of in New England banking market and results from Table 9.3 suggest that it should be eliminated from the analysis. If banks in New England were somehow insulated or operated differently from other regions, then equation (7) would not apply. I will initially eliminate the New England observations, but for completeness, present another set of estimates that include New England.

Ordinary least-squares estimates of equation (9), with and without the New England observations, are given by regressions 11 and 13 of Table 9.5 The New England observations lowers the explanatory power of the regressions considerably, with the R^2 falling from 93.3 percent to 78.1 percent. This further suggests that the New England region should be treated as a special case. Interpretation will therefore focus on the results that exclude the New England observations.[50]

Regression 11 shows that the estimated coefficients for *D1900–14* and [*D1900-14* $\times$ ($\sigma_i - \sigma_o$)] are not statistically different from zero. Regression 12 therefore drops the variables from the regression, and the remaining coefficients are statistically different from zero at a 1 percent significance level or better. We may interpret the results as indicating that the relation between profit premia and risk differentials was the same for the 1870–1884 and 1900–1914 periods, but a different relation existed for the 1885–1899 period. The estimated relation and the associated observations are shown in Figure 9.2. The line for the period 1870–1884 has an intercept that is statistically different from zero. For the same level of financial risk ($\sigma_i = \sigma_o$), profit rates for national banks in the other regions were on average about 1.8 percentage points or 22 percent (=1.8/8.28) higher than profit rates for Middle Atlantic national banks.

The regression results allow a decomposition of excess profits into various components. For example, the excess profit in the Western region of the US was 6.51 percent for the period 1870–1884. Of that, 1.8 percent can be attributed to the regional profit premium, 1 percent to prediction error, and the remainder, 3.7 percent, to regional financial risk. Based on this decomposition, much of the regional profit differential among national banks in this period can be attributed to financial risk.

---

[50] As can be seen from Table 9.5, however, the qualitative conclusions we can reach are not affected, and the quantitative results are similar, whether the New England observations are included or not.

Table 9.5. *Regression analysis of profit premia and financial risk*[a]

			Dependent variable: structural profit premia[b]					
			Independent variables[c]					
Regr. Number	Constant	Financial Risk Differential $(\sigma_i - \sigma_o)^d$	D1885–99 (D=1 for 1885–99, D=0 otherwise)	D1885–99 × $(\sigma_i - \sigma_o)$	D1900–14 (D=1 for 1900–14, D=0 otherwise)	D1900–14 × $(\sigma_i - \sigma_o)$	R^2	n
Without New England								
11	1.3949** (0.613)	1.7088*** (0.311)	−1.2034* (0.812)	−1.0230** (0.399)	0.3980 (0.718)	−0.4710 (0.653)	.933	12
12	1.7774*** (0.259)	1.5189*** (0.176)	−1.5859*** (0.552)	−0.8332*** (0.289)			.925	12
With New England								
13	0.1907 (1.060)	2.1193*** (0.592)	−0.7066 (1.321)	−1.1431* (0.718)	1.2002 (1.286)	−0.1426 (1.251)	.781	15
14	1.0201** (0.473)	1.7463*** (0.350)	−1.5360* (0.884)	−0.7700* (0.521)			.760	15

Notes: ***, **, and * indicate statistically different from zero at the 1%, 5%, or 10% levels in a one-tailed test.
[a] Coefficient estimates and standard errors are found using ordinary least-squares.
[b] Profit premia are from Table 9.4.
[c] Entries show coefficient estimates; standard errors are in parentheses.
[d] Regional financial risk is measured by the standard deviation of profit rates for each sub-period; the risk differential is the regional standard deviation minus the 1870–1914 standard deviation of profit rates for Middle Atlantic national banks.

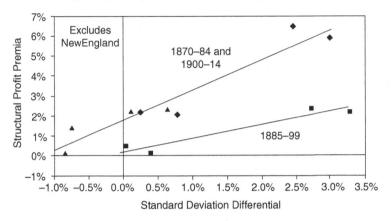

Figure 9.2 Structural profit premia and risk.

As Figure 9.2 shows, the line of best fit shifts down for the period 1885–1899 compared to the 1870–1884 period. For the 1885–1899 period, the intercept term is virtually zero ($1.7774–1.5859 = 0.1915$), so that financial risk can be completely explain any profit premia. These results are consistent with the DSJ hypothesis that monopoly power allowed risk-adjusted extraordinary profits for the 1870–1884 period, but competition eliminated these extraordinary profits by 1885–1899.

The picture for the period 1900–1914 presents a puzzle. The results suggest that risk-adjusted profit premia reemerged for the national banks in regions outside the Middle Atlantic and New England regions. For some reason, investors demanded a return to investments in regional banks over that required for banks in the Middle Atlantic region. Rockoff has suggested that differences in bank failure rates may explain profit rate differentials, but his analysis hints that rates of failure may have declined after 1900 compared to the 1885–1899, which provides little reason to think that the profit premia should have re-emerged.[51] An alternative hypothesis ties the profit premia to added risk in banking caused by bank entry and falling capitalization rates.

The number of national banks grew at an average annual rate of 5.3 percent from 1900 to 1914, compared to 3.2 percent and 2.1 percent for the 1870–1884 and 1885–1899 periods.[52] The boom was likely tied to

[51] Rockoff, "Regional Interest Rates." The periodization used by Rockoff does not coincide with that in this chapter. He shows that, compared to 1891–1904, rates of national bank failure for 1904–1914 increased in the Middel Atlantic regions but declined in the South, Midwest, West, and Pacific regions.

[52] While it is true, as James ("Development," pp. 889 and 893) notes, that in the period from 1900 to 1914 most of the growth of the overall number of banks in the US were

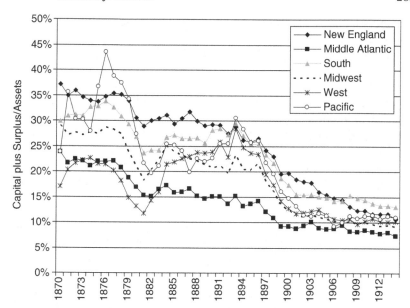

Figure 9.3 Capitalization of US national banks, 1870 to 1914.

lower capital requirements, which would have made it economical to establish smaller national banks in more sparsely populated and developing regions of the US.[53] According to Table 9.2, 3901 national banks entered the market outside of New England between 1900 and 1915. Only 629 of these were in the Middle Atlantic region. Indeed, James documents that most state banks that entered the market in this period had relatively little capital and were located in smaller towns, and this is likely true of national banks as well.[54]

Because capital acts as a cushion against unforeseen adverse financial results, the influx of new banks would not have had a major impact on risk among banks if they were sufficiently capitalized. However, as can be seen in Figure 9.3, average capitalization rates for national banks in all regions declined from 1870 to 1914. Capitalization rates fell by almost half over the entire period, and were at their lowest levels after 1900. Capitalization was generally bracketed by two regions, with New

due to the establishment of state chartered banks in the western and southern regions of the US, the period also saw fairly rapid growth among national banks.
[53] In fact the lower capital requirement was limited to banks in towns with a population of less than 3,000.
[54] James, "Development," p. 893.

England's national banks among the highest and the Middle Atlantic's among the lowest.[55]

The continued downward drift of capitalization after 1900 was not due to an influx of smaller national banks because the capitalization rate is not necessarily tied to the size of a bank.[56] While the level of capital for newly established banks was specified in minimum capital requirements, there were no capitalization requirements for ongoing operations for either state or national banks in this era.[57] Rather, capitalization was set by each bank according to their business needs and the downward trend may have been a response to competitive conditions pushing banks to improve returns to capital by increasing financial leverage.

In summary, the re-emergence of risk premia for investment in commercial banks after 1900 may be related to faster bank entry, falling capitalization, and the location of new entrants, all of which contributed to a higher average likelihood of bank failure. Research on modern banks shows that newly established banks tend to be more fragile than established banks.[58] Bank entry accelerated after 1900 and thus increased the proportion of young banks in the market. In addition, the increasing interdependence of banks, evidenced by the expanding interbank market, may have amplified systemic risk.[59] Competitive pressures to increase financial leverage added risk because declining capitalization increases the likelihood of default.[60] Finally, most of the new banks were in areas where local economic risk was significant. Research has shown that banks in developing regions of the US, where the economic base was undiversified and dependent on agriculture, were vulnerable to region-specific shocks.[61] Because these trends were most apparent in the southern and western regions of the US, investors may have required a risk premium to bank investments relative to that of banks in the Middle Atlantic region.

[55] The high capitalization rate for New England's national banks is another indication that it is a special case, given its conservative lending practices and a local economy was probably more stable than most other regions.
[56] In any case, the average size of national banks was relatively steady after 1900.
[57] There was a required reserve ratio for specie held against deposit liabilities but no specification on whether specie could be funded by liability or equity.
[58] DeYoung ("Birth, Growth, and Life or Death of Newly Chartered Banks," p. 24) found that this was because of high expenses for deposit funding and overhead.
[59] Redenius, "Bank Market Power."
[60] For an analysis of default risk in commercial banks, see Sullivan and Spong, "Managerial Wealth."
[61] Alston et al., "Why do Banks Fail?"

V.   Conclusion

This chapter has studied regional profit rates of national banks to examine the industrial dynamics of banking and identify periods where market power may have led to excess risk-adjusted profits. Using both time-series and regression techniques, I find support for the Davis–Sylla–James hypothesis that regional profit rate differentials were large in the 1870–1884 period, but fell substantially after 1884. I also find that differences in financial risk can completely explain these profit differentials for the 1885–1899 period but not for the 1870–1884 and 1900–1914 periods.

The strongest case for the DSJ hypothesis lies within changes seen in the Midwest, the South, the West, and the Pacific regions. Profit rate differentials in the period from 1870 to 1884 were large but diminished significantly after 1885. The profits of national banks were extraordinarily high where barriers to entry were effective, but when alternatives like commercial paper brokers and state-chartered banks became important, added competition eroded monopoly profits. Some regional profit differential remained for the 1885–1899 period, but was largely due to differences in financial risk.

Risk-adjusted profit premia re-emerged in the 1900–1914 period. This may be explained by the juxtaposition of two factors. First, spurred by lower capital required to start a bank, a large number of new banks entered the market. Because they were newly established, these banks were financially fragile. Moreover, they faced significant local economic risk because they were often in developing regions. Second, these banks entered at a time when capitalization rates among national banks were at historic lows, increasing the likelihood of financial failure. Risk-averse investors thus had good reason to demand higher returns to compensate.

Howard Bodenhorn and Hugh Rockoff have shown that regional rates of return to bank capital were fairly uniform across regions prior to the Civil War, and argue that the disruptions of the Civil War caused a divergence of regional rates of return.[62] This paper confirms the regional divergence in the period immediately after the Civil War and a convergence after 1885. This may have simply been a return to a pre-Civil War structure, but results of this study suggest a more complicated picture. The post-Civil War banking market development was punctuated by regulatory changes.[63] The National Bank Acts had great success

---

[62] Bodenhorn and Rockoff, "Regional Interest Rates," p. 181.
[63] See also White (*Regulation and Reform*), who makes it clear that competition between federal and state authorities led to continued changes in bank regulation.

in improving the quality of the nation's currency. But it also created minimum capital requirements giving established banks protected markets in some areas.[64] Along with disruptions caused by the Civil War, this local market power caused a divergence of regional profit rates. After 1885, however, competition by commercial paper brokers and/or by state banks led to more uniform levels of regional risk-adjusted profit rates. Further regulatory change was brought by the Gold Standard Act of 1900 which disturbed the banking market and may have contributed to subsequent bank fragility. Easing of entry barriers for national banks in 1900 allowed a flood of new, smaller banks that, by historical standards, had low capitalization rates. On average, banks in the south and west became more financially fragile and so commanded a higher risk premium. Rather than a picture of a financial market that was steadily becoming more competitive and contributing to economic growth, it is a picture of a mature market responding to significant exogenous regulatory changes by both innovation and market entry.

Appendix A
Testing for trends in national bank profit rates

A formal statistical test for trend in national bank profit rates can be based on the autoregressive formulation

$$x_t = a + \rho x_{t-1} + \eta_t \tag{A1}$$

where ρ is the first-order autocorrelation coefficient and η_t is a white-noise error term. If $-1 < \rho < 1$, then x_t is stationary, that is, it will fluctuate around a constant level (measured by $a/(1-\rho)$).[65] On the other hand, if $\rho = 1$, then the model reduces to $\Delta x_t = a + \eta_t$, and so x_t grows (or declines) in every period on average by the value of a, which suggests a trend to the data.[66]

---

[64] Other restrictions, such as prohibitions on branch banking, also contributed to local market power. But branching requirements did not change significantly in the 1870 to 1914 period and would not have influenced the changes we observe in bank profits and risk.

[65] Stationarity imposes restrictions on the variance and autocovariances of the time series; see Mills (*Time Series Techniques*). These restrictions would be violated if $\rho = 1$.

[66] The trend model discussed here is a stochastic trend; a deterministic trend would add quadratic functions of time as an explanatory variable to equation (1). In the initial test for stationarity I do not allow for a deterministic trend on the suggestion of Dickey *et al.* ("Unit Roots," p. 14 and p. 18), who note that if a does not equal zero, then tests for stationarity in a model with a deterministic trend have particularly low power.

Table 9A.1. *Stationarity tests for profit rates of regional national banks, 1870–1914*

		Tau statistic		normalized bias statistic	
Region	Sample autocorrelation $\hat{\rho}$	Dickey–Fuller	Phillips–Perron	Dickey–Fuller	Phillips–Perron
Middle Atlantic	.617	3.22**	−3.37**	−16.8**	−18.0**
Midwest	.752	−2.52	−2.71*	−10.9*	−12.4*
South	.728	−2.97**	−3.16**	−12.0*	−13.9*
West	.699	−2.75*	−2.82*	−13.2**	−13.3*
Pacific	.455	−2.19	−4.44***	−9.9	−25.4***
New England	.743	−3.01**	−3.06**	−11.3*	−10.8*

Notes: ***, **, and * indicate that the null hypothesis of $\rho=1$ (versus an alternative $\rho<1$) can be rejected at the 1%, 5%, or 10% levels.

Data source is Powlison, *Profits of the National Banks*, pp. 105–7; see Table 9.1 for definition of regions. The model is $x_t = a + \rho x_{t-1} + \eta_t$, where x_t are the profit rates for national banks from the various regions. The "tau" statistic is $(\hat{\rho} - 1)/s_{\hat{\rho}}$, where $s_{\hat{\rho}}$ is the estimated standard error for $\hat{\rho}$. The normalized bias statistic is $n(\hat{\rho} - 1)$. The Dickey–Fuller statistics assumes that a is not equal to zero, while the Phillips–Perron statistics allows a to be any value. Critical values to test the null hypothesis are −3.58, −2.93 and −2.60 at the 1%, 5% and 10% levels for the tau statistic, and are found using the method given in MacKinnon, "Critical Values." Critical values are −18.56, −13.14 and −10.60 at the 1%, 5% and 10% levels for the normalized bias statistic, and are interpolated from the values given in Fuller, *Introduction*, p. 371). In calculating the Dickey–Fuller statistics for the Pacific region, one lagged value of Δx_t was added to the regression to adjust for autocorrelated error terms.

Estimated correlation coefficients and statistics appropriate to test the null hypothesis $\rho = 1$ against an alternative hypothesis of $\rho<1$ are given in Table 9A.1. Two test statistics are presented, the "tau" statistic and the normalized bias statistic. Two versions of the test statistics (Dickey-Fuller and Phillips and Perron) are also presented.[67]

The statistics are designed to test for a unit root ($\rho = 1$). The "tau" statistic is $(\hat{\rho} - 1)/s_{\hat{\rho}}$, where $\hat{\rho}$ is an estimate of ρ and $s_{\hat{\rho}}$ is the standard error of $\hat{\rho}$. The normalized bias statistic is $n(\hat{\rho}\text{-}1)$, where n is the sample size. The "tau" statistic is less powerful than the normalized bias statistic, but the normalized bias statistic has size problems if the underlying data generation process is actually a higher-order autoregressive or a mixed autoregressive-moving average process.[68]

[67] Dickey and Fuller, "Likelihood Ratio Statistics"; Phillips and Perron, "Testing for a Unit Root."

[68] Dickey et al., "Unit Roots," p. 18.

The Dickey–Fuller test uses ordinary least-squares estimates of equation (A1) adjusted for serial correlation in η_t by adding to equation (1) one or more lagged values of Δx_t as regressors. Initial estimates of the error term in equation (1) suggested autocorrelation only for the Pacific region, and one lag term was needed for correction.

The Phillips–Perron procedure calculates the ordinary least squares estimates of equation (1) but adjusts the test statistics for autocorrelated and heteroscedastic error terms. The Phillips–Perron procedure also requires an estimate of the "long-run" variance of the error term η_t, which must be calculated using a number of the lagged autocovariances of $\hat{\eta}_t$. Three lagged autocovariances were used, based on the selection criteria given by Schwert.

The difference between the two test procedures is how the statistics depend on the "nuisance" parameter, a. The Dickey–Fuller version is parametric, and so critical values depend upon whether a is zero or not. The Phillips–Perron version is non-parametric, and so critical values do not depend on the value of a.

As long as a is not zero, critical values under the null hypothesis for each version of the test statistics are the same, but are not standard, and must be determined with Monte Carlo methods; the relevant critical values are also shown in the table.[69]

Schwert has shown that these tests are sensitive to the presence of a moving average component to the data generating process.[70] I examined the sample autocorrelation and partial autocorrelation coefficients, and found that only the Pacific region could potentially have a moving average representation. It is known that a pure moving average process is stationary and so I test to see if the autoregressive representation of the profit rates for the Pacific region is a stationary representation.

Schwert also argues that parametric tests are less affected by moving average components, and so the Dickey-Fuller tau statistic may be most relevant.

Identification for the Pacific region suggests that a two-lag auto-correlation (AR(2)) representation may be appropriate (all other regions were AR(1)). Thus a test for two unit roots is needed. Mills suggests testing for $\rho = 1$ in the model $\Delta x_t = a + \rho x_{t-2}$, and for the Pacific region, the null hypothesis can be rejected.[71] Moreover, estimated parameters of the AR(2) for the Pacific region are in the region of stationarity.

---

[69] The critical values for the "tau" statistic are from MacKinnon "Critical Values," and for the normalized bias statistic are interpolated from Fuller, *Introduction to Statistical Time Series*, p. 371.

[70] Schwert, "Effects of Model Specification."

[71] Mills, *Time Series Techniques*, p. 127.

Results in Table 9A.1 show that for every region at least one of the statistics would allow a null hypothesis of non-stationarity to be rejected at least at a 10 percent level. The strongest evidence is for the Middle Atlantic region, where every statistic allows rejection at the 5 percent level. The weakest evidence is for the Midwest, where the Dickey-Fuller tau statistic, at -2.52, would not allow rejection of the null hypothesis even at a 10 percent level, and where the other test statistics would not allow rejection at a 5 percent level. Other regions fall in between these extremes.

At a probability of 10 percent, these tests do not support the DSJ hypothesis in that a rejection of the null suggests that each of the profit rate series were fluctuating around a constant mean, so that profit rates were not converging between 1870 and 1914. But at a probability level smaller than 10 percent, a null hypothesis of non-stationarity cannot be rejected for at least some of the regions.

References

Alston, Lee, Wayne A. Grove, and David C. Wheelock. 1994. "Why do Banks Fail? Evidence from the 1920s," *Explorations in Economic History* 31: 409–31.

Atack, Jeremy, Fred Bateman, and Thomas Weiss. 1982. "Risk, the Rate of Return and the Pattern of Investment in Nineteenth Century American Manufacturing," *Southern Economic Journal* 51: 150–63.

and Peter Passel. 1994. *A New Economic View of American History*. Second edition. New York: W.W. Norton.

Barnett, George E. 1911. *State Banks and Trust Companies since the Passage of the National-Bank Act*. Washington, DC: Government Printing Office.

Binder, John J. and D.T. Brown. 1991. "Bank Rates of Return and Entry Restrictions, 1869–1914," *Journal of Economic History* 51: 47–66.

Bodenhorn, Howard. 2000. *A History of Banking in Antebellum America*. New York: Cambridge University Press.

Bodenhorn, Howard and Hugh Rockoff. 1992. "Regional Interest Rates in Antebellum America." In *Strategic Factors in Nineteenth Century American Economic History*, edited by Claudia Golden and Hugh Rockoff, 159–87. Chicago: University of Chicago Press.

Comptroller of the Currency. 1921. *Annual Report for 1920*. Washington, DC: US Printing Office.

Davis, Lance. 1965. "The Investment Market, 1870–1914: The Evolution of a National Market," *Journal of Economic History* 25: 355–99.

DeYoung, Robert. 1999. "Birth, Growth, and Life or Death of Newly Chartered Banks." Federal Reserve Bank of Chicago *Economic Perspectives*: 18–35.

Dickey, David A. and Wayne A. Fuller. 1981. "Likelihood Ratio Statistics for Autoregressive Time Series with a Unit Root," *Econometrica* 49: 1057–72.

Dickey, David A., William R. Bell, and Robert B. Miller. 1986. "Unit Roots in Time Series Models: Tests and Implications," *The American Statistician* 40: 12–26.

Fuller, Wayne A. 1976. *Introduction to Statistical Time Series*. New York: Wiley.

Granger, Clive W.J. 1991. "Developments in the Study of Cointegrated Economic Variables." In *Long-Run Economic Relationships*, edited by Robert F. Engle and Clive W.J. Granger, 65–80. Oxford: Oxford University Press.

Hansen, Lars P. 1982. "Large Sample Properties of Generalized Methods of Moments Estimators," *Econometrica* 50: 1029–54.

James, John A. 1976. "The Development of the National Money Market, 1893–1911," *Journal of Economic History* 36: 878–97.

———. 1976. "Portfolio Selection with an Imperfectly Competitive Asset Market," *Journal of Financial and Quantitative Analysis*, December: 831–46.

Johnston, J. 1984. *Econometric Methods*. New York: McGraw-Hill.

Lamoreaux, Naomi. 1994. *Insider Lending: Banks, Personal Connections, and Economic Development in Industrial New England*. Cambridge: Cambridge University Press.

MacKinnon, James. 1991. "Critical Values for Cointegration Tests." In *Long-Run Economic Relationships*, edited by Robert F. Engle and Clive W.J. Granger. Oxford: Oxford University Press: 267–77.

Mills, Terrence C. 1990. *Time Series Techniques for Economists*. Cambridge: Cambridge University Press.

Neal, Larry. Spring 1971. "Trust Companies and Financial Innovation, 1897–1914," *Business History Review* 55: 35–51.

———. June 1985. "Integration of Financial Markets: Quantitative Evidence from the Eighteenth to Twentieth Centuries," *Journal of Economic History* 45: 219–26.

———. 1990. *The Rise of Financial Capitalism: International Capital Markets in the Age of Reason*. Cambridge: Cambridge University Press.

Odell, Kerry A. 1989. "The Integration of Regional and Interregional Capital Markets: Evidence from the Pacific Coast, 1883–1913," *Journal of Economic History* 49: 297–310.

Phillips, Peter C.B. and Pierre Perron. 1988. "Testing for a Unit Root in Time Series Regression," *Biometrika* 75: 335–46.

Powlison, Keith. 1980. *Profits of the National Banks*. New York: Arno Press reprint edition (1931).

Redenius, Scott A. "Bank Market Power and Regional Differences in Postbellum U.S. Loan Rates." Working paper, Bryn Mawr College, 2003.

Rockoff, Hugh. 1977. "Regional Interest Rates and Bank Failures, 1870–1914," *Explorations in Economic History* 14: 90–5.

Rostow, Walt Whitman. 1960. *The Stages of Economic Growth*. New York: Cambridge University Press.

Schwert, G. William. 1987. "Effects of Model Specification on Tests for Unit Roots in Macroeconomic Data," *Journal of Monetary Economics* 20: 73–103.

Sharpe, William F. 1970. *Portfolio Theory and Capital Markets*. New York: McGraw-Hill.

Smiley, Gene. 1975. "Interest Rate Movement in the United States, 1888–1913," *The Journal of Economic History* 35: 591–620.

Solow, Robert M. February 1956. "A Contribution to the Theory of Economic Growth," *Quarterly Journal of Economics*: 65–94.

Sullivan, Richard J. and Kenneth Spong. "Managerial Wealth, Ownership Structure, and Risk in Commercial Banks." Working paper, 2005. Available at SSRN: http://ssrn.com/abstract=558684.

Sushka, Marie Elizabeth and W. Brian Barrett. 1984. "Banking Structure and the National Capital Market, 1869–1914," *Journal of Economic History* 44: 463–77.

Sylla, Richard. 1969. "Federal Policy, Banking Market Structure, and Capital Mobilization in the United States, 1863–1913," *Journal of Economic History* 29: 657–86.

White, Eugene N. 1982. "The Political Economy of Banking Regulation, 1864–1933," *The Journal of Economic History* 42: 33–40.

1993. *The Regulation and Reform of the American Banking System, 1900–1929.* Princeton: Princeton University Press.

White, Hal. 1980. "A Heteroscedasticity-Consistent Covariance Matrix Estimator and Direct Test for Heteroscedasticity," *Econometrica* 48: 817–38.

10 Anticipating the stock market crash of 1929: The view from the floor of the stock exchange[*]

Eugene N. White

On October 3, 1929, John D. Rockefeller sold his right to one-quarter of a new seat on the New York Stock Exchange for $125,000. Only a few days before, on September 26, 1929, J.P. Morgan and Junius S. Morgan, Jr. had sold their rights for the same price. These represented the highest real price that would ever be paid for a seat on the exchange.[1] Like other members of the exchange, Rockefeller and the Morgans had received these rights on February 18, 1929, as part of a plan to expand the capacity of the exchange and meet the flood of orders that flowed from the stock market boom.[2] While not active brokers, they, like at least another hundred wealthy men, reserved the option to appear on the floor of the exchange to intervene directly in the market if a merger, proxy fight or perhaps a panic loomed. These titans of industry and finance could have sold their rights at any time beforehand, but they had held on to them. Their sales seem to have been extraordinarily well-timed. The Dow Jones had reached its peak on September 3, 1929, and then began a slow decline. Rockefeller and the Morgans sold as the boom deflated and just ahead of the collapses on Black Thursday October 24 and Black Tuesday October 29, 1929, when the market lost 23 percent of its value.

[*] For the many useful comments, I thank the participants at the Conference in Honor of Larry D. Neal on the Occasion of his Retirement, "The Origins and Development of Financial Markets and Institutions" at the University of Illinois, Urbana-Champaign on April 28–29, 2006.

Eugene N. White is Professor of Economics, Department of Economics, Rutgers University, New Brunswick, New Jersey 08901 and Research Associate, NBER. Email: white@economics.rutgers.edu.

[1] The price of a seat for the purchasers Charles J. Collins and Andrew J. Fox, Jr. who put together four quarter seats was thus $500,000. Just before the distribution of the quarter rights in the week ending on January 24, 1929, the price of a seat first reached its peak $625,000; ex-rights, the price would have been $500,000.

[2] For details of this plan see Davis *et al.*, "Highest Price Ever."

While neither Rockefeller nor the Morgans left any hint of whether their timing was prescient or lucky, their sales raise the question whether the brokers knew something about the state of the market in September and early October 1929 that the investing public did not. Brokers would certainly be classified among the more informed participants in the market. An extensive literature in finance claims that brokers have valuable private information because they observe order flows, permitting them to profit strategically from timely trading or market making. Did the brokers suspect that there was a bubble in the market that was in danger of bursting? A quick sell-off of rights to a seat and a precipitous fall in the price of a seat on the exchange would be evidence that these insiders knew that trouble loomed ahead, while an "excessively" high seat price in the presence of declining share prices might be taken as an indication that brokers were exhibiting the same mistaken exuberance as their customers.

By examining seat prices and the abnormal returns to seat ownership on the NYSE, the New York Curb Exchange and several regional exchanges, this paper considers the possibility that brokers anticipated the crash. It appears that NYSE brokers became quite cautious by July 1929 and were paying far less for a seat than might otherwise seem justified by the rising volume of trading, higher securities prices and other positive indicators. In the months immediately preceding the crash, qualitative evidence suggests that buyers were increasingly very young and relatively inexperienced. Similarly, the prices paid for seats on the Curb Exchange in New York fell far short of forecast prices. Regional stock exchanges were also swept up in the 1928–1929 boom; but unfortunately, the seats on the regional exchange were too illiquid to adequately measure the determinants of their prices. Still, the prices of regional seats flattened after mid-1929 and sales were scant, suggestive of a worry that the buoyant market would collapse.

The sobriety of the 1929 brokers stands in contrast to findings that brokers were excessively optimistic in the months before the 1987 crash.[3] For the crash of 2000, inference is more difficult because the number of seats traded has diminished.[4] Nevertheless, it appears that brokers during the most recent boom were more like their brethren in 1929 and skeptical of the markets' advance so that NYSE seat prices reached a high in August 1999 and then fell 13 percent before the peak of the Dow Jones Index in December 1999, 25 percent before the peak

---

[3] Keim and Madhavan, "Predicting Returns."
[4] Many seats are owned by large publicly traded companies and turnover is less than when seats were owned by individual brokers.

of the Nasdaq in March 2000, and 37 percent before the August 2000 high in S&P500.

However, even though seats on the NYSE in 1929 appear to have signaled brokers' uncertainty about the future course of the market, this phenomenon did not provide the public with enough information to revise its judgment about share prices. Consistent with other studies, seat prices do not contain any information that would have allowed investors to forecast the behavior of the stock market.[5] Like other market anomalies, the lack of robust growth in seat prices on all exchanges as the stock market boom continued after mid-1929 should have given observant investors some second thoughts about pouring more money into the market. Yet, they may have just assumed that the flattening of prices was caused by the general increase in the number of seats and exchanges. Efforts by existing market institutions to restructure themselves via automated trading and extended hours to respond to the huge order flow probably rendered otherwise clear signals opaque. However, the econometric evidence in this chapter indicates that, given the prices brokers paid, these "insiders" were not sanguine about the markets' continued upwards climb.

I.   Bubbles and the price of a seat on the exchange

The debate over whether there are bubbles in the stock market has spawned a large literature. It has proven extraordinarily difficult to provide a tight case for or against the presence of a bubble in the market because fundamentals are difficult to identify. As Robert Flood and Robert Hodrick pointed out, any test for a bubble is troubled by the problem that the dynamics of asset prices with a bubble will not appear to be different from the dynamics when there is an omitted factor driving the fundamentals.[6] Studies which purport to find a bubble can be attacked for failing to find the missing fundamental, while results where the conclusion is that there is no bubble are highly sensitive to the choice of parameters.

While it is generally conceded that boom periods see an influx of new, often younger, and less informed investors, many models employ only a representative agent. Yet, we know that no matter how many optimists poured their money into the market, skeptics were also present and must also have voted with their dollars. Thus, one of the more potentially

---

[5] See for example, Schwert, "Stock Exchange Seats" and Keim and Madhavan, "Predicting Returns."
[6] Flood and Hodrick, "On Testing for Speculative Bubbles."

fruitful approaches is the identification of anomalies that may indicate the presence of a bubble. Avoiding the problem of misidentifying fundamentals, J. Bradford De Long and Andrei Shleifer examined the prices of closed-end mutual funds, where the fundamental value of a specific fund is simply the current market value of the securities in the fund's portfolio.[7] They found that the median seasoned fund sold for a premium of 37 percent in the first quarter of 1929, rising to 47 percent in the third quarter, before subsiding to 8 percent by December 1929. Contrary to the usual small discount generally observed for closed-end mutual funds, this huge premium is astonishing. Instead of buying a fund that was above its fundamentals' price, investors could simply have purchased a portfolio of the underlying stocks or entrepreneurs could have created new funds with the same stocks. The only consistent explanation for this phenomenon is that investors were excessively optimistic, suggesting the existence of a bubble. Peter Rappoport and Eugene White found evidence in the market for brokers' loans that lenders were very skeptical of the height that the market had attained in late 1929.[8] The extraordinary interest premia and margin demanded on these loans suggest that lenders felt they needed this protection against a potentially huge decline in the market. Casting brokers' loans as options written by the lender and bought by the borrowers, Rappoport and White extracted the volatility implied by pricing these loans as options, revealing the potential for a crash on the order of 25 to 50 percent well in advance of October 1929.

Like brokers' loans that carried high interest rate premia and margins, relatively low prices for seats on a stock exchange when the market was booming is additional evidence of contrarian expectations from individuals with their hand on the pulse of the market. Seats on the exchange are assets whose prices reflect stockbrokers' expected future profits from the special access to the market, which was provided by a seat. As such, seat prices are influenced by the volume, stock prices, technology, and the rules that govern trading on the exchange. Although seats are capital assets, the number is fixed and they cannot be sold short, making it more likely that a bubble can be observed.[9] A rapid run up in the price of a seat may thus reveal the sentiment of the holders regarding their trading for exuberant investors, while a depressed price may be an indicator of a bearish outlook.

[7] De Long and Shleifer, "The Stock Market Bubble of 1929."
[8] Rappoport and White, "Was The Crash of 1929 Expected?"
[9] Keim and Madhavan, "Predicting Returns."

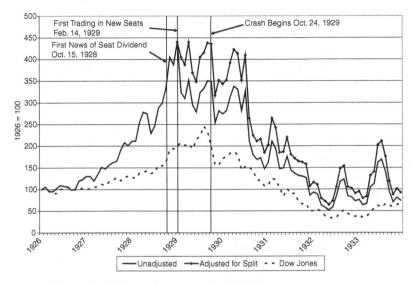

Figure 10.1 Price of a seat on the NYSE.

What did brokers expect in 1929? Figure 10.1 shows indices of the Dow Jones Industrial Average and the price of a seat on the New York Stock Exchange.[10] The value of a seat on the exchange roughly tracked the movement of stock prices through the mid-1920s. At that point, volume on the exchange began to rise rapidly and seat prices began their rapid ascent. On peak days, the exchange was flooded with orders and bid–ask spreads began to widen. The leadership at the exchange feared that investors would move to other exchanges and offered a modest proposal in 1925 to expand the 1,100 seat exchange by twenty-five new seats. This plan was rejected by the membership. Without any action, the problems had become chronic by 1928. On October 15, 1928, the president of the exchange put forward a new proposal to expand the exchange by giving each member a quarter-seat dividend that could be sold and bundled to create 275 new seats, thereby expanding the membership by 25 percent. Lance Davis *et al.* have shown that this bold plan eased the capacity constraint on peak load days, minimizing the widening

---

[10] There is higher frequency data. The NYSE Committee on Admissions (n.d.) recorded all transfers of membership from 1879 to 1971 for each week ending Thursday, giving the price but not the actual day of the transaction.

of the bid–ask spread.[11] This fact was appreciated by the membership who saw that the competitiveness of the exchange was thereby improved. In anticipation of sales of these seats, seat prices rose and yielded a cumulative abnormal return to seat holders of approximately 20 percent, when this type of plan should have had no perceptible effect on seat prices or the aggregate value of the exchange.

The publicly reported prices for NYSE seats did not adjust for the stock split and they were reported ex-right. Figure 10.1 corrects for this added value, showing the original and the adjusted series. Although adjusted prices did not sag as much as ex-right seat prices they do trend downwards from the beginning of seat sales until the end of June 1929. This movement is puzzling. Perhaps brokers did not correctly anticipate the effects of increased competition from a 25 percent increase in the number of brokers or perhaps there was now more competition from the expansion of other exchanges around the US. The stock market boom was still on and volume was high although the Dow-Jones' rapid rise had moderated, as seen in Figure 10.1. But beginning in June 1929 and continuing until the beginning of October, the price of a seat recovered all its lost value. Maybe the pessimism of the first half of the year turned into buoyant optimism? A simple model of the pricing of seats provides some insight into this question.

II.   Were NYSE brokers optimistic or pessimistic?

Seats on the stock exchange are capital assets whose price reflects the brokers' expectations about the future profits from the special access to trading on the floor of the exchange offered to them by a seat. The value of seats on an exchange is determined by the volume of activity on the exchange and the degree of competition among traders on the exchange and between the exchange and the rest of the market. The behavior of returns to a seat on the NYSE and the expectations of brokers before the 1929 crash can be studied by applying a basic capital asset pricing model and examining the cumulative abnormal returns.[12] Information from trading activity is measured by the current and lagged volume, both over the last thirty days and the change in the daily volume to capture both elements of trend and transitory factors. Additional factors, relative to size and value/growth from, are included to identify the non-diversifiable

[11] Davis *et al.*, "Highest Price Ever."
[12] Schwert, "Stock Exchange Seats," and Keim and Madhavan, "The Relation between Stock Market Movements and NYSE Seat Prices."

risk of an asset.[13] For this period, there are proxies for the former but not the latter factor. I estimated the following regression:

$$R_t - r_{f,t} = \alpha + \sum_{i=0}^{k} \beta_i (r_{m,t-i} - r_{f,t-i}) + \sum_{i=0}^{k} \delta_i \text{Vol}_{t-i}$$

$$+ \sum_{i=0}^{k} \theta_i \text{SizePrem}_{t-i} + \varepsilon_t \qquad (1)$$

where R_t is the return on a seat on the New York Stock Exchange over time t, and $r_{f,t}$ is the risk free rate, measured by the three to six-month rate on US Treasury notes and certificates or the four to six-month commercial paper rate.[14] The market return, r_m, is the return on the Dow-Jones Industrials. The figures for daily and monthly volume are for the NYSE, and the size premium is the difference in the returns between the Dow-Jones index, an unweighted index of twenty and later thirty of the very largest firms, and the Federal Reserve Board's Index, a weighted stock market index that includes several hundred stocks.[15] It is conjectured that the greater the difference, the greater the return on exchange seats as the business of the exchange focused on larger, more prominent stocks.

Table 10.1 reports the monthly results for 1920–1933 and two sub-periods.[16] Although only one lag is used, the results are quite robust to various lag structures and alternate periods for the purpose of estimating seat prices or abnormal returns. Splitting the sample at the end of 1927, before the boom, reveals that seat prices in this period responded to changes in market information, as embodied in the Dow-Jones, quickly but not completely, given that β_1 is less than one. After the crash, seat returns responded much more quickly. Yet, even in the pre-crash period, seat returns are much more sensitive than Donald Keim and Ananth Madhavan found for the period 1973–1994 and G. William

---

[13] They were a size premium, measured as the difference between a small stock return and a large stock return, and a value growth factor, measured, as the difference in a portfolio of high to low book-to-market returns. According to Fama and French (1993) firms that have high book-to-market ratios tend to have lower and persistently lower earnings. They also find that size is related to profitability, as small firms tend to have lower earnings on assets than big firms. Fama and French, "Common Risk Factors."

[14] Board of Governors of the Federal Reserve System, *Banking and Monetary Statistics*, 1943, pp. 450–1 and 460.

[15] Board of Governors of the Federal Reserve System, *Banking and Monetary Statistics*, 1943, pp. 480–1.

[16] Regressions with weekly seat prices, but more limited independent variables, yielded similar results.

Table 10.1. *Monthly returns to a seat on the New York Stock Exchange*

	1920–1933 Commercial Paper	1920–1933 US 4/6 Month Bills	1920–1927 Commercial Paper	1920–1927 US 4/6 Month Bills	1928–1933 Commercial Paper	1928–1933 US 4/6 Month Bills
Intercept	-0.002	-0.002	0.006	0.004	-0.012	-0.010
	(0.008)	(0.008)	(0.007)	(0.007)	(0.016)	(0.015)
$r_{m,t} - r_{f,t}$	0.973*	0.970*	0.639*	0.717*	0.964*	0.971*
	(0.128)	(0.128)	(0.203)	(0.261)	(0.178)	(0.179)
$r_{m,t-1} - r_{f,t-1}$	-0.312*	-0.336*	0.108	0.167	-0.486*	-0.487*
	(0.130)	(0.129)	(0.254)	(0.256)	(0.181)	(0.181)
Monthly Vol$_{t-1}$	0.051*	0.055*	0.008	0.008	0.085	0.088+
	(0.029)	(0.029)	(0.033)	(0.033)	(0.048)	(0.048)
Monthly Vol$_{t-1}$	0.063*	0.0677*	0.022	0.025	0.093	0.097*
	(0.027)	(0.027)	(0.031)	(0.031)	(0.044)	(0.043)
Daily Vol$_t$	0.038*	0.036*	0.003	0.01	0.062	0.056*
	(0.016)	(0.016)	(0.021)	(0.021)	(0.024)	(0.023)
Daily Vol$_{t-1}$	-0.015	-0.015	0.009	-0.001	-0.026	-0.028
	(0.016)	(0.016)	(0.021)	(0.021)	(0.026)	(0.025)
SizePrem$_t$	0.339+	0.364+	0.693	0.626	0.234	0.226
	(0.205)	(0.204)	(0.432)	(0.429)	(0.274)	(0.274)
SizePrem$_{t-1}$	0.104	0.090	0.325	0.385	0.083	0.064
	(0.174)	(0.173)	(0.367)	(0.365)	(0.235)	(0.234)
Observations	166	166	96	96	70	70
R–Squared	0.445	0.447	0.052	0.066	0.628	0.617

Note: The standard errors are reported in parentheses and * and + indicate significance at the 5 and 10 percent levels.

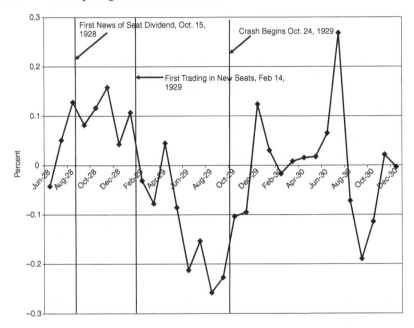

Figure 10.2 Cumulative abnormal monthly returns to NYSE seat, 1928–1929.

Schwert found for 1926–1972.[17] Recent changes in volume appeared to have information for brokers as seat prices responded to contemporary but not lagged changes in volume. The size factor often has a significant effect of seat returns, suggesting that seats exhibited lower liquidity like smaller stocks.

The cumulative abnormal returns to NYSE seats from the monthly regression in Column 3 of Table 10.1 are shown in Figure 10.2, measured as the cumulative residuals from the regression.[18] This figure reveals the rise in the returns for late 1928 and early 1929. In an earlier paper, Davis, Neal and White argued that the rise in the value of the NYSE was a consequence of the announcement that the NYSE would increase its capacity by 25 percent.[19] By easing the volume constraint, this expansion would help the exchange cope with its declining share of volume on the national market and on-the-floor capacity that drove up

[17] Keim and Madhavan, "The Relations between Stock Market Movements and NYSE Seat Prices"; Schwert, "Stock Exchange Seats."
[18] Weekly cumulative abnormal monthly returns show similar results.
[19] Davis et al., "Highest Price Ever."

bid–ask spreads and created delays on peak volume days. This optimism appears to have been justified because after the 275 seat increase the bid–ask spread moved much less when volume surged and the exchange regained some market share.

Although observed prices of NYSE seats moved upward in the summer of 1929, Figures 10.2 reveals that after February 1929, brokers slowly became less optimistic. Using monthly data, the cumulative excess returns turned negative and by the summer of 1929 they totaled over 20 percent, implying that actual prices were far below what would have been expected based on the surge in stock prices and volume. There was no recovery until after the crash in October.

This relative pessimism by potential brokers stands in contrast to Keim and Madhavan's finding for the period before the crash of 1987, when they found there were large positive abnormal returns to seats in the twelve months before the crash followed by large negative abnormal returns.[20] They argue that these findings are consistent with the behavioral finance interpretation that seats, which are in limited supply and cannot be sold short, exhibit occasional price bubbles. To take a closer look at 1929, Figure 10.3 calculates the forecast price of a seat with the actual price, revealing this widening dollar gap. By July 1929, the high share prices and ever higher volume implied that brokers should have been willing to pay $675,000 for a seat, when the split-adjusted price was only $575,000.

There are two possible explanations for the apparent pessimism in Figure 10.3. First, brokers might have erred in believing that the expansion of the exchange would increase its aggregate value. The increase in capacity may not have increased business sufficiently to overcome downward pressure on the bid–ask spread. Based on the results of Davis et al., the added increase in volume following the expansion appears to have outweighed the decline in bid–ask spreads. At the mean volume in their study prior to the expansion, the mean percentage bid–ask spread was 0.777 percent; afterwards it was 0.759 percent. Trading was consistently higher month-by-month in 1929 than in 1928. In July 1928, the market value of shares traded on the NYSE was $52,903 million; in July 1929, it was $77,264 million.[21] In a naïve calculation, the implied profits would have been $411 million for 1928 and $586 million for 1929, an increase greater than 25 percent. Thus, higher earnings should have propped up seat prices. On the other hand, if their

[20] Keim and Madhavan, "The Relation between Stock Market Movement and NYSE Seat Prices."
[21] New York Stock Exchange, Yearbook 1928–1929, p. 123.

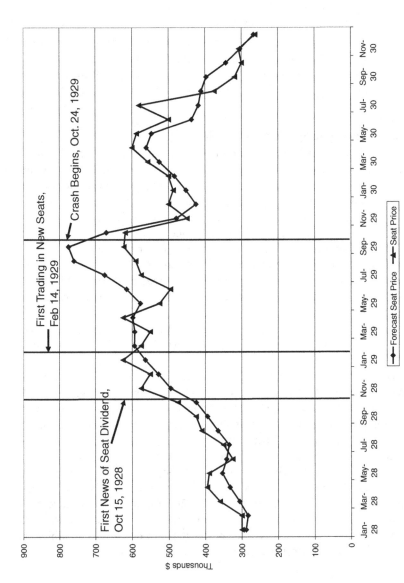

Figure 10.3 Actual and forecast monthly NYSE seat.

hopes were not disappointed, brokers may have thought that the market was excessively exuberant. This second explanation seems to be more credible as their negative feelings seemed to dissipate just after the crash. It may be hard to read much into later events, but brokers, like other businessmen, also seem to have become more hopeful of a recovery by late 1930.[22]

Could an investor on the street watching the prices of seats on the exchange have read this information, or was brokers' pessimism in the seat market unheeded Cassandra-like signals? It is well known that stock returns have been found to be predicted by a variety of observable market values, including the dividend yield, the Treasury bill yield, the Term Structure and the book-to-market ratio.[23] Using monthly data, Keim and Madhavan found that the information embedded in the innovations in the number of seats traded on the NYSE, but not the seat prices themselves, had predictive power for the S&P500 returns for 1973–1994.[24] Their approach is employed using the regression model in equation (2):

$$r_{m,t} - r_{f,t} = \alpha + \beta(r_{m,t-i} - r_{f,t-i}) + \sum_{i=1}^{3} \theta_i \text{Seat}_{t-i} + \delta_1 \text{SizePrem}_{t-i}$$
$$+ \delta_1 \text{TreasYield}_{t-1} + \delta_2 \text{TermPrem}_{t-1} + \delta_i \text{CallPrem}_{t-1}$$
$$+ \delta_i \text{DivYield}_{t-i} + \varepsilon_t \tag{2}$$

Information from the market for seats on the NYSE is measured both as the lagged innovation in the price of a seat and as the residuals from a regression of the number of trades on trades lagged, the log of the last seat price and the absolute seat return. The difference in returns between the Dow-Jones stocks and all stocks traded on the NYSE is used again. In addition, the yield on three to six-month US Treasury securities and the term premium, the difference between the long-term yield and the short-term yield are included.[25] Rappoport and White found that the premium on brokers' loans compared to bankers' acceptances or commercial paper represents the money market's heightened awareness of the risk in the market during the boom, and the difference between the call loan rate and the rate on bankers' acceptances is included

[22] See Klug et al., "How Could Everyone Have Been So Wrong?" for a survey of this literature on expectations of recovery.
[23] See Campbell and Shiller, "Stock Prices," Fama and French, "Dividend Yields," and Keim and Stambaugh, "Predicting Returns."
[24] Keim and Madhavan, "The Relation between Stock Market Movements and NYSE Seat Prices."
[25] National Bureau of Economic Research, Series 13029 and 13033.

Table 10.2. *Predictability of stock market returns monthly data, January 1920–June 1928*

	(1)	(2)	(3)	(4)
Intercept	0.063*	.059*	0.047	0.068
	(0.023)	(0.033)	(0.041)	(0.069)
$r_{m,t-1} - r_{f,t-1}$	−0.176	−0.207	−0.129	−0.151
	(0.160)	(0.167)	(0.156)	(0.162)
Seat Return$_{t-1}$	0.071	0.077		
	(0.064)	(0.067)		
Seat Trade News$_{t-1}$			0.003	0.000
			(0.004)	(0.006)
US Bond Yield$_{t-1}$	−0.008	−0.021*	−0.008	−0.024*
	(0.008)	(0.012)	(0.007)	(0.013)
Term Premium$_t$		−0.004		−0.009
		(0.016)		(0.019)
Call Premium$_{t-1}$	−0.027*		−0.029*	
	(0.014)		(0.013)	
Dividend Yield$_{t-1}$	−0.092	0.535	−0.086	0.606
	(0.580)	(0.677)	(0.594)	(0.690)
SizePrem$_{t-1}$	−0.263	−0.320	−0.222	−0.275
	(0.222)	(0.226)	(0.221)	(0.224)
Observations	98	98	98	98
R–Squared	0.112	0.074	0.104	0.061

Note: The standard errors are in parentheses and * and + indicate significance at the 5 and 10 percent levels.

in the regression.[26] Lastly, the dividend yield for Dow-Jones stocks is added.

Table 10.2 reports the results for the regressions for several variations on equation 2. Unlike Keim and Madhavan's findings for the last quarter of the twentieth century, neither changes in seat prices or news of seat trades appear to affect the returns on stocks. These results were robust to increases in the number of lags and curtailing the data at the end of 1927 to avoid the problem of the increase in the number of seats. The only significant variables are the yield on short-term US securities and the call loan premium. The yield on government securities would have signaled tighter monetary policy. The elevated rate on call loans which stood at an historic 300 basis points for a long period was a signal of the downside risk in the market. Nothing, however, could apparently be gleaned from the trading activity in seats.

[26] Rappoport and White, "Was There a Bubble," and Rappoport and White "Was the Crash of 1929 Expected?"

These results confirm the findings for the post-World War II period that seat returns did not predict market returns, although the latter found that seat activity does have information. Specifically, they found that lagged innovations of trading volumes in the seat market predict the monthly excess returns of the S&P500 after controlling for the dividend yield and book-to-market ratio. Whether the information contained in the number of seats traded in the 1920s is different, is not clear, as it may have been clouded by the big increase in the number of seats.

III.   Who bought the NYSE seats?

Even with 1,110 members, the brokers on the exchange constituted a large old boys' club. Although anyone in theory could buy a seat, a prospective member had to be presented by one of the existing members. The Committee on Admissions took a close and hard look at their character, rejecting those judged unfit by a blackballing process. Petra Moser has presented evidence that this process was sufficiently restrictive, for example, to permit some ethnic discrimination and effectively raise the price to those affected groups, especially during World War I when Germans and German-Americans were treated with great suspicion.[27]

The expansion of the exchange by an additional 275 seats began in February 1929, and although many seats were quickly formed from the quarter-seat rights, consolidations were unfinished by the time of the crash and dragged on through the early 1930s. Part of this delay is attributable to members holding on to their seats, hoping for a higher price; but there also may have been a relative dearth of qualified members who would not have been blackballed. It is unlikely that the expansion of the exchange did not lower the experience and quality of the brokers and reduce discrimination, introducing brokers perhaps more inclined to "irrational exuberance." Many of the new brokers were able to get on the exchange sooner than they had expected, being already experienced workers on the exchange or with partnerships whose members were active brokers.

Reports in the newspapers give a fairly detailed picture of some of the new members, even if they are impressionistic. The boom in the stock market was drawing in some men who appear to have had little or no prior market experience. Just before the seat dividend in January 1929, Lee-Adam Gimbel, thirty-two-years old, resigned as vice president of Gimbel Brothers, Inc. and bought a seat for $575,000; and though he remained a director of the department store he became an unaffiliated

[27] Moser, "War and Ethnic Discrimination."

floor trader.[28] As a floor broker, Gimbel traded on his own account, no doubt, hoping to quickly make a fortune.[29] Floor traders who had been in short supply (Davis *et al.* 2005) were the most adventurous as they had to hustle on the floor, risking their own capital, by matching incoming orders brought by other brokers, usually within the bid–ask spread set by the market maker at the post.[30] Two cousins Laurence C. Leeds and Robert L. Leeds, both directors of the Manhattan Shirt Company, also bought seats to become independent floor traders.[31] Others like Frederic L. Yeager obtained a seat to be a floor trader for the firm of Sutro Brothers & Co., a rapidly expanding brokerage house on the Pacific Coast with seats on the San Francisco and Los Angeles Stock Exchanges, as well as seats on the curb exchanges of those cities. Seeking to get in on the booming New York market, Sutro Brothers bought the business of Robinson & Co. in New York and transferred that firms' membership on the exchange to its New York representatives (*New York Times*, January 18, 1929, p. 38)

The seat dividend in February 1929 allowed more young men to move onto the floor of the exchange. George F. Hawkins, a telephone clerk became one of the youngest members of the exchange at the age of twenty-two when he was "rewarded" with a seat by his employer, Ira Haupt & Co.[32] Others came from off the exchange. On February 22, 1929, the *New York Times* noted that James Russell Lowell, a great-grandson of the poet bought four rights and became a member of Wrenn Brothers.

During the next several months, newspaper reports highlighted the arrival of young men on the floor of the exchange. Telephone clerk, William C. Pressman bought a seat, as did George Dolan of Maxwell & Co. who applied for membership after arranging to buy four rights.[33] Similarly, John Dempsey, a telephone clerk for Hoge Underhill & Co., put together a seat in March 1929. Thomas F. Kelly had been a page on the floor of the NYSE for fourteen years when he was able to buy four "rights" to acquire a seat in July 1929 and become a partner in the firm, Joseph & Co. that he had served. At the same time, Strother B. Purdy (a telephone clerk), James L. Slee (an advertising salesman), and Paul Pryibil (a customer's man with F.B. Keech), acquired seats. George C. Donelon, who had been a specialist's clerk for only six months and was

---

[28] *New York Times* (January 5, 1929), p. 15.
[29] Later, in July 1929, he was joined floor by Louis S. Gimbel Jr., also a director for Gimbel Brothers, Inc. in acquiring a seat.
[30] Davis *et al.*, "Highest Price Ever."   [31] *New York Times* (January 12, 1929), p. 14.
[32] *New York Times* (February 26, 1929), p. 42.
[33] *New York Times* (July 12, 1929), p. 35.

only twenty-two-years old, bought a seat in September 1929, but he was the son of George F. Donelon of the brokerage Milton E. Reiner. The elder Donelon had been active on Wall Street but he was not a member of the exchange.[34] However, there were some older men who took the risk of buying a seat, and Justin A. Morrisey, a tube man on the floor of the NYSE since 1911, bought a membership in September 1929.

Members of brokerages, such as Harry C. Schaack of Harris, Winthrop & Co. moved onto the floor.[35] Some new members of the NYSE had previously served as brokers on the New York Curb. David H. McDermott, a member of the New York Curb firm of Peter P. McDermott & Co., obtained a seat.[36] Similarly, in July 1929, Harry W. Asher Jr. a member of the New York Curb Exchange gave up his curb seat and obtained an NYSE seat. Out-of-town brokerages used the seat-dividend to gain direct access to the floor. For example, William H. Bixby, of George H. Walker & Co. of St. Louis, and John F. Betts, a member of John F. Betts & Co. of St. Louis, acquired seats. Other new brokers often came from non-brokerage firms, including Frederick T. Sutton and Harold W. Jennys, who were investment bankers.[37]

Older members of the exchange and those that held on to their quarter-seat rights may have been happy to relinquish their seats to more optimistic outsiders. If some members believed that they observed a bubble in the market that was not evident to others, this would have caused a downward shift in each broker's ask price. Even if potential buyers did become more exuberant, such a shift would result in more trades with brokers who had a lower reservation bid price. Moving down the schedule of bid prices one would encounter potential brokers who placed a lower value on their human capital. Consequently, we would expect to observe younger men buying seats if there was a bubble perceived by established brokers. While there is no data compiled on the age and experience of brokers, the limited journalistic evidence suggests an inflow of new and inexperienced younger men to the floor of the exchange.

IV.   The New York Curb and the regional exchanges

The New York Stock Exchange was by far the most active market for securities in the US and had the largest number of brokers. However, the sheer growth of trading and new listing in the late 1920s threatened

[34] *New York Times* (September 23, 1929), p. 50.
[35] *New York Times* (September 13, 1929), p. 43.
[36] *New York Times* (March 23, 1929), p. 32.   [37] *New York Times* (July 26, 1929), p. 31.

the NYSE's dominance. It struggled to handle the soaring volume of orders and was losing market share until it increased its capacity from 1,100 to 1,375 brokers in 1929 (Davis *et al.* 2005). In the meantime, the other exchanges eagerly expanded to capture orders for regional stocks and NYSE-listed securities.

The New York Curb Exchange, which later became the American Stock Exchange, was the second largest market. Its 550 brokers traded many securities that were not listed on the NYSE. The Curb brokers did not usually compete with the NYSE but cooperated and served as a market for non-NYSE listed securities, with NYSE members placing orders for unlisted stocks with Curb brokers. Thus, the Curb primarily complemented rather than competed with the NYSE. The Curb exchange's volume was only a fraction of the volume on the NYSE; its aggregate value (the total value of its seats) was at most 10 percent of the NYSE's aggregate value. Regional exchanges were even smaller and specialized in local stocks and competed for business with the New York exchanges in its listed securities. Trading volume was even lower on regional exchanges; taken all together their total volume approximated the volume on the New York Curb. The smaller number of seats and the lower level of activity on the regional exchanges and the Curb led to much thinner market for their seats with less frequent trading.

The *Commercial and Financial Chronicle* provides data on the last traded seat prices for both the Curb and the regional exchanges. Because of infrequent trading, some regional exchange prices in the paper were very stale, as they could have been transacted months before. The *Chronicle* sometimes also reported the bid–ask spread on the seats (information not available for the NYSE in this period). Figure 10.4 displays indices of volume and seat prices for the Curb Exchange and Figure 10.5 the seat prices for the six most active regional exchanges in the late 1920s with those for the Curb and the NYSE.

Paralleling trends on the NYSE, the Curb market also experienced a meteoric rise in the price of its seats, which climbed from $28,000 in January 1927 to a peak of $253,000 in August 1929. Through the early 1920s and well into 1928, the prices of seats generally followed the movement of volume on the Curb, as seen in Figure 10.4. Again resembling the NYSE, seat prices begin to rapidly outpace volume growth by late 1928, jumping in 1929. Indeed, Figure 10.4 suggests that the Curb market might have benefited from its complementary role by the expansion of the NYSE. The NYSE's increase in the number of brokers primarily served to manage the rise in orders, for which new listings contributed modestly. In contrast, the Curb, as well as the regional exchanges, added many new stocks to their boards during 1929; with the

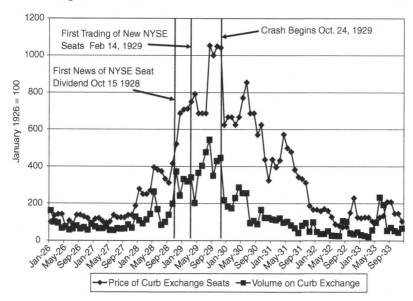

Figure 10.4 The Curb Exchange, 1926–1933.

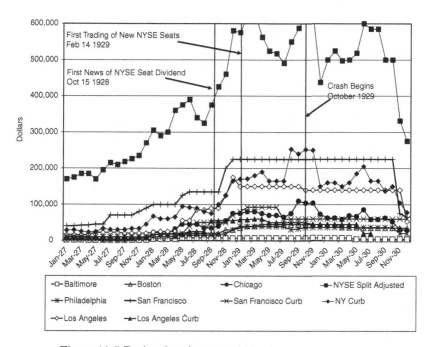

Figure 10.5 Regional exchanges, 1927–1930.

expectation of future trading income from these issues. Unfortunately, there is no monthly data on listings to adequately track these changes.

Business on the regional exchanges was also booming. The fastest growing exchanges were Chicago, San Francisco and Los Angeles; and the two California exchanges created their own curb exchanges to handle new start-up companies and less seasoned stocks. Chicago had 225 seats, raised to 470 in October 1929.[38] San Francisco had seventy seats and its Curb had 100 seats. Los Angeles and its Curb each had seventy seats, increasing to seventy-five and eighty-seven in 1929. The venerable Philadelphia exchange had 206 seats, and Baltimore and Boston had eighty-seven and 139 respectively. The markets for these seats were very thin, where trades were relatively rare. It is thus much more difficult to determine what the expectations of the brokers were in these markets given their illiquidity. This feature is reflected in the bid–ask spreads that were quite wide. For example, the bid–ask spread measured from mid-quote or the last transaction was 17 percent for Boston and Chicago and 25 percent for the New York Curb.

Except for Baltimore, seat prices rose on all the regional exchanges in 1929. However, the strong bulls were Chicago and the West Coast exchanges and their new curb markets. Although Figure 10.5 displays rising prices on the regional exchanges, it also shows the illiquidity of seats on these smaller exchanges, with few transactions for many months before and after the crash. In addition, Figure 10.5 strongly suggests that the bloom was off the rose by early 1929 for most brokers, as prices failed to rise or even fell. For the NYSE, as already seen, split-adjusted prices fell in the second quarter and then rebounded in the third. This recovery after a considerable period of pessimism is mirrored in the behavior of the Curb's seat prices. All the regionals appear to have been similarly affected by this pessimism, even though their prices did not decline. As in other thin asset markets, seat owners held on to their seats and waited for an improvement in price rather than try to sell them for a loss. The regionals' pessimism may also have reflected the fact that prices for smaller stocks had peaked in the first quarter of 1929 and the boom only continued in the larger stocks.[39] The only exception to this development was the Chicago market where seat prices rose to a new high just prior to the increase in the number of seats on that exchange in October 1929.

---

[38] In Figure 10.5, the prices for seats on the Chicago exchange and other exchanges where there were increases in the number of seat are adjusted for this "split."

[39] The Fisher index of stocks, which is equally weighted, began to fall in February 1929, while the Dow-Jones, composed only of large stocks, and the Federal Reserve index weighted by capitalization, continued to rise. Fisher, "Some New Stock Market Indexes."

Table 10.3. *Monthly returns to a seat on the New York Curb Exchange*

	1923–1933 NY Curb US 4/6 Month Bills	1923–1927 NY Curb US 4/6 Month Bills	1928–1933 NY Curb US 4/6 Month Bills
Intercept	0.028	0.021	0.024
	(0.185)	(0.031)	(0.025)
$r_{m,t} - r_{f,t}$	0.066	1.371	−0.035
	(0.270)	(1.540)	(0.277)
$r_{m,t-1} - r_{f,t-1}$	0.386	0.827	0.441
	(0.287)	(1.662)	(0.291)
$r_{m,t-2} - r_{f,t-2}$	1.499★	−0.613	1.497★
	(0.271)	(0.071)	(0.277)
Monthly Vol$_t$	−0.016	−0.061	0.099
	(0.037)	(0.071)	(0.043)
Monthly Vol$_{t-1}$	−0.23	0.023	−0.054
	(0.038)	(0.075)	(0.046)
Monthly Vol$_{t-2}$	0.043	0.036	0.045
	(0.037)	(0.074)	(0.043)
SizePrem$_t$	−0.675	−0.136	−0.697
	(0.338)+	(1.196)	(0.345)
SizePrem$_{t-1}$	−0.220	1.346	−0.344
	(0.397)	(1.128)	(0.409)
SizePrem$_{t-2}$	−0.622+	−0.030	−0.617+
	(0.361)	(1.131)	(0.372)
Observations	126	54	72
R–Squared	0.319	0.066	0.442

Note: The standard errors are in parentheses and ★ and + indicate significance at the 5 and 10 percent levels.

To examine whether the Curb or regional brokers may have exhibited excessive optimism or pessimism, the model of seat returns from equation (1) was applied to the New York Curb Exchange and the Chicago and Philadelphia exchanges and estimates are shown in Tables 10.3 and 10.4. Chicago and Philadelphia were selected because of the relatively large number of seats, which were traded more frequently than other regional seats. Volume data was available for the Chicago and Philadelphia exchanges from the *Commercial and Financial Chronicle*, and for the Curb Exchange from the New York Times; but there was no stock price index available for any of these exchanges. In its place the excess returns to holding the Federal Reserve's broad-based stock index was used for these exchanges.

The fit of the model for the Curb Exchange is somewhat weaker than it was for the NYSE, perhaps reflecting some of the data compromises and the fact that there is no volume data before February 1923. Two

Table 10.4. *Monthly returns to a seat on the Chicago and Philadelphia Exchanges*

	1920–1933 Chicago US 4-6 Month Bills	1920–1927 Chicago US 4-6 Month Bills	1928–1933 Chicago US 4-6 Month Bills	1920–1933 Philadelphia US 4-6 Month Bills	1920–1927 Philadelphia US 4-6 Month Bills	1928–1933 Philadelphia US 4-6 Month Bills
Intercept	0.036	0.011	0.080	0.012	0.007	0.014
	(0.022)	(0.016)	(0.051)	(0.016)	(0.012)	(0.016)
$r_{m,t} - r_{f,t}$	0.022	0.166	-0.008	-1.227*	-0.371	-1.226*
	(0.387)	(0.565)	(0.623)	(0.241)	(0.425)	(0.244)
$r_{m,t-1} - r_{f,t-1}$	0.637+	-0.531	1.059+	0.640*	0.107	0.635*
	(0.384)	(0.538)	(0.623)	(0.244)	(0.414)	(0.243)
$Monthly\ Vol_t$	-0.060	-0.067	-0.062	-0.400*	-0.016	-0.041*
	(0.054)	(0.048)	(0.095)	(0.020)	(0.013)	(0.019)
$Monthly\ Vol_{t-1}$	-0.041*	0.011	-0.093	-0.002	0.000	-0.002
	(0.054)	(0.049)	(0.098)	(0.020)	(0.013)	(0.020)
$SizePrem_t$	1.099+	1.275	0.965	-1.286*	0.102	0.206
	(0.619)	(0.949)	(0.969)	(0.409)	(0.691)	(0.319)
$SizePrem_{t-1}$	1.057*	0.590	1.213	0.521	0.308	-0.114
	(0.523)	(0.774)	(0.824)	(0.337)	(0.576)	(0.337)
Observations	167	95	72	167	95	72
R–Squared	0.037	0.045	0.011	0.146	0.000	0.182

Note: The standard errors are in parentheses and * and + indicate significance at the 5 and 10 percent levels.

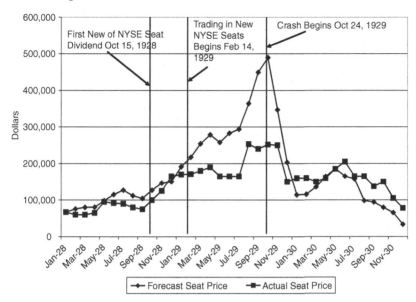

Figure 10.6 Actual and forecast monthly Curb seat prices, 1928–1930.

lagged values of the independent values are required here to capture their influence. Again the model is at its weakest for the period just before the stock market boom when there are fewer observations. Nevertheless, the estimation for the first period, 1923–1927, was employed to forecast seat prices out-of-sample, as was done for the NYSE. Both cumulative abnormal returns and forecast seat prices were constructed, and the latter are shown in Figure 10.6. The fit of the model is fairly good for 1928, and the expansion of the NYSE does not appear to be viewed as having any positive or negative effects on the business of the Curb, as the forecast remains on track when the information about the seat dividend on the NYSE was released. However, early in 1929, the forecast for seat prices moves well ahead of actual prices on the Curb exchange. Like their brethren on the NYSE, the Curb brokers appear to have become very skeptical about the rising market. Only after the crash do actual and forecast prices realign themselves, and the fit of the model improves.

Estimation of the determinants of seat prices on the regional exchanges fares less well in Table 10.4. There is comparatively little movement in regional seat prices and the Federal Reserve's stock market index may not accurately reflect events on these exchanges, dominated by local issues. Philadelphia's poor fit is perhaps not surprising given the stability of seat prices in the face of huge movements by the market.

Table 10.5. *News from the NYSE and monthly returns to seats on the Curb and regionals*

	1920–1933 Chicago US 4–6 Month Bills	1920–1927 Philadelphia US 4–6 Month Bills	1923–1933 NY Curb US 4–6 Month Bills
Intercept	−0.081	−0.055	0.016
	(−0.108)	(−0.075)	(−0.104)
$r_{m,t} - r_{f,t}$	0.091	−1.096*	0.037
	(−0.404)	(−0.247)	(−0.312)
$r_{m,t-1} - r_{f,t-1}$	0.537	0.492*	0.982*
	(−0.401)	(−0.247)	(−0.310)
Monthly Vol_t	−0.071	−0.042*	−0.061
	(−0.055)	(−0.020)	(−0.042)
Monthly Vol_{t-1}	−0.032	−0.012	−0.025
	(−0.055)	(−0.020)	(−0.042)
$SizePrem_t$	1.292+	−0.982*	−0.074
	(−0.663)	(−0.430)	(−0.390)
$SizePrem_{t-1}$	0.974+	−0.197	0.355
	(−0.553)	(−0.348)	(−0.408)
NYSE $Resid_t$	0.012	−0.024*	0
	(−0.016)	(−0.011)	(−0.013)
NYSE $Resid_{t-1}$	−0.009	0.001	−0.011
	(−0.015)	(−0.011)	(−0.012)
NYSE $Resid_{t-2}$	0.011	0.031*	0.014
	(−0.017)	(−0.012)	(−0.014)
Observations	166	166	127

Note: The standard errors are in parentheses and * and + indicate significance at the 5 and 10 percent levels.

Nevertheless, even the more active market for Chicago's seats does not yield an informative fit. Given the poor fit of these equations, attempts to extract abnormal returns to measure brokers' optimism or pessimism failed, as predicted seat price values scarcely moved.

As the stock market soared to new heights, was brokers' anxiety a generalized phenomenon or were the Curb and the regional exchanges influenced by the market for seats on the NYSE? Any excessive pessimism or optimism from New York, the dominant exchange, may have spilled over. To test this possibility, news from New York is extracted from the residuals obtained by differences between the actual and predicted prices for NYSE seats, using the coefficients for 1920–1927 in Table 10.1. This information contributes modestly to explaining the behavior of the returns for seats on the Curb and the regionals. For

Philadelphia, it appears that good news for the NYSE, a positive residual, was initially taken as bad news for this exchange given the negative coefficient on the first lagged residual. However, this opinion was subsequently overturned, as indicated by the subsequent coefficient of reserve sign and nearly equal value. For the Curb and the Chicago exchange, news in the form of changes in the price of a seat on the NYSE had little effect on the determination of their seat prices. Overall, the data does not suggest that optimism or pessimism from the New York market spread to other exchanges. If there was a feeling among brokers that the investing public was excessively exuberant, it appears to have been widespread.

V.   Wise brokers?

Spotting a bubble during the rise of a market or econometrically measuring it after a collapse is a hazardous enterprise because of the difficulty of properly identifying the fundamentals. Established brokers, familiar with their customers and the flow of orders onto the floor of the exchange might be thought to have a better view of the market than the average investor. There were enormous stakes for the brokers; while volume may surge during a boom and crash, it collapsed in the aftermath, driving down brokerage and trading profits. Members of the NYSE found their exchange's dominance threatened by the mid-1920s. It could no longer absorb more volume on peak days without higher costs arising in the form of greater bid–ask spreads and delays in processing orders. By expanding the exchange by 25 percent, the NYSE apparently eased the constraints while maintaining profits. Yet by the third quarter of 1929, the burgeoning market appears to have worried them and the prices of seats were well below what would have been expected. This concern also seems to have taken grip of the Curb and the regional markets. Furthermore, there is some journalistic evidence that younger men sought out NYSE seats and the quarter-seat rights to form new seats, as the older and perhaps wiser men abandoned the exchange. Other market anomalies corroborate brokers' anticipation of a crash. The willingness of investors to pay unprecedented premia on closed-end mutual funds is evidence of a rush by new investors into a bubble market. The extraordinarily heightened risk premia and margin on brokers' loans also reveals that lenders to the market were apprehensive and thought a big drop was imminent. Unfortunately, for the common investor this information was not appreciated and they continued to pay share prices that would, in retrospect, seem absurdly high.

References

Board of Governors of the Federal Reserve System. 1943. *Banking and Monetary Statistics 1913–1941*. Washington, DC: Board of Governors of the Federal Reserve System.

Campbell, John Y. and Robert J. Shiller. 1988. "Stock Prices, Earnings, and Expected Dividends," *Journal of Finance* 43, no. 3: 661–76.

Davis, Lance, Larry D. Neal and Eugene N. White. 2007. "The Highest Price Ever: The Great NYSE Seat Sale of 1928–1929 and Capacity Constraints," *Journal of Economic History* 67, no. 3.

De Long, J. Bradford and Andrei Shleifer. 1991. "The Stock Market Bubble of 1929: Evidence from Closed-end Mutual Funds," *Journal of Economic History* 51, no. 3: 675–95.

Fama, Eugene F, and Kenneth R. French. 1988. "Dividend Yields and Expected Stock Returns," *Journal of Financial Economics* 22: 3–25.

1993. "Common Risk Factors in the Returns of Stocks and Bonds," *Journal of Financial Economics* 33: 3–56.

Fisher, Lawrence. 1966. "Some New Stock Market Indexes," *Journal of Business* 39: 191–225.

Flood, Robert P. and Robert J. Hodrick. 1990. "On Testing for Speculative Bubbles," *Journal of Economic Perspectives* 4, no. 2: 85–101.

Keim, Donald B. and Ananth Madhavan. 2000. "The Relation between Stock Market Movements and NYSE Seat Prices," *Journal of Finance* 55, no. 6: 2817–40.

Keim, Donald B. and Robert F. Stambaugh. 1986. "Predicting Returns in the Stock and Bond Markets," *Journal of Financial Economics* 17: 357–80.

Klug, Adam, John S. Landon-Lane and Eugene N. White. 2005. "How Could Everyone Have Been So Wrong? Forecasting the Great Depression with the Railroads," *Explorations in Economic History* 42, no. 4: 27–55.

Moser, Petra. 2006. *War and Ethnic Discrimination: Evidence from Applications to the New York Stock Exchange from 1883 to 1973*. Unpublished Manuscript.

National Bureau of Economic Research, Historical Data Base, www.nber.org.

New York Stock Exchange, Committee on Admissions.

New York Stock Exchange. 1929. *Yearbook 1928–1929*. New York: NYSE Committee on Publicity. *New York Times*, various dates.

Rappoport, Peter and Eugene N. White. 1993. "Was There a Bubble in the 1929 Stock Market?" *Journal of Economic History* 53, no. 3: 549–74.

1994. "Was the Crash of 1929 Expected?" *American Economic Review* 84, no. 1: 271–81.

Schwert, G. William 1977. "Stock Exchange Seats as Capital Assets," *Journal of Financial Economics* 4: 51–78.

11 The development of "non-traditional" open market operations: Lessons from FDR's silver purchase program

Richard C.K. Burdekin and Marc D. Weidenmier[*]

Current Federal Reserve Chairman Ben Bernanke (2002) stoked interest in alternatives to conventional open market operations with his consideration of "non-traditional" monetary policy strategies that might be more effective in a low, or zero, interest rate environment. Under such circumstances, the interest rate transmission mechanism for traditional monetary expansion via purchases of government securities becomes less effective.[1] Moreover, if deflation is accompanied by banking crisis, as was the case in the US in the 1930s, then the hoarding of reserves and curtailed bank lending lowers the money multiplier and further emasculates monetary policy. This 1930s-type scenario once again came to the fore in Asia, and Hutchison (2004) ties Japan's declining money multiplier and reduced output effects of monetary expansion after 1997 to a credit crunch associated with banking sector difficulties and lending cutbacks. This has led to calls for broadened monetary policy that is not so dependent upon the interest rate channel and upon banks' willingness to actually lend out the extra reserves generated via traditional open market operations.[2] Fukao,[3] for example, has argued that "laws must be amended to allow the Bank of Japan to buy all securities, not just bonds, for its open market operations and purchase real assets . . . up to a few trillion yen per month."[4]

---

[*] The authors thank Jeremy Atack, Mike Bordo, Larry Neal, Scott Sumner, Pierre Siklos, David Wheelock, Tom Willett, Joseph Mason, Ida Whited and Claremont seminar participants for helpful comments.
[1] US overnight rates were essentially at zero during 1934–1939, for example – although this apparently did not preclude significant effects of reserve supply changes on longer-term interest rates. See Hanes, "The Liquidity Trap."
[2] See Buiter, "Deflation," for a theoretical analysis of the scope for non-traditional asset purchases and other alternatives for escaping deflation.
[3] "Financial Strains," p. 15.
[4] Indeed, the Bank of Japan did actually undertake limited direct stock purchases from banks. See Schwartz, "Asset Price Inflation," for a critique of this policy.

319

Bernanke (2002) cites the 40 percent devaluation of the dollar against gold in 1933–1934 under President Franklin D. Roosevelt (FDR), and the associated program of gold purchases, as a "striking example" of how rapid recovery from deflation can be achieved even with nominal interest rates close to zero. US money growth certainly accelerated sharply after the US left the gold standard on April 19, 1933, with the overall money supply rising by 9.5 percent from June 1933 to June 1934 (and then by 14 percent and 13 percent over the next two fiscal years).[5] The gold purchases were followed by large-scale silver purchases in 1934 – and Bordo and Filardo[6] argue that successful reflationary monetary policy through the gold and silver purchases "supports the cases both for conducting open market operations in assets other than short-term paper and for the use of monetary aggregate targeting in the case of severe deflation."[7] But, even though silver purchases became a key element of US monetary policy in 1934, their possible impact has often been heavily discounted in accounts of this period and never quantified empirically. In this chapter we provide new evidence on their significance that supports the potential effectiveness of such nontraditional monetary policy.

FDR's focus on silver in 1934 arose amidst persistent congressional pressure harking back to Populism and the 1890s experience. In the face of continued depression and deflation after 1930, net debtors like farmers suffered especially severely just as the western silver producers faced ruin as the silver price fell by more than 50 percent between 1928 and 1932. Both the farm lobby and the silver bloc gained strength after Roosevelt's sweeping electoral victory in 1932. The seven western silver states, accounting for fully one-seventh of the US Senate despite their small population, were newly unified behind twelve Democrats and only two Republicans – one of whom was a strong silver supporter.[8] Allied with the farm lobby and inflationists of all persuasions, the silver bloc

---

[5] Although Temin and Wigmore ("The End") also emphasize the devaluation's importance in helping dispel expectations of continued deflation, Eichengreen, *Golden Fetters*, p. 344n, points to disappointment with the course of the expansion in the second half of 1933 and a renewed fallback in industrial production pending sustained recovery in 1934. George Warren, architect of FDR's gold purchase program himself "understood that commodity prices in late January 1934 had already incorporated the anticipated impact of the devaluation, and that commodity markets were signaling that a gold price of $35/oz. was not nearly sufficient to produce the desired reflation." See Sumner, "Roosevelt," p. 165.

[6] See "Deflation and Monetary Policy," p. 832.

[7] See Burdekin, "Nontraditional Monetary Policy," for comparison with the US government's earlier 1890 silver purchase program as well as China's commodity-based stabilization policy during the 1940s and early 1950s.

[8] See Friedman, *Money Mischief*, Chapter 7.

put increasing pressure on President Roosevelt to honor his campaign pledge to restore silver's monetary role.[9] Unlike the first major silver purchase program under the Sherman Act of July 1890, the gold standard constraint was at least removed before the purchases began. The 1890 program had itself been repealed in 1893 in the face of growing gold outflows.

The May 12, 1933, amendment to the Agricultural Adjustment Act, sponsored by Senator Elmer Thomas of Oklahoma, initially authorized free coinage of both gold *and* silver. On December 21, 1933, FDR proclaimed that the mints should coin into silver dollars any silver mined in the US (after retaining half of it as seigniorage), and large-scale silver purchases were formally authorized under the Silver Purchase Act of June 19, 1934.[10] Under the terms of the 1934 Act, the silver certificates issued in exchange for the silver received were to "be placed in actual circulation . . . [and] be legal tender for all debts, public and private, public charges, taxes, duties, and dues, and . . . redeemable on demand at the Treasury of the United States in standard silver dollars"[11] By May 31, 1935, the Treasury had accumulated over 421 million ounces of silver – twenty-five million ounces of it newly-mined, 283 million from open market purchases and nearly 113 million from nationalization of pre-existing silver stocks.[12] Beginning on April 30, 1935, sales as well as purchases were made on the world market and the Treasury allowed silver prices to drop back down from their peak above eighty cents an ounce in April 1935 to forty-five cents, while still allowing US producers to sell at 64.5 cents an ounce.[13] The premium offered to US producers naturally facilitated continuing large silver accumulation.

As the Federal Reserve continued to issue circulating silver certificates in exchange for the silver it acquired, silver rose from less than 12 percent of total US currency in 1932–1933 to nearly 25 percent of total currency in 1938 (see Table 11.1). Meanwhile, domestic silver production more than doubled from thirty-three million ounces in 1934 to seventy million ounces in 1940, with most new silver output being "coined, and shipped for storage in Washington and at other government depositories" (Friedman 1992, p. 166). The proportion of the total change in US

---

[9] See also Blum, *Morgenthau Diaries*, Chapter V.
[10] For detailed discussions of the evolution of the US silver policy, see Westerfield, *Our Silver Debacle*; Brattner, "Silver Episode" and "Silver Episode II"; Paris, *Monetary Policies*; Leavens, *Silver Money*; Blum, *Morgenthau Diaries*; Friedman and Schwartz, *A Monetary History*; and Friedman, *Money Mischief*.
[11] From the text of the Silver Purchase Act of 1934 as reprinted in Leavens *Silver Money*, pp. 384–5.
[12] Blum, *Morgenthau Diaries*, p. 194.   [13] Blum, *Morgenthau Diaries*, Chapter V.

Table 11.1. *Composition of US currency before and after the 1934 Silver Purchase Act*

					Federal Reserve	Other
	(in millions of dollars)					
End of June	Total	Gold[a]	Silver[b]		Notes	Currency[c]
1932	5,408	882	640		2,780	1,107
1933	5,434	299	647		3,061	1,428
1938	6,461	78	1,612		4,114	655

Notes:
[a] Includes both gold coin and gold certificates.
[b] Includes silver dollars, silver certificates, Treasury notes of 1890 and subsidiary silver.
[c] Includes National Bank notes, minor coin, US "greenback" notes and Federal Reserve Bank notes.
Source: Friedman and Schwartz (1963, p. 492).

high-powered money accounted for by silver increased from 3 percent in 1934 ($47 million out of $1601 million), to 14 percent in 1935 ($202 million out of $1,440 million) and 41 percent in 1936 ($396 million out of $968 million) before dropping back in 1937 (see Table 11.2). In terms of M1, silver's share rose from 3.5 percent in January 1934 to 5.5 percent in December 1938. This almost certainly severely under-states the impact of silver money, however, given that silver certificates deposited in the banking system would immediately form the basis for creation of new non-silver money. Applying just the overall M1 money multiplier of 3.5 or so, a 2 percent increase in silver money would still translate into a far-from-trivial M1 shock of 7 percent.[14]

It seems unlikely that the fixed gold price of $35/ounce limited the scope of the silver purchase program. Indeed, Bordo *et al.* (2002) point to considerable room for monetary expansion even before the US exited the gold standard in 1933 given the large gold reserves held. Meltzer concludes that, if the Federal Reserve had "made substantial open market purchases, the administration's gold (and silver) purchase policy would have been unnecessary."[15] Both sets of policy initiatives appear to have been possible. But the effectiveness of traditional open market

[14] The actual ratio of M1 to the monetary base ranged from 3.69 at year end 1934 to 2.99 at year end 1938. See Friedman and Schwartz, *A Monetary History*. In light of the declining money multiplier we consider the effects of silver injections to base money as well as the M1 effects.
[15] Meltzer, *A History*, p. 463.

Table 11.2. *Source of change in US high-powered money,*
1932–1938

| | | (in millions of dollars) | | |
End of June	Total	Gold[a]	Silver[b]	Federal Reserve Operations[c]
1932	469	−1037	1	1409
1933	184	399	1	−263
1934	1601	1040	47	332
1935	1440	1239	202	−39
1936	968	1551	396	−286
1937	1794	1820	125	392
1938	1142	520	202	−40

Notes:
[a] Includes change in gold coin and gold certificates plus change in Federal
Reserve and Treasury monetary liabilities secured by gold.
[b] Includes Treasury silver purchases but no other Treasury operations.
[c] Includes change in Federal Reserve domestic monetary liabilities *minus* change
in Federal Reserve monetary reserves (i.e., holdings of gold, gold certificates,
and Treasury currency, plus bank note liabilities of national banks).
Source: Cagan (1965, p. 334).

operations in the very low interest rate environment of the time remains
imponderable given the Federal Reserve's actual inaction.[16]

Contemporary observers not only scathingly attacked the political
motivations for the Silver Purchase Act but also questioned its effectiveness.[17] Paris, for example, dismissed the silver purchases and issuance
of silver certificates as "just one of several 'currency-dilution' items."[18]
More recently, Romer (1992), while concluding that monetary expansion accounted for nearly all of the US economic recovery prior to 1942,
makes no mention whatsoever of the contribution of the silver purchase

[16] It is not clear that the instigation of the silver purchase program had any effect on
Federal Reserve willingness to undertake expansionary purchases of their own. The
myriad potential factors lying behind the passivity of Federal Reserve policy have, of
course, been much discussed. See, for example, Friedman and Schwartz, *A Monetary
History*; Wheelock, "Conducting Monetary"; Meltzer, *A History*.
[17] The negative effects of the US silver purchase program on other countries, particularly
China as the only remaining major nation on a silver standard in 1934, remain an
ongoing source of controversy. See, for example, Friedman, *Money Mischief*, Chapter 7.
Some confirmatory evidence on the accompanying silver outflow from both mainland
China and Hong Kong, and its adverse economic effects, is provided in Burdekin,
China's, Chapter 5.
[18] Paris, *Monetary Policies*, p. 109.

program. Finally, in an otherwise extensive review of alternative monetary policy proposals for a zero-interest rate environment (many of which have never been implemented in practice), Yates (2004) does not even recognize commodity-based open market operations as a policy option.

The role of the silver purchase program is noted by Friedman and Schwartz (1963), Eichengreen (1995), and Meltzer (2003). Meltzer takes the most negative view, concluding that the program "subsidized a small number of miners and companies at large cost . . . [and] achieved very little."[19] Friedman and Schwartz suggest that, although some net expansionary effect likely remained even after taking account of reduced gold purchases after the silver program was adopted, "the sums involved were small compared to either the total increase in the stock of money or the concurrent inflow of gold."[20] Eichengreen (1995, p. 346) notes an increase in currency in circulation as the silver purchases began in August 1934 and a temporary reversal of US gold inflows. The continuing tendency for currency in circulation to expand by much less than the overall gold inflows in both 1934 and 1935 is seen by Eichengreen, however, as evidence of the continuing "largely passive" nature of US monetary policy overall. While such criticisms have been widely shared, we show in this chapter that the Silver Purchase Act did itself make a real difference.

Estimation of a structural VAR provides a new look at silver's role in influencing overall money growth, inflation and our proxy for economic activity in non-silver and silver producing states over the 1934–1938 period. We find meaningful, consistent effects of silver on both prices and construction spending. Moreover, these effects persist and are not just a one-time blip associated with the initial purchases in the late summer of 1934. These results point to the potential relevance of non-traditional open market purchase programs in helping jump start an economy threatened with deflation and zero, or near-zero, interest rates. Our findings also suggest that, whatever the political machinations that produced the Silver Purchase Act, its practical effectiveness offers a precedent for considering broadened, non-traditional open market operations today.[21]

---

[19] Meltzer, *A History*, p. 462
[20] Friedman and Schwartz, *A Monetary History*, p. 488.
[21] This direct government involvement in the money supply process came in the midst of well-documented inconsistencies in Federal Reserve policy during the Great Depression, including the institution's apparent reactions to the stock market run up and collapse. See Siklos, "The Fed's Reaction."

I.   Data and empirical analysis

We use monthly financial and macroeconomic data for the period January 1934–December 1938 to assess the effectiveness of the silver purchase program.[22] We specify two four-variable vector autoregressions (VAR) to identify the effect of the silver purchase program in non-silver and silver producing states. Our basic model is similar to Sims' (1980) monetarist specification in his classic paper comparing business cycles in the interwar and postwar periods with two exceptions. First, we decompose the money supply into non-silver and silver components to isolate the effect of the silver purchase program. Second, we employ data on the aggregate value of construction permits reported in *Dunn's Review* to serve as a leading indicator for economic activity in the non-silver and silver regions (in the absence of monthly data on regional industrial production or aggregate output). The *Dunn's Review* series is a monthly index of the value of construction permits for 215 cities in the US divided into several different regions, including the Mountain region that encompasses the seven states (Arizona, Colorado, Idaho, Montana, Nevada, New Mexico and Utah) identified by Friedman[23] as the primary beneficiaries of the silver purchase program.

The value of construction permits for non-silver states, NSSTATES, was computed by taking the total value of construction permits in the US minus the value of permits in the Mountain (Silver) region, SSTATES. While the potential real effects of the silver purchase program at the local state level would not be confined to construction activity alone, the available construction permit series represent an area of the economy that is as a rule particularly sensitive to changes in financial conditions. If the silver purchase program was important for stimulating economic activity, then silver purchases should have a disproportionately large economic effect in silver states where the precious metal was important to the regional economy. Moreover, if shocks to the silver money supply help predict the value of construction permits in the Mountain region, then this would also imply that the silver support program had multiplier effects extending beyond mine production alone.

Figure 11.1 plots the value of construction permits in silver and non-silver states while Figure 11.2 depicts the trends evident in the available annual state personal income data over 1929–1938. The acceleration of

---

[22] Although the link between money and prices has certainly prevailed through wartime episodes, see Burdekin and Weidenmier, "Inflation," we end our sample prior to the outbreak of World War II given both the impact on world commodity markets and the consequences for the monetary policy regime.

[23] Friedman, *Money Mischief*, Chapter 7.

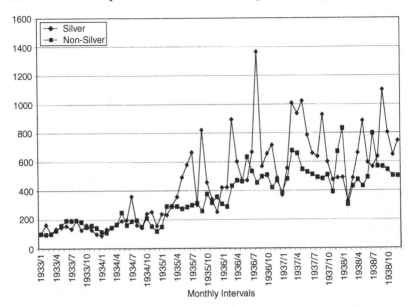

Figure 11.1 Construction permits in silver and non-silver states, 1931–1938.

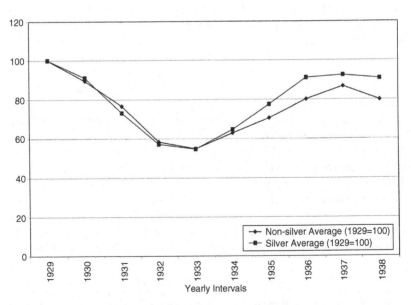

Figure 11.2 Personal income in silver and non-silver states, 1929–1938.

economic activity in the silver states after 1934 is evident in both figures, albeit subject to strong seasonal effects in the case of the permit data. Figure 11.1 reveals a contrast between the strongly rising value of construction permits in the silver states after 1934 and the flatter trajectory of permit activity elsewhere. Figure 11.2 shows that both silver and non-silver states faced essentially identical declines in personal income during 1929–1933. From that point on, however, state income in silver states rose by over 66 percent between 1933 and 1936 while state income in non-silver states rose by only 46 percent over that same period. Moreover, state income in the silver states was essentially back to 1930 levels by 1938 whereas income levels remained over 10 percent lower in the non-silver states. These trends add weight to the relevance of the similar movements evident in the construction permit data and also suggest that the Silver Purchase Act opened up an economically-meaningful disparity between silver- and non-silver state performance that did not exist before 1934.[24]

As for the other variables in our VAR system, we employ two measures of the money supply that are derived from Friedman and Schwartz's (1963) monthly estimates of M1 and original data from the Board of Governors of the Federal Reserve System (1943, pp. 412–13). The first measure, non-silver money (NSM), is defined as M1 minus the silver component of the money supply. The silver component of the money supply is the sum of standard silver dollars, silver certificates, and subsidiary silver, and silver money (SM) is defined as M1 minus the non-silver component of money.[25] Consumer prices – minus volatile food prices – (P) are taken from the NBER macro-history database. All variables are in natural logarithms. Figure 11.3 shows graphs of the money and price time series. Non-silver and silver money possess an upward trend over the sample period as a whole, with silver money continuing to expand after the initial burst in mid-1934 when large-scale purchases began. This uptrend in silver money is in keeping with the post-1934 increase in the value of silver-state construction permits and personal income seen in Figures 11.1–11.2. Consumer prices are flat for the early part of the sample period before rising significantly in late 1936 and early 1937.

---

[24] Silver-state personal income levels also likely benefited, to some extent, from the greater-than-average per capita new deal grants accruing to the Mountain region over 1933–1939. Early new deal spending in 1933–1935 probably had only limited short-run effects, however, given a primary stimulus that reflected the "direct transfer of relief benefits to unemployables." See Fishback et al., "Did New Deal," p. 63.
[25] This focus on M1 is in line with such prior studies as Romer "What Ended" and Christiano et al., "The Great Depression."

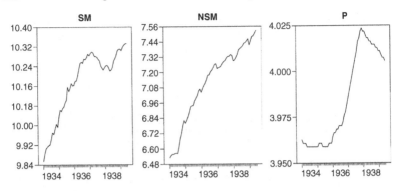

Figure 11.3 Silver, non-silver money, and prices, 1934:1–1939:6.

A p-th order dimensional vector autoregressive model with Gaussian errors can be written as

$$x_t = A_1 x_{t-1} + A_2 x_{t-2} + \cdots + A_k x_{t-k} + \gamma D_t + e_t, \quad t = 1, ..., T \quad (1)$$

where x_t is a p x 1 vector of stochastic variables, and D_t is a vector of dummy variables that captures seasonal fluctuations. The error term, e_t, is assumed to be a vector white noise process. Although the AIC and BIC criteria selected a lag length of one, we chose three lags for the VAR analysis to capture the dynamics in the system. We then identified the effects of the silver purchase program for the system including non-silver money (NSM), silver money (SM), the value of construction permits (SSTATES and NSSTATES), and consumer prices (P). Under the recursive ordering imposed on the variance-covariance matrix, non-silver and silver money are ordered first and second, respectively, to test the hypothesis that the US's recovery from the Great Depression was largely driven by monetary expansion.[26] Consumer prices are given the last ordering in the system to reflect slow price adjustment during the interwar period. We estimate VARs for the silver and non-silver states to compare the effect of shocks in non-silver and silver money on the value of construction permits in the two regions. Figures 11.4 and 11.5 display the impulse response functions for a one-standard deviation shock to each variable in the system. Sixty-eight percent fractiles, equivalent to one-standard-deviation error bands, are calculated for the impulse responses using the technique developed by Sims and Zha (1999).

[26] Romer, "What Ended."

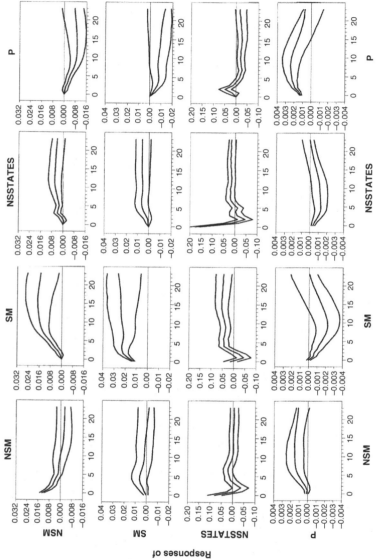

Figure 11.4 Non-silver-state impulse responses (ordering #1).

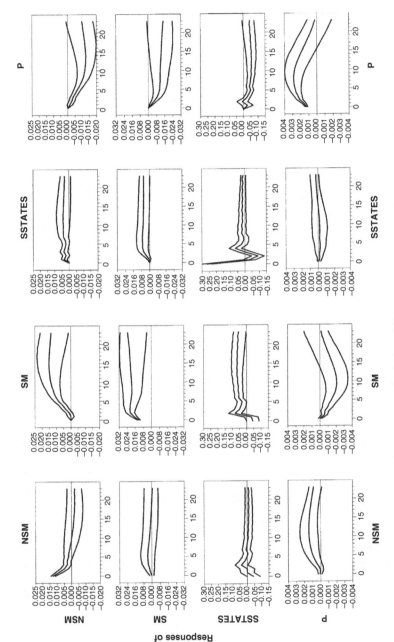

Figure 11.5 Silver-state impulse responses (ordering #1).

Figure 11.4 shows that a shock to non-silver money increased the value of construction permits in non-silver producing states and increased prices. A shock to silver money, while initially reducing the value of construction permits, still permanently increased their value over time. We also find some evidence of interaction between the Federal Reserve and the Treasury over our sample period. Federal Reserve money supply increases appear to follow shocks to silver purchases while it seems that Treasury silver purchases were marginally boosted following positive innovations in non-silver money.[27] Meanwhile, both silver and non-silver money decline in response to a shock in consumer prices.

Figure 11.5 shows the impulse responses for silver-producing states. A shock to silver money increases the value of construction permits. An innovation in non-silver money has no such statistically-significant effect on the value of construction permits, however. We also again find evidence that the Federal Reserve and Treasury responded to each other and that a shock to prices reduced the value of construction permits as well as money and non-silver money.

In Figures 11.6 and 11.7 the ordering of the variables in the Choleski decomposition is slightly changed with silver money given the first ordering and non-silver money the second ordering. Shocks to the silver and non-silver money supplies both have statistically significant effects on the value of building permits in non-silver-producing states. The Federal Reserve and Treasury are found to interact with each other as before. The basic tenor of the results remains unchanged with silver explaining approximately 31 percent of the movements in the value of construction permits in silver states at a two-year forecast horizon. Innovations in the non-silver money supply, on the other hand, do not have a significant effect on the value of construction permits in the silver states.

Although the VAR analysis is consistent with the hypothesis that the silver purchase program increased economic activity in the silver-producing states, it is important to guard against any possibility that the VAR analysis identified a spurious effect. Accordingly, we also estimated a historical decomposition of the value of construction permits using the identification restrictions used in Figures 11.6 and 11.7. This historical analysis decomposes a time series into a baseline and a baseline plus shock component. The baseline forecast component is computed by using all information in the system up to time t. The baseline plus shock

---

[27] This also suggests that the monetary effects of Treasury silver purchases were not necessarily offset by reduced printing of Federal Reserve notes as Friedman and Schwartz, *A Monetary History*, p. 488, for example, suggest.

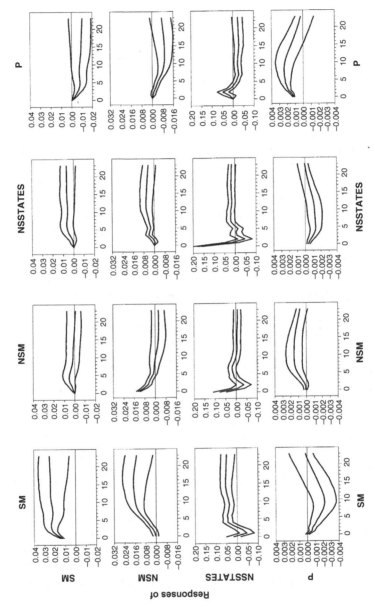

Figure 11.6 Non-silver-state impulse responses (ordering #2).

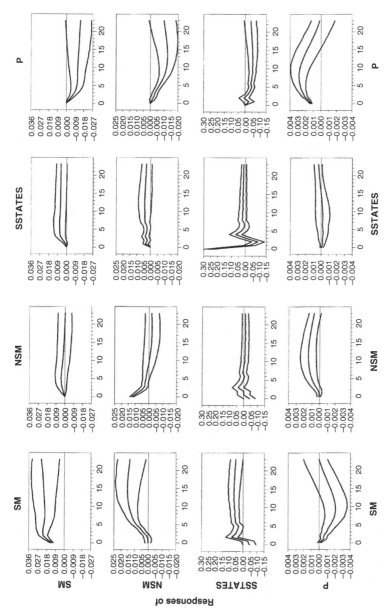

Figure 11.7 Silver-state impulse responses (ordering #2).

component shows the effect of an innovation in one variable on another (from the baseline forecast) in the VAR. For example, we would expect shocks to silver money to have their largest effect on the value of construction permits in 1934 and 1935, the two most important years of the silver purchase program. On the other hand, we should find that shocks to silver money have little effect by 1938 since the Treasury was no longer purchasing silver on the open market.

Figure 11.8 shows a historical decomposition of construction permits for silver-producing states. The baseline plus shock series for the figure labeled "Effect of SM" shows that silver money had its largest effect on construction permits in 1934 and 1935. The baseline forecast plus the silver shock closely follows the time series on building permits. This is especially true in the first six months of 1935. Later innovations in silver money appear to be much less important, as expected, and cannot explain movements in the construction permits over the last two years of the sample period. Rather, it appears that consumer prices and lagged values of construction permits do a better job of explaining movements in the leading indicator. The results from the decomposition support the inferences drawn from the preceding VAR analysis, therefore, and are quite consistent with the historical evidence on the timing of silver purchases by the US Treasury.

Another potential weakness of the VAR analysis, however, is that the results could simply be a figment of the atheoretical ordering scheme used to identify the shocks in the Choleski decomposition. As pointed out by Enders (1995), the Choleski decomposition imposes strong assumptions about the VAR's underlying structural errors. For example, we assume that prices do not have a contemporaneous effect on any of the other variables in the system. We also impose the identifying restriction that the value of construction permits only affects itself and consumer prices within a month. Thus, the two money variables do not respond to innovations in construction permits or consumer prices contemporaneously.

To address the possibility that our results are driven by an atheoretical ordering scheme, we add a series of structural VARs to provide some additional insight into the importance of the silver purchase program for our measures of economic activity and prices. We impose the following structure on the variance-covariance matrix to identify the effects of silver purchases on output and prices:

$$e_{1t} = a_1 \varepsilon_{SMt} + a_2 \varepsilon_{Pt} + \varepsilon_{NSMt} \tag{2}$$

$$e_{2t} = a_3 \varepsilon_{NSMt} + a_4 \varepsilon_{Pt} + \varepsilon_{SMt} \tag{3}$$

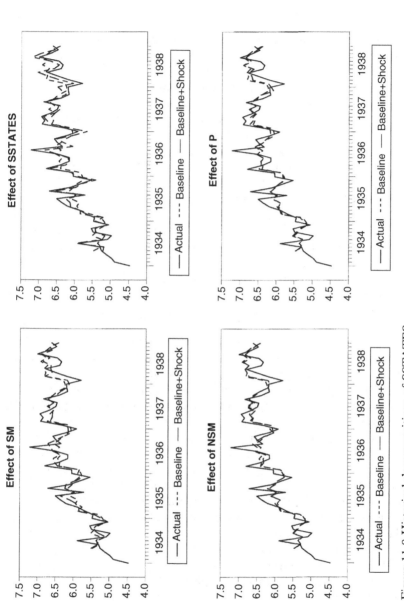

Figure 11.8 Historical decompositions of SSTATES.

$$e_{3t} = a_5 \varepsilon_{NSMt} + a_6 \varepsilon_{SMt} + \varepsilon_{(N)STATESt} \tag{4}$$

$$e_{4t} = \varepsilon_{Pt} \tag{5}$$

Equation (2) states that non-silver money responds to silver money and prices contemporaneously. In equation (3), silver money responds within a month to innovations in non-silver money and consumer prices. The contemporaneous reactions of silver and non-silver money are in keeping with the tug of war between the Federal Reserve and Treasury during the 1930s. Equation (3) allows construction spending to respond to innovation in the silver and non-silver money supplies within a month. Consumer prices, shown in equation (4), do not respond contemporaneously to the other variables in the system, however. This last specification is designed to reflect price stickiness during the Great Depression.

Figures 11.9 and 11.10 present the impulse response functions for a one-standard-deviation shock to each variable in the system along with the equivalent of one-standard-deviation fractiles for the non-silver and silver states. In Figure 11.9, the impulse response functions show that a shock to non-silver and the silver money stock significantly increases output. A one-standard-deviation shock to the non-silver money supply can explain a quite substantial share of the movements in the value of construction permits at the four, eight, twelve, and twenty-four-month forecast horizons, respectively accounting for about 14, 25, 29, and 35 percent of the total variation. A one-standard-deviation shock to the silver money supply can explain 9, 8, 9, and 14 percent of the fluctuations in output at the four, eight, twelve, and twenty-four–month forecast horizons. A shock to the non-silver money supply increases consumer prices. An innovation to the silver money supply initially lowers consumer prices but significantly increases consumer prices after about a fifteen-month forecast horizon. Both silver and non-silver money fall in response to a shock in consumer prices. Overall, shocks to the money supply have their maximum effect at a forecast horizon of one-year to sixteen-months. Non-silver and silver money can explain approximately 50 percent of the forecast error variance in consumer prices at a twenty-four–month forecast horizon.

Figure 11.10 shows the impulse responses for silver producing states. We find that a shock to the silver money supply increases the value of construction permits. An innovation to the silver money supply can explain 5, 8, 12, and 19 percent of the movements in the value of construction permits at the four, eight, twelve, and twenty-four-month forecast horizons. However, a shock to non-silver money supply does not significantly raise construction spending at the twenty-four-month forecast horizon. A shock to silver money increases non-silver money but an innovation in non-silver money does not significantly raise silver

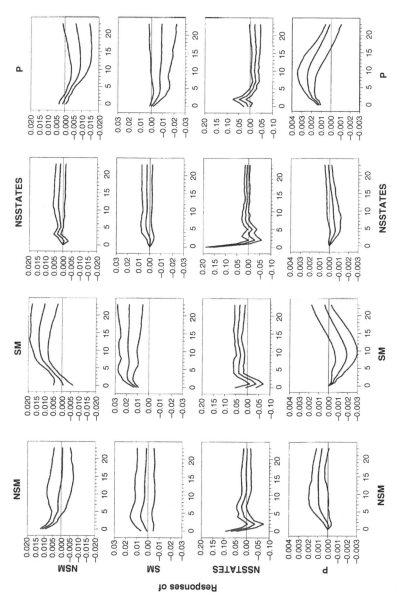

Figure 11.9 Non-silver-state impulse responses for structural model.

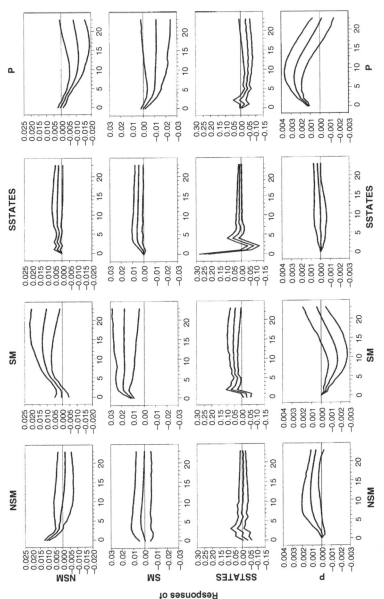

Figure 11.10 Silver-state impulse responses for structural model.

money. An innovation in non-silver money increases consumer prices as does a shock to non-silver money after a twenty-month forecast horizon. A shock to consumer prices decreases both non-silver and silver money. There is some evidence that a shock to building permits increases the non-silver and silver money supplies. Overall, we continue to see that shocks to silver have a statistically and economically significant effect on construction spending in silver-producing states while shocks to non-silver money do not have similarly significantly positive effects on economic activity in the region.

As an additional robustness check, we replaced the M1 measures of the silver and non-silver money supply with the silver and non-silver monetary base. The impulse responses for the non-silver-states and silver-states appear in Figures 11.11 and 11.12 using the same identification strategy employed in Figures 11.9 and 11.10. The essential pattern of the empirical results remains the same, with shocks to the silver and non-silver money supply increasing the value of construction permits in the non-silver-states. Innovations in silver and non-silver money can explain approximately 33 percent of the innovations in construction permits and 22 percent of the movements in consumer prices. In terms of the Mountain region itself, we find that an innovation in the silver monetary base increases construction spending in the area, but a shock to the non-silver monetary base does not have a statistically significant effect on building permits. A shock to the silver base can explain approximately 11 percent of the movements in the value of construction permits at the twenty-four-month forecast horizon.

Finally, we examined the effects of adding a measure of failed bank deposits, BANK, from Anari et al. (2005) to proxy for the effect of bank disintermediation on economic activity during the Great Depression. The identification scheme is altered in this case so that the silver and non-silver money supplies respond contemporaneously to the natural logarithm of the stock of failed bank deposits. The value of construction permits can now respond contemporaneously to shocks in silver and non-silver money as well as bank deposits. Failed bank deposits also respond within the month to innovations in construction permits. The basic results remain robust to the further changes in the identification scheme under our allowance for a credit channel effect via failed bank deposits. Silver money now explains more than 28 percent of the forecast error variance in construction permits in twenty-four months. Meanwhile, innovations in non-silver money also increase construction activity in silver states but the effect is quite small.[28] We find that the

---

[28] Results are available from the authors upon request.

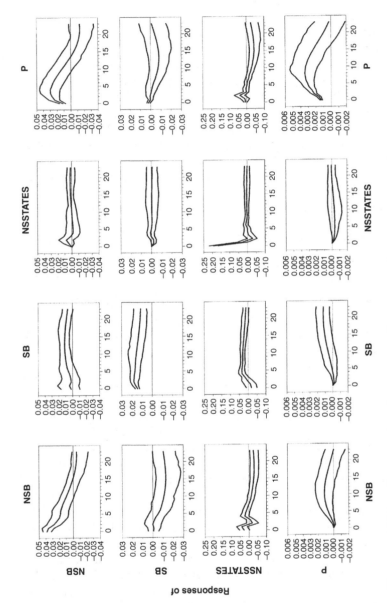

Figure 11.11 Non-silver-state impulse responses for monetary base.

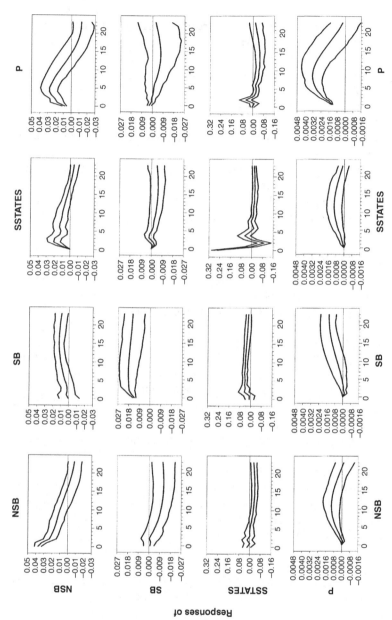

Figure 11.12 Silver-state impulse responses for monetary base.

stock of failed bank deposits does not itself have a significant effect on our proxy for economic activity in the two regions during this period, however. The insignificance of the bank deposits variable may reflect the fact that many of the financial sector problems had already been resolved through the banking restrictions imposed in 1933 and the establishment of the FDIC that commenced operations in 1934. The string of individual state and municipal bank holidays beginning in late 1932 that culminated in the national bank holiday of March 6, 1933, was closely followed by the US exit from the gold standard the following month. Although the 1933 reorganization ended the wave of bank failures that had begun in 1931, this was not, of course, sufficient to end the deflation. Our empirical results highlight the role that the silver purchases may have played in finally laying this trend to rest through, initially, jumpstarting economic activity in the silver states.

II.   Conclusions

Did Roosevelt's silver purchase program play a role in bringing the US out of the depths of the Great Depression? Our results strongly suggest so based on state income data as well as new data on the value of construction permits in the silver and non-silver producing regions of the US. The silver states recovered much faster from the Great Depression than the rest of the US as measured by state income estimates and the value of construction permits. By 1938, income in the silver states was very close to their levels of income in 1929–1930 whereas this chapter's empirical analysis also suggests that the value of construction permits in the Mountain region significantly increased in the wake of the silver purchase program. The time series of construction permits in the silver-producing regions shows a sharp increase coinciding with the Treasury's large-scale purchases of silver on the open market, whereas building in other areas of the country shows no such strong increase. A series of VARs confirms the significance of silver in stimulating economic recovery in the Mountain states while having a smaller economic effect in the rest of the US.

The significance of the silver effect detailed in the empirical work is not only of historical interest, but also represents a more longstanding lesson that purchasing government bonds is by no means the only way of achieving monetary expansion. Our study provides new insight into the potential usefulness of commodity purchase programs when very low interest rates and a liquidity-constrained banking system call into question the effectiveness of open market bond purchases – a scenario that applied to the US in the 1930s and recently returned to the fore in

Japan. Proposals for the Bank of Japan extending the range of its activities in buying land and stocks[29] to counter deflation are certainly not without historical precedent, and the US episode suggests that such non-traditional open market operations can potentially be quite effective.

References

Anari, Ali, James W. Kolari and Joseph R. Mason. August 2005. "Bank Asset Liquidation and the Propagation of the U.S. Great Depression," *Journal of Money, Credit, and Banking* 37, no. 4: 753–73.

Bernanke, Ben S. "Deflation: Making Sure 'It' Doesn't Happen Here." Remarks before the National Economists Club, Washington, DC, November 21, 2002.

Blum, John Morton. 1959. *From the Morgenthau Diaries: Years of Crisis, 1928–1938*. Boston: Houghton Mifflin.

Board of Governors of the Federal Reserve System. 1943. *Banking and Monetary Statistics, 1914–1941*. Washington, DC: National Capital Press.

Bordo, Michael and Andrew Filardo. October 2005. "Deflation and Monetary Policy in a Historical Perspective: Remembering the Past or Being Condemned to Repeat It?" *Economic Policy* 44: 799–844.

Bordo, Michael, Ehsan U. Choudhri and Anna J. Schwartz. January 2002. "Was Expansionary Monetary Policy Feasible during the Great Contraction? An Examination of the Gold Standard Constraint," *Explorations in Economic History* 39, no. 1: 1–28.

Brattner, Herbert M. October 1938. "The Silver Episode," *Journal of Political Economy* 46, no. 5: 609–52.

December 1938. "The Silver Episode: II," *Journal of Political Economy* 46, no. 6: 802–37.

Buiter, Willem H. "Deflation: Prevention and Cure," NBER Working Paper 9623, April 2003: http://www.nber.org/papers/w9623.

Burdekin, Richard C.K. 2007. "Nontraditional Monetary Policy Options and Commodity-Based Stabilization Policy," *International Economics and Finance Journal* 2, no. 1–2: 1–18.

2008. *China's Monetary Challenges: Past Experiences and Future Prospects*. New York: Cambridge University Press.

Burdekin, Richard C.K. and Marc D. Weidenmier. December 2001. "Inflation is Always and Everywhere a Monetary Phenomenon: Richmond vs. Houston in 1864," *American Economic Review* 91, no. 5: 1621–30.

Cagan, Phillip. 1965. *Determinants and Effects of Changes in the Stock of Money, 1875–1960*. New York: Columbia University Press.

Christiano, Lawrence, Roberto Motto and Massimo Rostagno. December 2003. "The Great Depression and the Friedman-Schwartz Hypothesis," *Journal of Money, Credit, and Banking* 35, no. 6, part 2: 1119–97.

Eichengreen, Barry. 1995. *Golden Fetters: The Gold Standard and the Great Depression, 1919–1939*. New York: Oxford University Press.

---

[29] Fukao, "Financial Strains."

Enders, Walter. 1995. *Applied Econometric Time Series*. New York: John Wiley.

Fishback, Price V., William C. Horrace and Shawn Kantor. March 2005. "Did New Deal Grant Programs Stimulate Local Economies? A Study of Federal Grants and Retail Sales During the Great Depression," *Journal of Economic History* 65, no. 1: 36–71.

Friedman, Milton. 1992. *Money Mischief: Episodes in Monetary History*. New York: Harcourt Brace Jovanovich.

Friedman, Milton and Anna Jacobson Schwartz. 1963. *A Monetary History of the United States, 1867–1960*. Princeton: Princeton University Press.

Fukao, Mitsuhiro. September 2003. "Financial Strains and the Zero Lower Bound: The Japanese Experience," Working Paper No. 141, Bank for International Settlements, Basel, Switzerland.

Hanes, Christopher. February 2006. "The Liquidity Trap and U.S. Interest Rates in the 1930s," *Journal of Money, Credit, and Banking* 38, no. 1: 163–94.

Hutchison, Michael M. 2004. "Deflation and Stagnation in Japan: Collapse of the Monetary Transmission Mechanism and Echo From the 1930s." In Richard C.K. Burdekin and Pierre L. Siklos (eds.) *Deflation: Current and Historical Perspectives*. New York: Cambridge University Press: pp. 241–68.

Leavens, Dickson H. 1939. *Silver Money*. Bloomington: Principia Press.

Meltzer, Allan H. 2003. *A History of the Federal Reserve: Volume I, 1913–1951*. Chicago: University of Chicago Press.

Paris, James Daniel. 1938. *Monetary Policies of the United States, 1932–1938*. New York: Columbia University Press.

Romer, Christina D. December 1992. "What Ended the Great Depression?" *Journal of Economic History* 52, no. 4: 757–84.

Schwartz, Anna J. March 2003. "Asset Price Inflation and Monetary Policy," *Atlantic Economic Journal* 31, no. 1: 1–14.

Siklos, Pierre L. April 2008. "The Fed's Reaction to the Stock Market During the Great Depression: Fact or Artefact?" *Explorations in Economic History* 45, no. 2: 164–84.

Sims, Christopher A. May 1980. "Comparison of Interwar and Postwar Business Cycles: Monetarism Reconsidered," *American Economic Review* 70, no. 2: 250–7.

Sims, Christopher and Tao Zha. September 1999. "Error Bands for Impulse Responses," *Econometrica* 67, no. 5: 1113–55.

Sumner, Scott. 2001. "Roosevelt, Warren, and the Gold-Buying Program of 1933," *Research in Economic History* 20: 135–72.

Temin, Peter and Barrie A. Wigmore. October 1990. "The End of One Big Deflation," *Explorations in Economic History* 27, no. 4: 483–502.

Westerfield, Ray B. 1936. *Our Silver Debacle*. New York: Ronald Press.

Wheelock, David C. May–June 2002. "Conducting Monetary Policy Without Government Debt: The Fed's Early Years," *Federal Reserve Bank of St. Louis Review* 84, no. 3: 1–14.

Yates, Tony. July 2004. "Monetary Policy and the Zero Bound to Interest Rates: A Review," *Journal of Economic Surveys* 18, no. 3: 427–81.

12　The interwar shocks to US–Cuban trade relations: A view through sugar company stock price data[*]

Alan Dye and Richard Sicotte

Recent work on the political economy of imperialism emphasizes how the imperial power can transform less-developed economies by setting up institutions that underpin modern financial markets, lower political risk, and benefit both the creditor and debtor nations. Kris Mitchener and Marc Weidenmier, for example, present the Roosevelt Corollary to the Monroe Doctrine (1904) as a natural experiment and demonstrate that Theodore Roosevelt's administration used the Corollary as a credible threat of military intervention that enforced sovereign debt contracts and suppressed political conflict in Central America and the Caribbean.[1] But natural experiments can be misleading: can one generalize from such findings to say that imperial powers set up "rules of the game" that underpin secure property-rights for international capital markets? In reality, the imperial power may choose to enforce or to violate the rules of the game when it is in its interest to do so.

In contrast, there is an extensive literature that declares the evils of imperialism and its US variety to be a source of internal political corruption and economic demoralization. This is a central theme in the historiography of Central America and the Caribbean, but nowhere is it more salient or more symbolic than Cuba, where even those who are critical of the Castro regime often see the anti-imperialism of the Cuban Revolution as justified.

Cuba was a prime example of US hegemonic rule-setting. As a condition of its military withdrawal after the Spanish–American War, the US required the Cuban constituent assembly to incorporate a set of provisions that handed over certain sovereign rights to the US, which were

[*] We wish to thank Lee Alston, Jeremy Atack, Charlie Calomiris, John Landon-Lane, Aldo Mussachio, Larry Neal, Hugh Rockoff, Richard Sylla, Mark Wasserman, Marc Weidenmier, David Weiman, and Eugene White for helpful comments, and the Smith Richardson Foundation for financial support.

[1] Mitchener and Weidenmier "Empire"; Ferguson, *Empire*.

written both into a treaty between the US and Cuba and into an amendment to the Cuban constitution of 1902. These provisions, known as the "Platt Amendment," formalized a unique relationship of tutelage between the two countries that included a legal commitment on the part of the US, precursor to the Roosevelt Corollary, to ensure political stability in the new Cuban republic, protect foreign investments against violations of property rights, discourage misuse of public debt, made credible by signaling a willingness to intervene militarily, if necessary, to enforce these aims. This institutional underpinning combined with a reciprocal trade agreement in 1903 propelled one of the most prosperous periods of economic growth in Cuba's history. Yet few scholars look favorably upon the Platt Amendment or the high volume of capital transfers that followed it. Instead, the historical literature maintains a convention of associating Cuba's long-run economic problems with the "penetration" of North American capital and identify it as an underlying cause of the Cuban Revolution of 1959.[2]

This chapter takes another look at the US's twentieth-century experiment with empire by examining the long-run performance of securities issued to finance foreign investments in Cuba, focusing especially on the interwar period, when the prosperity of the first two decades of the twentieth century ended, and the economy never fully recovered. More specifically, we examine the value of equity raised to finance investments in sugar, the dominant sector of the Cuban economy, as a way to assess the claims in the anti-imperialism literature of the damaging consequences of foreign investment in Cuba.

Although most historians attribute the mid-century economic and political turmoil to the adverse local effects from Cuba's integration into international financial markets, they typically base their views on evidence of the presence of presumed causes rather than of observed outcomes. Here, by contrast, we focus on outcomes by observing the performance of foreign-owned sugar companies operating in Cuba. The record of equity earnings in the dominant sector of the Cuban economy presents a puzzle that seems at odds with either the monolithic "institution-building" view or the "penetration" view of foreign capital in Cuba. We find that the failure of Cuban economic recovery in the interwar period, or the failure of the sugar industry to recover, was associated with market conditions that led to the cessation of new infusions of foreign capital. The evidence shows that, aside from enforcing

[2] Jenks, *Our Cuban Colony*; Guerra y Sánchez, *Azúcar*; Pino-Santos, *Asalto*; Ayala, *American Sugar Kingdom*.

property rights abroad, the adverse conditions were the result of domestic distributive politics of trade protectionism in the US. Aside from enforcing property rights abroad, the imperial power refused in a strict sense to defend the property rights of foreign investors against rent-seekers at home.

The chapter uses an event-study approach to identify influences on the share prices, rates of return, and systematic risk of sugar companies from 1921 to 1939. Sugar-company performance in Cuba is compared with competing companies operating in the mainland US and one of its insular possessions, Puerto Rico. The first section of the chapter presents a preliminary discussion of the history of US investment in Cuban sugar. The following two sections describe the structure of the US sugar market, introduce the data, and present indices of sugar-company equity by geographical supplier area. Questions raised in this section are further examined in the third section, which gives a "moving-windows" analysis of the pricing structure of sugar-company stocks, using the event-study method of Kristen Willard *et al.* (1996). We then explain some of the results of the event study, and consider their implications for the relationship between foreign capital, protectionism, and economic stagnation in Cuba in the 1930s.

I.   Preliminary discussion

Before 1898, American investments in Cuba were limited, but after the US military occupation following the Spanish-American War, unusual opportunities attracted American investors. Cuba's war of independence had been extremely destructive of productive property – burning of canefields, decimation of livestock and so on. Prior to the war, the Cuban sugar industry had a track record as a cost-leader in the global sugar industry with many talented entrepreneurs, but domestic capital sources were inadequate for the scale of the rebuilding job to be done afterwards.[3]

According to contemporary accounts, the Platt Amendment was instrumental in establishing the credible commitment to protection of foreign capital, necessary to mobilize the North American capital market to finance the rebuilding of sugar and other key export-related industries. After intervention in 1898, the US refused military withdrawal unless the new republic amended its constitution with a treaty popularly known as the "Platt Amendment."[4] What was most significant about the

---

[3] Jenks, *Our Cuban Colony*, pp. 128–74; Speck, "Prosperity"; Dye, *Cuban Sugar*, pp. 24–66.
[4] Pérez, *Cuba and the United States*, pp. 109–11, and *Cuba under the Platt Amendment*.

Table 12.1. *Foreign assets in Cuba ($US millions)*

Origin: US	1896	1906	1911	1927	1936	1946
Agriculture	–	96.0	75.0	645.0	264.6	227.0
Sugar	–	30.0	65.0	600.0	240.0	–
Other	–	66.0	10.0	45.0	24.6	–
Public utilities (incl. railroads and communications)		59.0	45.0	235.0	215.0	251.0
Mining and manufacturing	15.0	6.0	25.0	65.0	27.0	40.0
Services	30.3	50.5	95.0	275.3	274.2	35.0
Government	–	37.0	30.0	100.0	–	–
Other	–	13.5	65.0	175.3	–	–
Total	45.3	211.5	240.0	1220.3	781.2	553.0

Origin: UK			1913	1927	1939	1945
Railroads	–	–	125.6	147.6	142.2	127.1
Other	–	–	90.6	75.0	12.7	6.3
Total	–	–	216.2	222.6	154.9	133.4

Sources: Dickens, *American Direct Investment*; Lewis, *America's Stake*; Rippy, *British Investments*; US Dept. of Commerce, *Investment*.

amendment was that it ceded certain sovereign rights to the US, notably including the right to intervene militarily to protect "life, property and individual liberty" and to enforce sound public debt policy of the Cuban government. To further solidify the economic "ties of singular intimacy," the two nations signed a trade reciprocity treaty in 1903, which gave Cuba a 20 percent discount on the full duties for sugar and tobacco in the US in exchange for similar discounts (of between 20 and 40 percent) on a wide range of exports from the US.[5]

With the credible commitment to the security of foreign property rights and reciprocal trade, North American capital began to pour into Cuba, rising from $45 million to $211 million from 1896 to 1906 (See Table 12.1).[6] Within five years it was fueling one of the most prosperous periods of economic growth in Cuban history; and by World War I, Cuba had restored its position as a global sugar powerhouse among the world's sugar exporters, and the largest producer, supplying 25 percent of the world's sugar. Through 1914, Cuba was the most important destination in Latin America for North American foreign investment.

---

[5] The phrase "ties of singular intimacy" was used by President William McKinley in his State of the Union message on December 5, 1899. Jenks, *Our Cuban Colony*, p. 72; Pérez, *Cuba and the United States*.

[6] Figures are in constant US dollars of 1926.

Table 12.2. *Cuban sugar exports and the national economy*

Year	Sugar exports (thousands of short tons)			Sugar exports (millions of 1926 dollars)			Total exports (millions of 1926 dollars)			National income (millions of 1926 dollars)
	US	UK	Total	US	UK	Total	US	UK	Total	
1904	1212.4	0.0	1212.4	90.9	0.0	90.9	124.8	9.9	149.2	372
1909	1581.0	0.0	1581.0	117.1	0.0	117.1	161.9	7.4	184.6	444
1914	2385.8	260.5	2710.6	170.6	16.3	191.4	214.1	23.2	255.4	587
1919	3445.1	665.1	4374.3	285.8	53.4	362.4	317.4	59.5	414.6	622
1924	3714.2	490.9	4332.9	326.3	45.7	382.2	369.2	50.2	443.2	798
1929	4209.5	845.5	5400.8	169.7	32.0	214.9	219.0	35.9	285.8	599
1930	2488.5	773.7	3557.9	85.6	25.7	121.7	134.3	29.5	193.6	598
1931	2321.4	563.4	2972.6	85.7	18.6	107.6	122.0	22.7	162.8	537
1932	1870.1	720.4	2864.8	60.1	17.0	83.3	88.8	19.2	124.6	437
1933	1530.3	746.7	2501.8	59.4	21.5	87.8	86.6	24.8	128.0	446
1934	1736.9	534.9	2518.0	76.7	14.9	98.2	108.3	19.4	143.9	486
1939	2163.7	509.7	2997.9	106.8	16.4	137.3	144.2	23.3	191.6	633

Sources: Cuba, Ministerio de Hacienda, *Anuario Azucarero de Cuba*, 1959; Zanetti Lecuona, *Cautivos*; Alienes Urosa, *Características*.

The main beneficiary was sugar and the auxiliary sectors that serviced sugar, including transportation, communications, and public utilities.[7] From 1904 to 1920, Cuba experienced a thriving expansion of the sugar industry, when earnings from sugar exports grew at an annual average rate of more than 10 percent. Julián Alienes Urosa estimated real GNP growth during that period at an annual average of 4.5 percent.[8] As Table 12.2 indicates, sugar exports, which accounted for 80 percent of all export earnings, led this growth almost exclusively. Although interrupted by a sharp postwar financial crisis in 1920–1921, the phase of prosperity continued until the commodity crisis of the latter 1920s. However, by the time of the Great Depression, the Cuban economy fell into complete ruin. New foreign investment in Cuba vanished in the 1930s, and the prosperous times of the first quarter of the twentieth century were never restored.[9]

---

[7] Lewis, *America's Stake*; Winkler, *Investments*; US Dept. of Commerce, *Investment*. There was also substantial British investment in the country's relatively well-developed system of railroads. Zanetti Lecuona and García, *Sugar*; Rippy, *British Investments*; Stone, *Global Export*.
[8] Alienes Urosa, *Características*; Zanetti Lecuona, *Cautivos*.
[9] Wallich, *Monetary Problems*.

In spite of the foreign-capital-fed prosperity before the crisis, the predominant explanation among historians of Cuba's interwar economic difficulties is that the "penetration" of foreign capital was detrimental to Cuban economic development.[10] It hinges on the proposition that foreign ownership diverted the wealth-generating capacity of Cuba's national resources by permitting foreign capitalists to appropriate them. Oscar Pino-Santos captures the anti-imperialist tenor in the literature in the title of his important contribution, which is translated *The Assault on Cuba by the Yankee Financial Oligarchy*. According to Pino-Santos, although the major phase of foreign capital penetration came before and during World War I, the principal damage came after the crisis of 1921.

During the war, US interests expanded and became more concentrated. The catalyst was the interruption of European sugar due to the war. Cuba became the main alternative source for disrupted supplies of sugar. Cuban production capacity expanded from 2.8 million short tons in 1914 to 4.2 million in 1918. North American financial markets played a critical role in mobilizing the resources for this massive wartime expansion of sugar production in Cuba. Issues of new stock in Havana and New York became an important source of finance for building new sugar milling operations.

After the war, the lifting of wartime sugar price controls resulted in a sharp postwar crisis in Cuba. Figure 12.1 shows the movements of the price of sugar through the crisis in 1921. With sugar prices kept artificially low from 1917 through 1919, when controls were lifted suddenly in 1920, the market entered a speculative bubble, which peaked at a record price of 23.6 cents per lb. in May 1920, after which it plummeted to 4.5 cents on February 3, 1921.[11] When the bubble burst, a large share of the current Cuban crop was left unsold; and its holders, who had produced or purchased it at high prices, lost everything.[12]

A serious problem of imbalance of foreign ownership came about as a consequence of the fallout from the financial crisis of 1921. Table 12.3 gives estimates of the share of North American ownership and industrial concentration in the sugar industry. Fallout from the 1921 crisis caused a massive failure among mills and eighteen banks, including the two largest Cuban or Spanish-owned.[13] North American banks, which had owned about 0.5 percent of the Cuban sugar sector before 1920, suddenly found themselves in possession of 7 percent of Cuban sugar milling

---

[10] Pino-Santos, *Asalto*; Benjamin, *United States*.
[11] From January 1, 1917, to December 31, 1919, the sugar price had never exceeded 13.6 cents per lb.
[12] Collazo, *Pelea*.   [13] Cuba, Comisión Temporal de Liquidación Bancaria, *Compendio*.

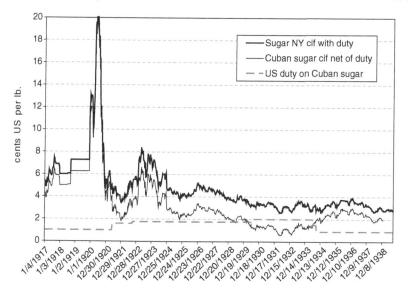

Figure 12.1 Sugar prices, *cif* New York.
Source: Journal of Commerce, Willett & Gray.

capacity from bad debt. This share grew to almost 12 percent by 1929.[14] From these figures, Pino-Santos's emphasis on the role of foreign banks appears exaggerated.[15] Nonetheless, American companies overall controlled 38 percent of the sugar manufacturing capacity before the war but acquired 65 percent by 1924. The top four firms, all American corporations, owned 49 percent of the industry's capacity by 1929.

Noteworthy in the 1921 fallout was that North American banks through foreclosure became direct operators in the sugar industry. National City Bank and the Royal Bank of Canada acquired sixteen Cuban sugar estates and made a fateful decision to retain ownership of these companies. The mills they acquired represented over $80 million in sugar-manufacturing assets in Cuba.[16] National City Bank's decision to keep the properties is well-documented because it later became the subject of a congressional investigation of lobbying activity in 1929. In 1921, Gordon Rentschler, hired in 1921 by National City as an adviser to assess the value of their recently acquired sugar properties, testified that he and his team concluded the properties were fundamentally

[14] Jenks, *Our Cuban Colony*; Wallich, *Monetary Problems*, pp. 66–7.
[15] Pino-Santos, *Asalto*, p. 93.
[16] Authors' estimates based upon ownership and capacity in 1924, as reported in the Cuba, Secretaría de Agricultura, Comercio y Trabajo, *Memoria de la Zafra*.

Table 12.3. *Nationality of ownership and industrial concentration in the Cuban sugar industry*

	Four-firm concentration ratio[a]	% Owned by North Americans[b]	% Owned by North-American Banks[c]	% Owned by North American Refiners[d]
1909	7.0	–	–	–
1914	11.2	38.3	0.0	0.0
1919	25.4	49.8	0.5	0.5
1924	35.3	64.5	6.8	5.2
1929	49.0	66.9	11.6	5.0
1934	39.6	68.4	12.1	5.4
1939	39.3	62.2	10.2	6.4

Notes:
[a] The four-firm concentration ratio for 1914 includes the Gómez Mena mills, which were Cuban-owned, and the Rionda mills, which were owned by a family with roots in both Cuba and the US. The Rionda mills are included among the top four firms in later years, but not the Gómez Mena mills.
[b] North American ownership includes mills owned by citizens of or companies based in the US or Canada. It also includes mills owned by companies that are "transnational," that is, the owners are members of a family that have roots in both the US or Cuba. It is the convention in the literature to include them as "American" mills.
[c] Bank-owned mills include all sugar properties owned by General Sugars Corporation, which was the operating subsidiary, wholly owned by National City Bank; the Sugar Plantations Operating Co., which was the operating subsidiary of the Royal Bank of Canada; The First National Bank of Boston; and Chase National Bank.
[d] Refiner-owned mills include only mills owned as subsidiaries whose core business was sugar refining. These include: the American Sugar Refining Co., the National Sugar Refining Co., and Warner Refining Co. The following are not included in the refiner-owned percent given here: the Cuban-American Sugar Co. owned a small refinery in Louisiana; the Rionda family acquired the McCahan refinery; but their chief business was raw sugar production. In both cases, the refining capacity they owned was small relative to their raw sugar producing capacity. Also, the Hershey Corporation owned a refinery, located in Cuba, also is not included in the refiner-owned figures in the table. For alternative views on the refiner and bank-owned properties, see Rowe, *Studies*; Pino-Santos, *Asalto*; and Ayala, *American Sugar Kingdom*.
Sources: To determine the ownership and nationality of sugar mills from Cuban official sources is less than straightforward. The lists usually used are incomplete and contain many discrepancies. The authors have compiled information to determine ownership from a wide array of sources including: Cuba, Secretaría de Hacienda, La industria azucarera y sus derivados, 1910, 1914; Pino-Santos, Asalto, pp. 45–7; Cuba, Secretaría de Agricultura, Memoria de la zafra, 1916–1929, Industria azucarera, 1930–1939; Farr & Co., Manual of Sugar Companies, 1922–1942; Santamaria, Azucar; McDowall, Quick to the Frontier; Jiménez, Empresas; García Álvarez, Gran Burgesía; McAvoy, Sugar Baron; USNA Record Group 59 Serial no. 837.61351/924 18 January 1935, and the Louisiana Planter and Sugar Manufacturer *passim*.

sound but needed to be "rehabilitated" and, in any case, could not be sold for what they were worth in the current depressed market conditions. National City, therefore, set up an operating company to "rehabilitate" the sugar properties and await a recovery in the sugar market before selling them, hoping to minimize the losses from bad debt. The Royal Bank came to an independent but similar decision.[17]

Pino-Santos and others argue that the American banks took advantage of their creditors' positions, and other American corporations took advantage of privileged access to credit, to take control of some of Cuba's most profitable properties, particularly in sugar and banking, at bargain-basement prices. The bank officials claimed they never intended to go into the sugar business; but rather, the decision to operate rather than sell the properties was a strategic one prompted by the depressed market conditions and the large share of the country's sugar properties in their hands that made it impossible to sell them off in the short run for anything near what they would be worth if the market were to recover, as was expected.

In all, twenty mills were acquired by North American banks, and another six mills were acquired by large eastern seaboard refineries. Also important, the increase in the milling capacity owned by North American corporations was due partly to acquisition and partly to an increase in size and capital intensity of mills as companies adopted the latest sugar manufacturing technology. For example, after 1921, banks acquired 32,600 tons of daily grinding capacity from existing mills and expanded them by 1928 to 51,000 tons.[18] The industry became considerably more concentrated. The four-firm concentration ratio, for example, was 11 percent in 1914 (with one of the four companies Cuban-owned), but after 1919, the top four were American-owned, or transnationally owned, corporations owning multiple mills, which by 1929 together owned 50 percent of Cuba's milling capacity.

The measures outlined here, although central to the standard argument, are factors in a presumed social process that has not been tested in the literature by observing outcomes. If North American companies were successful in appropriating the prime resources of Cuba's sugar industry, one might expect it to show up in performance measures. How did American corporations operating in Cuba perform after 1921 and particularly through the economic crisis?

[17] Cleveland and Huertas, *Citibank*; McDowall, *Quick to the Frontier*; US Senate Committee on the Judiciary, *Lobby Investigation*; US Senate Committee on Banking, *Stock Exchange Practices*.
[18] Effective days grinding each harvest season in the 1920s ranged typically between 100 and 130.

II.   The data

By 1909, the preferential tariff on Cuban sugar (combined with its capacity for expansion), had created a unique situation in the US market for sugar. Cuba had expanded so as to crowd out all other duty-paying sugar imports in the US market.[19] After this date, the US sugar market was served almost entirely by three groups of suppliers. Table 12.4 shows the source of sugar in the US market by "supplier area," as they were called. The three classifications are: domestic (mainland) beet and cane sugar; the insular possessions (Hawaii, the Philippines, Puerto Rico, and the Virgin Islands); and Cuba and other foreign suppliers. The insular possessions were not referred to as "domestic," but they all had rights of duty-free status.[20] Duty-paying supplier areas were Cuba, which paid 80 percent of the full-duty, and other foreign suppliers, which paid the full duty. Except for abnormal years, less than 1 percent of sugar consumed in the US in the 1920s and 1930s came from full-duty-payers.

The industrial structure of cane sugar production included two manufacturing stages – the processing of sugarcane into raw sugar, and refining raw sugar. Almost all imports from insular possessions or foreign countries were raw sugar, sold mainly to refineries in the mainland US (most located in the northeast). Beet sugar, on the other hand, was typically produced in a single stage as "direct-consumption" sugar – equivalent in quality to refined.

Our data are constructed from the weekly (end-of-week) prices of common stock of sugar companies. All the companies specialized in either raw cane sugar or beet sugar from Cuba, Puerto Rico, or US domestic beet sugar. Thus, each of the three supplier-area classifications in the US market is represented. The data were compiled from all common stocks of raw-sugar-processing companies operating in Cuba reported regularly in the *New York Times* and the *Wall Street Journal*. They include stocks traded on the New York Stock Exchange and the New York curb market, over-the-counter stocks and some regional exchanges.[21] Twenty

---

[19] Prior to that time, the net-of-duty price in the US market was above the price in the world market. After it, the protected US price was determined by the world price plus the tariff on Cuban sugar exported to the US.

[20] Imports from the Philippines, at times, were restricted, but not during the period we are discussing, until the enactment of the US Sugar Program in 1934, which established universal production and import quotas, discussed below. Ballinger, *History*.

[21] The main sources for the stock prices were the *New York Times*, and *Wall Street Journal*. Missing values were filled, where possible, from the *Commercial and Financial Chronicle*, and sugar trade journals, *Louisiana Planter*, and *Facts About Sugar*. Outstanding shares, descriptions of stock issues, and company histories were obtained from the annual

Table 12.4. *Sources of supply to the US sugar market*

	Volume (000s short tons)					
US mainland beet	Mainland cane	Hawaii	Puerto Rico	Philippines	Cuba	Total
1904	259	415	368	130	31	1410	3023
1909	348	332	511	244	42	1431	3530
1914	773	247	557	321	58	2463	4431
1919	777	122	579	364	88	3343	5352
1924	1166	90	677	393	339	3692	6463
1929	1089	218	882	507	711	4149	7587
1934	1562	268	948	807	1088	1866	6574
1939	1809	587	966	1126	980	1930	7466

	Value ($US of 1926 millions)					
1904	34.5	55.3	49.0	17.3	2.8	124.1	314.4
1909	41.1	39.2	60.4	28.8	3.4	112.1	327.6
1914	92.9	29.7	66.9	38.6	7.0	198.4	434.3
1919	82.5	13.0	61.5	38.7	9.3	306.5	518.6
1924	141.4	10.9	82.1	47.7	41.1	315.0	646.5
1929	86.0	17.2	69.7	40.1	56.2	174.2	444.5
1934	128.0	22.0	77.7	66.1	89.2	73.2	457.4
1939	134.5	43.7	71.8	83.7	72.9	98.5	508.4

Notes:
[a] Values are estimated using the product of volumes and the average annual price of sugar, net of duty for Cuba. Figures are deflated using the US Bureau of Labor Statistics Wholesale Price Index.
Source: US House of Representatives, Committee on Agriculture, *History*.

companies are represented: eleven prominent Cuban sugar companies, all American-owned; five major domestic beet sugar companies; and four major Puerto Rican companies. The companies in the data set owned multiple mills and were by and large among the largest and most technically advanced in each of their supplier areas. Out of Cuba's 160, or so, active mills, the companies in the sample owned forty-seven mills, which represented between 45 and 54 percent of Cuba's sugar production capacity. In domestic beet sugar, which was the most concentrated

Farr & Co., *Manual of Sugar Companies*, and dividend payments were collected from serial publications of the Standard Dividend Service, *Fitch Dividend Record*, and the *Commercial and Financial Chronicle*. The Havana Bolsa traded railroad, public utility, and various public and private debt issues (quotes are found in the daily *Diario de la Marina*), but in those years, it did not trade sugar-company stocks.

industrially, the companies in the data set represent between 67 and 71 percent of that supplier area's milling capacity. The four Puerto Rican firms represented were referred to in trade journals as the "top four," because they stood out in size relative to the rest of the industry, representing between 20 and 43 percent of Puerto Rican production capacity.

These data are used, in the next section, to construct indices of sugar-company equity by supplier area to give a graphical representation of sugar-company performance. In a later section, rates of return are calculated and assembled into three panels, one for each supplier area, to examine their risk-return profiles.

III.   Sugar-company equity indices

The indices shown in Figure 12.2 give estimates of the market value of the outstanding equity of sugar processors in each of the three supplier areas. The indices E_j are constructed as

$$E_j = \left(\sum_i [p_{ij}(s_{ij}^c + s_{ij}^p)] \right) \cdot a_j^{-1} \tag{1}$$

where p_{ij} is the share price of firm i in supplier area j; and s_{ij}^c and s_{ij}^p are the outstanding common and preferred shares, respectively, of firm i in supplier-area j.[22] The supplier areas represented are the US domestic beet sugar, Puerto Rico, and Cuba.

Often the levels of stock price indices such as these are presented as index numbers scaled so that all indices are equal to 100 on a specific date. Rather than doing this, we incorporate a scale factor, a_j^{-1}, which scales the indices to give a rough estimate of the relative total market valuation of sugar-company equity in each of the three supplier areas. The magnitude, a_j, is the share of the production capacity of all the firms in the sample for supplier area j relative to the aggregate production capacity of all firms in supplier area j. Production capacity is measured by the sum of daily per ton processing capacity at each factory.[23]

---

[22] Share prices are weighted by the sum of common and preferred shares outstanding to account for, and maintain continuity through, recapitalizations of some important companies that converted preferred to common shares. To put them on a comparable basis, outstanding shares were par-adjusted to render $1 par equivalent shares. Capitalization histories were obtained from Farr & Co., *Manual of Sugar Companies*.

[23] Records of the Puerto Rican index do not give daily grinding capacities per mill. As an alternative that makes the Puerto Rican figures comparable to the capacity figures available for the other areas, we take the historical maximum production of each mill as

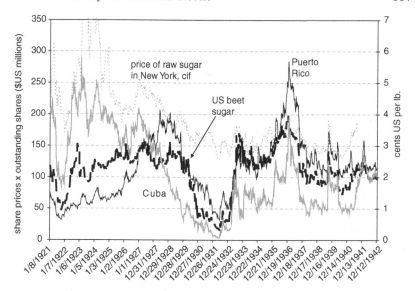

Figure 12.2 Sugar-company equity indices.
Source: see text.

The scale factor, a_j^{-1}, accurately rescales the expression inside the parentheses to cause E_j to reflect the total value of sugar-company equity in the supplier area if the value per ton of processing capacity of the firms in the sample was representative of all firms in the supplier area. Although the condition does not hold, the bias operates in the same direction for all three supplier areas. The firms in each supplier-area sample were among the largest and most profitable companies; therefore, the values shown in the figure overstate the actual aggregate market values. It is probably greater for the Puerto Rican index, which includes only the top four firms, and it is probably least for the beet sugar producers, where technical vintages were apparently somewhat more uniform. Therefore, although the levels of the indices shown in Figure 12.2 reflect relative aggregate supplier-area equity, they can only be taken as approximate.

We are more confident in the representativeness of the movement of the indices and the implied rates of return than in the levels. Observing

a measure of the production capacity. The aggregate supplier-area industry capacity figures are only observed annually. To prevent the annual observations from introducing discontinuities in the scale factor, we smooth the aggregate capacity series by interpolating between annual observations of shares of industry capacity represented in the sample.

the patterns of movement in Figure 12.2, three things stand out. First, comparing the supplier areas, the timing of the fall in the series over the period of the 1920s commodity crisis up to and after the NYSE crash is noticeably different. The Cuban sugar-company stock prices fall much earlier, beginning their descent in January 1927. The other two fall at or after the crash of the stock exchange. The Puerto Rican index turns downward by May 1929, but it takes a sharp plunge beginning in the week of October 29. The beet sugar index also drops sharply at the crisis, but it shows some recovery in the months leading up to the week beginning May 5, 1930.

Second, the recovery in each of the three supplier areas stands out. Most striking is the beet sugar industry, which recovered abruptly between January and July of 1933 to a level comparable, or slightly above, its pre-crisis level. Puerto Rico closely tracked beet sugar's ascent. Cuba's recovery was partial and with much greater instability.

Third, it is noteworthy that, in the 1920s, the market valuation of sugar-company equity in Cuba correlates closely with the price of sugar, but not in the other supplier areas. From 1934, all three correlate similarly, but moderately, with the price of sugar. One obtains a sense of the 1920s correlation by comparing the sugar-company equity with the price of sugar by inspection in Figure 12.2, but simple correlations confirm it. For the period from January 1921 to May 1934, before the adoption of production and import controls in the US sugar market, the Pearson correlation coefficient for the Cuban index against the price of raw sugar was 0.84; for the beet sugar industry, it was 0.38; and for Puerto Rico, it was −0.15.[24] In the period after 1934, production controls were in effect in both the US, under the New Deal Agricultural Adjustment Act, and in Cuba, under the Cuban Sugar Stabilization Institute.[25] By contrast, after 1931 when controls were in effect, the corresponding correlation coefficients are respectively 0.62, 0.66, and 0.62.

What explains these contrary movements in supplier-area stock prices, especially before 1930? Cuban sugar-company equity appears more sensitive to the short-run price of sugar than domestic beet and Puerto Rican companies. But why? The simple answer is that Cuba, which was the only significant supplier of duty-paying sugar in the US was dependent on the US tariff, and the tariff was endogenous to the price of sugar. The

---

[24] Sugar price data are end-of-week prices of raw sugar cif New York, duty-paid, taken from the *Journal of Commerce*.

[25] The Cuban controls were introduced earlier, in 1931, but production and export controls in the two countries were coordinated after the passage of the Jones-Costigan Act of 1934 made sugar a "basic commodity" under the AAA legislation. Álvarez Díaz, *Estudio*; Dalton, *Case Study*.

brief recovery in the price of sugar in 1926 reflects an attempt on the part of the Cuban government to stave off a threatened increase in the sugar tariff using production restrictions. Stock prices of sugar companies operating in Cuba turned upward with the price of sugar in 1926, but also followed it downward in 1927. The increase in the sugar tariff that would come about as part of the omnibus Hawley–Smoot tariff in 1930 began to be anticipated as early as 1927. Of course, as that expectation weakened stock prices of Cuban sugar companies, it strengthened share prices of companies in duty-free areas, as we observe in Figure 12.2. The next section outlines some of the main events that underlay these commodity and stock price movements.

IV.   The commodity crisis and tariff endogeneity

The tariff in those years was the single most prominent economic issue dividing the political parties in national politics.[26] It had been so since the end of the Civil War and remained so until the New Deal. During those years, the sugar tariff was often politically pivotal because it raised more revenue than any other customs item. Revenue aside, special interests differed on the issue of trade protection and created divisions that did not coincide with the party line. Beet sugar producers consistently called for increases in the tariff on raw cane sugar (discussed below); but refiners, who were the principal buyers of raw sugar, were opposed. American investors who had sugar properties in Cuba shared the refiners' view on the raw sugar tariff, but these two interests were geographically concentrated on the eastern seaboard. The refiners' sugar trust of the 1880s had had some influence against demands for protection. However, beet sugar expanded rapidly after about 1894, and geographically dispersed among twenty-one states by the 1920s, mostly in western and midwestern states. It could also count on support from cane sugar states, Louisiana and Florida. In many of these states, sugar was one of the most prominent, industrially concentrated industries in the state. By the 1920s, congressional support for the refining industry and American investors in Cuba was being seriously challenged and ultimately overshadowed by western beet sugar protectionists.

Although nominally a specific tariff (at the end of the war, the duty on Cuban sugar was set at 1.0048 cents per lb.), the sugar tariff was endogenous to the expected future price of sugar through political action on trade protection. The evidence for such endogeneity of the sugar tariff during the 1920s is abundant (more so than can be presented in

---

[26] Taussig, *Tariff History*; Goldstein, *Ideas*.

this chapter).[27] It begins with the US Congress' postwar deliberations over the 1922 Fordney–McCumber tariff act. A legislative battle broke out over the sugar tariff in late 1921. While eastern seaboard refiners and Americans with direct investments in Cuba lobbied in Washington for a lower sugar tariff, Secretary of Commerce, Herbert Hoover, and Senator Reed Smoot (R-UT), a high-ranking member of the Senate Finance Committee, pressured the Cuban government, on behalf of domestic beet sugar interests, to restrict Cuban sugar production. Smoot offered to lower the new sugar tariff in the Senate bill from 1.6 cents per lb., the rate recently passed in the House, to 1.4 cents.[28] When the Cuban government rejected proposals for restricting its sugar crop, Hoover tried to enlist the support of bankers in New York who had investments in both Cuban and western beet sugar. The bankers proposed, instead, to create a marketing pool to dispose of postwar sugar surpluses but refused to support production restriction in Cuba. Loathe to accept the roadblock against his state's principal industry, Smoot retaliated by negotiating an increase of the sugar tariff in the Senate bill to 1.84 cents. Publicly, he attacked the recalcitrant bankers and eastern refiners

---

[27] Industry participants and analysts were well aware of the tendency of countries with high-cost sugar industries to raise tariffs in response to a falling price of sugar. Gustav Mikusch, an Austrian sugar expert, published a report on tariff increases by eight European countries in 1925, in the US trade journal, *Facts About Sugar*, on February 20, 1926. Mikusch remarked, "The reason for these numerous advances in tariff rates undoubtedly is to be found in the low price of sugar during the past year. With imported cane sugar selling at prices below the cost of production in Europe the beet growing countries of this continent have felt the necessity of erecting higher barriers to protect their home industries." The minutes of meetings of the International Sugar Council, an exporting-country cartel formed in 1931, are replete with references to tariff endo-geneity (see minutes for the years 1931–1935 in the Cuban National Archives, Fondo ICEA [hereafter, CAN].); likewise, in the private business papers of Czarnikow-Rionda, the major New York sugar brokerage (see University of Florida at Gainesville, University Archives, Braga Brothers Collection, ser. 10c. [hereafter, BB]). The Java sugar industry faced an explicit endogenous tariff response in formulae established by the Indian Tariff Board. See India, Tariff Board, *Report*, 1931, 1933, 1938. US domestic sugar industry representatives increased demands for protection when prices were falling. In 1922, Louisiana sugar interests stated that if the price would stabilize at 2.9 cents, "they could live with the present tariff." Cable from W.R.M. (State) to Sumner Welles, February 24, 1922. United States National Archives, Department of State Records [hereafter USNA], 837.61351/347. In 1929, Stephen Love, President of the US Beet Sugar Association, argued that with the price at two cents, it was necessary to raise the tariff to prevent "huge" losses. *Facts About Sugar*, March 16, 1929. Congress considered a "sliding scale" that would tie the sugar duty directly to the price, but producers worried that it would not be sufficiently flexible (for further discussion see Smith, *United States*, pp. 57–66).

[28] The Harding administration raised the sugar tariff on May 27, 1921, to 1.6 cents per lb. from 1.0048 cents, in a stopgap emergency tariff law intended to halt the postwar recession. Smith, *United States*, p. 43; Ballinger, *History*, pp. 24–5.

accusing them of forming a "Wall Street Plot" to destroy the beet sugar industry.[29]

The pressure from protectionists was relieved by the high sugar prices of 1923 and 1924. J.W.F. Rowe explains that the high prices were caused by rapid increase in the world demand for sugar and the slow postwar recovery of the European beet sugar industry, interpreted at the time as a signal that expansion of world sugar production capacity would be needed. The downward movement from the end of 1924 was caused by greater-than-expected recovery of the European beet sugar industry in late 1924 into 1925, and increased production in the US insular possessions. European beet sugar production went from 5.6 to 7.8 million short tons. Also, stimulated by the recent tariff increase, US domestic production showed a slight upward trend while insular-possession sugar expanded greatly – production in Puerto Rico by more than 30 percent, and the Philippines by 80 percent from 1922 to 1925.[30] Then in 1925, Cuba had a record crop of 5.9 million short tons – 27 percent above 1924, itself a record crop. The consequence was that, by September 1, 1925, unsold physical stocks of sugar worldwide were 1.8 million short tons, almost double the usual end-of-crop-year carryover. Rowe says that "sugar producers of the world were stunned with surprise" by the accumulation of stocks. This was, however, just the first sign of a troubling market overhang that grew to four million tons by 1929.[31]

We know from Arthur Lewis and Charles Kindleberger that all major commodities markets exhibited similar patterns of falling prices and mounting physical stocks in the late 1920s.[32] In the case of sugar, the first signs of commodity crisis were an important turning point for Cuban sugar politics. As the problems of "overproduction" became visible, Cuban mill owners (especially those with older mills and less access to capital) argued that the aggressive expansion of American sugar mills was irresponsible in the postwar sugar market. Indeed, the American experts, who had been forecasting a slower recovery of European beet sugar production, were caught by surprise. National City Bank, for example, in 1919 had forecast a global shortage of sugar throughout most of the twenties, which was a factor in their strategy of

---

[29] The final rate of 1.7648 cents per lb. was a compromise between the House and Senate rates. Smith, *United States*, pp. 47–8.

[30] Authors' calculations; Rowe, *Studies*, p. 7; US Tariff Commission, *Sugar*, 1934. Data from Moreno Fraginals, *Ingenio*; Farr & Co., Manual of Sugar Companies; Willett and Gray, *Weekly Statistical Sugar Trade Journal*.

[31] Rowe, *Studies*, p. 7.

[32] Lewis, *Economic Survey*; Kindleberger, *World in Depression*, pp. 86–96.

investment and expansion.[33] Forecasts emerged that Cuba would have another record crop in 1926. The Cuban Hacendados (Sugar Mill Owners') Association recommended that Cuban President, Gerardo Machado, impose restrictions on the Cuban sugar crop using internal production quotas.[34] First implemented in May 1926, and later extended to 1927 and 1928, crop restriction was intended to boost the price of sugar, but the reasons behind the producers' call to limit production were motivated by concerns about threats of increased protection in the US market.

That the crop restriction was unilateral obviously put Cuba at risk because it invited competitors to expand. Producers understood this, but they also observed that, in Washington, representatives of the domestic industry were stirring fears that Cuban producers were trying to "eliminate the domestic sugar industry" and calling for an increase in the sugar tariff. Around the same time that the crop restriction was decreed in 1926, a group of US beet sugar company executives visited Cuba to discuss further remedies Cuban sugar producers might undertake to avoid an increase in the sugar tariff. In the months to follow, Senator Smoot emerged again as the key figure in Washington, advising representatives of the Cuban sugar industry that, if Cuba could manage to reduce its production enough to induce a recovery of the price, there would be no need for a revision of the tariff.[35]

Most industry participants saw the 1926 crop restriction as a temporary measure that would be unsustainable without international cooperation. So, in 1927, the Cuban government sponsored a mission to Europe to seek an agreement with major sugar exporters in Europe for a joint effort to reduce exports and halt the price decline. Although later, in 1931, the same parties came together and signed such an agreement, the initial attempt in 1927 failed. The sugar price weakened in part from realization that the international agreement would not materialize. By the summer of 1928, internal Cuban opposition to the crop restriction put its future in doubt. President Machado decreed to abandon it on December 27, 1928.[36]

---

[33] National City Bank, *Cuba: Review of Commercial, Industrial and Economic Conditions in 1919*, excerpts reproduced in Smith, *What Happened in Cuba?* pp. 149–51.

[34] Zanetti Lecuona, *Manos*, pp. 66–7; Rowe, *Studies*, p. 19.

[35] USNA, 837.61351/409, letter from Crowder to Sec. of State, May 12, 1926. Smith, *United States*, pp. 50–2.

[36] *Louisiana Planter and Sugar Manufacturer*, October 20, 1928; *Facts about Sugar*, December 29, 1928; Pérez-Cisneros, *Cuba*, pp. 15–21; Zanetti Lecuona, *Manos*, pp. 77–8, 83–5; BB.R.G. 2 Ser. 10c, Box 57 f. Gutierrez – Rentschler – Machado 1928, Letter from José Gómez Mena, a prominent Cuban millowner, to Viriato Gutierrez, President Machado's Secretary of the Presidency, August 1, 1928.

Cuban share prices plunged sharply beginning in June 1928, as observers forecast that the uncontrolled Cuban crop of 1929 would be another record crop. As this occurred in the sugar market, Herbert Hoover, in his 1928 presidential campaign, pledged to increase tariffs on farm goods for agricultural relief, while beet sugar growers' associations in the west called for an increase in protection against cheap Philippine and Cuban sugar. After his victory, Hoover called for immediate tariff reform, initiating the deliberations in Congress that led to the notorious Hawley–Smoot tariff. In another study, we show that Senator Smoot and the sugar tariff became a pivotal issue in the contest over the tariff.[37] With Smoot now as chair of the Senate Finance Committee, which had jurisdiction over the tariff, domestic sugar interests were well-positioned to demand new protection. After eighteen months in Congress, the Hawley–Smoot tariff act went into effect on June 17, 1930, and the sugar tariff was increased from 1.7648 cents to two cents per lb. Cuban interests, as they watched these events unfold, had predicted that a two-cent tariff would be ruinous for sugar producers in Cuba.[38]

The coincidence of falling values of sugar-company shares in Cuba and rising values in non-duty-paying areas from 1927 onward are explained by the same two underlying factors – an unstable sugar market and the endogeneity of protection in the US. Excess long-run production capacity and the accumulation of unsold physical stocks drove the price down and elevated the uncertainty over when it might recover. The falling sugar price, then, raised the probability of a revision in the sugar tariff in the US. In the US sugar market, to the extent that domestic producers could rely on Congress to adjust the effective level of protection to global market conditions, the risks of global sugar market instability were borne by producers in Cuba. Over the 1920s, as market conditions worsened and the threat of tariff revision in the US grew, Cuban sugar became a less attractive investment and the non-duty-paying insular possessions (especially Puerto Rico and the Philippines) became more attractive.[39]

V.   Sugar-company risk

If sugar market instability and the risk of tariff revision of the late 1920s explain the realignment of the market valuations of the three sugar supplier areas, then these same factors should be visible in the systematic

[37] Dye and Sicotte, "Institutional Determinants."
[38] Rowe, *Studies*; BB, R.G. 4, Series 10c.
[39] Hawaii had little remaining good cane land in which to expand.

risk of the assets in question. Investors would have updated their assessments of the risk of investing in sugar in one supplier area relative to another based on the news they received about changes, or possible future changes, in tariff protection, exposure to market instability, or other significant occurrences; and they would have incorporated them, in different ways, into the expected rates of return on Cuban shares, domestic beet sugar shares, or any other supplier area. If news of any of these events forecast an adverse effect on the perceived forward distribution of returns from equity in sugar companies, say, operating in Cuba, they would compensate for bearing that risk by demanding a higher expected rate of return.

The conditions described produce two predictions about changes in the structure of systematic risk between supplier areas. First, Cuba bore a greater burden of any downward shock to the price of sugar in the world market, while the US domestic beet sugar and Puerto Rico were insulated by selling entirely in the protected US market. Second, the risk assessed on sugar companies on the mainland and in Puerto Rico should have fallen as the progression of events signaled Congress's willingness to accommodate the domestic sugar industry's demands for protection. Similarly, risk assessed of Cuban sugar-company securities should have risen relative to US domestic and insular-possession securities as events signaled that increased protection would come at the expense of Cuba's market in the US, as Cuban sugar would have to sell a greater share of their crop in the unprotected world sugar market.

These predictions may also be used to distinguish the significance of the tariff from two other possible alternative explanations. One obvious alternative is that investors may have altered their risk perceptions in response to the New York Stock Exchange crash or other events associated with the onset of the Great Depression. A second alternative is the "financial penetration" hypothesis from the historical literature on Cuba, which emphasizes the monopoly power that North American-owned companies exercised in Cuba.[40] In either case, there is no reason to expect a pattern of divergence in the perception of risk in the different supplier areas in the pattern proposed above. In the first alternative, there is no reason to expect different supplier areas to behave differently. In the latter, one might expect the companies in our sample, all powerful North American corporations traded publicly on one of the New York exchanges, to perform well. If they had their way in Cuba, to the extent described in the literature, one would expect them to have lower perceived risk relative to the US domestic producers, where restraint of

---

[40] Ayala, *American Sugar Kingdom*; Ibarra, *Prologue*; Pino-Santos, *Asalto*.

trade faced stronger legal sanctions and political institutions were less subject to capture by sugar interests.

Assuming the market efficiently incorporated the news investors responded to into the prices of sugar-company securities, the timing of changes in perceived risk, inferred from price changes, should provide clues about the kinds of information investors responded to. One way to investigate these implications would be to conduct a conventional event study that examines the effects of a known event on prices.[41] A problem with this approach for our purposes is that the news of a declining sugar market and tariff endogeneity unfolded in a number of small events. Undoubtedly some news events were more significant than others to contemporary investors. Selecting the significance of events based on knowledge of the outcomes can be hazardous, since investors tried to anticipate the outcomes, when they responded, but did not know them. An endogenous approach to identify significant events is warranted to avoid problems of hindsight bias. We adopt a "moving-windows" event-study method proposed by Willard et al., which was devised precisely to identify "significant news" events over time using the information in asset prices.[42]

The premise upon which the method is constructed is the notion that prices in securities markets can offer a "running commentary" on broader historical processes. An iterative search for breaks in the underlying parameters is conducted using successive time intervals or "windows" of the full dataset. Unlike the parameters that describe the underlying structure of the economy (which are thought by many to be fairly stable, e.g., Pierre Perron [1989]), there are reasons to believe that the parameters that reflect the risk perceptions of investors may not be very stable, especially at times of great uncertainty, such as the period surrounding the Great Depression or the Cuban Revolution of 1933 (which began on September 4, 1933). Changes in risk assessments could occur at any moment investors received new information that they considered significant enough to alter their perceptions. In the analysis below, we employ moving windows in two forms. The first form, which follows Willard et al., seeks to identify "turning points," as they call them, that is, the timing of "significant news," which may exhibit breaks in the parameters, in our case, measuring relative perceived risk of sugar-company stocks in the three supplier areas. These should coincide with

---

[41] MacKinlay, "Event Studies."
[42] Willard, Guinnane and Rosen, *Turning Points*. Other applications of the moving-windows approach include Brown and Burdekin, "Turning Points"; Dye and Sicotte, "U.S. Sugar Program"; Oosterlink, "Bond Market"; Sussman and Yafeh, "Institutions"; Weidenmier, "Turning Points."

the significant changes in investors' information sets about the securities in question. The second form focuses, instead, on detecting the magnitudes of level changes in the same parameters. When there are multiple breaks, the second approach provides a sense of the cumulative or durable effects of multiple events. We find that observing the results of the two approaches together is informative.

As a structural model, we employ the Capital Asset Pricing Model (CAPM), modified to account explicitly for industry risk in the following way. Letting r_n be the average excess return (the market return minus the risk-free rate) for all sugar-industry securities, the usual CAPM relationship is

$$r_n = a_o + a_1 r_m + \varepsilon_n \tag{2}$$

where r_m is the excess return in the market overall, and a_1 represents the systematic risk of sugar-industry securities. The predictions at the beginning of this section, however, are about the systematic risk of sugar-company shares in one sugar supplier area, relative to the average for the sugar industry. These are not represented in equation (2), but they can be expressed by letting i represent sugar company i in supplier area j, and writing

$$r_i = \gamma_o + \gamma_1 r_n + u_i \tag{3}$$

as an expression analogous to equation (2). It expresses the relationship between the excess returns of the firm and industry risk, where γ_1 represents the risk premium on the firm's share relative to the average in the industry. Combining equations (2) and (3) produces the linear regression equation

$$r_i = \beta_o + \beta_1 r_m + \beta_2 \varepsilon_n + u_i \tag{4}$$

where β_1 is systematic risk associated with the market average, and β_2 is the additional systematic risk that relates firm i's risk to the average for the sugar industry.

To interpret, the standard CAPM distinguishes between two classes of risk – "market risk," which derives from events that affect all securities in the stock market, and "unique risk," which derives from events that are specific to i. Equation (4) identifies a third type of risk, relevant for our purpose – "industry risk," which derives from events that were specific to the sugar industry, commonly affecting all sugar-company stocks, but having no effect on non-sugar-related securities.

The data consist of a panel of twenty-two firms over 1,146 weekly observations running from January 15, 1921, to December 26, 1942. The regressions are performed by dividing the data into three separate panels, one for each supplier area, controlling for random effects. The coefficients are estimated assuming that the β_k coefficients ($k = 1, 2$) are identical within a given supplier area but differ across supplier areas. We thus obtain three sets of common within-area coefficients, β_1 and β_2, from equation (4), one for each supplier area, j, which are interpreted as average systematic risk estimates for each supplier area. (The same is also true of δ_k in equation (5) below.) The search for breaks is performed in two steps.

Step 1. The first set of tests is conducted iteratively within "moving-windows," in which a window is defined as a time interval of data of fixed length, say, $t_o, t_1, \ldots, t_w$. For each possible window of length w, a test for change in the parameters is performed by estimating a variant of equation (4) that includes a dummy variable to incorporate the possibility of a break at the midpoint of the window, in the form

$$r_i = \beta_o + \delta_o D + \beta_1(1 + \delta_1 D)r_m + \beta_2(1 + \delta_2 D)\varepsilon_n + u_i \tag{5}$$

where D is a dummy variable which is assigned zeroes for all observations preceding the midpoint and ones thereafter. The coefficient, β_1 , is the pre-break systematic risk associated with the market, and $\beta_1 + \delta_1$ is the corresponding post-break risk measure.[43] Our primary interest, however, is in the corresponding breaks and relative changes in systematic risk relative to the average in the sugar industry, captured by β_2 and $\beta_2 + \delta_2$. The test for each break is specified as a test of the insignificance of D, which is equivalent to a joint exclusion test on the coefficients δ_i ($i = 0, 1, 2$).

The chi-square statistics for the Wald tests for joint exclusion of all terms involving D in equation (5) are shown in Figure 12.3 mapped against the breakdate (midpoint) of each the corresponding window. Two series are shown, one for a 156-week window and one for a 208-week window. The econometrics literature on structural change has shown that, if the breakdate is unknown, assuming structural change takes the form of a sharp or immediate break, then the conventional chi-square critical values are too low, and standard tests infer breaks too often. A literature has developed which proposes alternative tests that try

---

[43] The regressions are estimated assuming an AR1 error structure. All pass standard goodness-of-fit tests and coefficients reject the zero null hypothesis at conventional significance levels.

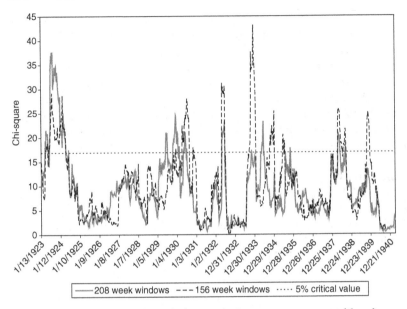

Figure 12.3 Moving-window exclusion tests on structural breaks.
Source: see text.

to eliminate this bias.[44] The tests follow suggestions in the literature to use the supremum of the chi-square.[45] Since the critical values for such tests are dependent on the breakdate, we use critical values for such test developed by Andrews. In step 1, the Andrews critical value is 16.92.[46] Test statistics below this level are unlikely candidates for breaks. Local peaks or intervals exceeding the critical value are candidates. However, as the overlay of chi-square series for 156-week and 208-week windows indicates, the tests lack robustness when the window length is varied.

The first interval indicated in step 1 is from April 7, 1923, to April 26, 1924, which coincides with the period of postwar adjustment during which there was uncertainty about the rate at which the European beet sugar industry would recover. The second is from June 8, 1929, to November 29, 1930, during which the revision in the sugar tariff under Hawley–Smoot was first debated, then decided and put into effect on

---

[44] See Andrews, "Tests"; Andrews and Ploberger, "Optimal Tests"; Christiano, "Searching"; Bai, "Estimating"; and Perron, "Great Crash."
[45] See Hansen, "New Econometrics of Structural Change."
[46] See Andrews, "Tests," and "Corrigendum." The critical values are dependent on the proportion of observations above or below the break. The tests in step one all have the same critical value because the breaks are in the same position in each window.

June 17, 1930. The October crash of the New York Stock Exchange also occurred in this interval.

After the 1930s, other intervals might be considered candidates as well, although the robustness in some cases appears suspect. We will not emphasize the post-1931 possible breaks in the current paper, but it is worth mentioning that each of these candidate intervals meets our prior expectations based on our knowledge of the history of sugar policy events during the period.[47] The interval April 23, 1932, to June 25, 1932 corresponds with a crisis in which Cuba used a brinkmanship strategy to force compliance of the international sugar cartel that operated from 1931 to 1935, which Cuba helped to organize. The period September 23, 1933, to February 3, 1934, coincides with two turbulent events for the sugar industry – the Cuban Revolution of 1933 and the political contest over the adoption of sugar quotas in the US as one of the New Deal agricultural stabilization policies, enacted finally in May 1934. It was highly contested because domestic sugar interests balked at the Roosevelt administration's insistence on compromising domestic protectionist objectives so as to use the policy to help restore political stability in Cuba as well.[48] The latter two intervals April 9, 1938, to October 1, 1938 and October 14, 1939, to December 16, 1939, appear to be associated with the conflict in Europe, which was expected to be disruptive to the world sugar industry. The latter interval coincides with a temporary suspension of the US sugar quota program in 1939 because the UK bought up all available sugar late 1939 to stockpile, making the quota restrictions temporarily unbinding.[49]

Step 2. The results from step 1 are sensitive to the act of dropping the first week of the series and picking up a new week at the end. Step 2 improves the robustness of the tests by fixing the window. Intervals that have statistically significant local peaks in step 1 undergo further investigation in the following way. The window of length w is kept fixed, and tests for breaks are performed iteratively by moving the hypothesized breakdate defined by D in equation (5) from t_o+26, t_o+27, . . ., t_w-26. A regression is estimated for each possible breakdate and joint exclusion tests are performed on all terms involving D, as in step 1. (The twenty-six-week buffer at either end is left to reduce distortions from too little variation in D.) Step 2 results are robust to the position and size of the window.

---

[47] In fact the authors have written papers about events occurring in two of these intervals, motivated independently, prior to doing this quantitative analysis. See Dye and Sicotte, "Brinkmanship" and Dye, "Cuba."

[48] Dye, "Smoot-Hawley"; Krueger, "Political Economy."

[49] Swerling, *International Control.*

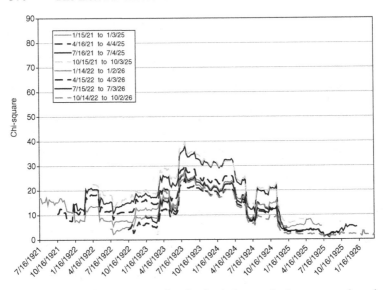

Figure 12.4A Successive fixed-window exclusion tests on iterative
structural breaks, January 1921–October 1926. (Each series represents
a 208-week window with iterative tests for breaks.)
Note: all series show have suprema that are statistically significant at the 0.05
level or better. *Source:* see text.

Figures 12.4A and 12.4B show tests for breaks over two intervals
identified as candidates in step 1 using 208-week windows. The intervals
examined are April 17, 1923, to April 26, 1924, and June 8, 1929, to
November 29, 1930. Concerned with robustness, we perform the same
test on series of windows all of 208 weeks positioned successively at
13-week intervals over wider intervals from July 1921 to March 1926 in
the first case, and July 1927 to June 1932 in the second. In each of
Figures 12.4A and 12.4B, the chi-square statistics for eight series of such
tests are shown. The combined results are unmistakably consistent. We
compare the test statistics against Andrews critical values of 5 percent
significance, which range between 18.56 and 25.47 depending on the
position of D in the window.

In Figure 12.4A, the series peak on August 4, 1923, and are consistently significant from July 7, 1923, to April 5, 1924. In Figure 12.4B,
they identify the weeks ending on November 2, 1930, and January 3,
1931. Tests using 156-week windows give similar results, showing
robustness to varying the length of the window. Neither interval is
precise enough to identify particular events, but the tests clearly single
out two intervals in which breaks were likely. The first is from late 1923,

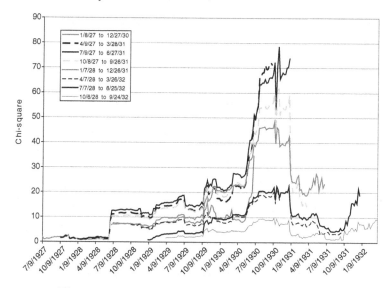

Figure 12.4B Successive fixed-window exclusion tests on iterative structural breaks, April 1927–December 1931. (Each series represents a 208-week window with iterative tests for breaks.)
Note: all series show have suprema that are statistically significant at the 0.05 level or better. *Source:* see text.

when forecasters began to receive information about a faster-than-anticipated recovery of the European beet sugar industry to recover. The second interval is from March 1930 to January 1931. This interval coincides with the period when the rates for the duty on sugar in the omnibus Hawley–Smoot tariff were settled. Debate in the Senate heated up in March 1930 and was resolved in June, just before the bill was passed. It went into effect on June 18, 1930. The evidence of a break in risk perceptions is strong, with differential effects on duty-paying and non-duty-paying suppliers. The tests suggest that one or more breaks occurred either during the period traversing the debate and passage of the tariff, or the aftermath, during which investors in sugar companies would observe how the industry dealt with the combined effects of the increased tariff and the crisis.[50]

---

[50] During the summer of 1930, representatives of the US beet sugar and Cuban sugar producers established a "gentlemen's agreement" to reduce production and exports to the US, respectively, in an effort to stabilize the falling price of sugar. A successful agreement would have been particularly beneficial for Cuban producers, but the self-

The tests performed may not identify all forms of structural change. Bruce Hansen observes that the tests in the literature to date focus only on the simple case of a sharp and immediate parameter shift when it is conceivable that structural change could take place gradually over a period of time.[51] That possibility seems particularly likely in our case. If news was revealed gradually, or if investors perceived an increase in the probability of an event based on piecemeal accumulation of relevant information, the resultant change in risk perception could "creep" gradually and may not be detectable as a sharp break. Furthermore, news that was misleading or misinterpreted could produce erratic behavior as investors received feedback and clarified mistakes. In principle, there is no reason to rule out small parameter shifts on a weekly, daily or even hourly basis. Studies of the stability of CAPM betas corroborate such prior expectations, as they show that betas are often not stable, particularly for individual securities or classes of securities, especially when deemed high-risk, such as sugar.[52]

It is informative to compare the results in Figures 12.3, 12.4A and 12.4B with Figures 12.5A and 12.5B. Here we estimate coefficients β_1 and β_2 in equation (4) for each window. Series for 208-week (bold) and 156-week windows are given. The figures give moving-window estimates of coefficients for β_1 and β_2 mapped against the midpoint of the moving window on the horizontal axis. This alternative use of the moving-windows technique permits identification of the cumulative effects of gradual or irregular parameter shifts.

Our primary interest is in Figure 12.5B, which gives estimates of the industry risk of each supplier area relative to the sugar industry average. It shows evidence of a change in the relative pricing structure of sugar companies in the three supplier areas represented. In particular, the moving-windows estimates of the betas indicate a convergence of risk assessments in the early part of the 1920s, but a divergence after 1926 or so, when Cuban sugar companies began to be perceived as riskier than the industry average. Puerto Rican companies, we see, came to be perceived as less risky than the industry average, and less risky that US domestic beet sugar after the Depression hit. The convergence followed by divergence in the moving-windows estimates of the β_2 in each supplier area are consistent with periods identified in Figures 12.3, 12.4A,

---

enforceability of the agreement was in serious doubt. By the end of the year, it had become clear that the agreement would not be honored by the domestic producers, Gutiérrez, *World Sugar Problem*, pp. 78–85; Álvarez Díaz, *Estudio*, p. 326.

[51] Hansen, "New Econometrics of Structural Change."

[52] Carpenter and Upton, "Trading Volume"; Ibbotson *et al.*, "Estimates."

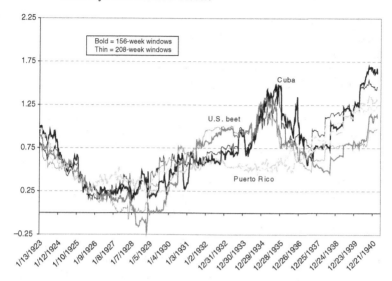

Figure 12.5A Market risk of sugar company stocks by supplier area.
Source: see text.

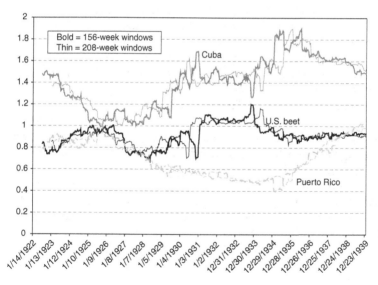

Figure 12.5B Industry risk of sugar company stocks by supplier area.
Source: see text.

and 12.4B over which breaks were more likely. One notes that the timing of fluctuations is sensitive to the window length, but the general pattern is robust.[53] We show below that the estimates before and after the period of structural change were statistically significant.

Neither the Depression story nor the capital penetration story is supported by the pattern of change of risk assessments revealed by the estimates of β_2. The pattern is, however, quite consistent with the proposition that the tariff was a significant factor in our risk measure. It also fits our prior expectations based on the history of the sugar market of those years. First, notice that investment in Cuban sugar companies was always risky, as expected, relative to US mainland and Puerto Rico. In 1922 and 1923, that gap was large. This is consistent with the story that J.W.F. Rowe tells about the uncertainty regarding how quickly European beet sugar would recover from the war, and the uncertainties in Cuba about the policies of recovery from the 1921 financial crisis. The decline in the Cuban β_2 coincides with the period when dealers in sugar obtained more information about the rate of the European recovery.[54] The perceived risk of Cuban securities, however, diverged upward during 1927 and 1928. Neither the moving-windows approach nor the fixed-windows approach allows us to identify the precise timing of structural change, yet the cumulative effect of structural change comparing the middle-to-late 1920s and the early-to-middle 1930s is distinctively visible. Table 12.5 gives additional information on two regressions on 208-week windows that bracket the period identified by the plateau in Figure 12.4B between November 30, 1929, and January 3, 1931. The results indicate the differences in the estimated β_2 coefficients, both between the supplier areas and within the same supplier area across time, are statistically significant.

Other patterns shown in Figure 12.5B are also consistent with our knowledge of the history of the three supplier areas. The perceived risk of Puerto Rican sugar companies falls below that of US mainland beet-sugar companies by 1929. The conclusion of the US Tariff Commission in an investigation of the relative costs of the sugar industry in 1933 offers a good explanation for why it happened. The average cost of producing sugar in Puerto Rico (without accounting for duties) fell between higher-cost mainland beet sugar and very low-cost Cuban producers. The Fordney–McCumber tariff of 1922, however, raised the sugar tariff sufficiently to make non-duty-paying Puerto Rican producers

---

[53] Shorter and longer windows were also tested without alteration of the patterns observed here.

[54] Rowe, *Studies*.

Table 12.5. *Pre- and post-break regressions*

208-week window	May 15, 1926 to May 3, 1930 est. coef. (std. error in parentheses)		Jan. 31, 1931 to Jan. 19, 1935 est. coef. (std. error in parentheses)	
Market betas				
Cuba	0.225 (0.082)	★★★	0.741 (0.148)	★★★
US beet	0.019 (0.117)		0.971 (0.182)	★★★
Puerto Rico	0.282 (0.142)	★★	0.545 (0.191)	★★★
Industry betas				
Cuba	1.171 (0.061)	★★★	1.495 (0.092)	★★★
US beet	0.787 (0.087)	★★★	1.036 (0.107)	★★★
Puerto Rico	0.693 (0.104)	★★★	0.500 (0.118)	★★★
Constants				
Cuba = 1	−0.009 (0.004)		−0.001 (0.020)	
Puerto Rico = 1	−0.002 (0.005)		0.001 (0.023)	
Constant	−0.001 (0.003)		0.003 (0.014)	
No. obs.	1809		2440	
Chi-square (9)	411.1		499.5	

Source: see text. ★★★ significance at 0.01, ★★ significance at 0.05.

more competitive with Cuban sugar production costs, after accounting for the tariff. The altered relative costs stimulated investment in modernization of Puerto Rican sugar production facilities and general expansion of the industry throughout the 1920s. When mainland beet sugar interests obtained the tariff increase under Hawley-Smoot, which went into effect on June 18, 1930, the main beneficiaries were the insular possessions, Puerto Rico and the Philippines. In a study conducted in 1933, the Tariff Commission found that the tariff could protect domestic beet sugar against imports from Cuba, but not against imports from the insular possessions. The primary effect of the increased tariff in 1930 was to give Puerto Rico and the Philippines a distinct cost advantage over Cuban sugar. The increased tariff gave less effective protection to its intended beneficiaries, the mainland sugar producers, than was intended. Beet sugar faced diminished competition from Cuba, but mounting competition from the duty-free insular possessions.[55]

VI.   The quality of Cuban sugar-company assets

The event study in the previous sections shows, above all, that the revision to the US sugar tariff in 1930, and its anticipation in 1929, was a major turning point in the expected profitability of Cuban sugar companies, relative to domestic beet and Puerto Rican companies, as reflected in the market performance of their securities. Investors clearly would not have placed their funds in Cuban sugar had they fully anticipated what transpired. So what was their reasoning when they formulated their investment strategy?

Cuban sugar production capacity had expanded significantly during World War I, but investment in new equipment was limited largely to what was necessary to meets demands for increases in the volume of production. Meanwhile, improvement in capital-embodied sugar milling technology during these years was dynamic and continuous. Because of this, the range of technical vintages of equipment that survived the war, in newer relative to older mills, especially in Cuba, was large. Consistent with the theory of vintage capital, high wartime prices made old vintages viable during the war; but as prices fell after the war, older vintages became obsolete.[56] The 75 percent increase in the US sugar tariff on Cuban sugar in 1922 was, naturally, a significant factor in the falling price margin as it stimulated the expansion of new mills in Puerto Rico, the Philippines, and US domestic producers. More recent vintages had a higher optimal scale of production; so when sugar companies with means invested aggressively after 1921 in new equipment to lower costs of production, they also greatly expanded the capacity of their sugar manufacturing operations.[57] This was especially true of companies in Cuba owned by large American banks or deep-pocketed, diversified corporations.

When Gordon Rentschler of National City Bank explained the perceived the decision to "go into the sugar business" and the need to "rehabilitate" their recently acquired sugar properties, it should be understood in the context of the competitive options they perceived.

---

[55] US Tariff Commission, *Sugar*, 1934. Hawaii, the other insular possession exporting sugar to the US, is not included in our statistical analysis because we lack the data. It is worthwhile to note that in comparison with Puerto Rico and Philippines, Hawaii had little room to expand production.
[56] Salter, *Productivity*.   [57] Dye, *Cuban Sugar*.

Although the banks had tried to work with beet sugar interests in 1921–1922 to reach a compromise on the tariff, in the end they felt misled by Smoot. After the 1922 tariff was passed, Robert F. Smith concludes that they decided to stop fighting the tariff and, instead, poured their efforts into lowering the costs of production.[58] In other work, we have observed that over the worsening market conditions of the 1920s, mills tended either to upgrade to more recent technologies or exit. Therefore, although the Cuban hacendados who did not have access to North American capital criticized the aggressive investment policies of the American corporations, the more technically sophisticated Cuban hacendados, who were able to raise capital in North America, adopted similar investment policies in order to survive.[59]

Contemporary experts in the sugar industry argue that it was the increase in the sugar tariff in 1930 that dealt the final blow to the Cuban sugar industry, including the most advanced American and Cuban properties. Rowe, for instance, said that few mills in Cuba broke even when the price of sugar was at 2.5 cents per lb., and none when it was two cents.[60] Before 1928, the evidence is overwhelming that investors in Cuban sugar were confident of the soundness of their properties. When the National City Bank found itself holding $66 million of non-performing loans in 1922, it could have auctioned them off, but instead, after careful study, "[it went] into the sugar business."[61] Despite the sugar tariff increase of 1922, investment in Cuban sugar was strong. Eighteen new mills were constructed, 112 out of 160 mills existing in 1922 expanded their production capacities by some amount by 1929, and twenty-four mills doubled their capacities. To finance the expansion, more than $150 million worth of sugar securities were floated in New York. Even as late as 1928, Standard and Poor advised the purchase of Eastern Cuba Sugar Corporation's 7.5 percent bonds, calling it "a good business man's investment."[62]

The underlying fundamentals, aside from the political economy of the tariff (we see with hindsight), were that Cuba had a distinct comparative advantage in the production of sugar. A League of Nations study of production costs in 1929 estimated that only Java could produce sugar at a comparable cost to Cuba.[63] With its climate and soils ideally suited

---

[58] Smith, *United States*, pp. 50–1.   [59] Dye, *Cuban Sugar, Cleansing*.
[60] Rowe, *Studies*, pp. 28ff.
[61] Gordon Rentscher testimony, US Senate Judiciary Committee, *Lobby Investigation*, p. 1326.
[62] Standard and Poor's *Industry Surveys*, November 9, 1928.
[63] Prinsen Geerligs, Licht, and Mikusch, *Sugar*; BB R.G. 2 Ser.10c Box 60, f. Java Sugars. Letter from Manuel Rionda to Col. John Simpson, March 13, 1929; Dye, *Cuban Sugar*.

to cane cultivation, Cuba's global cost superiority, alongside Java, was unquestioned. Geographically well-situated to supply one of the world's largest consumers of sugar, it was called "America's sugar bowl." In the US market, it was notably able to overcome a tariff of 1.7648 cent per lb. in the US market, with net-of-duty prices normally between two and four cents, even when its rivals all enjoyed duty-free status. The studies of the US Tariff Commission on the production and marketing costs of sugar in the major supplier areas in 1922 and 1933 indicated that Cuba produced sugar on average at between 40 and 70 percent of the cost of the other supplier areas.[64]

In Cuba, as noted, the technical diversity and range of production costs among the sugar mills was significant. Although many of the older mills were smaller and had higher production costs, the new investment was concentrated in the acquisition and expansion of mills to employ state-of-the-art technologies. The most outstanding examples were the giant sugar estates, such as American Sugar Refining Company's Jaronu, Cuban-American Sugar Company's Chaparra and Delicias, and General Sugar's (National City Bank) Vertientes. Among the largest and most efficient sugar factories in the world, these mills were thought to be viable investments, able to come out on top of almost any imaginable competitive scenario. Charles Mitchell, chairman of the National City Bank, stated that the bank viewed its sugar mills as "an excellent investment" so long as the market conditions were not unusually bad, "because these properties . . . are the lowest-cost producers, or among the lowest-cost producers, on the entire island of Cuba, and Cuba in itself is the lowest-cost producer in the world."[65]

The perception of the quality of their investments was reached after the increase in the US tariff in 1922. Mitchell, and others in control of these investments, were well aware of the possibility of further protectionism, but they did not countenance an increase in the tariff that would completely destroy the value of their properties. When the outcome of the 1930 tariff increase became foreseeable, the mood of investors in Cuban sugar became decidedly pessimistic. José Tarafa deemed the proposed House increase "fatal." National City Bank, in an official publication, stated that, as a result of the tariff increase, "the immediate blow would be fatal to perhaps most of the producers, for the credit of the industry and the stability of sugar properties would be affected at once." When the tariff was finally enacted, Cuban producers tried to use crop restriction

---

[64] Data are from US Tariff Commission, *Sugar*, 1926, p. 24, and 1934, p. 14.
[65] Charles Mitchell testimony, Senate Banking Committee, *Stock Exchange Practices*, p. 1796.

and international controls to salvage the situation. They cooperated with the US Sugar Program of the Roosevelt administration, even though it effectively froze the level of protection at its post-1930 level, expecting that any alternative would likely be worse for Cuban sugar.

American sugar producers in Cuba held onto their properties only to minimize their losses. In 1931, National City Bank wrote down its investment in Cuban sugar from $25 million to $1. National City's chairman explained, "When we saw the price of sugar drop to approximately half a cent a pound [in the wake of the tariff increase] it was perfectly obvious that, at that moment, that investment had no value. And it was written down accordingly on our books."[66] The chairman of the failed Santa Cecilia Sugar Co., Montgomery H. Lewis, wrote to the company's counsel, "The blow that killed Cuba was the tariff and Smoot was the man who struck it; while President Hoover looked on and permitted it without a gesture of dissent or word of regret."[67] The Cuba Cane Sugar Corp., its successor the Cuban Cane Products Corp., Punta Alegre Sugar Co., Cuban Dominican Sugar Co., Francisco Sugar Co., Manatí Sugar Co., Vertientes Sugar Co., and Camaguey Sugar Co., all defaulted on their debt and were reorganized. These companies owned some of the finest sugar mills in the world, their market capitalization was over $130 million and the face value of their outstanding bonds at time of default exceeded $80 million. Companies that escaped bankruptcy were unique. Cuban-American Sugar Co. and Guantánamo Sugar Co. were saved by having had uniquely conservative strategies of expansion during the 1920s, and American Sugar Refining and United Fruit's two sugar mills in Cuba were backed by the deep-pockets of the two most highly diversified companies with sugar concerns in Cuba.[68]

Overall, the destruction of the investment climate in Cuba was so complete that, by Henry Wallich's estimate, there was no net new foreign investment in Cuba from 1930 until World War II.[69] Rather than underpin international financial transactions, the policy of protection interfered with the ability to predict and appropriate returns, and it resulted in isolating Cuba from new foreign investment for several years.[70]

---

[66] Charles Mitchell testimony, Senate Banking Committee, *Stock Exchange Practices*, p. 1837; Cleveland and Huertas, *Citibank*, pp. 79, 105–10, 127, 165, 192.
[67] Letter from Montgomery H. Lewis to I. Howard Lehman, December 1, 1933, BB, R.G. 2 Ser. 10c Box 117 f. Tariff.
[68] Evidence of this is found in the papers of Manuel Rionda, BB, R.G. 2 Ser. 10c.
[69] Wallich, *Monetary Problems*, pp. 335–6.
[70] The collapse in the investment climate clearly contributed to the climate of revolution. See Dye and Sicotte, "U.S. Sugar Program," for an analysis of events in the 1950s up to the Revolution of 1959.

VII.   Conclusion

This chapter has re-examined the role of financial markets in the development, expansion, and crisis of the Cuban sugar industry in the interwar period. Most historians of Cuba view the large infusions of North American capital as causing "dislocations" that were at the root of the persistent crisis that began in the late 1920s. The economic stresses from the "penetration" of North American capital are thought to have established the underlying economic conditions for the Cuban Revolution in 1959. These arguments are informed by the evidence of the large share of foreign-owned properties, especially in sugar, and industrial concentration in the 1920s. However, these measures do not examine the outcomes of market power thought to result from foreign ownership and industrial concentration. We believe that if this argument centered on foreign capital penetration was truly at the core of Cuba's long-run economic problems, then it should be reflected in some way in the performance records of those companies.

To investigate North American companies' performance in Cuba in the interwar period, we look through the lens of share prices and risk-return profiles of publicly traded sugar companies in Cuba, compared with similar companies in the domestic sugar industry and insular possessions. The evidence from sugar-company market valuations and risk-return profiles does not support the conventional view. What we find instead, is unmistakable evidence that the protection of domestic sugar in the US was at the center of the story of Cuba's economic troubles in the interwar period. It began with an increase in the US sugar tariff after the First World War. That increase diverted some of the foreign capital flows away from Cuba toward the insular possessions. Nonetheless, even after 1922, the best sugar companies in Cuba continued to float securities in New York to finance a massive expansion, and the market performance of Cuban sugar-company securities remained satisfactory until 1927 or 1928.

The most critical turning point for the Cuban sugar industry, as well as foreign investments in Cuban sugar, was the anticipation and enactment of the 1930 increase in the sugar tariff in the US, as part of the Hawley-Smoot tariff act. Cuban and North American participants in the market agreed that it was the 1930 tariff that ruined them. National City Bank, forced to write down its $25 million investment in Cuban sugar, was shaken. Cleveland and Huertas argue that the bank's officers in the Havana branch exposed the bank unwisely to Cuban sugar.[71] But

---

[71] Cleveland and Huertas, *Citibank*.

even if they underestimated the risks of retaining and operating those properties, our findings incorporate estimates of relative costs by contemporaries, the US Tariff Commission, and our own research shows that price and cost risks had been well considered. It was the political risk that was underestimated – political risk that emanated from policy decisions of their own government.

Recent work in the political economy of empire argues that the hegemonic power tends to underpin international financial markets and enforce rogue nations to adopt sound investment practices. But we find a contrary result – hegemony, in this definitive case, led to the ruin and financial isolation of a country dependent on its markets for imports or finance. The US chose policies that protected rent-seeking domestic sugar producers even though it resulted in the almost complete destruction of otherwise sound foreign investments. We hear similar complaints about trade protection in recent rounds of WTO negotiations.

Yet in this case, domestic winners and losers also play a prominent part. If these acts of trade protection cannot be said to violate the property rights of citizens with assets abroad, they certainly did not enforce their security. Rather than underpinning financial development in Cuba, the trade protection of the hegemonic power distorted the market prices of sugar-company equity, relative to cost fundamentals, and caused foreign investors in Cuban sugar to flee one of the best spots in the world for making sugar. Contrary to the imperialist view, it was not the liberal policies of trade in sugar and finance that hurt Cuba's long-run economic prospects; rather, it was the US government's interference with them. If North American capitalists, powerful as they were, had been left unimpeded to reap the returns to their investments, Cuba's comparative advantage in sugar would have been maintained, and Cuba and the American consumer would have been better off.

Data Appendix

The dataset of sugar-company stock prices includes all common stocks of raw-sugar-processing companies operating in Cuba, Puerto Rico and the mainland US reported regularly in the *New York Times* and the *Wall Street Journal*. They include stocks traded on the New York Stock Exchange and the New York curb market, over-the-counter stocks and some regional exchanges.[72] This consists of eighteen companies operating

---

[72] Missing values were filled with records from the *Commercial and Financial Chronicle, Louisiana Planter*, and *Facts About Sugar*.

in Cuba, five beet sugar companies on the US mainland, and four companies in Puerto Rico. .

Companies that traded too infrequently or had very brief runs were eliminated. Also if one company came into existence as a result of a reorganization of another company in our dataset, both companies are referred to below as a single company, although, where necessary their stock issues were handled separately.

The supplier-area equity indices incorporate the prices of common stock of eleven companies that specialized in raw sugar production operating in Cuba, four in Puerto Rico, and five US beet sugar companies. In general, not all companies were listed throughout the period, so the numbers of firms represented in the indices vary accordingly.

The Cuban index consists of between seven and nine firms from 1921 to the beginning of 1930, representing between 40 and 54 percent of the total production capacity in the Cuban raw sugar industry. Coverage unfortunately becomes less representative in 1930. The numbers of firms in the sample drop from delisting often because of bankruptcy and reorganization. From 1930 to mid-1933, coverage includes four to five firms representing about 33 percent of the industry. From June 1933 to March 1934, only three firms are listed, representing as low as 12 percent of the industry. Afterward, the numbers rise to eight firms by early 1937, accounting for 40 percent of the Cuban industry (as measured by total grinding capacity).

The companies included are: Caracas (beg. January 7, 1928); Central Violeta (January 16, 1937–end); Cuba Cane Sugar Corp. (beg. March 1, 1930), succeeded by Cuban Cane Products Corp (March 8, 1930–June 4, 1932), succeeded by Cuban Atlantic Co. (March 6, 1937–end); Cuban American Sugar Co. (complete); Guantánamo (complete); the Rionda properties, Francisco Sugar Co. (January 2, 1937–end), and Manati Sugar Co. (complete); the New Niquero Sugar Co. (April 9, 1921–27 December 1930); Punta Alegre (beg. December 28, 1929); Vertientes-Camagüey Sugar Co. (March 27, 1937–end); Cuban-Dominican Sugar Co. (December 24, 1923–January 4, 1930), succeeded by West Indies Sugar Co. (March 30, 1935–end); Santa Cecilia (beg. November 22, 1924).

The index for US beet sugar producers consists of only three companies (for most years in our sample), but because of industrial concentration, these firms represent a large share of the US domestic beet sugar industry – up to 67 to 70 percent at the beginning and at the end of the period of study. Entry of smaller beet sugar companies in the 1920s causes the share represented in the sample to fall to 52 by 1929. From

July 1930, only two companies were listed, but together they represent 45 percent of beet-sugar production capacity. A third company reappeared in April 1933 and a fourth listed in October 1937, raising share of the industry represented in our sample to 67 percent of total beet slicing capacity. They are: the American Beet Sugar Co. (which acquires Amalgamated Sugar Co. and becomes American Crystal Sugar Co. in 1929) (complete), the Great Western Sugar Co. (complete), Holly Sugar Co. (beg. December 28, 1929), Michigan Sugar Co. (December 28, 1929–end), and Utah-Idaho Sugar Co. (October 2, 1937–end).

The four largest raw sugar companies in Puerto Rico were traded over the period, but no more than three at any given time, except from January 1928 through December 1929. For a brief period from January 2, 1935 to March 23, 1935, only one company, Central Aguirre Sugar Co., is listed. (We do not report an index for that interval.) They are: Central Aguirre Sugar Co. (complete); Fajardo Sugar Co. (beg. January 5, 1935; March 30, 1935–end); South Porto Rico Sugar Co. (beg. January 4, 1930); and United Porto Rican Sugar Co. (January 7, 1928–December 29, 1934), succeeded by Eastern Sugar Associates (March 30, 1935–end).

References

Alienes Urosa, Julián. 1950. *Características fundamentales de la economía cubana.* Havana: Banco Nacional de Cuba.

Álvarez Díaz, José, et al. 1963. *Un estudio sobre Cuba.* Coral Gables: University of Miami Press.

Andrews, Donald. 1993. "Tests for Parameter Instability in Structural Change with Unknown Change Point," *Econometrica* 61, no. 4: 821–56.

——— 2003. "Tests for Parameter Instability and Structural Change with Unknown Change Point: A Corrigendum," *Econometrica* 71, no. 1: 395–7.

Andrews, Donald, and Werner Ploberger. 1994. "Optimal Tests When a Nuisance Parameter is Present Only Under the Alternative," *Econometrica* 62, no. 6: 1383–414.

Ayala, César. 1999. *American Sugar Kingdom: The Plantation Economy of the Spanish Caribbean, 1898–1934.* Chapel Hill,: University of North Carolina Press.

Bai, Jushan, and Pierre Perron. 1998. "Estimating and Testing Linear Models with Multiple Structural Changes," *Econometrica* 66, no. 1: 47–78.

Ballinger, Roy. 1978. *A History of Sugar Marketing through 1974.* United States Department of Agriculture. Agricultural Economic Report No. 382. Washington, DC: GPO.

Benjamin, Jules. 1977. *The United States and Cuba: Hegemony and Dependent Development, 1880–1934.* Pittsburgh: University of Pittsburgh Press.

Brown, William, and Richard Burdekin. 2000. "Turning Points in the U.S. Civil War: A British Perspective," *Journal of Economic History* 60, no. 1: 216–31.

Carpenter, Michael, and David Upton. 1981. "Trading Volume and Beta Stability," *Journal of Portfolio Management* 7, no. 2: 60–4.

Christiano, Lawrence J. 1992. "Searching for a Break in GNP," *Journal of Business and Economics Statistics* 10, no. 3: 237–50.

Cleveland, Harold van B., and Thomas F. Huertas. 1985. *Citibank, 1812–1970.* Cambridge: Harvard University Press.

Collazo Pérez, Enrique. 1994. *Una pelea cubana contra los monopolios (Un estudio sobre el crac bancario de 1920).* Oviedo, Asturias, Spain: Vicerrectorado de Relaciones Institucionales, Universidad de Oviedo.

Cuba. Comisión Temporal de Liquidación Bancaria. Compendio de los trabajos realizados desde 17 de febrero de 1921, hasta 4 de agosto de 1924. Havana: Editorial Hermes, 1924.

Cuba. Ministerio de Hacienda. *Anuario azucarero de Cuba,* 1959.

Cuba. Secretaría de Agricultura, Comercio y Trabajo. *Memoria de la Zafra,* or *Memoria azucarera.* annual series. Name varies after 1930.

Cuba. Secretaria de Hacienda. *Industria Azucarera y sus Derivadas.*

Dalton, John E. 1937. *Sugar: A Case Study of Government Control.* New York: The MacMillan Company.

Dickens, Paul. 1938. *American Direct Investments in Foreign Countries – 1936.* United States Department of Commerce Economic Series No. 1. Washington, DC: GPO.

Dye, Alan. 1998. *Cuban Sugar in the Age of Mass Production: Technology and the Economics of the Sugar Central, 1899–1929.* Stanford: Stanford University Press.

———. 2005. "Cuba and the Origins of the U.S. Sugar Program," *Revista de Indias* 65.233: 193–218.

———. "The Smoot-Hawley Tariff and Crisis in Cuba." Working paper, 2005.

———. "Cleansing under the Quota: The Defense and Survival of Sugar Mills in 1930s Cuba." Working paper, 2006.

Dye, Alan, and Richard Sicotte. 2004. "The U.S. Sugar Program and the Cuban Revolution," *Journal of Economic History* 64, no. 3: 673–704.

———. "The Institutional Determinants of the Hawley–Smoot Tariff." Working paper, 2005.

———. 2006. "How Brinkmanship Saved Chadbourne: Credibility and the International Sugar Agreement of 1931," *Explorations in Economic History* 43, no. 2: 223–56.

Farr's. *Manual of Sugar Companies.* New York: Farr & Co., 1922–1942.

Ferguson, Niall. 2003. *Empire: the Rise and Demise of the British World Order and Lessons for Global Power.* New York: Basic Books.

García Álvarez, Alejandro. 1990. *La gran burguesía comercial en Cuba, 1899–1920.* Havana: Editorial de Ciencias Sociales.

Goldstein, Judith. 1993. *Ideas, Interests and American Trade Policy.* Ithaca: Cornell University Press.

Guerra y Sánchez, Ramiro. 1944. *Azúcar y población en las Antillas*. Havana: Cultural.

Gutiérrez, Viriato. 1935. *The World Sugar Problem 1926–1935*. London: Norman Rodger.

Hansen, Bruce. 2001. "The New Econometrics of Structural Change: Dating Breaks in U.S. Labor Productivity," *Journal of Economic Perspectives* 15, no. 4: 117–28.

Ibarra, Jorge. 1998. *Prologue to Revolution: Cuba, 1898–1958*. Boulder: Lynne Rienner.

Ibbotson, Roger, Paul Kaplan and James Peterson. 1997. "Estimates of Small-Stock Betas Are Much Too Low," *Journal of Portfolio Management* 23, no. 4: 104–11.

India, Tariff Board. *Report of the Tariff Board on the Sugar Industry*. Delhi: Manager of Publications, 1931, 1933, 1938.

Jenks, Leland. 1928. *Our Cuban Colony: A Study in Sugar*. New York: Vanguard Press.

Jiménez, Guillermo. 2001. *Las empresas de Cuba, 1958*. Miami: Universal.

Kindleberger, Charles. 1973. *The World in Depression, 1929–1939*. Berkeley: University of California Press.

Krueger, Anne O. 1996. "The Political Economy of Controls: American Sugar." In *Empirical Studies in Institutional Change*, edited by Lee Alston, Thráinn Eggertsson, and Douglass North. Cambridge: Cambridge University Press: 169–218.

Lewis, Arthur. 1950. *Economic Survey, 1919–1939*. Philadelphia: Blakiston.

Lewis, Cleona. 1938. *America's Stake in International Investments*. Washington: The Brookings Institution.

MacKinlay, A. Craig. 1997. "Event Studies in Economics and Finance," *Journal of Economic Literature* 35, no. 1: 13–39.

McAvoy, Muriel. 2003. *Sugar Baron: Manuel Rionda and the Fortunes of Pre-Castro Cuba*. Gainesville: University Press of Florida.

McDowall, Duncan. 1993. *Quick to the Frontier: Canada's Royal Bank*. Toronto: McClelland & Stewart.

Mitchener, Kris and Marc Weidenmier. 2005. "Empire, Public Goods and the Roosevelt Corollary," *Journal of Economic History* 65, no. 3: 658–92.

Moreno Fraginals, Manuel. 1978. *El ingenio: Complejo económico social cubano del azúcar*. Havana: Editorial de Ciencias Sociales.

Oosterlink, Kim. 2003. "The Bond Market and the Legitimacy of Vichy France," *Explorations in Economic History* 40, no. 3: 326–44.

Pérez, Louis A., Jr. 1986. *Cuba under the Platt Amendment, 1902–1934*. Pittsburgh: University of Pittsburgh Press.

1990. *Cuba and the United States: Ties of Singular Intimacy*. Athens: University of Georgia Press.

Pérez-Cisneros, Enrique. 1957. *Cuba y el mercado azucarero mundial*. Havana: Viñeta de Mariano.

Perron, Pierre. 1989. "The Great Crash, the Oil Price Shock, and the Unit-Root Hypothesis," *Econometrica* 57.6: 1361–401.

Pino-Santos, Oscar. 1973. *El asalto a Cuba por la oligarquía financiera yanqui.* Havana: Casa de las Américas.

Prinsen Geerligs, H.C., F.O. Licht, and Gustav Mikusch. *Sugar: Memoranda Prepared for the Economic Committee.* Geneva: Series of League of Nations Publications, No. C.148.M.57; Economic and Financial, 1929, II.20.

Rippy, J. Fred. February 1948. "British Investments in Latin America, 1939," *Journal of Political Economy* 56, no.1: 63–8.

Rowe, John Wilkinson Foster. September 1930. *Studies in the Artificial Control of Raw Material Supplies: No. 1. Sugar.* London: Royal Economic Society.

Salter, W.E.G. 1966. *Productivity and Technical Change.* Cambridge: Cambridge University Press.

Santamaría García, Antonio. 2001. *Sin Azúcar, no hay país: La industria azucarera y la economía cubana, 1919–1939.* Seville, Spain: Universidad de Sevilla.

Smith, Robert F. 1960. *The United States and Cuba: Business and Diplomacy, 1917–1960.* New York: Bookman Associates.

Speck, Mary. 2005. "Prosperity, Progress and Wealth: Cuban Enterprise during the Early Republic, 1902–27," *Cuban Studies* 36: 50–86.

Stone, Irving. 1999. *The Global Export of Capital from Great Britain, 1865–1914.* New York: St. Martin's Press.

Sussman, Nathan, and Yishay Yafeh. 2000. "Institutions, Reforms and Country Risk: Lessons from Japanese Government Debt in the Meiji Era," *Journal of Economic History* 60, no. 2: 442–67.

Swerling, Boris C. 1941. *The International Control of Sugar: 1918–41.* Stanford: Stanford University Press.

Taussig, F.W. 1901. *The Tariff History of the United States.* New York: Putnam.

United States. 1956. Department of Commerce. *Investment in Cuba.* Washington, DC: GPO.

United States. 1962. House of Representatives. Committee on Agriculture. *History and Operations of the U.S. Sugar Program.* Washington, DC: GPO.

United States. Senate. Committee on Banking and Currency. *Stock Exchange Practices. Hearings, Part 6.* Washington, DC: GPO, 1933.

United States. Senate. Committee on the Judiciary. *Lobby Investigation. Hearings.* Washington, DC: GPO, 1930.

United States. Tariff Commission. *Sugar.* Washington, DC: GPO, 1926, 1934.

Wallich, Henry. 1950. *Monetary Problems of an Export Economy: The Cuban Experience 1914–1947.* Cambridge: Harvard University Press.

Weidenmier, Marc. 2002. "Turning Points in the Civil War: Views from the Grayback Market," *Southern Economic Journal* 68, no. 4: 875–90.

Willard, Kristen L., Timothy Guinnane, and Harvey Rosen. 1986. "Turning Points in the Civil War: Views from the Greenback Market," *American Economic Review* 86, no. 4: 1001–18.

Willett and Gray. *Weekly Statistical Sugar Trade Journal.*

Winkler, Max. 1928. *Investments of United States Capital in Latin America.* Boston: World Peace Foundation.

Zanetti Lecuona, Oscar. 1989. *Los cautivos de la reciprocidad*. Havana: Ediciones ENPES.

2004. *Las manos en el dulce: Estado e intereses en la regulación de la industria azucarera cubana, 1926–1937*. Havana: Editorial de Ciencias Sociales.

Zanetti Lecuona, Oscar, and Alejandro García. 1998. *Sugar and Railroads: A Cuban History, 1837–1959*. Chapel Hill: The University of North Carolina Press.

13 Central bank reaction functions during the inter-war gold standard: A view from the periphery

*Kirsten Wandschneider**

The years between the two World Wars were ones of economic turmoil and crisis. The inter-war gold standard, created as an attempt to rebuild the pre-1914 gold standard, lasted a mere six years from 1925–1931 and failed to generate economic growth and prosperity. Many scholars have attempted to explain the fragility of the inter-war gold standard, focusing on different aspects of the regime, such as structural problems within the system, gold imbalances, the lack of an international hegemonic power, persistent deflation, and the changing social and political structures in the inter-war years.[1] One particular area of focus with regard to the operation of the system has also been the study of central banks within the system. Did they play by the rules of the game, supporting the international monetary regime with interest rate adjustment, or were their policies guided by domestic constraints and objectives?

This chapter sheds new light on the central bank reaction functions of four countries on the periphery, namely Austria, Czechoslovakia, Hungary, and Poland, by exploiting a natural experiment that was run throughout the inter-war years in eastern Central Europe. The four selected countries constitute an interesting mix of different institutions, as shown in Table 13.1. In Austria and Hungary the central banks were reconstituted under the auspices of the League of Nations to import credibility and establish stability following the hyperinflations of the early 1920s. Czechoslovakia and Poland in contrast, created monetary authorities without any external control. The four countries also differed

---

* This chapter is based on chapter six of my dissertation, completed at the University of Illinois in 2003. I thank Larry Neal, Lee Alston, Bill Bernhard, and Charles Kahn for comments on this work and guidance throughout the dissertation process. I also thank Jeremy Atack for extensive comments on this chapter.

[1] References include but are not limited to Feinstein *et al.*, *European Economy*; Triffin, "National Central Banking"; Kindleberger, *World in Depression*; Bernanke and James, "Gold Standard"; Eichengreen, *Golden Fetters* and Simmons, *Who Adjusts*.

Table 13.1. *Political and monetary institutions*

		Central bank independence	
		Yes	No
Democracy	Yes	Austria	Czechoslovakia
	No	Hungary	Poland

Source: author's classification.

with respect to their political regimes; Austria and Czechoslovakia were newly emerging democracies, whereas Poland and Hungary were ruled by authoritarian leaders. The variation in central bank design and political regimes makes these four countries particularly suitable for a comparison of central bank responses during the inter-war years.

Central bank responses were crucial for the stability of the inter-war regime. In the recent literature on central banking, central bank independence from domestic political pressure and the adoption of fixed exchange rates are often viewed as substitutes, as both present a solution to the problem of monetary credibility.[2] Either can avoid the inflationary bias that results from the time-inconsistency problem in discretionary monetary policy. They are permanent commitments to low inflation policies and thereby stabilize expectations. But central bank independence and fixed exchange rates can also be seen as complements which are chosen jointly and reinforce each other.[3] This complementary relationship stems from the observation that the conditions which lead countries to adopt fixed exchange rates are also those that bring about the design of independent central banks. The gold exchange standard of the inter-war years was a very unstable and fragile monetary arrangement of no high reputation. Therefore central bank independence and the commitment to the international monetary system at the time are better understood as complements. In fact, Simmons finds that higher degrees of central bank independence led to longer adherence to the gold standard.[4] Moreover, Smith argued that the rising monetary problems of the inter-war years enhanced the need for a central monetary authority, and that international monetary coordination would be facilitated through the role of central banks.[5] The establishment of an

---

[2] Broz, "Political System Transparency."   [3] Bernhard *et al.*, "Political Economy."
[4] See Simmons, *Who Adjusts?* The outlier for the set of countries investigated here is Poland, a country with a very politically controlled central bank that remains on gold until 1936.
[5] Smith, *Rationale.*

independent central bank was furthermore seen as a prerequisite for achieving financial stability and gaining access to the international capital markets. An independent central bank could send an important signal for commitment to sound financial practices. It was therefore a valuable tool to attract funds from outside investors. Nevertheless, central bank independence apparently did not guarantee the smooth working of the gold standard.[6]

Few studies have analyzed the central bank policies of the periphery countries during the inter-war years. Did the countries of the periphery follow the gold standard adjustment mechanism? Were domestic concerns important determinants of interest rate adjustments, or did periphery countries simply follow the policies of the larger center countries? Shedding more light on the mechanism of interest rate adjustments during the inter-war years can improve understanding of the fragility that characterized the gold exchange standard. To ensure the working of the gold exchange standard, countries needed to adjust interest rates to counter gold flows. But the goal of external equilibrium often conflicted with domestic policy goals and adjustments. If growing concern about domestic economic variables motivated the interest rate adjustments, this would be an important source of instability for the exchange rate mechanism.[7] Studying the inter-war periphery can also help us to understand the difficult exchange rate choices that countries today have to make between fixed and flexible rates. Often these choices are influenced by the nature of the political regime in the country.

The chapter begins by summarizing the key elements of the inter-war gold exchange standard and outlining the economic conditions in Central and Eastern Europe during the inter-war years. The following sections then focus on the bank rate policies of the four periphery countries. Following Eichengreen *et al.*, and Wheelock, I estimate the reaction functions in those four countries for the gold standard years 1925–1931, controlling for gold flows, domestic and international events, as well as bank rate adjustments in Britain and Germany.[8]

---

[6] For the purpose of this study, central bank independence refers to a combination of independent appointments and policy control, as outlined in Simmons, *Who Adjusts*. On a scale of 1–8, with 8 being most independent, the four countries studies here rank as follows: Austria, 4, Hungary, 3, Poland, 3, and Czechoslovakia, 2. In addition, independence from the domestic governments is strengthened though the involvement of the League of Nations in the case of Austria and Hungary.

[7] The notion of cooperative versus non-cooperative behavior during the gold exchange standard years goes back to Nurkse, *International Currency Experience* who compares gold flows with rate adjustments for a number of countries during the inter-war period. Nurkse concludes that the rules of the gold standard were frequently violated.

[8] Compare Eichengreen *et al.*, "Bank Rate Policy" and Wheelock, *Strategy*.

The results suggest a high correlation in bank rate adjustments among the four countries, as well as to the reference countries, Britain and Germany. Only for the cases of Austria and Hungary do I find some evidence that bank rate adjustments actually followed gold and reserve flows.

Furthermore, there is evidence that in Austria especially, the bank rate responded to domestic political events, a fact that highlights the struggles of the emerging democracies at the time. Understanding the mechanism of interest rate adjustments in the periphery during the inter-war years can improve the understanding of the fragility that characterized the gold exchange standard. This study furthermore provides insight into the relationship between monetary and political institutions under fixed exchange rates, and the problems related to external stabilization policy and institutional control.

I.   The inter-war gold exchange standard – a brief history

By the end of World War I, most countries had abandoned their peg to gold. Exchange rates were freely floating and extremely volatile. In the search for a new monetary order, governments and central bankers demanded an international currency system with stable exchange rates. There was a longing for the pre-war order of the classical gold standard that had promoted trade, financial integration, and prosperity.[9] But officials hesitated to reinstate the pre-war system out of fear that it would induce a global shortage of gold. Wartime inflation had shifted price levels so that, for many countries, a return to gold at pre-war parity would have implied an overvaluation of their currencies. Thus, the pressure to return to pre-war parities would induce deflation and delay reconstruction and the resumption of economic growth. A return at new exchange rates, in contrast, might have worsened a worldwide gold scramble and would have raised questions about the credibility of the new regime.[10]

The establishment of an inter-war monetary system was further complicated by the problem of post-war reparation payments.[11] Although the peace treaties held Germany and its allies responsible for

---

[9] An explicit discussion of how the classical gold standard promoted trade and financial integration can be found, for example, in O'Rourke and Williamson, *Globalization and History*.

[10] For an explicit discussion of the credibility of the inter-war gold exchange standard, refer to Bordo *et al.*, "Adherence."

[11] See Kindelberger, *World in Depression*.

the war and burdened them with reparation payments, the actual amount of the payments was negotiated country-by-country throughout the early 1920s. The insecurity about the size of outstanding payments delayed the reconstruction also in Austria and Hungary. The reparation demands by the 'winners' and the official judgment of what the 'losers' would be able to pay differed widely. For Germany, the large reparation demands, as well as the French commitment to extract them by force, led to a devastating budget situation and accelerated the hyperinflation.[12] Moreover, the war-torn economies of Europe were in dire need of international support to finance reconstruction, but the war had left the major powers entangled in a web of accumulated debts, delaying the suspension of international funds.

The emergence of the inter-war gold standard was linked to the adoption of gold by Britain in May 1925. By then, Britain felt pressured to return to gold as other countries were contemplating the stabilization of their currencies. Without Britain on gold, the adoption of gold as monetary anchor by other countries would have implied a further shift of gold reserves and deposits away from London and to New York. To halt the gold outflow, Britain returned to gold at the pre-war parity, a choice that was regarded as a key signal of stability and credibility for the new system. In fact, already by the end of the year 1925, a number of countries had adopted gold as their monetary anchor again. Regarding the countries at the focus of this study, Austria returned to gold in 1924, Hungary in 1925, and Czechoslovakia and Poland in 1926 and 1927, respectively.

The inter-war gold standard operated as an exchange standard system centered around key currencies. Adopting the gold standard brought stability to the international financial markets and introduced a brief period of economic growth. Nevertheless, the system could not repeat the classical gold standard success, and problems of operation soon became apparent. Difficulties with regard to the leadership and the balance of gold across member countries restricted the ability of the monetary system to respond effectively to worldwide economic problems. The system reached its height in the years 1927–1931 and fell apart in the 1930s.

II.   Bank rate policies

This chapter documents the policies of the national banks of Austria, Czechoslovakia, Hungary, and Poland during the gold exchange

---

[12] Holtfrerich, *German Inflation.*

standard years, 1925–1931.[13] The bank rate adjustments of these four countries are compared with those of Britain and Germany, and are related to domestic country-specific indicators.

For countries on the periphery, the choice of policies was whether to follow the gold standard adjustment process or give preference to domestic concerns. They worried about how to set rates with respect to the neighboring economies, or to the larger 'center' countries, and considered the need to attract foreign capital. For example, a report on the economic conditions in Austria to the League of Nations by W.T. Layton and Charles Rist recommended that "The Austrian bank rate had to stay above the rate of the countries that were granting the credit and maybe even above the German rate for Austria to get the international credits that the country needs."[14]

We can derive distinct hypotheses about how we expect the four countries to behave with respect to their bank rate adjustments.

Hypothesis I: countries that stabilized their economies with the support of the League of Nations and which were subject to League of Nations oversight (Austria and Hungary), should have been most concerned with keeping their policies aligned with the international monetary regime.

Hypothesis II: democratic countries (Austria and Czechoslovakia) should have been most concerned about gaining credibility and should therefore align their policies with the rules of the game, while autocratic regimes that relied on relatively little international support (Poland) should be least concerned with aligning their bank rates with the international monetary regime.

Hypothesis III: democratic countries (Austria and Czechoslovakia) which faced a re-election constraint should have been more responsive to domestic economic conditions than autocracies.

Based on these hypotheses we therefore expect Austria, being a democracy and under the auspices of the League of Nations, to align her bank rates with the international regime, while Czechoslovakia and Hungary should be a little less concerned with international alignment than Austria, since they are only subject to one rather than two constraints. Poland, in contrast, as an autocracy not facing external control, should be the most domestically oriented and least concerned with international alignment. To investigate these hypotheses, I test the determinants for bank rate adjustments in Austria, Czechoslovakia,

---

[13] The end of the gold exchange standard often defined as the devaluation of the pound sterling in September 1931. Austria, Hungary, and Czechoslovakia imposed exchange controls in 1931 and therefore effectively left the gold exchange standard, Poland remained on gold until 1936.

[14] League of Nations, Reports of the Commissioner 20, Vienna 1925.

Hungary, and Poland for the years 1925–1931, and with respect to the British and German bank rates.

Studies of bank rate policies during the inter-war years exist but mostly focus on the countries at the center of the international monetary regime. Eichengreen *et al.*, for example, estimate the bank rate policy of the Bank of England under the inter-war gold standard using a dynamic probit approach.[15] The central question in their paper is whether the interest rate policies of the Bank of England followed the gold standard adjustment mechanism. The authors stipulate that a better understanding of the bank rate policy of the Bank of England at the time can help explain the ultimate failure of the inter-war gold exchange standard. Indeed they find that the Bank of England only partially followed the "rules of the game," identifying an asymmetry in the bank's reaction to reserve gains and losses. The Bank apparently raised the rate in response to losses in reserves but failed to lower the rate following reserve gains. Moreover, they observed increased sensitivity to domestic economic conditions. The Bank furthermore reacted to changes in the cost of domestic credit. Both policies constitute violations of the strict "rules of the game" and show that the Bank of England was not solely committed to the stability of the exchange rate regime. The authors conclude that the Bank of England policies might have contributed to the instability of the inter-war gold exchange standard. Davutyan and Parke repeat the same study for the pre-World War I gold standard, again focusing on the Bank of England, and identify a similar asymmetry in the bank rate adjustments.[16] Consequently, they cannot explain the instabilities of the inter-war period. By 1930, however, these policies had become inappropriate in the face of the crisis, and the Fed failed to adjust promptly enough to avert further depression.

Looking at the set of fifteen countries, Simmons finds evidence of violations of the rules of the game during the inter-war gold standard, and she shows that countries with independent central banks placed more emphasis on domestic price stability than on the external adjustment process.[17] Therefore the rise of central bank independence led to deflation and might have contributed to the instabilities of the system. When comparing Simmons' central bank independence classifications with the actual inflation performance of the countries, though, the hypothesis can be rejected. In contrast to today, countries with independent

---

[15] Compare Eichengreen *et al.*, "Bank Rate Policy." The dynamic probit model outperforms OLS estimates by taking into account the discrete nature of the dependent variable as well as time series characteristics of the data.

[16] See Davutyan and Parke, "Operations."   [17] Simmons, "Rulers."

central banks did not display lower inflation rates during the inter-war years.

III.   Circumstances in Central and Eastern Europe after the war

What makes the study of central bank behavior for these four countries interesting is that the period between World War I and World War II was an especially turbulent time for Eastern and Central Europe. The first war and the peace treaties that followed it fundamentally changed the economic and political structure of the area. The collapse of three major empires, the German, the Russian, and the Habsburg Empire, brought about the creation of new states and the reorganization of existing ones. Compared with pre-war Europe, overall twelve new European states had been established by 1919. From the Habsburg Empire, Austria, Hungary, and Czechoslovakia emerged as independent successor states, and other parts of the secession areas merged into Italy, Romania, Yugoslavia, and the newly resurrected Poland.

Table 13.2 shows the consequences of the geographic shifts for the population of the successor states. The new republic of Austria, pro-claimed on November 12, 1918, had just 23 percent of its pre-war population within 28 percent of its pre-war geographic area.[18] Similarly, Hungary was reduced to 42 percent of the former population and 33 percent of the former territory. Czechoslovakia came into existence as an independent state; its geographic area was significantly larger than that of Austria or Hungary, but more sparsely populated. Poland, with an area of close to 400,000 square kilometers and a population of twenty-seven million, was the largest of the four states to be analyzed here.

With the political separation, the economic unity of the former empire was also destroyed. Prior to the war, the Habsburg Empire had been a well-functioning customs and currency union with regional concen-trations of agriculture and industry. Each region had specialized in the products in which it had a comparative advantage. Hungary had pri-marily focused on agricultural production, and the majority of the industries of the former empire lay in what was now Czechoslovakia. Vienna had been the financial center of the dual monarchy and was left with a large banking sector and a relatively developed financial market separated from its supporting industries.[19]

Prior to break-up, the Habsburg Empire had depended upon recip-rocal trade. For example, close to three quarters of Austrian and Czech

---

[18] Schubert, "Emergence."   [19] Feinstein *et al.*, *European Economy*.

Table 13.2. *Area and population before and after World War I*

Country	Area in sq. km		Population in 100,000	
	1914	1921	1914	1921
Austria-Hungary	676,443		51,390	
Austria		85,533		6,536
Hungary	325,000	92,607	20,900	7,800
Czechoslovakia		140,394		13,613
Bulgaria	111,800	103,146	4,753	4,910
Romania	137,903	304,244	7,516	17,594
Yugoslavia (Serbia)	87,300	248,987	4,548	12,017
Poland		388,279		27,184

Note: Austria-Hungary includes Bosnia and Herzegovina. Hungary refers to
the Hungarian Kingdom.
Source: Berend and Ranki, *Economic Problems*, p. 111.

manufactured textiles had been marketed in the agricultural regions of
the monarchy. In turn, 80 percent of Hungarian agricultural exports had
been sold in Austrian and Czech areas.[20] With the establishment of the
new borders, agricultural capacity, industrial production, and financial
service provision were now unevenly distributed. The new states suffered from the lack of imports and the loss of export markets. Economic
cooperation of the successor states was mostly hindered by domestic
political forces that were eager to establish economic independence and
self-sufficiency. The financial troubles of the successor states were
worsened by the disappearance of the common currency.

For Austria, credits of US $48 million furnished by France, the UK,
Italy, and the US in 1919 only provided short-term relief and failed to
improve the economic situation in the long-run. In Austria and Hungary
the deterioration of the economic situation, coupled with war-torn
domestic finances and rising budget deficits, led to hyperinflation.[21]
Hyperinflation also emerged in Poland in 1923, following the Polish–
Soviet war. In addition, Poland struggled with the unification of different currencies and financial systems. Czechoslovakia was the only
country of the four that managed to avoid post-war hyperinflation.
Immediately after the war, the Czech government stabilized the
domestic currency largely without foreign support. Because wages initially remained below pre-war levels and prices rose rapidly, the basis for
economic growth and recovery was laid, and pre-war levels of industrial

---

[20] Berend and Ranki, *Hungarian Economy.*
[21] Berend and Ranki, "Economic Problems."

production were already reached in 1924. Czechoslovakia was also the most industrialized country of the successor states and, according to the League of Nations, it ranked among the ten largest manufacturers of industrial goods and seven largest suppliers of arms in Europe.[22]

IV.   Financial reconstruction

By March 1921, it was widely recognized that Austria could not continue living on credits and charity, and that the relief payments had to be replaced by financial reconstruction. The lender countries, which, due to their reparation demands had a primary interest in the reconstruction of the Austrian economy, did not feel in the position to solve the problem on their own. They therefore referred it to the League of Nations in August 1922. The League's financial reconstruction of Austria constituted the first of the reconstruction programs administered by the League. After the initial success of the program in stabilizing the hyperinflation in Austria, Hungary followed suit in 1923. Both served as examples for the German reconstruction program that was administered by the US starting in 1924.

The reconstruction policies recommended by the League of Nations followed the general principles outlined at the Brussels financial conference in 1920. First and foremost, the League stressed the importance of a fiscal budget equilibrium as a precondition for financial stability. The equilibrium should be reached through a whole set of fiscal and administrative measures, such as the increase of taxes and revenues, the elimination of state subsidies, the adjustment of the size of the bureaucracy, and the gradual reduction of expenditures. To maintain the soundness of the state finances, the programs of the League also provided for the establishment of an independent central bank, as well as accounting and auditing offices. The central bank was to be constituted with private capital; it would hold the monopoly of note issue, control the money transactions of all public sector entities, and ensure the proper cover and reserve backing for note issue.[23] The preparation of a reconstruction plan by the League always followed the same five-step process. First, private conversations between the government of the aid seeking country and League officials would take place. Then, the respective country had to address a formal request for assistance to the Council of the League to be authorized by it. The third and fourth stages consisted of an enquiry in the appealing country, and a period

---

[22] See Teichova, *Czechoslovak Economy*, p. 20.
[23] Santaella, *Stabilization Programs*.

of discussion and negotiation between the Financial Committee of the League and government officials of this country. The preparation for the reconstruction plan ended with a final report of the Financial Committee, and the preparation of the formal documents to be approved and ratified by the League Council and the authorities of the recipient country.

Three direct instances of control guaranteed the enforcement of any League reconstruction scheme. The League appointed a Commissioner to the recipient country who reported regularly to the League on the progress of the reconstruction, and controlled the external loan and the securities revenues account. The external loan account was an account extended to the debtor government by foreign creditors, while the security revenue account contained any proceeds from specific revenues such as customs revenues, income from state monopolies, etc. that were set as security for the external loan. In addition to the Commissioner, the League also appointed an external advisor to the central banks of the debtor countries and established a board of trustees of the external loan who represented the interests of the foreign bond-holders.

V.   The Austrian reconstruction

In the case of Austria, the first protocol for the reconstruction was signed by the delegates and the Austrian government on October 4, 1922. The scheme was very careful not to infringe upon the political integrity and economic independence of Austria, and provided for a reform schedule that was to ensure the balance of the budget by the end of 1924.

The reconstruction scheme laid out the issue of long-term bonds in various currencies and denominations by the Austrian government in order to meet the excess of expenditure over revenue during the period of reconstruction. The proceeds of these loans were to total the equivalent of 650 million gold crowns, not including the expenses of the issue of the loan. To cover the period of negotiations until the long-term loan was issued the decision was made to precede the long-term reconstruction loan by a short-term loan of a smaller size, £3,500,000, backed by the UK, France, Czechoslovakia, Italy, and Belgium. This short-term loan was placed at the end of February 1923 in the form of one-year Austrian Treasury bonds.

Besides balancing the budget and providing liquid assets, an additional area of concern for the League was the establishment of an independent bank of note issue. Stopping money inflation was the fundamental condition of the economic reconstruction of Austria, and it was understood that inflation could only be brought to an end when monetary control could be separated from the government.

The reconstruction of Austria can largely be divided into four phases, as outlined in the official documents of the League: the period from October 4 to December 14, 1922 can be seen as the preparation phase in which negotiations were finalized and the scheme was put into execution. The second phase then went from the beginning of the control through the Commissioner General, Dr. Zimmerman, on December 14, 1922 until the successful issue of the long-term reconstruction loan in August 1923. This period was characterized by a quick financial recovery, leading up to a boom and rising stock exchange speculation.[24]

During all of 1924 and through the spring of 1925, Austria felt the effects of the trade depression following the stock market collapse in the fourth quarter of 1923. In an expert report by the Economic Committee in 1925, the League issued recommendations for the long term economic recovery of the area: Austria should increase her agricultural production to remedy the shortage of food supplies, and all former Habsburg states should negotiate to open their markets to lessen the distortions created by the establishments of new borders. Furthermore, all other countries were encouraged to extend the outlets for Austrian production and trade.[25]

In December 1924, the new Austrian currency, the Schilling, was introduced. It was first anchored to the Swiss Franc but after a few months the anchor was switched to the US dollar. By establishing a dollar exchange standard, the Austrian currency was effectively linked to gold, and the crown emerged as one of the most stable currencies in Europe between 1925 and 1931.[26] By September 1925, the economic situation had improved so much that the control of the League was modified with the prospect of a gradual removal. On June 30, 1926, the direct monitoring of the financial situation of Austria by the League of Nations came to an end, and the function of the Commissioner General ceased.

VI.   Financial aid for Hungary

In order to gain access to the League's support, Hungary filed a formal request to the Reparation Commission on April 22, 1923. Its objective was to lift the charges of the Treaty of Trianon, so these would be available as security for an external loan. The preparatory work for reconstruction by the League began in November of the same year.[27]

---

[24] See League of Nations, *Financial Reconstruction*.
[25] League of Nations, *Financial Reconstruction*.
[26] Van Walré de Bordes, *Austrian Crown*.
[27] Berend and Ranki, "Economic Problems."

As in the Austrian case, a reconstruction loan was proposed for Hungary in 1924 with the primary purpose of covering the budget deficit during the transition period. The League limited her responsibility exclusively to remedying the budget deficit. It was understood that the economic adoption to ameliorate Hungary's situation, primarily the improvement of the trade balance, had to be effected by Hungary. The League would only provide the stable basis for these adjustments. The main principles of the scheme were similar to the Austrian case, namely stopping inflation, the establishment of an independent bank of issue, and balancing the budget by June 30, 1926, although the loan took a slightly different form. The principles of control were also similar to those employed in Austria. The Commissioner General in Budapest had the main control over the reconstruction scheme and the revenues. A board of trustees represented the interest of the bond-holders, and a foreign adviser to the bank of issue was appointed on the nomination of the Commissioner General. The Committee of Control of the Guaranteeing Governments was replaced by a Committee of Control named by the Reparation Commission. Even after the end of the reconstruction period, the council could retake authority at any time during the duration of the loan whenever the equilibrium of the budget appeared to be endangered. The Hungarian remains of the Austro-Hungarian Bank were transformed into a new Hungarian central banking authority, independent of the government. With the help of the reconstruction loan, the Hungarian currency was stabilized in 1924, and the economy began to recover. As in Austria, the official control of the League of Nations ended on June 30, 1926. Preceding the loan, the Bank of England agreed to make an advance of £4 million to the National Bank of Hungary. This advance was also placed under the control of the League's Commissioner General and was to run for two years, until mid-1927. The advance was secured by six-month Hungarian treasury bills, which were exchangeable for the bonds of the long-term stabilization loan. So long as this advance remained outstanding, the Bank of England had considerable influence over the Hungarian National Bank, and could even recommend rises in the discount rate.[28]

In general, the reconstruction programs in Austria and Hungary during the inter-war period were relatively successful. The League was seen as a tough enforcer of programs that not only managed to provide the necessary financial means for reconstruction, but also lent the necessary credibility to the distressed governments.[29] Sargent points out the immediacy with which the price-levels and the foreign exchanges

---

[28] Cotrell, *Norman*.   [29] Santaella, *Stabilization Programs*.

were stabilized as a consequence of the League's reforms.[30] He emphasizes that after the stabilization the money stock continued to grow, but was backed by gold, foreign assets, and commercial paper. Schubert, in contrast, notes that the League's programs failed to address the underlying structural problems of the Austrian and the Hungarian economies.[31] Similarly, Wicker stresses the real economic costs in terms of unemployment that the stabilization programs imposed on both countries.[32] But the pressure exerted on the governments of the debtor countries to establish independent central banks also proved to be helpful and in the long-term interests of these countries.

VII.   Other financial aid schemes

Not all countries in need, during the inter-war period, relied on the financial assistance from the League. Some refused to sign an agreement, as they were not willing to accept the League's conditions (for example Portugal in 1928). Others did not want to be associated with the "losers" of World War I that the League helped to reconstruct. Importantly, German reconstruction mainly relied on bilateral loans from the US (the Dawes and the Young plan), while numerous other countries, e.g., Czechoslovakia and Poland, issued loans to finance the reconstruction after the war. From the perspective of the creditor countries, loans were often not only attractive because of the comparatively high interest rates, but were also seen as means to influence domestic policy. Examples are the US involvement in Germany and in Poland through the Kemmerer mission, and the French credits to Czechoslovakia. France extended a government loan to Czechoslovakia for military purposes, and at the same time intervened directly with military and political support, hoping to secure their military position against Germany.[33]

In Poland, a series of events led up to the stabilization loan in 1927. By 1923 it was clear that any further delay of monetary reforms would lead to political unrest or even revolution. On December 19, 1923, Wladyslaw Grabski was appointed head of the treasury, and he immediately began implementing financial reforms. The government was to cease using bank note issue to cover budget deficits. The Polish mark would be replaced with a new monetary unit, the Polish zloty, which was to be issued by the Bank Polski. The Bank began trading the zloty on April 28, 1924, and Polish marks were exchanged at a rate of 1.8 million

---

[30] Sargent, "End of Four Big Inflations."   [31] Schubert, "Emergence."
[32] Wicker, "Terminating Hyperinflation."   [33] Teichova, *Czechoslovak Economy*, p.74.

to one zloty. The new zloty was to be based on the gold parity of the Swiss Franc, and was secured by gold and foreign currency reserves equal to 30 percent of its circulation. In order to deal with the budget deficit, two new tax laws were implemented, burdening the various social groups according to their fiscal means. The propertied classes were to bear the highest burden in the form of a heavy property tax. Entrepreneurs and landowners were charged with an increased turnover tax and a higher land-value tax. In the first few months the reforms appeared to be successful, but soon the propertied classes refused to pay further taxes, and the problem of the budget deficit returned.

The financial situation improved after February 1926 with the general recovery of the market and increasing exports, but Pilsudski's "Coup d'Etat" in May 1926 once again led to an immediate fall of the zloty. The new regime, however, continued the previous financial policies and rates began to stabilize again. In 1927, the budget targets were finally achieved. But despite the full monetary stabilization Poland had just achieved, the government contracted a foreign stabilization loan to attract further foreign capital.

VIII.   Economic development following the reconstruction

In the years following the reconstruction programs, economic growth resumed. Nevertheless, each of the four countries continued to struggle with structural problems. Figure 13.1 plots the annual indices of industrial production for the four countries.

During the 1920s, Czechoslovakia shows the highest production index, as befits the most industrialized of the four countries. Austria, Poland, and then Hungary follow. All four indices show a sharp downturn after 1929, coinciding with the crash of the New York Stock Exchange in October 1929 and the beginning of the worldwide depression, which curtailed international lending, and depressed export prices for agricultural goods. The decline was most drastic for Austria and Poland and relatively mild for Hungary. Hungary and Poland reached the trough of the crisis in 1932 and began a steep recovery in 1933. For Austria, the recovery in 1933 was relatively weak, and production rates only started picking up in 1934. Similarly, for Czechoslovakia, the trough of the crisis was only reached in 1933 and the recovery was relatively slow.

In Austria, the financial difficulties, especially in the banking sector, continued. In October 1929, the second largest bank in Vienna, the Austrian Boden-Creditanstalt, failed and was merged with its former competitor, the Credit-Anstalt, Vienna's largest bank.

Table 13.3. *Return to exchange controls*

Country	Date
Austria	October 9, 1931
Hungary	July 17, 1931
Czechoslovakia	October 2, 1931
Poland	April 26, 1936

Source: Schubert, "Emergence."

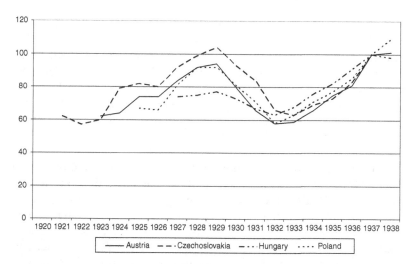

Figure 13.1 Index of industrial production (1938=100).
Source: Mitchell, *European Historical Statistics.*

The merger was initiated by the Austrian National Bank, hoping to minimize the effects of the Boden-Creditanstalt failure. Instead, the merger weakened the Credit-Anstalt, which collapsed only one and a half years later, in May 1931. The Credit-Anstalt failure triggered a banking crisis that quickly spread to the neighboring countries. The Austrian National Bank acted as lender of last resort and supported the Credit-Anstalt, but it soon became evident that the reserves of the central bank could not cover the losses. The lender of last resort function of the Austrian National Bank and the quick decline of international reserves undermined the credibility of the currency, and in October 1931 exchange controls were imposed to fight the outflow of specie and foreign currency (see Table 13.3).

In 1932, the Austrian government was forced to declare a virtual moratorium on transfer payments and withhold a portion of the revenues pledged for the service of the loan from the account of the trustees. The League of Nations reconstruction loan was finally restructured into a new loan in June 1935.

The Hungarian economy was predominantly agrarian. In 1925, a new tariff system introduced tariffs to protect the Hungarian infant industries, but the country remained an agrarian state. Gradually falling agricultural prices after 1925 and the failure to increase agricultural exports aggravated balance of payments problems.

The curtailment of international lending after the New York Stock Market crash in 1929 led to a financial crisis. The crisis worsened with the failure of the Austrian Credit Anstalt, which triggered a banking crisis in Hungary. The Hungarian government was the first of the four countries to introduce exchange controls (see Table 13.3), and declare a transfer moratorium on foreign credits. Though the League loan was exempted from the moratorium, its effects can be seen in the reconstruction bond prices. In the 1930s Hungary entered into bilateral exchange agreements with Nazi Germany which helped the economic recovery.[34]

Czechoslovakia, the most industrialized of the four countries, also depended on international trade and international demand for its goods. With 30–40 percent of the country's production sold abroad, Czechoslovakia was very vulnerable to fluctuations in the international economy. During the economic crisis of 1929–1931, Czechoslovakia suffered severely. While not initially affected by the decline in agricultural prices, Czechoslovakia did experience a severe drop in exports and industrial production. Even by 1938 the output and growth levels still fell short of 1929 levels. Foreign currency controls, which had been relaxed between 1928 and 1931, were re-established in 1931 and a high level of protection for agricultural goods was maintained.

Poland was in a situation that resembled Hungary's. Due to the strong agrarian orientation of its economy, Poland depended on the world export prices and suffered from the decline of agrarian prices. During the late 1920s Poland maintained strong ties to the US and was severely affected by the withdrawal of foreign credit and the decline in investments after 1929. Following the crisis, Poland did not immediately impose exchange controls, but remained as a member of the gold bloc until 1936. This slowed the post-crisis recovery, though Figure 13.1

---

[34] Neal, "Economics and Finance."

suggests that the Polish recovery was still stronger than that of Austria and Czechoslovakia.

IX.   Analysis

Figure 13.2 displays the bank rates over the years 1925–1931 for Austria, Britain, and Germany; and Czechoslovakia, Hungary, and Poland, respectively. The graphs show that the Austrian, German and Hungarian rates fell over the course of 1925. In all three cases, the rates had been high initially as the countries had overcome hyperinflation and stabilized their economies. The Polish rate remained high through 1926, and the British and Czechoslovak rates stayed comparatively low from the beginning, reflecting their relative economic stability. In the following years, all countries lowered the bank rates following the New York Stock Exchange crash in October 1929. The 1931 crisis was countered by steep rate increases, followed by gradual rate reductions. Comparing the levels of the bank rates one can see that the British rate was by far the lowest, followed by the Czechoslovak rate. The Polish rate was generally the highest except for the crisis period in 1931 where it remained constant at 7.5 percent while the other countries' rates increased. For the whole inter-war period, the Austrian rate stayed well above the British rate. Except for a short period in 1927 and 1928, the Austrian rate also stayed above the German rate. Thus, the Austrian central bank appeared to mostly follow the League's advice with respect to rate alignments to neighboring countries.

Figure 13.3 gives the frequencies as well as the magnitude of the rate adjustments. It becomes clear that rate adjustments were made more frequently in Germany, Austria, and to some extent Britain. The Czechoslovak rate in contrast remained the most stable. For all countries, rate increases frequently had the magnitude of one percentage point, while decreases were often more gradual and were made in one half percentage point increments. Germany showed the most extreme changes with adjustments of plus and minus 5 percent in response to the German banking crisis in August 1931.

Table 13.4 shows lags of the bank rate adjustments in London and Berlin, following the methodology used by Tullio and Wolters.[35] They use pairwise leads and lags in bank rate adjustments to analyze bank rate behavior during the classical gold standard. Their main question is whether the Bank of England was the primary "conductor of the international orchestra," or whether the bank also reacted to the rates of

---

[35] Tullio and Wolters, "Was London."

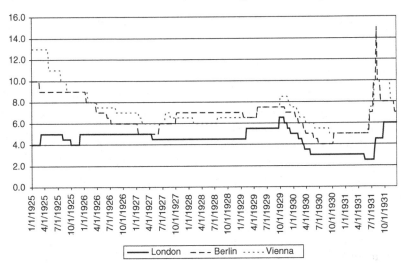

Figure 13.2A Bank rates for Britain, Austria, and Germany.

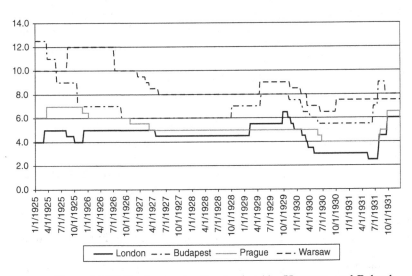

Figure 13.2B Bank rates for Czechoslovakia, Hungary, and Poland.

other central banks when making an adjustment. Tullio and Wolters' focus on the interest rate relationship between the UK, Germany, and France. Analyzing pairwise leads and lags as well as Granger causality between these rates, the authors document strong mutual feedback between the interest rates in London, Paris, and Berlin which suggests

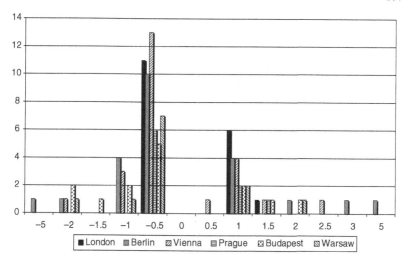

Figure 13.3 Frequency and magnitude of bank rate changes (January 1925–December 1931).

that the classical gold standard was a more decentralized system than previously assumed. In a more recent paper Tullio and Wolters analyze the influence of US interest rate changes on the Bank of England. Again the authors find strong feedback between the two rates.[36] This analysis allows a first assessment of the bank rate adjustments and their relationships.

For the four countries studied in this chapter, any rate adjustment that followed within one month of an adjustment in London or Berlin is counted. Table 13.5 indicates the number of adjustments, the average lag length in days, as well as the percentage of London or Berlin changes that were followed. It furthermore distinguishes whether adjustments were made in the same or in opposite directions. Generally same direction adjustments have a much shorter time lag than adjustments in the opposite direction. This difference shows that same direction moves are more likely to be concerted moves, whereas moves in opposite directions are more likely to be driven by other factors rather than by a response to the initial adjustment.

The results indicate a relatively strong leadership of London, but also the strong influence that Berlin had over the East-Central European countries. London also exerts direct influence over Berlin. Berlin followed seven of the eighteen London adjustments. These changes have a

[36] Tullio and Wolters, "Interest Rate Linkages."

Table 13.4. *Lags of discount rate changes*

By	Number of changes	Average lag length in days	% of London rate changes
London discount rate changes followed within one month			
Berlin			
Same direction	7	8.14	38.89
Opposite direction	3	21.33	16.67
Vienna			
Same direction	9	11.00	50.00
Opposite direction	1	25.00	5.56
Prague			
Same direction	4	11.00	22.23
Opposite direction	0	0	0
Budapest			
Same direction	6	10.83	33.33
Opposite direction	0	0	0
Warsaw			
Same direction	3	15.00	16.67
Opposite direction	1	6.00	5.56
Berlin discount rate changes followed within one month			
London			
Same direction	6	12.67	26.09
Opposite direction	3	18.00	13.04
Vienna			
Same direction	11	10.45	47.83
Opposite direction	0	0	0
Prague			
Same direction	6	7.70	26.09
Opposite direction	2	25.50	8.70
Budapest			
Same direction	10	10.60	43.48
Opposite direction	0	0	0
Warsaw			
Same direction	6	15.33	26.09
Opposite direction	0	6.00	0

Source: author's own calculations.

relatively short average time lag of eight days. Similarly, Vienna followed nine London adjustments with an average time lag of eleven days. Czechoslovakia, Hungary, and Poland followed with four, six, and again four adjustments.[37]

---

[37] For Poland a comparison with the French rate adjustments might be done in the future and prove fruitful in order to provide further insights into the policy objective of the

Table 13.5. *Reaction functions (OLS estimates)*

Variable	Austria	Czechoslovakia	Hungary	Poland
Local bank rate	0.5320***	0.8248***	0.6464***	0.7190***
(lagged)	(0.1124)	(0.0569)	(0.0724)	(0.1762)
London Bank	−0.0533	0.2300**	−0.4040***	−0.1477
	(0.2337)	(0.0942)	(0.0853)	(0.1954)
Berlin Bank	0.3696***	0.0620	0.1256**	0.4934*
	(0.1144)	(0.0430)	(0.0620)	(0.2588)
Vienna Bank	–	0.0576	0.1802***	−0.0463
	–	(0.380)	(0.0568)	(0.0754)
London Market	0.1799	−0.2084***	0.2989***	0.1127
	(0.1585)	(0.0770)	(0.0702)	(0.1606)
Berlin Market	−0.0132	−0.0206	0.0003	−0.1906
	(0.1011)	(0.0369)	(0.0480)	(0.1549)
Cover Ratio	0.0312***	−0.0064	−0.0057	−0.00001
(lagged)	(0.0097)	(0.0054)	(0.0056)	(0.0016)
Gold Inflows	0.0030	−1.87e-06	−0.0044***	−0.0001
(lagged)	(0.0064)	(0.0001)	(0.0006)	(0.0001)
Gold Outflows	0.0002	−0.00001	−0.0002	−0.0003
(lagged)	(0.0037)	(0.0001)	(0.0017)	(0.0009)
Stock Index	−0.0261***	0.0003	−0.0073***	−0.0026*
	(0.0068)	(0.0004)	(0.0014)	(0.0015)
Unemployment	−3.00e-06**	−7.19e-07	4.08e-06	−1.33e-06
	(1.43e-06)	(4.50e-07)	(4.47e-06)	(1.43e-06)
Cost of Living	0.0682**	−0.0446***	0.0327**	0.0045
	(0.0301)	(0.0158)	(0.0129)	(0.0037)
Adjusted R-squared	0.9303	0.9765	0.9608	0.9698
Number of Observations	70	70	66	60

*** indicates significance at 1%, ** at 5% and * at 10%
Source: author's own estimates. Standard error in parentheses.

Berlin exercised especially strong influence over Austria and Hungary. Vienna follows eleven of the Berlin adjustments and Budapest follows ten. Even Prague, which followed only four London adjustments, followed six Berlin rate changes. Warsaw also followed six Berlin adjustments, and London followed six of the Berlin adjustments. All this indicates that there was some feedback between London and Berlin, but the bilateral relationship was dominated by London. This preliminary analysis of the bank rates already provides some support for Hypothesis I

Polish central bank. Another possible direction for future studies is the analysis of the response after 1931, as Poland remained on the gold standard until 1936.

insofar as Austria and Hungary follow the London and Berlin rate adjustments, thus responding to the pressure of international alignment.

X.   Modeling reaction functions

The following analysis gives a detailed view of the determinants for bank rate policies in the countries of Central and East Europe, controlling for the feedback between countries as well as the domestic economic indicators.

The question of how monetary policy was conducted, and on which exogenous variables central bankers relied in order to determine a bank rate change, has frequently been addressed by estimating so-called reaction functions. Reaction functions serve as an attempt to formalize central bank behavior and link the instruments of monetary policy, namely interest rates and money growth, to exogenous variables such as output, inflation, unemployment, and general market indicators. Authors often try to replicate the policy making of the central bank by an econometric model, and though many existing models are based on a least squares approach, a wide variety of time series techniques has been used in order to model the existing relationships.

Following Eichengreen *et al.*, and Wheelock, I estimate country by country least squares regressions for the years 1926 to 1931, focusing solely on interest rate policies.[38] The dependent variables to be explained by the model are the monthly bank rates for the four countries, taken in basis points, and collected from *The Economist* and official documents of the Austrian National Bank.[39] The exogenous variables can be divided between international and domestic variables. The international variables are the bank rates and the three month market rates in London and Berlin. Market interest rates for the four countries in question are only available for Vienna, and even there only through May 1931. Therefore, the British and German rates were used as proxies and included in all regressions. In those regressions for Czechoslovakia, Hungary, and Poland the Vienna bank rate was included as explanatory variable, allowing for the possibility that Czechoslovakia and Hungary still regarded Vienna as the regional financial center, and, to some

---

[38] Eichengreen *et al.*, "Bank Rate Policy" and Wheelock, *Strategy*. Due to the lack of data the regression analysis only starts in January 1926 rather than in April 1925 when Britain returned to gold.

[39] For months in which a rate change occurred the monthly value is a weighted value of the two rates, according to the number of days where the different rates were in effect. This weighting smoothes the data series and moderates some of the statistical effects that are introduced by the discrete nature of the bank rates.

extent, followed the policies of the Austrian National Bank. Country specific variables that might have influenced the bank rates are the cover ratios, changes in the gold and foreign currency reserves (measured in domestic currencies), a stock market index, the number of unemployed, and a cost of living index.[40] To allow for an asymmetric response to gold flows, positive and negative changes in the reserves are coded as two separate variables (gold inflows and gold outflows). As a measure for general market activity, I include the Vienna stock market index for Austria. For the other three countries, the indices for Hungarian, Czechoslovak, and Polish stocks that were traded on the Vienna stock exchange were included.[41]

The estimation results, based on robust standard errors, are presented in Table 13.5.

As one can see, the Czechoslovak and Hungarian bank rates were affected by the British bank rate, whereas Austria, Hungary, and Poland reacted to changes in the Berlin rate. Moreover, Hungary followed Vienna's adjustments. Except for Hungary's response to the London bank rate, all coefficients are positive, which indicate that the periphery countries followed British and German adjustments. These results correspond to those from the previous section and lend support to Hypothesis I. The London market rate moreover affected the Czechoslovak and the Hungarian bank rates, even if showing an inverse relationship in the case of Czechoslovakia, strengthening the dominant influence of London.

Looking at the domestic variables, the Austrian central bank responded more actively to the domestic indicators. The bank rate was raised in response to an increase in the cover ratio, which indicates that the Austrian central bank was concerned about the cover and accumulated as many reserves as possible, rather than lowering the rate in response to increasing cover. A direct response to the gold inflows and outflows cannot be identified. The Austrian National Bank lowered the bank rate to fight growing unemployment and in response to increases in the stock market. This documents that to some extent domestic variables started to take precedence over the external adjustment. The Austrian National Bank was moreover concerned with the domestic price level, showing a positive relationship between price level changes and rate adjustments.

---

[40] Due to data constraints I use the number of unemployed, rather than the more commonly used unemployment rate.

[41] These indices were not available for 1926 and show missing values for 1931 when trading was interrupted due to the Austrian banking crisis. To avoid difficulties with missing data points I interpolated the series.

Hungary was the only country in the sample to counter gold inflows by decreasing rates, in accordance with the rules of the game. The Hungarian central bank furthermore responded to the stock index and the cost of living index in the same fashion that Austrian National Bank did.

For Czechoslovakia and Poland, gold flows appeared not to be significant for the bank rate adjustments. With regard to the domestic variables, Czechoslovakia only responded to the cost of living index, lowering the bank rate to counter increasing prices. Poland is the country that shows the least responsiveness to domestic indicators, only reacting to the stock market.

This analysis documents that Austria and Hungary showed a willingness to adjust the bank rates in response to the cover ratio and gold flows, thus providing additional support for Hypothesis I. In Austria, the influence of the League over the policies of the bank was the strongest. The Austrian National Bank still relied on a foreign adviser to the bank, beyond the official end of the control of the League in 1926. Through the foreign adviser to the Austrian National Bank, the League was able to influence the behavior of the bank, forcing it to comply with the rules of the gold exchange standard. Here again the different effects of the League's policies in Austria and Hungary become apparent. Hungary ended the function of the foreign adviser to the central bank with the end of the official League control. The League had no long term effect on the policies of the bank, as in Austria, and could not force Hungary to comply with the gold standard adjustment mechanism. Despite the formal independence of the Hungarian central bank, the authoritarian regime quickly took over and influenced the bank's policies. Czechoslovakia and Poland apparently also did not commit to adjustment mechanism of the gold exchange standard. In both cases the central bank was dependent on the political authorities.

Hypotheses II and III are most strongly confirmed with the contrasting examples of Austria and Poland, with Austria being most and Poland being least influenced by domestic indicators. Overall, the results provide limited support for all three hypotheses outlined in Section III: Austria, being a democratic regime and most under the influence of the League of Nations shows the strongest response, followed by Hungary and Czechoslovakia, and then Poland.

XI.   Conclusion

The four Central and Eastern European countries differed considerably with respect to their monetary and political institutions. During the gold exchange standard period, Austria and Czechoslovakia were parliamentary democracies, whereas Hungary and Poland were authoritarian regimes. In Austria and Hungary, the League of Nations constructed statutory independent central banks as part of the financial reconstruction schemes. In contrast, the central banks were politically controlled in Czechoslovakia and Poland.

The analysis of the bank rate adjustments provides insights into the behavior of the four banks. Only Austria responded to the cover ratio of the central bank, and only Hungary showed some willingness to adjust the bank rate as to offset gold flows. Czechoslovakia and Poland apparently did not commit to the adjustment mechanism of the gold exchange standard, confirming that the overall central bank independence in Czechoslovakia and Poland was very limited and that both countries were not subject to international control. All four Central and East European countries were subject to a relatively strong influence from London and Berlin.

The other important finding of this research is that democratic countries at the time were more responsive to domestic economic conditions than autocratic ones. In Austria, for example, bank rate adjustments followed the cost of living index, the stock market and the number of unemployed. In Czechoslovakia, the central bank was also responding to domestic prices. In contrast, Poland showed very little response to domestic indicators. This analysis thus highlights the challenges that new emerging democracies have to face when creating their monetary institutions.

For the inter-war period, central bank independence and commitment to the international monetary regime can be seen as complements. But very few countries of the periphery committed themselves to the international regime, thereby contributing to the instability of the system at the time.

References

Berend, Ivan T. and Györgi Ranki. 1985. *The Hungarian Economy in the Twentieth Century*. Contemporary Economic History of Europe Series, London: Croom Helm.
2002. "The Economic Problems of the Danube Region after the Breakup of the Austro-Hungarian Monarchy." In Ivan T. Berend, *Studies on Central and Eastern Europe in the Twentieth Century*. Variorum Collected Studies Series, Aldershot: Ashgate: Chapter 5, 110–20.
Bernanke, Ben and Harold James. 1991. "The Gold Standard, Deflation and Financial Crises in the Great Depression: An International Comparison." In Glenn Hubbard, ed., *Financial Markets and Financial Crises*. Chicago: Chicago University Press: 33–68.

Bernhard, William, J. Lawrence Broz, and William Roberts Clark. 2002. "The Political Economy of Monetary Institutions." *International Organization* 56, no. 4: 693–723.

Bordo, Michael, Michael Edelsein, and Hugh Rockoff. 1999. "Was Adherence to the Gold Standard a Good Housekeeping Seal of Approval during the Interwar Period?" NBER Working Paper No. 7186, Cambridge.

Broz, J. Lawrence. 2002. "Political System Transparency and Monetary Commitment Regimes." *International Organization* 56, no. 4: 861–87.

Cotrell, Philip. 1997. "Norman Strakotsch and the Development of Central Banking from Conception to Practice." In Philip Cotrell, ed., *Rebuilding the Financial System in Central and Eastern Europe*, Aldershot: Ashgate.

Davutyan, Nurhan and William R. Parke. 1995. "The Operations of the Bank of England, 1890–1908: A Dynamic Probit Approach." *Journal of Money, Credit and Banking* 27, no. 4: 1099–112.

Eichengreen, Barry. 1992. *Golden Fetters: The Gold Standard and the Great Depression, 1919–1939*. New York: Oxford University Press.

Eichengreen, Barry, Mark W. Watson, and Richard S. Grossman. 1985. "Bank Rate Policy in the Interwar Gold Standard: A Dynamic Probit Model." *The Economic Journal* 95, no. 379: 725–45.

Feinstein, Charles, Peter Temin, and Gianni Toniolo. 1997. *The European Economy Between the Wars*. Oxford: Oxford University Press.

Holtfrerich, Carl Ludwig. 1986. *The German Inflation 1914–1923*. New York: Walter de Gruyter.

Kindleberger, Charles P. 1976. *The World in Depression 1929–1939*. Berkeley: University of California Press.

League of Nations. 1926. *The Financial Reconstruction of Austria: General Survey and Principal Documents, 1923–1926*. Geneva: League of Nations.

Mitchell, Brian. 1975. *European Historical Statistics 1750–1970*. London: Macmillan.

Neal, Larry D. 1979. "The Economics and Finance of Bilateral Clearing Agreements: Germany 1934–1938." *Economic History Review* 32: 391–404.

Nurkse, Ragnar. 1944. *International Currency Experience, Lessons from the Interwar Period*. Geneva: League of Nations, Economic, Financial and Transit Department.

O'Rourke, Kevin and Jeffrey Williamson. 1999. *Globalization and History: The Evolution of a Nineteenth Century Atlantic Economy*. Boston: MIT Press.

Santaella, Julio A. 1992. "Stabilization Programs, Credibility and External Enforcement." Ph.D. Thesis, University of California, Los Angeles.

Sargent, Thomas. 1982. "The End of Four Big Inflations." In Thomas Sargent, ed., *Rational Expectations and Inflation*, New York: Harper and Row.

Schubert, Aurel. 1999. "The Emergence of National Central Banks in Central Europe after the Break-up of the Austro Hungarian Monarchy." In Carl-Ludwig Holtfrerich, Jaime Reis, and Gianni Toniolo, eds., *The Emergence of Modern Central Banking from 1918 to the Present*, Aldershot: Ashgate.

Simmons, Beth. 1994. *Who Adjusts? Domestic Sources of Foreign Economic Policy during the Interwar Years, 1923–1939*. Princeton: Princeton University Press.

1996. "Rulers of the Game: Central Bank Independence during the Inter-war Years." *International Organization* 50, no. 3: 407–43.

Smith, Vera. 1936. *The Rationale of Central Banking and the Free Banking Alternative*. Westminster: PS King and Son Ltd.

Teichova, Alice. 1988. *The Czechoslovak Economy 1918–1980*. Contemporary Economic History of Europe Series, London: Routledge.

Triffin, Robert. 1947. "National Central Banking and the International Economy." *The Review of Economic Studies* 14, no. 2: 53–75.

Tullio, Guiseppe and Jürgen Wolters. 1996. "Was London the Conductor of the International Orchestra or Just the Triangle Player? An Empirical Analysis of Asymmetries in Interest Rate Behavior during the Classical Gold Standard, 1876–1913." *Scottish Journal of Political Economy* 43, no. 4: 419–43.

2000. "Interest Rate Linkages between the US and the UK during the Classical Gold Standard." *Scottish Journal of Political Economy* 47, no. 1: 61–71.

van Walré de Bordes, Jan. 1924. *The Austrian Crown*. London: King.

Wheelock, David. 1991. *The Strategy and Consistency of Federal Reserve Monetary Policy, 1924–1933*. Cambridge: Cambridge University Press.

Wicker, Elmus. 1986. "Terminating Hyperinflation in the Dismembered Habsburg Monarchy." *American Economic Review* 76, no. 3: 350–64.

14 When do stock market booms occur? The macroeconomic and policy environments of twentieth century booms

Michael D. Bordo and David C. Wheelock[*]

Since the mid-1990s, many countries have experienced prolonged periods of rapid price appreciation in equity, housing, and other asset markets which have drawn the attention of economists and policymakers to the role of asset prices in the propagation of business cycles. Economists disagree about the appropriate response of monetary policy to such asset price booms. Some argue that financial markets are inherently volatile and that market prices often stray from fundamentals, suggesting that policymakers could improve welfare by deflating asset price booms, especially if sudden asset price declines are likely to depress economic activity. Other economists claim that financial markets process information efficiently or that policymakers usually cannot determine when assets are mispriced and, hence, that they cannot enhance aggregate welfare by reacting to asset price movements.

Such episodes have also fascinated financial historians, and research into these phenomena has yielded important information about the development of financial markets and the effects of financial regulation and macroeconomic policy on the stability of markets.[1] We believe that history can also inform the debate about the appropriate response, if any, of monetary policy to asset price booms. Accordingly, this chapter investigates the macroeconomic and policy environments in which stock market booms occurred among ten developed countries during the twentieth century. Our multi-country historical approach enables us to

[*] The authors thank Jeremy Atack, Hui Guo, Larry Neal, Maria Valderrama, and participants in conferences held at the University of Illinois and Universitat Pompeu Fabra (CREI) for their comments on a previous version of this paper, and Daniel McDonald and Joshua Ulrich for research assistance. The views expressed in this paper are not necessarily official positions of the Federal Reserve Bank of St. Louis or the Federal Reserve System.

[1] Among Larry Neal's important contributions in this area are his work on the South Sea Bubble, the development of European capital markets from the sixteenth to nineteenth centuries (Neal, *The Rise of Financial Capitalism*), and the British financial crisis of 1825 (Neal, "Financial Crisis").

explore the association between stock market booms and key macro-economic and monetary policy variables across a variety of policy regimes and regulatory environments.

We construct monthly, real (i.e., inflation-adjusted) stock price indexes for ten countries for which the data are more easily available over most of the twentieth century. We then identify extended periods of unusually rapid appreciation in the indexes for each country, which we have defined as booms. Finally, we use a simple event methodology to study the behavior of key macroeconomic and monetary policy variables during these stock market booms.

We find that booms generally occurred during periods of above-average economic growth and below-average inflation, and that they typically ended when monetary policy tightened in response to rising inflation. Most stock market booms were procyclical, arising during business cycle recoveries and expansions and ending when rising inflation and tighter monetary policy were followed by declining economic activity. We also find, however, that some twentieth century booms were not associated with rapid economic growth or low inflation, and that stock markets were often affected by changes in regulation and other events such as oil price shocks and political upheaval.

Although we are able to examine stock markets and macroeconomic conditions in a variety of settings, the limited range and frequency of historical data for many countries necessarily means that our study is more impressionistic than formal. For example, whereas the standard efficient markets model posits that stock prices reflect discounted expected future dividends, we lack the data to estimate expected dividend growth or changes in the discount factor with confidence. Hence, we do not address directly the question whether specific stock market booms degenerated into bubbles. However, policymakers are unlikely ever to have data that enable them to identify bubbles definitively as they arise, and a review of historical experiences can provide insights that help them respond to events in real time.

The next section briefly summarizes prior findings and presents information about the stock market booms in our data. Subsequent sections examine the macroeconomic conditions under which twentieth century stock market booms occurred among the ten countries. The final section summarizes our observations and conclusions.

I.   Stock market booms and crashes

Most studies of the relationship between asset booms and macro-economic conditions focus on the consequences of booms and, especially, market crashes for macroeconomic activity. Several have drawn policy lessons from crash experiences.

Michael Bordo finds that many, but not all, US and British stock market crashes of the nineteenth and twentieth centuries were followed by recessions. A serious decline in economic activity was more likely, he concludes, if the crash was accompanied or followed by a banking panic.[2] Frederic Mishkin and Eugene White come to a similar conclusion in their review of US stock market crashes in the twentieth century. They find that a severe economic downturn was more likely to follow a crash if the crash was accompanied by a widening of interest rate credit spreads. The key lesson for policy, Mishkin and White argue, is that policymakers should focus on the financial instability that can arise in the wake of crashes, rather than on crashes per se.[3]

Thomas Helbling and Marco Terrones examine median output growth across major stock market booms and busts of 1970–2001 and find that busts often preceded sharp slowdowns in economic activity. Echoing an observation of Bordo's about US and British crashes of the nineteenth and early twentieth centuries, Helbling and Terrones find that busts typically coincided with or followed a tightening of monetary conditions.[4]

Relatively few studies examine the conditions under which stock market booms arise or persist. In an earlier paper, we examined episodes of unusually rapid growth of US nominal stock prices during the nineteenth and twentieth centuries.[5] We found that many such episodes occurred when real output and productivity growth (both labor productivity and total factor productivity) were unusually rapid, suggesting that stock prices were at least partly justified by macroeconomic conditions. By contrast, we found no consistent relationship between the growth of *nominal* stock prices and inflation, but noted that inflation was usually low and stable during periods of rapid growth in *real* stock prices. Here we explore in more depth the macroeconomic conditions under which stock market booms have occurred in the US and nine other developed countries to gain insights about the macroeconomic conditions and policies that seem to foster booms, and determine whether experiences differ across countries.

[2] Bordo, "Stock Market Crashes."
[3] Mishkin and White, "U.S. Stock Market Crashes."
[4] Helbling and Terrones, "Asset Price Booms," also examine the effects of housing market booms and busts, and find that housing cycles have been more closely related to monetary policy, and that housing busts are associated with larger declines in economic activity than stock market busts.
[5] Bordo and Wheelock, "Monetary Policy."

A.   Defining booms

There is no precise empirical definition of an asset boom, and researchers have imposed a variety of filters to identify specific episodes as booms. We adapt the methodology of Adrian Pagan and Kirill Sossounov to identify prolonged periods of rapidly rising real stock prices in those countries for which monthly data on a nominal stock price index and a consumer price index are available from the early 1920s onward: Australia, Canada, France, Germany, Italy, Japan, Netherlands, Sweden, the UK, and the US.[6] We identify the maximum and minimum of the real stock price within rolling, twenty-five-month windows. We require that market peaks and troughs alternate, and so eliminate all but the highest maximum that occurred before a subsequent trough, and all but the lowest minimum that occurred before a subsequent peak. We classify as booms all periods of at least three years from trough to peak with an average annual rate of increase in the real stock price index of at least 10 percent. We also classify as booms a few episodes of exceptional real stock price appreciation shorter than three years.[7]

Table 14.1 lists the episodes that we have defined as booms for each country in our sample. For each boom, we include information about the average annual percentage increase in the market index from the market trough to its peak. Because several booms began as recoveries from market declines, we also note when the real stock price surpassed its prior twenty-five-month peak, and report the average annual percentage increase in the index after that date.

For comparison, Table 14.1 also reports information about long-run average annual rates of change in the real stock price index for each country. For example, the US real price index for stocks increased at an average annual rate of 2.4 percent during 1915–1940, and at an average annual rate of 4.4 percent during 1947–2004. Thus, the periods we define as booms were characterized by rates of appreciation that were substantially higher than long-run averages. Finally, Table 14.1 also includes information about the extent to which the real stock price index declined during the twelve months following a market peak, and from

---

[6] Pagan and Sossounov, "Simple Framework." We selected our sample countries based on the availability of historical data on a stock market index and key macroeconomic series, which obviously gives rise to possible sample selection bias. We are unsure of the extent to which our findings would differ if our sample included recently developed or emerging market economies. The appendix describes our data and sources.

[7] Helbling and Terrones, "Asset Price Booms," use a similar procedure to identify booms and busts. Specifically, they identify turning points in the log-level of real equity prices over five quarter windows, and define booms (busts) as the largest one-fourth of all price increases (declines).

Table 14.1. *Stock market booms*

Country	Boom start: local market minimum	Boom end: local market peak	Avg. annual % change from month after trough to peak	Boom start: when prior 25-month peak surpassed	Months duration after prior peak surpassed	Avg. annual % change from month after prior peak	Comparison avg. annual % change during period	Percent decline 12 months after peak	Percent decline to next minimum	
Australia	Dec. 1920	Feb. 1929	10.7	July 1921	91	9.1	3.6	-20.1	-41.0	comparison: Jan. 1915-Dec. 1940
	Sept. 1930	Mar. 1937	17.8	Oct. 1934	30	13.7	3.6	-12.2	-31.6	comparison Jan. 1947-Dec. 2004
	July 1956	July 1960	15.8	Aug. 1957	35	15.9	2.4	-11.6	-20.2[a]	
	Oct. 1966	Dec. 1969	21.8	Oct. 1967	26	17.5	2.4	-24.8	-42.2	
	Aug. 1977	Nov. 1980	21.9	Sept. 1979	14	32.1	2.4	-27.2	-47.2	
	July 1982	Sept. 1987	25.2	Mar. 1986	18	39.3	2.4	-35.8	-46.3[a]	
	Dec. 1990	Jan. 1994	18.9	Oct. 1993	3	36.9	2.4	-23.8	-23.8	
	Aug. 1998	June 2000	13.4	Jan. 1999	18	6.5	2.4	-0.8	-23.8	
Canada	Dec. 1920	Sept. 1929	17.4	-	-	-	3.7	-37.5	-75.1	comparison: Feb. 1920-Dec. 1940
	June 1932	Mar. 1937	28.0	-	-	-	3.7	-35.6	-35.6	comparison Jan. 1947-Dec. 2004
	Oct. 1953	July 1956	24.6	July 1954	25	23.5	3.4	-9.2	-32.4	
	Oct. 1977	Nov. 1980	22.1	-	-	-	3.4	-25.2	-52.5	
	July 1984	July 1987	17.9	July 1985	24	15.3	3.4	-18.5	-26.7[a]	
	Jan. 1995	Apr. 1998	19.2	Nov. 1995	29	20.1	3.4	-10.0	-28.2[a]	
	Aug. 1998	Aug. 2000	34.7	Dec. 1999	8	42.0	3.4	-36.0	-43.6	

Country								Comparison
France	Nov. 1920	July 1924	20.9	—	—	2.5	-16.1	-34.7	comparison Jan. 1920-Dec. 1939
	Nov. 1926	Feb. 1929	40.4	Dec. 1927 14	37.9	2.5	-12.0	-57.0	comparison Jan. 1947-Dec. 2004
	Dec. 1950	Apr. 1955	28.4	—	—	2.8	-17.4	-11.1[a]	
	Aug. 1958	Apr. 1962	20	July 1960 21	14.3	2.8	-18.7	-54.1	comparison Jan. 1950-Dec. 2004
	June 1981	Apr. 1987	24.4	Jan. 1985 25	36.2	2.8	-32.8	-45.0	
	Feb. 1995	Aug. 2000	23.6	Jan. 1997 43	26.8	2.8	-29.5	-60.1	
Germany	June 1957	Sept. 1960	43.6	Aug. 1958 25	54.1	6.0	-24.0	-49.3	comparison Jan. 1950-Dec. 2004
	Aug. 1982	Apr. 1986	31.8	July 1983 33	28.8	6.0	-18.4	-44.7	
	Mar. 1995	Feb. 2000	23.9	Sept. 1996 41	27.8	6.0	-25.4	-69.9	
Italy	May 1932	July 1935	27.5	—	—	0.4	-13.4	-20.0[a]	comparison Feb. 1921-Dec. 1938
	July 1950	Sept. 1955	18.5	Aug. 1952 37	22.7	3.1	-16.6	-22.2[a]	comparison Jan. 1950-Dec. 2004
	June 1958	Aug. 1960	56.4	Oct. 1958 23	58.7	3.1	-17.6	-17.6	
	Dec. 1977	May 1981	35.0	—	—	3.1	-46.8	-54.1	
	Dec. 1982	Aug. 1986	38.2	Mar. 1986 5	34.3	3.1	-26.7	-47.9	
	Nov. 1995	Feb. 2000	33.6	July 1997 31	34.9	3.1	-18.8	-56.5	
Japan	Oct. 1930	Feb. 1934	28.6	Feb. 1932 24	26.1	1.8	-12.0	-16.6	comparison Feb. 1923-Dec. 1940
	Jan. 1950	Jan. 1953	54.3	Jan. 1952 12	93.1	6.9	-30.0	-36.4	comparison Jan. 1950-Dec. 2004
Netherlands	Sept. 1982	Dec. 1989	23.9	Mar. 1983 81	22.5	6.9	-41.0	-47.6[a]	comparison March 1920-Dec. 1939
	July 1924	Feb. 1929	10.9	Jan. 1926 36	6.1	-1.8	-15.7	-71.8	comparison Jan. 1947-Dec. 2004
	June 1932	Mar. 1937	26.6	—	—	-1.8	-18.2	-31.5	
	Apr. 1952	June 1957	20.3	Nov. 1954 31	15.4	4.1	-19.8	-32.1[a]	

Table 14.1. (cont.)

Country	Boom start: local market minimum	Boom end: local market peak	Avg. annual % change from month after trough to peak	Boom start: when prior 25-month peak surpassed	Months duration after prior peak surpassed	Avg. annual % change from month after prior peak	Comparison avg. annual % change during period	Percent decline 12 months after peak	Percent decline to next minimum	
	Dec. 1957	Mar. 1961	22.2	May 1959	22	15.0	4.1	-10.5	-31.2	
	Sep. 1981	July 1987	22.0	Mar. 1983	52	20.1	4.1	-17.2	-36.7[a]	
	Jan. 1991	Aug. 2000	17.4	June 1993	74	19.6	4.1	-26.8	-65.4	
Sweden	Mar. 1922	July 1929	16.9	-	-	-	-1.8	-13.1	-73.3	comparison Feb. 1917-Dec. 1940
	May 1932	Mar. 1937	23.2	-	-	-	-1.8	-12.2	-12.2	
	Mar. 1958	Aug. 1961	15.1	Aug. 1958	36	13	5.7	-15.3	-20.2	comparison Jan. 1947-Dec. 2004
	Sept. 1980	Mar. 1984	36.8	May 1981	34	34.7	5.7	-24.6	-29.3	
	Sept. 1992	Feb. 2000	31.4	Sept. 1995	53	30.6	5.7	-31.2	-67.2	
United Kingdom	June 1932	Dec. 1936	15.4	Feb. 1936	10	5.4	-0.4	-23.6	-44.2	comparison Feb. 1916-Dec. 1939
	June 1952	July 1955	20.0	July 1954	12	16.4	2.8	-17.3	-31.4	
	Feb. 1958	Apr. 1961	25.4	Dec. 1958	28	19.6	2.8	-17.8	-31.0	comparison Jan. 1947-Dec. 2004
	Sept. 1981	July 1987	21.3	Oct. 1982	57	21.5	2.8	-23.4	-34.8[a]	
	June 1994	Dec. 1999	12.6	Apr. 1996	44	12.7	2.8	-10.6	-50.2	

United States	Oct. 1923	Sept. 1929 23.7	Dec. 1924 57	24.4	2.4	−30.1	−80.6	comparison Jan. 1915–Dec. 1940
	Mar. 1935	Feb. 1937 39.7	Oct. 1935 16	30.2	2.4	−39.0	−45.8	
	Sept. 1953	Apr. 1956 28.8	Mar. 1954 25	29.3	4.4	−9.6	−20.1	comparison Jan. 1947–Sept. 2004
	June 1962	Jan. 1966 13.3	Dec. 1963 25	10.3	4.4	−12.5	−20.1[a]	
	July 1984	Aug. 1987 22.9	Feb. 1985 30	21.6	4.4	−22.3	−27.5[a]	
	Apr. 1994	Aug. 2000 17.1	Mar. 1995 64	18.7	4.4	−22.8	−46.8	

[a]Market decline ended less than 12 months after boom peak.
Source: see the text and appendix.

the market peak to the next market trough. Almost all booms were followed by real declines of at least 10 percent within 12 months; however, not all booms ended with a spectacular crash, and the lengths and sizes of market declines after booms varied widely.

Comparison of stock price index growth rates is problematic because of differences in index composition across countries and over time. For the interwar period, cross-country comparisons are further complicated by differences in when monthly data on a nominal stock price index and inflation are first available, and in the nature and the availability of stock price data for the late 1930s associated with when countries became involved in World War II. For the post-World War II period, we report average growth rates for 1947–2004 for all countries in the sample except Germany, Italy, and Japan, which were still recovering from the immediate effects of the war and occupation. For these we report growth rates over 1950–2004. The real stock price indexes for these three countries exhibit rapid growth during the 1950s compared to average growth rates for subsequent decades. Among the other sample countries, we note considerable variation in average real stock price growth rates, ranging from 2.4 percent for Australia to 5.7 percent for Sweden. Again, however, such long-run cross-country comparisons are problematic because the performance of stock markets varied considerably over time within countries, as well as because of differences in the coverage of industries and firms in the stock market indexes of individual countries.

We find considerable coincidence in the occurrence of stock market booms across sample countries between January 1924 and December 2000 (Figure 14.1 – we omit the 1940s when the stock markets of several countries were closed for extended periods because of World War II). Several countries experienced a substantial increase in real stock prices during the 1920s and a market peak in 1929, as well as booms in the mid-1930s as their economies recovered from the Great Depression. Most countries in our sample also had booms in the late 1950s, in the mid-1980s and again in the 1990s. In contrast, there were almost no stock market booms among our sample countries from the mid-1960s to the early 1980s.

Additional information on the co-movement of stock markets among our sample countries is illustrated in Figure 14.2, which plots the rolling, five-year moving average correlation in the monthly percentage changes in the real stock price indexes of each pair of countries in our sample between 1920 and 1999. The figure illustrates that the average correlation in the monthly capital returns of the various stock markets varied widely over time. Periods of relatively high correlation included the late 1920s, late 1960s to early 1970s, the mid-1980s, and late 1990s. Except

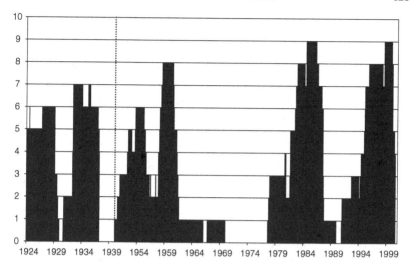

Figure 14.1 Number of countries with an ongoing stock market boom in given month, 1924–2000.

Figure 14.2 Five-year moving average correlation of cross-country returns.

for the late 1960s to early 1970s, each period of high correlation was marked by booms in several countries.

The pattern of average correlations of cross-country returns among our ten sample countries is largely consistent with the findings of studies of international financial integration. William Goetzmann *et al.*, for example, find that equity market returns were relatively highly correlated during the late nineteenth century, the interwar period, and in the late twentieth century.[8] And, from evidence on nominal and real interest rate differentials, Maurice Obstfeld and Alan Taylor conclude that international financial markets were highly integrated before World War I.[9] A brief period of high integration occurred again in the late 1920s (as our equity market data also suggest), but fell apart during the Great Depression. Markets gradually re-integrated in the late 1950s and 1960s before entering a period of disintegration associated with the breakdown of the Bretton Woods system of fixed exchange rates in the early 1970s. International financial markets became highly integrated once again during the 1980s and 1990s, again consistent with the high correlation among stock returns we find in this period.

II.   The macroeconomic environment of twentieth century booms

Changes in trend productivity growth are perhaps the best macroeconomic indicator of future growth of national output and corporate profits. However, except for recent years, even annual estimates of productivity are not available for most countries. We do, however, have estimates of current output growth (GDP) for several countries and, as a first step, we investigate whether stock price booms historically have occurred during periods of rapid output growth. Of course, current output growth rates are not necessarily good proxies for expected future growth unless investors simply extrapolate current output growth rates into the future.

Researchers have identified several channels by which monetary policy might affect stock prices. Monetary policy is often thought to operate through the short-term real interest rate and, thus, policy might affect the real interest rate that investors use to discount future profits, at least in the short run. Indeed, we find that booms typically have arisen when interest rates are low and/or falling, and end following increases in policy rates.

---

[8] Goetzmann *et al.*, "Long-Term."   [9] Obstfeld and Taylor, "Great Depression."

Monetary policy might also affect stock prices through inflation and/or inflation uncertainty. There have been several attempts to explain a negative correlation between the growth of stock prices and inflation observed in US data. Inflation uncertainty could increase risk premiums. By the same token, a policy commitment to a stable price level that investors view as credible might hasten a boom by reducing risk premiums or raising forecasts of future real growth. This suggests that stock prices could reflect the monetary policy regime. We investigate the association between booms, monetary policy actions, and inflation.

Finally, domestic or foreign shocks of various sorts, including political events, wars, and economic policies of other countries can affect stock prices. At times, countries have used capital controls and other policies to wall off their domestic markets from external forces, as well as to channel capital to specific uses. Various domestic financial regulations, such as margin requirements and ownership restrictions, may also affect the observed associations between stock prices and macroeconomic conditions and monetary policy. A thorough review of the myriad regulations imposed on equity markets over time, across the ten countries in our sample, is beyond the scope of this chapter. We note, however, several instances in which stock market booms appear to have been associated with changes in regulation or other policies.

We begin our study of the macroeconomic environments of stock market booms by examining annual data on real GDP growth and inflation across all boom episodes listed in Table 14.1. In the next section, we focus separately on stock market booms of the interwar, early post-World War II, and post-1970 periods.

For all stock market booms listed in Table 14.1, we computed real GDP growth relative to its long-run average for each market peak year and the eight years before and after each peak.[10] Real GDP growth exceeded its long-run average during a majority of stock market booms. Figure 14.3 plots the median real GDP growth rate (relative to its long-run average) in market peak years (year "0") and in the eight years before and after market peaks.[11] The chart illustrates that across all booms, median real GDP growth increased sharply relative to its long-run average during the two years prior to a stock market peak, and exceeded its long-run average by 1.5 percentage points in both the

---

[10] For the interwar period, we use the average over 1871–1939 as the "long-run" average GDP growth rate. For the post-World War II period, we use the average over 1960–2001.

[11] For all figures in the paper that show annual data, we define year "0" as the year the stock market reached a peak unless the peak occurred in the first half of a year, in which case we define year "0" as the year prior to the year of the peak.

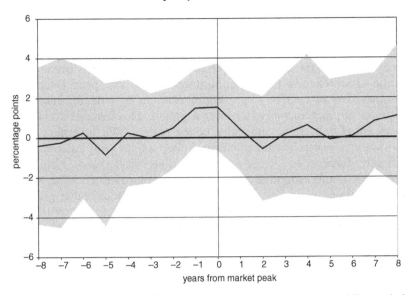

Figure 14.3 Real GDP growth (minus long-run average): All twentieth century booms (median ± mean absolute deviation).

market peak and prior years. Median growth also fell sharply during the two years following a peak. Thus, the typical boom arose when output growth was above average and rising, and ended when output growth stopped increasing. Median output growth fell sharply in the year following a market peak, and many booms were followed by a period of economic contraction.

Figure 14.3 also shows the mean absolute deviation of observations around the median, illustrating the dispersion in GDP growth rates across boom episodes. Observations of output growth are less dispersed during booms, which usually lasted for three to five years before a market peak, than before. Observations are least dispersed from about two years before a market peak year (year "−2") to about two years after a peak year (year "2").

Figure 14.4 plots median inflation (relative to its long-run average) during booms and their aftermath.[12] Booms tended to arise when inflation was below its long-run average and also falling. The median inflation rate was approximately 1 percentage point below its long-run

[12] For the interwar period, we use the annual average rate of consumer price inflation over the years for which we have data for individual countries, through 1939, as the long-run average. For the post-World War II period, we use the average rate for 1947–2004 as the long-run average.

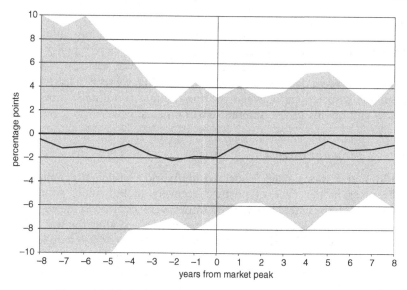

Figure 14.4 Inflation rate (minus long-run average): All twentieth century booms (median ± mean absolute deviation).

average between four and seven years before a market peak, and 2 percentage points below its long-run average during the two years prior to a market peak. Inflation tended to return slowly to its long-run average after a market peak. Figure 14.4 also illustrates the dispersion of observations around the median, as shown by the mean absolute deviation of observations around the median. As with GDP growth, the dispersion of inflation rates around their long-run averages declines over time toward the market peak year.[13]

III.   Monetary policy and twentieth century booms

Although a majority of twentieth century stock market booms in our sample countries occurred during periods of above average real output growth and below average inflation, many booms occurred when output growth was near normal, or even below normal, and/or when inflation

---

[13] Bordo and Wheelock, "Stock Market Booms and Monetary Policy in the Twentieth Century" compare GDP growth and inflation during US booms with the medians across the remaining nine sample countries. They find that the behavior of output and inflation were similar across US and non-US booms, but that, if anything, the association of booms with above-average output growth and below-average inflation was stronger across US booms than across the non-US median.

exceeded its long-run average. Moreover, booms occurred under a variety of macroeconomic and regulatory policy regimes. We next examine the association of macroeconomic and monetary policy conditions and stock market booms during the interwar, early post-World War II, and recent decades, separately. In so doing, we seek to learn more about the associations between macroeconomic conditions, monetary policy, and booms under different environments.

A.   The interwar period

World War I was a major shock to the world's principal economies. Differences in the pace of postwar recovery in individual countries reflected both the extent to which countries were involved in the war and in the economic policies their governments pursued after the war. The US, for example, experienced high inflation in 1918–1919 followed by deflation and a sharp, but short-lived recession in 1920–1921. The abrupt change in macroeconomic conditions reflected a shift from a highly expansionary monetary policy geared toward financing the government's debt at low interest rates, to a tight policy aimed at quashing inflation and protecting the Federal Reserve's gold reserves.[14] The Fed reversed course again in 1922 and the economy recovered quickly. The US economy enjoyed strong average growth and low, stable inflation throughout the remainder of the decade.

The US stock market ran a parallel course, with significant losses during the recession of 1921 followed by a strong recovery. After a brief relapse in 1923, the market turned upward and posted several years of rapid real price appreciation until the market peak in September 1929. Financial historians and other observers have long debated whether the US market was over-valued at its peak. Some, such as Irving Fisher (1930) and, more recently, Ellen McGratton and Edward Prescott (2004) argue that economic fundamentals could justify stock prices even at the market's 1929 peak.[15] Similar to the "new economy" stories that appeared to explain the stock market boom of the 1990s, advances in technology and management practices were often cited in the 1920s as reasons why US corporations could expect high earnings growth that justified the large increase in stock prices.[16] The 1920s saw rapid diffusion of electric power, the internal combustion engine, and other "great inventions" of the late nineteenth and early twentieth centuries in

[14] See Friedman and Schwartz, *Monetary History*, and Meltzer, *History*.
[15] Fisher, *Stock Market Crash*. McGrattan and Prescott, "1929 Stock Market."
[16] See White, "Bubbles."

American factories and homes.[17] US firms, especially in the manufacturing sector, experienced high average growth of labor and total factor productivity over the decade, though annual estimates suggest that productivity growth had slowed by the time the stock market boom was in full swing.[18]

Despite a highly favorable macroeconomic environment, many economists conclude that by 1929 US stock prices far exceeded levels that could be justified by economic fundamentals. J. Bradford DeLong and Andrei Schleifer, for example, compare prices and net asset values of closed-end mutual funds, and conclude that stocks were some 30 percent over-valued in 1929.[19] Peter Rappoport and Eugene White reach a similar conclusion from examining the premium on brokers' loans.[20] Other authors, such as John Kenneth Galbraith, emphasize the rapid growth of investment trusts and commercial bank securities affiliates in the 1920s, and their role in enticing unsophisticated investors to the market.[21]

The Federal Reserve did not directly address the question whether the stock market was over-valued, but Fed officials were concerned about the growth of loans used to purchase stocks, and the possibility that Federal Reserve credit was being used to support that growth. Federal Reserve policy tightened abruptly in 1928 through the market crash in October 1929 in an effort to choke off the flow of credit to the market. This policy was reflected in both a sharp increase in interest rates and a slowing of money stock growth, which preceded the business cycle peak, and it may have hastened the economic contraction of 1929–1933.[22]

Besides the US, five of the other nine countries in our sample experienced a stock market boom in the 1920s as their economies recovered from wartime disruption, and as international capital markets were reintegrated under the gold exchange standard. Several countries experienced a brief period of rapidly rising real stock prices during recovery

[17] David, "Dynamo," and Gordon, "Does the 'New Economy'?"
[18] Productivity change is most appropriately measured between business cycle peaks or other similar points in the business cycle. However, private domestic labor productivity (output/hours) and total factor productivity rose at average annual rates of 3.0 and 2.62 percent during 1920–1924, and at average rates of 1.74 and 1.32 percent during 1925–1929. In the manufacturing sector, labor productivity rose at an average annual rate of 7 percent during 1920–1924 and 3.90 percent during 1925–1929 (Private domestic productivity: Kendrick, *Productivity*, Table A-XXII; manufacturing sector: ibid., Table D-II).
[19] DeLong And Schleifer, "Stock Market Bubble."
[20] Rappoport and White, "Was there a Bubble?"   [21] Galbraith, *Great Crash*.
[22] See Friedman and Schwartz, *Monetary History*, Meltzer, *History*, and Wheelock, *Strategy*, for discussion and evidence on the Fed's reaction to stock market speculation. Based on a review of several measures of monetary conditions, Hamilton, "Monetary Factors," concludes that monetary policy tightened considerably during 1928–1929.

in the early 1920s, and a more sustained appreciation when their currencies were made convertible into gold or other hard currencies.

The experiences of France and the UK, for example, illustrate a close association between macroeconomic conditions and policies, and stock market performance. France had a market boom associated with a business cycle recovery in 1920–1924, though in real terms the stock market moved little beyond its previous cycle peak. Stock prices then declined rapidly as monetization of government deficits produced inflation and capital flight. The market decline continued until November 1926, when the government budget was brought under control and investors became convinced that inflation would not reignite.[23]

Restored fiscal discipline ended capital flight and brought investors back to the Paris market. The exchange rate policies subsequently pursued by the Bank of France further encouraged capital inflows. The Bank pegged the value of the franc against other currencies in December 1926, and restored full convertibility of the franc into gold in June 1928. That exchange rate, however, was pegged well below its prewar levels against the US dollar and British pound. Under the exchange rate pegs maintained by the Bank of France and the Bank of England, France tended to attract capital and the UK tended to lose capital. The Paris stock market boomed in this environment, with the real stock price index rising at a 40 percent average annual rate between December 1926 and February 1929. The London stock market rose at a much more modest pace. Between May 1925, when convertibility of the pound was restored, and August 1929, when the London market reached its peak in real terms, the real stock price index rose at an average annual rate of just 7.4 percent. Although above average, this rate of appreciation was well below the rates that the Paris and New York markets experienced over comparable periods.

The UK economy also grew at a much slower pace than did either the US or French economies. The Bank of England maintained a tight monetary policy throughout the 1920s, aimed first at restoring, and then maintaining convertibility of the pound into gold at the prewar parity. Persistent doubts about the viability of the peg discouraged capital inflows, however, and kept a brake on economic activity and the stock market. Thus, as in both the US and France, the performance of the UK stock market during the 1920s reflected underlying economic performance and macroeconomic policies.

The US and many other countries experienced a business cycle peak mid-1929, and the major stock markets crashed within a few months of

---

[23] On the French economic crisis, see Eichengreen, *Golden Fetters*, pp. 172–83.

one another. Several months of tight monetary policy, marked by high interest rates and slow money stock growth, preceded the US business cycle peak. Linkages through the international gold standard caused monetary conditions to tighten throughout the world, precipitating the Great Depression.[24] The Depression was hard on stock markets. For example, between its peak in September 1929 and low in June 1932, the Standard and Poor's index of US stocks declined 80 percent in real terms.

Economic recovery brought renewed vigor to financial markets in the mid-1930s, when stock market booms occurred in eight of our ten sample countries. As in the 1920s, the timing and extent of these booms were tied to economic recovery and the macroeconomic policies pursued in individual countries. Currency devaluation and/or the imposition of restrictions on gold convertibility was a precursor to economic recovery in many countries.[25] Britain abandoned the gold standard in September 1931, and several other countries quickly followed. Stock prices began to rise in the UK and other countries in mid-1932. Although stock prices posted gains in some countries that remained on gold, most countries did not have a sustained boom until they had abandoned the gold standard or at least devalued. The US, for example, experienced a financial crisis and market crash in early 1933, followed by a brief recovery after the Roosevelt Administration suspended gold convertibility and restored confidence in the US banking system. A sustained boom did not begin until the second quarter of 1935, however, when output growth stabilized and the economy began to grow consistently.[26]

Figures 14.5 and 14.6 illustrate the association between real economic growth, inflation, and stock market booms during the interwar period. Figure 14.5 shows median real GDP growth relative to long-run averages during interwar boom episodes, and the mean absolute deviation around the median in each year. Figure 14.6 shows similar data for inflation. The patterns are like those shown for all twentieth century boom

---

[24] Eichengreen, *Golden Fetters.*   [25] Ibid.

[26] Eichengreen, *Golden Fetters*, p. 344 notes that US industrial production and other measures of economic activity fluctuated widely in 1933–1934, and argues that the investor optimism created by the Roosevelt Administration's response to the financial crises in early 1933 "fell back substantially when it became apparent that America's departure from the gold standard had not inaugurated a new era of rapid monetary expansion." Among other sample countries, France, Italy, and the Netherlands remained on the gold standard until 1936, though Italy imposed stringent exchange controls in 1934. The Netherlands experienced a slow real appreciation of stock prices from a low point in June 1932, but a significant rise only when it abandoned gold in September 1936. France experienced a market crash in mid-1936, and recovery upon abandoning gold, but no sustained stock market boom.

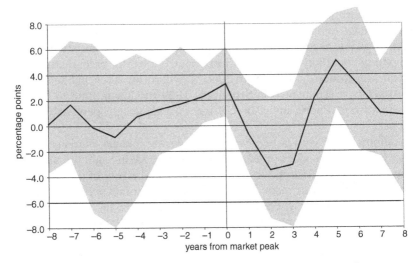

Figure 14.5 Real GDP growth (minus long-run average): Interwar booms (median ± mean absolute deviation).

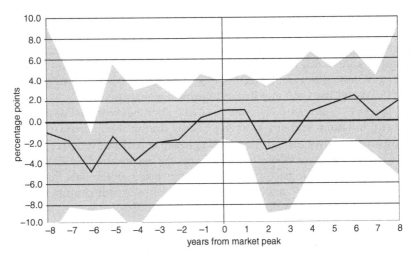

Figure 14.6 Inflation rate (minus long-run average): Interwar booms (median ± mean absolute deviation).

episodes in Figures 14.3 and 14.4: booms tended to occur during periods of above average output growth and below average inflation. During interwar booms, median GDP growth exceeded its long-run average by about 3 percentage points in market peak years, then fell sharply over the two years following market peaks. Median inflation was below its long-run average until the year before a market peak, but rose sharply in the months preceding a market peak.

Both US stock market booms in the interwar period ended within months of a shift in monetary policy. The boom of 1923–1929 ended in September 1929, some twenty months after the Federal Reserve began to stem the flow of credit to the booming stock market. Although consumer price inflation was minimal, Fed officials viewed speculation in stocks or other assets as a form of inflation that called for monetary restraint.[27] The US boom of 1935–1937 also ended when monetary policy was tightened. After largely staying on the sidelines as gold and currency inflows caused rapid growth of the money stock in 1933–1936, the Fed tightened abruptly with a series of increases in bank reserve requirements in August 1936, January 1937, and May 1937. Although the consumer price level had risen only modestly since 1933, the Fed hiked reserve requirements because officials viewed the large volume of reserves that banks held in excess of legal requirements as an inflationary threat. The stock market peak occurred in February, immediately after the second reserve requirement increase took effect on January 31, 1937.

B. Early post-World War II era

Stock market booms of the interwar period were closely associated with economic growth, inflation, and both domestic and international monetary policies. New regulations on securities markets and capital flows were introduced during the Great Depression, and intensified during World War II. We next examine stock market booms of the first two decades after the war, when controls on the allocation of economic resources were slowly eased and the international monetary system was re-established, but many markets remained tightly regulated and international capital flows were restricted.

International capital mobility hit a low point during and immediately following World War II as a result of exchange controls.[28] Capital mobility gradually improved during the 1950s, as the European Payments Union and other mechanisms were established to clear international payments and promote trade and economic recovery. Over time, countries eased restrictions on foreign exchange transactions and capital movements, and the Treaty of Rome, which created the European Economic

---

[27] See Chandler, *American*, or Meltzer, *History*, for discussion of the policy views of Fed officials at this time.
[28] Obstfeld and Taylor, "Great Depression," pp. 381–91.

Community in 1958, called for dismantling of all restrictions on the free movement of capital among EEC members.

In addition to restricting international payments and capital flows, many countries also tightly regulated domestic capital markets during the war and for several years afterward. In the UK, for example, all capital market issues were regulated by a Capital Issues Committee until 1959, when controls on domestic issues were relaxed.[29] Many other countries imposed similar restrictions on new capital issues in an effort to allocate the flow of national savings.

The US imposed comparatively few restrictions on either international payments or domestic capital markets. Still, both were more heavily regulated in the postwar period than they had been during the 1920s. The 1929 stock market crash and subsequent allegations of fraud, insider trading, conflicts of interest, and other financial improprieties led to new regulations and government oversight of US securities markets. Among the important laws enacted to regulate the issuance and trading of securities were the Securities Act of 1933, which required that investors receive material information about securities being offered for sale, and the Securities Exchange Act of 1934, which established the Securities Exchange Commission as the principal federal agency responsible for oversight and enforcement of federal securities laws. The latter act also authorized the Federal Reserve to set margin requirements on stock purchases. Finally, the Glass-Steagall Act of 1933 prohibited the commingling of commercial and investment banking activities.[30] The financial regulatory regime that was established in the 1930s remained largely in place throughout the remainder of the twentieth century.

Two waves of stock market booms occurred among our ten sample countries during the 1950s, one centered around 1952–1953, and the other around 1958–1960. Several countries, including France, Italy, Japan, and the Netherlands, had booms that began between 1950 and 1952, as postwar economic chaos gave way to recovery, and US aid, most notably the Marshall Plan, poured in. By 1951, the per capita incomes of the UK, France and (West) Germany exceeded their prewar levels by more than 10 percent.[31] DeLong and Eichengreen contend that the Marshall Plan was particularly important for European economic recovery. Although the $13 billion in aid transferred from the US to Western Europe was small relative to the size of European economies, this aid

---

[29] Dow, *Management*, pp. 235–6.
[30] The Glass–Steagall Act is the portion of the Banking Act of 1933 that concerns the activities of commercial and investment banks.
[31] DeLong and Eichengreen, "Marshall Plan."

was sufficient to give European countries breathing room to meet recovery needs without having to undertake contractionary policies to balance their international payments. Furthermore, DeLong and Eichengreen argue that the Marshall Plan promoted long-term growth by encouraging the establishment of mixed, market-oriented economies, and enabling the unwinding of controls over product and factor markets.[32] Thus, while the Marshall Plan contributed to economic recovery in the short run, it also helped lay the foundation for long-term economic growth by promoting a market-orientation and favorable investment climate. Although many restrictions on capital flows and investment remained, the combination of rapid economic growth and a foundation for future growth was an environment that proved conducive for booming stock markets.

A second wave of European stock market booms began in 1957–1958 as economic growth enabled European countries to gradually relax exchange controls and trade barriers during the 1950s. The signing of the Treaty of Rome in March 1957, which created the European Economic Community, and the re-establishment of currency convertibility by several countries in late 1958 were particularly noteworthy events. The timing of stock market booms among European countries suggests that investors viewed these steps as likely to produce rapid growth of corporate profits and national income.[33]

Figures 14.7 and 14.8 plot median real GDP growth and inflation (relative to their long-run averages) during stock market booms of the 1950s and 1960s among our ten sample countries. Similar to the patterns observed for the interwar period, median output growth was above average and inflation below average during the booms of the 1950s and 1960s. In market peak years, median real GDP growth exceeded its postwar average by approximately 3 percentage points before falling back after booms ended.[34]

As shown in Figure 14.8, median inflation rose toward the end of the booms in the 1950s and 1960s, as it had toward the end of interwar

[32] Ibid.

[33] See Neal and Barbezat, *Economics*, Chapters 2–3, for information about European economic recovery, integration and policies during 1945–1958, and for analysis of the economic effects of the formation of the European Economic Community on its members.

[34] Here we define long-run average GDP growth as the annual average rate during 1960–2001, and long-run average inflation as the annual average rate during 1947–2001. In Japan and many countries of Europe, real GDP growth was higher on average during the "Golden Age" of 1950–1973, and especially during 1947–1960 than in subsequent decades. See Crafts and Toniolo, *Economic Growth*, and the papers therein for analysis of European economic growth after World War II.

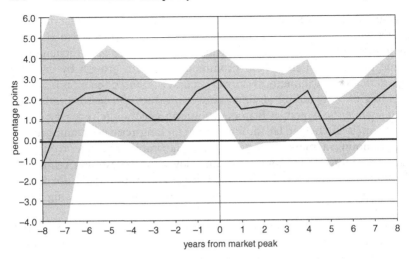

Figure 14.7 Real GDP growth (minus long-run average): Booms of the 1950s–1960s (median ± mean absolute deviation).

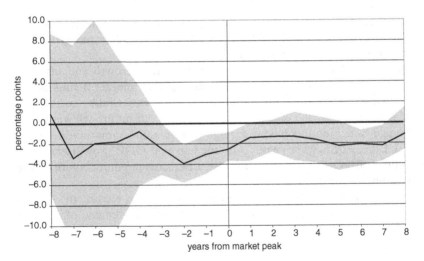

Figure 14.8 Inflation rate (minus long-run average): Booms of the 1950s–1960s (median ± mean absolute deviation).

booms. Interest rates also tended to rise toward the end of booms. Although the Fisher effect can explain why nominal interest rates rise when inflation increases, *real* (ex post) interest rates also rose and money stock growth fell during the last two years of most booms, indicating that monetary conditions tightened. Monetary policy tightening might snuff out a stock market boom by raising the rate at which investors discount expected dividend growth and/or by reducing the path of expected dividends. The Federal Reserve responded aggressively to inflation, especially during the 1950s, and both US stock market booms of the 1950s and early 1960s ended as the Fed tightened in response to rising inflation.[35] The behavior of median interest rate levels and money stock growth rates across all booms of this era indicates that the ends of many booms coincided with monetary policy tightening.

C.   Stock market booms of the 1970s–1990s

We have examined the stock market booms of the 1970s–1990s separately from those of the 1950s–1960s because the macroeconomic and regulatory environments of the two periods differ markedly, and because high frequency observations on a greater variety of macroeconomic series are available only for the period since 1970. The 1970s witnessed the breakdown of the Bretton Woods system of fixed exchange rates, two major energy market shocks, high inflation, and a worldwide slowdown in productivity growth. Only two of our ten countries experienced a stock market boom in the 1970s – Australia and Canada. In both countries, rising commodity prices brought improved terms of trade and a rising stock market. Energy and mining stocks have relatively heavy weight in the market indexes of both countries.

The 1980s and 1990s, by contrast, saw declining energy prices and inflation, higher average output growth, and buoyant financial markets in many countries. Several countries eliminated capital controls and deregulated financial markets and institutions in these years, and financial markets became more integrated across countries. All ten countries experienced a stock market boom during the 1980s, and all but Japan had a boom in the 1990s.

Advances in information-processing technologies that facilitated global financial transactions and innovations also encouraged financial deregulation. Countries adopted reforms to increase the efficiency of their domestic financial markets, tap foreign capital, and respond to various financial innovations, such as electronic trading and trading in stock market futures and options.

[35] Calomiris and Wheelock, "Was the Great Depression?" show that the Fed reacted to rising (falling) inflation by draining (adding) reserves from the banking system, and Romer and Romer, "Rehabilitation," find that during the 1950s the Fed's actions satisfied the so-called Taylor Principle in that policy resulted in changes in the real interest rate that exceeded changes in the rate of inflation.

The world's first electronic stock exchange, the Nasdaq market, was created in the US in 1971. The US deregulated brokerage commissions in the mid-1970s. Other countries followed suit in the 1980s and 1990s, abolishing minimum brokerage commissions and controls on the ownership of brokers and dealers, and establishing electronic trading and derivative securities markets.[36]

The UK removed exchange controls in 1979; Japan and Germany followed suit in 1980 and 1984.[37] Other European countries eliminated controls on capital in the late 1980s and early 1990s under the terms of the European Economic and Monetary Union.

In several countries, the removal of capital controls and deregulation of financial markets occurred as part of a sea change in economic policy. Tax cuts, especially on capital income, widespread deregulation of industry, and monetary policies that brought inflation under control produced a more favorable business climate in many countries than had prevailed in the 1970s. In the US, these policies were augmented by less aggressive anti-trust enforcement, which encouraged mergers and acquisitions and a booming stock market.[38]

Next, we identify the macroeconomic conditions under which stock market booms occurred during the 1970s–1990s. Figure 14.9 plots quarterly observations on median real GDP growth (relative to its long-run average) during boom episodes.[39] In contrast to earlier periods, when output growth typically exceeded its long-run average during booms, median output growth hovered near its long-run average across the stock market booms of the 1970s–1990s. The median, however, belies considerable variation in output growth rates across stock market booms. Several countries had a stock market boom in the mid-to-late 1990s. During these booms, output growth exceeded its long-run average in Australia, Canada, Sweden, the UK, and the US, but was near or below average in France, Germany, and Italy.

Figure 14.9 plots US real GDP growth (relative to its long-run average) during the twenty quarters before and after the third quarter of 2000, when the US boom of April 1994–August 2000 ended. US real

---

[36] For example, Japan permitted foreign firms to become members of the Tokyo Stock Exchange in 1982, and introduced domestic stock index futures trading in 1988. See Kato, "Japanese Securities." The UK abolished minimum brokerage commissions, permitted ownership of exchange member firms by outside corporations, and instituted electronic trading in 1986. France abolished fixed brokerage commissions and broke-up the brokerage and market-making cartels, and introduced futures and options trading on the Paris exchange in 1987.

[37] Yamada, "Japanese Banking."   [38] Wigmore, *Securities Markets*.

[39] Here we again define the long-run average as the average annual real GDP growth rate for 1960–2001.

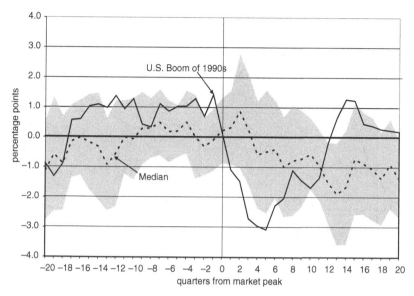

Figure 14.9 Real GDP growth (minus long-run average): Booms of the 1970s–1990s (median ± mean absolute deviation).

GDP growth exceeded its long-run average by about 1 percentage point over the eighteen quarters before the stock market peak. This boom was frequently attributed to an increase in productivity growth associated with advances in information technology. Although internet and other information-processing technology stocks experienced the largest price gains, the US stock market boom of 1994–2000 was broadly based as optimists expressed confidence in the prospects of accelerated earnings growth in the "new economy." Figure 14.10 shows that US labor productivity growth exceeded its long-run average by at least 1 percentage point in three of four years between 1996 and 1999. The figure also shows that across all booms of the 1970s–1990s median productivity growth was near its long-run average.[40] Thus, by occurring when productivity growth was above average, the US boom of 1994–2000 was unusual among booms of the 1980s–1990s.

Figure 14.11 plots monthly observations on US inflation (relative to its long-run average) during the boom of 1994–2000 alongside median inflation across all booms of the 1970s–1990s.[41] As in earlier periods,

[40] We define the long-run average as the average annual labor productivity growth rate for 1970–2004.

[41] Here we again define the long-run average as the average year-over-year rate of inflation for 1947–2004.

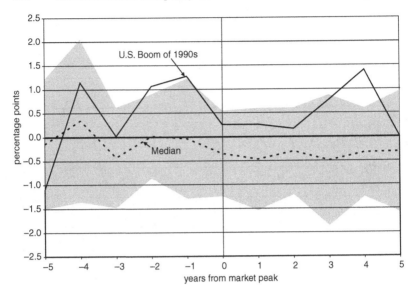

Figure 14.10 Labor productivity growth (minus long-run average):
Booms of the 1970s–1990s (median ± mean absolute deviation).

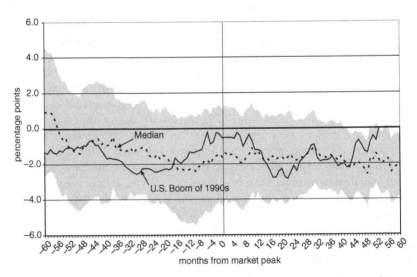

Figure 14.11 Inflation rate (minus long-run average): Booms of the
1970s–1990s (median ± mean absolute deviation).

inflation was typically below average during stock market booms of the 1970s–1990s, and rising as booms ended. The pattern held true during the US boom of 1994–2000. The increase in the rate of inflation before the August 2000 stock market peak occurred somewhat earlier, however, than the increase in median inflation across all booms.

As with earlier stock market booms, the ends of most booms of the 1970s–1990s were preceded by several months of monetary policy tightening. For example, the US stock market boom of 1994–2000 ended after just over a year of Federal Reserve tightening. Citing "a significant risk of rising inflation," the Federal Reserve began to tighten in June 1999, and then increased its federal funds rate target by a total of 175 basis points to 6.5 percent over the next 12 months.[42] As a result, the real funds rate, measured as the current month's funds rate minus the trailing year-over-year inflation rate, increased by about forty basis points, while spreads between short- and long-term Treasury security yields narrowed until the yield curve inverted in early 2000. The behavior of both nominal and real interest rates during other booms of the 1970s–1990s show a similar pattern, with median nominal and real rates increasing about 1 percentage point, and about 0.6 percentage points, respectively, within the last eight months of booms. Thus, we again find that booms typically ended following a period of monetary policy tightening associated with rising inflation.

IV.   Observations and conclusions

Our study of twentieth century stock market booms among ten developed countries finds that markets reflect both underlying macroeconomic conditions and specific economic policy actions. We find that stock market booms were an element of the business cycle, with booms typically arising during cyclical recoveries and other periods of rapid economic growth and ending when GDP growth slowed. Many stock market booms were followed by large declines in real stock prices, if not outright market crashes, and a slowing of economic activity. We also find an association between stock market booms and monetary policy. Booms typically arose when inflation was low and declining, and ended within a few months of an increase in the rate of inflation. Rising inflation tended to bring tighter monetary conditions, reflected in higher

---

[42] The target had been reduced from 5 percent to 4.75 percent on November 17, 1998. The target was raised to 5 percent on June 30, 1999, and elevated in five more steps to 6.5 percent on May 16, 2000. The quotation in the text is from the unpublished transcripts of the Federal Open Market Committee meeting of June 29–30, 1999.

real interest rates, declining term spreads, and reduced money stock growth.

During the interwar period, the timing and extent of stock market booms in several countries bore a close relationship to exchange rate policies. France, for example, experienced a stock market boom in 1926–1929, after its exchange rate was pegged at a level that encouraged capital inflows and fiscal and monetary policies were adopted that brought inflation under control. The UK, by contrast, pursued an over-valued exchange rate during the 1920s that resulted in capital outflows, slow economic growth, and only modest real stock price appreciation. Similarly, in many countries the timing of economic recovery and stock market booms during the 1930s was closely associated with devaluation or outright abandonment of the gold standard.

Stock market booms of the 1950s and 1960s reflected economic recovery and rapid growth after World War II. In Europe, actions to reopen markets to trade and capital flows also buoyed financial markets and contributed to two waves of stock market booms. We note in particular an apparent association between stock market booms in several European countries and the dismantling of trade barriers and exchange controls in the late 1950s. Finally, stock market booms of the 1970s–1990s were somewhat less commonly associated with rapid economic growth, though the US boom of 1994–2000 did occur during a period of rapid output and productivity growth, as well as low inflation. We speculate that financial deregulation and globalization weakened the links between domestic economic growth and stock markets in the 1980s–1990s.

Stock market booms tended to be roughly in sync across countries throughout the twentieth century. Several countries had booms in the 1920s, mid-1930s, 1950s, mid-1980s, and late 1990s, whereas few countries had booms between 1965 and 1980. Stock market returns were more highly correlated across countries during boom periods than at other times. The average correlation was especially high during the late 1920s and 1980s–1990s, when financial markets and capital flows were comparatively unregulated. In these decades, international financial markets were relatively highly integrated. Average correlation was relatively low, and booms were less in sync during the 1950s and 1960s when many of the financial regulations and capital controls imposed during the Great Depression, and strengthened during World War II, remained in force and interfered with international market integration.

By studying the behavior of financial markets under a variety macroeconomic and policy environments, financial historians can provide much needed insights that help in devising policies that promote the efficient and stable operation of financial markets. We find that stock market booms have been closely related to monetary policies, as reflected both by the level of inflation and actions to control inflation. Furthermore, we find that international economic policies, such as capital controls, exchange rate pegs, and financial regulation, affect the linkages between domestic economic performance and stock markets. A key lesson for policy, therefore, is that the effects of macroeconomic policies on asset markets are likely to be influenced by both the domestic regulation and the international integration of those markets. Thus, the efficient operation of financial markets would seem to hinge on both macroeconomic and regulatory policies, and how well those policies interact with one another.

Appendix
Data sources

Stock price index (nominal, monthly data): stock price data for all countries except the US are from Global Financial Data (www.glo balfinancialdata.com). The following lists the Global Financial Data series identifier and description for each country:

Australia:	AORDM, Australia ASX All-Ordinaries
Canada:	GSPTSEM, Canada S&P/TSX 300 Composite
France:	SBF250M, France SBF-250 Index
Germany:	FWBXXM, Germany CDAX Composite Index
Italy:	BCIIM, Banca Commerciale Italiana Index
Japan:	N225M, Japan Nikkei 225 Stock Average
Netherlands:	AAXM, Netherlands All-Share Price Index
Sweden:	SWAVM, Sweden Affarsvarlden General Index
UK:	FTASM, UK FT-Actuaries All-Share Index
US:	NBER Macro History Database, series m11025a (1871: 01–1920:12); Standard and Poor's 500 Composite Index (1941–1943 = 10), Monthly Average of daily data obtained from Haver Analytics (1921:01–2004:12)

Real Stock price (monthly): we used consumer price index data to deflate nominal stock prices to obtain a real stock price. Consumer price index data for all countries except the US are from Global Financial Data. The following lists the Global Financial Data consumer price index series identifier for each country. Monthly observations are available beginning from the month listed in parentheses.

Australia: CPAUSM (1912:01)
Canada: CPCANM (1914:01)
France: CPFRAM (1915:01)
Germany: CPDEUM (1923:12)
Italy: CPITAM (1920:01)
Japan: CPJPNM (1922:01)
Netherlands: CPNLDM (1919:01)
Sweden: CPSWEM (1916:01)
UK: CPGBRM (1914:01)
US: BLS, Series ID: CUUR0000SA0, CPI – All Urban
               Consumers, US City Average, All Items, not seasonally
               adjusted, 1982–84 = 100 (1913:01–2004:12)

General notes about the figures presented in the paper

We computed all growth rates using log first differencing, unless other-wise noted. For all figures displaying annual data we attributed the stock market peak to the prior calendar year if the peak month of a boom occurred in the first six months of a year. Otherwise, we attributed the peak to the calendar year that it occurred. For figures displaying monthly or quarterly data, we attributed the peak to the actual month or quarter that it occurred.

Real GDP: data are from Maddison, *World Economy*, Tables 1b, 2b and 5b for 1871–2001 and the OECD for 2001–2004. For booms ending prior to 1940, we defined the long-run average growth rate as the average growth rate for 1871–1939. For booms ending after 1940, we defined the long-run average growth rate as the average growth rate for 1960–2001.

Inflation: the sources for consumer price index data are listed above. We computed annual inflation rates by averaging annualized monthly growth rates. For booms ending prior to 1940, we defined the long-run average growth rate as the average growth rate from the first available observation through 1939 (first available observations: Australia, 1902; Canada, 1911; France, 1872; Germany, 1924; Italy, 1871; Japan, 1871; Netherlands, 1882; Sweden, 1871; UK, 1871; US, 1870). For booms ending after 1940, we defined the long-run average growth rate as the average growth rate for 1947–2004.

Real GDP: quarterly data downloaded from the OECDNEQ data-base of Haver Analytics. Data are available beginning in the quarter listed in parentheses: Australia (1960: 1); Canada (1961: 1); France (1978: 1); Germany (1991: 1); Italy (1980: 1); Japan (1980: 1); Nether-lands (1977: 1); Sweden (1980: 1); UK (1960: 1); US (1960: 1). We computed growth rates as year-over-year growth rates for each quarter. We defined the long-run average growth rate as the average growth rate for 1960–2001, calculated using the annual data from Maddison, *World Economy*, listed above.

Labor productivity: annual data on GDP per hour worked obtained from the OECD productivity database (July 2005). The data for all countries span the years 1970–2004. We defined the long-run average growth rate as the average growth rate for 1970–2004.

Inflation: monthly consumer price index data from Global Financial Data, listed above. We computed the inflation rate as year-over-year growth in the consumer price index. We defined the long-run average growth rate as the average growth rate for 1947–2004.

References

Bordo, Michael D. 2003. "Stock Market Crashes, Productivity Boom Busts and Recessions: Some Historical Evidence." Background paper prepared for IMF *World Economic Outlook*.

Bordo, Michael D., and David C. Wheelock. 2004. "Monetary Policy and Asset Prices: A Look Back at Past U.S. Stock Market Booms." Federal Reserve Bank of St. Louis *Review* 86, no. 6: 19–44.

2007. "Stock Market Booms and Monetary Policy in the Twentieth Century." Federal Reserve Bank of St. Louis *Review* 89, no. 2: 91–122.

Calomiris, Charles W., and David C. Wheelock. 1998. "Was the Great Depression a Watershed for American Monetary Policy?" In *The Defining Moment: The Great Depression and the American Economy in the Twentieth Century*, edited by Michael D. Bordo, Claudia Goldin, and Eugene N. White. Chicago: University of Chicago Press: 23–65.

Chandler, Lester V. 1971. *American Monetary Policy 1928–1941*. New York: Harper and Row.

Crafts, Nicholas, and Gianni Toniolo. 1996. *Economic Growth in Europe Since 1945*. Cambridge: Cambridge University Press.

David, Paul A. 1990. "The Dynamo and the Computer: An Historical Perspective on the Modern Productivity Paradox." *American Economic Review Papers and Proceedings* 80, no. 2: 355–61.

DeLong, J. Bradford, and Barry Eichengreen. 1993. "The Marshall Plan: History's Most Successful Structural Adjustment Programme," In *Postwar Economic Reconstruction and Lessons for the East Today*, edited by Rudiger Dornbusch, Wihelm Nolling, and Richard Layard. Cambridge: MIT Press: 189–230.

DeLong, J. Bradford, and Andrei Shleifer. 1991. "The Stock Market Bubble of 1929: Evidence from Closed-End Mutual Funds." *Journal of Economic History* 51, no. 3: 675–700.

Dow, J.C.R. 1964. *The Management of the British Economy 1945–60*. Cambridge: Cambridge University Press.

Eichengreen, Barry. 1992. *Golden Fetters: The Gold Standard and the Great Depression, 1919–1939*. New York: Oxford University Press.

Fisher, Irving. 1930. *The Stock Market Crash – And After*. New York: Macmillan.

Friedman, Milton, and Anna J. Schwartz. 1963. *A Monetary History of the United States, 1867–1960*. Princeton: Princeton University Press.

Galbraith, John Kenneth. 1955. *The Great Crash 1929*. Boston: Houghton Mifflin Company.

Goetzmann, William N., Lingeng Li, and K. Geert Rouwenhorst. 2001. "Long-Term Global Market Correlations." NBER Working Paper No. 8612, Cambridge, November.

Gordon, Robert J. 2000. "Does the 'New Economy' Measure up to the Great Inventions of the Past?" *Journal of Economic Perspectives* 14, no. 4: 49–74.

Hamilton, James D. 1987. "Monetary Factors in the Great Depression." *Journal of Monetary Economics* 19, no. 2: 145–69.

Helbling, Thomas, and Marco Terrones. 2004. "Asset Price Booms and Busts – Stylized Facts from the Last Three Decades of the 20th Century." Working Paper, International Monetary Fund, Washington, DC.

Kato, Takashi. 1991. "Japanese Securities Markets and Global Harmonization." In *Regulating International Financial Markets: Issues and Policies*, edited by Franklin R. Edwards and Hugh T. Patrick. Boston: Kluwer: 131–42.

Kendrick, John W. 1961. *Productivity Trends in the United States*. Princeton: Princeton University Press.

Maddison, Angus. 2003. *The World Economy: Historical Statistics*. Paris: Organization for Economic Cooperation and Development.

McGrattan, Ellen R., and Edward C. Prescott. 2004. "The 1929 Stock Market: Irving Fisher Was Right." *International Economic Review* 45, no. 4: 991–1009.

Meltzer, Allan H. 2003. *A History of the Federal Reserve, Volume 1: 1913–1951*. Chicago: University of Chicago Press.

Mishkin, Frederic S., and Eugene N. White. 2003. "U.S. Stock Market Crashes and Their Aftermath: Implications for Monetary Policy." In *Asset Price Bubbles: The Implications for Monetary, Regulatory, and International Policies*, edited by William C. Hunter, George G. Kaufman, and Michael Pomerleano. Cambridge: The MIT Press: 53–80.

Neal, Larry. 1990. *The Rise of Financial Capitalism: International Capital Markets in the Age of Reason*. Cambridge: Cambridge University Press.

    1998. "The Financial Crisis of 1825 and the Restructuring of the British Financial System." Federal Reserve Bank of St. Louis *Review* 80, no. 3: 53–76.

Neal, Larry, and Daniel Barbezat. 1998. *The Economics of the European Union and the Economies of Europe*. New York: Oxford University Press.

Obstfeld, Maurice, and Alan M. Taylor. 1998. "The Great Depression as a Watershed: International Capital Mobility over the Long Run." In *The Defining Moment: The Great Depression and the American Economy in the Twentieth Century*, edited by Michael D. Bordo, Claudia Goldin, and Eugene N. White. Chicago: University of Chicago Press: 353–402.

Pagan, Adrian R., and Kirill A. Sossounov. 2003. "A Simple Framework for Analysing Bull and Bear Markets." *Journal of Applied Econometrics* 18, no. 1: 23–46.

Rappoport, Peter, and Eugene N. White. 1993. "Was there a Bubble in the 1920 Stock Market?" *Journal of Economic History* 53, no. 3: 549–74.

Romer, Christina D., and David H. Romer. 2002. "A Rehabilitation of Monetary Policy in the 1950s." *American Economic Review Papers and Proceedings* 92, no. 2: 121–7.

Wheelock, David C. 1991. *The Strategy and Consistency of Federal Reserve Monetary Policy, 1923–1933.* Cambridge: Cambridge University Press.

White, Eugene N. March 2006 . "Bubbles and Busts: The 1990s in the Mirror of the 1920s." NBER Working Paper No. 12138, Cambridge.

Wigmore, Barrie A. 1997. *Securities Markets in the 1980s: The New Regime 1979–1984*, Volume 1. New York: Oxford University Press.

Yamada, Shohei. 1991. "Japanese Banking, Financial Markets, and Competitive Equality." In *Regulating International Financial Markets: Issues and Policies*, edited by Franklin R. Edwards and Hugh T. Patrick. Boston: Kluwer: 41–74.

15   Lessons from history for the twenty-first century

Larry Neal

Just before the sub-prime crisis broke in August 2007, an op-ed piece by David Hale in the *Wall Street Journal* boldly asserted that never in the history of the world has the human race enjoyed such material prosperity.[1] The facts back him up. With a record population of 6.6 billion and an average per capita income of $10,200 in 2006, the world's gross domestic product was still growing at over 5 percent annually in real terms and thus at 2–4 percent per capita.[2] Never has there been so many people living and never has their per capita income been so high. Moreover, never before have there been such bright prospects for the future. Driving this phenomenal achievement, most economists agree, is the rise of trade, starting with the industrialized West after World War II, including the oil producing countries in the 1970s, and finally encompassing the centrally-planned economies of China, India, and the former Soviet Union in the 1990s. Despite occasional tremors in the stock markets of the world, the global economy is awash in liquidity as a result of the unprecedented breadth and depth of prosperity, which has generated high profits in all the countries participating in increased trade.

The resulting savings, Hale argued, as have others,[3] are directed by the increasingly efficient financial markets of the world toward their most efficient investment opportunities. Global finance, in short, provides the basis for continued prosperity. The stock markets in New York, London, and Tokyo, and the international banks there allocate the world's savings toward their highest returns. Ironically, their favored destination turns out to be the US, far and away the largest capital importer in the world since the beginning of the 1980s, and still the

---

[1] "The Best Economy Ever," *Wall Street Journal*. July 31, 2007, p. A15.
[2] CIA, *World Factbook*, 2007.
[3] Mishkin, *The Next Great Globalization*, the Bank for International Settlements in its *Annual Reports 2003–2007*, and the International Monetary Fund in its semi-annual *World Economic Outlook* (July 2007).

richest country in the history of the world. Therein lies the potential pitfall for the future of global finance, not just in the rant of radical Islam or in the populist rhetoric of anti-globalization demonstrators, but also in the historical analysis of economists.[4] These distinguished economists draw upon the work of financial historians of the first age of financial globalization (1880–1913) to note that political forces reacting to the structural changes created by globalization in the nineteenth century led to "great reversals" in the twentieth century.[5] This same political dynamic could again thwart the new globalization of the twenty-first century, as even David Hale warned at the end of his op-ed piece.

As the US election campaigns for 2008 heated up, candidates in both parties called for further restrictions upon globalization, starting with restrictions on trade that benefit the usual constituencies: the steel producers, auto manufacturers, and textile mills. Complaints about immigration also escalated to new levels, not seen since post-World War I, even while more seasonal work in the US became dependent upon migrant workers whose legal status was at best indeterminate. No less important, albeit less well-publicized, were political initiatives to thwart further progress in the operation of financial markets. In the US, the Patriot Act of October 2001, which was renewed virtually unchanged in 2005, strengthened the regulatory powers and investigative authority of the US Treasury over the payments system to an unprecedented extent. The European Union quickly followed suit to enhance the cooperation among its member states for monitoring payments in order to prevent terrorist organizations and other enterprises from carrying out money laundering operations. The European Union even got the secretive banks of Switzerland to inform European governments of the taxes owed by their nationals on their Swiss earnings. The ultimate effect was, predictably, to increase the transactions costs of international payments in general.

With all these political forces at work in the twenty-first century to constrain the market forces driving globalization, especially financial globalization, readers will surely wonder whether the lessons of history presented above are pertinent to the present policy issues. Financial historians know that they are but, just as decision-makers in the past were convinced that their history was irrelevant in light of new innovations, so too are decision-makers today likely to spurn the insights

---

[4] For examples, Aghion and Williamson, *Growth, Inequality* and Rajan and Zingales, *Saving Capitalism.*
[5] Rajan and Zingales, "Great Reversals."

developed by historians, feeling that they are irrelevant in the context of modern technology and institutions.[6]

Indeed, if we review the recent history of developments in banking, capital markets, and government regulations, it appears that the initial mistakes have been recognized and rectified more quickly than earlier. At least by 2007, even financial historians can be cautiously optimistic about the future of global finance. In contrast, few people writing in 1907 were optimistic about the future of the gold standard or of British primacy in the world economy of the time. Events, as it happened, proved them right, but in terms much more draconian than imagined by the most dismal pessimist. To justify optimism now in light of the missteps of the past, we need to take a closer look at what mistakes were made then and those made more recently so as to compare the responses then and now. Our comparisons will touch first on international banking, then capital markets, and finally government interventions.

I.   Financial crises: then and now

The prevalence of financial crises in both the 1890s and the 1990s provoked financial historians to compare the sources of crises and their respective consequences. In work done with Marc Weidenmier, I found little evidence of contagion from the financial crises of the 1890s.[7] For the crises of the 1990s, the academic consensus appears to be that, at a minimum, the Asian crisis of 1997 and the Russian default in 1998 did provoke contagion.[8] A detailed analysis of the consequences of the financial crises in the respective three decades at the end of the nineteenth and the twentieth centuries was done by Bordo and Eichengreen.[9] They found that while the output losses were roughly the same in each epoch, there were many more crises in the 1990s.

The reason that crises in the 1990s were more frequent than in the 1890s, Bordo *et al.* concluded, was because peripheral countries trying to tap into global financial markets attempted at first to peg their currencies to one of the key currencies in the financial capitals (dollars, yen, or deutschemarks). While this was beneficial for attracting foreign savings into these countries, the currency pegs created excessive foreign

---

[6] A notable exception is Ben Bernanke, chairman of the Board of Governors of the Federal Reserve System of the US, whose latest book, *Essays on the Great Depression* summarized his decades of research into the banking crises of the 1930s, which were exacerbated by actions of the US Federal Reserve and the *Banque de France* in the 1930s.

[7] Neal and Weidenmier, "From Tulips to Today."

[8] Mishkin, *Next Great Globalizations* and Taylor, *Global Financial Warriors*.

[9] Bordo and Eichengreen, "Crises Now and Then."

currency exposures for their domestic banks. Lessons were learned, however, especially by IMF staff who shifted to recommending their client states to adopt flexible exchange rates rather than pegged, adjustable rates. These had been the standard under the Bretton Woods system until that system was finally abandoned in 1973, after collapsing in 1971. It took the IMF staff longer, however, to abandon their mindset. Furthermore, countries attempting to borrow in the international markets were encouraged to make explicit arrangements in case of default: the so-called "collective action clauses."[10] Finally, as reported in the IMF's July 2007 update to the *World Economic Outlook*, emerging market countries have been able to offer bonds in their own currencies to an increasing extent.

During the 1990s, these countries could not find an acceptable market for their bonds unless they were denominated in a major currency, a problem that economists labeled the "original sin" problem.[11] By 2007, however, this problem appeared on course for solution as well. The Central and Eastern European countries recently joining the European Union, or attempting to meet the requirements for admission, have adopted enough of the institutions of the European Union to make their own-currency debt marketable. This is happening even before they adopt the EU's euro as their own currency. Some Latin American countries have begun to find a market for their debt in their own currencies as well, provided they include the collective action clauses.[12]

By contrast, lessons from the crises of the 1890s had not really been learned even as the twentieth century began. Several major European countries simply abandoned the gold standard or delayed further joining it until the world supply of gold began to increase after 1897. The new supplies of gold from South Africa and the Yukon initiated a period labeled "gold inflation."[13] Thus, for example, after the easing of supply constraints on the world's monetary gold supply, Italy and Austria rejoined the gold standard club and Spain and Portugal managed to shadow it successfully.[14]

The one crisis that did occur in the ensuing period of monetary ease, the panic of 1907 that originated in New York, was severe and apparently did create contagion. This was in stark contrast to the previous crises in the 1890s according to the findings of Neal and Weidenmier.[15]

---

[10] Taylor, *Global Warriors*, p. 119.
[11] Eichengreen and Hausman, *Other People's Money.*
[12] IMF Research Paper, "Reaping the Benefits."
[13] By Friedman and Schwartz, *A Monetary History.*
[14] Bordo and Rockoff, "Good Housekeeping Seal."
[15] Neal and Weidenmier, "From Tulips to Today."

A key difference may have been that in this case the Bank of England abandoned Bagehot's rule for central banks in times of scrambles for liquidity ("lend freely at a penalty rate"). In response to an unusual outflow of gold from London in October 1906, primarily insurance payouts to the US for losses sustained in the San Francisco earthquake of April 1906, the Bank of England raised its discount rate sharply to 6 percent. But when that unusually high rate created financial distress in the London money market, the Bank lowered it and refused instead to discount any bills of exchange drawn from the US.[16] The Bank's novel action pushed the US demand for gold over to Paris and Berlin, with adverse consequences in turn for the reserves of the public banks in Italy and Austria-Hungary. Evidently, the easing of gold supplies at the beginning of the twentieth century reduced pressures as well for policy-makers to learn their lessons from history!

Even before the missteps of the Bank of England in 1906, however, there were signs that the first wave of financial globalization was ebbing away. The Inland Revenue service of the UK, in a confidential report on the eve of World War I to assess the possibilities for financing an increased armaments program, noted that the returns from the finance companies and stockbrokers had fallen off sharply in recent years, although profits in the banking and insurance companies remained healthy.[17] Membership in the London Stock Exchange fell continuously after 1907 as did dividends to the proprietors of the exchange.[18] Ranald Michie argues that the change in rules and regulations by the London exchange after 1907 decreased not only its membership, but also decreased its effectiveness as a capital market, the result of enforcing minimum commissions and restricting arbitrage operations with other exchanges, both domestic and foreign.[19] He also argues persuasively that similar restrictions imposed by the governments of France and Germany on the Paris and Berlin exchanges, restrictions designed to protect investors from the risks of defaults on forward contracts, decreased their effectiveness as well.[20] Even the Irish Stock Exchange lost its allure after 1897, reflecting in part the malaise of the London market as well as the increasing political frictions between the Irish and the British.[21] Consequently, even before World War I destroyed the global securities market its effectiveness was increasingly undermined even as domestic banking sectors expanded in all industrial nations.

[16] Odell and Weidenmier, "Real Shock, Monetary Aftershock."
[17] Inland Revenue, *Finance Bill*, 1914, p. 59.   [18] Davis and Neal.
[19] Michie, *London and New York*.   [20] Michie, *Global Securities Market*.
[21] Hickson and Turner, "Rise and Decline."

II.   "Overbanking" then and now

The monumental work of Lance Davis and Robert Gallman (2001), reviewed in Chapter 8, blames the various shortcomings of the capital markets in the UK, the US, Canada, Australia, and Argentina, on "overbanking." By this they meant the tendency of banks, especially in the frontier economies, to invest heavily in long-term, illiquid securities issued by agricultural and mining enterprises on the basis of deposits by distant investors, whether domestic or foreign. Given that returns from such enterprises were volatile, and that distant depositors could be fickle, crises had to occur from time to time. When they did, a country's capital markets either responded constructively (for example, Morganization of American railroads at the end of the 1890s in the US, bond houses in Canada) or not (Australia's governments creating land banks to send good money after bad, Argentina substituting regional banks for British banks). "Overbanking" in this sense was also a looming problem in the UK. The number of joint-stock banks with nationwide branches fell low enough (five) that an effective cartel could be formed.

Davis and Gallman argue that their analysis of the difficulties encountered by the emerging markets of the nineteenth century applies as well to more recent difficulties encountered by Japan during its lost decade of the 1990s.[22] Their masterly survey of the development of Japan's financial sector from the Meiji reforms to 1970 elicits a number of striking parallels with the various missteps in financial development that the authors uncovered particularly for Argentina and Australia. The imitation of the Japanese financial strategies by the Asian tigers in the 1990s also presaged the Asian crises in 1997 and the Latin American crises starting with the Mexican meltdown in 1995. Time and again, "overbanking" turned out to be the culprit. In each case, a country relied more on banks as their financial intermediaries for long-term capital investments rather than on capital markets. Capital markets can overcome the problem of mismatched maturities by providing outside sources of liquidity to companies, and they mitigate the asymmetric information problem by providing transparent prices to the public. For long-term intermediation, in short, capital markets have proven their superiority time and again. Excessive reliance on banks in Japan (and subsequently in South Korea, Thailand, and Malaysia) led to progressive mismatching between the maturities of banks' assets and liabilities by the beginning of the 1990s. The heavy investments of Japanese banks in the equity shares of their *keiretsu* manufacturing affiliates shrank in value as

---

[22] Davis and Gallman, *Evolving Capital Markets*, Chap. 9.

Korean, Chinese, and Malaysian exporters gained market shares at the expense of Japanese exporters to the US and European markets. Their depositors put their savings in the national Postal Savings Banks. Major Japanese multinationals began outsourcing their production to sites in Asia, central and east Europe, and even the US. The Bank of Japan, by reducing its interest rates to near zero, facilitated a "carry trade" in which investment banks borrowed at low rates in yen to invest in much higher rates in dollars, euros, or other Asian currencies, wherever Japanese overseas investment occurred. Japanese government debt, mostly issued to the Postal Savings banks, soared to record levels relative to Gross National Product.

"Overbanking" was not a term used to describe the Japanese dilemma since the end of the 1980s, but economists recognized that a major difficulty for Japanese banks in dealing with their backlog of non-performing loans was the lack of well-developed securities markets that could securitize their bad loans in some marketable fashion. Davis and Gallman concluded that the financial system of Japan that emerged after the Meiji Restoration of 1868, thanks to the guiding genius of the Finance Minister, Masayoshi Matsukata, eventually came to bear a striking resemblance to the Australian system of state-supported land banks and government-guided investment strategies that emerged after the 1890s crises. In both cases, governments tried to protect their citizens from the financial impact of a prior collapse in land values.[23]

The Asian financial crisis of the late 1990s was unfolding as Davis and Gallman were finishing their manuscript, leading them to conclude "that, although the past has provided valuable lessons, it does not appear that, even a century later, those lessons have been learned."[24] Since then, however, more by trial and error than by close reading of financial history, the basic problem of "overbanking" in financial globalization is well on course to being solved by the re-emergence of a global securities market.

III.   The global securities market then and now

Ranald Michie extols the virtues of a global securities market for the access it allows international banks to a much larger reservoir of savings in cases when they might confront a liquidity squeeze.[25] He argues that access to a wide range of pools of liquid assets enables financial

---

[23] Davis and Gallman, *Evolving Capital Markets*, pp. 900–2.
[24] Davis and Gallman, *Evolving Capital Markets*, p. 925.
[25] Michie, *Global Securities Market*.

institutions to find lenders of short-term funds rather than be forced to declare bankruptcy when they face a run on deposits and a falling market for their assets. If effective, such a global securities market could eliminate the need for an international lender of last resort.[26]

Forming such an institution, the Bank for International Settlements notwithstanding, has proven politically impossible. The US Treasury essentially played the role of international lender of last resort through the operation of the Bretton Woods system from 1944 until its demise in 1971, when its monetary gold stocks fell too low to meet the increasing demands from leading central banks. To financial historians, this was reminiscent of the US Treasury's role as domestic lender of last resort from the onset of the Civil War in 1861 until the establishment of the Federal Reserve System in 1914. Even when the Federal Reserve assumed the role of lender of last resort for National Banks in the US, it failed miserably during the Great Depression. It did not respond to the successive banking crises at the beginning of the 1930s, and actually precipitated another banking crisis in 1937 by raising reserve requirements for National Banks. This action nearly undid the efforts of the Treasury through underwriting the Reconstruction Finance Corporation to recapitalize the majority of the nation's banks from 1933 onwards.[27]

The savings and loan crisis of the 1980s in the US similarly required indirect action by the US Treasury through the Resolution Trust Corporation. Not until the terms of Alan Greenspan as chairman of the Board of Governors in 1986 did the Federal Reserve System truly act as a domestic lender of last resort. Greenspan's resolute actions succeeded in dampening the financial shocks of the stock market collapse in October 1987, moderating the widely anticipated shock of computer failures in banks at the turn of the year 2000, and enabling the New York money and capital markets to rebound from the terrorist attacks of September 11, 2001. The IMF, confronted with the unanticipated consequences of responding as a lender of last resort to the liquidity scrambles generated by the Asian crisis in 1997 and the Russian default in 1998, met the Argentine meltdown in 2004 with stolid resistance. It was backed up this time by the Federal Reserve System, still under Greenspan's leadership, and the US Treasury, now under more conservative leadership less responsive to the immediate needs of Wall

---

[26] In August 2007, the collapse of the sub-prime mortgage market in the US prompted (presumably coordinated) intervention by the central banks of the US, the European Union, and Japan with no mention of the International Monetary Fund.

[27] Calomiris and Mason, "How to Restructure"; and Mason, "Political Economy of the RFC."

Street investment banks. Only in nearby Uruguay was there any adverse effect on other countries, and this was probably due to ill-advised intervention by the IMF at the time.[28] In short, instead of having governments move toward forming an international lender of last resort, a variety of private reforms and innovations in the operation of the global securities market have managed to reduce the incidence of financial crises and moderate their influence on other countries.

IV.   Financial innovations and government intervention

While the pace of innovation in the global securities markets since 1980 has managed to quell calls for an international lender of last resort since the resolution of the Asian, Russian, and Argentine crises, government intervention has occurred elsewhere at the international level. Rather than intervene directly in credit or foreign exchange markets (at least until the meltdown of the sub-prime mortgage markets in August 2007), governments have found it useful and possible to regulate the international payments system. The events of September 11, 2001, motivated both the US and the European Union to cooperate in monitoring international payments to choke off the ultimate source of finance for terrorist groups. The attackers of September 11 had received regular payments while training in the US through the operation of various *hawala* currency exchanges and wire transfer services. These are informal currency exchanges created to allow foreigners in Europe or the US to remit earnings to family and friends in their home countries for a nominal fee. In effect, they operate much as the four-party bill of exchange did for making international payments in early modern Europe. As in the case of the four-party foreign bill of exchange in early modern Europe, a multitude of small payments made via various *hawalas* has to be settled eventually by an occasional large remittance through regular banking systems.[29] In the twenty-first century, these larger remittances can be picked up when they are recorded by the clearing system for international payments, SWIFT (Society for Worldwide Interbank

---

[28] Mishkin, *Next Great Globalization* argues that Uruguay had ample foreign reserves to maintain its exchange rate with the dollar, but that when the IMF forced it to float, investors took this as a signal that reserves were deficient and forced a severe devaluation that ruined the capital accounts of Uruguay's financial institutions with debts denominated in dollars and assets denominated in Uruguay's *peso uruguayan* (which had replaced the new peso in 1993, which in turn had replaced the peso in 1975 during the currency turmoil of the mid-1970s.

[29] See Chapter 1 of Neal, *Rise of Financial Capitalism*, and especially Neal and Quinn, "Networks of Information," for expositions of the four-party bill of exchange in early eighteenth century London.

Financial Telecommunication). While SWIFT is operated by private international banks for their convenience, it has cooperated with US and European authorities to monitor payments by particular individuals or organizations thought to be financing terrorist activities.[30] Such monitoring could, of course, also be useful to detect money laundering from illegal activities and tax evasion.

The banks responsible for reporting their international payments to the respective national authorities saw the new regulations as an opportunity to raise their service fees in general. This opportunity was especially welcomed within the euro-zone of the European Union where the introduction of a single currency in 1999 had eliminated the previously lucrative business of charging commissions on foreign exchange. The 2 percent fee that banks in the US and Europe imposed on any international transfer of funds thereafter exceeded by far the earlier recommendations of economists for a "Tobin tax" on speculative capital movements. The Tobin tax was supposed to throw a little bit of sand into the gears of currency manipulators such as George Soros, just to allow time for longer-term credit markets to adjust to changes in economic fundamentals. The 2 percent payments fee, by contrast, permanently raised transaction costs for international trade across the board despite citizen complaints and bank competitors. In contrast, the fees charged for clearing foreign bills of exchange through the payments system of the Amsterdam Exchange Bank in the eighteenth century, set by the municipal authorities of Amsterdam were only one-eighth of 1 percent!

In the US market, the Sarbanes–Oxley bill, passed in 2002 by overwhelming votes in the US Congress, also increased the transactions costs of publicly-traded firms. The increased reporting requirements of financial statements, combined with the legal liability of management and external auditing firms for their accuracy has led to renewed controversy over the role of government regulation. Do the expenses and uncertainties mean that startup firms will continue to be discouraged from going public in the future and that foreign companies will delist from US exchanges? Similar concerns were raised, of course, when the Securities and Exchange Act was enacted in 1934. The rise of private equity since 2002 and the corresponding fall in the number of initial public offerings by new firms may be attributable in part to the unforeseen consequences of Sarbanes–Oxley. But the increase in the supply of

---

[30] See Taylor, Chapter 1 for an explanation of SWIFT and its use by the US Treasury to monitor payments by terrorist support groups, at least until the *New York Times* made the program public in 2006!

cheap credit at the disposal of existing corporations and hedge funds has surely also played an important part. Economic historians remain divided over the earlier effects of the Securities and Exchange Act of 1934 as well. It may have discouraged new firms from going public then as well, and for much the same reasons. In the longer run, however, increased public confidence in the solidity of the remaining firms may have contributed to the rise of public participation in stock ownership after World War II. Perhaps the benefits of the increased transparency of financial reporting by public firms required by Sarbanes–Oxley will, in the longer run, outweigh the costs, which are certainly much higher in the immediate transition to the new set of regulations than they will be in a few years.[31]

Accounting standards to be followed by the public firms remain an issue as the European Union in 2005 required all public companies operating in Europe to adopt Internationally Accepted Standards (IAS). This was presumably in response to previous US legislation that required all public companies listing on US stock exchanges to provide financial accounts based on US Generally Accepted Accounting Practices (GAAP). These have been characterized as applying "rules" rather than "principles," which are the characteristic of IAS, given the diversity of enforcement agencies that the various European countries have created over the years. The US, and to a large extent the UK and other common law countries such as Canada and Australia, by contrast, have established specific rules that comprise Generally Accepted Accounting Practices. Finding mutually acceptable common ground for the two approaches to standardizing accounting for public companies has proven to be an arduous and ongoing process.[32] Fortunately for the future of the current global securities market, this task has been relegated to the private sector, the Financial Accounting Standards Board (FASB) in the US, and the International Accounting Standards Board (IASB) in Europe. The difficulties encountered in the US for extending branch banking among the various states and the similar difficulties that confront the EU in creating a single financial market demonstrate the dangers of leaving the resolution of such contentious issues to governments.[33] In

---

[31] Indeed, Thomas J. Healey, "Sarbox was the Right Medicine," former Assistant Secretary of the Treasury in the US, argues that costs of compliance to Sarbanes–Oxley fell sharply in the first three years, while the Securities and Exchange Commission has made compliance easier through modification of its enforcement procedures. Zhang, "Economic Consequences," however, argues that in those years the costs of compliance were substantial and stockholder value fell substantially as a result.

[32] See the special issue of *The International Journal of Accounting*, 38:2 (Summer 2003) devoted to the "rules" versus "principles" for accounting standards for the US and Europe.

[33] See the discussion in Neal, *Economics of Europe*.

2002, a Memorandum of Understanding between the two accounting boards was signed (the Norwalk Agreement) to work toward convergence of the two standards, creating a third set, the International Financial Reporting Standards (IFRS). By 2007, a great deal of progress had been made with cooperative research and decision making between the two, with the governments of over one hundred countries signing on to recognize and eventually enforce the IFRS as they emerge from the research, discussion, and decision-making of the IASB.[34]

The rise of standard accounting practices in the first wave of financial globalization created similar conflicts and concerns, both in the UK and the US. Firms that adopted more transparent accounting and issued annual reports found that their stock performed better than firms that did not.[35] American railroad securities found a worldwide market in the late nineteenth century, partly due to the ingenuity of American management in tailoring new security issues to the needs of each foreign market, but partly due to their eventual adoption of standard accounting practices, as well their payment of regular dividends.[36]

V.   Conclusion

From the perspective of the financial historians who have presented the case studies above, the specific issues today bear an uncanny resemblance to the issues confronted in the past whenever innovations occurred in financial capitalism. Fundamentally, each innovation in the past has created challenges to the separate institutions of government, banking, and capital markets to determine how they can incorporate and utilize the innovations to their mutual advantage. The responses have varied over time and across countries, but when success becomes apparent in one context, it must have spillover effects that, eventually, have led to the current triumph of global finance in the first decade of the twenty-first century. Even the usual voices of caution from the World Bank and International Monetary Fund acknowledge in their updates of July 2007 that the global economy has continued to prosper at unprecedented levels of growth for an unusually long-spell after the terrorist attacks of September 11, 2001. The possibility of derailing financial globalization appeared soon afterwards, first with the financial crisis in Turkey at the end of 2002, and then with the collapse of the Argentine commitment

---

[34] IFRS, *Annual Report*, 2007.
[35] John Turner, "Protecting Outside Investors," although Turner emphasizes the role of regular dividend payments in maintaining a firm's share price over time.
[36] Baskin and Miranti, *History of Corporate Finance*.

to a fixed exchange rate with the dollar in 2004. Unlike the financial crises that occurred during the 1990s, however, the loss of real output within each country at the time of the crisis has been restored within a few years. Furthermore, the possibility of contagion, spreading the crisis to neighboring or similar countries, was checked immediately.

Despite these desperate efforts to derail the process of globalization, dramatized by the destruction of the World Trade Center, the global economy has continued to prosper with the benefits of increased production of goods and services spread widely throughout the world and even within most countries. All of this, of course, has been driven by the renewed expansion of international finance. Clearly, some important lessons have already been learned and put into effect by leading policymakers. Nevertheless, as each historian in this volume has indicated for his particular case study, the possibility of reversals is always present, usually due to the response of governments trying to protect their perceived constituencies from dealing with foreign, impersonal market forces that are unleashed by innovations in financial capitalism.

References

Aghion, Philippe, and Jeffrey G. Williamson. 1998. *Growth, Inequality, and Globalization: Theory, History, and Policy.* Cambridge and New York: Cambridge University Press.

Bank for International Settlements, *Annual Report,* (BIS: Basel: 2003–2007), http://www.bis.org/publ/annualreport.htm.

Baskin, Jonathan Barron, and Paul J. Miranti, Jr. 1997. *A History of Corporate Finance.* New York: Cambridge University Press.

Bernanke, Ben S. 2004. *Essays on the Great Depression.* Princeton: Princeton University Press.

Bordo, Michael, and Hugh Rockoff. June 1996. "The Gold Standard as a 'Good Housekeeping Seal of Approval'," *Journal of Economic History,* 56:2: 389–428.

Bordo, Michael, and Barry Eichengreen. "Crises Now and Then: What Lessons from the Last Era of Financial Globalization," NBER Working Paper 8716, 2002.

Bordo, Michael, Barry Eichengreen, Daniela Klingebiel, and Maria Soledad Martinez-Peria. April 2001. "Is the Crisis Problem Growing More Severe?" *Economic Policy,* 16:32: 51, 53–82.

Calomiris, Charles, and Joseph Mason. 2003. "How to Restructure Failed Banking Systems: Lessons from the US in the 1930s and Japan in the 1990s," NBER Working Paper 9624.

Central Intelligence Agency, *World Factbook, 2007,* https://www.cia.gov/library/publications/the-world-factbook.

Davis, Lance E., and Robert Gallman. 2001. *Evolving Capital Markets and International Capital Flows: Britain, the Americas, and Australia, 1865–1914.* New York: Cambridge University Press.

Davis, Lance, and Larry Neal. December 2006. "The Evolution of the Structure and Performance of the London Stock Exchange in the First Global Financial Market, 1812–1914," *European Review of Economic History,* 10:3: 279–300.

Eichengreen, Barry, and Ricardo Hausman, eds. 2005. *Other People's Money: Debt Denomination and Financial Instability in Emerging Market Economies.* Chicago and London: University of Chicago Press.

Friedman, Milton, and Anna J. Schwartz 1963 *A Monetary History of the US, 1867–1960.* Princeton: Princeton University Press.

Grossman, Peter Z. January 1995. "The Market for Shares of Companies with Unlimited Liability: The Case of American Express," *The Journal of Legal Studies,* 24:1: 63–85.

Hale, David, "The Best Economy Ever," *Wall Street Journal.* July 31, 2007, p. A15.

Healey, Thomas J.. "Sarbox was the Right Medicine," *Wall Street Journal,* August 9, 2007, p. A.13.

Hickson, Charles R., and John D. Turner. April 2005. "The Rise and Decline of the Irish Stock Market, 1865–1913," *European Review of Economic History,* 9:1: 3–33.

IFRS. 2007. *Annual Report, 2006.* London: International Accounting Standards Committee Foundation.

Inland Revenue, United Kingdom, *Finance Bill 1914,* vol. 1, "Methods of Raising Revenue, Estimates and Statistics," National Archives, IR 63/46.

International Monetary Fund Research Department, "Reaping the Benefits of Financial Globalization," Discussion Paper, June 2007.

International Monetary Fund, *World Economic Outlook, July 2007,* Washington, DC: IMF.

Mason, Joseph R. April 2003. "The Political Economy of the Reconstruction Finance Corporation during the Great Depression," *Explorations in Economic History,* 40:2: 101–21.

Michie, Ranald S. 1987. *The London and New York Stock Exchanges, 1850–1914.* London and Boston: Allen & Unwin.

Michie, Ranald S. 2006. *The Global Securities Market: a History.* Oxford: Oxford University Press.

Mishkin, Frederic S. 2006. *The Next Great Globalization, How Disadvantaged Nations Can Harness Their Financial Systems to Get Rich.* Princeton: Princeton University Press.

Neal, Larry. 1990. *The Rise of Financial Capitalism.* New York: Cambridge University Press.

2007. *The Economics of Europe and the European Union.* Cambridge and New York: Cambridge University Press.

Neal, Larry, and Stephen Quinn. April 2001. "Networks of Information, Markets and Institutions in the Rise of London as a Financial Centre, 1660–1720," *Financial History Review:* 7–26.

Neal, Larry, and Marc Weidenmier. 2003. "Crises in The Global Economy from Tulips to Today: Contagion and Consequences," in Michael Bordo, Alan Taylor, and Jeffrey G. Williamson, eds., *Globalization in History*. Chicago: NBER and University of Chicago Press.

Odell, Kerry A., and Marc D. Weidenmier. December 2004. "Real Shock; Monetary Aftershock: The 1906 San Francisco Earthquake and the Panic of 1907," *Journal of Economic History* 64:4: 1002–27.

Rajan, Raghuram G., and Luigi Zingales. July 2003. "The Great Reversals: The Politics of Financial Development in the Twentieth Century," *Journal of Financial Economics*, 69:1: 5–50.

2004. *Saving Capitalism from the Capitalists*. London: Random House.

Taylor, John B. 2007. *Global Financial Warriors, The Untold Story of International Finance in the Post-9/11 World*. New York: W.W. Norton.

Turner, John D. 2007. "Protecting Outside Investors in a Laissez-faire Legal Environment: Corporate Governance in Victorian Britain," paper delivered at Business History Conference.

Zhang, Ivy Xiying. February 2005. "Economic Consequences of the Sarbanes-Oxley Act of 2002," unpublished paper.

Index